Also by
FREDERICK MERK

Economic History of Wisconsin During the Civil War Decade
   (1916; revised in 1971)

(Editor) *Fur Trade and Empire:*
   George Simpson's Journal, 1824–25 (1931; revised in 1968)

Manifest Destiny and Mission in American History (1963)

The Monroe Doctrine and American Expansionism, 1843–49 (1966)

The Oregon Question:
   Essays in Anglo-American Diplomacy and Politics (1967)

(Co-author) *Dissent in Three American Wars* (1970)

Fruits of Propaganda in the Tyler Administration (1971)

Slavery and the Annexation of Texas (1972)

HISTORY OF THE
WESTWARD MOVEMENT

HISTORY OF THE WESTWARD MOVEMENT

Frederick Merk

ALFRED A. KNOPF
New York 1978

Grateful acknowledgment is made for permission to reprint previously published illustrations from the following sources:

Atlas of the Historical Geography of the United States by Charles O. Paullin. Permission granted by Carnegie Institution of Washington.
The Expansionist Movement in Texas, 1836–1850 by William C. Binkley. Published in 1925 by The Regents of the University of California; reprinted by permission of the University of California Press.
Farms or Forests by Vernon Carstensen. University of Wisconsin Press, 1962. Used by kind permission of the author.
Geographical Review, Vol. 30, 1940, copyrighted by the American Geographical Society.
The Great American Land Bubble by Aaron M. Sakolski. Harper & Brothers, 1932. Used by permission of Harper & Row, Publishers.
Harper's Magazine. Copyright © 1937 by *Harper's Magazine*. Copyright © renewed 1964. All rights reserved. Reprinted from the February 1937 issue by special permission.
Historical Geography of the United States by Ralph H. Brown, copyright 1948, by Harcourt Brace Jovanovich, Inc.; renewed, 1976, by G. Burton Brown, Nancy Revsbech, and Laura L. Schrader. Reproduced by permission of the publishers.
A History of American Economic Life, 3rd. ed., Appleton-Century-Crofts, © 1960, 1967 by Edward Chase Kirkland; © 1969 by Meredith Corporation. All rights reserved.
Indians of North America by Harold E. Driver. © 1961 by The University of Chicago.
Life Magazine. Photo by Wayne Miller, Magnum Photos, Inc.
The New York Times. © 1956 by The New York Times Company. Reprinted by permission.
Our Landed Heritage: The Public Domain, 1776–1970, second edition, revised by Roy M. Robbins by permission of University of Nebraska Press. © 1942 by Roy M. Robbins; © 1976 by University of Nebraska Press.
The Range Cattle Industry by Edward Everett Dale. Copyright 1930 by the University of Oklahoma Press.
The United States 1830–1850 by Frederick Jackson Turner. Permission granted by Huntington Library, San Marino, California.

Complete information about all sources of illustrations may be found on pp. 639–641.

Library of Congress Cataloging in Publication Data

Merk, Frederick, 1887–1977
   History of the westward movement.
   Bibliography: p.
   Includes index.
   1. United States—Territorial expansion.
2. Frontier and pioneer life—United States. 3. The West—History. I. Title.
E179.5.M397 1978   973   77-20354
ISBN 0-394-41175-7

To Lois

CONTENTS

ILLUSTRATIONS xi
PREFACE XV

1 The Indian Background 1

2 Indian Culture 10

3 The Virginia Tidewater 15

4 Seventeenth Century Expansion of Virginia 26

5 The Massachusetts Bay Colony 33

6 Expansion of New England 39

7 The Piedmont and Great Valley 48

8 The French and Indian Barrier 55

9 The Seven Years' War in America 61

10 British Western Policy, 1763–75 67

11 Terrain of the Interior 74

12 Land Speculators and Settlers Enter the Allegheny Plateau 79

13 The West in the War of the
American Revolution and in the Peace Treaty of 1783 87

14 Land Cessions by the States 98

15 Land Policy and the Principle of Equality of States 102

16 Postwar Land Speculation 112

17 Advance Over the Allegheny Plateau 125

18 The Southwest in American Diplomacy, 1783–1803 134

19 The Northwest in American Diplomacy, 1783–95 143

20 The West in the War of 1812 153

21 Settlement of the Prairie and Lake Plains   163

22 Prairie and Lake Plains: Economy, Society, and Politics   173

23 Settlement of the Gulf Plains Province   181

24 Gulf Plains: Economy, Society, and Politics   196

25 The Slavery Issue and the Unification of the South   205

26 Internal Commerce and Internal Improvements   214

27 The Tariff as a Sectional Issue   223

28 The Public Lands, 1800–62   229

29 Physiography of the Far West   240

30 Trans-Mississippi Trade   252

31 The Mississippi Valley Frontier and
Its Outlets to the Far West   259

32 Texas   265

33 The Movement for Annexation and the Defeat of the Treaty   279

34 Annexation Achieved   293

35 The Oregon Question   309

36 The Mormons   330

37 California   347

38 The Bear Flag Revolt   353

39 The War with Mexico   359

40 The Issue of Slavery in the
New Territories and the Compromise of 1850   374

41 The Kansas-Nebraska Act and Bleeding Kansas   382

42 The Dred Scott Decision   394

43 The West and Slavery, 1856–60   399

44 Mining Advance Across the Cordilleran West   412

45 Plains and Mountain Indians and
the Dawes Act of 1887   419

46 Agriculture in the Middle West and
the Granger and Greenback Movements   431

47 Industrialization of the Great Lakes Region   447

48 Great Plains and Cattlemen   457

49 Farmers on the Great Plains   467

50 Populism   477

51 Dry Farming   484

52 Mining Techniques of the Twentieth Century   495

53 Early Irrigation and the Colorado River Projects   507

54 The Columbia Basin and Central Valley Projects   523

55 The Tennessee Valley Authority and
Its Role as Model for Western River Basin Development   533

56 The Missouri and Arkansas Basin Projects
and the Water Resources Planning Act of 1965   543

57 Soil Conservation   549

58 Agricultural Overproduction and Production Control to 1941   556

59 Agriculture and Farm Policy During and After World War II   563

60 The Kennedy-Johnson Years In Farm Policy   574

61 Farm Tenancy and Its Decline: A Century of Change   582

62 Migratory Farm Labor, 1900–75   591

63 American Indians, 1934–74   599

64 Land-Use Planning   604

Afterword   616

FURTHER READING   619

SOURCES OF ILLUSTRATIONS   639

INDEX   643

ILLUSTRATIONS

1. Indian Language Families   6
2. Town Plat of Enfield, Connecticut   35
3. New England Settlement, 1675, 1677   42-3
4. Eighteenth Century Expansion in New England   44-5
5. New England Vote on the Ratification of the Constitution   46
6. Colonial Population, 1760, 1780   52-3
7. Indian Boundary Line, 1768   70
8. Southern Appalachians   75
9. Cumberland Gap   76
10. Proposed Western Colonies, 1763–75   81
11. Fort Boonesborough   88
12. The West in the War of the Revolution   90
13. Proposal of France at the Peace Conference   94
14. British-American Negotiations, 1782   96
15. Land Cessions of the States   99
16. John Cartwright's Proposal   107
17. Thomas Jefferson's Plan for Future States   109
18. Treaty of Hartford   112
19. Land Speculation in Western and Northern New York   114
20. Land Speculation in Ohio   115
21. Presidential Election, 1804   120
22. Presidential Election, 1828   121
23. Presidential Election, 1832   122
24. Presidential Election, 1840   123
25. Presidential Election, 1844   124
26. Population Distribution, 1800   127
27. Population Distribution, 1830   128
28. Corn Crop, 1839   129

29. Tobacco Crop, 1839, 1849   129
30. Cotton Crop, Average of 1826 and 1833   130
31. Presidential Election, 1836   131
32. Treaty of Greenville   150
33. Population Distribution, 1810   154
34. Indian Cessions   155
35. Glaciation in the Middle West   164
36. Population Distribution, 1820   167
37. Wheat Crop, 1839, 1849   175
38. Wheat Crop, 1859   176
39. Corn Crop, 1849   177
40. Corn Crop, 1859   177
41. Sheep on Farms, 1840   178
42. Sheep on Farms, 1860   178
43. Population Distribution, 1840   191
44. Population Distribution, 1850   192
45. Slaves, 1810   193
46. Slaves, 1820   193
47. Slaves, 1840   194
48. Slaves, 1850   194
49. Cotton Crop, 1811   197
50. Cotton Crop, 1839   198
51. Cotton Crop, 1849   198
52. Cotton Crop, 1859   199
53. Presidential Election, 1848   204
54. Public Land Disposal   237
55. Physiographic Regions   243
56. New England in Texas   245
57. Annual Precipitation   246
58. Improved Land in Farms, 1920   247
59. Empresario Contracts   269
60. Texan Expansionism   277
61. House Vote on the Kansas-Nebraska Act   389
62. Congressional Election, 1854   403
63. Presidential Election, 1856   406
64. House Vote on the Tariff Act, 1857   407
65. Congressional Election, 1858   408

66. Presidential Election, 1860   409
67. Five Civilized Tribes, 1861   422
68. Indian Reservations, 1875   428
69. Indian Reservations, 1930   429
70. Corn Production, 1869   432
71. Corn Production, 1879   432
72. Wheat Production, 1869   434
73. Wheat Production, 1879   434
74. Sheep on Farms and Ranches, 1880   435
75. Railroads in Operation, 1860   436
76. Railroads in Operation, 1870   437
77. Cattle Trails   459
78. Cattle Industry, 1860, 1880   461
79. Population Distribution, 1890   468
80. Wheat Production, 1889   470
81. Wheat Production, 1899   470
82. Corn Production, 1899   471
83. Corn Production, 1909   471
84. Population Distribution, 1900   475
85. Cotton Prices Graph   476
86. Presidential Election, 1892   480
87. Population Distribution, 1930   485
88. Increase in Land in Farms, 1910–20   486
89. Winter Wheat, 1929   488
90. Spring Wheat, 1929   488
91. Grain Sorghum, 1939   490
92. Cotton Crop, 1889   493
93. Cotton Crop, 1929   493
94. Copper Mine, Bingham Canyon, Utah   496
95. Giant Terraces of the Bingham Canyon Mine   497
96. Early Irrigation   510
97. Hoover Dam   514
98. Colorado–Big Thompson Trans–Mountain Diversion   518
99. Colorado River Storage Project   520
100. Grand Coulee Dam   524
101. Pipes Raising Water to the Coulee Reservoir   525
102. Columbia Basin Project, Engineer's Relief Map   526

103. Profile of the Columbia Basin Project   526
104. Columbia Basin Treaty with Canada, 1964   528
105. Central Valley Project   530
106. Tennessee Valley Project   541
107. Missouri Valley Project   545
108. Arkansas Valley Project   547
109. Distribution of Erosion, 1934   551
110. Farm Tenancy, 1880, 1930   583
111. Crop Land Harvested on Tenant and Cropper Farms, 1934   587
112. Areas Unsuited to Farming, 1935   607
113. Michigan Cut-Over Area   608
114. Wisconsin Counties Having Rural-Zoning Ordinances   609
115. Federal Lands Unappropriated and Unreserved, 1923   610
116. Taylor Grazing Districts, 1936   612

PREFACE

This book is an account of one of the great migrations of mankind. It records a prolonged movement into the wilderness that is now the United States. The earliest of the migrants were from the British Isles. To them the Atlantic seaboard was the West. Their government at the outset was the British colonial system, which they ultimately turned against in a war for independence. A union of states was formed in which sectional differences developed between the Northeast, South, and West, over issues that were largely economic. Included was one that was primarily emotional—Negro slavery and its spread westward—over which the South and the North became embittered and ultimately fought a devastating war.

Beyond the Mississippi lay a wilderness possessed, in 1801, by European states. It continued to be held by them, however, only briefly. In the half century from 1801 to 1848 it passed into the hands of the new republic. The vast area of the Louisiana Purchase was the first to be acquired. It almost doubled the public domain of the Union. It opened vistas, moreover, of further territorial advance to the Pacific. In rapid succession, thereafter, came Texas, half of the Oregon Country, and a large part of Mexico, taken in a war of conquest. In half a century the young republic became a transcontinental power.

So swift an expansion intensified old sectional problems, especially that of the spread of slavery, which arose over the annexation of Texas and the organization of the Mexican Cession. Soon afterward the same issue was reopened over territory that had been earlier acquired. The outcome of the clash was the secession of the slave states and the Civil War.

A massive enrichment of national resources was one of the more enduring results of the territorial gains of the half-century. With the Louisiana Purchase came an immense addition of arable semi-arid plains and mountains. With it came, also, arteries of communication between East and West. The Father of Waters, with tributaries united, became a means of communication between the sections. The Texas accretion added a lush cotton country, together with an enormous domain of grazing land and rich, but arid soil that would some day be made productive by diverting to it irrigation streams and by pumping up to it water from the underground. The Oregon cession joined the great fur resources of the Pacific Northwest to those of the Great Lakes, and gave American pioneers title to land in the lovely Willamette Valley and in valleys that could later be rescued from aridity by the waters of the Columbia and its tributaries. No less significant was the harbor complex won in the treaty—the first harbors the nation acquired on the Pacific.

The Mexican Cession added the unrivaled harbor of San Francisco Bay and the river systems of the Colorado, the Sacramento, and the San Joaquin, which were to provide irrigation water to California's thirsty soils. Much of the land in the Mexican Cession seemed at the time hardly worth the taking. It consisted principally of semi-arid plateaus and inhospitable mountains. Yet it soon was found to contain immense resources. Its agricultural potentiality was revealed at once in Utah, where irrigation water was available. California's adaptation to grazing and agriculture were already apparent. Mineral deposits were promptly discovered, gold in the streams of California and silver in the even richer Comstock Lode.

The semi-arid lands west of the 100th meridian, acquired in the four cessions, were developed chiefly in the 20th century. They were redeemed in part by the arts of dry farming—by the hybridization of grains, by a worldwide search for grain species that were resistant to drought and pests, and by modes of cultivation that were conducive to maintaining moisture in the soil. For irrigation farming, technology provided the skills for reservoir construction, for piercing mountain ranges to permit transfer of water from one river system to another, and for control of salinity in streams whose flow had been polluted by the runoff of used irrigation waters.

Equally spectacular results were obtained in the 20th century in the upgrading of the lean ores found in the Cordilleran system—especially copper. By the process of flotation those ores were made profitable to exploit, and enabled the nation to retain first place as a producer of primary copper. In the same era the low-grade iron ores of the Lake Superior region were transformed and became a supplementary source in the output of American steel mills in World War II and thereafter.

The petroleum resources of the nation, found chiefly in Texas, Oklahoma, and California, gave evidence of depletion after a half-century of exploitation. A supplement to them was natural gas, present with petroleum in the wells. Another was coal. Immense resources of strippable coal, found in the West, have become the raw materials increasingly used to meet the current energy crisis. It is convertible into either oil or gas.

Comparable to the upgrading of low-grade mineral resources has been the renovation of the principal river basins of the nation. This was the product in large part of engineering advances. The initial enterprise was the Colorado Basin Project, begun by the federal government in 1928. It was followed by a project undertaken by the state government of California for its Central Valley, but given reality by the federal government after the launching of the Tennessee Valley Project in 1933. In that project the basic concept was the renovation of a run-down society by harnessing the might of a turbulent and destructive river. Concepts of similar scope, altered in administrative form, animated the Columbia, Missouri, and Arkansas basin projects.

The outcome of the Westward Movement was the conversion of a raw wilderness into a nation that is a world power. The process was unplanned, and could hardly have been otherwise. But the planlessness brought penalties, especially in the domain of land use, and these became increasingly evident with the growing national maturity. The evidences were impoverishment and even destruction of the soil, rivers that were a flood menace to lowlands, and societies stranded on impaired lands that had become a burden to the states and to the nation to maintain. These consequences manifested themselves in the opening quarter of the 20th century in a series of dramatic disturbances of nature in major areas. The result was the inception of a program of land-use planning, participated in by the federal and state governments. The application of the program was directed, at the outset, to the vast western lands remaining in the possession of the federal government. It was intended, also, to be extended to government purchases of private land needing to be retired. Initiated in the 1930's, this program was a road to the future.

In preparing this book I have had generous help from many persons and institutions. I wish I could express my thanks by name to each of the friends who assisted me. But space does not permit it. I must single out, however, the name of Frederick Jackson Turner, who was the initiator of a famous course of lectures on the History of the Westward Movement. In 1921 he proposed to me at Harvard University that we share the lectures, he taking the first half of the course and I the second. This arrangement, which I gratefully accepted, continued until his retirement from teaching. Thereafter, the course as a whole fell to me. My special interests lay in the areas of American territorial expansion over the Far West—the Oregon Country, Texas, and the region of the Mexican Cession. In deepening my knowledge and extending it, backward and forward in time, I incurred obligations to numerous libraries and especially to their administrative staffs. Among the libraries, the ones most steadily used were those of the Harvard University system, especially Widener and Houghton of the College Library, Littauer of the Kennedy School of Government, and the libraries of the Business School and the Law School. Outside this system I sought and received frequent help from the Massachusetts Historical Society Library and the Boston Public Library. In New York I obtained much help from the New York Public Library and the library of the New-York Historical Society. In Washington I was the recipient of repeated assistance and courtesies from the Library of Congress and the National Archives. In Worcester, Massachusetts, the massive collection of newspaper materials at the American Antiquarian Society was placed at my disposal. The State Library, in Augusta, Maine, and the Maine Historical Society, in Portland, opened their special manuscript materials to my use. In Canada, at the Ottawa National Archives, diplomatic materials on Canadian-American relations were made available with unfailing promptness and courtesy.

I have obligations to a number of persons and publishers for permission to republish maps and other illustrations scattered throughout the text. Identified by a number, each is described briefly in an introductory list and is more fully identified and explained in the text. A section at the back of the book provides full information on the sources of all types of illustrative material. I am indebted also to the Harvard University Press for permission to republish a section of a lecture I gave at the Massachusetts Historical Society, which was published with others under the title *Dissent in Three American Wars*.

For guidance concerning problems arising in the publication of illustrations I am indebted to my son, Dr. Frederick Bannister Merk. I am indebted to him also for several photographs that were taken by him. My greatest obligation is to my wife, Dr. Lois Bannister Merk, who has been my collaborator during most of the years of preparation of this book in research, analysis, and criticism, and who has been its inspiration.

June 1, 1976   F.M.

HISTORY OF THE
WESTWARD MOVEMENT

The Indian Background

THE PRIMITIVE RACE OF MAN found in the New World by Christopher Columbus in 1492 seemed to him to be Asiatic, necessarily so, since he had reached the Indies by sailing west. He christened the race "Indian." It could not protest, and has lived with the name ever since. The reasoning and the name were not erroneous. Columbus had found Asiatics as he expected, though not on the coast of Asia. North America had been an appendage of Asia in the Ice Age, connected by a causeway across Bering Strait, and the Indians whom whites later encountered in the Westward Movement were descendants of those who had crossed to America twenty or twenty-five thousand years or more earlier.

The crossing is accepted universally by scholars as a fact. In the New World no race of man originated; thus the one Columbus met must have come by migration. In the Old World skeletal remains of remote antiquity have been uncovered, which exhibit man rising from brute ancestry. Such remains have appeared in Asia, Africa, Melanesia, and elsewhere. None have ever been found in the New World, nor are there in the New World evidences of any species of hominid from which *Homo sapiens* could have evolved.

In north central Asia two races matured into *Homo sapiens*—the Mongolian and Caucasian. They reached that stage forty or fifty millennia in the past. They were not as distinctly segregated then from each other as they later became. They presently expanded in all directions—eastward, westward, northward, and southward. Of those moving eastward, part made their way into North America. They were principally Mongoloids, though Caucasians may have come also.

The route taken by them is likely to have been across Bering Strait from the northeasternmost tip of Siberia to the westernmost extension of the Seward Peninsula. The crossing could have been by raft. The waters separating the continents of Asia and North America at that latitude are only 56 miles wide and three islands divide the distance, so that the longest single water stretch is 25 miles. This could easily have been crossed in a day by the rafts or hide boats of fifteen or more thousand years ago. In good weather the view from island to island and thence to the mainland is clear.

If the crossing was on foot it probably occurred near the end of the Ice Age. The waters of the earth's oceans were then in considerable part piled up in ice glaciers a mile or more in height over much of the northern part of the earth's surface. Ocean waters were accordingly several hundred feet lower than they are now. At Bering Strait the bottoms, now several hundred feet under water at the line of the islands, would have been above water. Not only at the island line but for a hundred miles southward, the bottoms are likely to have been dry land between the continents during the closing stages of the Ice Age.

The forces creating this causeway would also have closed the continent of North America at the Far North. If a massive cover of glacial ice lay over all the approaches to the causeway for hundreds or thousands of miles on either side, primitive man, who relied on game and fish for a living, would have been unable to reach, or to leave the causeway. Climatologists, however, dispose of this possibility by pointing out that, although lofty sheets of ice extended from the centers of ice accumulation over regions at long distances from the centers, frayed edges and extensive corridors were formed at the extremities. The regions of eastern Siberia and western Alaska were the extremities and were warmed, besides, by the Japan Current. Much of eastern Siberia, as well as the coastal region of western Alaska, was never touched by glaciation. Across central Alaska, moreover, and through the interior from north to south, ran broad bands of unglaciated country along the valleys of the Yukon and the MacKenzie. Alongside the spine of the Rocky Mountains, on the eastern side, ran a corridor offering migrants passage southward.

Corroborative evidence of the Asiatic origin of the American Indians is the marked resemblance, facially and otherwise, of living representatives of the two racial strains. The prominent high cheekbones, the broad flattish face, frequent incidence of dental peculiarities, straight, coarse black hair, sparse beard, and, a feature especially noticeable, slant eyes (an appearance given by a fold of skin over the inner corner of the eye) point to a common origin. The American Indians most pronouncedly Mongoloid were the later arrivals in the New World and this corresponds with a growing predominance of the Mongoloids in northeastern Asia. The Athapaskans and the Eskimos were latecomers to America and are more notably Mongoloid.

Whether migration was by land or by water it occurred in small groups and over thousands of years. Advances could have been in response to pressures from behind, or to the pull of open land ahead, or to the attraction of abundant game in the New World. No deterrent of clashes over hunting grounds could have kept the first hunters from spreading out, inasmuch as the New World then was without other inhabitants.

The migrants drifted southward by the corridor on the eastern side of the Rocky Mountains until they were beyond the area of glaciation. They moved into New Mexico, into Middle America, and presently into South America. A segment went eastward across the Great Plains and skirted the edge of the glacial lobe of the Wisconsin ice sheet in what is now the Old Northwest. They pressed on to what is now the shores of the Atlantic Ocean, indeed beyond. A continental shelf—now submerged—then extended eastward as a low-lying plain a distance of 250 miles in the latitude of New England and New York, and 100 miles in the latitude of

Chesapeake Bay. This was a feeding ground for mammoths, mastodon, and other big game, as indicated by skeletal remains occasionally brought up in fishermen's drag-nets, and it constituted a hunting ground for early Indians.

Culturally, early man in North America was in the Paleolithic Age at the time of crossing. He knew the arts of chipping stone to his needs; he manufactured utensils such as stone knives and scrapers for butchering and skinning game, spear points for projectiles that were hurled by an atlatl, and choppers used in a variety of work. He did not know the arts of the bow and arrow or the polishing of stone. He had not yet domesticated animals such as horses or cattle, though he had the dog. He knew the fishing arts and used them when near the water. He understood the uses of fire and the means of producing it. He knew nothing of the arts of the wheel.

In the portion of the New World now held by the United States, evidences of the presence of Paleolithic man are most impressive in the Far Southwest. They are also the most indisputably ancient. Artifacts are found in excavations ten or more feet below the earth's surface and in caves containing successive layers of Indian debris, exhibiting successive stages of cultural advance. Spear points, stone scrapers, and stone knives, used in the Paleolithic Age, have been found associated there with the bones of species of animals that, until their extinction, were the primary food of the hunters. The most revealing discoveries are those at so-called kill sites, where hunters drove big game over cliffs, or into arroyos, in which the beasts were dis-patched and butchered preparatory to being carried off to Indian lodges. Such sites have been excavated in the High Plains of the Southwest, where bones of mastodon, mammoth, and great bison have appeared in close association with artifacts known to date back ten thousand or more years.

The dating of artifacts is a highly technical and sophisticated art. It requires the skills of geologists for analyzing and dating strata of soils, and for identifying rock debris containing artifacts. It calls into use climatology—the science of historic changes of climate. It employs knowledge of zoological structure to identify and reconstruct skeletal remains of extinct animal types. It uses typology—the science of artifact types and their changes—time-wise and space-wise. It calls into service modern chemistry and physics to apply radioisotope techniques to the dating of organic matter found in association with artifacts, especially the carbon 14 technique, which permits dating samples as old as thirty thousand years. This technique was devised in 1955, and has been steadily improved since, most recently by the technique of racemization, which carries the system of dating back many thousands of years more. Tree-ring dating has also been developed, which permits determining the age of less ancient sites and has added detail to vistas opened by the carbon 14 test. The combination of these arts has revolutionized the study of prehistoric man.

Among the artifacts uncovered from the High Plains of the Southwest the earliest are the type known as the Clovis fluted spear points. A discovery of them in unmistak-able association with mammoth remains was made near Dent, Colorado, in 1932. Such points have been found southward as far as Mexico, and eastward through the Middle West and the Ohio Valley to the Atlantic seaboard.

Points more fully fluted but smaller in size, and representing an apparently later culture, were found in 1926 at a famous site near Folsom, New Mexico. Here a point was found firmly implanted in the fossil ribs of an extinct species of great bison, common then in that area. Similar projectiles have since been discovered distributed over the United States, but most numerously and in most ancient sites in the Far Southwest.

In the Pacific Northwest spearheads of a different kind, but also of great antiquity, have been uncovered. They have the shape of a willow leaf and are without stem. How they were attached to a shaft is still uncertain, but shaft splints, tree gum, and binding twine could have been the means. Such points are also found in refuse heaps of animal and fish bones, notably along the Dalles of the Columbia River, a favorite salmon-fishing ground. In sites on the coast of the Pacific Northwest have been discovered harpoon heads made of bone, indicating a society in which not only game but also fish and marine animals were primary sources of food. The name applied by archaeologists to this culture is "Old Cordilleran," and it is dated from about 9000 to 5000 B.C.

By 9000 B.C. the two Americas were occupied by a scattered hunting population. The southern continent was occupied less fully than the northern, and finds are correspondingly few there. On the Peruvian coast projectile points have turned up similar to those of the Old Cordilleran and dated at about 8500 B.C. At the tip of South America, in Patagonia, points were found of date c. 8700 B.C., exhibiting Cordilleran traits but with stems somewhat pronged, and labeled "Magellan" by archaeologists. Ancient sites in Brazil have also been excavated.

At southwestern sites in North America the economy was herd hunting—the stampeding of game in herds over cliffs or into dead-end arroyos, and dispatching them at leisure. In coastal areas, as in the Pacific Northwest, fishing was a main reliance, salmon runs offering food in especial abundance. Hunting and fishing were normally accompanied by gathering of seeds, roots, berries, fruits, and nuts in season.

Cultivation of wild plants occurred, in incipient stages in some areas. The center of this advance was Middle America. Origins are dated at about 5000 B.C. by scientists applying carbon 14 tests. Experimentation consisted of transferring from a wild state plants of generous seed, such as sunflowers, vines producing beans and squashes, and roots and tubers, into tended plots and sustaining or even increasing the yield by a minimum of care.

Among the forces stimulating experimentation was a change of climate in Middle America. Temperatures rose and rainfall became less plentiful in a period extending from 5000 to 2500 B.C. In parts of Middle America temperatures became tropical and heat was accompanied by semi-aridity or aridity. Aridity, greater than that of the present, prevailed then in the Far Southwest of what is now the United States. In this period the mammoth, mastodon, and great bison, sustained earlier by the lush vegetation of the pluvial age, vanished. Their disappearance, and the decrease of smaller game, encouraged experimentation in plant cultivation.

Experimentation was stimulated also by the presence in Middle America of a large assortment of wild plants. In addition to those already mentioned, there were gourds, rhizomes, fibers, and grasses, including the one from which maize was developed. Here also were peoples of progressiveness and capacity for organized effort who were to show abilities in fields outside of agriculture—in the fields of art, architecture, and science.

In all the early stages of culture, except those of the frozen North, the simple gathering of wild food was a supplement to that acquired in other ways. The people of the forest learned to rely on its fruits. In some areas gathering was central to subsistence. In parts of California, for example, acorns were collected. From them a mash was made which was subjected to a leaching process, to rid it of tannic acid, before cooking or baking. Where gathering was an important part of the economy it was accompanied by the development of basketry as receptacles for food. Pottery was another cultural advance made in the period after 1000 B.C. It was an accompaniment of agriculture and spread to what is now the United States from Middle America or South America.

Migrations of Indians on a continent-wide scale had ceased thousands of years before the discovery of America by Europeans. In parts of North America Indian cultures of a high degree of advancement had become established. In Middle America the Maya, by A.D. 1000, had made advances in science, in the arts, and in the modes of life.

Language is a measure of residential stability. In 1492 there were 2000 Indian languages established in the New World, each unintelligible except to those who spoke it. By ethnologists these have been reduced to basic languages by the study of word roots and forms. For the part of America north of Mexico the number of basic languages used to be set by ethnologists at 56. The number was later reduced to about 18 for the whole of North America.

The most widespread of the linguistic stocks was the Algonquian, as indicated on the map (1). It embraced several scores of tribes, speaking dialects of the basic language. Their area extended with interruptions from the Atlantic Ocean to the Rockies and from Hudson Bay to the Tennessee. They encompassed all the New England tribes and some of the tribes of the Middle Atlantic states. They also included the tribes of Virginia—for example the Powhatan Confederacy—and the tribes of the Great Lakes region. They extended westward to the Rocky Mountain area. All these Indians spoke dialects of the same basic tongue. This does not mean that they were necessarily friendly to each other. They might be bitter enemies. In the Great Lakes area were the Ojibwa, wild-rice gatherers, the Ottawa, who were the center of Pontiac's uprising, and the Menominee. In the Illinois country lay the Illinois Confederacy, and west of them, the Sauk and Fox, ancient enemies of the French and later implicated in the Black Hawk War. At the base of the northern Rockies were the Blackfoot, the terror of the fur traders, and to the south of them, the Cheyenne and Arapaho, whom Custer crushed at the Battle of the Washita. The Cheyenne were cut off from the main body of Algonquians by a wedge of Sioux. The map shows that there were considerable migrations of tribes even after languages had become established.

Another powerful Indian stock, though much less numerous and widespread than the Algonquian, was the Iroquoian. It comprised a main body in the north, and two smaller southern groups. The northern one consisted of the Five Nations of New York, the famous People of the Long House, and, in addition, the Neutral or Neuter Nation, the Erie, and the Huron. The two southern groups of the Iroquois were the Cherokee—the largest single tribe of Iroquois—and the Tuscarora of North Carolina. The Cherokee must have become separated from the northern tribes at a very early day, judging from the great divergence of their dialect from that of the

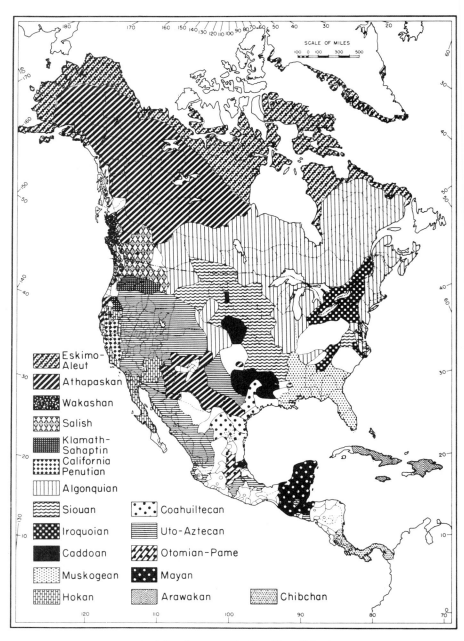

1. Indian Language Families (from Driver)

northern Iroquois. Some students of Iroquois history think that the parent stock was southern; others believe that it was northern, with an ancestral home in the lower St. Lawrence Valley.

Among the northern Iroquois a famous league developed—the League of the Iroquois, which was a confederation of the five New York tribes. It was organized about the middle of the 16th century. It was the most advanced political organization among the Indians north of Mexico. Its governing organ was a League Council, in which each tribe had one vote. Every decision had to be approved by all tribes, so that every tribe had a veto power in the League Council. The local government of the individual tribe was the tribal council, where sat the sachems, who represented the tribe in the League, and, in addition, local war chiefs.

The League proved of great military value to the Iroquois. Previously its tribes had hardly been holding their own in a seesaw warfare against their Algonquian neighbors. After the formation of the League the Iroquois took the offensive in every direction. First (1648–49) they crushed their own kinsmen, the Huron, with whom they had been at war for generations, and related tribes who had befriended the Huron—the Neutral Nation (1653), the Erie (1653), and the Susquehanna (1675).

Then they turned on the Algonquians. They sent the Ottawa flying to the west. They decimated the Illinois (1682) and broke the Delaware (1720). They overawed the New England tribes, regularly collecting tribute from them. In the days of the Massachusetts Bay colony their tribute collectors came regularly to the New England tribes through the passes of the Berkshires and the Mohawk Trail. The League in its best days lorded it over all the country from the Kennebec to the Tennessee and from the Hudson to the Mississippi. It was a factor even in international politics because of its early and normal hostility to the French.

This dominant position was held with a fighting force incredibly small. The total League population in 1600 was only about 5500 souls. A century later it had doubled, for the tribes had a practice of incorporating beaten foes into their ranks, especially in the case of cognate people. But the League could never have had in its palmiest days more than 12,000 population, or 2500 warriors. Its astounding military success was due to a number of factors—its effective organization; the lack of organization of its foes; and its early acquisition of firearms from the Dutch. Its strategic location was important. The League could send out war parties by way of the Allegheny and Ohio rivers to the Illinois country. They could go southward by way of the Susquehanna to the back country of Pennsylvania, Virginia, and the Carolinas. They could move eastward from the Hudson into New England. The League held a central, a key position. It controlled the fur trade of the interior. It served as a middleman in the trade to the Europeans. It crushed the Huron largely in order to consolidate its hold on the fur trade. It showed exceptional political astuteness.

Culturally the northern Iroquois were less advanced than they were politically. They were a ferocious people. They took a sadistic delight in torture of prisoners, which they carried to a high state of refinement, as well with women as with men. The southern Iroquois also showed great political astuteness. The Tuscarora, after trouble with the whites in 1722, moved north, and joined their New York brethren. Then the League became the League of the Six Nations. The Cherokee also showed astuteness. In 1820 they adopted a written constitution under the influence of missionaries, a constitution modeled on that of the United States.

A third powerful linguistic stock in the East was the Muskogean. This group lived in the region of the Gulf Plains. It consisted of the Creeks, the Choctaw, the Chickasaw, the Seminole, and others. It had a central location in the struggle between England, France, and Spain for the control of the Gulf of Mexico and the lower Mississippi. Its members were culturally well advanced. They lay within the cultural influence of the Caribbean tribes.

But they did not have the political aptitude of the Iroquois. They allowed themselves to be divided against each other by European powers. The Creek vacillated between the English and the Spanish. The Chickasaw took the English side; the Choctaw were normally aligned with the French. The Muskogean had the further misfortune of occupying lands destined to become the cotton kingdom of the world, which the whites were increasingly determined to have. They were already under some pressure to move by the time of the American Revolution. In the presidency of Andrew Jackson they were for the most part forced to leave their homes and settle in the region that became the Indian Territory.

Another great linguistic stock was the Siouan, now regarded by ethnologists as being basically the same as the Muskogean. It comprised an eastern and a western wing, with the bulk of its strength west of the Mississippi. The eastern wing comprised the Catawba tribe in the Carolinas, and a tiny tribe, the Biloxi, in Mississippi. How the Siouan stock came to be so widely scattered and which wing was the wanderer from the ancestral home are questions that are obscured in the mists of the past.

The Indian population north of Mexico was relatively sparse when the Europeans arrived. It was estimated by James Mooney of the Bureau of Ethnology in 1928 to have been not more than a million. His estimate was based on a detailed examination of the members in individual tribes gathered from the testimony of early traders, explorers, and missionaries. Later estimates, by scholars using the techniques of archaeology and ethnology, were higher. In 1969 they placed the number north of Mexico as three million or more.

The Indian population north of Mexico was not merely sparse but, what is equally important, it was not growing. The reasons for this failure to increase have to be guessed at. Probably two important reasons were the constant warfare among Indian tribes and the frequent epidemics of disease. These reasons were stressed by all early American scholars of Indian history. They are, however, not a complete explanation. Persistent warfare and devastating epidemics of disease have not prevented a vast increase of European populations.

Probably a more fundamental reason for the failure of the Indian population to grow was that a larger number could not have found food to live on in North America. The Indians north of Mexico were a primitive people. They could do no more than scratch the surface of nature's resources. A continent that in 1975 supported about 226,400,000 people north of Mexico could not have provided food for more than 3,500,000 Indians. The more primitive a civilization, the more the land needed to support it. The inability of the Indian to effectively exploit his resources is illustrated in the case of the countless buffalo of the western plains. The Indian could not effectively hunt the buffalo until he got the horse, and the horse came only with the Spaniards.

The fact that the Indian population north of Mexico was so sparse and was so primitive in culture was of major significance to the frontier. It gave the frontier the opportunity and the justification needed for brushing the Indian society aside and supplanting it with a European society. If the Indian population had been greater and had been at a higher stage of development, the process of simply supplanting it would not have been feasible. In Central America, in Mexico for instance, Indians could not be brushed aside. They were too numerous per square mile, and on too high a level of development. They had to be allowed to remain, and Mexican society is today basically an Indian society. It is an Indian society with a veneer of Spanish civilization. Genetically it is about 85 percent Indian and only 15 percent Spanish or mixed blood. The same is true of other Spanish-American states. Within the zone of the United States, where Indian population was sparse and at a low level of culture, it could be simply brushed aside by the frontier.

Indian Culture

INDIAN SOCIETY ROSE stage by stage at varying rates in different parts of North America during the thousands of years preceding the advent of Europeans. This evolution, which is the domain of the archaeologist, lies outside the sphere of the historian dealing with the process whereby Indian cultures were supplanted. Only the closing stages of the evolution, as revealed within the area now the United States, can be chronicled here.

In 1492 Indian society was a mosaic of cultures in United States latitudes. Each culture was a product of such forces as regional environment, development at different rates from Paleo-Indian origins, and divergences of tradition and language. In the eastern part of this territory, in the woodland extending from approximately the line of the Great Plains to the seaboard of the Atlantic, the cultures were basically alike. They centered on primitive villages and represented a stage in culture dating back to about 2000 B.C. They are classified by archaeologists and anthropologists as "eastern woodland." In some areas a later development known as "Mississippian" was found, which included the tradition of the "Mound Builders."

Within these cultures economic life consisted still of hunting, fishing, gathering, and agriculture. Hunting was with weapons more advanced than those of the Paleo-Indian. The chief instrument was the bow and arrow, which is thought to have come to the Indians in a process of diffusion from Siberia at some time between 2000 and 1000 B.C. The bow and arrow was more effective for hunting than the spear and atlatl. It had greater range and accuracy, and was usable in bringing down winged game, as the spear was not. Reliance was still widely placed on organized drives in hunting. A favorite procedure was to drive game by forest fires upon concealed hunters, a method adopted by whites in the colonial period. Individual hunters made use of snares and traps cunningly devised.

Along streams and upon the shores of lakes and sea, fishing was a major occupation. The means employed were bone-made hooks. Where shellfish grew in abundance, as at Muscle Shoals, on the middle Tennessee, they were exploited in the season of sluggish waters, when the stream bed could be invaded safely. Shell beds at Muscle Shoals were worked as early as 5000 B.C., as indicated by shell middens at the Eva site on the Tennessee. The middens were the refuse of millennia of Indian life, and they form, for the anthropologist, storehouses of historical data. The gathering of shell foods was the work of entire communities. So also was the gathering of berries, roots, and nuts, which gave women and children congenial employment.

In the eastern woodlands farming was increasing in importance by 1492. The major crop was Indian corn, which was a plant indigenous to America. It is one of the major contributions of the Indians to the world's agriculture. It was developed from a primitive Mexican grass, *Zea mays,* that grew tiny ears of pod corn. Drill cores driven 200 feet beneath the present level of Mexico City have brought up cobs, and ancient pollen, exhibiting the species in its origins. Evidence found in Bat Cave in New Mexico indicate that a cross was effected, about a thousand years ago, of this grass with a native Mexican grass, teosinte, and the result was corn of the modern type. This spread rapidly across Middle America, northward into New Mexico, and eastward across the whole region of the eastern woodlands. It became a major food reliance of the Indians of the eastern woodlands, supplementing what was obtained from hunting and fishing and from gathering wild fruits and berries.

The appearance of corn in the eastern woodlands has been placed by archaeologists at about the year A.D. 1000. The plant arrived there by infusion from Middle America. What its travel route was—whether by way of the Gulf Plains or the Great Plains or the West Indies—is a question concerning which archaeologists differ. In Illinois, excavations at the Koster site reveal that it had become a major food reliance of the Indians by the year A.D. 1000, supplementing what was obtained from hunting, fishing, and gathering wild fruits and berries. European travelers among the Iroquois at a later day reported large fields of Indian corn and gardens of beans, squashes, and tomatoes. Travelers among the southern Indians reported similarly on extensive cornfields. By the time of the advent of Europeans, corn was sufficiently at home in the eastern woodlands to be part of mythology and ceremonial. It was considered a gift of nature to nature's children and two festivals—the winter festival and the green corn dance—were tributes paid to it.

Corn became for successive frontiers of whites a major food reliance. One of its attractions was that it could be raised on unplowed land. A hole was merely cut into the ground with an axe, the seed dropped into it, and the soil hilled up over it. Its growth in unplowed land was of major importance since cultivation of land still full of stumps was impossible. Another allurement of corn was its generous yield. Its yield was far higher per plant than that of wheat, rye, or barley, which Europeans were accustomed to grow. A third attraction was that its tops and leaves made excellent cattle fodder, so that cattle and human food were provided at the same time.

The taste of corn was something the first American frontiersman had to get accustomed to. Ultimately Americans learned to like it and Indian corn is still widely used in America for bread. But in Europe the taste for it was acquired much more slowly, and for several centuries it was grown there only as cattle fodder. Even today it is less accepted in Europe for human food than in America.

Corn was not the only great contribution of the Indian to the white man's agriculture. The Irish potato, mistakenly so called, was another. The Irish potato was actually a contribution of Peru, from where it spread northward. It was then carried by the Spanish explorers to Europe, where it transformed the food economy of the poor, especially the poor in Ireland.

On the Northwest coast salmon was a chief food of the Indian. Salmon were caught with nets in great quantity as they ascended and descended the streams of the Pacific Northwest. The fish were dried and pulverized and stored for the winter in large moisture-proof baskets. The fish diet was supplemented by wild roots of various sorts and wild berries. In California and in the Great Basin wild seeds and nuts, especially acorns, were a major food asset.

In the Southwest there were areas of intensive agriculture, chiefly of corn and vegetable production. Irrigation was widely practiced. Evidence has been found of hundreds of miles of irrigation canals that had been in use among the Indians of the area before the coming of the white man. Irrigation called for a high degree of social organization. The highest social cultures among the American Indians at the time of the discovery of America were in the Southwest and in Middle America.

On the Great Plains a principal food reliance was the buffalo. It was hunted with bow and arrow and by organized drives. The purity and rarity of the atmosphere were relied on for the curing of the meat. The lean of the flesh was cut up into slabs and hung to dry in the sun or before a fire. When dried, the slabs were sweet and wholesome. In favorable portions of the Plains agriculture was practiced to supplement hunting.

Tobacco was a third great Indian contribution. Many other plants developed by the Indians were of importance to the world—for example, tomatoes, beans, pumpkins, and peanuts. It is estimated that four-sevenths of the present production of world agriculture, in terms of value, is derived from plants developed by the Indians.

The shelters of the Indians were evidence of stability. They varied from region to region. In the Northeast they were constructed of saplings and were covered with skins and mats. The rectangular residences of the Iroquois, the famous "long houses" of the clans, were of such construction. Others, common on the Northwest coast, were lean-tos, built of a framework of poles, covered with hides or skins. On the Great Plains tipis, covered with buffalo hides, were widespread. The difference in the character of housing helps to account for a more determined resistance to white encroachments by the woodland Indians than that of the Great Plains Indians.

The degree of civilization of any society is indicated not only by its food reliance but also by its trade. Extensive trade is an indication that the production of a people has become large enough and specialized enough to allow for exchanges of goods.

The Indians of North America were for the most part self-sufficient. But some trade was maintained by them, in every case resting on the possession of some special tribal asset. The Iroquois asset was a strategic location. The League controlled the Lakes route, the Hudson route, the Ohio route, and the route of the upper Susquehanna. They became persistent traders—the most notable in America. Iroquois history was largely shaped by considerations of trade. The Huron were destroyed in order to take over their tribal trade. In the case of other tribes trade was a result of owning an important natural resource. A tribe, possessing a quarry with flint that flaked well and produced good arrow and spear points, made a business of manufacturing and trading them. Famous quarries of that kind were at Flint Ridge in Ohio and

Hot Springs in Arkansas. The obsidian rock of the Yellowstone Park area was another valuable resource for the manufacture of spear points.

Trade was sometimes the outcome of the possession of salt. The Shawnee were famous salt traders as the owners of salt springs in Ohio and Kentucky. Sometimes a special skill acquired by a tribe or a family, such as in the manufacture of baskets, pottery, or blankets, was the basis of trade, especially in the Southwest. The persons carrying on trade were frequently women. Often a woman in a tribe would be sent for marriage to a neighboring tribe in order that she might establish a trading base.

In some regions trade had developed to the point where an annual trading fair was held, to which came tribes from a considerable distance. During such fairs Indian traders were protected against violence by a system of guest friendship. Western localities which were famous centers of such fairs were Cheyenne, Wyoming, and Colorado Springs.

Partly for trade purposes, a sign language was in existence in the West—a kind of Indian Esperanto. This reached its highest development in the region of the Great Plains, but it was understood in elementary form as far eastward as the Appalachians.

The Indian trade was the base on which that of the frontier was built. The habits of trade, the trade trails, and personal connections of native traders all served the frontier. They became the mechanism for white exploration of the interior. Virtually without exception frontier explorers made use of the Indian knowledge of trade trails. When the Lewis and Clark expedition moved across the continent from St. Louis it was guided from one tribe to another by Indians. The guide part of the way was a woman, Sacajawea.

The frontier trade, transferred from Indians to whites, became a force disintegrating and breaking down the ancient structure of Indian life. Firearms brought by traders to Indians set them back on the ladder of civilization. Many eastern Indians who had advanced in farming tended to become hunters again. Firearms, moreover, revolutionized the relations between tribes. When the Iroquois obtained guns from the Dutch they became a scourge upon neighboring tribes for a thousand miles around. Tribes in flight from them pressed upon others, who in turn pressed upon still others.

Traders also brought the Indians European diseases previously unknown to them, especially smallpox, cholera and gonorrhea. These diseases played havoc with Indians, who had not built up resistance to them. Epidemics decimated the tribes. The Indians gave as good as they got. In exchange for gonorrhea they gave syphilis to the Europeans. The sailors of Columbus brought back syphilis from the West Indies to Spain. In the 1490's there was a dreadful syphilis epidemic that ran with explosive force through Europe for eight or ten years. The disease was known in some regions as West Indian measles, in others as the French disease. The transfer of syphilis to Europe, considering its toll through the centuries, was one of the greatest catastrophes that Old World society suffered—worse than the Black Plague.

In addition to new diseases Indians acquired rum from traders. The disruptive effect of the rum trade on Indians runs all through this book. Also, Indians obtained from white traders the implements of European origin—kettles, knives, blankets, and beads—which broke down Indian self-sufficiency. Finally, the traders ensnared the Indians into the wars of rival European powers.

The touch of the white trader and of white society was withering to the Indian. In some cases it was not immediately destructive—it was often constructive at first. It was stimulating in matters of art forms and culture. But not long after whites established close contact with any tribe the latter would drop to half its former size in population. It would decline partly for the reasons mentioned above, but also for the reason that the old tribal equilibrium of habits, the equilibrium of old ways of life, which had served as a protection, had broken down. Disorganization of habit and outlook would appear perhaps the most destructive of all the factors in the breakdown of Indian society.

The Indians north of Mexico were a backward society. They remained in their primitive state longer than the Indians of Middle America. They were idealized almost out of recognition by James Fenimore Cooper. They appear in truer light in Francis Parkman's writings. His *History of the Conspiracy of Pontiac* and *The Oregon Trail* are admirable accounts of Indian psychology and society. But even Parkman overstresses the dramatic and the romantic in Indian life. His eloquent prose casts a glamour over Indian society. A truer picture appears in the journals of explorers such as Lewis and Clark, and in the writings of missionaries and the accounts of traders as gathered in *The Jesuit Relations* and *Early Western Travels,* both edited by Reuben G. Thwaites. In these sources Indian life appears as an existence that was recessive and harsh.

Indian society north of Mexico was not merely backward, it was less adaptable than that of Middle America. The northern Indians were slow to accept forced change in their mode of life. They were likely to break before they bent. In the case of Negroes, brought to America from the wilds of Africa, there was relatively quick adjustment to new conditions and new needs. Negroes yielded more easily to force in accepting a new order. They accepted the discipline of regular work, and even, while in a state of slavery, rose steadily on the ladder of civilization. Northern Indians were less adaptable than Negroes. If the attempt was made to change their life by force, they perished. Such northern Indians as were enslaved in colonial times, and forced to work in slavery, usually died quickly.

It was the tragedy of Indian history that the most progressive centers of Indian culture, those in Middle America, were the ones that were crushed first by the Spanish conquest. They were broken in the dramatic episode of the expansion of Spain early in the 16th century. The Indians north of Mexico were of less progressive spirit. Their society was brushed aside and displaced for the most part by a white society. It was the tragedy of the displacement, brought about by the frontier, that it was so rough and callous. In that tragedy not only the Indian, but the frontier, suffered greatly.

The Virginia Tidewater

ON APRIL 10, 1606, an era opened in the history of English colonization of America. On that day James I, Queen Elizabeth's successor on the throne of England, chartered a company for the colonization of Virginia. The charter conferred on two groups of English colonizers the entire North Atlantic seaboard from the 34th to the 45th parallels of latitude—roughly the area between Nova Scotia and the southern line of North Carolina. It ignored the claims of Spain and France to that area.

The groups named in the charter were the London and Plymouth companies. The London Company was given the area between the 34th and the 38th parallels; to the Plymouth Company went the area between the 41st and 45th parallels. The intervening space was left to be developed by either. Inland the grant included all territory within 100 miles of the coast, all rights of trade with the natives, and the exploitation of any gold, silver, or copper mines. A fifth part of any gold or silver and a fifteenth part of any copper produced were reserved to the Crown. Christian consideration was expressed for the natives, who were conceived of as savages and infidels living in darkness and in miserable ignorance of the true knowledge and worship of God. They were to be offered true religion and were to be won to human civility and to a settled and quiet government. Their lands in the meantime passed to the two companies.

The London group was the more active of the two. It dispatched a fleet to Chesapeake Bay in December 1606. The fleet did not match the one sent by Spain to Hispaniola more than a century earlier. There were three ships, compared with seventeen of Columbus's second expedition to the New World. The largest was of 100 tons, the other two were 40 tons and 20 tons, respectively. The ships were manned by 120 men and boys, compared with 1200 of the Spanish fleet. The passage proved stormy and in the course of its four months sixteen persons perished. The remainder effected a settlement 50 miles up the James River, a reflection of fear of Spanish interference. Though peace had been made by James I with Spain, it included no recognition of England's rights to plant colonies in North America. The site also

15

reflected hope of developing trade with the Indians and of finding gold mines and a passage to the western sea.

None of these hopes materialized. Trade with the Indians was meager, no gold mines were discovered, and the passage by river or strait to the western sea proved a delusion. The colony barely survived the winter. Its site, chosen, contrary to instructions, on low ground near swamps, was beset by malaria and diseases carried by impure drinking water, which proved more destructive than Spaniards or Indians. The colonists consisted of gentlemen, artisans, and common laborers. They had little incentive to work. They produced insufficient food and were saved from starvation only by the activity of Captain John Smith, through whose efforts a quantity of maize was grown and more was obtained from the Indians. The number of settlers fell off within a year to 53 and only the arrival of rescue ships sent out from England saved the colony from disappearance.

In 1609 the London group obtained a charter separating it from the Plymouth group and came to be called the Virginia Company of London, or simply the Virginia Company. The charter provided an improved corporate structure and enlarged boundaries. Its coastal boundaries were drawn to run 200 miles north and 200 miles south of Old Point Comfort. They ran in the interior "west and northwest" to the South Sea. The company structure took on the form of a joint-stock enterprise, its members including 56 guilds or companies and, in addition, 659 persons. Additional membership and an increased capital were sought in a vigorous campaign to sell stock to the public.

Stock was offered at a price of £12½ per share. A purchaser of one or more shares became an Adventurer of the Company—he adventured his capital. Anyone who undertook to migrate to Virginia, paying his own way, was a Planter, entitled to a share of stock. All the costs of the enterprise were to be borne by the company; all produce and profits were to go to the company. Profits were to be distributed at intervals to the Adventurers and Planters in proportion to their stock and to services rendered. The date of the first distribution was left unspecified, which was prudent, considering the uncertainties of the enterprise. Control of the company was made to rest with the so-called general court, attendance at the sessions of which was open to all shareholders. The latter were entitled to participate in debate, to vote on issues of policy, and to choose officers, who would implement policy. The reorganization was an improvement over the first charter, and remained Viginia's basic constitution until it became a crown colony.

In order to increase the sale of stock in the company, Robert Johnson, a leader in it, published unofficially and anonymously, but authoritatively, a pamphlet entitled *Nova Britannia*, describing in glowing terms the public and private benefits to be gained from joining the enterprise. To those having religious leanings, he emphasized the uplift purposes of the company with respect to the heathen; for the patriotic, the advance of empire interests by providing raw materials, creating an outlet for the unemployed, and opening a vent for English manufactures. For those hankering after returns on investment, he stressed the likelihood of attractive dividends, both in cash and in virgin wilderness lands. Dividends were definitely forecast, which in the charter had been only vaguely promised. They would begin at the end of seven years both in cash and in lands. The pamphlet suggested that encouragement be given to wealthy groups of shareholders to establish at once six or more plantations besides

Jamestown, in the valley of the James. In other pamphlets of the day the public was invited to join the venture which the Crown had so attractively initiated.

But more was required than a new charter to ensure survival and prosperity for the colony. An economy was needed that would support an expanding population in the wilderness. A landowning system was necessary that would give incentive to the landless in England to cross the ocean to become owners of farms. Political institutions were requisite also that would ensure to emigrants the basic rights of liberty which Englishmen had at home. These had been merely foreshadowed in the charter.

The company undertook to meet these requirements. It gave up the search for gold, or a passage to the western sea, or the lure of trade with the Indians. It turned to the more prosaic pursuits of farming, for which Virginia seemed especially well suited. To Captain John Smith, who served for a time as acting governor, the colony was a veritable New Arcadia. He described it in 1612 as

> a country that may have the prerogative over the most pleasant places of Europe, Asia, Africa, or America, for large and pleasant navigable rivers: heaven and earth never agreed better to frame a place for mans habitation being of our constitutions, were it fully matured and inhabited by industrious people. Here are mountaines, hils, plaines, valleyes, rivers and brookes all running most pleasantly into a faire Bay, compassed, but for the mouth, with fruitful and delightsome land.

A blanket of forest extended over the tidewater of Virginia when the white man arrived. It presented a problem of clearance to early settlers. But it was less a problem than the forests of the interior. Those of the tidewater were light and free of underbrush. They were like an English park; the trees were scattered comparatively widely over the land, and the forest floor was relatively clear of underbrush. The absence of underbrush was probably the result of Indian hunting operations, of driving game toward concealed hunters by setting fire to the underbrush. This did not, in the moist tidewater climate, destroy older trees, it merely cleaned out the growth below.

The estuaries of tidewater Virginia, mentioned by John Smith, extended deep into the interior. They were important factors in the economic life of the early settlers. They were navigable by the small ships of the colonial period far into the interior—as far as the so-called fall line. What is equally important, they offered excellent landing places for oceangoing vessels at frequent intervals. On the James, good landing sites occurred about every half mile—tidewater Virginia was a kind of forested Venice.

The estuaries gave every planter in tidewater Virginia convenient access to the sea. Often his produce could be shipped to England and the supplies he needed could be received on his own wharf. Marketing of the annual crop occurred on the planter's wharf. Trading centers did not rise in tidewater Virginia as they did in the North, tying society together. The contrast between this dispersion of life and the close-knit unity of New England was marked. Some of the consequences of the dispersion appeared in the marketing of Virginia tobacco.

The population which flowed into Virginia was of mixed character, reflecting the classes of English society. A large number were rural middle-class, elements of the type that later flowed into New England. These people had means to pay for their passage in cash. Often they were prosperous tenants, or younger sons of landowners who had little hope of obtaining land by inheritance, because of their juniorage, and expected to acquire it in the New World. Some were merchants or the sons of merchants, accompanied by servants who paid for their passage by signing contracts of indenture. Many of the middle-class migrants were artisans who hoped to find in the New World fuller employment and better wages than in the Old. They proved to be more independent in America than bonded servants, and less inclined to remain long in uncongenial employment. Such elements are estimated to have constituted a third to a fourth of the total number who came to Virginia. They rose in the New World to a property-owning status and to leadership earlier than did bonded servants.

The bulk of the population flowing from England to the New World were the poorer tenants and laborers on the estates of the well-to-do, and artisans chronically unemployed. They were a part of a redundant population in England in the 17th century. Their removal was regarded with favor since it would correct dislocations in the economy, would create an overseas empire, and would mean for the unemployed a happy future. But how was the removal to be financed? The voyage to the New World was costly. Poor people by definition could not afford it, nor could they borrow the money. No commercial lender would think of making loans to the penniless, especially if the loans were to be used to take them out of reach of collection.

The answer to the problem was offered to the commercially minded. Every man or woman had assets—a body, two good arms, and freedom to sell these for a brief span of years. The sale could initially be made to a ship captain or merchant, or agent of one or the other. It would be registered in a written contract that would be negotiable, and that would set forth the terms of the transaction with a clarity beyond the possibility of later dispute. The ship captain would carry the migrant and the contract to Virginia and there the two would be offered for sale to a purchaser, who would pay all the incidental costs of the contract, the passage itself and its risks, and a profit to the seller. An incidental cost would be a decent outfit of clothing provided prior to embarkation. The risks would include possible sickness or death of the migrant en route. The contract would be comparable to an English apprenticeship indenture. The migrant, delivered safely to an employer in Virginia, would become an indentured servant.

Surrender of freedom for years to an unknown master in a distant country was a considerable price to pay for escape from England and arrival in the dreamland of the New World. It required imagination, ambition, and a certain amount of courage on the part of the migrant. In a sense the migrant was an adventurer, though hardly in the sense in which the term was used for a stockholder in the Virginia Company. As for the concept of using bonded immigrants to build an empire in North America, it was a contribution of the Virginia Company. It originated with stockholders seeking laborers for their colonial estates in 1617. The idea accorded well with the laws of supply and demand—oversupply in England, undersupply in America. The imbalance could be righted by converting free men temporarily into bonded servants.

Not all the poor in England were attracted by the idea of migration as bonded servants. The utterly indigent and the vagrant preferred to remain at home, wary of major risks. They found life in England hard, but not hard enough to drive them into the terrors of the unknown. They found refuge from starvation by going onto poor relief. Such an existence was bearable, though complained of as intolerable. These elements in the population would willingly have been contributed to the colonies by the local and Crown representatives, if that could have been done without compulsion. Occasional indigents did stray into indenture contracts, but proved to be the least satisfactory servants in America.

Historical sources of information concerning migration to America in the colonial period are the passenger lists kept by local authorities at the chief English ports of embarkation. Such lists, maintained at Bristol for the years 1654–86 and at Liverpool for the years 1697–1707, are of special value inasmuch as they concentrate on indentured servants and cover fairly long spans of years. The Bristol list, kept by order of the municipal authorities, shows that 36 percent of those on the list considered themselves farmers or husbandmen, 22 percent were in the artisan class, 10 percent were honest enough to say they were unskilled laborers, 1 percent thought they were gentlemen, about 25 percent were women. Young people formed a large fraction of those on the list, including numerous children whose parents or guardians thought their offspring would be best started in life overseas.

Registration offices for recording indenture contracts were maintained in the chief English ports of departure. In 1664 Parliament adopted a law requiring the recording of indenture contracts in those offices, partly as a means of discouraging the kidnapping of children. Immigrants bonded but without evidence of written contracts were required upon arrival and sale in the colonies to be taken to a local court to have verbal agreements recorded.

The length of indenture varied in the contracts, a four-year term being the most common. This went to workmen whose qualifications were thought favorable. Contracts requiring five or six years went to the less advantaged. Some well-situated artisans were able to specify that they were to be employed in America only at their own trades. Children consigned to indenture in the New World drew the longest term—seven years. These were the terms required, also, in apprenticeship contracts in England, but in the latter the master agreed to teach the youth a trade.

Merchants and ship captains found the trade in indentured servants a profitable form of business. The cost of transport of a servant was £5 to £6. This included food and drink in passage. Clothing and equipment, which were incidentals, came to £2 or £3. Agents, who recruited the servants and assumed responsibility for lodging them while they were waiting for ship departure, had to be reimbursed. The total outlay of the merchant or ship captain might be £10 or £12 per head. The sale price received by the ship captain from the Virginia purchaser depended on the need for labor and the quality of the servant. It might be as high as £20 or £30.

In the minds of shipmasters and merchants the flow of bonded servants was a movement of cargo. A two-way flow was necessary to ensure profit. The greater the flow each way, the greater the profit. The outflow was servants. The inflow was the product of their labor, which in Virginia was tobacco. The outflow was kept steady by propaganda of various kinds. It might take the form of brochures such as *Nova Britannia,* or less pretentious broadsides or handbills depicting the plenty and the freedom to be had in the overseas Paradise. For those who could not read, vocal pressures supplemented the printed. They consisted of dazzling accounts of life in the New World by agents in the employ of the shipmasters. The agents mingled with the poor in the byways and taverns of the cities or in depressed areas in the countryside. Paid at a rate per head of those induced to sign up, they were known in the 17th century as "spirits," from their habit of lurking in the shadows of the trade. Their name was an equivalent for rogues and cheats. They were charged with plying youths with liquor to induce signing indentures, then holding the victims in virtual imprisonment on board ship until the vessel departed for America.

Convicts were part of the flow to America, though their number was contemporaneously overdrawn. They were individuals who had been convicted of felonies and sentenced to long terms of imprisonment or death, had won reprieve to the colonies, and went out on seven-year indenture terms. In Virginia they were sold for use on exposed frontiers, where planters did not risk employing slaves. The importation of convict labor was objected to in the colonies. In 1670 it was forbidden by the Virginia Assembly, but the act was overriden by Parliament in 1717. The total of convicts sent to the American colonies was estimated to be about 50,000.

From continental Europe emigrants came in large numbers, the so-called redemptioners. They came usually in better circumstances than did indentured English migrants. Often they were able to raise part of the funds needed to emigrate by selling ancestral farms. They usually brought families, which increased the costs of passage. They paid whatever they had to a ship captain, who carried them to the New World with the understanding that the balance of their passage would be paid on arrival. It would be paid by an indenture arrangement with a planter, who cleared accounts with the ship captain. The length of service depended on the amount paid by the purchaser to the ship captain. Many of the redemptioners ended up in the tobacco colonies, though the bulk of them settled in the middle colonies.

The total of bonded servants was a large fraction of all the emigrants to the colonies prior to the American Revolution, estimated to have been from two-thirds to three-fourths of those who came. The flow was larger than normal in the disturbed period of civil war in England. It fell off during the first half of the 18th century, but increased in the years immediately preceding the American Revolution. The preference of these migrants for the southern and middle colonies over New England was that these offered large-scale commercial agriculture, which New England lacked.

The quality of life of the bonded white servant was a reflection of the character of the master. It reflected, also, the custom of the community. In the tobacco colonies the service might be hard; it might be harder than that of the Negroes. A callous master, with rights to only four or five years of a servant's time, was under temptation to make the most of the contract. He might be less exacting of a slave, bound for life and representing a larger capital investment. In each of the colonies bonded servants were protected by codes of law, but a servant, obliged to remain with a master, would be slow to take him to court. The insecurity of the servant was increased by the fact that he could be sold or transferred by bequest from one master to another.

The bonded servant was restricted in his freedom in various ways. He could not leave his master's premises or marry without consent, or engage in buying or selling, or frequent the local tavern. For disobedience he laid himself open to his master's lash; for infractions of the law he received heavier penalties than those imposed on free men. The penalty for an offense as serious as running away was an increase in the length of service.

The servant was entitled, on the expiration of his contract, to a departure payment known as ''freedom dues.'' This differed from colony to colony. It was established by custom or by law or by the terms of the indenture. In Virginia in the 17th century it was food and clothing for a year, and, in some cases, seed and tools. In Maryland it was 50 acres of land.

White bonded labor was preferred to black slave labor in Virginia during the greater part of the 17th century. It was cheaper and was available in great abundance in England during much of the century. The first half of the century was a period of severe unemployment in England and the unemployed were a burden to parish tax-payers. The taxpayers were eager to lighten the load and the unemployed were willing to escape intolerable living conditions by selling themselves as servants in America. Another factor was that some well-to-do English hoped to build great estates in Virginia worked by white servants or tenants.

In the latter half of the 17th century, however, the flow of white bonded servants to the colonies fell off. One of the causes for this was a change in attitude in England toward emigration after the Stuart restoration of 1660, a growing appreciation of the value to England of an expanding population.

But a more important reason was that white bonded labor was proving unsatisfactory in America, chiefly because it lacked the element of permanence. The good and reliable servants at the end of their term of indenture went off to the frontier and became independent farmers. An informed estimate is that 30 to 40 percent became independent farmers. The less reliable servants often ran away before the completion of their terms and were hard to recapture. A favorite refuge for runaway servants was North Carolina, which was attractive because land titles there were in a state of great confusion and land could be obtained for almost nothing.

The greatest weakness, however, in the system of white bonded labor was the ease with which land could be obtained on the edge of the plantation area. This drained off bonded servants—the desirable as well as the undesirable. It was the frontier factor that in the last analysis made white bonded labor in the South unfeasible and that made Negro slavery attractive to the planters. For planters slavery had the great advantage that it was servitude for life.

Negro slavery did not become a major force in Virginia until relatively late. While a few slaves arrived as early as 1619, it was not until the latter part of the 17th century and the early years of the 18th that Negro slavery became a vital part of the Virginia economy.

A combination of forces was responsible for the tardy arrival of slavery. One was the initial popularity of white bonded labor. Another was the relatively high cost of slaves resulting from the insatiable demand for them in the West Indies during the 17th century. Another was the inefficiency with which the slave trade was carried on by English entrepreneurs. A monopoly of the British trade was conferred by Parliament in 1662 on a corporation known as the Adventurers Trading to Africa. The corporation was mismanaged and was unsuccessful. In 1672 Parliament transferred the monopoly to the Royal African Company, but this was also unsuccessful. In 1698, in an overturn of policy, Parliament opened the trade to private adventurers on the condition that royalties be paid to the Royal African Company on all slaves brought into the English colonies. This was successful. The supply of slaves mounted and the needs of the southern colonies were more nearly met. Until well into the 18th century, however, Virginia planters preferred slaves trained to plantation life in the West Indies to those brought raw from Africa. This was true, also, elsewhere in the South.

The slave trade was objected to in some southern colonies, and import duties on slaves were levied in several of them. Such limitations were defended, not on moral grounds, but because of the loss of specie in payment of slaves and fear of insurrections. All restrictive laws were disallowed, however, by the imperial government. Later, in the Declaration of Independence, the English government was rebuked for its insistence on continuing the flow of slaves into the colonies.

The economy of tidewater Virginia for several years after the founding of Jamestown was directed chiefly to the production of food. Food needed to be imported to supplement what was grown or obtained from the Indians. An export crop was necessary, however, to meet the financial commitments of the Virginia Company, and was found in the form of tobacco.

Tobacco was indigenous to the New World. A variety of it was grown in the West Indies that was pleasing to the taste of the smoker. It was mild and sweet. Introduced to English society by the Elizabethan privateer and slave trader John Hawkins, it caught hold quickly in England and on the continent of Europe, and a market for it soon grew up there.

Tobacco was native to tidewater Virginia. But it was a variety inferior to the West Indian. It bit the tongue of the smoker. In 1613, however, John Rolfe, famous in American folklore as the husband of the Indian princess Pocahontas, carried the seed of the West Indian plant to Virginia, where it grew well. Within a dozen years it was established in Virginia, and its best grades were commanding prices on the English market not far below those of the Cuban varieties. Cultivation of it brought such profits that a veritable craze of production followed, to the disgust of James I, who frowned on tobacco smoking as injurious to the lungs until he himself acquired the habit. It also dismayed leaders of the Virginia Company who wished a diversified economy to become established in the colony. Virginia became an area of one-crop agriculture, dependent on the export of its great staple to England. So much did tobacco dominate the James Valley that some planters imported food for their own needs. Virginia and Maryland became the greatest tobacco producers in the world, so successful that they drove British competitors in the West Indies out of tobacco cultivation and into the production of sugar.

The advent of tobacco cultivation brought to fulfillment the promise of land dividends to Adventurers and Planters that had been held out in the charter of 1609 and in *Nova Brittania*. The first such dividend was authorized in 1618. To Adventurers went an initial installment of 100 acres for each share of stock held, and a second of the same amount after the first had been settled. Like dividends were to be paid to Planters who had come to Virginia prior to 1616, provided they had paid their passage. If Planters had come at company expense they were to receive, after having served the company seven years, a full land dividend, but were to pay annually a quitrent of two shillings for each 100 acres. Ordinary settlers who had come after 1616 at their own expense were to receive 50 acres initially and 50 acres more after the first allotment had been brought under cultivation.

For a short time Virginians enjoyed immense prosperity. They sold their tobacco in England at high prices. They rapidly expanded the area of tobacco cultivation. Virginia became dependent on the export of a single staple to England. After a time, price declines set in, and by 1660 the level was at a depression low which hung on year after year. From 1660 to the end of the century Virginia planters were in a state of chronic depression, with alternations only between years of greater and less calamity. They suffered one of the most prolonged farm depressions of American history.

The Virginia depression of the 17th century has been attributed to British governmental policy, specifically to the Navigation System, which was the heart of British colonial policy. This was a control system imposed on the export of certain commodities, including tobacco. Rice and indigo were others. The tobacco of Virginia or Maryland, if exported, had to be sent to England, even if its ultimate destination was the continent of Europe. Also, it had to be sent in vessels built and owned within the empire, and manned by sailors of whom three-fourths were subjects of the Crown. The purpose of this legislation was to confer a middleman function on British merchants in the sale of colonial tobacco, and on the British marine as carriers.

When Virginia tobacco entered England a customs duty had to be paid on it, which amounted in 1660 to 2*d*. a pound. This was a high duty, but only a third of what was imposed on Cuban tobacco entering England, a duty that was heavily restrictive. Any duty collected was, of course, ultimately paid by the British consumer. But Virginia producers considered it harmful to the Virginia tobacco interests in that it reduced consumption in England by raising the price.

Of the tobacco sent to England somewhere between a half and two-thirds was re-exported to the continent of Europe. British merchants were the middlemen in the re-exportation and sale. They earned the profits and commissions of the trade. When tobacco was re-exported part of the duty that had been paid was returned. It was a refund known as a "drawback," which, after 1660, was 1½*d*. a pound. Thus only a ½*d*. of the initial duty was retained by the Treasury. The question raised by this system was whether its burdens were responsible for the chronic depression that existed after 1660 in the Virginia tobacco industry.

One school of opinion among historians has been that it was responsible for the depression. According to this view, the market for tobacco in England was narrowed by the increased costs to British consumers which British policy entailed. The duty collected at the customs and passed on to the consumer was part of the increase. Another part was the middleman cost of handling tobacco re-exported to the Continent. This was mostly refunded, to be sure, but a halfpenny a pound was retained, and was a handicap in sales on the Continent. Additional cost stemmed from the expense of double shipment. Finally, the obligation to ship in British or colonial vessels was a handicap. Dutch shipment would have been much cheaper, since Hollanders were the most efficient carriers in the world. All these handicaps raised the price of tobacco so much, it is averred, that the colonial product could not be sold in competition with Cuban tobacco in Europe. According to this view, the market for Virginia and Maryland tobacco remained circumscribed from 1660 to the end of the century. It was not regained until so great a mass of unsold tobacco was piled up in England that the dumping of it on Europe at almost any price was resorted to. Only so was the continental market regained.

This view is challenged by historians who defend the British Navigation System. The argument made by this school is that under the Navigation System, a virtual monopoly of the English market for tobacco was given to Virginia and Maryland. Cuban tobacco was virtually excluded. This enabled Virginia to get established, and once established it could compete with any tobacco producers in the world. Also, the market in England was a large one, even though it was narrowed somewhat by price increases due to the duty. It was not narrowed very much, for tobacco smoking was and is a habit that is indulged at any cost, even at the sacrifice of essentials of life.

It is also maintained that the British middleman service in Europe was of major advantage to Virginia and Maryland. The British were experts in grading tobacco; they decided just where the different grades should be sent—a highly technical service. Such a service might have been performed by the Dutch in peacetime, but Amsterdam could not have been depended on in wartime.

Other advantages were gained by this system. British credits were given Virginia planters; British convoys were provided in wartime; British ambassadors acted as trade envoys on the continent of Europe, as salesmen of tobacco. These services, it is argued, were more valuable than the halfpenny duty retained by the English Treasury. After 1723, moreover, a further liberalization occurred in the drawback. The entire duty was given back as a refund when tobacco was re-exported to Europe.

The high costs of shipping tobacco to Europe were not, it is claimed, as much the result of high freights on British or colonial vessels as of the dispersed system of tobacco collection in Virginia. Ships of 200 to 400 tons went up and down Virginia rivers collecting small parcels from every big planter's own wharf, doing what river boats might as well have done. A fleet of 150 vessels was engaged in the collection and shipping of Virginia and Maryland tobacco, a much greater number than was necessary. This was an effect of the dispersion of Virginia's economic life produced by the river estuaries.

A reform in this method of collecting tobacco was urged on Virginia by the British Board of Trade. This was to centralize Virginia exports in a few cities within the colony, but that reform was never adopted since competing English ship captains were always glad to come to a planter's wharf for the tobacco.

The conclusion reached by historians who take this position is that the British Navigation System was not the cause, or was not a major cause, of the chronic depression in Virginia and Maryland agriculture after 1660. The thesis of this school is that no long-term loss of the continental market for Virginia tobacco took place. In some years there were declines of exports to the Continent; in other years, increases. But certainly no such steady decline as has been alleged. Unfortunately there are no continuous series of British statistics of exports of tobacco, or of price statistics for the tobacco trade. There was no centralized agency in England that recorded tobacco exports, and the press gave only scattered information.

The effect of the Navigation System on the economy of Virginia is an issue that arose again at the time of the American Revolution. The Navigation System is said to have been an important factor in producing that conflict. In 1951 O. M. Dickerson's *The Navigation Acts and the American Revolution* set forth the view that the Navigation Acts were not objected to in the colonies and were not a major factor in producing the Revolution. The evidence for this view is strong. After the Revolution, when American tobacco planters no longer had a privileged status in the British market, their economy for years was in a state of collapse.

Probably a major factor in the depression of the 17th century was simply overproduction. Virginia and Maryland raised more tobacco than the English and European markets could absorb. Overproduction is likely to occur wherever an area as large as Virginia and Maryland follows a one-crop system. Overproduction entails falling prices and these stimulate still greater production, since farmers raise increased crops in order to make up for low prices. That has been the record of single-crop agriculture throughout American history.

The early Virginia tobacco plantations were relatively small. Their acreage steadily grew during the second half of the 17th century. By the end of the century a few well-to-do planters on the lower James had estates of about 3000 acres. The forces producing this enlargement were, in part, the requirements of tobacco culture. The sweetest tobacco is grown on virgin soil. But the plant is soil-devouring, especially if the methods of conservation are as little known and as little practiced as they were in colonial Virginia. Every tidewater planter, therefore, sought to have a reserve of land, which made for large plantations. More effective use of labor could be made on large plantations than on small. Subdivision of labor was possible, which permitted routine work to be done effectively by slave labor. Also the buying of supplies and the selling of tobacco could be done to better advantage on a large plantation than on a farm. A social consideration made for the enlargement of plantations—an ambition to match the life of the British aristocracy. Large plantations, once established, were protected by the laws of inheritance—of primogeniture and entail. The tone of Virginia society was set by the big planter, as was the character of the government.

Seventeenth Century
Expansion of Virginia

A NUMBER OF INSTITUTIONS basic in southern history were brought into being in Virginia in the 17th century. They were introduced to the economic, social, and political life of the colony and for an understanding of this narrative a description of them is essential. One was the plantation. Its first form was Jamestown itself. For more than a decade it was a jointly owned property with no individually owned land or housing. The funds used to establish it were provided by the Virginia Company — raised by sale to the public in England of shares of stock at £12½ a share. Purchasers of shares were designated Adventurers of the Company. They normally resided in England. The labor provided for Jamestown was also a company matter, consisting in part of persons who paid their costs of transportation to the New World. A paid-up individual was known as a Planter of the Company, entitled to one share of stock. Other labor was expected to be provided by common workmen sent out by the company. Labor was on a community, not an individual, basis. All supplies, including food, were company-provided. All profits earned by the plantation were to go to the company.

In the 1609 charter provision was made for the introduction of private ownership. The profits that would accumulate in the enterprise after seven years were to be divided per share among the stockholders—both Adventurers in England and Planters in the colony. Part of the profit was to be a land dividend—100 acres per share, and a second 100 acres as soon as the first had been put under cultivation. (This was the first appearance of individual ownership of land in Virginia.)

While the company profits were presumably accruing, six more plantations were established in the James Valley higher up the river. All seven, Jamestown included, proved in the end to be financial failures. The reason for failure was that the company system of operation offered no incentive for hard work. Whether a Planter was industrious or lazy, whether he was efficient or otherwise, he was entitled to share alike in the profits at the end of seven years. And the infection spread to all workers. For this reason the company type of plantation was doomed to failure from the outset.

A second type of plantation—the particular plantation—was experimented with during the same period in the valley of the James. Particular plantations were those established by groups of shareholders in the Virginia Company who pooled their shares. They obtained land from the company in return for undertaking to send out at least 100 persons to work the land and to pay all the costs of the enterprise. They obtained for the enterprise a certain amount of self-government. Altogether 44 grants for particular plantations were obtained from the company. They were readily obtained because the company fell into financial difficulties and lost the means of directly pressing the colonization of Virginia. Some of the grants were on as large a scale as 200,000 acres. They were known as "hundreds," a term derived from an Anglo-Saxon designation of a community of a certain size. They are perpetuated on Virginia maps in such names as Southampton Hundred and Bermuda Hundred. Ultimately all the particular plantations were converted to private ownership.

Private plantations, in the usual sense in which the term is used, came into existence in 1619. They had been authorized under the charter of 1612 and again in 1618 when the company declared its first land dividend. In instructions issued to Sir George Yeardley, the new governor of the colony, the dividend was ordered paid, and in 1619 private ownership of land in Virginia became established.

Provision was made in the Yeardley instructions, also, for "glebe" lands for ministers in the colony. Educational grants were likewise ordered. Precedents were thus set not only for the colonies but for the nation after independence was won. A grant was also authorized for the education of Indian children and this was located at Henrico.

In addition the government was democratized under the instructions issued to Yeardley. The charter of 1609 had promised that all persons becoming Planters of the Company, and their posterity, would have the liberties and immunities of English subjects to the same extent "as if they had bine abidinge and borne within this oure Kingdom of England." Among such liberties one was especially precious— representation in a legislative body of their own choosing. Yeardley's instructions authorized a legislature, to consist of two supreme councils, one a council of state, chosen by the company in England, the other a general assembly, of which a constituent part should be a body elected by the people of Virginia, consisting of "two Burgesses chosen out of each Town, Hundred, or other particular Plantation." This order was acted upon soon after Governor Yeardley's arrival in Virginia, in January 1619, and the first representative assembly in the history of English colonization met on July 30, 1619. Another promise thus materialized which gave migrants to Virginia a stake in the colony's future. The Yeardley instructions, which carried all these concessions, promptly became known as the "Greate Charter."

These reforms were the result of a change in leadership in the Virginia Company in 1618. Sir Thomas Smith, who for years had shaped the company's policy, was voted out of office. He was replaced by Sir Edwin Sandys, leader of the democratic forces in Parliament and in the company. But under Sandys factional disputes in the company continued. In part they were the result of developments in the colony. More emigrants were sent than could be absorbed, which led to charges of incompetence. The company had never been able to pay cash dividends, though it was committed to paying land dividends. A deadly epidemic struck the settlers, which carried off nearly 4000 persons. In 1622 an Indian massacre added its horrors, and 347 settlers lost their lives. An Indian war followed which ran on for a dozen years.

Problems raised by the preoccupation of the colony with tobacco culture proved disruptive. Sandys wished diversification of production. Under accepted theory the English colonies were supposed to complement the needs and interests of the homeland. Sandys and others felt that tobacco did neither. It merely encouraged an evil habit, which the Crown and even the company deplored. The company endeavored to develop other staples—silk, wine, tar, and flax—but these could not be effectively produced, or at least as effectively as tobacco. Attempts at restriction of tobacco planting were tried and failed.

The Virginia Company wished a monopoly of all tobacco entering England as recompense for the duties it paid. This was resisted by the Crown. A special commission was appointed by the Privy Council in 1623 to examine the company's affairs. It reported that the company was hopelessly divided and bankrupt, and that the mortality rate among emigrants was startling. Three out of four of the those sent in the period 1619–24 had died. The only feasible answer to the company's failure to meet its charter obligations seemed to be dissolution, and this was ordered in 1624 by the Court of King's Bench in an action sponsored by the Privy Council. The company had achieved great ends, but had failed to meet empire needs and at the same time the hopes of stockholders for dividends.

With the dissolution of the company, Virginia became a royal colony. The company's unallotted land reverted to the Crown, and land distribution became the responsibility of the Crown representatives in the colony. Distribution was carried out under the so-called headright system.

A headright was a right to 50 acres of land in Virginia accorded to anyone who would finance the transportation of a settler—one head—to the colony. A headright was given on the condition that cultivation of the land would begin within three years after the headright had been granted—the land had to be ''seated,'' as the phrase went, within three years. The holder could locate his 50 acres wherever he chose on ungranted land. The theory of the headright was excellent. Wilderness land in Virginia, which was valueless without settlers, was to be used to attract colonists from England.

But the headright system was much abused. If a Virginia gentleman went to London for a vacation, on returning to America he would apply for, and get, a headright. He swore he had financed the transportation of one person to Virginia. Captains of ships sailing for Virginia would take out headrights for their sailors and even their passengers. Sailors touching at Virginia ports took out headrights. Three different persons might take out headrights for the transportation of one indentured servant to Virginia—the shipmaster who carried out the servant, the broker in Virginia who bought the servant from the shipmaster, and finally the planter who bought the servant from the broker. By such fraud any person who got a headright had a claim to 50 acres of land. If the person to whom the headright was issued did not wish to use it to take up land, he could sell it.

Frauds on the headright system could have been checked if the provision requiring seating of the headright within three years had been enforced. But enforcement of that provision was impossible because the Virginia public was complaisant about frauds practiced on the London government. Throughout American history the frontier has winked at land frauds practiced on an absentee government.

The chief beneficiaries of the system were land speculators. Headrights obtained fraudulently were sold cheap. Speculators bought them up, located them on desirable land, and built up large speculative holdings in desirable areas. The lands were held for later sale to incoming settlers at a high rate. It was characteristic of American frontier history that the purposes of theoretically excellent land systems were defeated by the activities of land speculators.

Ultimately headrights were sold on a purely commercial basis by Crown authorities in Virginia. The requirement that the cultivation should begin within three years was abandoned. In 1705 an act for the purely commercial sale of headrights was passed by the Virginia legislature. A definite price of five shillings for a 50-acre headright was fixed, the sum being payable in tobacco or corn. Other methods than headrights were used to build up speculative holdings in Virginia. Large grants of land passed from the Crown to court favorites or to influential colony politicians.

As a result of such activity the high ideal of using the wilderness as a fund with which to settle America was defeated. Great grants of land, held by speculators, became an actual hindrance to settlement, for these men derived their profits from holding back the choicest land until settlement around it had increased the sale value.

Another institution that was established after the era of the Virginia Company was the quitrent. This was something very different from what its name indicates. It was not a rent, but an annual land tax. The term originated in England at the end of the feudal period. In England a quitrent was actually a rent paid by a tenant to a feudal lord in order to be relieved—to be quit—of all feudal obligations and services. In America it was never a rent but a tax of a special sort paid by a landowner. The amount of the tax was relatively small. In Virginia it was one shilling for every 50 acres, paid annually.

Originally the Crown received the quitrent. But where a tract of land was given by the Crown to a court favorite, the right to the quitrent accompanied the gift. In that case the court favorite was the recipient of the quitrent. If land was then sold to a settler, the quitrent was paid to the court favorite or his heirs for all future time, no matter how often the land changed hands.

In a proprietary colony, such as Maryland, the right to the quitrents lay with the proprietors and their heirs—the Calverts in Maryland. The quitrents were regarded as a more important source of revenue by these proprietors than the money derived from the sale of the land.

The quitrents might have been, if reserved by the Crown, of enormous importance. If the Crown had reserved to itself quitrents on all lands that went to court favorites and others, and had carefully collected them, the revenue would have been large enough to defray all costs of colonial administration. If quitrents had been thus collected no dependence by Crown authorities on colonial legislatures would have been necessary. The power of the purse would have remained in Crown hands all through the colonial period instead of passing to legislatures. There would have been no need for a Stamp Tax in 1765 or for the Townshend duties. The history of the American colonies might have been different if the quitrents had been carefully reserved and collected by the Crown.

The quitrents might have been made a means of regulating land speculation. If they had been collected every year on land held by speculators, the latter would not have found it profitable to hold great tracts of wilderness land idle for long periods. But neither the British government in the colonial period nor the state or federal governments later had the vision to use the quitrents or a land tax in this way.

Quitrents, moreover, proved almost uncollectable. They were contrary to the spirit of the frontier. In Virginia, where they were supposed to be collected by the county sheriffs, these officials never took the duty very seriously. Most of them were themselves land speculators on a big scale. In every colony where attempts were made to collect quitrents, there was trouble with the collections. Only in Maryland was there ever any degree of success in making collections. In Pennsylvania, where quitrents were payable to the Penn family, pioneers dodged payment by refusing to buy land; they simply became squatters on the land. In 1726 there were nearly 100,000 squatters on Pennsylvania frontier lands.

In 1774–75, just before the outbreak of the American Revolution, the British government tried to rehabilitate the quitrent system in the royal colonies. It attempted to turn the quitrent on remaining wild land into a real revenue producer. But the attempt came too late—it was cut short by the American Revolution. At the outbreak of the Revolutionary War every one of the revolting colonies which had experienced the quitrents passed legislation abolishing them, and they were never revived in America after the Revolution.

Tidewater Virginia was settled with rapidity in the 17th century. The valley of the James was the first to be overrun. Then the valleys to the north, the York and the Rappahannock, were taken. Land between the valleys was more slowly occupied, because the soil was inferior in quality for the most part. These lands became the home of a run-down people—the piney woods element—whose life was in stark contrast to that of the river valleys where the plantations were.

The tidewater section into which settlement most rapidly moved in the second half of the 17th century was the Northern Neck, the region between the Rappahannock and the Potomac. The whole of it had been granted by Charles II in 1673 to Lord Culpeper and a group of associated favorites, from whom it passed to a son of Culpeper and later to Lord Fairfax. Land could be bought there for five shillings per 100 acres, plus yearly quitrents of two shillings. This was half the price at which land could be obtained elsewhere in the tidewater, and settlement was swift.

As the tidewater became occupied, two distinct societies emerged. The older along the lower James was a plantation society of big-scale operations, resting increasingly on Negro slavery. The other was the frontier society higher up the James and in the Northern Neck, consisting of yeomen farmers, often men who had been squeezed out of the lower James by the spread of slavery. It was a society of primitive conditions and of democracy, as compared with the increasing aristocracy of the lower James. The two societies were persistently at odds with each other.

The new society had many grievances against the old, especially taxation. The poll tax was the chief reliance of the colonial government—so much per head or poll. It was levied on all white males over sixteen, on white females of that age who tilled the land, and on all slaves old enough to work. By the large planters it was paid easily enough, but it placed undue weight on farmers in new communities or on inferior soil. More equitable would have been a real estate tax, specifically the quitrent, which would have taken into account the extent of plantations and the holdings of speculators. But quitrents belonged in theory to the Crown; their collection was costly and widely evaded by large landowners; and they were subject to frauds by sheriffs in reporting the collections and disposal of the tobacco.

Equal discontent was generated by the government of the colony, which after 1660 became increasingly reactionary, in harmony with the temper of government in England under the restored Stuarts. The governor of Virginia was then Sir William Berkeley. By a judicious distribution of jobs to members of the Burgesses, the lower house of the legislature, he managed to obtain control of it. Then he refused to call new elections from 1661 to 1676. He also obtained control of the upper house, the Council. His control there came from his right to fill vacancies, a privilege obtained from the Crown in 1660. He used his control over the legislature to carry out a program of reaction. In 1670 he succeeded in pushing through the legislature a restriction on voting, by which only freeholders were thereafter permitted to vote.

At the same time local government in Virginia—the government of the counties and of the parishes—became reactionary, partly as a result of the governor's power of appointment. The county court, consisting of eight justices of the peace, appointed by the governor, came to consist almost entirely of big planters. The sheriff, appointed by the governor on nomination of the county court, was also normally a big planter.

A subdivision of the county was the parish. It was both a civil and a religious unit. It oversaw the moral and religious welfare of the community since Virginia maintained an established church. The controlling body of the parish was the vestry, which was at first elected by the parishioners. But in the period of Governor Berkeley vestries gradually became self-perpetuating, and consisted chiefly of the great planters of the parish. Local offices became the possession of selfish cliques, plural officeholding was general, and there was no real check on maladministration.

The Indian trade of the interior passed under the control of the governor. It did so as the result of a legislative act passed in 1676 requiring Indian traders to be licensed. Only a limited number of licenses were authorized. Those which were issued were all granted by the governor to his political adherents.

In 1675–76 an Indian war harassed the Virginia frontier. The Susquehanna Indians, themselves pressed southward by Iroquois attacks, were raiding the frontier counties of Virginia. The settlers demanded a vigorous offensive against the Indians. Instead, Berkeley adopted a passive policy of building forts. This was attributed to his personal interest in the Indian trade, and to his determination not to interrupt its profits. The outcome of this accumulation of grievances was a rebellion in 1676 on the part of the frontiersmen—Bacon's Rebellion—the first armed uprising in American history.

The revolt was successful for a time. The governor was forced to dissolve the Long Assembly and permit election of a new legislature. A long list of reforms was forced through. The property limitation on the suffrage was abolished, restrictions were placed on plural officeholding, and some democratization was effected in local government.

But the rebellion got out of hand. Its leader, Nathaniel Bacon, a recent arrival in Virginia, was irresponsible. He permitted the capital of Virginia, Jamestown, to be burned and talked wildly of establishing an independent republic in Virginia. He has been rather grandiloquently described as the "Torchbearer" of the American Revolution. At the height of the rebellion he died, and the rebellion died with him. The governor was able to regain control and took a savage vengeance on Bacon's follow-ers. The gains of the rebellion were lost and the Virginia government became as reactionary as it had ever been.

This was the first of a series of armed frontier uprisings in American history. It was followed by such outbreaks as the War of the Regulation in North Carolina, just prior to the American Revolution, Shays's Rebellion in Massachusetts after the Revolution, and the Whiskey Rebellion in Pennsylvania. In all these collisions the frontier lost, partly because of its numerical inferiority, but also because, in every one, the frontier had rash and inexperienced leaders.

The Massachusetts Bay Colony

IN THE COLONIZATION of Massachusetts the objectives sought were more idealistic than those which shaped the settlement of Virginia. They were the winning of freedom of worship and the opportunity to build a community of the godly. These ends were to be achieved by use of the public lands of the wilderness. The modes of doing so appear in the early history of Plymouth and Boston.

Plymouth was founded on December 21, 1620, the first permanent English settlement made at the north. Its founders were the Pilgrims, religious leftists who considered the established Church of England so tainted with Romish tendencies that it could not be reformed. They were separatists who preferred to find refuge for themselves by migration to a foreign land. In 1609 they migrated to Holland, where for ten years they lived in exile. They became fearful, however, of losing their identity in a foreign land and determined to migrate to the New World. They obtained from Edwin Sandys, the head of the Virginia Company, a grant of land to establish a particular plantation in the valley of the James. Lacking the means to finance their crossing, they obtained a loan from a group of sympathetic English merchants. They made their crossing of the Atlantic in the *Mayflower* late in the season of 1620. The journey was stormy and a winter landing was decided on—far short of the James—at Plymouth. There they remained, never gathering much strength either in numbers or in means. Ultimately, in 1671, the settlement was taken over by the Massachusetts Bay Company. Its inhabitants at that time numbered only 7000.

The Boston community was stronger in every respect. Its members were Puritans, who represented the powerful middle class in England, which, within a decade, was to take control of the government and retain it through the Cromwellian period. Many of them were people of means, who were discontented members of the Anglican Church. They had longed to remain in it only to purify it. They wished the Church to be cleansed of its Romish tendencies. Also, they wanted to abolish the Book of Common Prayer, indeed, all set prayers. These reforms they hoped to accomplish within the Church. Later their desire was a church government, not by bishops, but by federated congregations. Their numerical strength and economic means account in part for the rapid growth of Boston and the Massachusetts Bay colony. Intellectually they were outstanding, with ties to the Cromwellian leaders, which was important for the colony.

The Boston settlement was an enterprise of the Massachusetts Bay Company, which had obtained a grant of land from the Council for New England in 1628. The grant was confirmed the following year by Charles I. It extended along the New England coast from a point three miles south of the Charles River to a point three miles north of the Merrimac, and, between these points, everything westward to the South Sea. The grant was free of any quitrent obligation to the Crown, so that the land could be distributed free of quitrents by the company.

With the confirmation of the grant came a royal charter incorporating the Massachusetts Bay Company. The charter contained no clause binding the company to maintain headquarters in England. A group within the company decided to turn the charter and the government of the colony over to the settlers who would move there. In 1630 a fleet of vessels carrying passengers to the number of about 900, and John Winthrop as governor, crossed the ocean and founded Boston, together with several other towns nearby. This was the vanguard of a migration of 15,000 to Massachusetts in the next decade. The migrants were Puritans who had in mind establishing communities of their own faith in the New World. They also were moved by a desire to acquire free land in the wilderness.

The method of distribution of land was directed by the General Court of the company. A grant would be made to members of the Church desiring to form a settlement in the wilderness, either members in Boston wishing to move westward or groups arriving fresh from England. The grant would then be located by a committee which would go out to choose the site. The committee, known as the "viewers," would consist of representatives of the General Court and of the petitioners. The location agreed upon would be submitted to the General Court for approval. Normally it had to be a location adjoining an older town. Compactness of settlement was insisted on. The chief reasons for this policy were religious and cultural, though the factor of defense against Indians was also important. Compactness of settlement would mean that churches and schools in new towns would be always in close touch with their counterparts in the old towns. There would always be good company for the godly. Such a policy contrasted sharply with the dispersion of settlement in Virginia.

Ordinarily the size of a town grant was about six miles square. The group that obtained such a grant was known as the town proprietors. They became owners of all the town land, and were a kind of landowning corporation. They are not to be confused with the town fathers who were the town government, though usually members of the one body were also members of the other.

The town proprietors were expected by the General Court to divide the grant partly among themselves and partly among later comers. They were expected to admit later comers who were in good church standing to their ranks until the total number would be 60 to 80 heads of family.

As soon as the town proprietors had received a grant they would move out to the land together. They would lay out the plan of the town as they wished it. The site for the central village would be selected—a place easy to defend. Its plan would then be drawn, its roads, its central common, and its church. A sawmill and a gristmill would be authorized on some eligible stream within the town limits. Then the farmlands would be laid off into fields. The settlement, in other words, was a planned community. A good example of such a town was Enfield (Map 2). It was settled in 1674 by people from Springfield and was considered a part of Massachusetts until a boundary agreement was made in 1713, when it became part of Connecticut. Such a town could belong equally well in either Massachusetts or Connecticut.

The nucleus of the town was the village, with its main street, lined with house lots, a village green, and a conveniently located church. Each lot in the village contained five to ten acres of land, which gave every proprietor enough for a house, a garden, and an orchard. The lots were laid out so that all were equal in value as nearly as possible.

Then a distribution of the village lots would be made. It would be by a system of chance, such as drawing numbers out of a hat. One lot in the distribution was always

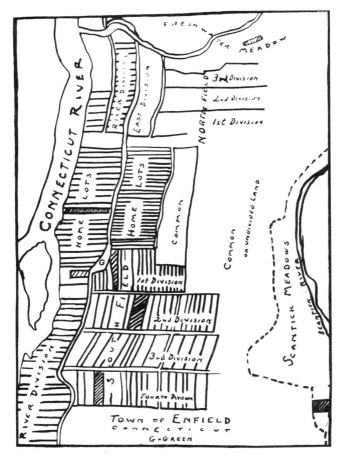

2. Town Plat of Enfield, Connecticut (from Allen)

reserved for a church, one for the minister, and one for a school. Some lots were always set aside for later comers.

The farmlands adjacent to the village would then be laid off in a pattern of divisions and the divisions were cut into strips. Each strip was made equal in value to every other. This was followed by a distribution of the strips by chance. That process of distributing the farmland was repeated division after division, new ones being distributed as soon as old ones had been brought under cultivation.

In these successive land distributions not all proprietors fared alike. Some were allowed to draw from the hat two or three times at each distribution, others only once. The number of drawings each proprietor was entitled to was determined at the first distribution. It was done under the supervision of a committee of the General Court. Any town proprietor permitted to have two or three drawings at the first distribution had the right to the same number of drawings at every later distribution.

Why were some proprietors allowed to have two or three drawings at each distribution while others were to have only one? The criteria differed from town to town. In many towns it was the amount of property a proprietor brought with him when he migrated—the quantity of his taxable goods.

The theory was that men of property and respectability should receive land according to their station. "To him that hath shall be given." But this principle was often varied, so that a poor man, if he had a large family, could receive more land than his humble status might otherwise entitle him to. In a few of the more democratic towns the basis of distribution was the size of a man's family. In no towns did the most favored proprietors get more than two or three times as much land as the poor proprietors. The purpose of this system was not to build up great estates, but rather to create communities of small landholders. The first minister of the church and the magistrates were always among the most favored proprietors.

In all these divisions the strip system was used so that each proprietor would get some strips of a better sort and some of a poorer. Each would receive some plowland, some woodland, some pastureland; also some meadowland on which hay was cut for the winter.

Under this system a proprietor would come to have a half dozen strips of land in different places. The map shows the holdings of an individual proprietor of Enfield (John Pease) in crosshatch shading—five scattered strips in all. If the map had revealed the divisions of the North Field in detail, it would have shown him possessing, perhaps, as many more. It was something of a nuisance to a proprietor to be the owner of many scattered strips and therefore after each distribution exchanges of strips among proprietors were made to consolidate holdings.

As has been indicated, the wish of the General Court was that rights of proprietorship in each town should be reserved for later comers until the number of proprietors reached 60 to 80 heads of family. But the willingness of the town proprietors to take in later comers diminished as the amount of undistributed land decreased. Sometimes later comers were given only partial rights—a right, for instance, to share in a single division. Sometimes they were taken in inadvertently—a careless record would be kept as to just what rights had been given, and in the absence of clear records full rights would be later claimed. Sometimes a laborer was given a right to build a cottage on the town land—just a house site without any adjoining land.

The right of a proprietor to share in the successive divisions of land was a legal, a property right that could be passed on by will. It could not be forfeited, except for tax delinquency. It could be sold or given away, but the right of sale was subject to restrictions. In Watertown, for instance, a town proprietor could not sell his rights to foreigners. Foreigners were probably any non-Puritan English. If these early Watertown proprietors could see the names on Watertown store signs now, the Irish, French-Canadian, and Polish Catholic names, they would turn in their graves.

In any Massachusetts town of the 17th century there would always be some land held in common. This was of three kinds. One was the village green, intended to be preserved forever as a common. A second form was a common field where cultivation was a community enterprise. Normally a field so cultivated was a temporary thing, intended to meet necessity. Sometimes it was a pasture where each proprietor was entitled to put cattle in accordance with his proprietorial rights. Each proprietor was responsible for a section of the fence of a common pasture. An official of the town, the hogreeve, looked after the cattle while they were there. In Concord, Ralph Waldo Emerson was at one time appointed an honorary hogreeve. Common fields and pastures were normally broken up in the end and distributed. A third variety of common land was the undistributed or undivided land, which was intended for division as fast as it could be put into cultivation.

Such was the land system of the Massachusetts Bay Company. Its basis was land donation, and title to such property without any encumbrance of quitrents. Land was used for the purpose of building communities of small freeholders of the Puritan faith and adherents of the congregational form of church organization. The land system was a foundation upon which was built the Puritan ideal of a biblical commonwealth.

The advantages of this land system over that of Virginia were many. One was compactness of settlement. On Massachusetts frontiers social and cultural values could be maintained. On southern frontiers, where settlement was permitted to scatter widely, frontiersmen were likely to degenerate socially and culturally. In 1855 Josiah G. Holland, in his *History of Western Massachusetts,* wrote:

> The influence of this policy [community settlement] can only be fully appreciated when standing by the side of the solitary settler's hut in the West, where even an Eastern man has degenerated to a boor in manners, where his children have grown up uneducated, and where the Sabbath has become an unknown day, and religion and its obligations have ceased to exercise control upon the heart and life.

Other than social values flowed from the Massachusetts compactness of settlement. One was protection from devastating Indian attack. Such attack did not come until the expansion of New England settlements gave assurance of survival. Another value was the elimination of land speculation, which played so large and influential a part on other American frontiers. Land speculation appeared in New England only at a later day.

The land system of Massachusetts became that of New England, just as Virginia's became characteristic of the South. In some respects it served as a model for the land system of the federal government. And the habit of community planning and settlement, which became ingrained in New Englanders, was carried to the West, even to the Far West. It was eventually carried into the Mormon communities of Utah.

There were less desirable features, however, in the New England land system, which became apparent during the later 17th and early 18th centuries. In every town the time arrived when the proprietors refused to admit newcomers to their ranks. It came as soon as the undivided lands had nearly all been distributed. In Watertown and in Dorchester the town proprietors voted in 1635 not to add any more to their numbers; in Cambridge that step was taken in 1664.

The proprietors, when they voted not to add to their numbers, became a privileged landholding group. They became an upper class, working hand in glove with the Congregational clergy. Later comers had to accept positions as laborers or renters unless they could afford to buy a proprietor's land. In some towns the landless became a majority of the population and resented this condition. They had to bear the dangers and costs of life on the frontier without any of its compensations. Their feeling is shown in a protest from the town of Newbury. ''We think it hard to be deprived of the right of commonage. We pay according to our property as much as freeholders for the support of public worship, the support of schools, the repairing of roads, and our equal proportion of all other taxes, and some of us have served as soldiers for your defence.''

Another defect in the New England land system was absentee proprietorship. Absentee proprietors had all the rights of town proprietors but were not required to go out with their fellow town proprietors to a new town. Such men might be named by the General Court merely to give supervision to the settling of a new town, receiving rights of proprietorship as compensation. Church leaders and political leaders were often named for this purpose. These men got the benefit of increasing land values in a new town without incurring any of the hardships and dangers of the frontier. They shared in division after division of land, though persons actually in the town got nothing. Absentee proprietorship of this sort existed almost from the beginning of settlement in Massachusetts and it became increasingly common in towns that were founded in the later 17th and early 18th centuries. These defects of the town system as well as its merits were significant in New England history. They were a force driving the dissatisfied to new areas of town settlement.

Expansion of New England

THE EXPANSION INTO the New England interior began five years after Boston was founded. It was initiated by the community of Cambridge, or Newtowne, as the place was then called. In 1634 a group of its inhabitants petitioned the General Court to be allowed to migrate to the Connecticut Valley, explaining that they wished to go because of lack of sufficient meadowland to produce hay for their cattle in winter. Cambridge was then a cattle country. What is now Harvard Yard on the east side was lined with cow pens. The petitioners hungered, they declared, for the beautiful meadowlands of the Connecticut Valley. To reinforce the argument they urged that the valley be promptly occupied to keep it out of the hands of the Dutch or the non-Puritan English. Their petition concluded with the sentiment that they were drawn to emigrate by the strong bent of their spirits. This was the wanderlust, a true western motif.

Not urged in the petition as a reason for wishing to go was dissatisfaction with the government of the colony. Thomas Hooker, the pastor of the First Church in Cambridge and the chief promoter of the migration, was more democratically inclined than John Winthrop and John Cotton, the Boston leaders who controlled Massachusetts policy. His sentiments were shared by his congregation and this was a factor in the desire to leave.

In the General Court the petition was anxiously debated. It ran counter to the colony's basic principle of compactness of settlement. Opposition to granting the petition was expressed on the ground that the migration would weaken the colony. It was phrased in the biblical terms in which debates were then carried on. "The removing of a candlestick is a great judgment."

Ultimately, after a year's delay, the petition was granted when it became evident that the migration would in any case be made by individuals. Accordingly, in 1635, the Cambridge petitioners went out and founded Hartford. Shortly afterward, Windsor, Wethersfield, and Springfield were settled by migrants from the greater Boston area. By 1637, 800 persons were living in the Connecticut Valley.

This expansion was an intrusion on the hunting grounds of the Pequot Indians. It led to the first Indian war in New England, the Pequot War of 1637. The Pequots occupied the area between Narragansett Bay and the Connecticut River. They were being encroached on from every side, on the east by the Narragansett settlements of Roger Williams, on the northwest by the new river settlements of the Connecticut Valley, on the west by the hostile Mohicans.

In the war the Connecticut River towns and the Boston area cooperated in a joint campaign. The plan was that the river towns would send their troops floating down the Connecticut and into Long Island Sound, where they would be joined by the Boston forces. The joint army would strike the Pequots from the south. The Pequots were not looking for attack from that direction and were caught by surprise. Their main village, a palisaded circle, with openings at two sides, was surrounded. The torch was put to it. Then the troops withdrew to a safe distance, and watched the Indians—men, women, and children to the number of 500—roast to death in the flames. Any Indian that broke out was caught on the swords of the troops. This branch of the Pequots was practically exterminated. For 40 years there were no further Indian troubles in New England. The extermination of the Pequots also opened up the New London area to settlement.

By 1675, because of the rapidity of settlement, a new conflict arose with the Indians. It was King Philip's War. In this clash the tribe that took leadership was the Wampanoag, which had befriended the Plymouth Pilgrims in their early adversities and had helped them to survive. Philip was the son of Massasoit, the chief who had saved the Plymouth settlers. He had an alliance with two other tribes, the Narragansetts and the Nipmucks of central Massachusetts. That triple alliance attacked the whole New England frontier from Rhode Island to Maine.

The war continued until 1676. Half the towns of Massachusetts were raided, sixteen were destroyed or abandoned. Terror was spread throughout New England. Ultimately Philip was brought to bay in a great swamp fight and was defeated and killed. His wife and nine-year-old son were captured and sold into slavery in the West Indies. The maps of illustration 3 show the destructiveness of the war. Much of the occupied area of the interior was destroyed or abandoned, and settlement was thrown back on the coastal regions.

With the return of peace the abandoned towns were reoccupied and a new expansion began. But this was achieved under harsh conditions. For in 1689 began a long series of Indian hostilities known as the French and Indian Wars, which extended with only short intermissions for three-quarters of a century. During that period New England experienced the horrors of Indian massacres, inspired and often led by the French.

This danger was met by a new defense institution, the military town, a frontier community designated by the Massachusetts legislature as an outpost. Eleven towns were so designated in 1694–95. In these the inhabitants were forbidden to desert during Indian crises except by express permission of the governor and Council. The penalty for desertion was forfeiture of land and imprisonment. These towns were expected to serve the frontier function of rampart for older communities. In Connecticut similar action was taken. Seven such towns were designated in 1704. In New York like action occurred in 1689, when Albany and Schenectady were made military towns.

In spite of the constant menace of Indian attack, settlement kept pressing into the interior. By 1713 Boston's hinterland was again occupied as far westward as Lancaster. In the Connecticut Valley settlement had crossed into New Hampshire, and along the New England coast, as far as Penobscot Bay.

These thrusts into the wilderness were invasions of the Indian country. Frontier towns were expected to serve as defense for the older towns, and as a cutting edge for a further advance of the frontier. At the beginning of the 18th century, settlement in New England was at a stage comparable to that of Virginia. The lowland areas had all been occupied, including the coast and the fertile interior valleys of importance.

During the remainder of the century expansion was chiefly across uplands, across hills and mountains. It was, on the whole, northward rather than westward. It is shown on the pair of maps in illustration 4. The advance is up the Housatonic Valley into the Berkshires; up the Connecticut Valley into Vermont; into New Hampshire far up the Merrimac. During the war of the American Revolution the frontier line lay in northern New England. Vermont was in process of occupation from Connecticut. Southern New Hampshire had been occupied in part by settlers from Massachusetts, in part by Scotch-Irish from the British Isles.

The forces that produced this 18th century expansion were comparable to those at work in the 17th century. But a number of new forces had been added. Speculation had become a major force in the movement. To an increasing extent town tracts were being sold commercially by New England legislatures to land speculators. Such sales became almost normal after 1715 in Massachusetts. In 1762 the last of the Massachusetts western towns, those in the Berkshire Hills, were sold to speculators.

In Connecticut the last of the wilderness towns was sold to speculators in 1737 at public auction. In northern New England, in the royal colony of New Hampshire, a more sophisticated form of speculation appeared. The colony asserted claim to the Vermont region and also to northern New York. In the period 1749–64 Governor Benning Wentworth made no less than 129 township grants to groups of proprietors in the claimed area, as well as 18 more in New Hampshire itself. In each he thriftily reserved 500 acres for himself. In 1770 the New York grants came before the New York Supreme Court for adjudication and were annulled, which led to years of controversy thereafter.

The willingness of New England authorities to sell town tracts was the result in part of a great need for more revenue. In all the New England colonies revenue was desperately needed to pay the military costs of the French and Indian Wars. Land policy became shaped by fiscal necessities resulting from war, as has often occurred in American history. Another important element in the willingness of legislatures to sell tracts was a decline in the religious fervor which had once shaped land distribution.

During most of the period of expansion across the uplands—from 1689 to 1763—Indian wars ran on. The pioneers of interior New England were constantly exposed to tomahawk and torture. This produced a characteristic frontier attitude toward Indians. Indians were thought of as wild beasts. In all the New England colonies bounties were given for Indian scalps, bounties that were graded according to whether the scalps were those of warriors or squaws or children. In the Seven Years' War, Massachusetts paid bounties of £200 to £220 each for scalps of warriors,

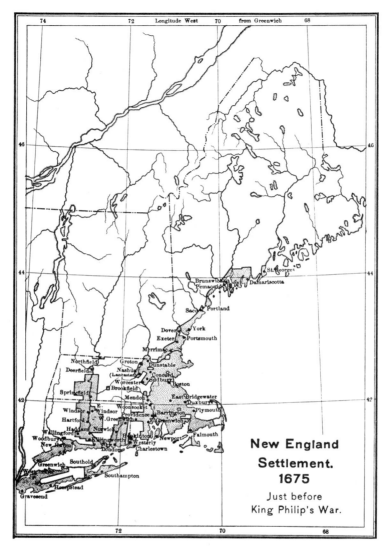

3. New England Settlement, 1675 (from Mathews)

and £100 to £110 for scalps of non-military individuals. A tidy sum could be earned gathering scalps. The famed Rogers Rangers went in for such work.

This was a frontier temper throughout American history. But in the 19th century, when a similar attitude toward the Indians developed in the Far West, the people of New England were horrified. They denounced the Far Westerners as little better than savages. In Congress, New Englanders became associated with the policy of humanitarianism toward Indians, and Senator Henry L. Dawes of Massachusetts was the great exponent of reform in the treatment of them.

By the end of the 18th century, as a result of the northward expansion, New England contained two societies—an older society and a newer one on the frontier.

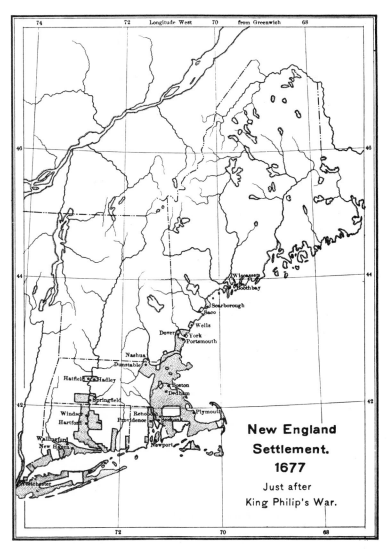

New England Settlement, 1677 (from Mathews)

The two differed sharply from each other. The older society was located in the lowlands, occupying the coastal area and the big river valleys—the Housatonic, the Connecticut, and the Merrimac. Along the seacoast prosperity reflected commerce and shipping, and the markets opened there for local agricultural produce. In the big river valleys prosperity was the result of soil fertility. In politics the lowlands gave their majorities to conservatives, especially on economic issues such as banking and currency. They looked with favor on the Federalists when that party was organized in the Washington administration. In religion the lowlands tended to be conservative. They remained faithful to the old Congregationalism. They were the area where ideas of a state-supported church had deep roots. Their centers of religious education were

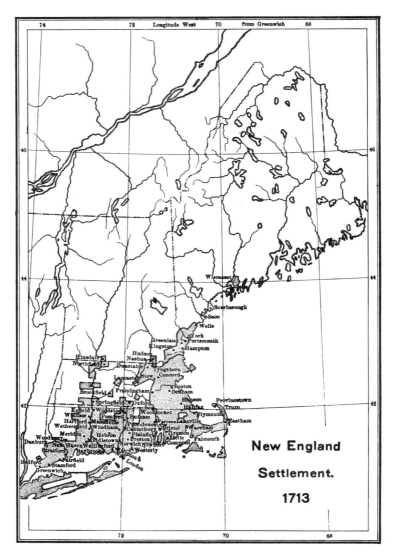

4. Eighteenth Century Expansion in New England (from Mathews)

Yale and Harvard. Yale was the school to which fathers sent their sons if they wanted to be sure of their orthodoxy. Harvard was becoming tainted with Unitarian heresies by the time of the American Revolution.

The newer and less prosperous frontier society was situated in the hill and mountain areas settled in the 18th century. The soil, which had initially seemed good, proved to have only surface fertility. The first crops were excellent, and for a generation or two the land was fruitful, but the real character of the soil had become evident. The greater part of the hill country was unfit for any kind of agriculture except pasture or forest. Today a large part of upland New England has reverted to forest.

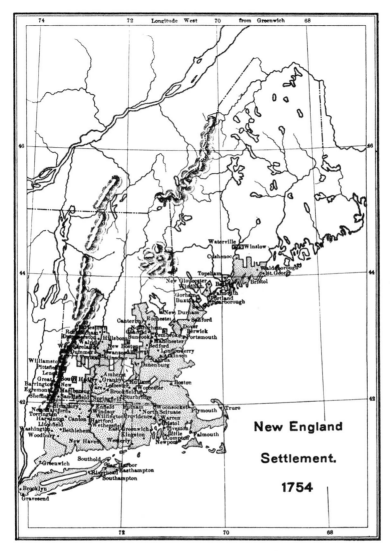

Eighteenth Century Expansion in New England (from Mathews)

    In settling the hill country the pioneers had in many cases chosen the worst land first. They had chosen hilltops and hillsides in preference to the intervales. The hilltops were selected partly because they were dry and healthful, whereas land in the intervales was likely to be insufficiently drained and swampy. Hilltops were also less liable to early frosts than lower land. But they were chosen chiefly because they were easier to defend against Indians.

    After these areas had ceased to be fruitful the enterprising moved to the intervales or migrated westward. Those who remained on the tops and sides became poorer. The hills generated economic and political discontent. They became areas of

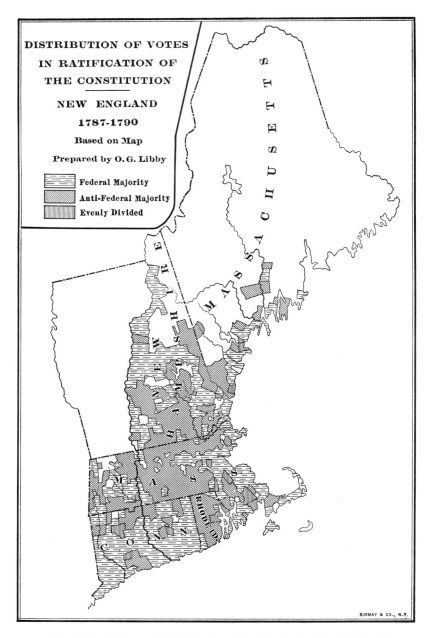

**DISTRIBUTION OF VOTES
IN RATIFICATION OF
THE CONSTITUTION**

NEW ENGLAND

1787-1790

Based on Map

Prepared by O. G. Libby

Federal Majority
Anti-Federal Majority
Evenly Divided

BORMAY & CO., N.Y.

5. New England Vote on the Ratification of the Constitution (from McLaughlin)

debt and paper-money heresies. In Massachusetts they were the centers of Shays's Rebellion in 1786. In New Hampshire they were the region of the Exeter riots. In religion the hill areas rejected Congregationalism. They preferred the emotionalism of the Baptists and Methodists to the cold intellectualism of the older church. They objected to the union of church and state, and demanded equality of religions.

This correlation prevailed in the period of the Confederation. It is found in the vote of New England on the ratification of the federal Constitution, as shown on the map (5). It is a well-known fact that the people who favored ratification of the Constitution were the prosperous, propertied classes, the trading classes, and the conservative classes, while those who opposed ratification were the debtor classes and the paper-money elements.

On the map the areas voting for the Constitution were the seaboard, the older, commercial, prosperous sections—Plymouth, Boston, Gloucester, Portsmouth, and Portland. In the interior, the Housatonic, Connecticut, and Merrimac valleys, all of them regions of good soil and prosperity, were Federalist. The anti-Federalist areas lay in the hill country—the Worcester area, which had been a center of Shays's Rebellion, the interior of Rhode Island, and the hill country of New Hampshire.

The same correlation appears in state politics in Massachusetts in the period of the 1790's and the early 1800's. The fertile Connecticut Valley voted Federalist consistently. So did the prosperous commercial and fishing centers—Plymouth, Boston, and Gloucester. In the cities, however, the proletariat were defecting to Jefferson. The poorer farm areas in the Berkshires stood out sharply for Jefferson, and, likewise, the impoverished upland region between the Connecticut watershed and the coastal plain.

For New England as a whole during the period of the 1790's and early 1800's the same correlation holds. The rich and prosperous valleys—the Housatonic, the Connecticut, and the Merrimac—were consistent areas of Federalist majorities. In 1801 the conservative Federalist editor of the Boston *Columbian Centinel* observed with satisfaction that the Connecticut River was a stream that "like the Nile in Egypt, fertilizes its banks from its source to the ocean, and causes them to produce abundant harvests of Federalism and unwavering attachment to right principles." The coast towns, Plymouth, parts of the Boston area, Gloucester, Portsmouth, and Portland were likewise Federalist. The areas that were Jeffersonian lay in the interior uplands. The Berkshires were unwaveringly Jeffersonian; so were the Green Mountains in Vermont, the White Mountains of New Hampshire, and the hill country between the Connecticut Valley and the seaboard. In New England, as in Virginia, geography thus stamped its influence on the economy and on the political and religious views of society.

The Piedmont and Great Valley

BY THE LATTER HALF of the 17th century the society of tidewater Virginia had become sufficiently mature to be ready for expansion into the provinces of the Piedmont and the Great Valley of the Appalachians. These lands have a northeast-southwest axis, and expansion across them was due west. In 1671 two explorers, Thomas Batts and Robert Fallam, penetrated to the Blue Ridge Mountains and the New River. That river was part of western waters, a tributary of the Great Kanawha and, therefore, of the Ohio. The explorers made an unabashed claim, in the name of the king of England, to all the territory drained by the river to the sea, which was a portent of the future.

The base from which exploration and trade into the interior was carried on was the fall line, a line dividing the tidewater from the Piedmont throughout Virginia and the South. It was the boundary at which waters from streams rising in the Blue Ridge dropped precipitately on their way to the sea. It marked the limit of navigation to the interior from the seaboard. At this line stood a row of forts serving the fur and peltry trade with the Indians.

The most important in the row was Fort Henry, established in 1645 at the falls of the Appomattox, a branch of the James. Its commander for thirty years was Captain Abraham Wood, a notable Virginia frontiersman and fur trader. At the falls of the James stood Byrd's Fort, commanded by Colonel William Byrd, ancestor of a famous Virginia family.

From these forts a considerable trade with the Indians was carried all across the Virginia Piedmont and, from there, through the back country of the Carolinas and beyond. From Fort Henry went out each year a caravan of 100 horses (15 traders), loaded with trade goods, which went to the Indians and brought back deerskins and furs in exchange. This trade flourished through the 17th and into the 18th century, when it was taken over by Charleston in South Carolina.

After the fur traders came cattlemen. Early in the 18th century they established themselves on the meadows of Virginia and Carolina, the so-called pea-vine pastures and savannas, which had been created by Indian burnings in the forests. There a very considerable cattle industry grew up, devoted to the raising of half-wild steers and horses. It was a predecessor to the later cattle industry of the Great Plains. Its techniques of operation were much like those of the Great Plains—the annual round-ups, cowboys, and cattle brands. The industry was temporary, but an evidence of its existence still remains in such a place name as Cowpens in South Carolina.

A third stage in the development of the Piedmont was the arrival of pioneer farmers. These came from two directions. From the tidewater flowed a stream of native Virginians, a strain exemplified by the father of Thomas Jefferson. From the tidewater came also foreign elements—Germans largely. In 1714 a group of German redemptioners was sent beyond the falls of the Rappahannock by Governor Spotswood to work his iron mines. This colony, Germanna, was the beginning of a considerable flow of Germans into the province.

Stimulation to this movement came from land speculators in the tidewater, often influential politicans, who had obtained grants from the legislature on the condition that a specified number of settlers be brought to them. Also, after 1720, under an act passed by the Virginia legislature, tracts of 1000 acres of land were given free to any who would settle in certain exposed frontier counties of Virginia. Such grants were not only free but free of quitrents for a period of years. They were made to yeoman farmers in the tidewater and to ex-redemptioners who had completed their service.

Another stream of population into the Piedmont flowed down from Pennsylvania, which during the 18th century was a reservoir. It was constantly filling up with population and constantly pouring it out again. The process by which the reservoir became filled may be dated as early as 1683, when Germans began to come to Germantown on the outskirts of Philadelphia. That was almost as soon as William Penn came into possession of Pennsylvania. Germans were attracted by Penn's advertising literature and by his Quaker views. They arrived in such numbers during the 18th century that by the time of the American Revolution they constituted a third of Pennsylvania's population, about 100,000. They were prominent in such river valleys as the Delaware and the Susquehanna, and also in the Great Valley. Many of them were Mennonites and Pietists.

Another stream was the Scotch-Irish. They were Irish only in the sense of having resided some generations (since the early 17th century) in the Ulster counties of Ireland. They began to emigrate to America early in the 18th century (1718) as a result of discontent over rising rents and the repression of their woolen industry by the British Parliament in 1699. They spread all over western Pennsylvania, concentrating in the valleys of the Cumberland and the Monongahela.

The flow southward of these elements began early. In the case of the Germans, it commenced with Justus Hite, who in 1732 led a group of his countrymen from York, Pennsylvania, to Winchester, Virginia, in the beautiful valley of the Shenandoah. The movement was so rapid that by the time of the American Revolution Germans were thick all through the Shenandoah Valley and farther down. It was possible to talk German from Pennsylvania to Georgia. The Scotch-Irish were more numerous, however, than the Germans, and formed the backbone of the population in the Valley, the Piedmont, and the interior of the Carolinas.

The two elements differed widely in their characteristics as settlers. The Germans were excellent farmers. They knew good soils and how to preserve them. They took pride in long residence in one place, handing down farms in good condition to their descendants for generations. The Appalachian Valley as a result of their farming became the granary of America, displacing the Connecticut and Delaware valleys in this respect. Another characteristic of the Germans was their great stone barns, superior to other American barns of that day. They built good barns for their cattle before they built good homes for their families. The Germans were famous for their canvas-covered wagons, built to an Old World pattern for them at Conestoga, Pennsylvania. These became the overland means of transport to the West, carrying American pioneers clear to the Pacific. They have been aptly termed the "wagons of empire" in the United States.

The Scotch-Irish tended to be individualistic as settlers. They did not cling together in ethnic communities. They preferred to scatter out as much as the Indians would let them. They needed lots of air and elbow room. They felt crowded when neighbors got as close as five miles. They had a passion to be on the move, and they had an intense land hunger. They thought the best land was that lying just a little farther on. They were a militant people, a fine physical stock, quick to learn from the Indians, and easily becoming superior to them in the arts of border warfare. They were the cutting edge of the frontier all the way to the Pacific.

In matters of land title the Scotch-Irish were pests. They had a habit of settling where land was in dispute between colonial proprietors or governments, and playing off one against the other. They became squatters on the soil wherever they settled. In 1726 there were estimated to be 100,000 squatters in Pennsylvania, and most of the complaints of Penn's land agents were directed against what he called the "saucy Scotch-Irish."

In this stream of southward-moving people were a large number of outlaws and ne'er-do-wells, who gave an unsavory reputation to the interior, particularly to interior North Carolina. In self-defense against them, protective vigilante organizations were formed, such as the North Carolina Regulators, to whom reference will be made later. On nearly every American frontier outlaws and ne'er-do-wells were prominent.

An acceleration occurred in the second half of the 18th century in the southward flow of the population from Pennsylvania. It was stimulated by the high price charged for land in that colony. The price was £10 to £15 per 100 acres, with quitrents of 2 to 4 shillings per 100 acres. Land could be obtained more cheaply in the Virginia Piedmont and in the Carolinas.

Another force in the southward movement was Indian pressure upon the Pennsylvania settlements during the last of the French and Indian Wars. After Braddock's defeat in 1755 a regular drive of Indians, led by the French, was let loose on the western Pennsylvania frontier. Even the Scotch-Irish did not relish quite so much exposure, and drifted southward.

The southward movement occurred on both sides of the Blue Ridge, on one side by way of the Great Valley, on the other by roads of the Piedmont. The result was that by the beginning of the American Revolution, the Great Valley and the Virginia Piedmont were fairly well filled, and a surplus was spilling over into the trans-Allegheny West—into the great interior.

In 1700 population had reached the fall line in Virginia—at the edge of the Piedmont. By 1760 the Virginia Piedmont had been occupied. The North Carolina Piedmont was also in the process of settlement. By 1770 the big advance was in the North Carolina and South Carolina Piedmont. Settlement was up against the Blue Ridge Mountains. Population was also moving down the Great Valley of the Appalachians and out into the upper waters of the Tennessee (Map 6). Thus, at the time of the American Revolution, a new upland society had come into existence in the South, as it had in New England. It extended south into the Carolinas and west as far as the upper waters of the Tennessee. It was a society of yeoman farmers and of strenuous democracy.

Tidewater Virginia had in the meantime become completely dominated by the planter aristocracy. Even that part of the tidewater which had once been the center of Bacon's Rebellion was, by the time of the American Revolution, an area of big plantations and slave labor. The older society and the new were out of touch with each other.

One of the insulators was the break in river communication where the rivers from the Piedmont drop into the lowland of the tidewater—where all navigation from the seaboard was interrupted. Vessels coming up the rivers with cargo or going down stopped there to break cargo. The fall line was a kind of insulator between the provinces. Another was a belt of poor, sandy soil, a zone of pine barrens, between the tidewater and the Piedmont, a belt that is quite wide in Virginia. It is even wider in the Carolinas, where it is 80 miles from east to west.

Clashes of interest, growing out of differences in economic maturity, exacerbated the relations between the sections. One was over the apportionment of representation in the legislature of Virginia. The Virginia rule of apportionment was that every county had two Burgesses in the legislature regardless of the size of its population. That rule favored the tidewater counties, for these were always kept small in population by legislative action. As soon as a tidewater county got large in population it was cut in two, and each of the divided parts was assigned two representatives in the legislature. But the Piedmont and Valley counties were not cut in two when their population grew because the legislature, which the older area dominated, objected to increasing the voting strength of the radical western counties. The refusal to divide the western counties led to great discrepancies in representation, described by Thomas Jefferson in his famous work *Notes on Virginia*. They are indicated by the statistics on the chart, which are taken from Jefferson's work.

	Fighting Men	*Burgesses*	*Upper House*
Tidewater	19,012	71	12
Piedmont and Valley	30,959	78	12

The refusal of the legislature to divide the big interior counties had the effect not merely of depriving those counties of fair representation but of paralyzing their local government. In the big counties so much work piled up in the courts that they were overwhelmed and ceased to function properly. This evil was accentuated by another. Where the interior counties were large, the courts were likely to be a long distance

6. Colonial Population, 1760 (by Herbert Friis from the *Geographical Review*)

from parts of the population. The whole judicial and executive machinery of local government suffered as a result. Similar conditions existed in North Carolina and South Carolina. In the North Carolina legislature there were, prior to the Revolution, only two Piedmont representatives. In the South Carolina legislature, before 1773, there were no separate Piedmont representatives.

Clashes over the issue of representation in southern legislatures occurred at just the time of the more famous quarrel between the colonies and Parliament over the Stamp Tax. In that dispute the tidewater planters, facing Parliament, took the position that taxation without representation was tyranny. But in dealing with the Piedmont and the Valley, the planters took an opposite stand. They withheld adequate representation.

The argument used by the tidewater planters in justifying their position was that population alone was not a good basis for representation, that a mixed basis of

Colonial Population, 1780 (by Herbert Friis from the *Geographical Review*)

population and property was better. Even if the Piedmont counties had a large population, this was more than counterbalanced by the higher property values of the counties of the tidewater—the higher values of plantations and slaves. An age-old issue was raised by this argument—the issue of the rights of man as against the rights of property, the rights of democracy as against the rights of vested interests.

Another argument of the tidewater pertained to the quality of the population in the counties of the interior. The population of those counties was largely alien; it spoke English badly, if at all. It was regarded as an ignorant, turbulent rabble by the planter class, as little better than savages. Why should those who had built up the colony hand over control of it to nondescript immigrants, who would make use of it to levy heavy taxes on property and slaves?

Other issues besides representation and taxation embittered the relations of the two societies. Religion was a very sore issue. A state-supported Anglican establishment was maintained in all the southern colonies by the tidewater planters. In the frontier counties society consisted largely of dissenters. They demanded religious equality, the separation of church and state. But they were powerless because of the control of the legislature by the tidewater.

Clashes of a like nature divided the sections in other southern colonies. In North Carolina they occurred over issues of a special nature, though all were part of the general problem of unequal representation. One issue was taxation. The principal tax was the poll tax, which had to be paid in specie. It could not be paid, as in Virginia, in the form of tobacco. County sheriffs performed the service of collection, but did not properly account for what they collected. More than half the collections, according to a report of Governor Tryon in 1767, stuck to the fingers of the sheriffs. The sheriffs were also charged with being overzealous in declaring forfeit the property of tax delinquents. The fees taken for legal services by local attorneys and court officers were excessive. The proper amount was specified by law, but the law was evaded by dividing the services and charging a separate fee for each part. In performing marriage ceremonies clergymen of dissenting faith operated under legal restrictions and a reform of these was blocked because of unequal sectional representation.

A protective organization, known as the Regulators, served the frontiersmen in North Carolina. It was directed at first chiefly against outlaws. But it took on political functions in the clash with the tidewater by sending its representatives to the legislature. In 1769 a legislature was chosen favorable to the reforms demanded by the frontier. A series of reforms was in process of enactment when the legislature was dissolved by the governor because of its adopting radical resolutions against the Townshend Acts of the British Parliament. A year later reforms of various kinds were adopted. But in the meantime rioting took place on the part of the Regulators and court proceedings at Hillsborough were interrupted. Several thousand Regulators began a march to the seaboard to free one of their leaders who was held in prison. They were met by the militia and a pitched battle was fought—the Battle of the Alamance. The Regulators were defeated and dispersed, and their leaders were captured. A dozen of them were convicted of felony; six were executed. The movement collapsed and the only recourse of those who were unwilling to accept defeat was to move over the mountains to western waters.

In all the southern colonies, and also in Pennsylvania, such sectional clashing occurred between the Piedmont and the tidewater. The clashes continued long after the American Revolution. In the southern Atlantic states they continued even into the 1850's, notably over the issue of apportionment of representatives in the legislatures. Then, partly as a result of the westward expansion of slavery, constitutional changes were agreed upon by which the Piedmont attained a large measure of equality.

By the middle of the 18th century a frontier society occupied the hill and mountain country all the way from the uplands of New Hampshire and Vermont to those of the Carolinas. It was not merely discontented, it was expansive. In the South it was ready to leap over the ranges of the Appalachians into the great interior of the continent and to seize it from the Indians.

But the interior was part of New France in the middle of the 18th century. It was a barrier possessed by a European power that also had visions of territorial expansion in the New World.

The French
and Indian Barrier

THE BUILDING OF NEW FRANCE began a year after the founding of Jamestown. It began in 1608 with Samuel de Champlain's founding of Quebec on the St. Lawrence. From this beginning the French, with characteristic dash, raced across the interior. While the English were plodding slowly and painfully across the tidewater of Virginia, the French were exploring and taking preliminary possession of the whole interior valley of the continent. Their possession seemed a bar to further English expansion into the interior.

A few dates will suggest the speed of the French advance. In 1613 Champlain discovered the Ottawa River route—a shortcut to the upper Great Lakes. In 1634 Jean Nicolet established himself at Green Bay, an arm of Lake Michigan. In 1659 Radisson and Groseilliers discovered the Grand Portage, which gave France the means of connection from Lake Superior to the Far West. In 1671 St. Lusson was at the Sault Ste. Marie, taking possession, in an elaborate ceremony, of the whole interior in the name of the king of France. This was the year Batts and Fallam were standing on the banks of the New River in the Appalachian Valley taking formal possession of the whole interior in the name of the king of England. In 1673 Marquette and Joliet, moving from the Great Lakes by way of Green Bay and the Wisconsin River, reached the Mississippi and descended it as far as the Arkansas. In the years 1673–87 La Salle was pressing his immense scheme of empire, vividly described by Francis Parkman. In 1699 Louisiana was organized as a French colony, with Biloxi on the Gulf Coast as its administrative center. In 1718 New Orleans was founded, and the dream of La Salle came true.

By the end of the 17th century, while the English were entering the Piedmont, the French were at the heart of the continent and were in preliminary possession of it. They controlled the gateways to the St. Lawrence and to the upper Mississippi, and all the strategic points between: Fort Frontenac (1674), Niagara (1678), Detroit (1686), Green Bay (1685); and, in the Illinois country, Chahokia (1698) and Kaskaskia

(1700). This outrunning of the English in the race for empire is to be explained partly by the fact that the French had a great open road into the interior—the St. Lawrence —acquired by them early; partly by their characteristic verve and spirit; and finally by the superficiality of their occupation.

Their chief economic interest in this vast wilderness was the fur trade. This they exploited on a large scale. By the end of the 17th century (1693) their fur exports from Montreal were worth 800,000 livres. The method employed in this trade differed from that of the English to the south. It was monopoly as contrasted with the English system of free enterprise.

As soon as New France was established, a monopoly of its trade, together with all rights of colonization, was conferred by the Crown on a promoter commanding the necessary capital. In 1611 the monopoly was transferred to the Company of Associates, a group of capitalists and court favorites. This remained French policy to 1663, with changes merely in the beneficiaries. In 1663 the policy was modified to the extent of turning over the trade to the merchants of Montreal. But monopoly privileges were still granted by the Crown to favored individuals. Thus La Salle obtained such a privilege at Fort Frontenac in 1674 and a monopoly of the whole Mississippi Valley in 1683. In 1712 Sieur Antoine Crozat, a capitalist, obtained a fifteen-year monopoly of the trade.

French policy was marked also by greater concern than the British for protection of the Indians against one of the abuses of the fur trade—the traffic in liquor. French policy kept fur traders as much as possible out of the interior. It left to the Indians as much as possible the trapping of the furs and their transportation to a central market at Montreal.

Each spring the furs taken in the Great Lakes country were brought eastward by a fleet of Indian canoes to Montreal. The fleet was always large and picturesque, numbering 400 or 500 canoes and manned by 1000 to 1500 Indians. It was composed of sections from different parts of the Great Lakes region. From Lake Michigan would come one section, from Lake Superior would come another. All sections would join at a rendezvous and would move in a body to Montreal. Accompanying the fleet would be guards of hundreds of half-breeds and *coureurs de bois*. The entire catch of furs taken in the forest the preceding winter would be brought in this way.

The route of the fleet was normally the line of the Great Lakes and the St. Lawrence, with a portage around Niagara Falls. If, however, the Iroquois were on the warpath against the western Indians, the route was the interior one, the Ottawa River to the Great Lakes, discovered by Champlain.

By midsummer Montreal would be reached. A great fair would be held at which the furs brought by the Indians were exchanged for French goods. The fair would last a fortnight. Then the Indian fleet would return to the Great Lakes bearing the goods obtained in exchange for the furs. Upon the success of this annual expedition to Montreal, and on the success of the fair, the prosperity of eastern New France depended. If the Indians were prevented by fear of the Iroquois, or by some other cause, from coming east to Montreal, New France was on the verge of bankruptcy.

As a corollary to the concentration of trade at Montreal, Frenchmen were forbidden by royal decree to enter the interior. Such posts as were permitted there were only for the purpose of moving the furs of the Great Lakes region to Montreal in the regular channels.

The French policy was excellent in theory. It gave protection to the Indians from the abuses of the fur trade and especially from the abuses of the liquor traffic. At Montreal the traders could be kept under the eye of the French authorities. In the forests they were uncontrollable.

Another important advantage in the policy of centralization was the preservation of the fur-bearing animals from rapid extermination. In the breeding season, and in the season when the young were being reared, the Indians were not trapping. Their leaders were on the way to Montreal. The Indians were happy to make the trip to Montreal. They had no feeling that time was lost. They loved the excitement of the expedition, and the fun of the fair.

Compared with the trade in the English colonies the French fur trade was, on its face, more respectable. In the English colonies traders gathered wherever the Indians were congregated. Rum was a major item in the traffic. Indians were demoralized. They were removed from the protective equilibrium of former habits, encouraged to trap out of season, which meant extermination of the fur-bearing animals.

The French program of trade centralization was, however, breached by a variety of exceptions. Favored French fur traders often obtained special dispensations to carry on the trade in the interior. Thus in 1674 La Salle got the right to trade with the Indians at Fort Frontenac. The understanding was that he would purchase only the furs of such Indians as did not regularly come to Montreal. But he gave little attention to this restriction, which accounts in part for the desperate hostility of the Montreal merchants toward him.

In 1681 a more general departure from the centralization policy was initiated. Special licenses to the number of 25 were authorized by royal order to be given to traders operating in the interior. Such licenses were conferred as special favors on henchmen or friends by French colonial governors. Or they were sold to traders. Each license entitled the holder to take four canoeloads of goods into the interior. By partition of such licenses and by other subterfuges, a single license could be made to cover as many as 40 canoeloads of goods.

The greatest breach in the centralization policy, however, was illicit trading, which took place on a large scale despite the severe penalties of the law. It was carried on by the lowest and the highest in Canada, even by the governors of New France. The unauthorized traders in the interior were the so-called free traders or *coureurs de bois*. They operated either independently or under the protection of an influential French official to whom a share of the profits was kicked back. Half the population of Canada was said to be connected in one way or another with this trade. Contraband furs were sold almost openly in Montreal. If a conscientious Montreal official occasionally cracked down on it, the result was that the furs were diverted to the English at Albany.

One of the major problems of this trade was brandy. If brandy was sold to Indians in exchange for furs, it was certain to demoralize the Indians. It broke down Indian morale faster than the French missionaries could build it up again. That was fully realized by the French court, which was genuinely interested in the redemption and Christianization of the Indians. It was realized by the Montreal authorities also. One of the prime purposes of the centralization policy was to keep the brandy trade out of the interior. But that humane purpose was defeated to a large extent. It was almost impossible to keep brandy out of the Indian trade. Brandy was sold to Indians almost openly.

The use of brandy was defended by the Montreal merchants on the ground that it was the only way of meeting English competition at Albany. If brandy was forbidden in the French trade, the furs would go to Albany, where rum could be got in exchange. The rum was obtained from Boston, the greatest distillery center in the colonial period in North America. The Indian would merely get a different form of alcohol. Moreover, if brandy was withheld, French influence over the interior Indians would be supplanted by English influence. French control of the interior would be imperiled, and even the souls of the Indians would go to the heretic English. The brandy trade was therefore winked at by the French authorities. Even at Montreal the annual fair often ended in a spree. Still the brandy evil was never as unregulated as the rum evil in the English trade, since at Montreal at least some oversight of traders was possible.

French policy gave prominence to missionaries as well as to fur traders. The missionaries had functions of major importance. The French court relied on them to hold the interior since any large scale colonization by Frenchmen on the English pattern was not occurring. Frenchmen did not easily leave home. At the end of the French regime in 1763 their total number in Canada was not more than 65,000 or 75,000. By contrast there were 1,250,000 pioneers in the English colonies at that time.

Since Frenchmen would not readily migrate to New France the Indians had to be left as occupants of the soil. The Indians were the foundation on which French policy was built. The agency to win them and hold them to French loyalty was the Roman Catholic Church. But the extension of Catholic Christianity to the Indians was not solely a matter of policy on the part of the French court. It was also a matter of missionary zeal. Louis XIV was interested in saving the souls of the Indians, in winning the heathen to the true faith.

The order chosen to carry religion into the interior was the Jesuits. They were given a monopoly of the interior field, because they were the most militantly aggressive of any of the Catholic missionary orders. Another Catholic order, the Récollets, a branch of the Franciscans, also was permitted to work in the New World, but only in the maritime provinces of New France. Exceptions to this rule were allowed, and some Récollets went into the interior. They went, for instance, with La Salle, who disliked the Jesuits and was disliked by them in turn.

The work of the missionaries was chiefly spiritual, winning the Indians to Catholicism and performing for them the rites of the Church. The crusade the Jesuits carried into the wilderness for this purpose is one of the most thrilling and heroic episodes in the history of missionary enterprise. The story is magnificently told in Francis Parkman's *The Jesuits in North America* and in the writings of the Jesuits themselves in the monumental series of volumes edited by Reuben G. Thwaites, *The Jesuit Relations*.

The Jesuits ministered to the Indians also as teachers of the practical arts. They gave much time to this labor. They also served as doctors, giving such medical care as the jealousy and hostility of Indian medicine men permitted. They also kept the fur trade of the interior moving as much as possible toward Montreal, in the effort to tie the western Indians to Montreal by trade alliances. They were an important factor in the diplomacy of the forest, in committing the Indians militarily as much as possible to the French and against the English.

Parkman believed the Jesuits were a failure as spiritual guides of the Indians, that in spite of their prodigious and heroic labors they never converted a single normal Indian to Christianity in the sense that the Indian understood the theology and ethics of the Church. Indians were too steeped in their own ancient culture and mythology, too unbending, too stubborn in their adherence to old ways to be promising material for missionaries in the spiritual realm. The Jesuits sought to protect the Indians from the fur traders, especially from the brandy traffic, earning thereby the bitter hostility of the traders; but even in that attempt they were unsuccessful, because of the disintegration brought about by the traders. Some Jesuits, moreover, were charged with being themselves traders of brandy to the Indians.

As long as the valley of the St. Lawrence and the Great Lakes were the limits of the French advance into the interior, the English were not alarmed. The French were at a safe distance; the English colonies on the seaboard were well established, and the whole interior was open to them. But when Louisiana was set up as a French colony in 1699 and New Orleans was founded in 1718 on the lower Mississippi, the attitude of the English colonies, and of London, took a new turn. The governors of the southern colonies wrote home in anxiety about the threat of French power in the heartland of the continent, the possibility of a French encirclement, and a cutting off of English expansion.

The English counteroffensive began as a fur traders' advance into the interior, a contest for empire in which the weapons were at first trade goods and alcohol—rum against French brandy. It went on in every latitude from Hudson Bay to the Gulf of Mexico. At the Far North the English contestant was the Hudson's Bay Company, organized in 1670 in the reign of Charles II. It had its origin in a report made by two disgruntled French *coureurs de bois,* Radisson and Groseilliers. They had been engaged in illegal fur trading in the Great Lakes area. Their activity had been discovered by the Montreal authorities and a valuable fur cargo of theirs had been confiscated. Soon after, they became aware of the fur wealth of the Hudson Bay region. They had carried their knowledge of it to merchants in Boston, whom they sought to enlist in it. On failing, they resorted to London, where they received welcome and immediate support.

On the basis of the information thus obtained the Hudson's Bay Company was formed. It was given an enormous principality by the Crown—all the land whose waters drained into Hudson Bay from the crest of the Rocky Mountains to Labrador—the greater part of what is now Canada. It was named Rupert's Land in honor of Prince Rupert, a cousin of Charles II, who was one of the leaders of the company. The grant conferred full title to the soil, a complete monopoly of the trade of the area, and extensive rights of government.

The region was claimed by the French and a clash followed the grant. This coincided with rivalries of European origin and escalated into wars. The first, the War of the Palatinate, or King William's War, ran from 1689 to 1697. It was without outcome in the colonies though the fighting, especially in the New England uplands, was savage enough. A second war—that of the Spanish Succession, or Queen Anne's War, extending from 1701 to 1713—was more decisive. It ended with the Peace of Utrecht, in which British sovereignty was recognized over all of Rupert's Land. That vast area proved fabulously rich in furs. The Hudson's Bay Company became the greatest fur-trading corporation in the world.

Thereafter the British thrust into the interior went forward in the latitude of the

Great Lakes and the country south of them. This country was considered by the French especially their own, for it was they who had explored and exploited it, with Montreal as its base. The British base was Albany, which controlled the route of the Mohawk River, the route of the Iroquois, who were the intermediaries in the trade with Indians of the Great Lakes basin. The Iroquois connection was inherited from the Dutch in 1664, after the conquest of New Netherland, and it proved of great advantage both to the Iroquois and to the British. It brought the Iroquois plentiful supplies of cheap and high-quality trade goods—English woolens, kettles, and trinkets—half as costly as the French and better made. In the 18th century the English were the most efficient manufacturing power in Europe. Also English rum was much cheaper than French brandy and created intoxication quite as fast.

To the English, the Iroquois alliance was also of great advantage. It made available to them not only western furs but the trade routes of the Iroquois and their military prowess. On the other hand, the Iroquois were in some respects a liability to the Albany traders. The terror they inspired among the western tribes induced many of these to move closer to the French. Yet from the Iroquois base at Oswego on Lake Ontario, the English could press westward themselves and divert to Albany some of the French furs intended for Montreal. Ultimately, after a half-century, the English were able to dispense with the Iroquois partnership. In 1727 they persuaded the Iroquois to let them build a fort near Oswego and thereafter carried on a direct trade to the western tribes. In the latitudes of Pennsylvania and Virginia the English counteroffensive was pressed into the Ohio Valley. This achievement, the work of traders of Pennsylvania, Maryland, and Virginia, was a major threat to peace.

In the South the counteroffensive proceeded out of Charleston, which had become the successor to the primacy once held by Fort Henry in Virginia. Control of this trade had initially been a monopoly of the eight Carolina proprietors. But the monopoly could not long be sustained against interlopers, and outposts were established at Forts Augusta and Moore, on the Savannah River, and Okfuskee, on the upper Alabama. Westward the traders penetrated to the Creeks in Tennessee and Alabama and to the Chickasaw on the Mississippi. They competed there with the French operating out of New Orleans and the Spanish from Pensacola. The exports of Charleston increased from 65,000 deerskins in 1699 to 225,000 in 1731, in addition to quantities of other pelts and furs.

Thus in every latitude from the Far North to the Gulf of Mexico the fight for empire was waged. It went on over the counters in rival fur-trade posts, in the villages of opposing tribes, in the rum distilleries of Boston and the brandy presses of France, in the counting rooms of Montreal and Albany, and in the council chambers of London and Paris. It could not be limited to trade and degenerated into military duels. In 1744 it sank again into war, King George's War, the American counterpart of the War of the Austrian Succession, which preceded the final clash of the Seven Years' War.

The Seven Years' War in America

OF THE INTERCOLONIAL WARS fought between 1689 and 1763 for the mastery of the continent of North America and its trade, the first two produced little change in America, though the Treaty of Utrecht in 1713 brought England commercial advantages and French recognition of its sovereignty over Rupert's Land, Newfoundland, and Nova Scotia. The third war, the War of the Austrian Succession or King George's War (1744—48), was, like its predecessors, European in origin, and was indecisive in America.

The final war of the series, the Seven Years' War, differed from the previous clashes both in origins and in the conclusiveness of its results. In Europe it was true to its title, extending from 1756 to 1763. But in America—where it was known as the French and Indian War—it was longer. It began either in 1752 or in 1753, depending upon one's choice among frontier episodes. Its American origins lay in controversies between the French and British frontiers, from Nova Scotia in the east to the upper waters of the Ohio in the west.

In Nova Scotia the controversies emanated from the Treaty of Utrecht. Under that treaty the peninsula of Nova Scotia became British and was dominated from Halifax. Its inhabitants were Acadians, loyal to France for the most part. Connecting the peninsula with the mainland was a neck of land separating the combatants. On one side of it stood a British fort—Beaubassin. On the other was a French fort—Beauséjour. Between the two a tug-of-war went on over the issue of the allegiance of the Acadians.

Another zone of incessant friction was the valley extending from New York City to Montreal. At the south it was English, with Schenectady and Albany as strong points. At the north it was French, with a fortress at Crown Point, which had connection with Montreal via Lake Champlain and the Richelieu River. For many years Crown Point had been used as a base for Indian raids against the New England and New York back country.

The region of greatest friction, however, lay in the trans-Appalachian West. In the country between Lake Erie and the upper waters of the Ohio was a natural passageway for connecting the two great French provinces of Quebec and Louisiana, and their seats of government at Quebec City and New Orleans. The route ran from Lake Erie up Elk Creek, a stream emptying into Lake Erie. Then it passed to French Creek, one of the tributaries of the Allegheny, which in turn was a tributary of the Ohio. This route was the shortest and most convenient passageway from the Lakes to the Mississippi.

In 1749 and in 1750 the French undertook to fortify the passage. They had wished to do so sooner but had met a formidable obstacle, the Iroquois, who possessed it and had been hostile to the French since the days of Champlain. In 1749 and 1750 the Iroquois were persuaded to relent and the French moved to seize and fortify the route.

This was just the period when English fur traders were advancing into the area of the upper Ohio. Traders from Pennsylvania and Virginia were establishing connections with the Indians and acquiring furs. Among the traders were such famous frontier figures as George Croghan and Christopher Gist, who had been pressing the English trade throughout the upper Ohio region.

Their favorite Ohio rendezvous was Pickawillany, a town of the Miami tribe on the Miami River in what is now western Ohio. It was one of the greatest Indian trade centers in the West with a population of some 2000 persons. It had a fortified trading post where sometimes as many as 50 English traders could be found at one time. They were solid with the Miami, for they brought English trade goods that were cheap and good. Their standing with the tribe is indicated by the fact that their chief was known as Old Britain.

The French hated the town. No other place except Oswego gave them such alarm. Its trade with the British was in defiance of French claims to sovereignty in all this wilderness. Also its trade lanes ran athwart the route to be opened to New Orleans.

In 1749 the French sent a military expedition, under command of Jean B. Le Moyne, Sieur de Bienville, to the upper Ohio region. It was designed to overawe the Miami, to proclaim French sovereignty over the whole country, and to drive out English fur traders. The expedition moved from Lake Erie, down French Creek and the Allegheny to the Ohio, down the Ohio to the Miami, then up the Miami to Pickawillany. Wherever the force went it proclaimed French sovereignty and left lead plates, containing formal French proclamations of ownership and warnings to the English to get out. The plates were usually buried at the mouths of streams emptying into the Ohio. Burial would seem at first thought a strange way of issuing a proclamation, but nothing else was feasible. If lead plates were nailed to trees the Indians would consider them gifts and would melt them down for bullets.

One of the plates was buried at the junction of the Muskingum and Ohio rivers, at the place where Marietta now stands. It was found half a century later by boys at play. The boys were not history-minded, and before the plate could be rescued from them part of it had been melted down for bullets. The rest of it was saved and was deposited in the American Antiquarian Society at Worcester, Massachusetts. It is one of the treasures of this Society, and indicates the character of all the proclamations.

When the expedition arrived at Pickawillany it encountered a good many English traders. Bienville warned the traders off but did not dare do anything more, for the Miami and Old Britain were determined that no harm should befall their friends. In fact, the Indians so threatened the expedition that Bienville hurriedly returned to Canada, having only partly fulfilled his mission.

In 1752 a new French expedition moved out against Pickawillany from Michillimackinac on the Great Lakes. It was led by a Michillimackinac Frenchman, Charles de Langlade, who later planned the ambuscade that destroyed the Braddock army in 1755. His force consisted chiefly of Ottawa Indians. The expedition overwhelmed Pickawillany, plundered it of a great store of trading goods, and destroyed the post. Five of the English traders were captured and carried off into captivity. Old Britain was killed. In accordance with an Ottawa custom he was cooked until tender and eaten. The destruction of Pickawillany was a first blow struck in the Seven Years' War.

In 1753 the French constructed a row of four forts from Lake Erie to the forks of the Ohio. The first of them was Fort Presque Isle on Lake Erie. The most formidable of the four was Fort Duquesne, built at the commanding site of the forks of the Ohio.

This activity brought Virginia, which claimed that country, to take countermeasures. Its governor, Robert Dinwiddie, sent a messenger, George Washington, to the Ohio country in 1753 to warn the French off. Washington at this point emerges into history. He gave warning to the French. On the way back he engaged them in a skirmish—called the Battle of Great Meadows—which set off the fighting in America three years before the opening of hostilities in Europe. Washington hurriedly built Fort Necessity on the Monongahela River, but the next year the French captured the fort.

News of the defeat caused British officials to send to America two regiments of regulars under General Edward Braddock, an able but aged general, accustomed to the art of European, not American, warfare. He and his troops landed in Virginia and ascended the Potomac to Fort Cumberland, Maryland. A road had to be built inland through the wilderness, wide enough for his supply trains. His men were exhausted by the time they reached a point seven miles south of Fort Duquesne. They were unaware of an ambuscade of French and Indians, planned by the same Charles de Langlade who had overwhelmed Pickawillany. Braddock's force was overwhelmed in the attack, Braddock was killed, and the survivors fled back to Fort Cumberland. The French success emboldened the Indians to side with the French, and they ravaged the frontiers of Pennsylvania and Virginia. These raids sent Pennsylvania Scotch-Irish and Germans southward.

From this woeful start the English went forward to a succession of tremendous victories in the war under the inspiring leadership of William Pitt. They overwhelmed the combined forces of the French and the Spanish. They took Canada from the French; also the whole of the trans-Appalachian West to the Mississippi. They captured East and West Florida from the Spanish. At sea they seized Martinique and Guadeloupe from the French, and Havana from the Spanish.

But the war was costly and burdensome. By 1761 its unending casualty lists and oppressive taxes had become almost unbearable. The English king and Parliament desired to have peace by negotiations with the French. Pitt, who was not ready for peace, was obliged to resign as Prime Minister. In 1761 negotiations began, with the understanding that England would restore to France and Spain some of its conquests. The question before the English was which of the gains should be retained, which should be restored. Over that issue a division of opinion developed in the English cabinet and public.

One group, the continentalists, desired that Canada, the trans-Appalachian West, and the Floridas be retained. They represented the fur-trading and land-speculating elements in England as well as leaders who believed that the newly won lands on the North American continent would be of considerable, if not immediate, profit to England. They foresaw greater markets for British manufactures and sources of raw materials. Benjamin Franklin, the colonial agent in London, stood with the continentalists.

The insular group believed the tropical sugar islands should be held and that part of the continental conquests should be returned. It valued the immediate profitability of the sugar islands, their commercial potentialities, and the strategic values of Guadeloupe, Martinique, and Havana. It believed Canada, the Floridas, and the trans-Appalachian West would prove to be administrative burdens. They would cost more than they would bring in revenue. The group also believed French Canada should be left to France as a matter of imperial prudence. If French Canada were allowed to be French, the spirit of self-assertiveness and independence in the American colonies would be held in check and they would remain permanently in a state of proper subjection to the British Crown. This argument was countered by Franklin's assurance that the American colonies were so divided against each other that they would forever be in need of British support.

The victory in the debate went to the continentalists. In the Treaty of 1763, Canada, the trans-Appalachian West as far as the Mississippi River, and the two Floridas were retained by England. The important sugar islands were restored by the treaty to France and Spain. Thus all the country lying between the Appalachian Mountains and the Mississippi, except the city of New Orleans, passed to England. As part of a Franco-Spanish settlement, Louisiana, including the city of New Orleans, which is on the east side of the river, became Spanish. It was given to Spain by France in compensation for the loss of the Floridas to the English.

As a result of these arrangements France disappeared altogether from the continental part of North America. She retained only some small islands in the Atlantic. The French barrier that had once seemed so formidable to the English colonies dissolved, just at the time the frontiersmen in the Virginia and Carolina uplands were ready to overleap the mountains into the great valley of the interior.

As soon as the English government had completed the peace settlement it was faced with the problem of forming a policy for the West. It had never squarely faced that problem as long as the crucial issue of ownership was in dispute. It had simply left the trans-Appalachian region to the care of the colonies which had claims there. The immediate problems to be faced in this area were the unregulated fur trade and uncontrolled settlement. The fur trade especially needed regulation. It was carried on usually by the most hard-boiled elements in colonial life, men at the level of the Indian in their outlook. Fur traders had to have a certain amount of obtuseness to engage in a business in which rum played so large a part.

When a fur trader came to an Indian village he usually began his operations by opening his kegs of rum. His arrival was the signal for what the traders called a "frolic," a polite name for a wild carouse. In such a spree Indian bucks would go on a shooting or stabbing rampage and drunken mothers would strangle noisy children. John Long, a fur trader who carried on business in the trans-Appalachian West after 1763, gave graphic descriptions of such a frolic in his published journal. He considered his own method of dealing with Indians a model of thoughtfulness and self-restraint. First, he liberally watered down the rum he intended to distribute; second, he added laudanum so that when the Indians had got drunk enough to be at the fighting stage, the laudanum would put them to sleep.

Fur traders not only brought demoralization into Indian life, but those of one colony or one company would stir up the Indians against the traders of another colony or company as a matter of trade competition. Traders would represent their rivals as spies of hostile Indians or land grabbers in disguise. The result was that the Indians would presently go on the warpath not merely against the traders but against the frontier settlements.

An even more serious problem than abuses of the fur trade was the problem of the unregulated advance of settlers into the Indian country, the constant loss of hunting grounds to white intruders. That was an evil disturbing the Indians more than the rum trade and producing most of the Indian wars of American history. The Indians who were especially uneasy under these conditions were those north of the Ohio, the Shawnee, the Delaware, and the Ottawa. They lay directly in the path of the expansion of settlement.

The expansion was especially swift in the closing years of the Seven Years' War and in the postwar years. It brought a rush of frontiersmen, largely Scotch-Irish and Germans, to the region around the forks of the Ohio in western Pennsylvania, as soon as Fort Duquesne had been captured in 1758. In the Virginia latitude the movement began even sooner, in response to a Virginia law of 1754 offering 1000 acres of land free, and free of quitrents for 10 years, to anyone who would locate on Virginia's western waters. The law had the full approval of the London government. It was in a sense a war measure to attract settlement into an area in dispute with the French. In addition to the free land offered, Virginia had by 1757 disposed of 2 million acres of land to speculators on her western waters. The settlement that followed was especially alarming to the Indians.

Another source of discontent, particularly to the Indians north of the Ohio, was the loss of bargaining position they had enjoyed during the war, when they had been able to play off the French against the English and get presents and flattery from both. After the war they were at the mercy of the English. They were misled by false reports, spread by French traders, that a new French army was coming which would support an Indian uprising against the British.

These Indians were brought to a fighting pitch by the blundering policy of Lord Geoffrey Amherst, the British commanding general in America. In a fit of economy in the demobilization period after the war he abruptly cut off all annual presents to which the Indians had become accustomed. Amherst detested Indians and had no idea how to deal with them. His attitude is revealed by a suggestion made in one of his letters home that the only good solution of the problem of the interior was to distribute to the Indians blankets that had been thoroughly infected with smallpox.

As a result of their grievances the northwest Indians organized a great intertribal uprising. On a single day in the spring of 1763, they surprised and destroyed every British post in the West except three, and then carried the tomahawk to the exposed settlements. More than a thousand persons were massacred on the Pennsylvania, Maryland, and Virginia frontiers, and terror was spread throughout the area.

This uprising—known as Pontiac's War—is graphically described by Francis Parkman in his *History of the Conspiracy of Pontiac*. Researches that have been made since Parkman's day have tended to diminish somewhat the stature ascribed to Pontiac and the central role he played in the uprising, but the story is still basically sound history and it is one of the great works of American literature. Pontiac's uprising thrust upon the British government abruptly and dramatically the need for the formulation of a new policy for the West.

British Western Policy, 1763–75

WITH THE ACQUISITION of the great interior of the continent the English government acquired formidable problems. One of them was the Indian question, highlighted by the uprising of Pontiac. A swift response was made to it. British regulars were sent to quell it and succeeded in doing so after several years of fighting.

A more basic problem was the preservation of peace with the Indians in the future, which required a policy of orderly administration of the whole area. The initial answer given to that problem was the Proclamation of 1763. It converted the entire trans-Appalachian region to the Mississippi into a temporary Indian reserve. The reserve was marked off at the east by a boundary that ran from the southern limit of the province of Quebec down the watershed of the Appalachian Mountains to Florida. West of that line no further land grants were to be made by colonial authorities. Speculators were ordered to stay out of the region. So also were prospective settlers. Settlers already there were ordered to return to the East.

The fur trade was put under restriction also. Traders were not to operate there except those holding licenses from colonial authorities, backed by bonds to make sure that orders from the English government would be obeyed. The trade was to be carried on only at designated posts where it could be kept under observation. The rum trade, the old evil, was strictly forbidden; also forbidden was trade in certain military rifles. At every trading post three representatives of the imperial government were to be stationed—an Indian agent, an interpreter, and a blacksmith.

Land speculation was also put under imperial control. Purchases of land from Indian tribes by private speculators were prohibited. Every negotiation for land was to be under the direction of one of the two Indian superintendents to be appointed by the Crown, acting in cooperation with the colonial governors. The program of converting the new West into an Indian reserve was intended to be temporary. Closure of the region was to continue only until an orderly advance into it could be worked out.

In the 1763 Proclamation the English government gave preliminary organization to other areas brought into the Empire in 1763. It did so for Quebec, whose boundaries were reduced to a fraction of what they had been. This reflected the British policy of not giving a hostile population too much room to expand over. The southern and western boundaries of the province were made especially confining. The southern line ran from the Bay of Chaleur parallel to the St. Lawrence as far as the 45th parallel, then due west to the St. Lawrence and out to Lake Nipissing. All the area south and west of this line which had once belonged to Canada was made part of the Indian reserve. The two Floridas, East and West Florida, were also given organization and boundaries. The confining principle was applied to them since they were also occupied by an alien population.

A year after the Proclamation a detailed plan of government was issued for the Indian reserve by the Board of Trade. The Plan of 1764 became the basis for British administration of the Indian reserve for a period of four years, though it was never formally adopted by the British cabinet. It divided the trans-Appalachian country into two Indian superintendencies. The two were marked off from each other by the line of the Ohio River. Each was put under the charge of an official experienced in the management of Indians.

The northern superintendency was assigned to Sir William Johnson, an Indian trader of great ability residing in Albany. He was chosen because he was high in the confidence of the Iroquois. One of the reasons for his popularity was that his mistress, Caroline, was the niece of a leading Mohawk chief. He was a widower, so that he could afford this luxury. By her he had three children. After her death he took Molly, the sister of the famous Mohawk chief Joseph Brant, as his mistress.

The southern superintendency was placed under the headship of Colonel John Stuart, who was well liked by the Cherokee. He was less able than Johnson. He was encumbered with a wife, so he could have no Indian mistress, but his deputy had a girl friend among the Cherokee.

One of the major assignments of the Indian superintendents was to mark out a line that should be the limit of white settlement in the West. It was to be drawn by treaties negotiated with the tribes, and would replace the temporary Proclamation Line of 1763, which had been proclaimed off the cuff to meet the emergency of Pontiac's uprising. It had been a rigidly geographic line—the crest of a mountain system. Its one and only merit was that it was easily defined and recognizable and could be described without a survey.

The chief weakness of the Proclamation Line was that it was out of accord with the facts of existing settlement. It lay in some regions so far west of settlement that it was meaningless as a check on frontier advance. This was so in the latitude of New York. The same was true in the latitude of South Carolina and Georgia. On the other hand, in Pennsylvania, Virginia, and North Carolina it lay so close to the frontier settlements that it allowed hardly any room for the expansion of their population.

The directions given the two Indian superintendents were to negotiate agreements with groups of tribes. Each piece of the line was to be drawn after preparation of the tribes. For the northern section Sir William Johnson in 1768 called an Indian conference at Fort Stanwix on the upper waters of the Mohawk River. It was one of the most notable gatherings of the colonial period, attended by all the important

Iroquois chiefs and by delegations from many of the tribes north of the Ohio. About 3400 Indians were there and the presents distributed amounted to 200 canoeloads. Among the notable whites in attendance, other than Sir William Johnson, were the governor of New Jersey and representatives of other colonies. Agents of the big fur-trading and land-speculating interests in the colonies were likewise present.

At the conference an Indian line was agreed to that was to run from a point near Oneida Lake in New York. This starting point was chosen because Johnson thought it would not be prudent to try to draw the line through northern New York. From Oneida Lake the line ran to the headwaters of the Delaware River, thence across Pennsylvania to the forks of the Ohio, and down the Ohio to the mouth of the Great Kanawha (Map 7). In Pennsylvania and Virginia a considerable tract of land was thus opened beyond the line of the Proclamation of 1763. A large part of what is now southwestern Pennsylvania and western Virginia became available for settlement.

Another conference to draw the line in the South was held in 1768. It was with the Cherokee at a village called Hard Labor in South Carolina, and presided over by Colonel John Stuart. The line agreed upon carried the Stanwix boundary southward. It ran from the mouth of the Great Kanawha to Chiswell's Mine in southern Virginia. From Chiswell's Mine it ran irregularly southward to the Reedy River, a tributary of the Santee River in northern South Carolina.

A third conference was held in 1768 in the Far South to establish the southernmost part of the line. It took place at Savannah with the Creek tribe. The line drawn there ran from the Reedy River through eastern Georgia toward the coastline of Georgia, thence along the perimeter of Georgia and Florida to about Mobile in West Florida. In the peninsula of Florida it opened only some coastal towns to white settlement.

As a result of all these negotiations a boundary of racial demarcation, a line of segregation, was established that ran all the way from New York to Mobile in West Florida. The line had Indian acceptance and permitted some expansion of white settlement.

But the line was no sooner drawn than the process of breaking it down began. Throughout American history treaties with Indians have taken effect only against Indians, for the frontier could never be brought to respect such treaties. The process of breaking down the 1768 line began even while the treaty-making process was going on. At the Congress of Fort Stanwix a curious cession of land was made by the Iroquois in addition to the cession described. All the area shown on the map between the Ohio and Tennessee rivers was given away by the Iroquois. That area was not within the right of the Iroquois to cede. It was a country to which the Cherokee and the Shawnee had the best claim. But the Iroquois insisted on relinquishing it to prove that they controlled it.

The cession ought not to have been accepted by Sir William Johnson. It invited trouble later with the Cherokee, the bitter enemies of the Iroquois. In accepting it Johnson was violating his instructions. At a later time he was accused of having been bribed by Pennsylvania and Virginia land-speculating interests and of having adroitly induced the Iroquois to make the cession by casting doubt on their right to do so. Johnson indignantly denied the charge.

This curious cession was permitted by the British authorities to stand, chiefly for

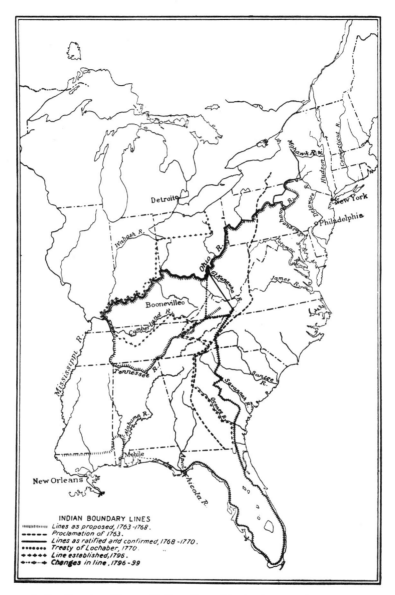

7. Indian Boundary Line, 1768 (from Farrand in the *American Historical Review*)

the reason that if it had been rejected a whole new negotiation with the Iroquois would have become necessary. The result was a wide opening through the treaty line for speculators.

The second break in the line occurred in Virginia, as a result of the urgings of Virginia land speculators. They wanted more land made available to them than had been obtained at the Hard Labor conference. They kept up an agitation for a new treaty and finally in 1770 had their way. In that year a new agreement was obtained from the Cherokee, the Treaty of Lochaber, by which the Hard Labor line was shifted westward to a new anchor on Long Island in the Holston River. From Long Island the line was to run due north to the mouth of the Great Kanawha, opening a big new triangle of land to speculators.

To reduce the expense of surveying the line northward from Long Island, another agreement was made with the Cherokee. The surveying would be carried only as far as the Louisa River, a branch of the Big Sandy. When the line reached the Louisa it was to follow the channel of the Louisa and the Big Sandy to a junction with the Ohio, and then the channel of the Ohio around to the outlet of the Great Kanawha. Finally, an error was made—a rather extraordinary one, though perhaps bona fide. The name Louisa River was used sometimes in the colonial period to designate the stream now known as the Kentucky. When the survey was run in 1771 by John Donelson, the line was run down the Kentucky to the Ohio and around to the Great Kanawha. It is suggestive that these shiftings and errors all occurred at the section of the line of 1768 where the pressure of population was greatest into the Indian country.

British policy in the West between 1763 and 1774 was vacillating. Whenever a new ministry came into office in England there was a change in western policy. In general, the Whigs of the Shelburne type, who were friendly to the colonies, tried to give them as much control of the West as possible. The less friendly Whigs wanted control to be centered in London.

As a result of a change of ministry in 1768 all detailed administration of the Plan of 1764 was abandoned. The fundamental reason for the change in policy was that the cost of administration under the Plan was proving burdensome. The expectation of the British government had been that the cost of administration would be borne in part at least by taxes collected in the colonies, such as the Stamp Act and the Townshend taxes. But that expectation was defeated by the colonial resistance to parliamentary taxation. All thought of collecting from the colonies the costs of administering the West were given up, and the British government felt unwilling to attempt placing the burden on the British taxpayers. Therefore in 1768 the new ministry restored administration of the West to the colonies, including the control of the fur trade. The two Indian superintendents were kept at their posts, but stayed only in a supervisory capacity. British troops were withdrawn from most of the scattered posts in the West, and concentrated on the seaboard, where they could be more cheaply supplied, and where the need for them was increasing, in view of the bitterness of the colonial quarrel with Parliament over taxation.   *note following discussion*

In 1774 Parliament adopted the Quebec Act. The province of Quebec, inhabited by a French population numbering approximately 65,000, had been since 1763 under the British flag and subject to the administrative provisions of the Proclamation of that year. This meant English forms of law. The inhabitants had asked for a restoration of the French code. As Roman Catholics they especially demanded freedom of religion. An ambiguous promise had been extended to them in the Treaty of 1763 that they should have the right to worship as Catholics "as far as the laws of Great Britain permit." That provision, strictly interpreted, gave no rights to Catholics at all. Catholic worship in England was forbidden under law. However, there was an informal toleration in England, and the same informal toleration had been extended, after 1763, to Quebec. But Quebec Catholics wanted something more than this—equality of religion including the right to collect tithes for the support of their church and the right to hold office, neither of which was allowed Catholics in England.

These desires were, in part, granted in the Quebec Act. The French code was restored for all civil cases. The English criminal code, which was milder than the French, was retained for criminal cases. The act also granted equality of religions. Quebec Catholics could collect money for their church and were made eligible to hold office. They were also given the form of government they wanted—a governor and council appointed by the Crown. The Quebec people did not want an elected assembly. They were accustomed to paternalism. The act was an enlightened piece of colonial legislation, a landmark in the history of progressive colonial administration.

But a major provision of the act related to the boundaries of the province. All the region between the Great Lakes and the Ohio River, reaching to the Mississippi, which had been cut away from Quebec by the Proclamation of 1763 and had been thrown into the Indian reserve, was restored to Quebec. That area, the hinterland of the eastern colonies, was reassigned to a province which, though British-held, was alien in population and in outlook.

What were the motives animating this provision? One answer was the record of excessive colonial land speculation, some of it illegal, in this hinterland. It had been overrun by Virginia and Pennsylvania speculators. In 1763 a group of Virginians, including the Washingtons and the Lees, had organized the Mississippi Land Company and were seeking from Virginia authorities a tract of 2,500,000 acres in the upper Mississippi Valley, part of it in the Illinois country. Three years later a group of Pennsylvanians was seeking to set up three new colonies, all in the Northwest. It included the prominent Philadelphia fur-trading firm of Baynton, Wharton and Morgan. Benjamin Franklin was part of it and so, also, was a prominent Englishman, Lord Shelburne. In 1773 another Philadelphia firm, David Franks and Company, organized the Illinois Wabash Company and bought from the Illinois Indians a huge tract of land lying along the Illinois and Mississippi rivers. This was in flagrant violation of law and of the principles established in the Proclamation of 1763. One of the reasons for restoring the Northwest area to Quebec was to bring the area again under the control of the imperial authorities.

Another purpose was to return the fur trade of that area to imperial authorities. In the Quebec Act the governor of Quebec was directed to reapply to this region all the detailed regulatory trade features of the Plan of 1764.

A third intention of the Quebec Act was to unite for governmental purposes the 7000 French and half-breed elements in the Illinois country with the French in Quebec. The western French had been left under military government since their separation from Quebec under the Proclamation of 1763. They were restored to civil government.

All these provisions offended the public of the seaboard colonies. They offended especially Massachusetts, Connecticut, and Virginia, all of which had claims to the Northwest region. Also, they offended the land-speculating interests in Virginia and in Pennsylvania. The rich trade of the region north of the Ohio was likely to gravitate under the act to Montreal. A fourth cause of resentment was that executive government was applied to an area which would have had popular government under Massachusetts, Connecticut, or Virginia.

Finally, the Quebec Act meant the extension of Roman Catholicism over the Northwest, which gave the greatest offense. In Puritan Massachusetts and Connecticut it seemed an extension of idolatry. This sentiment was graphically expressed by a Boston clergyman who in a sermon declared that the Quebec Act was greeted with a jubilee in hell. In Massachusetts the popular belief was that the Quebec Act was a punitive measure of Parliament in reply to the Boston Tea Party of 1773.

The religious intolerance of the New England colonies on this occasion soon exacted its penalty. In the ensuing war the thirteen colonies hoped that Quebec could be induced to join them as a fourteenth colony in fighting the British. But the Catholics of Quebec remained cold to the cause of the rebels.

The British purposes were essentially benevolent in the measures adopted for the West in the years 1763 through 1774. They were designed to ensure an orderly occupation of the western wilderness. But these purposes were subverted by colonial forces too powerful to be controlled—land speculation, the fur trade, and dispossession of the Indian. These forces were, moreover, not merely colonial, they were also British, especially land speculation and fur trading. They were reinforced by the reluctance of the British taxpayers to pay the costs of detailed imperial administration of the newly acquired wilderness. When the attempt was made by Parliament to impose on the colonies part of the costs of imperial administration, it led to controversy over the right of Parliament to tax the colonies, and that controversy became steadily more explosive. Finally, when Parliament in 1774 voted to restore the area north of the Ohio to the Quebec province, the religious emotions of the colonists, especially in New England, became aroused to the fury pitch, and the Quebec Act became one of the sparks that set off the explosion of the American Revolution.

Terrain of the Interior

THE TERRITORY ACQUIRED by Britain in 1763 and brought under administrative control the next year was separated from the eastern seaboard by three chains of mountains, all lying along a northeast–southwest axis. In each chain was a mountain wall presenting its own set of obstacles to pioneers trying to cross.

The first of these was the Blue Ridge Mountains (Map 8), extending all the way from Pennsylvania southward to Georgia. They consist in Pennsylvania and in Virginia of a single high ridge. They widen out gradually and become the club-like mass which includes the Great Smoky Mountains. They were an especially formidable barrier at the south, where they were, for the early pioneers, an almost insuperable barrier.

West of the Blue Ridge Mountains lay the "linear ridges" or parallel ridges of the Appalachians. These were especially formidable in the Virginia latitude, rising up 4000 feet from the floor of the valley of the Appalachians. They were so abrupt that they could be crossed only where rivers had cut transverse valleys through them.

West of the linear ridges is the Allegheny Front. This is the steep edge of the geographic province known to geographers as the Appalachian or Allegheny Plateaus, later described. The Front runs all the way from New York to Alabama. It goes by different local names in different latitudes. At the north it is the steep eastern slope of the Catskill Mountains. At the south it is the Cumberland Escarpment. It was everywhere one of the most formidable of all the hurdles to the West to be scaled.

What made this whole mountain system so difficult to pioneers was that it was a combination of three barriers. Where an opening existed through one of them, the passageway was closed in the others. Together they were a tremendous obstruction. In every mountain system there are useful passes and gaps, and the Appalachians were no exception in having passes through single walls. What the pioneers needed were ones nearly opposite each other in all three walls.

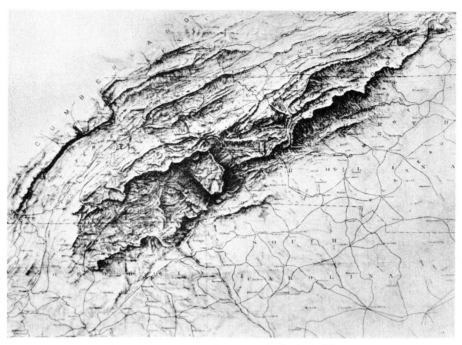

8. Southern Appalachians (from the U.S. Geological Survey)

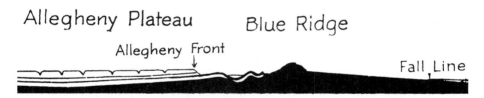

Allegheny Plateau   Blue Ridge

Allegheny Front

Fall Line

Cross Section (from Lobeck)

One such series does exist, however, in the South just where the mountains are most massive. The map shows its eastern and western openings. The eastern is Saluda Gap, a pass through the Blue Ridge, where the Saluda, an east-flowing river, cuts through the Blue Ridge just on the boundary of North and South Carolina. Saluda Gap ties in with a second pass in the series, the valley of the French Broad River, one of the mountain tributaries of the Tennessee River. The French Broad has cut a transverse valley across the Great Smoky Mountains. A third pass in the series is Cumberland Gap, a pass through the Cumberland Escarpment just on the border between Tennessee and Kentucky. Pictured in illustration 9, it is one of the most significant of American passes—the equivalent of South Pass in the Rockies. Near the center of the picture lies the village of Cumberland Gap. Higher up is the pass, and beyond it in the distance, the relatively open plateau country of Kentucky.

9. Cumberland Gap (from the National Park Service)

This series of passes has a general southeast–northwest axis. Together they opened a way from the seaboard to the West in the direction pioneers desired to go. If the pioneers were from the Piedmont they used the entire series. If they were from the Great Valley they used part of it. They got into the valley in Pennsylvania, flowed southward in the trough as far as Cumberland Gap, and then out through the Gap into the West.

The Saluda–Cumberland opening was more than a mere pioneers' entrance to the West. It became, when Kentucky and Tennessee had been occupied, a means of sending surplus produce back to the seaboard. From Kentucky and Tennessee droves of cattle, horses, mules, and hogs went by this route to the cotton plantations of South Carolina and Georgia. It is still one of the most used mountain openings in the United States. It is a major outlet for the tobacco of eastern Tennessee and eastern Kentucky to a seaboard market. From Tennessee and Kentucky, the leaf goes in great quantity by this highway to tobacco factories in North Carolina.

In the latitude of the middle colonies openings through the mountains were also found. One of them lay between the upper waters of the Potomac and the upper waters of the Ohio. That opening was converted into a road in 1755 by the Braddock expedition. An even better-known northern opening is the route of the Mohawk Valley in New York.

The problem of crossing the mountain barrier was by no means solved in the pioneer days. It became a greater and greater problem after the West had become settled and had a surplus to exchange with the East. In the 1820's, 1830's, and 1840's it led to a major program of internal improvements and the issues arising out of it. In the railroad age it was again a problem. It called forth spectacular marvels of railroad engineering. An example is the climb of the Pennsylvania Railroad up the Allegheny Front at Altoona in Pennsylvania—the famous Horseshoe Curve—built in 1854 and regarded at that time as one of the engineering wonders of the world. The problem is equally illustrated on the Pennsylvania Turnpike today, where there are seven tunnels through mountains, seven miles of tunnels all told. Five tunnels are needed to cut through the linear ridges, two are necessary for the Allegheny Front.

The problem of the mountains was intensified in the pioneer age by the Indian problem. The mountain passes were closed in pioneer days by Indian tribes, or aggregations of tribes. In the latitude of the Saluda-Cumberland Gap, the opening through the mountains was blocked by the fighting tribe of the Shawnee. In the New York latitude where the mountains could be passed by way of the valley of the Mohawk, was the League of the Iroquois. In the far South there was no mountain problem. The Appalachians could be skirted there. But in this latitude lay the formidable Creek confederacy. This combination of mountain and Indian barriers was a profound influence shaping the flow of population from the seaboard into the interior.

The country lying to the west of the mountains is the province of the Appalachian or Allegheny Plateaus. This takes its name from the fact that in a remote geologic age the province was actually a series of plateaus sloping off toward the Ohio and Mississippi rivers. They later became, by ages of weathering, the broken and irregular hill and mountain country, which is referred to later in this history as the Allegheny Plateau.

From the point of view of farming the province was of uneven value. It contained some areas of wonderful attractiveness, some of the finest soils in the United States. It also contained a good deal of very poor land. One wonderfully attractive area was the Kentucky Blue Grass region. This is a limestone region of great fertility, especially the part known as the Inner Blue Grass or the Lexington Plain. Another inviting area was western Kentucky, which had good soil well adapted to tobacco and corn growing. Other such areas were the Nashville Basin of Tennessee, sometimes called the Tennessee Blue Grass, and the Huntsville region in Alabama within the big bend of the Tennessee. Some of the river valleys of the province were also attractive, especially those of the Great Kanawha, the Kentucky, the Cumberland, and the Tennessee.

The greater part of the Allegheny Plateau province is not especially fertile. It is a hill area and has been called the province of 100,000 hills. Much of it is actual mountain country in eastern Tennessee, eastern Kentucky, and West Virginia. One of the most unpromising sections is the so-called Highland Rim, a ring of sterile hills that hems in the Nashville Basin of Tennessee. It is a rough stone wall surrounding a garden.

A heavy hardwood forest of oak, hickory, and chestnut covered the Allegheny Plateau. Its timber was a burden to clear away, yet was welcomed by pioneers. They felt that land covered by hardwood was necessarily good soil. Also it had an important advantage over pine land, since the stumps of hardwood trees rot faster than those of pine, which are full of pitch.

The Blue Grass region of Kentucky was one of the less heavily timbered areas of the province. It was an alternation of groves and open land, like an English park and beautiful to look upon. Its sparseness of forest growth was a great attraction to settlers because the job of clearing the land was not a killing one.

The Blue Grass region was a land without Indian residents when the white man arrived. It had recently been evacuated by the Shawnee, who had drifted northward across the Ohio before whites crossed the mountains. Not only did the Shawnee evacuate the Blue Grass country, they left the gateway to the province—the Cumberland Gap—open, which helps to explain why Daniel Boone was able so easily to bring his settlers into the area and to get established there. A wedge of settlement was inserted into this vacant area. Later the wedge simply spread out north and south.

But Kentucky was unoccupied only in the sense that no Indian tribe was in residence. It was a hunting ground of Indians, used by both southern and northern tribes—by the Cherokee, whose homes were in the Tennessee area, and by the Shawnee and Miami, who came from the north side of the Ohio. It was, moreover, a battleground—an Indian no-man's-land, crisscrossed by warrior paths. Among Indians it was known, even before the whites arrived, as a dark and bloody ground. It had been fought over especially by the Iroquois from the north and the Cherokee from the south. It became even more a bloody ground during the War of the American Revolution, when raiding parties of Shawnee and Miami were sent down into the Kentucky settlements by the British in Detroit. However, the fact that no tribe was actually resident in the Blue Grass region did much to ease the problem of the early white entrance.

That influx took place in a number of stages. First came hunters and trappers, including figures destined to achieve fame in American folklore and in frontier history—such colorful figures as Dr. Thomas Walker, Christopher Gist, John Finley, and Daniel Boone. They were known to Indians as the ''Long Knives,'' from the long hunting knives they carried. They were masters of the arts of the hunt and of Indian fighting.

Some of them were explorers of note, who revealed the Allegheny Plateau province to Easterners. In 1750 Dr. Thomas Walker discovered Cumberland Gap. In the same year Christopher Gist traversed the whole of Kentucky to the Miami River. In 1752 John Finley saw the falls of the Ohio, where Louisville now stands, and came back with such glowing reports of Kentucky that Daniel Boone got interested in the Kentucky area. In 1769 Daniel Boone reached the beauties of the Blue Grass.

The Blue Grass region was attractive partly because it was a hunter's paradise, especially the Lexington Plain section of it. It carried a luxuriant, tall, nutritious grass, producing an abundant blue seed, which gave the grass and the region its name. That grass, and the salt licks of the region, attracted whole herds of deer, wood buffalo, and elk. They had done so even before the arrival of the Indians. Paleontologists have found in the area deposits of bones of species long extinct—the mastodon and the related mammoth.

But these lands had been the hunting grounds of the Indians from time immemorial. The wildlife nourished on the grasslands—together with that found in the forests and streams—were the essentials of their survival. The wilderness and all its bounty were sanctified by their mythology. These were ties not easily broken by the Long Knives.

Land Speculators and Settlers Enter the Allegheny Plateau

THE ALLEGHENY PLATEAU PROVINCE contained a number of regions of unusual attractiveness. These were discovered not only by explorers but by speculators, who were ever a jump ahead of the ordinary settler. The speculators operated on a vast scale, comparable to such colonizing ventures of an earlier period as the Virginia Company and the proprietary principality of Pennsylvania. Their enterprises in many cases represented combinations of American and English capital and energy.

One of the earliest was the Ohio Company. This was a Virginia enterprise launched in 1748 under the leadership of such prominent families as the Fairfaxes, the Washingtons, and the Lees. It received from the Virginia government a grant of 200,000 acres of land—with promises of more to come—at the forks and south of the forks of the Ohio, on the condition of colonizing it. The grant was cheerfully confirmed by the British Crown, which was eager in 1748 to settle the West in order to close it to the French. The company was unable, however, to meet the conditions of the grant, partly because of the Seven Years' War, and the concession lapsed.

In 1749 the Loyal Land Company, another Virginia enterprise, received a grant from the governor and Council of 800,000 acres in western Virginia "from the North Carolina line, westward and northward." In 1751 a third Virginia group, the Greenbrier Land Company, was given 100,000 acres on the Greenbrier River, a branch of the Great Kanawha in present-day West Virginia. For both of these companies, the grants were conditioned upon making surveys. In the case of the Loyal Land Company, surveys had been made before war broke out again in 1754.

In 1769 a major new venture—the Grand Ohio Company—was organized. This was a Philadelphia venture with heavy Pennsylvania backing. Its head was Samuel Wharton, of the ubiquitous fur-trading firm of Baynton, Wharton and Morgan. Wharton was an aggressive Quaker, able and adroit and none too scrupulous. He gathered into his company such prominent colonials as Benjamin Franklin, Joseph Galloway, and Sir William Johnson. As a means of building strength he absorbed various

Virginia and Pennsylvania speculative companies such as the first Ohio Company of 1748.

Wharton also signed up big British land speculators: Thomas Walpole, a great London banker, George Grenville, a minister of the Crown, Lord Camden, the famous jurist, Lord Hertford, and others. His company undertook to obtain from the Crown a tract of 20 million acres in what is now eastern Kentucky and West Virginia, the tract shown on the map as Vandalia (10). The tract included part of the Blue Grass region of Kentucky. It comprised the whole area that had been opened up to settlement in this latitude by the Treaty Line of 1768. The price offered the Crown for this principality was £10,000.

The tract was to be used to establish the first transmountain English colony. The colony was to be partly proprietary, partly of the royal type. Its governing officials were to be appointees of the Crown. The name Vandalia proposed for the colony was a bid for the favor of the royal family. The queen of England was supposed to have an ancestry that went back to the Germanic tribe of the Vandals. Her lineage had been traced back to princes of that tribe by devices known to genealogists. A book written on the subject had been published in London in 1770.

After much backstairs diplomacy the project won the approval of the British Privy Council in 1772. But it encountered legal objections thereafter. Before these could be removed the shot was fired at Concord, Massachusetts, marking the outbreak of the American Revolution. Because of this development, the colony was never launched.

While that project was slowly maturing, another was started which was also directed partly to Kentucky, partly to Tennessee. This was the Transylvania project (Map 10), a North Carolina enterprise. Its leading spirit was Judge Richard Henderson. He had received reports from Daniel Boone extolling the beauties of the Blue Grass region. He organized a company in 1774 and the next year bought the immense tract marked "Transylvania" on the map from the Cherokee Indians. The tract included the Kentucky Blue Grass. The price given the Cherokee was £10,000. This seems to have been a stock price for principalities, only this was paid in Indian trade goods, worth a good deal less. The purchase was in direct violation of the Proclamation of 1763 and the laws of Virginia and of North Carolina. It was contrary not only to law but to the prevailing theory of the acquisition of land in the wilderness.

The theory was that title to land in the wilderness was held initially by the Crown and could be passed on to private parties only by the Crown. The Crown was owner by virtue of the fact that in its name the wilderness was discovered or conquered. Any Christian prince was the owner of land in a wilderness discovered or conquered in his name, and occupied only by heathen.

The heathen on the land ceased to be the owners. They were, after the Christian prince had discovered or conquered it, merely occupants of the land. If at any time thereafter they made a cession by treaty to a representative of the Christian prince, all they ceded was the right to occupancy of the land.

This theory, if rough on Indians, was the only one that was workable. Any other would have led to anarchy in land titles. Indians did not understand European concepts of land title. They could be persuaded to sell the land they occupied as many times and to as many different whites as would offer kegs of rum.

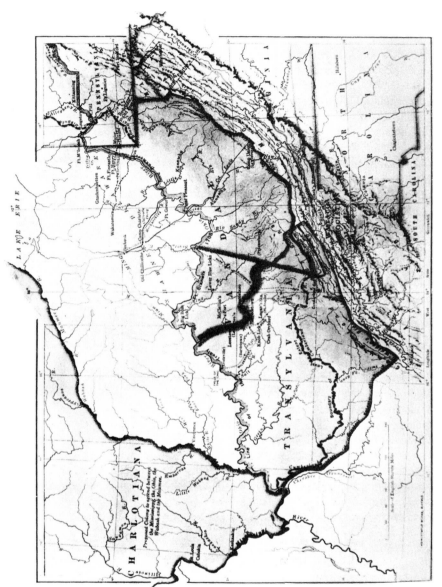

10. Proposed Western Colonies. 1763–75 (from Avery)

The theory that only the Crown could give valid title to wilderness land was not only British; it was the theory of every European colonizing power in America. It was the theory of the American government after independence was won. It was upheld by the Supreme Court in the case of *Johnson v. McIntosh* in 1823. The Court ruled that the British Crown acquired title to the wilderness by discovery or conquest and that it was from the Crown that title passed to the American states or to the federal government when independence was achieved. When an Indian tribe made a cession to the federal government by treaty, all it gave up was a right of occupancy. In purchasing Transylvania from an Indian tribe Henderson was acting on a different theory, that a valid title could be taken directly from Indians without any consent of the Crown.

A theory so out of accord with accepted views and law needed a legal crutch to bolster it. The crutch was a lawyer's informal opinion given in London in 1757, in reply to a request from the East India Company. The question was whether, after the British conquest of India, its princes retained title to their land which could be passed on. The answer given by Attorney General Charles Pratt (later Lord Camden) and Solicitor General Charles Yorke was that, even after the conquest, Indian princes would retain title to their land, inasmuch as they had organized governments and civilized populations. Where a conquest was made of an area that had an organized government and a civilized society, title to the land was not acquired by the Crown.

During the period 1773–75, when Vandalia and other speculative enterprises in western land development were on foot in America—and British authorities delayed confirmation of such projects—a garbled version of the 1757 Camden-Yorke reply to the East India Company gained currency. Its inference was that Indian tribes in America had the right to transmit title to land without reference to the Crown. This version put uncivilized tribes of North America on the level of the civilized princes of India. It was without government sanction in England or America.

Henderson learned of the later version of the Camden-Yorke opinion. He seized upon it to bolster the purchase he wished to make from the Cherokee Indians. This was a typical lawyer's trick to gain the color of law for an illegal transaction. The ploy did not impress the Crown representatives in either Virginia or North Carolina. They at once denounced the purchase as illegal, and the Revolutionary state governments soon afterward took the same position. Despite this stand, these states later maintained that the Cherokee had abandoned their rights to the Transylvania area. Henderson refused to recognize the denunciation of his title by the two governments. He appealed from their verdict to the Continental Congress. Throughout the War of the American Revolution he beseeched the Congress to validate his title, but never succeeded.

His claim to ownership of Transylvania and his attempt to sell land there to settlers was ridiculed by most pioneers in Kentucky. It was scoffed at especially by settlers in Harrodsburg led by George Rogers Clark. In the end the project collapsed, and Henderson left Kentucky in discouragement, complaining that the Kentuckians were a set of scoundrels who had no faith in God or fear of the devil. He eventually obtained from the legislature of Virginia a gift of 200,000 acres of land, to compensate him for his expenditures. He got a similar gift from North Carolina.

The Transylvania project was a characteristic frontier land speculation. It illustrates the ceaseless search by land speculators for ways and means of circumventing land law. It differed from the circumvention by other speculators only in that it was more wholesale and barefaced. The Transylvania project was typical also of the persistence with which speculators carried appeals from one government authority to another—from colonial and state governments to the Continental Congress in this case.

Throughout American history speculators were active in searching for loopholes through land law, frequently with success. Henderson was defeated, if the generous settlements made with him can be called a defeat, because he was rash enough to make a frontal assault on land law.

Following the land speculator came the advance of the settler. This began in the wake of the Loyal Land Company. Between 1750 and 1754 purchasers from that company made settlements in the Powell and Holston valleys, upper tributaries of the Tennessee in southwestern Virginia. After the Seven Years' War, between 1768 and 1773, settlers as squatters moved farther down the Holston, making settlements along it, and in the lovely valley of the Watauga, a branch of the Holston. Others moved into the valley of the Nolichucky, a branch of the French Broad. These "Watauga settlements" were farther west than any English settlements up to that time, yet they were still within the great Appalachian trough through which the Tennessee flows for miles.

The first settlements beyond the escarpment—out onto the plateau country, broken by eroded hills—were in the North, in areas more easily reached from the East. In the Pennsylvania latitude settlement commenced while the Seven Years' War was still in progress. In 1758, as soon as Fort Duquesne, at the forks of the Ohio, had been captured by the British, settlers began to appear there. By 1764 their number had increased so greatly that Pittsburgh was laid out as a town. In the latitude of West Virginia settlement began in 1763. The first settlements were made in the valleys of the Greenbrier and of the Monongahela.

The first settlers came to Kentucky in the early months of the Revolutionary War. The Blue Grass region was the center of earliest occupation. Harrodsburg was founded in March 1775. Boonesboro, Henderson's settlement, was organized the following May. The big push into Kentucky came in 1780. By 1783 there were 15,000 to 20,000 settlers in Kentucky. The Nashville basin in middle Tennessee, another blue grass region, got its first settlers in 1779. By the close of the Revolutionary War the settlers in these prize areas of the trans-Appalachian West numbered 25,000 or 30,000. Considering the fact that this occupation occurred in a period of almost unbroken Indian wars, the growth was surprisingly swift.

One explanation for the swiftness was the surpassing agricultural attractiveness of the areas occupied. Another was the improvements being made in the highways of westward migration. In Pennsylvania, where the mountain barrier was circumvented more readily than elsewhere, two highways were built during the Seven Years' War. Braddock's Road, connecting the Potomac River with the Ohio, was laid out as a military road in 1755. Forbes's Road, tying Philadelphia to the forks of the Ohio, was constructed in 1758. These military thoroughfares, which opened the water route to the West by way of the Ohio River, were of major significance in opening the Allegheny Plateau province to settlers.

In the South the great road into the interior was the Wilderness Trail, marked out by Daniel Boone in 1775. It ran from the gateway of Cumberland Gap to the Blue

Grass region of Kentucky. At first the Wilderness Trail was a mere packhorse path, but in 1796 it became a regular road, and a notable highway to the interior.

Two major streams of population flowed into the interior by way of the Wilderness Trail. One moved from Pennsylvania and Maryland into the trough of the Appalachian Valley, and flowed down it and out into the interior at Cumberland Gap. The other came up by way of Saluda Gap from the Piedmont of the Carolinas.

The swift growth of the transmountain settlements was a response also to the cheapness of land in the West during the Revolutionary War. Under a 1779 Virginia law land could be bought on her western waters at the rate of £40 per 100 acres or $1.33 an acre. This price was quadrupled the next year because of the disordered state of the currency when it became £160 per 100 acres or $5.33 an acre. But payment could be made in the paper money of either the Continental Congress or Virginia. That of the Continental Congress was accepted at 1/40 of its face value. The actual worth of that money in 1781 was somewhere between 1/100 and 1/1000 of its face value. So the real price of land was about 25 cents an acre.

More favorable terms were given to early arrivals in Kentucky. A settler who had raised a crop of corn on any of Virginia's western waters prior to January 1, 1778, received a gift of 400 acres and, in addition, a pre-emption right to buy 1000 acres more—at the regular price. Poor settlers got special concessions as to price. They were permitted to buy 400 acres at the rate of 20 shillings in specie per 100 acres under an act of 1781. Soldiers of Virginia were given free land in the form of warrants. Privates who had served three years got 200 acres; officers were given land proportionate to their rank—a colonel was entitled to 5000 acres.

On North Carolina's western waters land could be bought even cheaper. Under a 1777 law land could be bought there for £2 1/2 per 100 acres or about 6 cents an acre An unmarried man was allowed to buy 640 acres at that rate. A married man was allowed to buy even more, 100 acres for his wife and 100 for each child. In 1783 there was an increase in price to £10 per 100 acres or about 5 cents an acre. But payment could be made in North Carolina certificates, worth 1/6 to 1/7 their face value, so that the actual price was 3 to 5 cents an acre. The limit of a single purchase was 5000 acres. To soldiers free lands were given. Under a 1780 law privates of the North Carolina line got 640 acres free. Officers received warrants according to rank, as much as 7200 acres for a colonel.

The chief beneficiaries of such legislation were the land speculators. They had abundance of depreciated currency and were ceaselessly active. They were usually a jump ahead of settlers in buying up the choicest locations. They acquired large amounts of soldiers' warrants and settlers' pre-emption rights from recipients who did not wish to use them, and located them in the best locations.

The Blue Grass region of Kentucky was largely engrossed by speculators who later sold to settlers. Robert Morris, the financier of the Revolution, held 600,000 acres there in 1796. Thomas Marshall, father of the later Chief Justice of the United States, held 140,000 acres there in 1784. This region by reason of its extraordinary promise became a speculators' paradise. Elsewhere in Kentucky and Tennessee immense speculative holdings were erected. Possessions of a half million acres were not at all unusual.

The extent to which soldiers' warrants were acquired by others and used for speculative purposes is indicated by the fact that of the Kentucky lands acquired under soldiers' warrants, 60 percent were in tracts of from 1000 to 5000 acres. The opinion of some historians is that the wartime legislation of Virginia and North Carolina regarding their lands was put through by lobbies of land speculators who planned the engrossment of the state lands. Whatever the facts may be, it is true that the fantastic currency inflation of the Revolutionary War period was an important element in transferring lands to private hands and stimulating the flow of population into the trans-Appalachian West.

Government in the new communities came with settlement. Ordinarily it began on an informal and an irregular basis. In Kentucky the first government was that of Richard Henderson, who conceived of himself as head of a proprietary colony. In the spring of 1775 he summoned a legislature consisting of delegates from the settlements in Kentucky. This legislature met under an oak tree, listened to a speech by Henderson, adopted some laws, and adjourned. The Henderson government and its laws were laughed at by most of the settlers in Kentucky and were ignored by the state of Virginia. In December 1776, the whole of the Kentucky area was erected into one great county by Virginia. It was governed in county form throughout the years of the American Revolution. Its erection as a county was bitterly objected to by Henderson, who appealed against it, unsuccessfully, to the Continental Congress.

In the Watauga area of eastern Tennessee the first government was an irregular squatters' association, which came into being in a characteristic frontier fashion. When the area was first occupied by settlers, the western boundary between Virginia and North Carolina had not yet been surveyed. The settlers were under the impression that they were on the Virginia side where Indian rights had been extinguished by the Treaty of Lochaber. In 1772 when the line was finally surveyed, it appeared that the Watauga settlers were on the North Carolina side—on land to which Indian rights had never been extinguished.

When this fact became known, the settlers, instead of vacating, formed the Watauga Association. They drew up a compact which was designed to prevent eviction by the Indian superintendent of the South. The Watauga Compact was, in part, an anti-horsethief agreement. No copy of this famous document exists. It is known to historians only from secondhand accounts. It is rather grandiloquently described by Theodore Roosevelt, in his *Winning of the West,* as the first written constitution adopted west of the Appalachian Mountains. It was actually a conspiracy to resist the law authorities and an agreement to fight horse thieves. One of the functions of the Association was to keep a record of land titles. As a further means of protecting themselves against eviction the settlers entered into an arrangement with the Indians. Since purchase from Indians was illegal, a leasing arrangement was made with them for their lands. Ultimately, when it became safe to do so, the leases were converted into purchase by making additional payments to the Indians.

In 1776 the Watauga settlers made contact with the revolutionary state convention of North Carolina which had assembled to frame a state government. They succeeded in obtaining recognition and took part in the framing of the state government. This constituted a validation of their settlement. The next year the legislature of North Carolina erected the whole of their western waters into one big county— Washington County—which became the legal government.

In the Nashville Basin the earliest local government was the so-called Cumberland Compact, an agreement framed in 1780 by all the settlements in that basin. It closely resembled the Watauga Compact. In 1783 all the Nashville Basin settlements were organized as a county, which was cut off from Washington County and named Davidson County. Thus in all the new settlements the same pattern of governmental development appeared—an irregular, often illegal, squatter government at the outset, followed in a few years by legal forms.

The area beyond the mountains that was being overrun by land speculators and settlers from the East seemed no less attractive to the Indian inhabitants than to the intruders. The land was essential to them, whether for farming, or hunting and fishing, or gathering the fruits of the forest. Alarmed by the extent and swiftness of the intrusion, the Indians attacked, producing a succession of Indian wars from the close of the Seven Years' War through that of the American Revolution. These wars, in turn, gave new form to the mode of life and institutions on the frontier.

The West in the War of the American Revolution and in the Peace Treaty of 1783

THE PROVINCE OF THE ALLEGHENY PLATEAU gained settlers throughout the years 1758 to 1783, a period of almost continual warfare. In some latitudes the earliest settlements were made during the Seven Years' War, in the face of fighting that was not confined to conventional forces but was a brutal conflict between frontiersmen and Indians. After the close of the war fighting was continued in Pontiac's uprising, though chiefly north of the Ohio. It flared up again in the Shawnee War of 1774, locally known as Lord Dunmore's War, which will be later described. Most widespread was the Indian fighting of the War of the American Revolution. Its horrors were as much a feature of the occupation of the Allegheny Plateau as they had been of the occupation of upland New England, and they called forth an institution of defense and advance of a special variety—the "frontier station."

The frontier station was a stockade or community shelter or fort of the kind pictured in the illustration (11), which is here Fort Boonesborough in Kentucky. Such a structure was usually built by the firstcomers to a wilderness area. It consisted of a series of log houses joined. Its outer walls were palisaded, with the logs well dug into the ground, and the upper ends sharpened to a point. Often a palisade would consist of a double row of such logs.

A station would be big enough to provide living accommodations for a whole community. It might consist of as few as 10 or as many as 40 cabins, arranged in a rectangle, and flanked by blockhouses. A station might provide accommodations not only for families but for cattle. It was built on elevated ground, if possible, so that it could not be shot down into by Indians. It was built adjacent to water—sometimes around a spring. At Harrodsburg in Kentucky such a station has been restored and is now a tourist attraction in the Blue Grass area.

A station was normally impregnable to direct Indian attack. It could be captured only by surprise or by setting it on fire. It was not built to withstand a long siege. It did not need to be, since Indians on a raid did not have food for a long siege and did not have artillery.

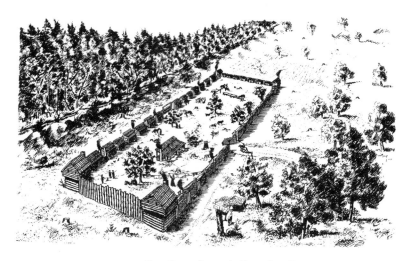

11. Fort Boonesborough (from Ranck)

A station was normally the only residence of the community, while its settlers were few. It would house women and children day and night and the men at night. During the day the men were outside the station, hewing out their farms from the wilderness. As soon as a community had become numerous enough so that pioneers dared to establish homes on their lands, they would erect log cabins and bring their families to them. Then the station would be a place of refuge only in time of crisis. If word came that Indians were approaching, the family would hurry into the station. At such a time, if warning was ample, some of the cattle would be driven into the station until the crisis had passed.

The site used for station purposes was at first community land. It was given to the community for that purpose by the legislature. In Kentucky, under a law passed by Virginia in 1779, a 640-acre tract was conferred on any group desiring one for station purposes. When the protection of the station was no longer needed, the land allotted for it would be divided among those of the settlers who had built it. Each such settler would receive what was known as an ''in lot''—a lot inside the stockaded area—and also an ''out lot''—a somewhat larger parcel lying within the 640 acres of the grant. Thus the station would evolve into a kind of central village for a community.

The station was a characteristic southwestern mode of advance and defense. It arose in response to an acute danger in the wilderness, just as the New England military town had evolved. It was intended to be temporary, in contrast to the permanent character of the New England military town. By its ephemeral nature the station indicated the dispersed character of settlement on the southern frontier, just as the New England military town by its permanent character revealed the compactness of settlement in that region.

Of the Indian wars in the period when the Allegheny Plateau was being occupied the first, the Seven Years' War, has already been described. The second, the Shawnee or Lord Dunmore's War of 1774, was spearheaded by the Shawnee, who had moved out of Kentucky and across the Ohio River in the years before the Kentucky settlements were made. The tribe was a fighting aggregation. Its whole history was a record of clashing with the American frontiersmen. In 1763 it had been part of the coalition that Pontiac had put together against the English. It had been humbled at that time. In 1773 the tribe was again in a fighting mood. It had the usual grievances. Its hunting grounds in Kentucky, like those of its neighbors, the Delaware and the Miami, were being intruded on by the Long Knives. Its game was being destroyed. Settlers were crowding into the upper region of the Ohio, and also into the upper waters of the Tennessee in violation of the provisions of the Indian Treaty Line of 1768.

At the forks of the Ohio, a region in dispute between Pennsylvania and Virginia, there was a provocative situation. In 1773 the royal governor of Virginia, Lord Dunmore, marched troops into the area, in disregard of imperial instructions, and built a fort at the forks. He left a deputy there who was rash and offended the Indians coming to the forks to trade. Virginia and Pennsylvania traders had been inciting the Indians against each other. The result was a succession of murders of settlers and retaliations against the Indians.

The Delaware, who were neighbors of the Shawnee, had an additional grievance. A depraved white trader, in company with some others, brutally murdered the entire family of the Delaware chief, John Logan, in a drunken spree. The result of all these forces, and of incendiary proclamations by the deputy of Dunmore, was the flare-up of the Shawnee War in 1774.

The war was marked by the pitched Battle of Point Pleasant, one of the major Indian battles of frontier history. Indians had normally avoided such encounters, relying on surprises and ambuscades. But in this war they were so stirred that under a fiery chief, Cornstalk, they crossed the Ohio and attacked a formidable force of frontiersmen at the mouth of the Great Kanawha. They were beaten off only with great difficulty and loss of life. When they retreated to their own side of the Ohio they were pursued to their villages. It was autumn. The villages and cornfields of the Shawnee and the Delaware were systematically destroyed. The Indians were compelled to sue for peace.

The peace signed in 1774 brought the usual treaty of cession. The two tribes agreed to surrender all their hunting rights in Kentucky, and not to molest white travelers on the Ohio. The Shawnee and their neighbors north of the Ohio were thus humbled and for three years, from 1774 to 1777, they kept the peace. Those were just the years when the frontiersmen were moving into the Blue Grass region of Kentucky. By 1777, when the Shawnee had recovered sufficiently to go to war again, the Blue Grass settlements were strong enough to beat them off.

Following closely upon the Shawnee War came the War of the American Revolution. That conflict, in the West, was an Indian war almost altogether, in which nearly all the western Indians fought on the British side. They willingly joined the British, because they were under the influence of the Indian superintendents. On the northern frontier, Guy Johnson, the successor to Sir William Johnson, brought the Iroquois over. On the southern frontier Colonel John Stuart brought over the Cherokee. His deputy and successor, Alexander Cameron, lived among the Cherokee and was almost indistinguishable from them. Another reason for the alliance of the Indians with the British was resentment at the land grabbing of the Americans.

In the fighting of this war the Indians were often led by Tories and some of the most ferocious massacres were in their presence. The western Tories were often the scum of society. Unlike the eastern Tories, who were likely to be members of the

ruling class, the western Tories were often broken-down traders or squaw men—
whites living with squaws in Indian villages. Outstanding among them were Simon
Girty, Alexander McGee, and Colonel John Butler, who had no scruples about
leading the Indians to butcheries.

Of the three principal theaters of Indian attack during the Revolution (Map 12),
one was in the frontier areas of central New York and northeastern Pennsylvania,
another was in the Kentucky region, and the third in Tennessee. In the New York and
Pennsylvania theaters the most destructive fighting was done by the Iroquois. They
entered the war as individual tribes, not as a league, because the Oneida and Tuscarora insisted on remaining neutral.

A series of frightful raids was staged by the Iroquois in the summer of 1778. The
war parties followed the Susquehanna River eastward—a favorite route. Their leader
was the Tory Colonel Butler, and associated with him was the famous Mohawk chief
Joseph Brant. The savages destroyed two entire frontier communities, that of Cherry
Valley in New York and Wyoming Valley in Pennsylvania, both part of the Susquehanna watershed.

Retaliation of the usual sort came in 1779. An American army under General
John Sullivan moved from Cooperstown, New York, along the Susquehanna—
following the same road westward that the Iroquois had taken eastward. The Indians
were met and defeated at the Battle of Newtown, now Elmira. Then Sullivan's army

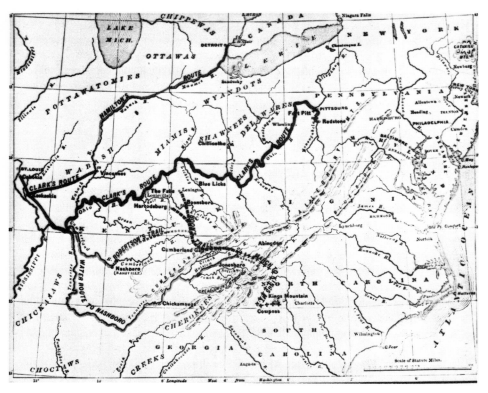

12. The West in the War of the Revolution (from Roosevelt)

systematically proceeded to destroy the Iroquois cornfields and towns. Forty towns were wiped out, and an entire season's harvest of corn, an amount estimated at 160,000 bushels. The power of the Iroquois was broken. At the end of the war the Mohawks, and some small bands of other Iroquois, led by Brant, fled to the valley of the Grand River north of Lake Erie in western Ontario, where they had been given a generous grant of land by the British. Here their descendants are still to be found. Brant continued for many years to be an influential figure in Indian-white relations.

The significance of the Sullivan campaign was even wider than the defeat of this formidable power. Sullivan's soldiers were impressed by the agricultural attractiveness of the Iroquois lands, especially those in the Finger Lakes region. After the war American settlement moved early into that region and especially into the valley of the Genesee.

In Kentucky, the Indians who gave the most trouble were the Shawnee, who were thirsting for revenge after their defeat of 1774. In 1777 they were induced by the British commander at Detroit, General Henry Hamilton, to join the fighting. They brought along their neighbors, the Miami and the Wyandots. These Indians became the wasps of all the West. Their sting was felt by the frontier from Kentucky to Pennsylvania. Kentuckians had to fight for bare survival in the years from 1777 to 1782. Those were the years when Kentucky once more earned the name of a dark and bloody ground.

Victory in that merciless war finally went to the Kentuckians, inasmuch as they not only survived but expanded their settlements. Their advance, however, went forward like the flow and ebb of a tide. The flow occurred in periods of relative quiet. The ebb came when the pressure of the Indians got too fierce and men fled with their families back across the mountains.

In 1778 a counteroffensive was organized by Virginia into the Indian homeland north of the Ohio. It was intended to be a diversionary attack that would deter them from raiding Kentucky. George Rogers Clark, its leader, headed first for the French settlements in the Illinois and Indiana country, which had been used as bases to outfit many of the Indian raids. Their population, however, was expected in 1778 to be friendly to Clark, inasmuch as France in that year had become an ally of the United States. The French settlers did welcome Clark, and he was able in 1778 and 1779 to make himself master of the Illinois region. From Illinois he led a famous attack on Vincennes, Indiana, where he captured the British leader in the West, General Hamilton, the so-called "hair-buyer." As a result of these operations, the Indians were overawed, and remained quiet until Clark withdrew to the falls of the Ohio. Then the attacks on Kentucky began again.

In the Tennessee country the Cherokee proved the most ferocious. They had long been restless because of white encroachments on their lands, and especially because of the spread of the Watauga settlements. In 1776 they entered the war through the influence of the British Indian superintendent, Colonel John Stuart.

Their first objective was to wipe out the Watauga settlements. They planned to overwhelm them by a coordinated surprise attack patterned after Pontiac's thrust in 1763. The plot, however, did not succeed, for warning of it was given to the Watauga people by a Cherokee squaw, Nancy Ward, who had a white man as husband, and the settlers were able to get into their stations. The war fanned out into savage raids over the whole southern frontier, from Virginia to Georgia.

In retaliation the southern states sent forces into the Cherokee country in the autumn of 1776. They went through the villages of the Cherokee, which were vulnerable because they were close together, with fire and sword, destroying all of them and the standing corn. The Cherokee were temporarily humbled, and in 1777 they made peace, ceding 5 million acres of their lands.

In 1780 they went on the warpath again. Once again they were heavily punished, this time by one of the great Tennessee heroes, John Sevier. In 1785 they signed a new treaty—the Treaty of Hopewell—by which they gave up still more of their lands. In the Nashville region, the Indians who were most troublesome were a wing of Cherokee that had seceded from their eastern compatriots and were known as the Chickamauga. They took up the hatchet against the Nashville settlements in 1779, but were defeated by the frontiersmen under another famous leader, Evan Shelby. All the tension and drama of this Indian fighting is recaptured in Theodore Roosevelt's *Winning of the West*. This is not a great work of scholarship, but it is a fine piece of narration.

The War of the American Revolution was a bitter and merciless one in the West, as Indian wars inevitably were. It was a war of horrid atrocities, of massacres of whole communities, including women, children, and the aged; of fiendish tortures of prisoners, the burning of prisoners to death at the stake. The West nursed against the British bitter memories of those atrocities for generations, and this became an important force later. It accounted for the western war-hawk push against England in the War of 1812.

In the Indian fighting of the Revolutionary War victory went to the frontiersmen. It went to them by virtue of their survival. At the end of the war there were 25,000 to 30,000 settlers living in the Allegheny Plateau. This victory was of major importance in the peace negotiations which ended the war.

At the peace conference in Paris two members of the alliance that had defeated the British coveted the trans-Appalachian country: the United States and Spain. To the United States it was an indispensable outlet for its expansive forces. Without it the new nation would remain a minor power clinging to the seaboard.

But Spain aspired to at least a portion of trans-Appalachia to round out her American empire. She had conquered the two Floridas during the war with forces operating out of New Orleans. She had recovered what she had lost to the British in the Seven Years' War. At the close of that war she had acquired from France all of Louisiana west of the Mississippi. She had ancient possession of Mexico and claims to the Pacific Northwest extending far to the north. She hoped, with French aid, to acquire the trans-Appalachian country northward to the Cumberland River. If this hope were to be realized New Spain would further dwarf in dimension the territory of the new republic.

Spain had entered the war at the instance of France. She had been promised help from France to recover the Rock of Gibraltar, lost to England in 1704. She had been promised that no peace would be made until the Rock had been restored. But the Rock could not be reduced even by the combined efforts of France and Spain. The compensation Spain demanded for this disappointment was part of the trans-Appalachian region.

The French came into the peace conference without interests of their own in the trans-Appalachian region. They had given the United States a pledge on entering the war that they would claim none of the British territory on the North American continent in the peace settlement. Their primary interest, after humbling the British, was to get the war over with. They were ready, in lieu of their Gibraltar promise, to support the Spanish claim to some of the trans-Appalachian country.

The French court felt under no obligation to assist its American ally in winning the trans-Appalachian region. It had pledged itself to winning independence for the United States, which would apply to the territory east of the Appalachians. The territory west of the mountains had been severed from the American colonies by the Proclamation of 1763 and, therefore, constituted a separate entity of the British Empire which was subject to any disposition the peace conference might decide for it. Under these circumstances the presence of 25,000 American settlers in that region was of basic importance. A population of that size could not be overlooked by the diplomats at the peace table. This was the significance of the presence of these pioneers in the Kentucky region.

The American negotiators in Paris were Benjamin Franklin, John Jay, and John Adams. Adams was late in arriving at the negotiation. These were able men and they had wide powers. But they were under restrictions in two respects. One was the treaty of alliance with France, by which the United States and France had pledged that neither would ever make a separate peace with England. The other restriction was a set of instructions drawn by Congress in 1781 in which the negotiators were directed to be guided at the conference by the advice and opinion of the French court and to undertake nothing in the negotiations without French knowledge and concurrence.

When the conference began in 1782, delegations were present from all the powers in the coalition. In order to simplify and hasten the preliminary proceedings, the delegations agreed that each would do business with one section of the British peace commission—Americans with one section, French with another, and Spanish with a third section. It was also agreed by the allies that the separate negotiations should all go forward together at the same pace so far as possible, in order that no one ally in the coalition would get the jump on the others in coming to terms with England. The Americans and the French further agreed to keep each other constantly informed of the progress of their separate negotiations.

The actual proceedings are a familiar story and require telling only in bare outline. Jay was suspicious of the good faith of the French government. He believed it was intent on selling out American interests at the peace table to satisfy Spain. His suspicions were increased by various episodes that occurred while the bargaining proceeded, and also by a map prepared by Gérard de Rayneval, secretary to Count Vergennes of the French Foreign Office, proposing a division of the trans-Appalachian country, which was shown to him (Map 13). Under this plan Spanish territory would extend from the Gulf of Mexico to the Cumberland River. Great Britain would retain the area which in 1774 she had reintegrated into Quebec province, and which, presumably, she would prolong the war to hold. The United States would acquire only the area between the Ohio and Cumberland rivers—roughly Kentucky—and a tongue of land behind Georgia where American settlement was beginning. Such a division of the West left little room for future expansion by the people of the United States. It gave Spain the bulk of the Southwest and England the greater part of the Northwest. The United States would at no point have touched the Mississippi River.

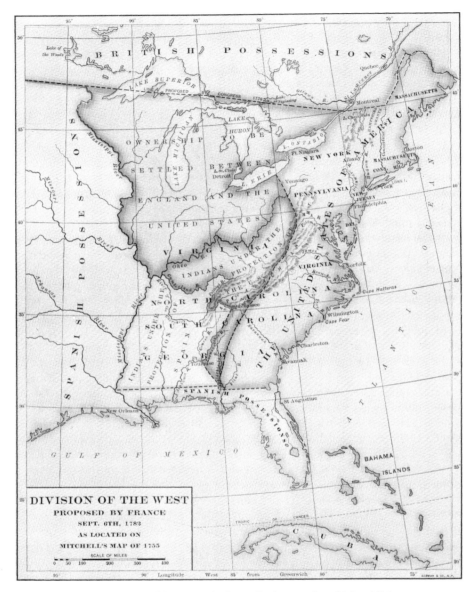

13. Proposal of France at the Peace Conference (from McLaughlin)

This apportionment probably reflected the long-range strategy of the French court. If Spain remained strong in the Southwest and England was strong in the North and Northwest, and the United States touched the Mississippi at no point, the latter would remain a relatively weak power, and be forever dependent on France. If, on the contrary, the United States acquired the transmountain area to the Mississippi, it would be powerful enough to stand alone, and the need for a French connection and for dependence on France would disappear.

Jay became so convinced of French duplicity that he secretly communicated with Lord Shelburne, the British Prime Minister. He let Shelburne perceive his suspicions and intimated that if the British government would show a disposition to deal liberally with the United States at the peace table he would be prepared to go forward with England separately as far as possible, and leave the French and Spanish to fend for themselves. Jay took this step while Franklin was seriously ill and before Adams had arrived in Paris.

The British Prime Minister had been friendly to the Americans throughout his career. He now saw an opportunity to win them away from their allies at the peace conference—to break the solidarity of the coalition. He seized the opportunity. He sent instructions to the British delegation in Paris that gave promise of a generous peace with the United States. Thenceforth the Anglo-American negotiations were pressed forward separately, and as secretly and rapidly as possible.

The opening proposals of the American negotiators were those relating to the northern boundary. The Americans suggested that the northern boundary should be the same as that established by England as the southern boundary of Quebec in the Proclamation of 1763—along the highlands south of the St. Lawrence to a point near the headwaters of the Connecticut River, and thence to Lake Nipissing (Map 14). From that lake it would go directly to the source of the Mississippi. That line would have given the United States a large part of what is now Ontario. This proposal the British balked at.

The Americans then proposed two alternative lines. Both would follow the southern boundary of Quebec to where the upper Connecticut crosses the 45th parallel. One would follow the 45th parallel all the way to the Mississippi. That line, as in the case of the initial American proposal, if accepted by the British, would have given the United States a large part of present-day Ontario. On the other hand, it would have left to the British the Keweenaw Peninsula of Michigan, which was later found to contain an immense wealth of pure copper. More important, it would have given the British the whole southern and western shores of Lake Superior, which were later discovered to contain iron-ore deposits unsurpassed in the world. This proposal the British also turned down.

The second alternative offered by the Americans was the line of the 45th parallel from the upper Connecticut River to the St. Lawrence, thence down the middle of the St. Lawrence and the middle of Lakes Ontario, Erie, and Huron to Lake Superior. Passing north of Isle Royale, it would follow a water passage from Lake Superior to the northwestern corner of the Lake of the Woods, and from there due west to the Mississippi River. This line the British accepted. It was a very favorable line for the United States, but it was ill-informed. A line drawn due west from the Lake of the Woods would never hit the Mississippi. It would lie far north of the source of the river. The negotiators were drawing lines concerning a wilderness that they knew little about, that had not been well explored.

The western boundary was to be the line of the Mississippi River from its supposed junction with the northern boundary "until it shall intersect the 31st parallel."

The negotiations on the southern boundary were complicated by the fact that the Anglo-Spanish negotiations were not yet complete and that Spanish troops were occupying West Florida. On the assumption that the Floridas would go to Spain the

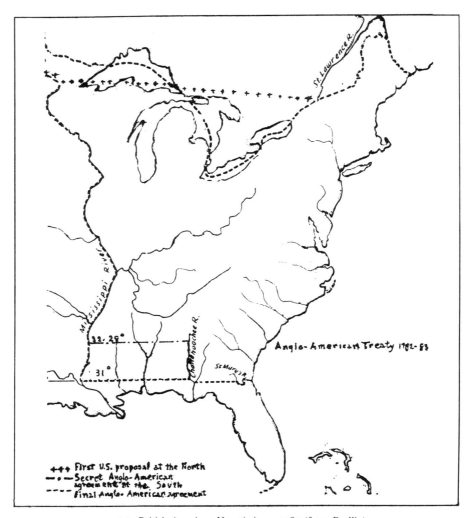

14. British-American Negotiations, 1782 (from Paullin)

Americans and British agreed that the boundary between the Floridas and the United States would be the 31st parallel from the Mississippi to the Apalachicola, then that river to the Flint, then in a straight line to the head of the St. Mary's River and down that river to the sea. Concurrently in a separate article they agreed: ''In case Great Britain . . . shall recover . . . West Florida, the line of the north boundary between said province and the United States shall be a line drawn from the mouth of the Yassous where it unites with the Mississippi, due east to the river Apalachicola'' [32° 28']. This was the boundary between West Florida and the trans-Allegheny area when the Floridas had been British from 1763 to the war. The secret article was an indication of the degree to which the Americans had thrown in their lot with the British as against their Spanish ally.

In the Anglo-Spanish treaty both Floridas became Spanish. But that treaty had failed to define the boundary of West Florida. The existence of the secret article leaked to the Spanish and made them doubly unwilling to accept the line of 31°, especially since the treaty they had signed with the British did not define the boundary of West Florida.

With regard to the navigation of the Mississippi River, the Americans were also successful. The British conceded to the United States the right to navigate the river from its source to the ocean. This concession, however, made trouble. Spain came out of the peace conference holding both banks of the lower river, and Spain denied that Britain could confer on the United States the right to navigate a river ''to the ocean'' both banks of which, at its mouth, Spain controlled.

These were the western terms of the preliminary Anglo-American agreement. They were signed on November 30, 1782, seven weeks ahead of the preliminary agreements made between Britain and its other adversaries. The United States did just what the coalition had wanted to avoid; it got the jump on the others in obtaining terms from England. The terms constituted a tremendous diplomatic achievement for the United States.

The preliminary terms were converted into a definitive treaty after the French and Spanish, on January 20, 1783, had each concluded preliminary negotiations with the British. Finally, on September 3, definitive treaties were signed all around, and the war came to an end. The territory the Americans had won included all the trans-Allegheny hinterland ever operated in by them. It included even the region between the Ohio and the Great Lakes which had been incorporated before the war into Quebec by the Quebec Act of 1774.

The success of the Americans was due to a number of factors. One was the sharp diplomacy of their negotiators, their willingness to play the game of cynicism that characterized the diplomacy of the period. Another was the proximity of the United States to the principal conquest of the war—in the trans-Appalachian region. A third factor was crucial—the presence of American settlers in the area that was the subject of negotiation, the presence there of 25,000 to 30,000 American frontiersmen, the victors in the Indian fighting of the war. This is the significance also of the George Rogers Clark expedition into the Illinois country. That expedition, though it remained only temporarily in the Illinois country, served, while there, to divert Indian attack from the Kentucky settlements, and helped the Kentucky settlers to survive.

Land Cessions by the States

As soon as the ownership of the trans-Appalachian West had been transferred to the United States, the task of formulating a land policy had to be undertaken by the Continental Congress. It was a problem of major dimension, one that had never been effectively dealt with while the area had been in the care of the British Parliament.

The immediate question to be decided was whether that great area was to be state or federal property. Prior to the War of the Revolution it had been claimed by seven of the colonies. It continued to be claimed by them during the war (Map 15). All the claims except that of New York rested on colonial charters. They were sea-to-sea claims which in 1763 had been sheared off at the Mississippi when England made the agreement with France and Spain which closed the Seven Years' War.

The claims in some cases overlapped. That of Virginia, for instance, overlapped those of Connecticut and Massachusetts. New York's claim was another overlapping one, because it rested on treaties made with the Iroquois. Wherever the Iroquois had taken a scalp New York had a claim. The largest and one of the best claims was Virginia's. It covered all the trans-Allegheny region north of the latitude of her southern boundary, and conflicted with the western claims of every state north of Virginia.

Six of the American states had no western claims. As soon as the Revolutionary War broke out, the landless states began an agitation in the Continental Congress for the cession of all the state claims in the West to Congress. They felt that any western lands won by the war would represent the exertions of all the states and should therefore become the joint property of all. But the landed states refused to make cessions. They wrote instead into the Articles of Confederation—framed in 1777—the provision that no state should ever be deprived of its territory for the benefit of the United States. That angered the landless states, especially Maryland, which refused for four years to sign the Articles. Since signature by all the states was required, the nation was without a constitutional government until near the close of the Revolutionary War. In 1780 the state of New York yielded its flimsy claim. On the day in 1781

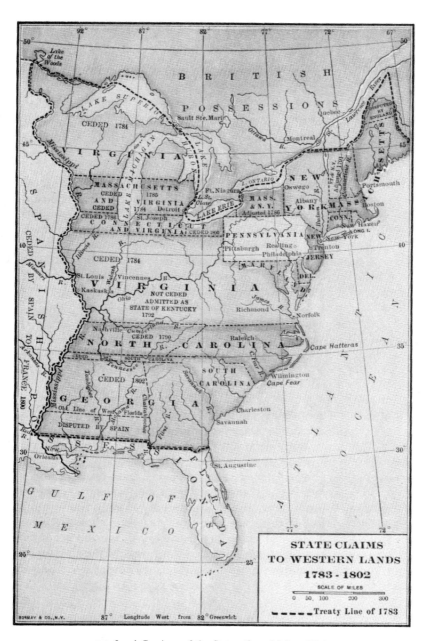

15. Land Cessions of the States (from McLaughlin)

when Congress accepted it and the prospect brightened that all the state claims, including Virginia's, would be surrendered, Maryland signed the Articles of Confederation.

Why was it that Maryland exhibited such determination to extract from the landed states their claims to western land? The answers once were that Maryland was national-minded, wished the nation to be strengthened by ownership of the western lands, and, as a small state, was unwilling to permit the large states to carry off the territorial prize of the war which had been won by the sacrifices of all.

But another and more realistic explanation of Maryland's determination was land speculation. Maryland's state government was dominated by a powerful group of speculators. It included the governor of the state, Thomas Johnson, the two Maryland representatives in Congress, Charles Carroll and Samuel Chase, and other state politicians of less prominence.

Allied with this group was a powerful Pennsylvania circle of land speculators: Robert Morris, the financier of the American Revolution, Samuel Wharton, of the Philadelphia firm of Baynton, Wharton and Morgan, James Wilson, one of the biggest speculators of the period and later a justice of the United States Supreme Court, and Benjamin Franklin. These men had made immense purchases of western lands from Indians in contravention of the Proclamation of 1763 and of colonial laws. One was in the area that is now Illinois. It had been bought in 1773 from the Illinois Indians. A second lay in the Wabash Valley, purchased in 1775 from the resident Indians. These two had been merged in 1779 into one vast project, the Illinois Wabash Company, of which James Wilson was president.

The same group was interested in another great tract in what is now West Virginia, obtained from the Iroquois at Fort Stanwix in 1768. This tract had been absorbed into the Vandalia project, and had become defunct when that project collapsed at the outbreak of the American Revolution.

All these purchases and cessions lay in country to which Virginia had the best claim. The aim of the speculators was to obtain a transfer of those lands from Virginia to Congress. Virginia had made clear its attitude regarding purchases by speculators of lands from Indians. It had done so in the Transylvania case and had reaffirmed this position in 1778, when its legislature had declared that any private purchases of land on its western waters from Indians were illegal. While Virginia retained the lands, the Maryland and Pennsylvania speculators had no hope of obtaining validation of their accessions. If, on the other hand, Virginia could be brought to cede its western claims to Congress, the purchase might be validated by a giveaway Congress. This explains why the spokesmen of Maryland in the Continental Congress made so determined a fight to get the western claims transferred to Congress, why the state objected so stubbornly to the clause in the Articles of Confederation guaranteeing the claims of the landed states, and why it blocked the adoption of the Articles.

In 1781 Virginia made an offer to cede its western claims to Congress. The state performed a genuine act of patriotism—a real sacrifice of its interests. But it attached to the offer a stipulation that, in the area ceded, no validation should ever be made by Congress of purchases of land privately obtained from Indians. That stipulation was attached to make sure that the beneficiaries of its sacrifice should not eventually prove to be the land speculators of Maryland and Pennsylvania.

When Virginia's offer, hedged about by this stipulation, was received by Congress, the Maryland and Pennsylvania interests demanded that it be rejected. They kept it from being accepted for three years. In the meantime, however, Maryland's representatives in 1781 had signed the Articles of Confederation.

Ultimately, all the claims of the states to western lands were ceded to Congress. The last to be ceded, that of Georgia, was made in 1802. All the cessions were on a partial basis, or subject to reservations.

The Virginia cession in 1784 comprised only the area north of the Ohio. It had already sold or given away almost all its land in Kentucky. It kept only political jurisdiction there, and this it ceded to Kentucky on Kentucky's becoming a state. Virginia was obliged to reserve even territory north of the Ohio to satisfy its outstanding soldiers' warrants. The reserved region was known as the Virginia Military Tract—an area between the Scioto and the Miami rivers. North Carolina made a limited cession, having almost no land left in Tennessee to hand out. It ceded to Congress only political jurisdiction.

Georgia's cession in 1802 comprised the bulk of what is now Alabama and Mississippi. The state yielded to Congress political jurisdiction over the area but the state's title to the land ceded had been clouded. Its legislature had sold the whole to four land-speculating companies that had bribed members of the legislature to approve the deal. When the truth was discovered there was an outcry in Georgia and the next legislature revoked the sale, leaving title to the land unclear. The legal aspects of Georgia's title to the western lands she ceded are more fully described in connection with post-Revolution land speculation.

In spite of all these reservations and complications, an immense area passed to Congress—an area of over 200 million acres of land. The ownership of this domain imposed on Congress the responsibility of working out an orderly system of distribution and occupation, something that had never been accomplished during the British regime. Congress had to work out a system more or less *de novo*.

Land Policy and
the Principle of
Equality of States

THE CONTINENTAL CONGRESS assumed a major obligation in accepting the western claims of the landed states. The obligation was to frame an effective administrative system for this immense public domain. It was not merely a responsibility, but a challenging opportunity. No adequate administrative system had been developed for that area by France or Great Britain, nor could it be while the region was contested. It would have required surveying of land, formulation of the mode and terms of sale, and establishing the method of recording title. Preliminary steps to the creation of such a system had been taken by the British government in the Proclamation of 1763 and the Plan of 1764. But in 1768 the fulfillment of them had been abandoned and the administration of the area had been restored to the colonial governments possessing claims, each of which had maintained its own pattern of survey, sale, and recording of title. The result had been chaos.

The response of Congress was the Land Ordinance of 1785, adopted while the cessions were still coming in. This was one of the most important and admirable measures ever enacted by an American legislature. It established basic principles that were to apply to the region north of the Ohio. Later the same principles were extended to all the western country coming into federal possession. A first principle was that survey must precede sale in any federal wilderness. The wilderness was to be laid out in a pattern of straight lines and rectangular blocks. This would minimize the danger of surveying errors and overlapping boundaries.

A starting point was fixed for the survey. It was at the geographic point where the Ohio River cuts across the boundary of Pennsylvania west of the Virginia panhandle. From this point a so-called base line was to be drawn due west, on which range lines were to be laid off at right angles, at six-mile intervals. Within the range lines townships were to be erected, each six miles square, and numbered in a specified order. Then each township was to be cut into 36 sections which were to be numbered in an order prescribed by law. This was the checkerboard pattern of land division.

The chief merit of rectangular survey was the avoidance of errors likely to occur in marking irregular angles in an era when surveying instruments were crude. The recording of title to land by number rather than by a description of markers left on trees or rocks had a like merit of avoiding errors. The reservation of land for educational purposes was an added virtue of the Ordinance. In every township one section was reserved for such purposes. Country schools throughout the West owe their inception to that provision. The principle of reserving public land for education was later much extended. In the Dakotas and in Montana two sections of land were reserved in every township for common schools. Also, later, the reserving of public lands for higher education was added.

The merit of the 1785 ordinance can be fully realized only when compared with the cumbersome and complex system followed on Virginia's western waters. There the first step in acquiring public land was to purchase a warrant from the Virginia land office, which was a certificate stipulating the number of acres the purchaser had paid for. Location of the warrant was permissible wherever wilderness land had not already been pre-empted or settled or restricted. It was made simply by marking off the boundaries of the tract desired on rocks or blazing it on trees. The person making the markings had no means of knowing whether the land had already been pre-empted by a speculator or a prospective settler. The next step was to call a county surveyor to make a plat of the land. If a county surveyor was not available a private surveyor was used. The plat was then registered in Virginia's land office. Finally, after a wait of six months, a deed or patent to the land was issued, provided that no counterclaim or "caveat" had been filed in the meantime. This was the system used for Kentucky by Virginia and for Tennessee by North Carolina.

An essential feature of this system was survey after a warrant had been bought and paid for. Location of the warrant could be made wherever in the wilderness Virginia had land. The shape of the tract purchased was normally irregular, which resulted in difficult surveying angles. The recording of boundaries was in terms of perishable symbols such as blazes on trees or marks on rocks.

A multitude of errors crept into titles acquired in this way, errors of surveying, overlapping boundaries, and of recording. The result was endless litigation later in the courts. Litigation of disputed land titles filled the courts of Kentucky and Tennessee beyond the close of the 19th century. When the Tennessee Valley Authority was established and title to land for reservoirs was sought by the federal government a mass of confusion was dredged up.

In land-title litigation frontier lawyers in Kentucky and Tennessee found a golden opportunity. Nearly all had in reserve some cases of disputed land title to be worked on in spare hours. In such cases the fee of the lawyer depended on winning the case, since retainers could not ordinarily be paid by frontiersmen. A lawyer would be tempted to win the case by any device. The tone of frontier legal practice as a result was low and had its effect on frontier politics, since politics was largely left then, as now, to lawyers. These evils were minimized by the principles prescribed in the Land Ordinance of 1785.

The principles of the Ordinance applied only to the area possessed by the government north of the Ohio. Later they were extended by Congress to other areas acquired in the West. They were also later copied from the United States by other countries—by Canada, Australia, and New Zealand.

The origins of the Ordinance were colonial. What Congress did in drawing up the measure was merely to select and combine the best ideas of various colonial systems. The idea of township tracts, laid out in orderly fashion before settlement, was taken from the New England town-planting system. The rectilinear form of the townships came, also, from the New England towns, though they were seldom exactly six miles square. Concord was the first town six miles square. The idea of reserving land for public uses, such as education, emanated also from the New England town system. The size of sections of land—640 acres—came from the North Carolina pre-emption laws and from the grants made by Virginia to Kentucky stations. The Ordinance combined the best of colonial diversities.

The financial terms for sale of public land under the Ordinance were far less generous than those in effect in the states during the Revolutionary War. Purchase was to be by bidding at public auction. The lowest bid permitted—where bidding was to begin—was a dollar an acre. Once land had been offered at auction in a given district, it could be bought at the minimum price fixed by the law. Payment had to be made in hard money or its equivalent.

These stiff terms were established because the federal government was desperately in need of revenue. Revenue considerations had to be put ahead of social considerations in the disposal of the public domain, and that continued to be the case until the federal debt was paid off.

Other illiberal features of the Ordinance of 1785 related to the size of the parcels of land to be sold. Every alternate township had to be sold in quarter townships—in blocks of nine square miles—which meant, in effect, to speculators. The smallest parcel of land that could be bought was a square mile (640 acres). In subsequent land legislation three issues recurred: what should be the size of the minimum allowable purchase; what should be the price per acre; and what form should the payments take—cash or otherwise?

Actual surveying of land under the Ordinance of 1785 was delayed. The delay was due in part to the lack of means of Congress to pay for surveying, partly to Indian disturbances in the West. In the meantime, land-speculating companies were eager to buy land direct from Congress in big blocks. This was a period of feverish speculation in public lands. Many of the nation's leaders, including George Washington, were in it. Robert Morris held millions of acres of western land. James Wilson was heavily involved. Alexander Hamilton was so involved at the time of his death that he was virtually insolvent.

One of the largest of the land-speculating ventures was the Ohio Company, a Massachusetts organization, centered in Boston. It was headed by General Rufus Putnam, who had done surveying for Congress under the Ordinance of 1785. Putnam had noticed the beauty and the fertility of the lands in the Muskingum Valley of Ohio, and in 1786 he formed the Ohio Company for the purpose of buying a big block of them direct from Congress.

In order to obtain capital Putnam sold shares of stock of the Ohio Company to New England investors. Payment for the shares could be made in certificates of indebtedness, special securities that had been issued by Congress during the Revolutionary War. In this way a large quantity of certificates of indebtedness came into the possession of the company. Then the Reverend Manasseh Cutler, a clergyman from

Ipswich, Massachusetts, was chosen as agent to make a proposition to Congress. He was not a genius as a clergyman, but as a lobbyist he proved a wonder. He went to New York, where Congress was meeting, and made a proposition to buy 1,500,000 acres of Muskingum Valley lands. The price he offered was a dollar an acre, the minimum at which bidding could begin under the terms of the Ordinance of 1785. But Cutler asked for a special discount of 33⅓ percent because, as he said, much land in the Muskingum Valley was swampy. That would bring the price to 66⅔ cents per acre. Then he proposed that, instead of paying hard money for the lands, as the law required, he be permitted to make payment in certificates of indebtedness, which were worth at the time about 12 cents on the dollar. This would bring the offer to 8 or 9 cents per acre.

Congress hesitated. It looked as if the deal would fall through. Then Colonel William Duer, the Secretary of the Treasury Board, made a call on Cutler. He was a big and reckless speculator, the head of a large venture known as the Scioto Land Company, including influential members of Congress. The company was eager to buy land from Congress on the terms Cutler was proposing. But such a purchase could not be openly made, for if it became known that a company, headed by the Secretary of the Treasury Board and including members of Congress, was buying a huge tract of public land at 8 or 9 cents an acre, there would be an outcry.

Duer therefore proposed that Cutler enlarge the project he had offered Congress. Instead of a mere 1,500,000 acres, Cutler was to ask for 5 million acres at 8 or 9 cents an acre. The enlarged deal would be put through Congress. Then the Scioto Company would buy from the Ohio Company the surplus 3,500,000 acres at 8 or 9 cents an acre.

Cutler agreed to the whole scheme. He enlarged the project to 5 million acres. It now went through Congress without a hitch. But it brought the Duer group no profit. Duer himself went into bankruptcy, and the greater part of what his company had acquired reverted through the Ohio Company to the government.

The land purchase of the Ohio Company was a stimulus to the Confederation Congress to meet a second obligation in taking over the trans-Allegheny West—that of providing for the government of the area. Land speculators needed to have in the West a liberal form of government as an inducement to Easterners to buy from them land for new farms. Congress met this requirement in the Northwest Ordinance of 1787. Like the Ordinance of 1785, it established principles that were expected to apply to the remainder of American territory westward to the Mississippi and that might apply, some day, as far westward as the Pacific Ocean.

The authors of the act were acquainted with history. They had learned from it that any government which extended its authority over an area of continental proportions was likely to degenerate into an autocracy in which the people lost their freedom. This was the danger to be avoided. The problem was how to extend the authority of their government over a continental interior without repeating the errors of the past. The solution found to the problem was the Northwest Ordinance.

This Ordinance provided that the region north of the Ohio be divided into not more than five, nor less than three, territories. So long as any of the territories had a small population it was to have a purely executive government—a governor, secretary, and three judges, all appointed by Congress. When the population had reached

5000 adult males it was to have an elected assembly, and when it had grown to a population of 60,000 inhabitants it was to have the right to statehood in the Union on a basis of complete equality with the original thirteen states.

This system of government carried none of the trappings or potentialities of colonialism. Its terminology was meaningful. It described the future communities as "territories," not as "colonies," and it assured them, in advance, of a gradually increasing autonomy as they grew in population and maturity. It prepared for them a position of full equality with the founding states—a full partnership in the governing Union.

The Ordinance also contained the equivalent of a bill of rights. It guaranteed to the communities to be established in the Northwest Territory religious freedom, the right of habeas corpus, the right of jury trial, and other freedoms sacred to Englishmen. A concluding article declared that in the Northwest Territory "there shall be neither slavery nor involuntary servitude . . . otherwise than in the punishment of crime whereof the party shall have been duly convicted."

The area south of the Ohio was not organized during the Confederation period. Virginia had retained jurisdiction in Kentucky, governing it as a county until 1792, when it consented to the county's becoming a state of the Union, without ever having passed through the territorial stage. North Carolina retained the Tennessee region throughout the Confederation period, ceding it to Congress only in 1790, when Congress organized it as the Territory Southwest of the Ohio River. The basis of organization was that of the Northwest Territory, with the exception of the provision prohibiting slavery. The territory became the state of Tennessee in 1796.

Of the region south of Tennessee, the bulk was claimed by Georgia. But a portion—between 32° 28′ and 31°—was in dispute between the United States and Spain until 1795. In 1798 Congress organized the Spanish cession as Mississippi Territory under the principles of the Northwest Ordinance except for the clause prohibiting slavery. In 1804, after Georgia had ceded its claim to Congress, that area was added to Mississippi Territory.

Thus by 1804 all the trans-Allegheny area to the Mississippi—which came to the nation as little more than an inchoate wilderness in 1783—had either achieved statehood or acquired territorial status under the principles enunciated in the Northwest Ordinance. In 1803 Ohio became a state. The same year the United States acquired the Louisiana Purchase. In this great extension of sovereignty, and in later extensions of it to equally vast regions, the system went along. The United States is today a republic of 50 equal partners. Of the 50, 31 have come into the Union under the principles of the Northwest Ordinance of 1787.

The elevation of new settlements to a position of equality in the partnership of the Union was a surprisingly advanced concept for the 18th century, so advanced that two questions arise at once: where did it originate, and how did it evolve? These used to be answered by ascribing them to Thomas Jefferson or James Monroe. Actually the Ordinance was the brainchild of no individual. It was a product of gradual evolution.

The first stage in the evolution emerged from the clash of the American radicals with the British Parliament in 1774, following the Boston Tea Party. Parliament responded to the riotous party by adopting the Coercive Acts, which aroused the radicals throughout the colonies. They took the stand that Parliament had no power to pass such legislation, that it lacked the right to legislate for them at all. The American colonies, the radicals argued, had a position of autonomy in the British Empire. They were autonomous dominions of the King. They had a status of equality in the British Empire with the realm of England. They were under the King, but not under Parliament. This doctrine of autonomy, of equality with the realm of England in the Empire, was developed especially by such colonial radicals as Sam Adams, John Adams, and Thomas Jefferson.

In England, that thesis had few defenders. It was not taken seriously even by liberals of the Pitt school. It was, however, justified by a handful of extreme radicals in England. One of these, John Cartwright, wrote a pamphlet in 1774 defending the idea of colonial autonomy. He referred to autonomy as a kind of independence under the Crown. The pamphlet was republished in America in 1776.

Cartwright suggested that not only the thirteen colonies already established along the seaboard, but future western colonies built up in the interior, should have a status in the Empire of equality with the realm of England. He thought that nineteen new colonies might be established in the future in the interior. All of these, as soon as they had a minimum of population, should become autonomous dominions of the Empire, with a status of equality with the realm of England under the King. He published a map as a frontispiece to the pamphlet which is reproduced here (Map 16). It shows the new dominions Cartwright had proposed in the interior which should have equality with England inside the Empire. This proposal was a foreshadowing of the Northwest Ordinance of 1787.

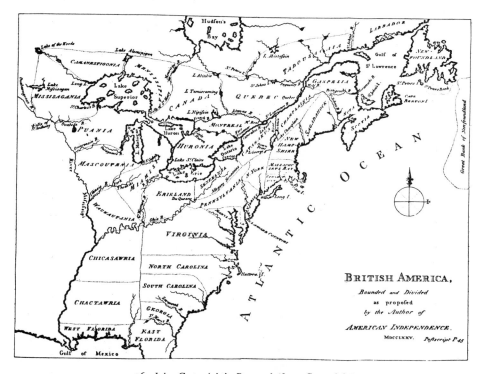

16. John Cartwright's Proposal (from Cartwright)

The next step in the evolution of the great principle was a pledge the Continental Congress made in October 1780 to the landed states during the Revolutionary War, when it was trying to persuade them to cede their western claims to the nation. The pledge was that if the western lands were ceded they would be used for the common benefit, and when settled, would be divided into states which would be admitted to the Union on a basis of full equality with the older states.

The third step in the evolution of the principle was an ordinance, drawn up by Jefferson and adopted by Congress in 1784 for the government of the West. Under it sixteen territories were to be laid off in the trans-Appalachian West (Map 17). As soon as any one of the sixteen had a sufficient population, it was to have the right to enter the Union on the basis of equality with the older states. The Ordinance was provisional. It was to go into effect only when all the landed states had ceded their western claims to Congress. It never went into operation because it was superseded within three years by the Northwest Ordinance of 1787. But it is significant as the first legislative formulation of the principle of equality of the new states with the old. The Northwest Ordinance of 1787 merely gave detailed and final form to the crude legislation of 1784.

An important element in the evolution of the equality principle of the Northwest Ordinance was the clamor of frontier communities for statehood. All the frontier communities from Vermont to Tennessee were demanding statehood in the Union in the years after the Revolution and demanding it belligerently. Vermont, whose territory was claimed by New York and New Hampshire, was demanding statehood. When Vermont was refused by Congress, out of deference to New York and New Hampshire, its leaders, Ira and Ethan Allen, turned to the British authorities in Quebec for support, asking for a treaty with England.

Another frontier area that demanded equal statehood was the one that called itself Westsylvania—the region of western Pennsylvania, western Virginia, and eastern Kentucky. It wanted separation from Virginia and equal statehood. When this was delayed, it flirted with the Spanish authorities at New Orleans. Another was eastern Tennessee, calling itself the state of Franklin. It maintained its right to statehood under the provisional Ordinance of 1784, drew up its own constitution, and flirted with Spanish authorities at New Orleans when independence was denied. North Carolina quelled this separatist state in 1789, shortly before ceding its claims in Tennessee to Congress. The pressure of these frontier communities was an important force in the adoption by Congress of the Northwest Ordinance with its great principle of equal statehood in the Union.

A few weeks after the adoption of the Northwest Ordinance, the Constitutional Convention, summoned to draw up a new framework of government for the Union, assembled in Philadelphia. It met next door to the Congress of the Confederation. The Convention was at once confronted by the question whether the great principle just approved for the Northwest would be made to apply to the whole of the western country. In view of the clamor which Kentucky, Tennessee, and Westsylvania were making for statehood, this issue was one of the most pressing before the Constitutional Convention.

A sharp division of opinion at once appeared over the issue. One element, led by Madison, wished to apply the principle of the Northwest Ordinance to all the West, as fast as the cessions of lands came in, and to any future areas acquired. This group

17. Thomas Jefferson's Plan for Future States (from Barrett)

wrote into the first draft of the Constitution the provision: "If the admission be consented to, new states shall be admitted on the same terms with the original states." That provision was a clear triumph for the equality principle of the Northwest Ordinance. It was a mandatory extension of the equality principle to any new states admitted into the Union.

But another element in the Convention, led by Gouverneur Morris of New York and Elbridge Gerry of Massachusetts, objected to such a provision. They believed that if it were approved and made to apply to all the West, it would lead to a future domination of Congress by radical majorities from the West. They advocated a plan that consisted of two ideas. One was that a limit be set to the number of new states admitted to the Union in the future. The limit should be low enough so that the new states would never outnumber the original thirteen. The West was to have power in the future only in safe proportions. The second proposal was that Congress should have the right, in admitting new states, to decide whether equality should be the basis of the admission, or something less than equality. These ideas represented a retreat from the principle of equality of new states that the Ordinance of 1787 had just established for the Northwest.

The Convention finally adopted a compromise between the proposals of the two groups. It consisted of scrapping Madison's mandatory equality proposal and replacing it with the neutral and colorless statement which is now in Article IV, Section 3, of the Constitution: "New states may be admitted by Congress into this Union." This was agreed to by a vote of 9 states to 2.

In this compromise nothing at all was said as to the basis on which new states were to be admitted, whether on a basis of equality with the older states or something less. But the fact that Madison's mandatory equality provision had been rejected would seem to indicate that the framers intended Congress to have the right to admit new states on a basis of less than equality.

In the exercise of its powers, however, Congress regularly admitted new states on a basis of full equality with the older states. Vermont, in 1791, and Kentucky, in 1792, were admitted as complete and entire states. In the case of Tennessee, which was admitted in 1796, the words used were "on an equal footing with the original states in all respects whatsoever."

In 1820, however, the issue of equality for new states became a matter of controversy, when the slavery problem arose in the fight over the admission of Missouri. The issue was raised by Senator James Tallmadge of New York, who proposed that a condition be attached to the admission of Missouri—an agreement to gradually do away with slavery within its boundaries. That condition was objected to by Missouri and by the slave states of the South.

The objection to it was best stated by Senator William Pinkney of Maryland, one of the great constitutional lawyers of his day. He argued that no condition could be imposed in admitting Missouri that would make it less than equal to the older states of the Union; that since the older states had the right to maintain slavery, Missouri must have it also. Any restriction imposed on Missouri which made it less than equal to the older states would be contrary to the Constitution, and if this were attempted by Congress, Missouri could ignore the restriction as unconstitutional, once safely in the Union. This argument was allowed to prevail in the settlement of the Missouri question. The state was admitted, under the Missouri Compromise, without restriction as to its right to have slaves.

Thereafter no state seeking admission to the Union was in danger of restriction as to slavery. All had the right to establish it or not. In 1851 in *Strader v. Graham* the Supreme Court ruled that Ohio as a state could have permitted slavery, despite having been under the restriction of the Northwest Ordinance while a territory. And this right continued until the adoption of the Thirteenth Amendment, which abolished slavery in all the states.

But the issue of equality of new states arose in different forms after the Civil War. When Utah applied for admission to the Union in 1896, it was required to write into its constitution a provision prohibiting polygamy. Its legislature complied. After the state was admitted, the legislature could, theoretically, have re-established polygamy, but it did not do so. Congress considered that possibility, but dismissed it with the rather strange argument that if Utah ever did re-establish polygamy, it could be excluded from Congress on the ground that it would have ceased to have a republican form of government.

In 1911 Arizona applied for admission to the Union with a constitution permitting the recall of judges. Congress complied, but coupled its resolution with a condition that a referendum be held by the people of the territory on the recall provision. This was vetoed by President Taft, who as a former judge objected to even a referendum on the issue. While the problem was before Congress, the Supreme Court in *Coyle v. Smith* rendered a decision which re-echoed the thesis developed by Senator Pinkney a century earlier that, if a state was admitted, it must be on the basis of full equality with the older states, and that any political restrictions or conditions imposed would have no binding force on it, once it was in the Union.

Arizona, encouraged by this ruling, amended its constitution by taking out the recall of judges. Congress then voted to admit the state without conditions, and the state was formally admitted in 1912. But no sooner was it safely in the Union than the recall provision was put back in the state's constitution and left there.

Postwar Land Speculation

IN WESTERN NEW YORK a tale unfolded in the closing years of the Confederation and the early years of the Constitution that was a microcosm of American frontier history. It began as a dispute between two powerful states of the Union over territory, which ended in a treaty of partition, followed by immense land speculation and colonization. The colonization ended the designs of a foreign nation on the area.

The region of this development lies between the parallels of latitude 42° and 44° 15′, and between the longitude of the western tip of Lake Ontario and the point at which the southern boundary of New York is intersected by the Delaware River. All that area was claimed by Massachusetts and New York. None of it had been ceded to Congress. The two states quarreled over it until 1786, when they reached an agreement locally known as the Treaty of Hartford (Map 18). This awarded jurisdiction

18. Treaty of Hartford (from Winsor)

over the entire area to New York. It divided title to the land between them. To New York went the area lying between the point where parallel 42° is cut by the Delaware River and the northwesternmost shore of Seneca Lake. To Massachusetts went the area from this line to the meridian of the western tip of Lake Ontario, a territory embracing more than 6 million acres of land. In addition Massachusetts received the "Boston Ten Towns" on the Chenango River.

In 1788 the Massachusetts legislature sold the whole tract in one deal to a prominent Boston land-speculating company, Phelps & Gorham. The price was nominally a million dollars. But payment could be made in state certificates of indebtedness worth only 20 cents on the dollar. The specie price thus was $200,000. Part of the price was the extinction by Phelps & Gorham of Indian rights of occupancy, which was achieved by small payments to the Indians.

But the bargain proved more than the company could carry. A first installment, a third of the purchase price, was met, but the company was unable to raise the money to pay the rest. So an arrangement was made whereby the company kept the eastern third of its purchase and allowed the western two-thirds to revert to the state of Massachusetts.

The eastern third retained by the company was laid off in 100 townships. Of these the eastern 50 were gradually sold to small speculators. The western 50, including the rich Genesee Valley, were sold in one block in 1790 to Robert Morris, the financier of the Revolution. Morris did not long hold his purchase. After a few months he sold out to an English capitalist, Sir William Pulteney. The profit on the deal was a pleasant one. Morris got twice as much for the land as he had paid.

The land that had been reacquired by Massachusetts from Phelps & Gorham was, in the meantime, resold in 1791 to Robert Morris. The price was $333,000 (£100,000 in Massachusetts currency). In 1792 Morris disposed of the whole of it, except a twelve-mile strip west of the Genesee Tract, to a Dutch company—the Holland Land Company. Morris got about three times what he had paid for it.

Thus by 1793 two European land companies—the Sir William Pulteney estate and the Holland Land Company—owned the greater part of New York west of Seneca Lake. These two companies were engaged for the next half-century in parceling out the area to minor speculators and settlers.

Meanwhile New York's share of the Treaty of Hartford—the land from the Delaware intersection to the west side of Lake Seneca—also passed to land speculators. The region known as the Finger Lakes country had been earmarked by the New York legislature for its soldiers who had fought in the Revolutionary War. It was distributed in the form of military land warrants, which were transferable. Most of the warrants passed to speculators who bought them up at a low price. The Finger Lakes region as a result became an area of great speculative holdings.

In northern New York the same process went on. In 1785 a land commission was created by the state legislature with power to dispose of the northern lands. The head of this commission was Governor George Clinton; another member was Aaron Burr. The policy adopted by the commission was to sell the land to speculators in great blocks.

In 1791 a tract of 3,675,000 acres on the eastern shore of Lake Ontario was sold to a group of speculators headed by Alexander Macomb (Map 19). The tract, which became known as Macomb's Great Purchase, was sold at a price of 16 cents an acre

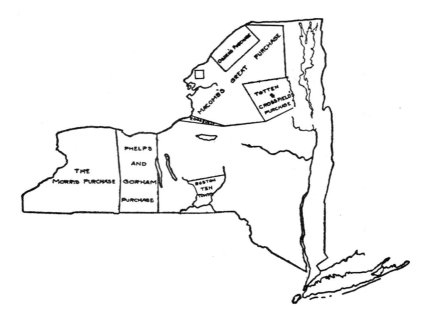

19. Land Speculation in Western and Northern New York (from Sakolski)

with long credits and no interest. Associated with Macomb were William Constable, Gouverneur Morris, and General Henry Knox. Other big sales were made by the New York commission to Samuel Ogden, to Totten & Crossfield, and to James Roosevelt of the Roosevelt connection. The amount of land sold by the commission to speculators in the years 1785 to 1792 was 5,542,000 acres, and the total sale price for it was $1,030,433. This reckless dispersion of the state's lands led to an outcry. Governor Clinton, head of the commission, was charged with being personally interested in these sales, which he denied.

In other parts of the Union speculation on a like enormous scale went on. In Maine the chief speculators were General Knox and Colonel William Duer, head of the Scioto Land Company. In northwestern Pennsylvania great tracts were sold to the Holland Land Company.

In Ohio (Map 20), Connecticut had a land claim under her old colonial charter, of which she ceded a part in the Confederation period to Congress. But a large part, containing nearly 3 million acres, she reserved—the region that came to be known as the Western Reserve. In 1796 the bulk of this region was sold by the legislature to Oliver Phelps, of Phelps & Gorham, and a group of associates, at the price of $120,000 or about 40 cents an acre. The state set aside a small portion of the Reserve, the Firelands Tract at the western end, to recompense Connecticut citizens who had suffered from British raids during the American Revolution. Congress carried further the wholesale parceling of the Ohio region to speculative interests. In 1787 it made the great sale, earlier described, to the Ohio Company, and in the same year sold the big

Symmes Tract, at the other end of Ohio between the Great and Little Miami, to a New Jersey speculator.

In Georgia, as already noted, the greatest speculation and the greatest legislative scandal in American land history took place. Practically all the state's western land in what is now Alabama and Mississippi—about 35 million acres, much of it exceptionally rich—was in 1795 sold by the legislature to four land-speculating companies for the sum of $500,000. Every member of the legislature except one had been bribed to make the sale. When the corruption became known, the next legislature passed a measure revoking the sale, accompanied by a public burning of the contract of sale. But in 1810 the revocation fell foul of the U.S. Supreme Court. Chief Justice John Marshall, who had a strongly developed sense of the rights of private property and who was a land speculator on a big scale, led the Court in ruling in the case of *Fletcher v. Peck* that Georgia could not revoke a sale once made, since the land had already passed out of the hands of the corruptionists and into the hands of innocent third parties. The decision was a peculiar one in two respects. In the first place there were few, if any, genuine innocent third parties. The whole nation knew of the scandalous process by which the land had been bought. In the second place the case was not a bona fide lawsuit. It was trumped up to obtain a decision of the Supreme Court. It should have been thrown out of court on that ground alone. Ultimately the United States government, to which Georgia had yielded the lands in 1802, had to buy off the alleged innocent third parties. The amount paid them to quiet their rights, under an act of 1814, was close to $5 million.

20. Land Speculation in Ohio (from Brown)

All this frenzied speculation in the state and federal lands was part of a universal fever that marked the period following the American Revolution. Great wars in American history have normally been followed by widespread speculation, and one of the principal media of it after the Revolution was public land.

But there were special reasons for this fever. State governments and Congress were eager to sell big tracts in order to clear away the staggering debts incurred in the war. Financial considerations became the chief motive in the land policy of the state and federal governments. Another explanation is that exciting opportunities of profit seemed present in big land deals as measured by the difference in values between land in the settled parts of the East and those in the wilderness of the West. In the worn-out hills of New England land was $20 to $30 an acre. In the wilderness of western New York the price at which speculators could buy fertile land was 20 to 30 cents an acre.

A further prospect of profit lay in the installment system of paying for public lands, which could be spread out over a number of years. The currency in which they could be met was state or federal certificates—usually greatly depreciated. The expectation of speculators making installment payments was that before the final ones fell due the currency in which they had to be paid would have depreciated even more. Finally, relatively little capital was needed by speculators, many of whom operated on a shoestring. They borrowed money to meet even their first installments. They hoped to be able to sell at an enhanced price in a few months or in a year.

Because speculators operated so largely on borrowed capital, they were usually eager to unload on European capitalists, from whom immediate cash payments could be obtained. This helps to explain the big sales to Europeans.

Speculators often employed fraud to effect their sales. They used it especially on ill-informed capitalists in Europe and on inexperienced immigrants. The frauds were of various kinds. In some cases speculators would sell lands to which they did not have complete title. An example is the Scioto Land Company, which obtained a large tract in Ohio in the transaction already described. The company never completed its payments yet it sold 150,000 acres of land to refugees from the French Revolution, chiefly middle-class Parisians. When some 600 hopeful French arrived in 1790 and looked for their land, the Scioto Company had none to give them. It tried to obtain land from the Ohio Company in repayment of a loan but was unsuccessful. The head of the company, Colonel Duer, went bankrupt, and the French emigrants lost everything. Finally Congress had to intervene and pass relief legislation for these people.

A variety of fraud often employed by speculators was to misrepresent the quality of the land for sale. This technique is described by John Bernard, a famous English actor visiting the United States in the 1790's. It is described half humorously:

> The most amusing species of scum on the surface of New York society were the land speculators, who prowled about the wharves and hurried, like so many alligators, to pounce on the unwary emigrant. Everybody arriving with a ruddy, round, moneyed-looking aspect they conceived must necessarily want to buy land, and they forthwith produced a list of soils, like a tailor's pattern book, which they had to sell cheap; land possessed of such wonderful properties as would turn all the poetry of the Fortunate Islands into poor prose, all the golden coloring of Oriental fertility into mere barrenness. It was capable not merely of growing everything . . . from a pumpkin to a buffalo, but it

emitted various kinds of effluvia which contributed to skill in all kinds of trade, the atmosphere being impregnated with an indescribable something which made a man cleverer there than in any other part of the Union. One of their rogueries was to plant hickory-trees, which will grow only on the best soil, about the edges of the worst, the fact of their production being considered a guarantee of good soil. What a world of new ideas would a Hogarth have received from observing the speculator grasping his victim by the collar, and pouring into his ears a torrent of talismanic sounds; and the good, easy, innocent English farmer rumbling the money in his pockets, and gloating with his eyes half-unsocketted on the vision of fairyland set before him. These worthies were in the habit of selling the same land to two or three different customers, and emigrating before the parties could make discovery of the fraud.

Most speculators of the type described here were mere brokers, regarded by the settlers as parasites on society. They bought public land, held it for a time so that its value might be raised by the advance of settlement, and then sold, gathering an unearned increment. They made no real contribution to new communities.

But a few speculators were developers, who made some contribution. An example is the syndicate of Sir William Pulteney, which bought land in western New York from Robert Morris. It prepared the way for settlement in the Genesee Valley by constructing roads, one from the Genesee Tract to the Susquehanna; another from the Genesee River to the Niagara. It improved the navigation of the upper Susquehanna. It laid out cities and built taverns, sawmills, gristmills, distilleries. The American agent of the company, Charles Williamson, spent close to a million dollars in development schemes. He spent money so freely that he brought his European principals to financial embarrassment.

The Holland Land Company was another of this type. Its chief contribution was not development, but long extensions of credit to settlers, a service of great importance to a new country. Judge William Cooper of Cooperstown, famous as the father of James Fenimore Cooper, was a speculator who performed services of this kind for settlers to whom he sold land. He tells of his activities in a pamphlet, *Guide in the Wilderness*. He maintained that speculators were useful servants of society, performing indispensable services to the frontier, and that the federal government should not enter into competition with them by giving credit on land purchases to settlers. The development speculators were continuing on the New York frontier, in modified form, the old New England town-proprietor tradition. The laying out of towns, the building of roads, mills, and churches, was in the normal New England pattern.

In a later generation the development tradition was still maintained in the West. In Kansas the New England Emigrant Aid Company of the 1850's began its work as a development company. Still later, some of the land-grant railroads in the West carried this tradition forward to the Great Plains.

Many of the more reckless land speculators of the post-Revolutionary War period came to grief as a result of Alexander Hamilton's measures for restoring the credit of the state and national governments. Speculators who bought public land, paying in installments and in depreciated certificates, expected that before the final installments were due the certificates would have depreciated still further. But Hamilton's assumption of the state debts abruptly raised the value of state certificates and his measures for the restoration of the national credit did the same for national certificates. The speculators were caught short. If they were fortunate they were permitted to return part of their purchases, as were Phelps & Gorham, the Ohio Company, the Scioto Land Company, and Symmes.

In 1792 the land bubble burst, and many of the more reckless speculators, such as Duer, went into bankruptcy and had to go to debtors' prisons. In 1796 an even worse crack-up occurred as a result of the Wars of the French Revolution, which drained off English and French capital formerly available for speculation.

One of the famous speculators who went bankrupt was James Wilson of the U.S. Supreme Court. He spent the remainder of his years dodging creditors and a debtor's jail, a curious situation for a Supreme Court justice. An even more celebrated speculator who actually went to a debtor's jail was Robert Morris. He stayed in prison until a bankruptcy law was passed by Congress in 1801.

Even the conservative land-development companies in the long run made only slight profits. The profits of the Pulteney estate amounted to no more than a low rate of interest on investment over a long period of years. The Holland Land Company had to struggle for more than half a century to dispose of its lands and to make collections from settlers to whom it had extended credits.

The population that was brought by speculators to western New York was, to a large extent, of New England origin. It was drawn partly from Massachusetts and Connecticut, but a large part was also drawn from northern New England, where farms on hillsides were beginning to show signs of soil deterioration. The number of New Englanders migrating to western New York after the Revolution amounted each year to from 10,000 to 20,000 persons. The flow was accelerated by Wayne's victory over the Northwest Indians at the Battle of Fallen Timbers, which made western New York a safer place than it had been for pioneers.

In Ohio a regional pattern of population became established. In the area of the Seven Ranges the predominant strain was from Pennsylvania—Scotch-Irish and Germans to a large extent. In the region of the Connecticut Reserve and the Muskingum Valley the predominant element was from New England; in southern Ohio, Virginians and Kentuckians; in the Symmes Tract a good many New Jersey people. This regionalism of population was a reflection to some extent of the eastern recruiting grounds in which the speculators happened to be operating. It soon appeared in the economic life which emerged in the western New York and Ohio societies. It appeared, also, in their social and political outlook. Those areas became a microcosm of life of the different sections of the eastern seaboard.

In western New York a one-crop economy developed. Wheat was the primary reliance. This was especially true of the Genesee Valley, which became the greatest wheat producer in the country, supplanting the Delaware Valley of Pennsylvania. Wheat growing brought flour milling. Rochester, at the falls of the Genesee River, became the great flour manufacturer of the nation. The market to which the wheat and flour were sent was Baltimore, which was reached by way of the Susquehanna River. It remained the chief market until the middle 1820's, when, as a result of the building of the Erie Canal, New York City acquired primacy. In eastern Ohio a mixed economy was established. In the Western Reserve dairying was prominent at an early day—butter and cheese and eggs were notable exports.

The social life of these western communities was a transplanted version of what existed in rural New England. But it was more materialistic and more frankly so. The gauge of success was to get ahead financially; the ideal was the self-made man. Less emphasis was given to education than in New England, though education was seldom wholly neglected. On no frontier settled by New Englanders was illiteracy ever a major problem.

The religion of New England settlements was like that of upland New England. The churches having the biggest membership were the emotional ones—the Methodist, the Baptist, and the Presbyterian, in the order of importance named. Congregationalism was not a major sect on these frontiers. It lost out as a result of an agreement made with the Presbyterians—the so-called Plan of Union of 1801. Under this plan the Presbyterians and the Congregationalists agreed that in the West neither church would invade territory that had been pre-empted by the other. Since the Presbyterian Church managed to get into the field first in western New York and eastern Ohio, it became the abiding place of many Congregationalists.

New religions easily became established in western New York. It was the region where the golden plates of the Book of Mormon were found, on which was built the Church of Jesus Christ of the Latter-Day Saints. In western New York, the Millerites, believers in the immediate second coming of Christ, the Disciples of Christ or "Campbellites," and the Spiritualists either got their start or received their major impulse.

This mushrooming of new religions was probably the result of the New England origin of the population. A New England upbringing, whether in the homeland or on this frontier, often generated high religious intensity and mysticism. It was likely to produce introspective personalities—persons eager to get into direct touch with God, to see God in person, to hear His voice from on high.

In the New England homeland, high-strung religious people often had visions; they would hear heavenly voices. They would become almost neurotic on the subject of religion. There is frequent evidence of this kind of religious intensity in the diaries, letters, and family histories of colonial New England. Still, such persons were likely to be kept in restraint by the strong forces of orthodoxy and conservatism in religion. But on New England frontiers restraints were off.

In western New York and particularly in the Genesee Tract new social isms were common—such as prohibitionism, abolitionism, feminism, bloomerism, Grahamism. Every social ism of the western world swept over western New York. Social and religious isms so often ran like wildfire over the region that it became known to the rest of the country as the "Burnt-Over-District."

In politics this region combined conservatism on economic issues with a crusading spirit on moral themes. Its conservatism on economic issues was a natural expression of prosperity, which in turn was an outcome of good soil, of an easy access to market, and of an industrious and thrifty population. In elections the majorities tended to go to the political party that responded to the interests of property. This was especially true of the Genesee Tract, and it was also true of Ohio areas of New England settlement, such as the Western Reserve and the Marietta District of the Muskingum Valley.

The political party to which the majorities in these areas first turned was the Federalist, and it held their loyalties as long as it lasted. After its disintegration these people gave their majorities, successively, to the National Republican party and to the Whig party, which carried forward the Federalist gospel on such issues as currency and the protective tariff. After the Whig party broke up, the majorities went to the Republican party.

These habits of voting are exhibited on the next series of maps, which reveal the influence of population origins and economic prosperity in producing political majorities in a rural society. The first map is of the presidential election of 1804 (21). The black is the area of Federalist majorities, the white is Democratic-Republican. The Federalist candidate is Charles C. Pinckney; the Democratic-Republican, Thomas Jefferson. Notice that the western New York area is solidly Federalist. It votes with the New England homeland for the Federalist candidate.

The next map is of the presidential election of 1828 (22). The white shows

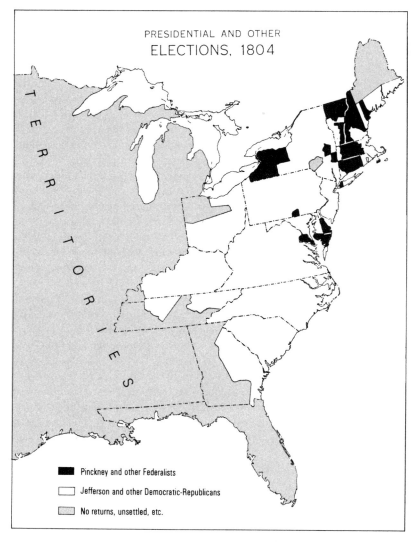

21. Presidential Election, 1804 (from Paullin)

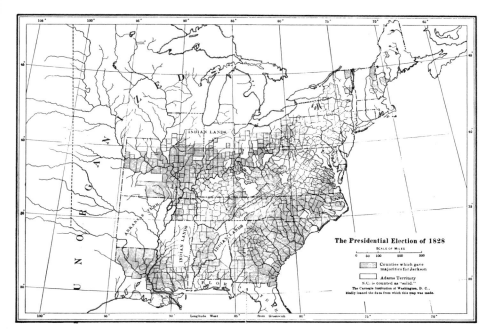

22. Presidential Election, 1828 (from Dodd)

National Republican majorities, the gray Democratic. The candidates are John Quincy Adams for the National Republicans, Andrew Jackson for the Democrats. Western New York gives its majority to Adams. So does the Western Reserve of Ohio; so does the Muskingum Valley (Marietta)—all areas of New England population.

The next map is of the presidential election of 1832 (23). The white is the Henry Clay vote; the checkrow is the Andrew Jackson vote. The slanted broken lines show the Anti-Masons. The Anti-Masons were a splinter party, a political freak. They proposed to protect America against secret societies, especially against the Masons, since Masons were believed to be atheists and to be undermining American institutions. A murder committed in New York, supposedly by Masons, precipitated the formation of the Anti-Mason party. Notice that western New York, the Western Reserve of Ohio, and the Marietta region of the Ohio Land Company, all areas of New England moralists, are centers of Anti-Masonry. They presently gravitated into Henry Clay's Whig party; Anti-Masonry was the bridge by which they crossed.

The next map shows the presidential election of 1840 (24). White is Whig; checkrow is Democratic. Notice that western New York and the Western Reserve and the Ohio Company area are now safely Whig.

The presidential election of 1844 is shown on the next map (25). White is Whig; checkrow is Democratic. Henry Clay is the Whig candidate. James Polk is the Democratic. This election turned on a slavery issue—the annexation of Texas. Clay was believed to be against annexation, though he hedged. Polk aggressively favored annexation. Notice that western New York, the Western Reserve, the Marietta region

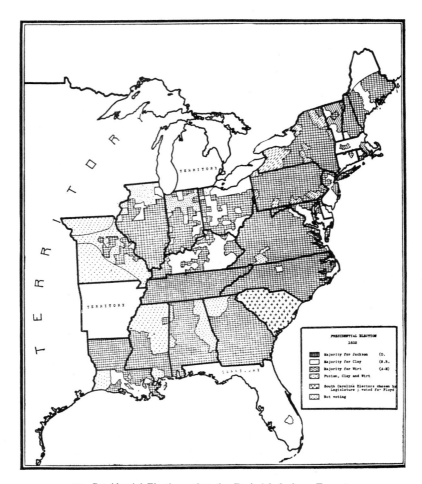

23. Presidential Election, 1832 (by Frederick Jackson Turner)

all voted Whig. On the moral issue of slavery these people were of one mind. The habit of voting Whig was established here, and that habit was itself a force in politics.

By 1848, as a result of the growth of antislavery and abolition feeling, the New England elements in western New York and in Ohio had become dissatisfied with the Whig party, which they considered too compromising on the issue of slavery. They shifted their allegiance, turning first to the Free Soil party, and later to the Republican party. They later became rock-ribbed Republican areas. On these maps the regional segmentation of society is illustrated, the segmentation that was a product of population origin, which was, in turn, a product of land-speculator activity in the years following the American Revolution.

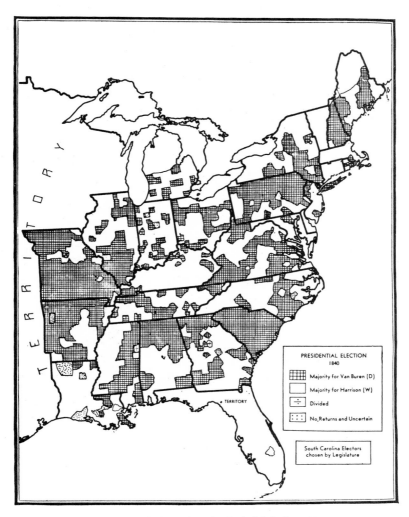

PRESIDENTIAL ELECTION
1840

Majority for Van Buren (D)

Majority for Harrison (W)

Divided

No Returns and Uncertain

South Carolina Electors
chosen by Legislature

24. Presidential Election, 1840 (by Frederick Jackson Turner)

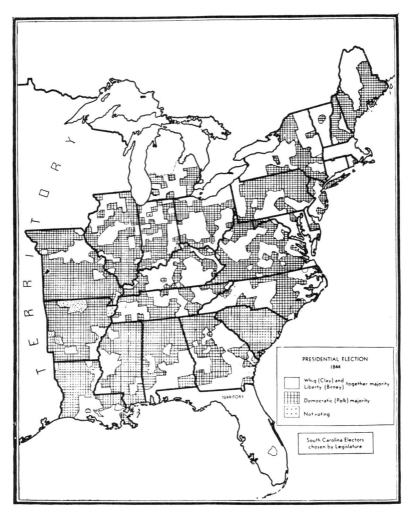

25. Presidential Election, 1844 (by Frederick Jackson Turner)

Advance Over the Allegheny Plateau

FOLLOWING THE CLOSE of the War of the American Revolution the frontier swiftly advanced into the southern half of the Allegheny Plateau. It carried to fulfillment the hope of John Jay that American pioneers would take possession of that country and force the hand of Spain. The migrants moved into uplands, into the hills and mountains of Kentucky, western Virginia, and Tennessee. Earlier pioneers had taken the attractive lowlands. The areas from which the later comers came were the Piedmont, the valley of the Appalachians, and even the Kentucky and Tennessee Blue Grass. Frontiersmen who during the war had ventured into those exposed lowlands gave up such equities as they had, for reasons of lack of thrift or restlessness, and took cheaper lands in the hills. The movement into newer country spilled over the Ohio River into the southern parts of Ohio, Indiana, and Illinois. It went as far north as the latitude of the later National Road. That road formed a line of demarcation between southern and northern population elements in the Old Northwest.

A dense hardwood forest extended over all the hill country of the Allegheny Plateau. Such a forest was looked upon with favor by the pioneers. It was believed to be a guarantee of good soil. But clearance of the forest had to occur before farms could be made. A special type of timber clearers developed to perform that labor. They were specialists in the arts of the axe. Astonishingly skillful, they could clear as much as ten or twelve acres of hardwood a season. In addition to clearing they usually did some desultory farming, and some hunting and trapping. Their major work, however, was done with the axe. They were likely to be the semi-vagrant type of pioneers, forever on the move. They would start a clearing and stay at work on it for a few years. As soon as population had begun to press in around them they would sell out and move forward to a new frontier. When neighbors got as close as five miles, they felt crowded. Often they moved three or four times in a lifetime.

The equity sold by the migrants was usually nothing more than a squatter's title, or a pre-emption claim, plus the improvements made—a clearing and a cabin. Such men would be followed by farmers of a more stable sort who would buy up the half-finished clearings and carry the labor of making farms to completion.

The process of making farms was in one sense destructive, for it involved destroying the timber on the land. The timber was burned in large part, and converted into potash. From the potash was made lye and pearl ash, both considerable articles of frontier export.

The most laborious part of clearance was getting out the roots and stumps. This was slow work, much slower than clearing the forest. It had to wait until the roots had rotted a little in the ground and had come loose.

The first crop to be planted was corn. It was planted between stumps, where cultivation would have been difficult. But corn could be grown with a minimum of cultivation. It continued to be the staple crop of this hill country until the revolution effected by the Tennessee Valley Authority reduced its relative importance in this region.

Corn became cornmeal mush or was baked into corn pone. It was fed also to cattle and hogs. In Kentucky and Tennessee whiskey was also made from it. Kentucky Bourbon began to be manufactured in the outer Blue Grass area and moved into the hills after the American Revolution.

Between 1785 and 1850 two levels of society became established south of the Ohio River in the Allegheny Plateau. One was the society on the rich and enduring soils of the Kentucky and Tennessee Blue Grass regions and the Watauga region of the upper Tennessee Valley. The other was the society of the uplands. The two levels appear in terms of population density on the following maps.

The first map shows population in the province as of 1800 (26). In the Blue Grass regions and in the Watauga Valley of the upper Tennessee, heavy concentrations of population appear. Settlement is also under way in western Kentucky, where the soil was well suited to tobacco, though less rich than that of the Blue Grass region. The upland areas are the Highland Rim, surrounding the Blue Grass, a sterile country, and the mountain regions of eastern Kentucky and eastern Tennessee. The next map shows settlement in 1830 (27). It shows greater density of population in the rich-soil areas and sparsity in the upland areas.

The next series of maps shows the crops of these areas. The first shows the corn crop of 1839 (28). A heavy concentration appears in the Lexington Plain of the Kentucky Blue Grass region. This meant hogs and farm stock, including work horses and riding horses—a special interest of Henry Clay. In Tennessee, in the Nashville Basin and Watauga regions, similar concentrations of corn appear on the map, while the mountainous areas of eastern Kentucky and Tennessee and the Highland Rim show little productivity. The same areas of concentration and of sterility appeared on crop maps for later years.

The next map shows tobacco production for the years 1839 and 1849 (29). Western Kentucky stands out. It also produces a good deal of hemp and flax. On the seaboard tobacco is concentrated in Maryland, Virginia, and North Carolina.

On the next map the cotton crop of the West appears in 1826 and 1833 (30). It is concentrated in the Nashville Basin of Tennessee, and also in the rich Memphis area adjacent to the Mississippi.

The markets to which the tobacco and cotton surpluses of the region went were those of the lower Mississippi. They were reached, as earlier, by raft or flatboat,

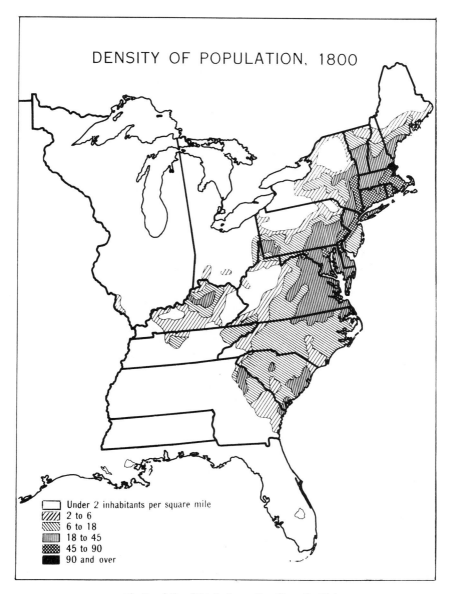

26. Population Distribution, 1800 (from Paullin)

normally as community ventures. The market for the sale of the cattle of eastern Kentucky and eastern Tennessee was the cotton-growing region of South Carolina and Georgia. It was reached by droving herds via the old Wilderness Road to Cumberland Gap and across the mountains to the seaboard via the Saluda Gap.

In politics the areas of fertile soil and prosperity were likely to give their majorities to parties that were conservative on economic issues. The mountain areas, where soil was poor and communication with the outside world was difficult, were

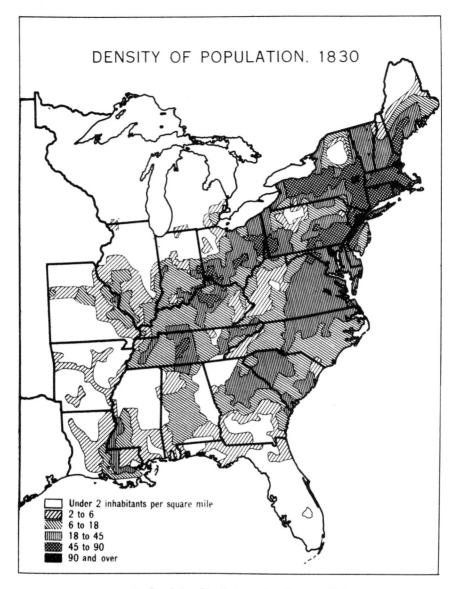

DENSITY OF POPULATION. 1830

Under 2 inhabitants per square mile
2 to 6
6 to 18
18 to 45
45 to 90
90 and over

27. Population Distribution, 1830 (from Paullin)

centers of political unrest. Areas of prosperity gave their majorities to the Whig party, whose banking, currency, and internal improvement policies were pleasing to them. The Democratic party was preferred in the uplands. These correlations of economic status and voting appear in a succession of presidential elections. They are especially evident in the map of the election of 1836 (31). On it the broken-line areas are Whig; the checkrow, Democratic. There were three Whig candidates that year; the Democratic candidate was Martin Van Buren, heir to Andrew Jackson. The vote in Tennessee is particularly revealing. The cotton areas around Nashville and Memphis are solidly Whig; so are the Watauga settlements in the rich upper valley of eastern Tennessee. The sterile Highland Rim and the mountains of eastern Tennessee are Democratic. In Kentucky, the Lexington Plain and the prosperous western tobacco area are Whig. But personal factors shaped the equation, especially the great local popularity of Clay in the mountains of eastern Kentucky, which would normally have

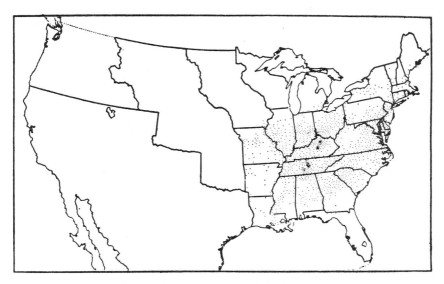

28. Corn Crop, 1839 (from Bidwell & Falconer)
Each dot represents 300,000 bushels.

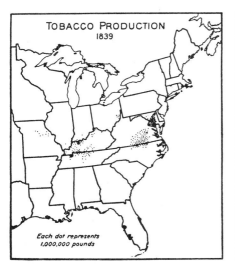 

29. Tobacco Crop, 1839, 1849 (from Gray)

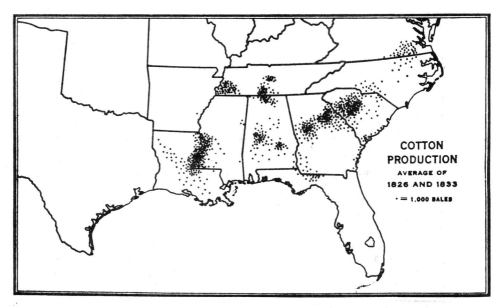

30. Cotton Crop, Average of 1826 and 1833 (from Gray)

gone Democratic. Western Virginia contains a Whig area—the fertile valley of the Great Kanawha.

The same pattern was repeated in the election of 1840 (Map 24, page 123). This was the election in which William Henry Harrison alone led the Whig ticket. Van Buren, though discredited by the depression following the Panic of 1837, was again the Democratic candidate. The vote was a triumph for Harrison. Its pattern was nearly a copy of that of 1836. Kentucky was overwhelmingly Whig.

An apparent contradiction to a geographical interpretation of voting is found east of the mountains in the Carolinas. Local politics probably accounts for the contradiction. In North Carolina the tidewater, which theoretically should have voted Whig, voted largely Democratic. The explanation was a tidewater brand of Democracy, a highly conservative brand. It was pro-bank, pro-slavery, and pro-states' rights, at the opposite pole from Jacksonian Democracy.

The interior—the Piedmont and the mountains—voted Whig, which is also explainable on local grounds. The mountain area had been in feud with the tidewater, a clash dating back to before the Revolution, which was as bitter as ever. Because the tidewater was Democratic, the mountain region was Whig. But its Whiggism, at least on local issues, was a liberal variety.

In South Carolina there was an even stranger picture, with the entire state voting one way, a result of the fact that its electors still were being chosen by the state legislature rather than by popular vote. The legislature was completely dominated by the ideas of John Calhoun. On economic issues his ideas were highly conservative. They were pro-bank, reactionary on issues of apportionment in the state legislature, and extreme on the issue of slavery. A deadly feud existed between Calhoun and the Jacksonian radicals, led by Martin Van Buren. The feud was so bitter that the electoral vote of the state was withheld from Van Buren and thrown away on Willie Mangum, a states' rights, pro-bank man allied with Calhoun and opposed to Jackson.

The pattern was again repeated in the election of 1844 (Map 25, page 124). The pattern is the same west of the mountains and in the region of the Carolinas. A habit of voting had become established, and it persisted until the 1850's, when new forces developed as a result of the westward movement of slavery which reshaped all earlier alignments.

What generalizations do these maps illustrate regarding party voting in this period? Do they illustrate determinism in American politics, based on geography, or soil, or markets, or prosperity? They do not. They suggest that soil and markets and prosperity were important. But other factors were also important—population origins, personality of leaders, and habits of voters.

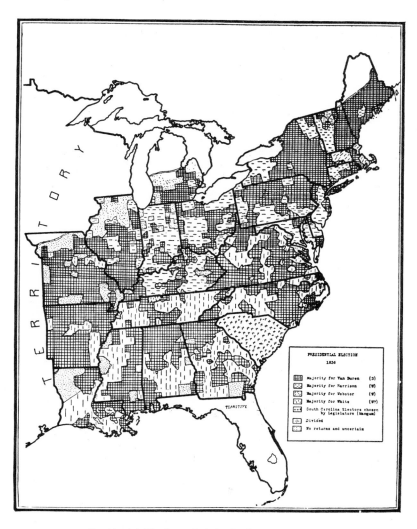

31. Presidential Election, 1836 (by Frederick Jackson Turner)

Socially the hill and mountain society of the southern Allegheny Plateau was primitive and backward. Education was much neglected. A high illiteracy rate was characteristic of the hill areas of the province, and also of southern Ohio, southern Indiana, and southern Illinois. A graphic account of Indiana conditions of illiteracy is found in a novel by Edward Eggleston, *The Hoosier Schoolmaster*. Book learning was not highly regarded. It was even scorned by some. But other forces were important, such as difficulties of communication and the poverty prevailing in the upland country. Illiteracy became subsequently one of the exports of the area. It was carried into the southern part of the Old Northwest, and to every later frontier, until the new states, with federal land grants for education, were able to lessen its impact.

The religious life of the hill and mountain people was highly emotional, even more so than that of the New York and Ohio frontiers. The denominations most numerous were the Baptists, Methodists, and Campbellites. The preaching was a call to repent of sin and to recover faith in God.

The most characteristic of the preachers were circuit riders, rugged evangelists, like the Methodist Peter Cartwright, who traveled thousands of miles with rations in their saddlebags, preaching repentance for sin and consigning unbelievers to hellfire and everlasting damnation. The most characteristic church gatherings were revivalist meetings, where the attendance often numbered hundreds or thousands of people, who listened for weeks to exhortations and prayer and reached a high state of religious excitement.

The entire nation was swept by revivalism in the early years of the 19th century. The eastern seaboard and the western interior partook of what was known as the Great Revival, or the Blessed Revival. This emotionalism was a reaction against the rationalism and agnosticism that had marked the later years of the 18th century, spread by the French Revolution.

In the frontier regions of Kentucky and Tennessee it led to strange religious manifestations. The congregations at revivalist meetings would get worked up, under the spur of circuit riders of strong personality, into such a frenzy of religious emotion that they would break out into the holy laugh, the holy groan, the holy bark, or the holy growl. There were such symptoms of muscular Christianity, also, as the jerks, the holy trance, and the holy roll. A graphic account of a revivalist meeting of this sort is given by Cartwright in his *Autobiography* (1856). The account is of the so-called Cumberland Revival at the turn of the century. Cartwright did not regard a little exaggeration as a serious sin.

> Just in the midst of our controversies . . . a new exercise broke out among us, called the *jerks,* which was overwhelming in its effects upon the bodies and minds of the people. No matter whether they were saints or sinners, they would be taken under a warm song or sermon, and seized with a convulsive jerking all over, which they could not by any possibility avoid, and the more they resisted the more they jerked. If they would not strive against it and pray in good earnest, the jerking would usually abate. I have seen more than five hundred persons jerking at one time in my large congregations. Most usually persons taken with the jerks, to obtain relief . . . would rise up and dance. Some would run, but could not get away. Some would resist; on such the jerks were generally very severe. To see those proud young gentlemen and young ladies, dressed in their silks, jewelry and prunella, from top to toe, take the *jerks,* would often excite my risibilities. The first jerk or

so, you would see their fine bonnets, caps, and combs fly; and so sudden would be the jerking of the head that their long loose hair would crack almost as loud as a waggoner's whip.

Frontier revivalism of this sort was more than robust religion. It was an escape from the loneliness and monotony of frontier life. Revival meetings were the equivalent of concert, church, theater, and chautauqua, all rolled into one.

In the mid-twentieth century the hill and mountain areas of the southern Allegheny Plateau remained centers of religious emotionalism and intensity. They were also centers of fundamentalism in religion. Concepts of religious modernism, of higher criticism of the Bible, of Darwinism and the doctrine of evolution, were regarded there with distrust. In Tennessee the teaching of the doctrine of evolution in the schools was long forbidden by law. The great hold William Jennings Bryan had on these hill and mountain people was the result largely of his own religious fundamentalism, though his democracy and the humanitarianism of his ideas were also important.

The Southwest in American Diplomacy, 1783–1803

FOREIGN PROBLEMS RELATING to the trans-Appalachian territory pressed for solution while those of its government absorbed the attention of Congress. They reflected the sober reality that foreign troops still occupied the periphery of the acquired area. Most immediate were the problems growing out of the peace treaty. One was the boundary of West Florida, seized by Spanish troops from the British during the war. In the preliminary Anglo-American negotiations a secret agreement had been made that if the province were restored to England the boundary would be where it had been before the war, at the line of 32° 28'. But if Spain held on to the province the line would drop to 31° in favor of the Americans. Spain won the province in the final Anglo-Spanish treaty, but without specification of the boundary. In the final Anglo-American treaty, the line was set at 31°. Spain refused to recognize that line for a dozen years, and her troops held the disputed strip.

The navigation of the lower Mississippi had been accorded the United States, from the river's source "to the ocean" in the Anglo-American agreement. But Spain held both banks of the lower river at the end of the war and its government denied that the British could confer upon the United States the right of navigation on the river "to the ocean" when it (Spain) controlled the river's mouth. This proved a particularly stubborn issue.

American settlers in the up-country clamored for navigation to get their surplus to market. They did not yet have much surplus, most of which was absorbed by incoming settlers, but they were thinking of the future. The Americans wished also a place of deposit on the lower river for transfer of their produce from rafts or flatboats to oceangoing vessels. They asked for this not as a right, but as a privilege. They wished another privilege—admission of their surplus to the local New Orleans market, which was the distributing center for about 40,000 people in lower Louisiana. It was also a major tobacco market, some two million pounds of upriver tobacco were annually bought there on behalf of the Spanish government. Such concessions had been given Americans during the war, when the United States and Spain were fighting England.

After the war the normal Spanish mercantile policy came back into force. In 1784 the lower river was declared closed, and in 1786 an American flatboat, loaded with provisions, was seized at New Orleans by the local authorities. Spanish ambitions had been enhanced by the gains of the war. The Gulf of Mexico had become, with the recovery of the Floridas, a kind of Spanish lake, conceived of as the center of the vast empire of New Spain, including Louisiana and extending to the Pacific. That center would not become infested by the rude frontiersmen of the North if the lower river were kept closed.

Yet an airtight closure was inexpedient and might become unsafe. At New Orleans food shortages sometimes occurred and it was necessary to import the cheap food of the up-country. Also, a tight closure would inconvenience and irritate the residents of that region, nearly all of whom were French and restless under Spanish rule. If they were too greatly pressed the French government would be troubled and France was the ally of Spain. Also, the Kentucky and Tennessee frontiersmen were unlikely to accept calmly a closing of the lower river. They were likely to make a descent of the river and seize New Orleans, either by themselves, or, in case of a European war, in cooperation with some European fleet. That possibility haunted the Spanish mind.

In the spring of 1785 the Spanish government sent Don Diego de Gardoqui to Philadelphia, empowered to negotiate a treaty with the American government. He carried instructions to offer to the Americans trade to the ports of Spain and the Canary Islands, to propose the Ohio River as the boundary of West Florida at the north, to agree, if necessary, to the line of 32° 28', and to gain American recognition of Spain's exclusive control of the lower Mississippi where the river flowed between Spanish banks.

To deal with him the American government named John Jay, who had known Gardoqui in Paris. He was instructed to establish the line of the 31st parallel as the West Florida boundary and to obtain the navigation of the lower Mississippi. As a New Yorker, he was impressed by the eagerness of the northeastern states for trade with Spain and the West Indies, and he believed that, to obtain it, the American government would be wise to agree to a temporary yielding of the navigation of the lower Mississippi. He acutely realized the feebleness of the American government under the Articles of Confederation. Time would permit migration of Americans to the West in sufficient numbers to force the hand of Spain. For the present, Southerners in Congress would vote to maintain the river rights of their constituents who had migrated to the West and a compromise would be the best solution of that problem. He therefore formulated a plan whereby the American government would forbear pressing for twenty-five years the issue of navigation of the lower river in return for a liberal commercial treaty with Spain.

The plan was submitted to Congress on August 3, 1786. Debate on it ran to the end of the month. In the final vote seven states approved the plan, five opposed, and Delaware was absent. The favorable votes were all northern, the unfavorable southern. The plan failed inasmuch as nine votes were necessary for ratification of a treaty. George Washington was one of the few southern leaders favoring the plan. He believed the closing of the lower river would produce agitation to build a Potomac-Ohio canal which would tie the West to the East.

The size of the aye vote alarmed and angered the West. Only a slim margin had averted a sellout to Spain by the East. The West felt betrayed by the seaboard, both North and South. The North was willing to surrender the birthright of the West to a foreign power. The South on other scores was equally culpable. It was withholding separate statehood to western communities, and its speculators were preying on western pioneers. The Union seemed to be going to pieces; the West must look after itself.

Politicians in Kentucky and Tennessee spread such views in electioneering for local office. They emphasized the resistance of Virginia and North Carolina to their separate statehood, and muted the contribution the southern states had made in defeating the Jay-Gardoqui plan. In Kentucky politicians attributed the withholding of statehood to Virginia's opposition, rather than to the differences in the Continental Congress over the conditions attached by Virginia to the cession of her western claims. Some Kentucky politicians resorted to a threat of secession and a connection with Spain as a spur to Virginia to concede statehood.

Especially adept at such tactics was James Wilkinson. He had come to Kentucky in 1784 with the rank of brigadier general in the Revolutionary army. In the autumn of 1787, a year after the failure of the Jay-Gardoqui plan, he appeared in New Orleans with a cargo of up-country produce to sell, for which he sought a license from Governor Don Esteban Miró. He was able to ingratiate himself with the governor and with the intendant, Martín de Navarro, and obtained the license. Wilkinson drew up a memorial to the Spanish court in which he outlined a river policy that would be advantageous to Spain and safe to apply. The river should be kept closed to American navigation. The up-country settlements would then remain subordinate to, and seek protection from, the power which could give them this precious privilege. But indulgences in trading should be offered to men of influence in the settlements; these indulgences would attach them to Spain and prevent acts of hostility against its possessions. Such a system would serve as a transition from leaving the Union and entering a negotiation with the Spanish court. Wilkinson swore allegiance to the king of Spain and offered to serve as agent of the Kentucky settlers in negotiations in New Orleans. The memorial, which went to the Spanish court, bearing warm recommendations of Miró and Navarro, was promptly accepted there as policy.

Wilkinson was given a monopoly of the up-country trade with New Orleans. In 1788 he brought down to New Orleans a flotilla of flatboats loaded with produce which netted him a profit of $5000. He became a secret business partner of Miró, from whom he obtained a loan of $7000. In 1792 he obtained an annual pension of $2000, which continued until 1800, though in 1796 he had become the commander in chief of the American Army of the West. But he was not altogether trusted by the Spanish government, and another Kentuckian, Judge Benjamin Sebastian, was given an annual pension of $1000 to keep an eye on him. Other Kentuckians who engaged in flirtations with Spain were Judge Harry Innes, General John Adair, and John Brown, later a senator.

In Tennessee, in the Watauga area, John Sevier, embittered against North Carolina because of the failure of his Franklin statehood scheme, dallied with alliance with Spain, and applied to Spanish authorities for a loan. James White, an American

agent to the Indians, took money from Spain and was referred to in Spanish correspondence as "our Don Jaime." At Nashville, James Robertson, in a letter to Miró,
expressed willingness to become a Spanish subject. At his suggestion the region
around Nashville was named "Miró District." These leaders were as ready to derive
profit from a tortuous situation as were the Spanish authorities. Some of them may
have intended merely to lead the Spanish authorities by the nose. But Wilkinson,
whose career was a prolonged record of rascality, would doubtless have moved
wherever self-interest lay.

Enforcement of closure by the Spanish at New Orleans was vacillating and
inconsistent. In 1788 trade on the lower river was opened to Americans generally,
breaching Wilkinson's monopoly. Also the market at New Orleans was opened
generally to upriver produce on payment of a duty of 15 percent. Holders of special
licenses, such as Wilkinson, had to pay only 6 percent. In 1793 all upcountry produce, regardless of sender, was admitted to New Orleans at a 6 percent duty. But if the
produce was later re-exported from New Orleans, an additional 6 percent was required as an export duty. However, more advantageous terms could always be obtained by a judicious distribution of bribes. This system continued at New Orleans for
the remainder of the period of the Spanish regime.

Under this system New Orleans became an important exporter of flour, bacon,
and tobacco. The city also began exporting sugar and cotton. By 1800 it was coming
to be regarded as a great future seat of commerce. Its rapidly growing trade attracted
the attention of Napoleon, which helps to explain his eagerness for a return of
Louisiana to France.

Colonization in Louisiana and West Florida by trusted persons was an added
facet of Spanish policy. In Louisiana one region seemed especially desirable to
colonize. It was upper Louisiana, now Missouri. Colonization there was deemed
desirable by Spain, not merely as a development matter, but as a means of defending
New Orleans against the danger of a sudden raid down the Ohio and the Mississippi
from Kentucky. The precise area to be colonized was the part of Missouri which lay
opposite the point where the Ohio flows into the Mississippi, where a Kentucky force
descending the river could be intercepted. The concept of a defensive colony of this
sort, and also its particular location, had been suggested to the Spanish government by
Wilkinson in his memorial of 1787.

The persons used to set up this colony were to be partly Europeans and partly
trustworthy Americans, the latter only the most responsible of frontiersmen. They
were to be attracted to the cause of Spain by liberal treatment as to land, religion, and
government, and converted into loyal Spanish subjects. Their settlement was to serve
as a buffer—a semi-military outpost—defending New Orleans. An incidental advantage in attracting Americans to this region would be that it would weaken Kentucky
settlements by draining off their best elements.

In 1788 a start was made on the program. Don Gardoqui in Philadelphia made an
offer to Colonel George Morgan of the Philadelphia firm of Baynton, Wharton and
Morgan. It was of an extensive tract of land in Missouri opposite the mouth of the
Ohio River, subject to the approval of the Spanish Crown. It was jumped at by
Morgan. He acted on it just as if approval had already been given by the Spanish
Crown. In 1789 he laid out the site of a colony opposite the confluence of the Ohio and
the Mississippi, naming it New Madrid. He brought there a group of 70 selected

persons, gathered at Pittsburgh and floated down the Ohio. The colonists were offered land virtually free, up to an amount of 320 acres, as well as assurances of freedom of worship and, what was more important, access without payment of duty to the New Orleans market for their surplus. They were expected to become loyal Spanish subjects.

The project, however, did not turn out well. It ran into difficulties raised at New Orleans by James Wilkinson and his partner, Governor Miró, who were annoyed because they had not been consulted. Also, in 1790 the whole New Madrid area was overflowed by an unusually high flood of the Mississippi River. The settlers in discouragement gave up their land and returned to the East. Morgan went with them, so completely discouraged that he never tried to retrieve the project.

Some permanent colonization of the Missouri area was, however, achieved by grants of land to individuals. Daniel Boone was given a grant and became a Spanish citizen for a time. Moses Austin, of later fame as a Texan, was given another. A Dutchman, Baron Bastrop, was given a grant on the Washita River (lower Louisiana). Baron von Steuben of Revolutionary War fame applied for a grant. A considerable amount of settlement was made also in West Florida.

The idea of using Americans as colonists in upper Louisiana for the defense of New Orleans was fatuous. It was the idea of using Gauls to defend Rome, as James Madison observed. The same idea was later adopted in Texas with disastrous consequences to Mexico.

The Spanish government gave military support to the project of colonization. It carried out a program of fortification on both sides of the lower Mississippi. The forts were constructed where possible on bluffs overlooking the river. On the east side one was built at Chickasaw Bluffs, the site of present-day Memphis, on territory indisputably American. Another was built at Walnut Hills, the site of present-day Vicksburg. On the west side of the river fortification directly on the banks was not feasible. The banks were too low and unstable. The one fort erected was near the entrance of the Arkansas River into the Mississippi. It was not very effective as an interception of forces coming down the river. Equally ineffective was the manning of the forts. Not more than a regiment of troops was maintained along the wide arc from Chickasaw Bluffs to New Orleans and from New Orleans eastward via the "inner lakes" to St. Marks in West Florida.

A supplement to land defense was a freshwater fleet patrolling the river. It consisted at first of two or three galleys or "galiots," gradually increased to eleven, which operated between New Orleans and the Gulf. It was used to coordinate administration and defense.

Defense was also sought by means of alliances with Indian tribes. This was a substitute for settlement by Spaniards, who were few in Louisiana and fewer in West Florida. The Europeans in Louisiana were predominantly French, none of them too loyal to the Spanish Crown. The most powerful of the Indian allies were the Creeks in Florida, who were able to put 4000 warriors in the field. They were drawn to Spanish alliance by fear of the land-grabbing Americans. Part of their domain was in the region of West Florida which the United States was claiming.

Their leader was Alexander McGillivray, a half-breed, the son of a Scotch father and a Creek mother. He was a man of ability and education, who led a dissolute life. He was completely unscrupulous and he hated Americans. His father, who had been a

Tory, had lost his property to Georgia by confiscation in the War of the American Revolution.

One of the means by which the Creeks were held steadfast in loyalty to Spain was a fur-and-peltry-trade partnership—Panton, Leslie and Co., located at Pensacola on the Gulf of Mexico. It dated back to the years prior to the American Revolution, when the Floridas were British. Its head was William Panton, a Scotchman, who had been a Tory in the American Revolution, had lost property to Georgia by confiscation, and now hated Americans. In the firm Alexander McGillivray was a junior partner. With the return to Spain of the Floridas, the company enjoyed a special favor. It was exempt from the normal mercantile requirement that any goods used in trade to Indians must be of Spanish origin. It was allowed to use British goods, which were preferred by the Indians, and it could bring them into the Floridas at a low rate of duty. The whole setup was designed to keep the Indians loyal to Spain.

Another means by which the Indians were held in allegiance was the giving of annual presents of arms and supplies. The annual presents to the Creeks were on a considerable scale, as much as $40,000 to $50,000 a year. The Cherokee, Choctaw, and Chickasaw were also held by such means to the side of Spain.

In 1793 this Indian program was expanded. All the southern tribes were organized into a great confederation, and a defensive and offensive alliance was made with them in the Treaty of Nogales. As a means of implementing the program a Spanish fort, Fort Confederation, was built on the Tombigbee River among the tribes. Like the fort at Chickasaw Bluffs, it was north of 32° 28′ on indisputable American territory. The Spanish official who particularly pressed the confederation program was the governor at New Orleans, Barón de Carondelet, who had succeeded Miró in 1791, and was much more hostile to the United States than his predecessor.

Carondelet's ultimate objective was to bring southern and northern tribes into one grand alliance, forming a solid wall of Indian resistance to American advance from the Great Lakes to the Gulf of Mexico. The Shawnee, who had once been associated with the southern tribes, were to form the junction between the two segments. The project was big and farsighted, but it was too big. The Indians were too separatistic and shortsighted for such a plan, and it failed. A good deal later, in 1810, the great Shawnee chief Tecumseh tried again to effect such a confederation and he also failed.

The United States government at the time was feeble in meeting the problems of the Spanish and the Indians. Exemplifying the weakness that troubled John Jay, it left the defense of the Southwest to the settlers. Attacks were made on the middle Tennessee communities by the Upper Creeks; on the Oconee frontier in Georgia by the Lower Creeks; on the Cumberland settlements by the Creeks and the Cherokee. General Henry Knox, the rotund Secretary of War, who was charged with Indian affairs, lacked the means or the energy to bring these tribes to terms.

In 1790, at the invitation of Knox, McGillivray was invited to New York for a peace conference. He came attended by a delegation of 23 befeathered subchiefs, and accorded a flattering reception. He became an honorary chief of Tammany Hall and a brigadier general in the American Army. He was already a colonel in the English Army and a general in the Spanish Army. He swore allegiance to the United States and signed the Treaty of New York, which pledged perpetual peace and drew a boundary for the Lower Creeks along the valley of the Oconee. Presents to the value of $10,000 were provided the tribe and the salary of the brigadier general was set at $1200 a year.

But the treaty was without much effect. One reason was that on the sidelines of the New York negotiation had been William Augustus Bowles, a Maryland-born Tory adventurer, who had established himself among the Lower Creeks as "Director General of the Creek Nation." He had means, for he was backed by capitalists in Nassau. He was a rival of McGillivray and considered the latter's peace a selling short of the Lower Creeks. Also, McGillivray, on his return home from New York, was granted a greatly enhanced pension by Carondelet, which restored his allegiance to Spain. The result was that the boundary of the Creek cession under the Treaty of New York was never even drawn.

In Kentucky the Spanish conspiracy culminated in a convention of the settlements meeting at Danville in 1788. All the grievances of Kentucky were aired there—the failure of statehood, the river issue, and the Indian menace. Wilkinson was at the convention ready for mischief if conditions were favorable. Enough of his relations with the Spanish at New Orleans had become known, however, to put him under suspicion. By June 21, 1788, the new Constitution of the United States had been framed and ratified. Virginia had consented to Kentucky's statehood and action by Congress was awaited. Kentuckians were hopeful that their problems would be solved by a stronger federal government. The convention, therefore, took no action other than to send an urgent request to Congress for a speedy solution of the problems of the West.

In 1789 a new era opened for the United States and for Europe. In the United States the government of the Constitution was organized, with George Washington at its head, bringing strength and stability to the nation. In Europe the French Revolution broke out, which was destined to be followed by a quarter-century of warfare and to subject Spain to increasing isolation and weakness. By this reversal of fortune the conditions were created which induced Spain to agree to a treaty with the United States, the Pinckney Treaty of 1795.

In the treaty Spain conceded the major demands of the United States. She accepted the boundary line of the 31st parallel for West Florida from the Mississippi River to the Apalachicola. She agreed to the free navigation of the lower Mississippi by United States citizens. She granted for three years the privilege of deposit at New Orleans—a permission to transfer cargoes from the river to seagoing vessels—and a renewal of it thereafter either at New Orleans or some other convenient locality on the riverbank. Finally, she undertook to use her influence to restrain the southern Indians. Everything the United States had been demanding since 1783 was granted. The treaty was such a capitulation as only the menacing European situation and the fear of an American assault on New Orleans could have brought. It proved a stimulus to migration to the Mississippi Valley. By 1800 the census reported nearly 300,000 white persons in the trans-Allegheny area as compared with about 30,000 at the close of the American Revolution. This was in spite of the fact that the Spanish dragged their feet in implementing the treaty and kept troops in the ceded area until 1798.

With the turn of the century new problems arose in the Southwest. In the autumn of 1800 the Spanish government retroceded Louisiana to France, including New Orleans on the east side of the Mississippi. The Treaty of San Ildefonso, by which this was done, was secret, but evidence of it reached the American government within a few months. The treaty provided that the actual transfer of the province would occur as soon as the promises Napoleon had made to Spain in the document were fulfilled. This meant that the United States had acquired a far more formidable neighbor at New Orleans than before.

In recovering Louisiana, Napoleon also had in mind West Florida, which contained harbors on the Gulf—especially Mobile—that would serve as naval bases for the defense of New Orleans. Included in his plan, as well, was the welfare of the French sugar islands in the West Indies. Sugar islands were prize possessions in European empires. The service of Louisiana would be to provision them and supply them with timber.

Louisiana was retroceded without excessive pressure on Spain. It had been an unprofitable possession to hold. Its administrative costs had been greater by far than its revenues, and the population was predominantly French. The quid pro quo offered by Napoleon was the Kingdom of Tuscany for the Prince of Parma, the nephew of the Spanish king, Charles IV, who was an admirer of Napoleon. The King had been won by a further argument of Napoleon, that Louisiana had been of value to Spain primarily as a shield for her older possessions against American aggression. France, with greater military might, would be a much more effective shield. Delay in the transfer of Louisiana occurred only because of delay in delivery of the promised Kingdom of Tuscany to the Prince of Parma.

When the Treaty of San Ildefonso became known to President Jefferson he wished to give Napoleon warning, indirectly, of the dangerous consequences of a French take-over of New Orleans. To a personal friend in Paris, Pierre Du Pont de Nemours, he sent, unsealed, a letter addressed to Robert Livingston, the American minister in Paris, the nature of which he asked the friend to convey to Napoleon. The letter ran in part as follows:

> There is on the globe one spot the possessor of which is our natural and habitual enemy. It is New Orleans, through which the produce of three-eighths of our territory must pass to market, and from its fertility it will ere long yield more than half of our whole produce and contain more than half our inhabitants. France, placing herself in that door, assumes to us the attitude of defiance . . . It seals the union of two countries who in conjunction can maintain exclusive possession of the ocean [England and the United States]. From that moment we must marry ourselves to the British fleet and nation.

Du Pont de Nemours felt that such a message would be unwise to convey to Napoleon, that it would be counterproductive. He wrote Jefferson that a better tactic would be to offer to buy New Orleans and the Floridas, a course Jefferson already had in mind. The Secretary of State, James Madison, had written Livingston to inquire the price for which France would sell New Orleans and the Floridas, if France obtained them.

In November 1802 two items of exciting news arrived in Washington. One was that the king of Spain had ordered the formal transfer of Louisiana to France, the other that the Spanish intendant at New Orleans had withdrawn the right of deposit guaranteed in the Pinckney Treaty, and had not designated an alternative. The news of the closing of the deposit produced a storm in the United States, where it was attributed to Napoleon, who was believed to have inspired it in order that he might take over New Orleans unencumbered by American rights. Eastern Federalists, eager to embarrass

Jefferson, cried for immediate seizure of New Orleans and the Floridas, with negotiations afterward.

Jefferson was more prudent. He had knowledge of the exertions of the Spanish minister in Washington for a restoration of the deposit right, which had been withdrawn because of abuse of it by American smugglers. He permitted that issue to ride, and sent James Monroe, instead, to Paris in 1803 with instructions to seek a purchase of New Orleans and the Floridas, which Napoleon was believed to have acquired. If such a purchase could not be effected, and if France were to attempt to close the lower river to Americans, Monroe and Livingston were authorized to seek an alliance with England. Monroe was popular in the West and his appointment calmed excitement there.

In the ensuing Paris negotiations it became clear that Napoleon actually had nothing to sell on the east side of the Mississippi except the island of New Orleans. The Floridas, which he had sought, had not been obtained. Before Monroe arrived in Paris, Napoleon had decided to offer the United States not New Orleans alone, but the whole of Louisiana. Monroe and Livingston accepted this proposal, though without authority to do so, and the only issue was the terms. Napoleon would have accepted 50 million livres. His minister asked 100 million. A compromise was finally reached on 80 million ($15 million), of which three-fourths was to go to France, the rest to Americans having damage claims against France.

The sale of Louisiana was a typically cynical Napoleonic act. It repudiated a pledge that France would never alienate the territory unless to return it to Spain. It was sold to the one power Spain most feared to have there. The sale was also a violation of the French Constitution, defended by Napoleon on the ground that he could not hold the province in case of renewed war with England. The true explanation of the sale was that his scheme of a sugar empire in the West Indies had collapsed. The island of Santo Domingo, linchpin of the scheme, had succumbed to Negro insurrectionists led by Toussaint L'Ouverture, and the army of General Leclerc, sent to subdue them, had been decimated by yellow fever. The heart of Napoleon lay in his ambition to dominate Europe, which meant the renewal of war with England and an immediate need of the money which the sale of Louisiana would bring. The sale brought the final solution to the problem of the European hold on the mouth of the Mississippi.

19

The Northwest in American Diplomacy, 1783 – 95

A MAJOR DIPLOMATIC PROBLEM of the new nation after the close of the war was the British presence in the "Northwest Posts." This was not a boundary dispute. The northwest boundary had been defined in the peace treaty as running up the St. Lawrence River from its intersection by the 45th parallel to Lake Ontario, and thence, by the middle of the Great Lakes and their connecting waters, to a specified point on the western shore of Lake Superior. South of that line the British relinquished to the United States all claim to territorial rights and government. They also agreed to withdraw, with all convenient speed, troops, garrisons, and fleets from every port, place, and harbor within the United States. On the eastern seaboard these promises were fulfilled without delay. But in the Northwest Posts, which were undeniably on United States soil, British troops remained for thirteen years after the treaty was signed.

The posts numbered seven, of which four were on the shores of the Great Lakes, one was on the St. Lawrence, and two were on Lake Champlain. In character they were partly military and strategically important. They were the key to the navigation system of the Great Lakes. All were fur-trade centers. They preserved Montreal's historic connection with the tribes of western New York and the Old Northwest. Montreal's fur trade in 1785 was worth £180,000, of which £100,000 came from territory within the boundaries of the United States. The economic life of all the area between the Great Lakes and the Ohio River turned about these posts.

Historically the Old Northwest had been part of, and had rendered service to, the power possessing Montreal and Quebec. It had given France interior connection with the Gulf of Mexico via the Ohio and the Mississippi, and had served the British, after 1763, in the same way. It was not an easy province to give up. If a neutral Indian state could be maintained there, and if the American Confederation were to dissolve, it might gravitate back into the old orbit. This was a dream nursed by British imperialists in Canada and in England throughout the period of the Confederation and later.

The justification offered for postponing evacuation of the posts changed with changing circumstances. At first it was that the Indians in the Northwest must be reconciled to the new situation and that British traders must have time to make an orderly withdrawal. Otherwise the Indians would turn in rage against an ally that had deserted them. Later the argument was that the American government had failed to fulfill its obligations under the treaty. Under Article IV the treaty provided that British creditors were to meet no lawful impediment to full recovery of prewar debts; in Article V, that Congress should earnestly recommend to the state legislatures restitution of all confiscated Loyalist estates and properties; under Article VI, that there should be no future American confiscations because of the part taken by Loyalists in the war. All these provisions had been violated. Congress had made the recommendations; the states had ignored them, and had even continued to pass confiscatory legislation.

The Indians loyal to England in the war were enmeshed in this tangle. Some were fragments of tribes mauled by American frontiersmen. In the upper valley of the Wabash and on the Maumee were the Wabash "confederates" and parts of the Shawnee. On the upper Miami were the Miami, and, east of them, the Shawnee and the Wyandot—the "wasps" of the Kentucky frontier. In the upper Muskingum Valley were the Delaware, and in western New York the nations of the Iroquois. With the exception of the Oneida and Tuscarora, who were neutral, the Iroquois League had joined the British under the leadership of the Mohawk, and had staged the frightful massacres in New York's Cherry Valley and in Pennsylvania's Wyoming Valley. They had met retribution in the Sullivan campaign of 1779, and their zest for fighting had been broken. The Mohawk especially had been humbled. Exposed to swift punishment for any new misdeeds from the white settlements rising on their flanks, they were satisfied to keep the peace. Their great leader, Joseph Brant, had become a consistent advocate of peace, and even sought to use his prestige among the Indians to restrain aggressions against the United States by the western tribes.

In the Confederation period Indian affairs north of the Ohio were the assignment of a special committee of Congress. On October 15, 1783, the committee, in an interim report, outlined what should be done about the Indians under its jurisdiction. It was not as vengeful as the public in the United States. It considered a summary punishment of them inexpedient, and recommended drawing a veil of clemency over what had happened in the war. Still, its program was not unduly merciful. It suggested sending commissioners to meet delegates from all the northern tribes at some designated site for a peace settlement. The commissioners should seek to obtain from the Indians an agreement to open to white settlement a portion of the territory inhabited by them. The portion was extensive—all the region eastward of a line up the Great Miami River from the Ohio and joining the Maumee River, which flows into Lake Erie; in other words, the greater part of the present state of Ohio, together with western New York and western Pennsylvania. As recommended by the committee, commissioners were appointed by Congress to convene a grand council for this purpose and they did their best to induce the Indians to assemble for it, but without success.

On March 19, 1784, Congress concluded that grand councils with the northern tribes were not effective means of obtaining wide cessions. It shifted to piecemeal negotiations with groups of tribes at designated rendezvous. Councils were held with three groups of those tribes, from all of whom land-cession treaties emerged. In chronological order the treaties were: Fort Stanwix (October 22, 1784) with the Six Nations; Fort McIntosh (January 21, 1785) with the Wyandot, Delaware, Chippewa, and Ottawa; and Fort Finney (January 31, 1786) with the Shawnee. In these treaties cessions were made of all the area that is now eastern and southern Ohio as far as the Great Miami. The cessions were made without payment and were regarded as reparation for damage done to the United States in the war.

Tribes absent from the negotiations, but whose lands had been included in the cessions, denounced the treaties. In 1786 ten of them, including the tribes signatory to the treaties, petitioned Congress to cease land surveys. Sporadic fighting occurred.

In 1787 Congress became mellower toward the Indians. In the Northwest Ordinance it declared in Article 3: "The utmost good faith shall always be observed towards the Indians; their lands and property shall never be taken from them without their consent; and in their property, rights and liberty, they shall never be invaded or disturbed, unless in just and lawful wars, authorized by Congress; but laws founded in justice and humanity shall from time to time be made, for preventing wrongs being made to them, and for preserving peace and friendship with them." A like spirit was shown by Congress in instructions the same year to Governor Arthur St. Clair of the Northwest Territory. He was to endeavor to extinguish Indian possession of lands as far west as the Mississippi River. But this was to be done by treaties with the Indians and payments were to be made for any lands ceded. The principle of retribution was abandoned.

In conformity with the new policy St. Clair held a council with the Indians at Fort Harmar. In January 1789 he obtained treaties with two groups of tribes. One was with the Six Nations, the other was with the Wyandot, Delaware, Chippewa, and Ottawa. In each case earlier treaties with these tribes were confirmed, but a new element was added. Payment was made for the lands ceded. This was a reversion to colonial principles which recognized that Indians had rights of occupancy in the lands they used for farming and hunting—rights which the sovereign could acquire, but for which he must pay.

The new treaties did not produce peace, however. They were denounced by the northwestern tribes as worthless, as not having been made with the entire Indian community of the North, and as granting away hunting lands of tribes other than those present at the council. In the closing years of the Confederation trouble was brewing in the Northwest over the series of treaties made from 1784 to 1789.

In 1789–90 an episode occurred in the Pacific Northwest which revealed, as in a flash of lighting, the dangers of the British presence in the Old Northwest. A Spanish naval unit seized a British fur-trading vessel and adjacent harbor property at Nootka Sound. The seizure was in enforcement of Spain's claims to sovereignty in the Pacific Northwest, which impinged on British claims. The incident expanded almost to the point of a general European war, with England and her allies lined up on one side, and Spain and her allies on the other. It drew a memorandum of inquiry to President Washington from the governor-general of Canada, Lord Dorchester, on July 8, 1790:

Would the United States grant permission for a passage of British troops through American territory from Detroit to the Mississippi? The memorandum was presented indirectly, via Alexander Hamilton, who had received it from Dorchester's agent in Washington, George Beckwith, with whom Hamilton was maintaining confidential relations.

Washington was alarmed by it. If British troops were to cross American territory, with permission or without, and were to overrun St. Louis, lower Louisiana, and the Floridas, the neutrality of the United States would be questioned in a subsequent European war. The British were showing no great respect for American neutrality. British power would encircle the United States in a war. At the north it would be in Canada and the Great Lakes; at the west, in Louisiana; at the south, in the Floridas; and at sea, by the British fleet.

Washington sought advice from his cabinet and received conflicting opinions. Hamilton would have tolerated a British crossing of American territory. Jefferson would not; he would simply have declined a reply to the inquiry. In the end the perils of an Anglo-Spanish war were averted by a Spanish capitulation in the Nootka Sound affair. But the crisis brought a new dimension to the problem of British occupation of the Northwest Posts and reinforced American eagerness to get it resolved.

In 1790 a full-blown Indian war in the Northwest added to apprehension over the British presence in the Northwest Posts. The war was pressed by the tribes in the Maumee Valley and was the sequel to Governor St. Clair's Fort Harmar treaties. In the autumn of 1790 a United States army of 1500 men, commanded by General Harmar, moved from its Ohio River base against the Maumee hostiles. The force penetrated to their villages, which were found vacant, and destroyed them with their stores of corn. Then it beat a not very valorous retreat, with the aroused Indians harassing its rear.

In 1791 a second army, numbering 2000 troops, many of them recruited from the offscourings of eastern cities, was sent against the Maumee. Its supplies were inadequate and belated. Led by St. Clair, it moved into the Indian country without adequate precautions against a surprise attack. It was caught in a sunrise assault and disastrously defeated. Almost half the force was killed; only 50 remained unwounded. The retreat became a rout, artillery and supplies abandoned, and even rifles thrown away. The army had spent a month to march from its base to the scene of battle. The survivors got back in twenty hours. An especially serious casualty in the disaster was the new government's image of competence in military affairs. This became evident in the attitudes of the British government, the northwestern Indians, and the administration's critics.

In April 1793 Europe became locked in war. England and Spain laid aside their old grievances against each other and joined in fighting revolutionary France. The conflict spread to the West Indies, where the French colonies were major producers of tropical staples. France at once opened its hitherto restricted trade to neutral vessels as a means of assuring safe shipment of French exports to its colonies and safe arrival in Europe of their exports in exchange. The chief neutral carrier in the world was the United States, whose shipowners made full use of the opportunity, but in doing so they fell foul of the British Navy. The French government had no illusions that the British government would readily concede the validity of this war-born trade. It calculated that British measures in suppressing the trade would embroil Anglo-

American relations, as, indeed, they did. Fleets of American ships began carrying American produce to the islands, loading in exchange colonial produce for Europe. In June the British government ordered seizure of all vessels encountered in the trade, for adjudication in the Admiralty courts.

These orders were carried out with zest by the British Navy and courts in the British island colonies. Hundreds of American ships were taken into these ports for adjudication and confiscation. Seamen and even passengers on the ships were held in prison and browbeaten by island subordinates. In European waters ships transporting food were hauled into British ports, where the food was purchased, inasmuch as it was not clearly contraband, and was paid for, but at British prices. The June orders were followed, on November 6, by an Order in Council authorizing the seizure of any ships caught at sea transporting the property of French subjects. This was an extreme measure, designed to paralyze the shipping of neutral states.

In Congress the followers of Jefferson proposed to meet the British measures by punitive restrictions on British trade with the United States. Early in 1794 James Madison submitted to Congress a series of resolutions proposing such restrictions. In the ensuing debate the followers of Hamilton pointed out that, since nearly seven-eighths of American imports arrived in British vessels, to exclude them would be ruinous to the economy and crippling to the new government. Congress was induced to postpone voting on the measure.

In March 1794 news arrived of the hated Order in Council of November 6, 1793. At the same time news came of an extraordinary speech by the governor-general of Canada, Lord Dorchester, to a delegation of Indians, predicting that war with the United States would soon come and that the Indians would then be aided to recover their hunting grounds. The speech was repudiated by London authorities as soon as reported, and Dorchester was privately rebuked for making it, but it created a sensation in the United States. About the same time came news of the impressment of American seamen into the British Navy. The response of Congress was a thirty-day embargo on all ships leaving American harbors for foreign ports. Resolutions were offered also for the sequestration of debts due to British subjects. Preparations were made for war.

The British cabinet, in the meantime, drew up a plan to resolve the issue of the Northwest Posts and the related problem of control of the Indians. An Indian neutral barrier would be created between the frontiers of the United States and Canada, embracing all the area between the Ohio River and the Great Lakes, and extending eastward to the shore of Lake Champlain—in other words, the zone of influence of the Northwest Posts. The future inviolability of this Indian reserve would be guaranteed by the British and the American governments. If this plan were accepted by the Americans, the British government would evacuate the Northwest Posts. The plan was conceived shortly after the arrival in London of news of the St. Clair disaster.

The proposal was not wholly new. It had been outlined to the cabinet by the governor-general of Canada in 1783, after the terms of the peace treaty with the United States became known. It had also been privately proposed in January 1791 to Hamilton by George Beckwith, the British agent, and had been rejected. In 1792 it was offered to Jefferson, Secretary of State, by George Hammond, the newly appointed British minister to the United States, and had been spurned.

Hammond had then offered Jefferson a new proposal. He had discovered a major error in the treaty of 1783. The treaty described the northern boundary as extending from the most northwestern point of the Lake of the Woods "on a due West Course to the River Mississippi." The Treaty's authors believed that the source of the river was north of the line so described, and that the river's magnitude at this line was such as to entitle Great Britain and the United States to equal rights of navigation on the river. Hammond's discovery was that a line due west from the most northwestern point of the Lake of the Woods would not touch the Mississippi at all, that the river's source was south of that line, and that a "boundary gap" was actually embedded in the treaty. He intimated to Jefferson that a bargain might be struck in rectifying the error, that a boundary might be drawn so as to give Great Britain access to the river, and that in return the Northwest Posts would be evacuated. Jefferson declined to listen to the bargain, seeing in it only a sly maneuver to acquire from the United States additional territory.

Hammond's mind was a fountain of ideas. Bubbling up from it came another notion, that a British mediation in the Indian war might be agreed to by the American government if a "spontaneous" demand for it should arise among the Indians. The idea was communicated to John G. Simcoe, lieutenant governor of Upper Canada, on July 11, 1792, who embraced it. He realized that all the Indians—western and eastern—would favor British mediation, and a grand council was called together on the Maumee. But the Indians were less interested in British mediation than in the boundary and over it divisions developed. The western Indians insisted that in a negotiation the boundary between red and white be the Ohio River. They were fired—especially the Shawnee and Miami—by memories of their triumph over St. Clair. The Iroquois tribes hesitated to have an ultimatum issued over so radical a demand, but consented to it after being taunted that they were under American domination. Agreement was reached in October 1792 that a negotiation be held with the American government the next spring at Sandusky and that, until then, the hatchet be laid aside. It was hoped that Simcoe would be recognized as mediator in the negotiation.

The American government agreed to the negotiation without much expectation of success. It named three commissioners whose instructions were drawn by Secretary Knox. The instructions affirmed humane principles and offered minor adjustments in the Fort Harmar cessions. Major concessions were, however, ruled out. Certainly none were feasible concerning land already granted by the government to land companies and to settlers. The government could make additional compensation for land ceded at Fort Harmar to the extent of $50,000 in treaty goods, and annuities to the amount of $10,000 thereafter. Payments could also be made to tribes whose hunting grounds had been ceded in their absence. No countenance was to be given to a concept of an Indian confederacy, or of rights claimed by a confederacy over lands of individual tribes. Care should be taken to maintain the existing good understanding with the nations of the Iroquois. No British agents were to be recognized as mediators or umpires, but their presence at the council (including members of Governor Simcoe's family) could be permitted. The outcome of the council should be communicated to Major General Anthony Wayne, now in charge of the army in the Northwest, by August 1, 1793. The instructions clearly offered a choice to the Indians between the olive branch and the sword.

The commissioners bearing these instructions reached Niagara in mid-May 1793. They were held there six weeks by Governor Simcoe while awaiting news of the arrival of the tribes at the Maumee. Some tribes were expected to come from west of Lake Michigan; others from Canada. The final attendance totaled about a thousand persons.

The aims of the Sandusky council became, in the meantime, an issue on the Maumee between the radicals and the conservatives, headed by Brant. To the western radicals Brant seemed an eastern traitor. Simcoe absented himself, but his Detroit subordinate, Alexander McKee, attended and inconspicuously shaped decisions. In the meantime, Wayne, on orders from Knox, remained quiet.

The American commissioners arrived at the mouth of the Detroit River on July 21, while the Indians were still on the Maumee. Communication between the two camps was carried on by Indian runners. When the commissioners received the Indian ultimatum that the Ohio River be made the dividing line, they replied that the Fort Harmar line, with liberal payments and minor modifications, would be the limit of American concessions, that the area demanded by the Indians was already occupied by settlers. Back came the Indian response that the liberal payments proposed by the commissioners could be used to ease the removal of the settlers. The commissioners were told they had wasted their time in traveling West if they carried no authority to concede the Ohio River line. On that note communication between the camps ceased. The council projected at Sandusky never materialized, and the prospect of a negotiated peace evaporated. So did the halt imposed on Wayne by Knox in April 1793.

Wayne had been appointed to command the northwestern army in April 1792, after the St. Clair disaster. His reputation for recklessness, acquired in the Revolutionary War, was not exhibited in this war. He took a year to train his men in methods of Indian fighting. Then he marched northward into the Indian country from his base on the Ohio River. Lord Dorchester believed an assault was contemplated, not merely on the Indians in the Maumee Valley but on the Detroit post. As a defensive measure he ordered Simcoe to erect a fort at the Maumee rapids, twenty miles inside American territory.

Wayne learned of the failure of peace negotiations with the Indians too late for a reopening of his campaign and went into winter quarters. He resumed the campaign the next summer, moving in August to the Maumee, where he encountered the Indians at Fallen Timbers, four miles from the fort Simcoe had built. In the ensuing battle the Indians, and 60 Canadian militia reinforcing them, were heavily defeated. They sought safety in the fort but the commanding officer refused to take the grave step of admitting them. They disappeared into the forest, with less respect for the British and more for the Americans. Wayne concluded the campaign by systematic wasting of the villages and cornfields of the hostiles. They were reduced to despair and sued for peace.

Wayne was as deliberate in peacemaking as in warmaking. He set the date for a peace conference far ahead so as to have time for preliminary discussions with individual tribes and to assemble as wide a representation of them as possible. In discussions with the tribal representatives he informed them that the basis of the coming peace settlement would be the Fort Harmar treaties, sweetened by added payments for the lands ceded. Acquiescence to these terms was won in other ways known to negotiators with Indians. The latter were informed that a treaty had already been made with the British, and that British troops were about to depart from the Northwest Posts. One after another of the tribes was brought to recognize reality. On August 3, 1795, at an assembled council, they signed the Treaty of Greenville, ceding the immense area shown on map 32—two-thirds of the present state of Ohio, plus a slice of Indiana known as the "Indiana gore." In addition, within the remaining "Indian country," they relinquished sixteen scattered tracts of limited acreage, but otherwise of importance, including lands adjacent to the Northwest Posts, lands strategically located at the mouth of the Illinois River, and lands at the mouth of the Chicago River. Also they gave up lands adjacent to Vincennes on the Wabash, lands earlier ceded to George Rogers Clark at the rapids of the Ohio, and others adjacent to Fort Massac near the mouth of the Ohio.

For these concessions the tribes were given payments amounting to $20,000 in treaty goods. In addition, designated tribes were given annuities amounting to $9500. The annuities, in amounts of $1000, were granted to seven designated tribes, including the Shawnee, Miami, Wyandot, and Delaware, and, in amounts of $500, to a number of other tribes. Thus was the mellow Indian policy, recommended by the Congress of the Confederation in 1787, implemented in 1795.

In the history of the westward movement the Greenville Treaty had meaning beyond that of the immense land cessions. It unlocked a major route to the West by assuring safety of travel on the Ohio River. For eastern migrants the river became an outlet to the northwestern wilderness and to Kentucky and Tennessee. From Pitts-

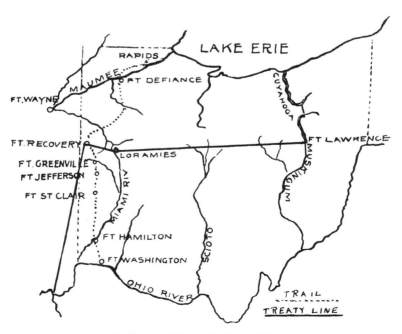

32. Treaty of Greenville (from Wilson)

burgh and Wheeling migrants could now float down the river without fear of Indians, and fan out northward into Ohio, Indiana, and Illinois, or, alternatively, into the upper South. They had now only to fear the perils of the river itself.

During the period of Wayne's preparation for his northwestern campaign, relations between the British and American governments deteriorated almost to the point of rupture. After news reached the United States in 1794 of the wholesale capture of American vessels in West Indies waters, of Dorchester's inflammatory speech to the Indians, of Simcoe's building of a fort on American territory, and of the harsh Order in Council of November 6, 1793, war seemed inescapable.

Yet to the Federalists war seemed suicidal. Not only would it drag the nation into the European war, but, worse yet, on the side of revolutionary France. An amelioration of tension providentially came early in April 1794 with the arrival of word of a British decision to exempt from the Order in Council of November 6, 1793, American ships bearing French property from the French West Indies to the United States. Washington seized upon this concession to initiate a special mission to England with instructions to seek a peaceful solution of the whole series of Anglo-American conflicts. To head the mission Washington nominated Chief Justice John Jay.

Jay's instructions, which he himself helped to write, were to obtain fulfillment of the 1783 treaty. This would mean British evacuation of the Northwest Posts. He was also to obtain protection of American neutral rights at sea, as understood in the United States, and compensation for seizures of American vessels and cargoes in violation of those rights. He was to secure a favorable treaty of commerce, if possible. The instructions were drawn before Wayne's triumph over the western Indians.

After four months of negotiation, during which news of Wayne's victory arrived, a treaty was concluded in London favorable to the West. It promised evacuation of the Northwest Posts not later than June 1, 1796, a promise that was fulfilled. It permitted subjects of either country to pass and repass the boundary in prosecution of the fur trade, which favored Montreal. It authorized a joint survey to ascertain whether a boundary line drawn due west from the Lake of the Woods would intersect the Mississippi River, and, in case it did not, proposed an amicable negotiation to establish the boundary.

With regard to other issues that had become entangled with those of the West, the treaty resorted to joint commissions. One was to adjudicate claims of British subjects against Americans for unpaid pre-Revolutionary debts, the awards to be made by the American government. Another was to adjudicate American claims for irregular or illegal British seizures of vessels engaged in the neutral trade. On these scores the American government ultimately paid $2,664,000 for the debts, and the British government paid $11,656,000 for the seizures. Under the treaty American commerce with Great Britain was accorded a most-favored-nation status. Also, under Article XII, American trade with the British West Indies was opened, but on so unsatisfactory a basis that the Senate withheld it in approving the treaty.

The treaty was of major significance in that it removed British garrisons from the soil of the Northwest. It accomplished what the Pinckney Treaty of the next year was to accomplish in the Southwest with respect to Spanish garrisons above parallel 31°. But the British influence over the Indians of the Northwest was not eliminated. It was exerted in the future from Fort Malden, across the narrow strait from Detroit, and also via the fur traders from Montreal. In Indiana territory two Shawnee braves, Tecumseh and his brother, Laulewasika, the Prophet, envisaged a grand confederation of Indian tribes, and in Great Britain imperialists still nursed dreams of an Indian barrier state separating the territories of the United States from those of Upper Canada.

The West
in the War of 1812

IN THE DECADE and a half following the Treaty of Greenville a wave of population flowed over southern and central Ohio and southeastern Indiana, so that the treaty line of 1795 and the population line of 1810 became virtually identical in those two states (Map 33). This swiftness of occupation reflected the pacification of the Indians and the safety of travel on the Ohio. The migrants came primarily from western Pennsylvania, western Virginia, and Kentucky.

In 1800 William Henry Harrison was appointed governor of Indiana Territory, after having served in Wayne's army at the Battle of Fallen Timbers. He personified the philosophy of that era regarding the Indians, the lands they occupied, and their destiny. The Indians should cease to rely on hunting, should devote themselves to farming, and thus become peaceful. This conversion would reduce their need for wide-open spaces. The land they had hunted over would no longer be needed by them and they would be relieved of it by sale to the American government. Such a process of thought had for a time shaped President Jefferson's Indian policy. Prior to 1803—when the province of Louisiana was a pawn in the game of European power politics and a threat to American security—he was especially prone to such thinking. He conceived of absorption of the Indians into the white race as their ultimate destiny. As a matter of national safety he wished American settlement to reach the Mississippi as quickly as possible. Later, when Louisiana had been acquired, his solution of the Indian problem was the removal of the tribes to that wilderness.

In the Treaty of Greenville scattered tracts of land in Indiana beyond the ''gore'' went to the government. One tract, adjacent to a post at Vincennes, was alleged to have been ceded by the Indians to the Wabash Land Company in 1775. The validity of the cession had never been recognized by the British or American authorities, and it was denied by the Indians. It was, however, recognized by Harrison and used as a wedge to pry from the Indians the Treaty of Fort Wayne of June 7, 1803, by which a cession estimated to contain more than 2 million acres was obtained. Part of the price paid took the form of annuities to the principal chiefs of the tribes.

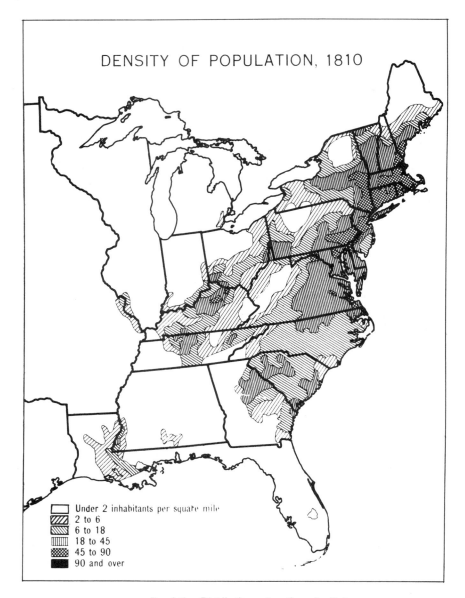

DENSITY OF POPULATION, 1810

	Under 2 inhabitants per square mile
	2 to 6
	6 to 18
	18 to 45
	45 to 90
	90 and over

33. Population Distribution, 1810 (from Paullin)

A long series of cessions followed. By the Treaty of Vincennes of August 13, 1803, 7 to 8 million acres of land in lower Illinois were obtained from the Kaskaskia. Two treaties, one with the Delaware on August 18, 1804, and one with the Piankashaw on August 27, 1804, brought cessions in Indiana of nearly 2 million acres. A Treaty of St. Louis, on November 3, 1804, with the Sac and Fox, brought an estimated 9,803,000 acres. The recent addition of the province of Louisiana had made possible cessions on both sides of the Mississippi—in northern Missouri, northern

Illinois, and southern Wisconsin. A treaty concluded with the Delaware, Potawatomi, Miami, and other tribes on August 21, 1805, at Grouseland, the governor's palatial home, brought 1,500,000 acres in Indiana. Another treaty with the Piankashaw on December 30, 1805, brought about 2 million acres in southeastern Illinois. A climax in this succession of treaties was reached on September 30, 1809, in a new Fort Wayne agreement (primarily with the Miami), whereby two areas were obtained, one in the valley of the Wabash, and another adjacent to the Indiana "gore," totaling 3,250,000 acres (Map 34). That treaty finally touched off a last-ditch resistance among the Northwest Indians, similar to that produced a decade earlier in Ohio by the Fort Harmar treaties of St. Clair.

The center of the excitement was the Shawnee. The tribe had earlier been conspicuous in resisting the white advance into the Indian country. The Shawnee War of 1774 had ushered in the Indian fighting of the Revolutionary War. After the war

34. Indian Cessions (from the Dept. of the Interior)

many Shawnee had withdrawn to the South, joining the Creeks; others had gone to Missouri. Those remaining north had been part of the problem facing St. Clair in the Fort Harmar councils. After the Treaty of Greenville part of the tribe moved to the river Auglaize, and a faction agreed in 1803 and 1805 to two treaties of cession desired by Harrison. When the Fort Wayne treaty of 1809 was concluded the tribe was a shell of its former self.

The spirit of the Shawnee was embodied in two remarkable brothers, Tecumseh and Laulewasika, the Prophet. They were half Shawnee, half Creek. Tecumseh was a visionary who had caught the meaning of the unending series of treaties extracted from individual tribes or groups of tribes. Indian society would come to an end, he believed, unless such treaties were halted. Indians were helpless against the wiles of white negotiators and the power brought to the enforcement of treaties. The one hope of survival was the formation of a confederation of all tribes bound by agreement to resist any further cessions of land. Tecumseh conceived of this as a message from the Great Spirit, for whom he was the spokesman. He regarded himself as leader of all Indians. In view of the migration history of his tribe he considered his special mission to be the formation of a nationwide confederation.

Laulewasika, Tecumseh's brother, was a mystic. He appears to have been an epileptic, and his trances were believed by his followers to be periods of communication with the Great Spirit. The message he spread was that the salvation of the Indians required a return to the simple ways of earlier Indian life, reliance on the hunt, abstinence from whatever the white man brought, especially strong drink, and refusal to agree to further land cessions. At the invitation of the Potawatomi he established the headquarters of his flock at the junction of the Tippecanoe and Wabash rivers, and there Prophetstown grew up. It became the center, also, of Tecumseh and his followers, and attracted many wanderers of other tribes. It was the headquarters of the movement for a great Indian confederation.

A year after the conclusion of the Fort Wayne treaty, and a long campaign against it, Tecumseh made a visit to Vincennes at Harrison's invitation, escorted by 300 warriors. A confrontation with Harrison followed at a formal council, in which he denounced the treaty as invalid. He declared it had been signed by a few village chiefs who were without authority to sell the lands, and who would be killed if the lands were not returned. He listened impassively for a time to Harrison's reply, which was devoted to proving that the government had used justice in dealing with the Indians. Then he leaped to his feet in anger and told the governor he lied. This broke up the session. On the next day he apologized, and the meeting ended peacefully. But Tecumseh remained tireless in his travels, eastward as far as the Iroquois, westward as far as the Chippewa, and southward for an extensive tour.

To the American government Indian confederation was anathema, particularly one to halt land cessions. As has been seen, Secretary Henry Knox, in instructions issued in April 1793 to the commissioners to negotiate with the northwestern tribes, ordered that no countenance be given to any idea of a confederation. This was the foundation of the government's relations with Indians.

In 1811 Harrison decided to take measures against the Shawnee agitation by striking at its source—the village of Prophetstown. In September, after learning that Tecumseh was on his way south, Harrison led an army up the Wabash from Vincennes and pitched camp provocatively near the village. In the absence of Tecumseh the younger braves could not be restrained. They made an early-morning attack, which Harrison, with great difficulty and loss of life, beat off. Harrison then destroyed the village and returned in triumph to his base. He was hailed as a military hero and in 1840 was rewarded by election to the presidency of the United States. The affair marked the opening of a full-scale Indian war, which the next year became part of the War of 1812.

Tecumseh's tour through the South in 1811 carried him to the Chickasaw and the Choctaw on the west, and to the Upper Creeks on the Alabama. He may also have visited the Lower Creeks in Georgia. To all these tribes he came at the head of a cavalcade of warriors in full regalia. He was a gifted orator and his speeches were translated for his southern audiences, enlivened by pantomimes comprehended by all. An especially effective pantomime, emphasizing the need for union, was to hold his war club with outstretched arm aloft, then open the little finger and the next and the next till the club fell to the ground. The tour was, however, without effect. The Indians were too separatistic and localistic to embrace a plan contemplating union. Southern Indians, like the northern, were troubled by white intrusions on their lands, especially the Upper Creeks. But their hunting grounds produced none of the profusion of game enjoyed by the Northwest Indians. The climate was less vigorous. The tribes turned to agriculture for part of their sustenance earlier than the northern tribes. The agents of the federal government, especially Benjamin Hawkins, encouraged farming. These Indians were provided with plows, hoes, and other farm implements, and blacksmiths to keep them in repair.

From the east and from the west whites were intruding on Creek lands. The intruders on the east were organized parties of hunters from Georgia, who sought deer for their skins. They hunted efficiently at night, by firelight, which frightened off other game. Squatters were numerous, also, whose cattle, hogs, and horses ranged the woods consuming forage that would have attracted game. Creek meetings with federal agents in the 1790's were filled with complaints of this kind. The area of the most friction was the valley of the Oconee, which had figured as a boundary in the Creek treaty of New York of 1790, the line of which had never been marked.

The western zone of friction lay in present-day Alabama, along the lower Tombigbee and Alabama rivers. There a settlement was growing during the first decade of the new century at the confluence of the two rivers and extending southward to the Spanish boundary at the 31st parallel. One lobe of the settlement adjoined Fort Stoddert, built in 1799 just below the confluence and garrisoned by federal troops. Another lobe adjoined a ferry, a little to the north, on the Alabama, which Sam Mims, a half-breed, operated. The ferry was the terminus of a road from Georgia which in 1805 the Creeks had given the government permission to build through their country. The permission was for a "horse road," but was interpreted to become a wagon road. Even before its completion in 1811, it was filled from end to end with migrants to the west from Georgia.

Migrants came also from Kentucky and from Tennessee. They came via the Mississippi to the Iberville River and thence eastward by the Iberville and the inner-lake route to Mobile, where they turned northward through Spanish territory. Another stream came from the American community at Baton Rouge. By 1810 the settlement above Mobile had become large enough to appear on the census map as a sizable island in the Creek homeland. A stockade was built in 1811 around the Mims establishment, which was named Fort Mims. This expanding frontier society—part of Mississippi Territory—troubled the Upper Creeks.

The Spanish at Mobile and Pensacola were also troubled. They recollected the loss to the United States of Spanish territory between the latitudes 31° and 32° 28′, and feared that remaining narrow strip along the Gulf would also be lost. A portion of it—the region between the rivers Mississippi and Perdido—was already claimed by the American government as part of the Louisiana Purchase. That claim, resting on the ambiguous language of the two treaties by which Napoleon acquired Louisiana from Spain and then sold it to the United States, was so flimsy that it has never found a defender among American historians. The strip had high value, however, because rivers from the up-country flowed through it to the Gulf, and because the harbors at their estuaries held the keys to the defense of New Orleans. Jefferson and Madison, therefore, aggressively pressed that claim.

In 1804 Congress extended the revenue laws of the United States over West Florida to the Perdido. This brought angry protests from Spain, but nothing more, for she was helpless because of the war situation in Europe. In September 1810, Baton Rouge inhabitants, nine-tenths of whom were Americans, revolutionized the area as far as the Pearl River, converting it into the Republic of West Feliciana, at the same time petitioning Congress for admission to the Union. They justified the revolt on the ground that the area had to be saved from the British, who were thought to have designs on it.

President Madison had wider ambitions. He gave the governor of Orleans Territory, who was in Washington at the time, orders to take possession not only of the rebellious district, but of the rest of the area claimed by the United States. The governor was not to use force, and none was necessary. The revolted district was added to Orleans Territory and the remainder of the area to the Perdido was taken over as part of Mississippi Territory but without disturbing the Spanish troops holding Mobile, who were simply enveloped. For a time the troops were a source of friction to migrants wishing to pass through the city to the settlements above. However, in April 1813, after war with England had opened, American troops under General Wilkinson, on orders from Washington, took over the city and remained there.

The Indians of the Gulf region, and especially the Upper Creeks, were angered by these seizures of Spanish territory. Their relations with the Spanish in West Florida, in the days of Alexander McGillivray, had been friendly. They had received trade goods, arms, and ammunition, subsidized by the Spanish government, in generous quantity. The situation resembled that in the Northwest, in the period before the Battle of Fallen Timbers, when American Indians were receiving support from British traders under the protection of British troops in the Northwest Posts.

In the autumn of 1812, Tecumseh, on a second visit to the South, brought word to the Upper Creeks of American defeats at the hands of the British and Indians in the Great Lakes area. The younger Creek warriors dreamed of expelling the Americans from their hunting grounds with the aid of the British and Spanish. A band of them joined Tecumseh on his way home, and served with him for a time in fighting the Americans. On their way back, in passing through Chickasaw country, they murdered some whites. The Chickasaw were fearful of being held responsible for the murders and requested that the Creeks undertake punishment of the guilty. At the request of the American agent, Benjamin Hawkins, the elder Creeks in council ordered executions, which were carried out in April 1813. Factional fighting among the Creeks was the result.

One faction was the Red Sticks, the young warriors, stirred against Americans by Tecumseh and by local prophets. Another was the elders, determined not to be dragged into war against their will. A band of Red Sticks, in need of ammunition, visited the Spanish governor in Pensacola, from whom they obtained ammunition and firearms. They were intercepted on the way home, near Fort Mims, by a party of whites, led by two half-breeds. In the succeeding fight the whites made off with part of the mule train carrying the ammunition. The leaders of the successful party then took refuge at Fort Mims, which was an invitation to Red Stick reprisal.

A motley assembly of whites, half-breeds, and Negroes was already gathered at Fort Mims for safety. On August 30, 1813, a force of 800 Red Sticks, drawn from thirteen Upper Creek towns, and led by William Weatherford, who was seven-eighths white, surrounded the stockade, which was carelessly guarded, and stormed it. In the ensuing massacre 500 men, women, and children were slain and scalped. The affair horrified the American public and three armies of retribution were called up. One came from Georgia, another from Mississippi Territory, a third from Tennessee.

Retribution was a major undertaking. It entailed war on a foe that could muster 4000 warriors, most of whom, however, lacked firearms. A greater difficulty was carrying the war to them, for their center of strength was deep in the wilderness. No supply base was closer than 150 miles for the invading army, and the troops to be used were mostly militia, serving short terms and impatient to get home once their service was over. On these accounts the movements from Georgia and from Mississippi Territory against the hostiles were ineffective. But despite all obstacles the army from Tennessee was effective, for it was commanded by a soldier of iron will and great resourcefulness, Andrew Jackson.

Jackson moved south from the great bend of the Tennessee in the winter of 1813–14, establishing bases of supply and fighting indecisive battles. In February he was reinforced by the arrival of regulars. On March 27 he came upon the entrenched Indians at Horseshoe Bend on the Tallapoosa River, and crushed them. The body count afterward was 550 dead, which did not include those drowned in the river. The spirit of the Indians was broken.

The aftermath was, as usual, a treaty of land cession. The Treaty of Fort Jackson of August 9, 1814, was as grim as the campaign preceding it. It took from the Creeks 23 million acres of land in a great L-shaped tract comprising three-fifths of later Alabama and one-fifth of Georgia. It spared the friendly Lower Creeks no more than the hostiles. It isolated the Creeks from the Spanish at the south, and from the Chickasaw and Choctaw at the west. Whatever unity the southern Indians might have enjoyed was ended. The only problem they now presented was how soon they could be ejected from the Gulf area and moved out to the Great Plains.

The foe on whom Jackson next turned was the British, who had allied themselves with Spain in fighting Napoleon. In the summer of 1814 their fleet appeared outside the harbors of West Florida, ready to occupy them for use as bases for an attack on New Orleans. In November, Jackson occupied Pensacola without authorization. The British fleet commander, unwilling to subject a city of an ally to bombardment, withdrew after blowing up an outer fort guarding the harbor. Jackson also withdrew, marching swiftly to Mobile, where he added to its formidable harbor fortifications. The plan of the British to use Gulf ports for a sea attack on New Orleans was foiled.

The British strategy in the campaign against New Orleans was not to reach the city by ascent of the Mississippi but by the shortcut of Mississippi Sound. The sound was a body of shoal waters near the shore that extended from Mobile Bay to Lakes Pontchartrain and Borgne at the west. The western shore of Lake Borgne, where debarkation of troops was possible, lay only nine miles from New Orleans. The shallow craft accompanying the British fleet could thus be used to transport British troops to within striking distance of New Orleans. Jackson foresaw the design and prepared his defenses to counter it.

The only route to New Orleans from Lake Borgne ran through a swamp that, on both sides, was impenetrable. That route was blocked by Jackson. Across it, at a strong natural position, he constructed a barricade of earth entrenchments, bristling with artillery and manned by troops of unexcelled marksmanship. On January 8, 1815, the British force reached the barricade, after preliminary fighting, and launched a frontal assault on it. The disastrous failure of the assault is attested to by the casualties. On the British side there were 291 killed, 484 missing, and 1262 wounded. In addition, in the preliminary fighting, 450 had been killed. Among the dead were General Pakenham and the next two in command. The American loss was 13 killed, 19 missing, and 39 wounded. The British army, withdrawing to its transports after the battle, had been decimated.

Another threat to American security was Spanish East Florida on the Atlantic seaboard just south of Georgia. It might be transferred to Great Britain in payment for military aid in freeing Spain from Joseph Bonaparte, brother of Napoleon. If it should become British, the entire southern flank of the United States would lie exposed to British naval power. That was a prospect haunting the Madison administration and in January 1811 it called forth an act of Congress.

The President was authorized to take possession of East Florida under either of two contingencies. One would be a request from local East Florida authorities to the President to take possession of the province. The other was evidence reaching the President that East Florida was about to be transferred by Spain to some other foreign power. The authority to the President to act in the case of the second contingency was the initial formulation of the well-known "no transfer" precept in American foreign policy.

General George Mathews, a veteran of the American Revolution and a former governor of Georgia, was sent to East Florida. He organized a party, consisting of local dissidents and "patriots" from just across the St. Mary's River in Florida and troops from a garrison on the American side, to surprise St. Augustine. In this he failed. Mathew's only success was the seizure of Fernandina, a smugglers' haven on Amelia Island at the mouth of the St. Mary's River, which was done in the presence of American gunboats. This activity was denounced by Federalists in Congress, and in April 1812 Secretary of State James Monroe, who had tacitly approved it, disavowed it and dismissed Mathews. In May 1813 the troops that had followed Mathews into East Florida were withdrawn.

In Europe the war came to an end in May 1814 with the defeat of Napoleon and his exile to Elba. Peace negotiations between Great Britain and the United States were concluded by the Treaty of Ghent, signed the day before Christmas 1814. The war, which had been singularly inconclusive, was ended by a treaty that settled none of the issues over which it had been fought. The war had grown out of maritime issues. It stemmed from a European struggle, opening in April 1792, between revolutionary France and Austria, which had expanded to include Great Britain and most of the Continent, and was destined to endure for nearly a quarter-century. Each of the belligerents had struck at the commerce of the other by blockade and arbitrary sea rules. The United States, with the greatest neutral carrying trade in the world, was a victim of the crossfire. The American government had sought to protect its shipping by every conceivable means short of armed conflict. Ultimately it had reached the conclusion that not only its national honor but the very heart of the republican form of government was in peril, and that war against the British aggressor was necessary to save it.

The war vote in Congress on June 18, 1812, had been more than a product of anxiety and pride, however. It grew out of an effort to reopen world markets to American farmers that had been closed by British decrees. American farmers—eastern, southern, and western—were in a severe economic depression as a result of British measures to forcibly redirect the flow of American staples to the British Isles. John C. Calhoun voiced the feeling of all sections of the Union in addressing Congress on behalf of the planters of his section on December 12, 1811: "They see in the low price of their produce the hand of foreign injustice; they know well, without the market of the Continent, the deep and steady current of supply will glut that of Great Britain; they are not prepared for the colonial state to which again that Power is endeavoring to reduce us. The manly spirit of that section of our country will not submit to be regulated by any foreign power."

A contemporary charge was made in Congress that the War Hawks in the nation longed for war with Great Britain because they lusted after the provinces of Canada. A thesis has been advanced that a sectional bargain was struck by expansionists hoping to acquire both Canada and the Floridas in war. But expansionists lacked the voting strength in Congress to swing such a vote. The same weakness lies in the thesis that the war vote was a response to frontier demands to end British influence with Indians and Indian attacks in the Northwest. The war, in its origins, was not a "western war."

As to results, if the terms of the Treaty of Ghent alone are to be relied upon, the outcome was negative. The treaty was silent as to the maritime issues which had produced the war. It made no mention of impressment or of British sea rules overriding the rights of neutrals in wartime. Regarding territorial conquests made during the war a formula was adopted which ran: "All territory, places and possessions whatsoever, taken by either party from the other during the war, or which may be taken after the signing of this Treaty . . . shall be restored without delay." The prewar status was what the treaty was designed to restore.

But restoration of the *status quo ante bellum* was not completely attainable. Especially in the West, events had occurred that were irreversible. The western Indians had been defeated and their spirit broken. In the Northwest, on October 15, 1813, Tecumseh was slain in the Battle of the Thames, in which his Indian contingent was covering the retreat of a disorganized British force. The tribe had no land left to pay the penalty of defeat and the concept of Indian confederation perished with him. Jackson's victory over the Creeks at Horseshoe Bend and the ensuing Treaty of Fort

Jackson brought to an end all thought of Indian resistance to white expansion in the Southwest.

The problem of clandestine British influence through trade with the Indians of the Northwest came to an end with the close of the war. It ended as a result of one of the silences of the Treaty of Ghent. The Jay Treaty had given British fur traders with Indians the right "freely to pass and repass by land or inland navigation" across the northern boundary of the United States. With the outbreak of war in 1812 the right had lapsed. At Ghent the British made a determined effort to get it renewed, but the American negotiators would have no more of it. In 1816 Congress adopted a measure at the instance of John Jacob Astor, prohibiting, under severe penalties, foreign trade with American Indians. The Indians finally lost the tie to the British in the Northwest that had meant so much to them, and this rendered them more amenable to removal to the trans-Mississippi West.

In the Southwest the process of separating American Indians from foreign influence was also achieved in the war. The Creek tribe, broken in the war, was separated from the Spanish in East Florida by the cession exacted of it by Jackson, though the separation was not complete because of the migration of the dissident Red Stick faction to East Florida, where they joined the hostile Seminole.

Another outcome of the war in the Southwest was the success of American expansion eastward in West Florida from the Mississippi to the Perdido River, claimed since the Louisiana Purchase. Though, under the terms of the Treaty of Ghent, no territorial gains could be made at the expense of Britain, American expansion in Spanish West Florida was a product of the war, justified by the wartime ties between the Spanish and the British. This expansion not only enlarged the area of the United States, but opened an important outlet from the Southwest to the Gulf through Mobile.

By the end of the war only East Florida and the easternmost segment of West Florida containing Pensacola remained in Spanish hands. Before long, depredations on American settlements by the Seminole and dissident Red Stick Creeks from these areas necessitated negotiations with the Spanish, by which these remaining parts of the Floridas were acquired by the United States in 1819.

In the Pacific Northwest the war effected a transformation of the American claim to the Oregon Country. The claim stemmed from the discovery in 1792 of the mouth of the Columbia River by an American. It was strengthened by the Lewis and Clark explorations, and by John Jacob Astor's founding of Astoria in 1811-12. The Astoria establishment symbolized the American claim to the Oregon Country. During the war an agent of Astor sold it to a Canadian fur company to prevent capture by a British war vessel. Technically the sale became a seizure as a result of the British commander's ceremonial changing of the flag. The British government subsequently recognized that this constituted a capture and entitled the United States to a restoration of the *status quo ante bellum*. The restoration ceremony had been intended by the British government to be merely a restoration of the flag. But the document accompanying the restoration was not so limited, and the error became a basis later for the acquisition of the Oregon Country.

Settlement of the Prairie and Lake Plains

In the period following the War of 1812 two geographic provinces of the Northwest—the Prairie Plains and the Lake Plains—were opened to settlement. They had been made inviting to settlement by the prehistoric process of glaciation. During a million or more years they had been periodically covered by huge masses of ice, a mile or more in height, moving south out of centers of ice accumulation in the Far North and passing over the Lake and Prairie Plains, as well as New York and New England. In the Old World, portions of Europe and Asia had been similarly overrun. Six times the process was repeated, interspersed with periods of warmer climate and melting ice. The surface over which the glaciers moved was ground down, hilltops and mountains were leveled, valleys were filled with glacial debris, the course of streams was changed; in short, the land was profoundly altered. This alternate advance and melting of the glacial ice is estimated to have continued until about 10,000 years ago. As has been noted earlier, the crossing of the Indians to the New World from the Old is believed to have occurred between the closing phases of the last glacial advance.

In the Prairie and Lake Plains a single area was left untouched by glaciation, the part of southwestern Wisconsin and northwestern Illinois known to geographers as the Driftless region. It is devoid of glacial drift and rougher than the surrounding land. The reason it was never overrun is probably that the moving ice was deflected by the depressions of the Great Lakes.

A major consequence of glaciation was that the rock of the earth's surface was ground into soil. The soil of every glaciated area is principally the residue of pulverized local rock. About 10 percent brought to the prairie and lake plains was, however, of Canadian origin. Ninety percent was the product of pulverized local rock.

The local rock of the prairie plains was primarily limestone, which made an incomparably rich soil. The region is one of the richest large-soil areas in the world.

By contrast, New England soil, though glacier-ground, is by and large poor, because the original rock was sandstone and granite.

Mechanically pulverized soil is richer than soil which is the product of ages of weathering. It retains more of its valuable minerals and salts. Soil that is the product of leaching has lost many of those elements. The principal gift of glaciation, however, was the leveling of the terrain over which the glaciers moved. That was significant from the beginning of settlement and became steadily more so with the advent of mechanized farming.

A generalized view of the glaciated portions of the Old Northwest is shown on map 35. Shown also is the southern limit reached by two of the glacial sheets. The southern limit of the last of them, marked on the map as Wisconsin Drift border, is of special interest. It is the line separating the freshest of the glacial soils, and therefore

DIAGRAMMATIC REPRESENTATION OF THE OUTLINE OF THE ICE BORDER AT SEVERAL SUCCESSIVE POSITIONS AND THE DIRECTION OF ICE MOVEMENT IN CONNECTION WITH EACH POSITION.

35. Glaciation in the Middle West (from Leverett)

the richest, from the less good soils. This border is easily traced in the field in the form of moraines or hills of debris left by this glacier when it melted. This border is conspicuous in the neighborhood of Shelbyville, Illinois, and the name given it is the Shelbyville moraine. This line, separating soil of exceptional richness from soil less good, appears again and again on the political maps to be shown later. Another area that stands out on this map and on political maps is the Driftless region of western Wisconsin, northwestern Illinois, and northeastern Iowa. Also shown, in stippled gray, are exposed portions of the earlier Illinoian drift, where the topography is uneven and the soil less fertile.

The climate of the Middle West is favorable for farming. The rainfall is adequate in normal years and the rain is well distributed over the growing season. But it is not really abundant, only 30 or 40 inches a year, not equal to the exceptional capacity of the soil. If it were more abundant the province would dominate American agriculture even more than it does. As it is, the region became the wheat kingdom, the corn and hog kingdom, and later the dairy kingdom of the United States.

In regard to forest covering, the prairie province was transitional between the heavily wooded condition of the Allegheny Plateau and the treeless state of the Great Plains. It was a region of thousands of prairies, big and small, with forested ribbons running along streams separating the prairies. In Indiana and in southern Illinois the prairies were small and scattered and forests were almost continuous. On the other hand, in central and northern Illinois, prairies predominated. In northern Illinois lay the very extensive Grand Prairie. In Iowa, in the valley of the Red River of the North, and in eastern Nebraska and eastern Kansas prairie predominance increased until the treeless Great Plains were reached.

This alternation of forest and prairie is explained as a product of repeated burnings of forest by Indians in hunting operations. Full-grown timber was destroyed. By contrast, in the humid tidewater province only underbrush was destroyed by burnings. After repeated fires grass became established on the burnt-over areas, and this prevented reseeding of the forest.

Tall grass was one of the prominent features of the province, growing as high as wheat when young. In wet places, and especially in the Far Southwest, it grew as high as a horse. In the Far Southwest it was so high as to astonish the Spanish explorers who first encountered it. It seemed like the surface of the sea in the wind. It was a continuous grass, a sod grass, in contrast with that of the Great Plains, which, for the most part, was scattered bunch grass.

Prairie grass was excellent fodder. It came up each spring in young and tender shoots after the old grass had been burned off by the Indians in hunting. The young grass attracted deer and wood buffalo in their movements north, in the spring and in the summer.

The earliest pioneers to the Northwest did not look with favor on the prairie land. It was untimbered. Since it supported no hardwood, it must be poor land. Southerners especially entertained that view. James Monroe described the prairie province to Jefferson in 1786, after a visit there, as follows:

> A great part of the territory is miserably poor, especially that near lakes Michigan and Erie, and that upon the Mississippi and Illinois consists of extensive plains wh. have not had from appearances and will not have a single bush on them for ages. The districts

therefore within [which] these fall will perhaps never contain a sufficient number of Inhabitants to entitle them to membership in the confederacy.

But the objection to the prairies was based on more substantial grounds than absence of hardwoods. The sod was thick and tough and plowing it under was a major problem. Also, the land was often flat and poorly drained. Early in spring it was likely to be covered with water, requiring expensive drainage. It was infested with mosquitoes and produced malaria, the "miasma" of the frontiersmen. Where prairies were extensive, timber for houses and barns was costly to obtain. Large prairies were exposed, moreover, to prairie fires in the late summer or autumn and to high winds in the winter. All these liabilities accounted for the reluctance of southern pioneers to locate on prairies.

In southern Michigan and southern Wisconsin "oak openings"—crosses between prairie and forest—were found. They were parklike in appearance. As described by James Fenimore Cooper, they were areas lightly covered with low oak, growing "with much of that air of negligence that one is apt to see in grounds where art is made to assume the character of nature." The trees were burr oak principally, "and the spaces between them, always irregular, and often of singular beauty, have obtained the name of 'openings'; the two terms combined giving their appellations to this particular species of native forest, under the name of 'Oak Openings.'" Much sought, these areas proved often to have less permanent fertility than the prairies.

Northern Michigan, northern Wisconsin, and northern Minnesota carried a heavy growth of white pine. The stand was the finest to be found anywhere in the world, and was to be the resource for a great lumber industry. Over wide areas, however, the soil was sandy and poor. It gave little support to the farming that had developed as an adjunct to lumbering. It became, with the passing of lumbering, one of the problem areas of the Middle West.

The movement of population into the prairie-lake province began after the close of the War of 1812. Settlements already established north of the Ohio at the outbreak of the war were in the province of the Allegheny Plateau. By 1820 settlers were at the edges of the prairies in Ohio, Indiana, and Illinois (Map 36). By 1830 the line of population was far advanced in them. An island had formed in the Driftless region of southwestern Wisconsin. That region contained lead deposits lying close to the surface since they were not covered by an overlay of glacial debris. They had already been discovered in the French period, but were more energetically exploited by Americans. The miners were mostly Southerners who came up the Mississippi from the Missouri mines.

By 1850 densities of population were appearing in parts of the prairie province. The greatest density was in areas of forest predominance in southern Ohio and in southern Indiana; also in the forested ribbons of the valley of the Illinois. There was also substantial population in the oak openings of southern Michigan, in the forested lakeshore counties of Wisconsin, and along the timbered shores of the Mississippi in Illinois and Iowa. The lighter shadings were in areas of prairie predominance—in the big prairies especially. In northeastern Illinois the Grand Prairie was almost unsettled until the late 1850's. By 1860 the Grand Prairie of Illinois had finally been conquered. The pioneers had learned to manage the special problems of the prairies.

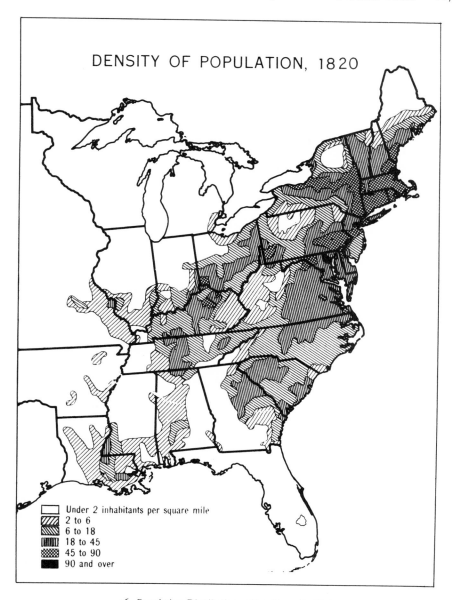

DENSITY OF POPULATION, 1820

Under 2 inhabitants per square mile
2 to 6
6 to 18
18 to 45
45 to 90
90 and over

36. Population Distribution, 1820 (from Paullin)

The population strains moving into the province were diverse. In the southern parts the people were of southern origin—Kentuckians and Virginians, who simply crossed the Ohio River. Into southern Indiana came North Carolinians—the so-called Hoosiers; into southern Illinois, Kentuckians and Tennesseans; into southern Iowa, Kentuckians in large numbers.

In upper latitudes of the province the diversity of population was even greater. New Englanders pressed into northern Ohio, northern Indiana, southern Michigan, northern Illinois, and southern Wisconsin. A good many New Yorkers moved into southern Michigan and Wisconsin. Pennsylvanians came to Ohio and Indiana in large numbers. The forces producing this flow from the East were the normal ones of westward expansion.

But special forces were also at work. In 1825 the Erie Canal was completed. It opened an easy water route via the Great Lakes to the Middle West. At the same time it brought the full impact of western grain growing upon the East, and further stimulated the movement of New England migrants to the virgin lands of the prairies. In the 1830's and 1840's the hill farms in New Hampshire and Vermont were becoming sheep pastures, and displaced farmers were moving West or into the cities of the East.

The mode of migration to the West was normally that of individuals or families. But the old tradition of communities moving in a group—town planting—was continued. Such western towns as Oberlin, Beloit, and Vermontville were the product of community migrations. Eastern neighborhoods were re-established in the West also by a reassembling of old friends.

Foreign elements flowed to the northern part of the prairie province. Germans established themselves in the lakeshore counties of Wisconsin and in northern Illinois. Many settled in the Missouri Valley and in the Belleville region of southern Illinois. German artisans came to the cities of the West, particularly to Milwaukee, St. Louis, Cincinnati, and Cleveland. By 1850 there were 300,000 Germans in the Middle West.

The forces producing the German migration were largely economic. The German economy was changing from the handicraft to the factory stage in the 1820's and 1830's, which produced dislocations. Crops in the Rhine Palatinate and in Württemberg failed repeatedly in the middle 1840's. Political discontent, caused by the failure of the 1848 revolution, sent refugees to America such as Carl Schurz, Henry Villard, and Eduard Schroeder, who became leaders among the Germans. Hollanders also arrived in considerable numbers, establishing themselves in western Michigan.

Irish immigrants came in growing numbers in the 1840's and 1850's. They tended to remain in the eastern cities, but many went West. They settled along lines of transportation—rivers, canals, and railroads—where they served as laborers. Many worked on river steamboats as roustabouts. By 1850, 150,000 Irish were in the Middle West. In the lead-mine region the Cornish were a substantial element.

The forces producing Irish migration in the 1840's and 1850's were chronic famine conditions. The migration was, to a large extent, assisted—to get the poor off the parish rates. It was also stimulated by steamship companies as a matter of providing traffic.

Few Scandinavians came prior to the Civil War. Wisconsin drew those who came, especially the Fox and Rock river valleys. More significant numbers after the Civil War went into Minnesota and the Dakotas. By 1856 foreign elements comprised 12 percent of the population of the Middle West. The melting pot worked in this area surprisingly well.

To make way for the settlers, Indians in the prairie province had to be removed. They went to the trans-Mississippi country, peacefully for the most part, because they had become aware of the might of the federal government, of the undependability of British aid, and the hopelessness of resistance, by confederation, to loss of their lands. In an earlier period some of the tribes had agreed to treaties containing the seductive promise that they could remain on the lands they were ceding until a future day when the lands had been surveyed and opened to settlement by the federal government.

Such a provision was inserted in a treaty of cession with the Sac and Fox Indians concluded by Governor Harrison at St. Louis on November 3, 1804. The treaty had been signed by five chiefs who were part of a band of hunters on Sac and Fox lands in Iowa, near St. Louis. The area ceded was a broad crescent of tribal lands in Illinois, extending from Cairo at the southern tip to the headwaters of the Illinois River. The price given for this great tract was $2234.50 in trade goods and an annuity of $1000. The tribal debts to traders were to be subtracted from the annuities. The Indian signers were alleged to have been drunk at the time. Two other big cessions in Illinois were obtained by Harrison—one from the Kaskaskias in August 1803, and another from the Piankashaw in December 1805. The three comprised almost the whole of present Illinois and much of southern Wisconsin.

The one serious Indian disturbance marring the peaceful clearance of the prairie province was the Black Hawk War of 1832. Its leader, Black Hawk, was an elder chief of the Sac tribe, a contemporary of Tecumseh, at whose side he had fought in the War of 1812. His views regarding land cessions to the federal government closely resembled Tecumseh's. He objected particularly to the St. Louis treaty of 1804, which he held to be invalid, though he himself had signed a confirmation of it in 1816 under a misapprehension.

The center of the disturbance was the village of Saukenuk, the principal seat of the tribe, a settlement of 500 families near the junction of the Rock and Mississippi rivers in Illinois. The soil was unusually fertile and produced abundant crops of corn, beans, and pumpkins to supplement the returns of hunting on the west side of the Mississippi. If the treaty of 1804 had been enforced against whites, squatters would not have been allowed to intrude on lands where the Sac and Fox were permitted to remain until they were sold. But squatters filed sham pre-emptions in the area around Saukenuk, even in the village itself, and had the support of Governor John Reynolds of Illinois.

The Sac were a divided tribe. One faction, led by a young realist, Keokuk, saw wisdom in supporting the plans of the federal government. His standing had risen when Black Hawk allied with Tecumseh in the War of 1812. By 1830 Keokuk had withdrawn to the west side of the Mississippi and his followers were settled in new villages along the Iowa River. Black Hawk and his followers insisted on remaining in their ancient Illinois home.

In the spring of 1830 notice was served on the Sac and Fox by the federal government that it intended to survey and sell to settlers the lands in Illinois they had ceded in the treaty of 1804. Black Hawk resolved to ignore both the treaty and the notice. In the spring of 1831, after the winter's hunt, he was back at Saukenuk with 300 warriors. This was enough to frighten off the squatters, and the women of the tribe planted their corn. News of the return sent a wave of consternation through the state. The Illinois governor proclaimed an Indian invasion and called out the militia. Federal troops went into action. The combination was too much to defy, and Black Hawk and his followers abandoned the village by night and returned to the Iowa side of the river. Summoned to the army post at the mouth of the Rock River by the commander of the federal troops, Black Hawk appeared and signed an agreement not to recross to the Illinois side.

An impulse to return came, however, with news of a successful Sac and Fox raid against the Menominee up the Mississippi, in revenge for Menominee murders of Fox chiefs the preceding year. The raiders found a party of Menominee in a drunken state on an island opposite Prairie du Chien and killed and scalped 28, creating the danger of an Indian war that would imperil white frontier settlements. Black Hawk refused an order to surrender the murderers, which added to his standing in the tribe. He was summoned to a council and declined to attend. President Jackson ordered reinforcements to the disturbed area to maintain quiet while the accused braves were arrested and brought to trial. As a result of the forced abandonment of the Saukenuk lands, and insufficient food, Black Hawk had an invitation from the Rock River Winnebago, whose lands lay north of Saukenuk, to visit them and raise a crop of corn. In May 1832, a year after his promise not to cross the Mississippi to the Illinois side, he did so, with about 450 warriors and 1500 women, children, and old men. He may have toyed with visions of the future. He had friends among the Winnebago and Potawatomi who held out prospects of aid in recovering the ancient Sac and Fox domain. He also had hopes of aid from the British at Malden, with whom he was in touch.

The recrossing of the river brought a peremptory order to return from General Henry Atkinson at Fort Armstrong, and induced the governor of Illinois to summon the state militia, from which 1600 mounted men responded. Offended by the tone of General Atkinson's letter, and protesting that his mission was peaceful, Black Hawk refused to obey. He moved up the Rock River, skirting Saukenuk, to the Winnebago village, pursued by the mounted militia and the federal infantry. At the Winnebago village his reception was cool. The tribe was divided and had no taste for meeting the combined forces hurrying to overtake the outnumbered fugitives. The Potawatomi were similarly reluctant to involve themselves in a war. The project of "making corn" collapsed. So also did the visions of the future. Black Hawk was ready to surrender to Atkinson and his disciplined infantry. But the mounted militia were well in front.

In the midst of a parting council with the Potawatomi, Black Hawk learned of the approach of a company of the mounted militia. He dispatched three men with a white flag to meet them and to arrange a council. He also sent five scouts to observe from a distance the reception of the peace party. The militia caught sight of the flag-carrying party and the scouts at the same time and suspected an ambush. The peace party and the scouts were fired on. Three were killed, and others were made prisoner. The survivors made their way back to Black Hawk.

To Black Hawk it was now clear that a war was on. With 40 of his warriors he concealed himself across the path of the oncoming militia and met them in a surprise charge. The militia were frightened and fled, spreading panic to the forces behind. A rout occurred and when the militia was reassembled a majority insisted on returning home. A new militia levy had to be made.

The war expanded beyond the area of its inception. The Winnebago and Potawatomi in northern Illinois and southern Wisconsin, infected with the restlessness of Black Hawk, carried the war to outlying regions and massacres occurred. For

Black Hawk the war became a prolonged flight from state and federal troops, interspersed with rearguard actions. The flight for a time was northeastward, toward Milwaukee, where ammunition and supplies from the British at Malden were hoped for. The hope, however, proved vain. Then the direction of the flight became northwestward, to the Wisconsin River. The country west of the Wisconsin was a little-known wilderness, and might not be ventured into by the pursuers. If the Mississippi could be reached and crossed, a safe return might be made to the Sac settlements in Iowa. Among the pursuers were more than 3000 mounted state militia; 1000 were federal. Ahead, on the west side of the Mississippi, was a force of Sioux, ancient enemies of the Sac, who had been alerted to the coming of the Black Hawk refugees and had visions of scalps easily gathered.

The refugees reached the bluffs on the east bank of the Wisconsin late in the afternoon of July 21, 1832, where they were overtaken by forward elements of their pursuers, and the Battle of Wisconsin Heights was fought. With determination and skill Black Hawk beat back the attacks until nightfall, and his people were able, under cover of darkness, to cross the low waters of the river. On the west bank canoes and rafts were obtained from friendly Winnebago and some of the women, children, and old men started down the river in the hope of being permitted, as noncombatants, to pass the garrison at Fort Crawford and reach the Iowa shore. They were attacked, however, by a company of regulars. Those not captured or drowned were driven ashore, where they were massacred by a band of Menominee led by white officers.

The remnant of Black Hawk's band kept barely ahead of the pursuers on the flight to the Mississippi. Its progress was encumbered by what remained of old men, women, and children, the weakest of whom were dying of starvation. The Mississippi was reached just ahead of the pursuers on August 1, and part of the band was able to cross on makeshift rafts and canoes. The transit was interrupted, however, by the appearance of a war steamer. Black Hawk sought to surrender but the troops on the steamer opened fire.

The ensuing Battle of Bad Axe, in which the Indians were caught between the river and the combined force of militia and regulars who had caught up with them, was a massacre. One hundred and fifty Indians, including fighting men, women, and children, were killed or drowned; the remainder were captured. Those who had managed to cross the river found the Sioux waiting for them, and 68 lost their scalps.

With the Battle of Bad Axe the war came to an end. Of the force that had crossed the Mississippi a few months earlier not more than 150 returned to Iowa. Black Hawk was caught east of the Mississippi by a party of renegade Winnebago and was delivered to the Indian agent at Prairie du Chien. He was imprisoned in Jefferson Barracks, Missouri, and in Fortress Monroe, Virginia, for a time in irons. Later he was released to make a tour of the eastern cities under the supervision of Keokuk. The idea was to impress upon him the might of the government he had defied. He was then released, shorn of all tribal powers.

The Sac and Fox tribes were forced to sign a punitive treaty shortly after the capture of Black Hawk. It resembled the one submitted by Andrew Jackson to the Creeks after the Battle of Horseshoe Bend. It treated friend and foe in the tribe alike, opening with the stern declaration that desperate tribal leaders had levied upon the frontier an unprovoked and brutal war, which had spared neither age nor sex. As an indemnity and to secure the future safety of the frontier the treaty required the cession of the Iowa tribal lands, with the exception of a 400-square-mile reservation in the valley of the Iowa River. As a gesture to the Keokuk faction it granted an annuity of $20,000 for a period of thirty years, with the provision, however, that $40,000 from the total amount was to be withheld for payment of the tribe's debts to traders. The treaty was signed by 33 chiefs, headed by Keokuk. Four years later, in 1836, the tribe surrendered the new reservation with the understanding that another would be given in Kansas, which was done in 1842.

From 1815 to 1845 the federal government concluded some threescore treaties with Indian tribes north of the Ohio in which lands were ceded in whole or in part. Normally treaties were obtained with the help of traders who had accounts to settle with Indians for furnishing them with supplies, tools, or whiskey on credit. The treaties always included clauses for the discharge of tribal debts to traders out of the annuities.

In the treaties where tribes retained part of their lands, special provision was often made for chiefs and headmen who had supported the arrangements. They were allowed to reserve lands in fee simple in amounts varying from several sections to as much as ten or more. Like favor was shown to relatives of the tribal leaders. Lists of the privileged sometimes covered pages of the treaties, with the amounts reserved to each individual specified, and attested to by the individual's signature (his cross). In some cases payments in lieu of land reserves were listed. It was normal for individuals—with land rights so reserved—to transfer privately their rights in advance to speculators, traders, or even in some cases to government agents. Already established prior to the 1830's, such practices became prevalent in the 1830's. They were deplored by Calhoun in 1836 as productive of speculation, gross frauds, and injustice to the Indians. Hundreds of thousands of acres in the prairie province passed thus by treaty into speculators' hands without ever having been part of the federal land system.

Prairie and Lake Plains:
Economy, Society,
and Politics

IN THE PROCESS of building a new society in the prairie province the sod was a problem comparable to that of the forest in the eastern provinces. It consisted of a thick and tough mat of grass roots, interlaced often with "red root," a bulbous residue of tree root. "Breaking sod" was a labor almost as heavy, and as costly in time, as clearing the forest. It required a season's labor for a quarter section of land, even with the help of improved implements. Professionals were available to do it, but the cost was high, $1.50 to $2 an acre, which was more than the price of the land.

The implement relied on for the work in the 1830's and 1840's was a heavy wooden plow, the mold board of which was covered by a sheath of wrought iron. The sheath was a protection against splitting of the plow. Plowing was feasible only in the spring when the sod was softened by rain. But wet earth was sticky and made scouring more difficult. The power needed for plowing was two or three yoke of oxen or horses. In the late 1840's a steel plow was put on the market, the steel for which was imported from England. It was a lighter instrument than the old plow, its polished mold board scoured more effectively, and it required less motive power.

Before the prairie sod was subdued, however, further decomposition was necessary. The prairie farmer began the process by walking alongside the upturned furrows, cutting gashes into them at intervals with an axe. Seed corn was dropped into the gashes and covered. Cultivation was not possible because of the presence of sod clumps. The resulting crop was a half crop, a so-called sod crop, which sufficed for home use for the winter. Its chief virtue was that it effected a disintegration of the clumps. In the second season the soil was friable and could be cultivated. Two good crops, after the sod crop, paid for the land and for improvements, provided a market was not too distant.

On the larger prairies lack of lumber was a problem. The walls of the first house of many pioneers consisted of piled-up layers of thick sod. Lumber was brought in for doors and windows, and in some cases for the roof. On the roof a sod thatching was relied on for protection from the cold, even if not against leaks. Such a house was lived in for several seasons, and then relegated to the stock. The sod house was common west of the Mississippi.

The size and location of the prairies were important elements in their selection and in their conquest. Small prairies adjacent to forested land along streams were normally preferred, for timber for building and fuel were at hand. The ideal prairie was one high enough to drain well and limited enough in size to reduce the dangers of grass fires in the heat of the summer and blistering winds in the winter. A house was built near the shelter of forest and on the margin of the prairie.

The raw prairie was put to use at once as pasture for cattle. As a protection against grass fires, 40 or 50 furrows were plowed into the prairie. Bare ground was an efficient fire check. The plowed land was seeded to a sod crop. The next season it was planted with a view to systematic cultivation, and the fire check was extended into the prairie. Year after year the plowing moved deeper into the prairie until a meeting occurred with the land of a neighbor, worked from the opposite side. In this process settlers learned of the incomparable richness and durability of prairie soil and old prejudices against it were dispelled.

In the conquest of the larger prairies railroads were an important agency. They cut the costs of lumber and other supplies purchased at a distance, and also those of reaching a market. They were especially crucial in the conquest of the Grand Prairie of east central Illinois in the middle 1850's.

Wheat was the crop that became established in the northern part of the province. It was spring wheat, for which the climate in those latitudes was ideal, providing plentiful moisture at planting and dry weather in the period of harvesting. If harvesting is delayed because of wet weather the grain tends to shatter. The northern portion of the prairie province had this favorable weather and it soon became the wheat kingdom of the United States.

A series of maps prepared by the Department of Agriculture represents this development for the years 1839 to 1859. The maps illustrate the migration of wheat (both spring and winter wheat) from the East to the West in these years. In 1839 Ohio, with its crop concentrated in the east and the south, is the greatest producer in the Union (Map 37). Older areas of concentration were in New York and in the Appalachian Valley of Pennsylvania and Virgina. The New York production is concentrated in the Finger Lakes region and the Genesee Tract. In the Appalachian Valley German farmers had been wheat farmers since the colonial period. They knew how to grow wheat without exhausting the soil. In New England wheat growing had nearly ceased by 1839. Population was moving from Vermont and New Hampshire to the West.

In 1849 the great western developments were in the oak openings of southern Michigan and the Rock River valley of Illinois and southern Wisconsin. Ohio, New York, and the Appalachian Valley were still major producers.

In 1859 the Rock and Fox valleys of Illinois and Wisconsin were the great producers (Map 38). Illinois ranked first in the Union. Indiana and Wisconsin were second and third. Southern Michigan was maintaining its production. But the eastern areas had thinned out. The prairies of the Middle West were the nation's breadbasket during the Civil War.

Corn was another of the great staples of American agriculture that migrated to the Middle West in this period. It is a southern plant in origin and natural habitat; its

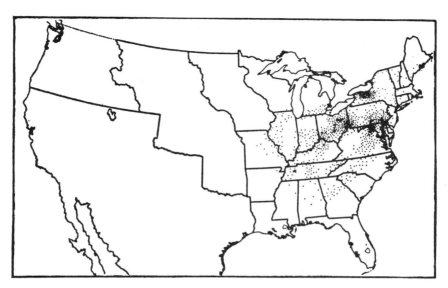

Wheat Crop, 1839

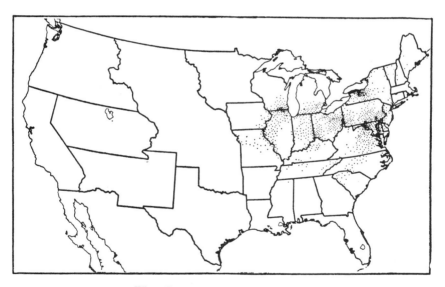

37. Wheat Crop, 1849 (from Bidwell & Falconer)
Each dot represents 100,000 bushels.

climatic needs are abundant moisture after planting and hot days and sultry nights in maturing. It thrives especially along the northern limit of a southern climate—in other words, in the Ohio Valley.

In 1839, as seen on map 28 (page 129), the corn belt lay in southern Ohio, Indiana, and Illinois, while across the Ohio is was noticeably concentrated in parts of Kentucky and Tennessee. By 1849 corn had become more heavily concentrated on

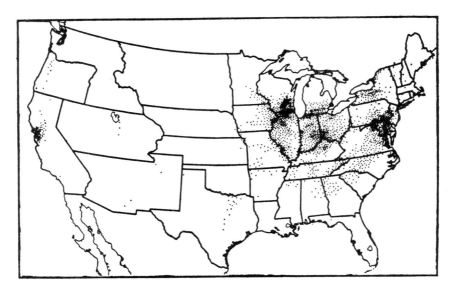

38. Wheat Crop, 1859 (from Bidwell & Falconer)
Each dot represents 100,000 bushels.

both sides of the Ohio River (Map 39). By 1859 this region, together with Iowa and Missouri, had become the corn kingdom of the nation (Map 40).

Wool also moved into the Middle West in the quarter-century preceding the Civil War. Its migration is shown on the next maps. In 1840 its centers of concentration were Vermont, the Finger Lakes region of New York, and Ohio (Map 41). Production there represented a departure from wheat farming. In Ohio the area of principal production was the hill region of the southeastern part of the state—the Allegheny Plateau region. By 1850, after the Mexican War, the wool-producing areas in New Mexico and California had been added to the national production.

By 1860 Ohio was the premier wool grower in the Union. The area of concentration was the hill region of Ohio, also southwestern Pennsylvania. Michigan has also become important (Map 42). The Middle West was thus providing the wool that went into the uniforms of northern troops in the Civil War, or rather, that should have gone into them. Much that went into them was shoddy provided by army contractors.

Two societies had become established in the prairie province at the outbreak of the Civil War, one with a northern orientation, the other a southern. They differed from each other in population origins, economic output, and social structure. Ohio was peopled by northern and foreign stock; Indiana was more nearly divided between Northerners and Southerners, with a large German contingent in its cities; northern Illinois was prevailingly northern, with a heavy foreign concentration, while the southern half of the state was prevailingly southern. Wisconsin and Michigan were northern in their population, each reinforced by large foreign admixtures. Across the Mississippi, Iowa contained a southern population in the south and people of northern origins in the north.

The line of separation between the northern and southern societies in the region north of the Ohio was approximately the Shelbyville moraine. The National Road from Wheeling on the Ohio to Vandalia in southern Illinois and on to St. Louis was

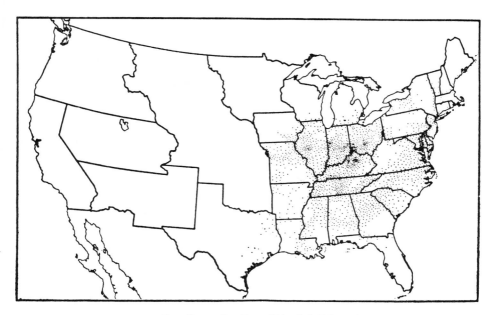

39. Corn Crop, 1849 (from Bidwell & Falconer)
Each dot represents 300,000 bushels.

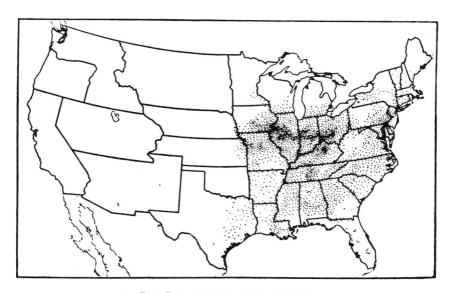

40. Corn Crop, 1859 (from Bidwell & Falconer)
Each dot represents 300,000 bushels.

more popularly regarded as the line. The area to the north of the line consisted of rich and level land ideal for farming, except where it was low and waterlogged. It produced abundant crops and gave every evidence of prosperity. Its houses were substantial and well kept, its land values high, its livestock well fed. Its educational standards were good, and the illiteracy rate was low.

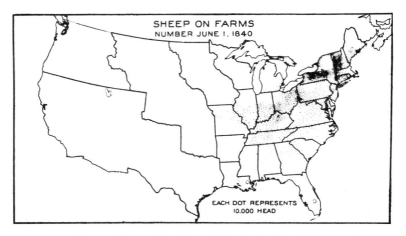

41. Sheep on Farms, 1840 (from the *Yearbook of Agriculture*, 1923)

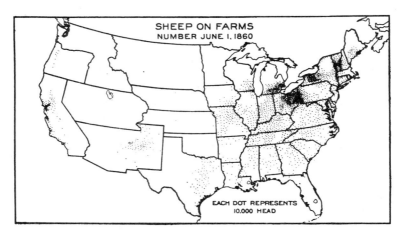

42. Sheep on Farms, 1860 (from the *Yearbook of Agriculture*, 1923)

The society south of the Shelbyville moraine was less prosperous. The land was rougher in topography and was less fertile; real estate values were lower; farm buildings were unpainted; there was less energy and enterprise than in the north. This difference was marked enough at the time of the Civil War to draw comment from travelers.

The forces producing this difference have already been mentioned in part. One was the soil factor, including glaciation. Another was population characteristics. Northerners, especially Yankees, were popularly considered more hard-working, more enterprising, more frugal than the southern farmers in the province. Foreigners, especially Germans, were even more hard-working and frugal; the women worked beside the men in the fields.

The comparative well-being of the Northerners was partly due to the greater capital and credit they normally brought to the West. This was true also of the German emigrants to the province. The Germans were not the redemptioner type of the colonial period. They were able to pay the cost of the ocean voyage to New York from Bremen, and normally worked their way westward. In the West they were likely to serve as hired hands until they had acquired the means to purchase land and equipment. Southerners, on the other hand, normally arrived in the province with little means and began as squatters on the public lands.

The affiliations of the two parts of the province in terms of markets were of importance in shaping their views. The northern part of the province was tied to the East and principally to New York City. Its two chief cities were Chicago and Milwaukee. By 1853 Chicago was connected by rail with the Mississippi River and at the east with New York City. The National Road also gave the province, north and south, connection with the eastern seaboard. The southern portion of the province had access to New Orleans by way of the Ohio and Mississippi rivers. These differences of outlet produced differences in point of view between the two parts of the province on issues separating the North and the South. But they also produced compromise views, especially regarding the problem of slavery.

All the great compromises on the slavery issue came from corn-belt politicians. An Illinois senator, Jesse B. Thomas, introduced the Missouri Compromise of 1820. A Kentucky senator, Henry Clay, worked out the Compromise of 1850. Another Illinois senator, Stephen A. Douglas, was the champion of the compromise doctrine of popular sovereignty. A Kentuckian, John J. Crittenden, worked out the Crittenden peace plan of 1860, which failed. Abraham Lincoln was governed as President by the compromise temper of the Ohio Valley. He moved slowly and warily regarding the Emancipation Proclamation, but moved too fast for the Ohio Valley, and, in the election of 1864, the Republican vote there fell off dangerously.

Such conclusions are supported by the evidence of the maps in Chapter 43. On map 63 (page 406) the presidential election of 1856 is shown. In the election the Republican candidate was John C. Frémont; the Democratic was James Buchanan; the candidate of the Whigs and American party was Millard Fillmore. The Republican area is shown in black, the Democratic in white, and the Whig-American in shades of gray. In the Middle West the Republican area corresponds with the area of glaciation; the Democratic lies south of it. In the prairie region the lakeshore counties of Wisconsin, occupied by Germans, go Democratic; so does the lead-mine region in the Driftless area, occupied by Southerners. The center of strength of the Whig-American party is in Kentucky and Tennessee—the Ohio Valley—which wished to compromise on the slavery issue.

Map 66 (page 409) shows the presidential election of 1860, the election which made Lincoln president. The black is Republican. The gray in various forms is compromise: the vertical lines show Douglas Democrats, the clear gray is the Constitutional Union party, the parallel lines are fusion against Lincoln. The white is the radical southern proslavery vote, which went for Breckinridge. In geographic terms the pattern of the vote is like that of the preceding election. The arc of the Shelbyville moraine across southern Illinois and southern Indiana is there, the line separating the northern and southern elements in these states. In the lakeshore counties of Wisconsin the German vote is Democratic, though not as consistently as earlier. The lead-mine region of Lafayette County, Wisconsin, and Dubuque County, Iowa, with their southern population, votes Democratic. Iowa, which up to 1850 had been a southern community—a child of Kentucky—has come by 1860 to be a northern community. However, southern Iowa still reflects its southern population. Northern Wisconsin and Minnesota are still a vast forest, with practically no vote. Pennsylvania, in 1860, gave Lincoln its vote, which was decisive in electing him and in precipitating the Civil War. The compromise parties—the Douglas Democrats and the Constitutional Union party—are strong in the Ohio Valley.

The prairie province is an example of one of the dualities of nature. Its connections were south and east. To the south it was united by the mighty Mississippi and the Ohio. To the east it was tied by the immense system of the Great Lakes. A like duality marked the population elements flowing into the province. Those occupying the region south of the National Road were predominantly southern in extraction, accustomed to slavery and tolerating its extension.

Those occupying the region north of the National Road were predominantly northeastern and foreign in extraction. They carried with them the moral values of the northeastern seaboard, and especially the conscience of New England and New York regarding slavery. Willing to abide by the compromises of the Constitution as to slavery in the states, they objected to its expansion into the territories of the trans-Mississippi West. Increasingly, as a result of the spectacular achievements of internal improvments by water and by land, they became allied with the Northeast and its moral outlook on slavery. Ultimately they took the lead, in the mid 1850's, in framing the Republican program of restriction of the advance of slavery. In cooperation with the Northeast they elected Abraham Lincoln President in 1860. In the Civil War which followed, they joined their young strength to that of the Northeast and together saved the Union.

Settlement of the Gulf Plains Province

THE GULF PLAINS PROVINCE is a counterpart to the prairie province of the North—the resemblance is marked as to shape, size, and the variety of its soils. In shape it is a pyramid with its base resting on the shore of the Gulf of Mexico. It extends along the Gulf from Florida to the lower banks of the Rio Grande, and its apex is at the point where the upper Mississippi and the Ohio meet.

It contains stretches of soil that are exceptionally rich, others that are less so, and others, very poor. An exceptionally rich zone is the Alabama Black Belt, an arc conforming to the terminal arc of the Appalachian mountain system. It swings from northeastern Mississippi southward to the state's middle latitude, then, in that latitude, moves across Alabama and extends into Georgia. It consists of prairies, with soils once comparable in richness to the northern prairies, but which proved to be less enduring.

An even richer and much larger soil region is the Mississippi River floodplain, which extends on both sides of the river from the southern tip of Illinois to the Gulf. In an earlier geologic age it was altogether under water, the bottom of a long estuary of the sea 30 to 60 miles wide. The estuary was gradually filled by great deposits of silt that came with the melting waters of the glaciers. The silt originated partly in the rich limestone soil of the prairie province. It was deposited to a depth of 150 to 200 feet, and part was distributed by winds beyond the region of deposit. The plain resembles in extent and in fertility the floodplain of the Nile.

As land emerged in the estuary three independent rivers—the upper Mississippi, the Ohio, and the Missouri—became linked as the single great stream that formed the drainage system of the whole interior. A combination was thus created of a rich soil area and a navigable river giving easy access to world markets.

The river also created banks for containment of its waters. The banks were constructed by the silt of the river, which even in postglacial years was an immense quantity. An average year's deposit was equal to a foot of soil spread over a space of

275 square miles. As long as the river remained in its channel the silt was carried in suspension by the force of the current and went out to the Gulf. But in time of flood the waters spread out over the banks, and, having lost their momentum, the silt sank. The bulk of it came to rest at once on the banks, which as a consequence rose higher than the level of the backcountry. These were the natural banks of the river, but they were not high enough in time of record flood to contain the river. They had to be raised by artificial banks or levees built on them to protect the backcountry from inundation in exceptional floods.

At New Orleans levee building began with the founding of the city in 1718. Higher up the river, in the Yazoo delta, a few plantations were protected by levees by 1840. But inundations periodically swamped the low-lying interiors of the southern basin and most of the Yazoo delta remained unoccupied. In 1842 a flood of exceptional height occurred and stimulated the formation of levee districts on a countywide basis. In 1858, after a disastrous flood, the local districts were consolidated to form a single district, including virtually the whole of the Yazoo delta. The levees constructed at that time withstood the great floods of 1861 and 1862, but were disrupted in the military operations that led to the capture of Vicksburg by Union forces.

On the west side of the river the flood problem was more serious than on the east side. The natural banks were lower and less stable than on the east side, and major tributaries, pouring their floods into the main stream, were more numerous. Fortunately the tributary floods did not all peak at the same time. In 1849 and 1850 floods of unprecedented destructiveness occurred on the main stream, which finally brought the federal government into action. In 1849 a Swamp Land Act was adopted by Congress whereby all federally owned wetlands in Louisiana were granted to the state, to be sold and the proceeds used for levee construction. A like act was passed for the benefit of the other states of the lower river the next year. Both acts were failures. As administered by the states they produced little more than land speculation.

The problem of flood control was linked by engineering specialists with a serious navigation problem—low water in seasons after high water. This linkage was made in 1853 in a notable report prepared for the War Department by Charles Ellet, an eminent civil engineer. Ellet believed that the ever rising level of floods and the related problem of low-water navigation were the result of deforestation and settlement on the upper waters of the Mississippi and the Ohio, and were likely to be aggravated in the future. He advocated a program of coordinated control of the upper waters to meet these problems. Included in the program were: reservoir storage of waters on the tributaries of the Mississippi; enlargement of the Mississippi's natural outlets, one of which was considered to be the Atchafalaya; creation of an artificial outlet via Lake Borgne; cessation of labors to straighten the turnings and twistings of the river; and finally, a vigorous and coordinated program of levee building. The report was an admirable analysis of a major national problem, but its recommendations were ahead of its day. Only in the second quarter of the 20th century were its principles resurrected and its proposals, in new combinations, acted upon.

The eastern portion of the Gulf Plains consists, for the most part, of soil of intermediate or low fertility. The intermediate soil was found in valleys of the sand hills, in ridges and plateaus of central Mississippi and north central Alabama. Here grasses and vines provided food for the cattle and hogs of early settlers, and corn was raised for further fattening. The poorest lands of the region lay in the swamps and tidal marshes of southern Mississippi and Alabama.

Timber was a valuable resource of the whole eastern half of the Gulf Plains. It was hardwood at the north, longleaf and shortleaf pine (yellow pine) at the center, and cypress, mixed with pine in the tidal marshes adjoining the Gulf. Mixed cypress and pine were also found in the wetlands of the Yazoo delta. Adjacent to Natchez, for example, was a prosperous cypress lumbering and sawmill industry with New Orleans as its marketing center. But the heart of the prosperity of Mississippi and Alabama lay in the rich soils of the Alabama Black Belt and the portions of the Mississippi floodplain that were protected by levees.

The climate of the Gulf Plains was a major asset to agriculture, especially in cotton cultivation. The growing season for cotton is about 200 days, free of frost at either end. In the spring, when the young cotton plant is having its most rapid growth, the weather should be moist and warm. In the summer, when the bolls are ripening, the weather should be hot and dry. This is the weather of the Gulf Plains.

But the wetness of the low-lying sections was a serious health hazard. Myriads of mosquitoes bred there, and were carriers of diseases such as malaria, dengue, and other maladies. Malaria, or miasma, or ague, as it was variously known, was a scourge of the region. It was a greater scourge there than in any other part of the United States. It was a force shaping the history of the Gulf area. Malaria, which produced fever and anemia, afflicted pioneers almost as soon as they came into the province. It was especially prevalent among residents of low or swampy land.

Another disease, prevalent in areas of wet and sandy soils in the Gulf Plains, was caused by the hookworm. This parasite was brought to the region from Africa, probably in the blood of slaves. In Negroes the disease was usually mild. But in whites it was disastrous. The chief areas of southern infection were those in which the soil had become polluted by human waste. The disease was common where children and adults went barefoot. The larvae entered the body through the pores of the feet and got into the bloodstream, lungs, and intestinal tract.

The manifestations of the hookworm disease were gastric disturbances. The victims developed a craving to eat dirt, and were known as clay eaters or dirt eaters. Other manifestations were extreme emaciation, anemia, and mental retardation. The disease was a factor in producing the sluggishness and inferiority complex among poor whites and the run-down condition of their society.

The identification of the cause of the disease was made by a medical scientist, Charles W. Stiles, in 1902, and a campaign to eradicate it was organized and financed by the Rockefeller Foundation. A cheap and effective remedy was developed. An antihelminthic drug destroyed the parasite, permitting the rebuilding of the victim by improved diet, and the disease was stamped out early in the 20th century. Stiles won the reputation as ''the professor who had discovered the lazy bug.'' The discovery and the resulting remedy are estimated to have rescued 15 to 20 millions of sufferers from a life of debilitation.

In the opening stages of the settlement of the Gulf Plains the eastern half was the home of four Indian tribes mentioned earlier—the Creeks, Cherokee, Chickasaw, and Choctaw. In 1830 they numbered altogether some 60,000 persons, a meager population for the great area occupied. The Creeks and Cherokee resided partly in the state of Georgia, partly in the region Georgia had once held as her western claim. The two tribes occupied 9,500,000 acres in Georgia, much of it the state's best land. They also occupied nearly 6 million acres in Alabama. The Chickasaw and Choctaw held about 1,250,000 acres in Alabama, and in Mississippi they had nearly 16 million acres more.

These Indians were rising steadily on the ladder of civilization, and were moving toward farming for their subsistence. The farming was done chiefly by women, but men tended the cattle and hogs without loss of standing. Cornfields were cultivated in common, but families had private gardens producing food adjacent to their lodges. Cotton was raised by some tribes—Negro slaves providing the labor. Within tribal domains, chiefs, headmen, and traders who had married into the tribes owned fenced farms of considerable size. Much use was made of implements and techniques of civilization. Spinning wheels and looms were operated by women, trained by missionaries.

The Cherokee made notable advances in education and in tribal economy. According to an enumeration made in 1824, there were 18 schools in the nation attended by 314 pupils. The economy included 36 gristmills, 13 sawmills, 762 looms, 2468 spinning wheels, 172 wagons, 2923 plows, 7683 horses, 22,531 black cattle, 46,732 swine, 2566 sheep, 430 goats, 62 blacksmith shops, nine stores, two tanyards, and a powder mill. Public transport included several roads, turnpikes, and ferries. Among the Choctaw there were similar economic advances. In 1826 at a tribal council a constitution was adopted and powers were delegated to a committee, whose acts, when approved by the chiefs, became law. Among the Chickasaw there were like evidences of improvement. Most backward were the Creeks, who were beset by factionalism and an addiction to drink that was notorious.

The advances toward civilization of these Indians were alarming to the state governments and their citizens, who had designs on the tribal lands. Civilization threatened to make those Indians fixtures on the land. Georgia, which had ceded its western claims in 1802, was especially troubled. The federal government, in accepting the cession, had agreed to extinguish Indian rights to such lands as Georgia retained, as soon as this could be done peaceably and on reasonable terms. The federal government had obtained from the Indians considerable cessions, but not enough to satisfy Georgia, whose authorities had become clamorous for fulfillment of the government's agreement.

In 1825 the Monroe administration obtained from a faction of the Creeks—the Lower Creeks, headed by a half-blood, William McIntosh—a cession of all Creek lands in Georgia. The treaty was a product of gross bribery, and the Upper Creeks repudiated and denounced it. McIntosh was sentenced to death by a tribal council and, with an associate, was executed. The treaty went, however, to the Senate and was approved. An internecine war in the tribe became imminent, and early in 1826 a new treaty was negotiated in Washington superseding that of the preceding year. Full title to the Creek lands in Georgia thus passed to the state. The price paid for the cession was $217,000 plus a perpetual annuity of $20,000. Also, a present was made to the chiefs and warriors of the old McIntosh faction to the amount of $100,000. In addition, the federal government agreed to purchase a new home for the faction west of the Mississippi, to which it would remove. The treaty marked a new scale of prices as compared with the trifling sums paid by Harrison for cessions earlier in the century.

In the same years the Cherokee of Georgia were pressured to cede their lands and move. They were unwilling to do either. With the aid of missionaries they framed a written constitution, modeled on that of the United States, in which they declared themselves an independent nation. They relied on principles adopted in Indian relations by the government of the Confederation and on the treaty mode of dealing with Indian tribes under the Constitution. The Georgia legislature met the challenge by declaring all Indians within the state subject to its jurisdiction and all tribal usages and customs null and void after June 30, 1830. Anyone deterring a tribal chief or other officer from ceding tribal lands was made subject to imprisonment for from four to six years. An appeal for protection from the law was sent by the tribal leaders to President Jackson. His sympathies lay with Georgia, however. He considered it wrong that fine arable land, which was needed by whites, should be held by a few Indians to hunt over. He was troubled, also, by the conviction that contact by Indians with a white society resulted in Indian degradation rather than civilization. As a soldier he had taken a huge penalty in land from the Creeks in 1814. The penalty was exacted not only from the Upper Creeks, who had fought him, but from the Lower Creeks, who had aided him. Now as President he gave answer to those appealing to him that they must either remove beyond the Mississippi, where ample lands would be set aside for them, or accept the authority of Georgia.

The Cherokee leaders applied to the Supreme Court for an injunction against the enforcement of the Georgia laws. Their counsel maintained they were an independent nation within the United States and not subject to state authority. The Chief Justice, John Marshall, deeply sympathized with the tribe and with Indians generally. But in the case of *Cherokee Nation v. Georgia* the Court reluctantly ruled that it lacked jurisdiction, that Indian tribes were neither foreign nor domestic states, but rather "domestic dependent nations" not authorized to bring suits in the federal courts. Justice Marshall pointed a finger of accusation at Andrew Jackson for not curbing aggressive states' rights in this case, though against the nullifiers of South Carolina he was active enough. "If it be true that the Cherokee nation have rights, this is not the tribunal in which those rights are to be asserted. If it be true that wrongs have been inflicted, and that still greater, are to be apprehended, this is not the tribunal which can redress the past or prevent the future."

A new case to test the Georgia laws came before the Supreme Court in *Worcester v. Georgia*. It was brought by Samuel A. Worcester, a missionary, who had been assigned to the Cherokee by the American Board of Commissioners for Foreign Missions, and who held an appointment from President Adams to a postmastership in a Cherokee town. The case was a challenge to a state law requiring white residents in Cherokee areas to take an oath of allegiance to the state and to acquire a license to remain. Worcester refused compliance with the law, was arrested, and jailed. He appealed to the Supreme Court. Marshall wrote the Court's decision, which pronounced the Georgia legislation void as a violation of the Constitution, laws, and treaties of the United States. The Georgia governor flouted the decision and the President defied it. Jackson was reported to have said: "John Marshall has made his decision: now let him enforce it."

Without action from the federal executive, Georgia, Mississippi, and Alabama added to their pressures on Indians. Georgia already had legislation forbidding Cherokee chiefs, headmen, or warriors to interfere with the cession of tribal lands to the federal government. Mississippi and Alabama extended their jurisdictions over resident tribes. Under a Mississippi statute of 1830 resident Indians were made subject to suit in state courts for the payment of debts they had incurred. They could be required to pay state taxes, participate in road building, and muster in the state militia. A fine of $1000 and imprisonment for twelve months was imposed on persons convicted of acting in the office of chief, mingo, or headman under any tribal law that the state did not recognize. In Alabama the legislature in 1832 abrogated the authority of tribal chiefs and imposed penalties on whoever was convicted of opposing tribal cessions of land or discouraging enrollment of Indians for removal. The Indian policy of these states was now a federally sanctioned expulsion.

Expulsion seemed a righteous policy to at least parts of the American public. It conformed with the principle of the greatest good for the greatest number. By Providence the wilderness had been given to mankind to improve. Yet the Indians who merely roamed over it as hunters were not improving it. The biblical injunction to ''be fruitful, multiply, and replenish the Earth'' was beyond the capacity of uncivilized redskins. In war they were savages; in peace, drunken and degraded. Under approved legal code they were mere temporary occupants of the wilderness. The purposes of Providence would be fulfilled if they were removed to make way for civilized man.

Even John Quincy Adams, as President, leaned to such views. His Secretary of War, James Barbour, on December 28, 1825, brought before the Cabinet a benevolent plan for incorporating Indians into their respective states, as a means of civilizing and protecting them. Henry Clay, then Secretary of State, was skeptical of civilizing Indians, and opposed the scheme as impractical. As paraphrased by Adams in his diary, Clay's observations were these:

> . . . . There never was a full-blooded Indian who took to civilization. It was not in their nature. He believed they were destined to extinction, and although he would never use or countenance inhumanity towards them, he did not think them, as a race, worth preserving. He considered them as essentially inferior to the Anglo-Saxon race, which were now taking their place on this continent. They were not an improvable breed, and their disappearance from the human family will be no great loss to the world. In point of fact they were rapidly disappearing, and he did not believe that in fifty years from this time there would be any of them left.

These dour opinions shocked the Secretary of War. But Adams felt unable to disagree with them. He added in his diary: ''I fear there is too much foundation'' for their validity.

Yet Clay's observations contained a major weakness—the assumption that the racial element which would displace the Indians in the Gulf states would be Anglo-Saxons primarily. The race that did become the tillers of the best lands in the province was African—the chattels of Anglo-American cotton planters. The sequence was redskins, who were free, replaced by blacks who were unfree. This was the sequence, also, of the recent rise of Missouri to statehood which had become a ''firebell in the night,'' warning of coming controversy in the Union. It was no mere coincidence that the later opposition in Congress to the removal of Indians from the Gulf Plains was centered in the same section of the country that had resisted the westward extension of slavery in 1820.

The removal campaign took on a new vigor with the election of Andrew Jackson. The owner of a slave-operated plantation in Tennessee, the new President saw less evil in slavery than in the Indian occupation of the fertile lands of the South. He thought the removal of the Indians would be a boon to them, and would at the same time prepare the land for a better society. Like Clay, he professed kindly feelings for the Indians, but his election was based on the understanding that he would seek to free the region east of the Mississippi of its Indian occupants. In his annual messages to Congress he repeatedly referred to the civilized tribes of the South as savages.

Executive proposals for Indian removal had preceded Jackson's. As early as December 1817, President Monroe had suggested such a program to Congress. Monroe had recommended it more forcefully in December 1824, and again in a special message of January 1825. The latter was based on a report by the Secretary of War, John C. Calhoun, who maintained that removal was an obvious and easy solution of a major problem, because Indians were few and their numbers were declining, while whites, needing their lands, were many and civilized.

Jackson's first annual message to Congress warmly advised Congress to set aside an ample district west of the Mississippi beyond the limits of any organized state or territory, as a home for the stranded eastern tribes. He especially had the Gulf Indians in mind, and reminded Congress that he had discouraged the attempts of those tribes to set themselves up as Indian entities within the sovereign states.

Early in 1830 a bill appeared in each house of Congress for Indian removal. The Senate bill, ultimately adopted, provided that districts be laid off in the unorganized territory west of the Mississippi for the reception of such nations or tribes of Indians as desired to exchange their eastern for western lands. The President was authorized to give solemn assurances to such tribes that the United States would guarantee to them and their heirs and successors "forever" such lands as they would receive. Any improvements they had made on ceded lands were to be appraised and paid for. The emigrants were to have aid in their removal, and whatever aid was necessary for their subsistence in the year following removal. They were to be protected after removal from any tribe or nation of Indians and from any other persons. The sum of $500,000 was to be appropriated by Congress to meet the costs entailed in the act.

In anticipation of such legislation treaties had already been made with tribes resident in the country west of the Missouri-Arkansas line, whereby their hunting lands were ceded to the federal government for locating intruded eastern Indians. In 1825 treaties had been obtained from the Great and Little Osage and from the Kansa tribe for such use. The areas ceded—all good for hunting—were in part also good for farming, and would answer the mixed needs of the civilized tribes.

The removal bill was debated in Congress through the months of April and May 1830. Following Jackson's recommendation it was designed to apply to all the tribes east of the Mississippi, though the southern tribes were the focus of it. In the debate the whole Indian-white history, colonial and national, was drawn upon for fact and argument. Supporters of removal were the adherents of Jackson and their arguments echoed his views. Removal of the tribes would be voluntary and their segregation from whites in that area would permit them to develop as they liked.

Debate on the bill was also on sectional lines. Opposition came chiefly from the northeastern and middle Atlantic states. Approval was general in the South. Outstanding congressional opponents were Peleg Sprague of Maine, Edward Everett of

Massachusetts, H. C. Storrs and W. W. Ellsworth of Connecticut, and Theodore Frelinghuysen of New Jersey. The opponents were nascent Whigs—Federalists, Anti-Masons, and National Republicans. They were philanthropists, educators, religious leaders, and objectors to the extension of slavery. Everett denounced state pressures on the southern tribes and the justification that those Indians were savages. He cited statistics, gathered from Indian sources, to prove their civilization. Frelinghuysen was a prominent religious leader, president for years of the American Board of Commissioners for Foreign Missions, head of the American Tract Society, and president of Rutgers College. He was closely associated with Henry Clay, whose running mate he became in the presidential campaign of 1844. He held Senate attention for six hours, with an eloquent survey of colonial and national Indian policy in which he urged that the aborigines had more rights than mere occupation of their lands.

The vote following the debate was a victory for Jackson's removal program. It reflected the President's recent triumph in the election. In the House the margin was narrow—102–97. The Senate vote was more decisive. The affirmative House vote was a coalition of Jackson Democrats, states' rights adherents, and believers in Anglo-Saxon expansion. The negative vote was prevailingly from the North—78 of the 97 votes, and reflected the New England conscience.

The language of the Removal Act indicated that the removals were to have Indian consent. The President was authorized to set aside districts in the West "for such tribes or nations of Indians as may choose to exchange the lands where they now reside and remove there." The means of obtaining consent were not, however, spelled out. They were left to the treaty negotiators. The likelihood was that the civilized tribes would be loath to cede and move. They were attached to their farms and hunting grounds and venerated the graves of their forefathers. To obtain consent substantial inducements as well as state pressures would be necessary. The carrot and the stick were both needed. The inducements had to be of a new order. Normally a showering of favors on tribal leaders had been sufficient. Now the commonalty also would have to be won over.

In the treaties made with the civilized tribes both the leaders and the commonalty were to be given allotments of land from the tribal holdings. These were to be located after federal surveys, which were expected to be completed in five years. Then the allotments were to become patents in fee simple. Allotments to leaders of tribes had figured in earlier treaty negotiations. They had passed quickly into the hands of traders and speculators. In the treaties with the civilized tribes this was likely to happen again, for Indians were notoriously shortsighted. But the cessions would at least be voluntary.

The Choctaw were the first to exchange their eastern lands for a reservation in the West. In September 1830, they surrendered in the Treaty of Dancing Rabbit Creek all their lands east of the Mississippi (about a sixth of the state of Mississippi) and agreed to move to a reservation west of Arkansas Territory. In compensation each chief obtained an allotment of four sections of land, an annuity, and other specified gifts. All tribal heads of family desiring to remain in Mississippi were allowed an allotment of one section, with an adjoining half section for each child over ten and a quarter section for each child under ten. The allotments, in due time, were to be converted into patents in fee simple. Actually these patents went to speculators. Few of the Indians receiving allotments persevered in the intention of settling down in Mississippi. From 80 to 90 percent sold their allotments promptly to speculators.

In 1832 the Creeks ceded their lands east of the Mississippi (the eastern fifth of Alabama). As compensation each of the 90 chiefs received a section of land and every head of family obtained a half section. The allotments were to be located where the allottee had made improvements. After five years they were to be exchanged for patents in fee simple. The tribe was paid $100,000 to clear its debts and given an increase in annuities of $12,000 to be paid for five years. The tribe was expected to move west to join the McIntosh faction already there. The boundaries of the new reservation were yet to be fixed. The allotments provided in the treaty went quickly to speculators, as in the case of the Choctaw.

The Chickasaw treaty, concluded in 1834, ceded the northern sixth of Mississippi. It gave the chiefs of the tribe allotments ranging from one to four sections. Heads of families received allotments scaled to the size of families—four sections to families of ten or more persons, three to families of five to nine persons, and two to families of less than five. Owners of slaves received added sections. The residue of the lands was to be sold by the federal government with the proceeds going into a tribal trust fund. The price of the lands sold was to start at $1.25 an acre and was to decline, year by year, on a graduated basis, such as was being urged in Congress for all public lands. Removal of the tribe to the West was assumed. From 80 to 90 percent of the allotted lands passed into the hands of speculators and settlers.

In 1835 a treaty with the Cherokee was concluded ceding all but a fraction of the tribal lands east of the Mississippi for $5 million. The treaty was made with a minority faction of the tribe and was at once repudiated by the majority. In contained no allotment provisions, that program having come into disrepute. The tribe was granted a spacious new home west of the Missouri-Arkansas line, where a few tribesmen already were resident, with an extensive outlet "as far west as the sovereignty of the United States extends." Removal was to occur within two years after ratification of the treaty. The treaty was not agreed to by a dissident majority of the tribe and their removal had to be implemented by force.

The last tribe enmeshed in Jackson's removal program was the Seminole of Florida. The tribe was a composite of remnants of indigenous Indians and separatist Creeks. It included a considerable population of runaway slaves from Georgia who were employed in farming. The tribe clashed frequently with slave catchers from Georgia and with border intruders on its lands. In 1823 it had been induced to agree to a treaty, accepting a reservation in south central Florida and agreeing to no longer receive runaway slaves. In 1833 this treaty was replaced by another, obtained from a faction of the tribe, whereby the reservation was exchanged for one in the trans-Mississippi West within the area occupied by the Creeks.

The new treaty was repudiated by the majority of the Seminole who executed the chiefs signing it, and defied an army sent to effect a forced removal. The ensuing war lasted seven years, costing the lives of nearly 1500 troops and an expenditure of $40 million. The leader of the resisters was Osceola, who had been a Red Stick among the Creeks in the War of 1812. He eluded the troops sent to round him up, hiding women and children in the great Florida swamps and fighting a skillful guerrilla war. He was ultimately captured, when he trusted a flag of truce in going to a peace conference, and was imprisoned until his death. The war was bitterly criticized in the North for its bungling and its evident design to safeguard the slave system of the South.

The promise of voluntary removal, held out to all Indian tribes in the act of 1830, was fulfilled in the case of only two of the southern tribes. The friendly Choctaw and Chickasaw were removed peacefully, though they suffered in the process. The Creeks, torn by dissension over the removal, were forced to migrate after a tribal war in 1835–36. The majority faction of the Cherokee had to be forced, and a quarter perished on the way. When the majority faction arrived in the West, it ordered the execution of the minority leaders already there, who had signed the treaty. The Seminole war, which was necessary to remove that tribe to the West, was merely the climax of Jackson's policy.

The sequel to the removal of the Indians from the Gulf Plains was the westward advance of population from the southern seaboard. This occurred in the same period as the westward advance over the prairie province. It marks the culmination of the frontier advance in the decades 1810–50.

In 1810 the frontier line lay in Georgia and in Tennessee. It fronted, in Georgia, on the lands of the Cherokee and the Creeks. In Tennessee it hung like a spout over the province. In Louisiana, near New Orleans, was a population of French extraction, dating back to the colonial era.

By 1820 the Tennessee hydrant had released its flood, following the crushing of the Creeks in the War of 1812. Population had flowed southward and westward, coalescing with that in West Feliciana. A decade later the Indians were surrounded and the Jacksonians were demanding their removal to the Great Plains. The Cherokee and the Creeks were under the greatest pressure, but the Choctaw and the Chickasaw were also in the way. The presence of these Indians meant that the wonderful cotton country was closed to the frontier.

By 1840 the Indians were gone except for remnants and except for the Seminole in Florida territory (Map 43). The removed tribes were lined up west of the Missouri-Arkansas border in reservations promised to be theirs forever. By 1850 the Seminole in Florida had been subdued and removed.

In the 1850 census map (44) densities of population are shown in the shaded areas. These are found in the areas of the Black Belt extending from northeastern Mississippi, and across Alabama, into Georgia, and in parts of the floodplain of the Mississippi. The lighter shadings are in the lowlands of the Yazoo-Mississippi delta not yet protected by levees, in the hill country of eastern Mississippi and northern Alabama, and in the pine barrens of south central Georgia. The marshy coastal areas of southern Mississippi, southern Alabama, and western Florida, which were used for lumbering, stand out. The fertile valleys of the Mobile and Alabama, however, were a region of rapidly growing population.

The eastern recruiting grounds from which the migrants to the Gulf Plains were drawn were Virginia, South Carolina, Georgia, and Tennessee. From Virginia and South Carolina especially came planters obliged to migrate because of the depleted state of their soils and seeking the rich earth of the Black Belt. A major element in this great migration of population was black—Negro slaves.

In 1810 the Gulf Plains were just beginning to be populated by slaves (Map 45). There were slaves in the West Feliciana area of the lower Mississippi and the valley of

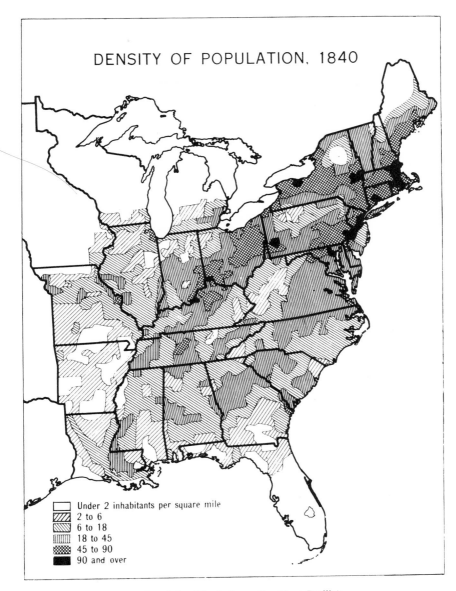

DENSITY OF POPULATION, 1840

Under 2 inhabitants per square mile
2 to 6
6 to 18
18 to 45
45 to 90
90 and over

43. Population Distribution, 1840 (from Paullin)

the lower Alabama. On the west side of the Mississippi, the Red River valley begins faintly to stand out.

In 1820 the Tennessee hydrant had let out its flood (Map 46). The Creeks had been crushed by Andrew Jackson in the War of 1812 and by the treaty of cession extorted from them after the Battle of Horseshoe Bend. Another area of development was lower Louisiana. No great concentration of slave population had yet appeared in the Alabama Black Belt. Pioneers were slow to take up this region, partly because its

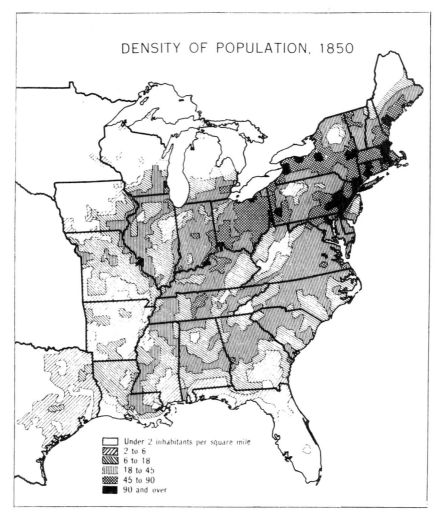

44. Population Distribution, 1850 (from Paullin)

soil was sticky and hard to work. Not until the 1830's did the marvelous fertility of the Black Belt become widely known. Then planters and their slaves went into it with a rush. The slave population of Alabama rose by over 35 percent in the decade 1830–40, while the rise in South Carolina, the source of most of it, was only a tenth of that rate.

By 1840 a striking correlation had appeared in the Gulf Plains province between rich soil, slave concentration, and Indian disappearance (Map 47). The great slave rushes went into the Black Belt of Alabama, the floodplain of the Mississippi, the Red River valley in Louisiana, and the Huntsville region in the bend of the Tennessee. The

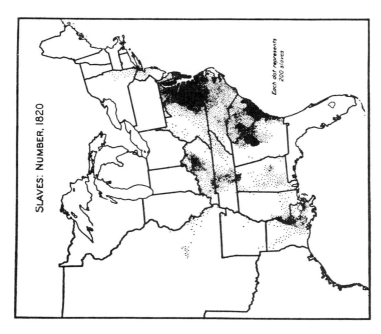

46. Slaves, 1820 (from Gray)

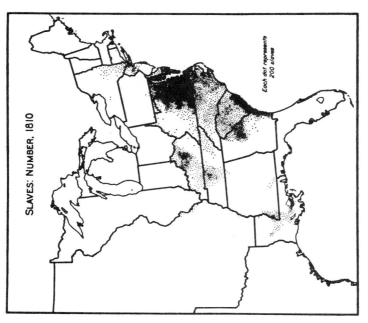

45. Slaves, 1810 (from Gray)

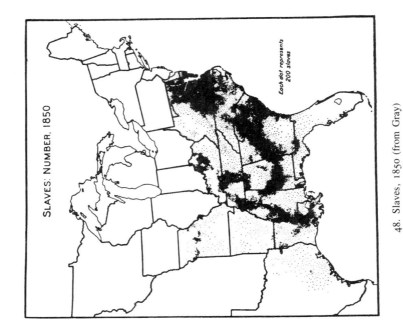

48. Slaves, 1850 (from Gray)

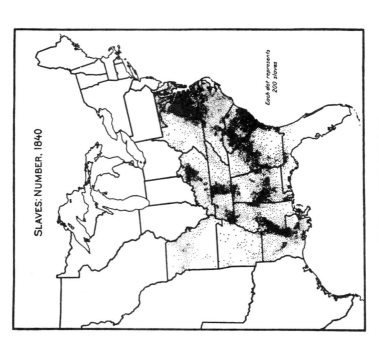

47. Slaves, 1840 (from Gray)

alluvial plain of the Mississippi was not yet fully occupied because the rich Yazoo country, as noted on the population map, was not yet protected by adequate levees.

In 1850 the pattern of slave society in the South is fully revealed (Map 48). Slaves are in occupation of all the rich-soil areas—the Black Belt of Alabama, with its extension into Georgia, the alluvial plain of the Mississippi, with the Red River as a side spur, the Nashville Basin, and, to the north, the Kentucky Blue Grass area. The black belts were now black in a double sense—in their soil and in their labor. They might serve as a soil map of the area. They were the areas of a plantation economy and of plantation capitalism.

Gulf Plains: Economy, Society, and Politics

TWO TROPICAL STAPLES shaped the development of the Gulf Plains province in the period between the War of 1812 and the Civil War. They were cotton and sugar. Cotton, the more valuable of the two, appears for 1811 on the map in terms of dots, each representing 1000 bales. The centers of the crop are on the Atlantic seaboard, in South Carolina and Georgia (Map 49). In the lower Mississippi floodplain the growth was slight—a little in Louisiana and in Tennessee, where Andrew Jackson was a planter. By 1821 cotton planters had arrived in Alabama. They had come from Tennessee and the seaboard. Some production occurred in the lower Mississippi floodplain.

In 1839 the great development was in the lower Mississippi floodplain (Map 50). Each heavy dot means 10,000 bales. The Alabama Black Belt had begun to take form. A big development was in northern Alabama in the Huntsville bend of the Tennessee River. The result of this expansion was a flooding of the world market with cotton, and a decline in the price to the ruinous level of 10 cents a pound or less. In the early years of the decade many South Carolina planters were going bankrupt. The Nullification crisis was a protest against a high protective tariff which increased costs of planters already suffering from low prices.

In 1849 the Alabama Black Belt stands fully revealed (Map 51)—also the Mississippi floodplain, except for the Yazoo area, which was subject to flooding. Cotton production in these newer areas equaled that of the Old South.

In 1859 the Alabama Black Belt and the Mississippi floodplain, except for the Yazoo region, were congested with cotton production (Map 52). The Gulf region was overwhelming in its productive power, while South Carolina was fading out. The Gulf states were shipping huge cotton surpluses to England for manufacture. A connection had been established with the British textile industry, which the South relied on in case of war over the slavery issue, and which the North correspondingly dreaded.

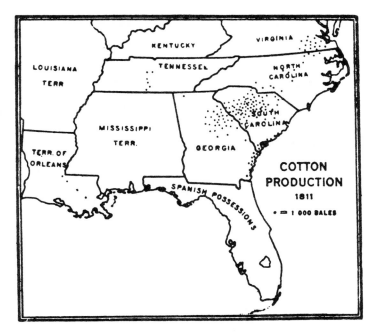

49. Cotton Crop, 1811 (from Gray)

Sugar, another major crop, was second in value only to cotton. It was produced chiefly in southern Louisiana. It grows best where the soil is a fertile silt or alluvium, where the climate affords a maximum period for maturing, free of frost, and where ditching for irrigation or drainage can be cheaply done. That combination was found in southern Louisiana. Good sugar land is also good cotton land and often a planter raised cotton until he had accumulated sufficient capital to turn to sugar, which needed much capital, but was also more profitable. The labor force required for sugar per acre was larger than for cotton and the slave population had risen by 1860 to 60 percent of the population in the sugar country.

The forces contributing to the success of cotton and sugar agriculture in the Gulf Plains were more than fertility of the land and abundance of cheap labor. They were the acquisition of superior varieties of plants from foreign lands. In the case of cotton, a superior variety was found in the West Indies in the colonial period, the Sea Island type. It had a long fiber and could be spun into a strong thread. The fiber was silky and cloth made of it had a satiny appearance. The seed was a large glossy black variety which was only loosely attached to the fiber and was easily separated out. It was fed into a roller resembling an old-fashioned clothes wringer. The fiber easily passed through; the seed fell off behind. This variety of cotton required, however, a Sea Island climate. It could not be grown in an inland climate and its range was limited to the islands off the coast of the Carolinas and Georgia.

In 1734 a short-staple variety was found in the West Indies that would grow in an inland climate. Its fiber was short and its seed was fuzzy, which made it stick to the fiber like a burr. A day's labor was required to clean out a few pounds. Also, it was subject to the fatal cotton rot. It was grown inland, but only for family use.

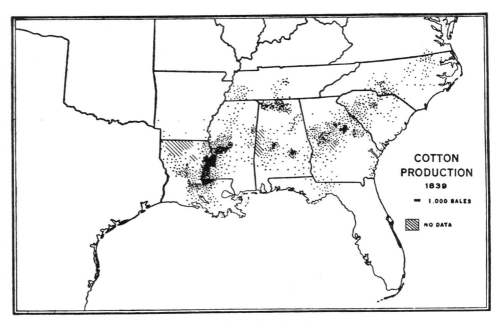

50. Cotton Crop, 1839 (from Gray)

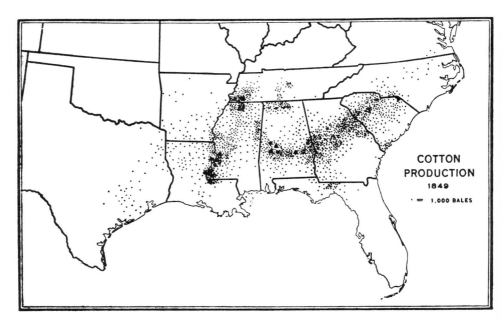

51. Cotton Crop, 1849 (from Gray)

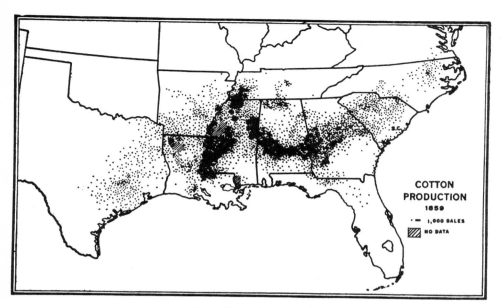

52. Cotton Crop, 1859 (from Gray)

In 1791 Eli Whitney invented the cotton gin, which separated seed efficiently from any variety of cotton. Turned by hand, it cleaned as much as 50 slaves could. Harnessed to steam, it cleaned 1000 pounds a day. It opened the uplands of the Gulf to cotton production.

In 1805 a new upland variety reached the seaboard states from Mexico and was known as Mexican upland. Greatly superior to the old upland, its fiber was almost as long as that of Sea Island cotton and produced a thread nearly as strong. It had another virtue. Its pods opened up widely and generously, so that a quicker and cleaner picking job was possible. Also, it was resistant to the cotton rot. It was improved by a Natchez planter between 1805 and 1810, and thereafter was steadily developed by breeding in the plantations of that area, which became a great seed producer. Within a few decades Mexican upland became the only variety grown in the inland South, and nearly all the cotton produced there is now of this type. The best varieties have a fiber almost an inch long. From an economic point of view, the introduction of this hybrid was as important to the South as the invention of the cotton gin.

Other factors responsible for the swift spread of the cotton plant across the Gulf Plains were two inventions emanating from the English textile industry near the end of the 18th century. One was a device by which the spinning of fiber into thread was revolutionized, the achievement of Samuel Crompton and Richard Arkwright. The other was an invention of Edmund Cartwright by which the weaving of cloth was refashioned. As a result of these improvements, the cost of manufacturing cotton textiles was enormously reduced. These textiles became the articles of cheap wear for the masses throughout the world, largely displacing woolens. An almost unlimited market was opened for the raw cotton of the South.

A like advance transformed the growing of sugarcane. In 1796 a strain that would mature in the limited growing season of Louisiana arrived from Santo Domingo along with the refugees from the Negro uprising on the island. In 1817 another important advance occurred with the appearance of Batavian ''striped'' or ''ribbon'' cane, which had a built-in protection against cold weather in the form of a thick bark. To such improvements was added tariff protection in the legislation of 1816 and later, which offset the costs of draining large plantations, purchasing more slaves, and erecting mills for converting cane into raw sugar. By such improvements 95 percent of all the sugar produced in the United States was grown in Louisiana, and the quantity of molasses—a side product of sugar making—was correspondingly high. By 1860 the Gulf Plains province had become the cotton kingdom of the world and an important sugar and molasses reliance of the nation.

A conspicuous feature of the cotton and sugar economy of the Gulf Plains was the large scale of its plantations. The census of 1860, in its agricultural statistics, illustrated this phenomenon. In the Black Belt county of Dallas, Alabama, which specialized in cotton production, the average acreage of all farm holdings, large and small, was 770 acres. By contrast the average acreage of all holdings in a typical northern Alabama county, such as Blount, was 94 acres.

The building of big plantations was a process differing from region to region and from period to period. It began with the sale of worn-out eastern plantations and the transportation of their personnel and equipment to the West. In the 1830's picturesque caravans were crowding the roads from South Carolina and Georgia to the Gulf Plains. An example is the migration of the James Lides family to the Black Belt of Alabama from Springville in South Carolina late in the autumn of 1835. A large force of field Negroes went out ahead, in charge of an overseer, to prepare a house for the master and family and to begin clearing the land for the spring planting. The master and family took up their journey later, traveling by horseback and coach, accompanied by plantation carts carrying household goods and servants. They took an established route across western Georgia where the larger rivers were spanned by bridges. The smaller streams were at low stage and could be forded. At night the party camped in tents. The road ran through Creek country, which was considered not altogether safe, but the Indians proved more friendly than anticipated. The destination of the party, Pleasant Hill, in the Black Belt not far from the Alabama River, was reached near the end of the year, and charmed the travelers. Plantations thus established were enlarged later by consolidations. A planter of unusual energy and ability, who was making big profits in cotton, would buy out less successful neighbors and consolidate the whole. An acceleration in this process occurred in the late thirties and early forties, as an outcome of the great depression that hit cotton planters after the Panic of 1837. Cotton prices fell to a level of 5 or 6 cents a pound, staying there throughout the early forties. At such prices only big, efficient plantations were able to survive because of their large-scale economies.

The economies resulting from large-scale agriculture were of various sorts. Labor was reduced to routine operations, the kind best performed by slaves. Big plantations were virtually factories in the field and they gained all the advantages of subdivision of labor. They had, also, better discipline than did the small plantations because of the less personal relations of master to slave, which meant better order, more effective cultivation, and greater profits. Large plantations had advantages, also, in the purchasing of supplies and the marketing of crops, and in their reserves of virgin land that could be held for such time as old fields were worn out.

In the Louisiana sugar region the scale of operations was even larger. In 14 parishes in 1860, given over principally to sugar production, there were then 1618 plantations ranging in size from 100 acres to more than 1000. Of these, 115 ranged from 100 acres to 499; 364 from 500 acres to 999; and 139 ran over 1000 acres. The scale of operations on a successful plantation was of capitalistic proportions. Each stage in sugar production required a major investment. The acreage had to be extensive and suitable in soil, location, and slope for cane growing. It had to include reserves of agricultural land to expand over, and wood lots to fuel furnaces for boiling cane juice in kettles, until it was converted from syrup to raw sugar. The work force had to be especially large, to grow the cane and man the machinery for grinding it, as well as to attend the process of reducing it from juice to sugar and molasses—all in the limited number of days that nature allowed. The capital invested in a big sugar plantation, and in its grinding mill and sugar houses, amounted to a million or more dollars.

In the states of the lower South the raising of stock for food and for traction was a major industry. Stock found sustenance on the open range, on the grasses and pea-vine pastures. In central Mississippi and in north central Alabama they grazed on the plateaus, ridges, and valleys. They also found forage in the parishes of southwestern Louisiana and in the tidal marshes adjoining the Gulf.

In all these areas swine had forage and were fattened on corn, where that was possible. Sheep were raised likewise, though primarily for wool, as mutton was not savored in the South. The census of 1860 showed 1,500,000 head of cattle in Alabama and Mississippi; in adjacent Georgia nearly that total was found, and in Louisiana, 516,000 head. Cattle production was everywhere a meat industry—milk and butter were minor by-products. Of swine there were over 5 million in Alabama, Mississippi, Arkansas, and Louisiana. A total of 9,732,000 was raised in the lower South, which was nearly half the entire southern production and nearly a third that of the United States.

Meat imports were relied on by the planters in the lower South as well. These originated in the upper South and came by way of the Mississippi. Also, from the vast prairies of Texas came herds of cattle on the hoof. Years before the famous "long drives" of cattle to the North from Texas, herds were sent to the cotton and sugar regions.

Even on cotton and sugar plantations corn and meat were produced in quantity when the prices of staples fell to low levels. Planters then turned a larger part of their acreage to corn for cattle and swine. When cotton and sugar prices were high more purchases of meat occurred and less was raised. The same practices prevailed with regard to animals for traction—horses and mules. But a large majority of the planters in the lower South bought all or nearly all the meat their work force consumed in the periods when their staples brought high prices.

Socially the society of the Gulf Plains was highly stratified. Its top layer was the cotton and sugar planter class, constituting the "establishment" of the province, and occupying the richest soils. A second layer was the yeoman farmers, who occupied land good for farming, but not exceptionally rich or adapted to large-scale production. Such farmers raised corn and marketed hogs, and sometimes a little cotton. They often owned a few slaves, beside whom they worked in the fields. A third class was the poor whites, who were found in portions of eastern Mississippi, northern Alabama and Georgia, and in the coastal swamps of the Gulf region. They lived in degrading poverty, a debilitated and defeated class, ignorant and superstitious, quick to engage in brutal brawls, and prone to drunkenness and low sexual standards.

In southern Louisiana lay a small farming class of Creoles and Acadians. The latter, known as Cajuns, were descendants of Nova Scotian French, who during the Seven Years' War refused to swear allegiance to the British Crown, were rounded up, and deported to the American colonies, to the West Indies, and to Louisiana. In Louisiana they cultivated narrow holdings lining streams in the French colonial pattern, and some of them became growers of sugar on a small scale. Easygoing and unenterprising, they or their children ultimately sold their fertile plots to the Anglo-Saxons crowding in on them. They were content thereafter to lead a relaxed life of fishing, hunting, and growing corn for livestock.

The artisan class was essential to the society of the Gulf Plains. The engineers, carpenters, coopers, blacksmiths, wheelwrights, and mill hands kept the economy functioning smoothly. They were by no means all city residents. They were found wherever planters needed craftsmen. Not all of them were whites. Many were free Negroes or even slaves let out, in some cases, for hire. On sugar plantations, where skilled craftsmen were an essential part of the work force, trained slaves were a normal constituent of it. Common labor was likely to be left to the Irish to perform. The Irish were numerous on routes of transportation, on levees, as roustabouts on steamboats, or laborers on railroads. On sugar plantations they were employed as ditch diggers. Planters were reluctant to risk the health of valuable slaves in employment injurious to health.

At the bottom of the scale was the great mass of the slaves, increasing in the Gulf states in number more rapidly than in any other slave states. Between 1840 and 1860 the slave rate of increase in Mississippi was 62 percent, in Alabama 71 percent, in Louisiana 94 percent. By way of contrast the rate of increase in Kentucky and in South Carolina was 23 percent, and in Virginia 9 percent.

This stratification of society was reflected in the politics of the region. The cotton and sugar planters were political conservatives. They were Whigs in outlook when that party was formed. On such economic issues as banking and currency, and internal improvement, they accepted the leadership of Henry Clay. On the tariff issue the sugar planters favored protection at a high level, at least on sugar and molasses. They wanted protection against Cuban imports.

On the slavery issue the planters were, on the whole, satisfied with Clay's leadership. They were compromisers with regard to slavery and its extension, as exhibited in the issues of the annexation of Texas and the Mexican War. They wished to remain in harmony with the northern wing of the party, realizing that in a violent clash over slavery large property owners in the South would have the most to lose. They led in the effort to keep Louisiana from seceding in 1860–61.

The fact that the planter class in the rich-soil areas was normally attached to the Whig party was a commonplace of southern politics. The saying was: "Wherever you have black soil you have black labor; wherever you have black labor you have white cotton; wherever you have white cotton you have Whigs''—a kind of house that Jack built. According to the southern press, in 1850 Whigs were the owners of three-fourths of the slaves in the South.

The yeoman whites and the poor whites voted Democratic. They were believers in the economic ideas of the Jacksonian wing of the party. But on the slavery issue they were adherents of the Calhoun wing of the party. The poor whites were the most extreme and aggressive of any of the classes of southern society in their proslavery attitude. They wanted the Negro to be kept in slavery as a matter of their own sense of racial superiority. Their level of economic and social life was as low as that of the slaves, in some cases lower. The one badge of superiority over the Negro they could wear was that they were free and the Negro was in bondage. They were determined to keep that differentiation. Also they had a strong dislike for and contempt for the Negro, a feeling that the Negro returned. The Democratic party was thus a union of conflicting, often incompatible, ideas.

The differences in attitude of the classes of southern society were reflected in the presidential elections of 1840, 1844, and 1848. In this series of maps the Whig vote is in white, the Democratic in checkrows. In the election of 1840, shown on map 24 (page 123), the Whig candidate was General William H. Harrison; the Democratic was Martin Van Buren, the incumbent President. The Whig vote was everywhere large, the outcome of the Panic of 1837, which brought the Van Buren administration into discredit. The vote in the alluvial plain of the Mississippi was overwhelmingly Whig. So was that of the rich valley of the lower Arkansas, and of the Alabama Black Belt with its extension into Georgia. In Louisiana the Whig vote reflected the demand of sugar planters for tariff protection on sugar and molasses. The Democratic areas were in the uplands of eastern Mississippi, in northern Alabama and Georgia, and in the "cracker" area of south central Georgia.

The presidential election of 1844 is shown on map 25 (page 124). The Whig ticket was headed by Henry Clay, and the Democratic by James K. Polk. This is the election that turned on the issue of the annexation of Texas—on expansion of slavery. Clay took an evasive stand on this issue. Polk, on the other hand, came out aggressively for the annexation of Texas. The Whig areas—the areas of moderate views on annexation—were those of the great plantations and of slave concentration—the Black Belt and the alluvial plain. Even though many planters desired Texas they did not want it at the cost of collision with the North. Plantation Whigs in the South, on the Texas issue, voted with New England and western New York.

The Democratic vote lay in the hill region of eastern Mississippi, northern Alabama, and northern Georgia, the areas of the small farmers of the Gulf Plains. They were more aggressive on issues involving the expansion of slavery than the big planters. They were ambitious to be planters themselves and voted for Polk, who was pledged to acquire Texas, where land could be cheaply obtained.

In the 1848 election the pattern of voting was repeated (Map 53). The Mexican War had been fought and a vast cession of territory had been acquired from Mexico by the Treaty of Guadalupe Hidalgo. The Whig candidate was General Zachary Taylor, a war hero and a Louisiana planter, but a moderate on the issue of slavery expansion. The Democratic candidate was Lewis Cass, who represented expansionist extremism. The vote in the Gulf Plains followed the earlier pattern. The areas of rich soils, of slave concentration, and of plantation economy reflected moderation on the

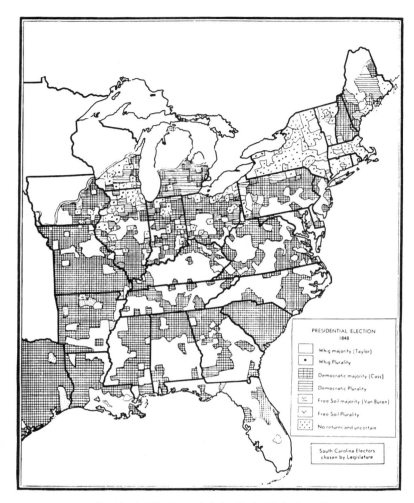

53. Presidential Election, 1848 (by Frederick Jackson Turner)

issues arising out of expansionism. The hill regions supported the doctrines of Manifest Destiny. By 1848 Florida had come into the Union. The Whig areas in northern Florida were cotton areas. The Tallahassee region was a rich area of Sea Island cotton.

A variety of forces thus shaped the destiny of the Gulf Plains province. Some were age-old—those fixing the character of soils and of transportation systems. Others were man-made—the expulsion of the Indians and the supplanting of them by white and black migrants. Still others were the migration and improvement of crop specialties; the creation on this basis of economic and social stratifications; and eventually the transformation of them into political divergencies. The final process was the sectional unification of the South on the issue of slavery, and the resultant series of clashes with the North, which rent the Union.

The Slavery Issue and the Unification of the South

THE PROBLEM OF NEGRO SLAVERY had troubled the conscience of the American public in the era of the Declaration of Independence. The Declaration attributed responsibility for its existence in the colonies to the policy of the British government. During the War for Independence northern and southern leaders alike expressed their objection to it. In the generation following the war, full emancipation or gradual emancipation measures were passed in all the northern states, but none was adopted in the southern states, though a bill was debated in Virginia as late as 1830.

The obstacles to emancipation were formidable in the South, because of the large number of slaves there. In South Carolina, for example, slaves almost equaled the free population. An uncompensated emancipation would have meant an enormous financial sacrifice. It would have wiped out a large part of accumulated capital. Great hazards of other kinds were also present. If emancipation were to be gradual, only a portion of the blacks would be free at the start, and their presence was likely to seduce those still in bondage. The fear of a slave insurrection hung over southern white society like a nightmare. There were, indeed, several minor uprisings that were suppressed. Another hindrance to gradual emancipation was the likelihood that unscrupulous planters would unload, under this guise, their sick and aged slaves on the public.

But the most serious of the obstacles to gradual emancipation in the South was the race problem. Blacks were acceptable as a race while they were in a state of slavery. But most whites felt it unendurable to have among them free blacks with equal social and, perhaps, political rights.

A type of legislation common in the slave states reflected this attitude toward gradual emancipation. It provided that any person emancipating his slaves must see to it that they were removed from the state. Residence restrictions against Negroes existed in some northern states. In Illinois, for example, the entrance of free Negroes for the purpose of establishing residence was forbidden by law. Such legislation was considered even in Massachusetts. In northern cities Negroes were considered a charity problem and, also, a crime problem.

The weight of race feeling as an obstacle to gradual emancipation in the South is indicated by southern leaders who deplored slavery. Thomas Jefferson observed, at the time of the Missouri crisis of 1820:

> There is not a man on earth who would sacrifice more than I would to relieve us from this heavy reproach [slavery]. . . . The cession of that kind of property, for so it is misnamed, is a bagatelle which would not cost me a second thought, if in that way a general emancipation and *expatriation* could be effected. . . . But, as it is, we have the wolf by the ears, and we can neither hold him, nor safely let him go. Justice is in one scale, and self-preservation in the other.

James Madison remarked near the close of his life that if he had the power to work a miracle, there was just one he would like to perform: turn all Negroes white. Then the slavery question would be solved in a day.

Like testimony was given by Abraham Lincoln during the Civil War in answering a proposal by free Negroes for expatriation to Africa. In expressing his approval he observed: "You and we are different races. We have between us a broader difference than exists between almost any other two races. Your race suffer very greatly, many of them, by living among us, while ours suffer from your presence."

One early plan for dealing with the problem was the expatriation of Negroes as soon as they were freed. The American Colonization Society was organized for that purpose in 1816. It was primarily a southern project, widely supported by southern leaders. The Liberia area of the west coast of Africa was acquired to that end and some cargoes of Negroes were sent there. But after fifteen years of effort and the expenditure of $800,000, the Society succeeded in expatriating only as many Negroes as the number of slave babies born in the South in four months. The project failed. Steam-powered ocean transport was not yet available. Also, the Negroes, taken to Africa, found readjustment there difficult, and came near to dying of starvation.

In the meantime slave labor became increasingly useful to the South. The discovery that varieties of upland cotton could be profitably produced in the Gulf Plains, the widening of the world market for cotton following the textile inventions of Crompton and Arkwright, and the removal of the Creek from the Gulf Plains in the wake of Jackson's triumph over them at Horseshoe Bend—all contributed to this result.

For slave labor cotton was the ideal crop. It offered a succession of routine jobs to which slaves could be set: planting, chopping, cultivating, picking, and baling. Also, slave labor in a cotton field could be well supervised. Upland cotton grows only knee high, and an overseer on a horse could overlook a gang of slaves and see to it that every member of it kept steadily at the job. In a cornfield supervision was less easy. A shirker could hide and go to sleep.

As a result of such factors, slavery took on new vitality in the South's economic structure and way of life. The attitude toward it was transformed. At the time of the American Revolution the institution was deemed by most southern leaders an unmitigated curse. By 1820 it was apologized for as an evil to be alleviated by spreading it out thin over the West. This was Henry Clay's position in the debate on the Missouri question. By 1837 Calhoun and other southern writers were defending slavery as a positive good. By the 1850's southern clergymen were eulogizing slavery as a divine institution, sanctioned by the Bible and approved by God. The prospect of dislodging it by gradual emancipation vanished.

The first serious sectional clash over slavery occurred in 1819, when Missouri applied to Congress for admission to the Union as a state. Slavery was then still common in the North. In 1819 there were 10,088 slaves in New York, 7557 in New Jersey, 211 in Pennsylvania, and some even in New England.

A factor in the debate on the admission of Missouri was the control of Congress. The North dominated the lower house because of its large population. In the Senate the North and the South were balanced, each with 22 votes. If Missouri were to be admitted as a slave state this balance would be upset—the South would hold control. As a preventive measure James Tallmadge of New York proposed two restrictions on the admission of Missouri to the Union, which would have had the effect of ultimately converting Missouri into a free state. One was that no further slaves be admitted into Missouri. The other was that children born to slaves already in Missouri should become free at the age of 25. These proposals produced a congressional crisis. They raised the basic issue of whether Congress has the right, under the Constitution, to impose any political restrictions on a state when admitting it to the Union.

In the debate William Pinkney, an eminent constitutional lawyer, advanced the doctrine that became definitive. He maintained, as earlier noted here, that to impose a political restriction on a state as a condition of admission would render it less than equal to the older states, and would be unconstitutional. Since older states had the right to maintain slavery, a restricted Missouri would be less than equal to them. If Congress were to approve the Tallmadge amendment Missouri could ignore the restriction, once in the Union. That thesis seemed to Congress conclusive.

As a solution to the problem, Congress adopted a political compromise. Missouri was given statehood without restriction; the remainder of the Louisiana Purchase north of the line of 36° 30' was closed forever to slavery; and Maine was admitted as a free state. An issue later raised was whether a territory could be closed to slavery by Congress. But at least the dangerous crisis over the Missouri issue was peacefully ended.

The larger issue of slavery had two aspects which divided the North from the South. They were economic and moral. The economic question was whether slavery was a profitable form of labor. This issue had far-reaching implications. If slavery was a profitable form of labor it was likely to be maintained in the South. It could, in that case, be extirpated only by outside pressure. If, on the other hand, it was unprofitable, it was likely to disintegrate of its own self, and the Civil War might have been unnecessary.

This complex issue has continued to divide American historians. One school was led in the early 1930's by a prominent southern historian, Ulrich B. Phillips. He believed that slavery was an inefficient and unprofitable form of labor and that it would have collapsed of its own weight if it could have been kept out of the hands of northern abolitionists and politicians.

Phillips contended that Negroes were, by and large, ineffective workmen, that they were naturally unenergetic and irresponsible. If they had been of the white race slavery might conceivably have been profitable. Also, in slave labor the great incentive of self-interest, which made free labor successful, was lacking. Because of these defects the costs of slave labor, direct and indirect, were too high to permit a profit.

Of direct costs, the first, if the slave was purchased, was the price. This was swiftly rising in the second quarter of the 19th century. In 1790 it was about $300 for a prime field hand; in 1840, $1000; in 1850, about $1500. This price rise was the result of the great demand for slaves created by the opening of the Gulf Plains. In the case of a slave reared on the plantation, the first direct cost was his maintenance in childhood. The second, whether the slave was purchased or reared, was his keep and that of his family during working years and during illness and old age; the third was interest on the capital the slave represented; the fourth was the risk of permanent incapacity or premature death, which in financial terms would be insurance against these risks. If all these direct costs were added, their total, according to the Phillips school, was larger than the total production of the slave during his lifetime.

A number of indirect costs, according to Phillips, heightened the expensiveness of slave labor. He believed that only a single type of farming could be taught to the slave. The consequence was that a one-crop system was imposed on the planter, whether in the cotton, sugar, or tobacco area. This was especially damaging to the planter of cotton. That staple had to be continuously raised even when its price had fallen below the cost of production. A further indirect cost attributed to slave labor was the impoverishment of the soil, since that was an inevitable consequence of a single-crop system.

Related to all these items of cost was the price at which the staple products of slave labor were sold. To be sure, this was not determined by the kind of labor used, but by world conditions. Still, the price commanded by cotton, sugar, and tobacco in Liverpool profoundly affected the profit of the planter. The average annual price of cotton in Liverpool steadily declined in the first half of the 19th century. In 1800 it was 40 cents a pound; in 1830, 10 cents; in 1845, 5½ to 6 cents. The conclusion of this school was that for these reasons slavery was an unprofitable form of labor.

This judgment was challenged by a later school, led by Lewis C. Gray, an eminent economist in the Department of Agriculture. His view was that slaves of the Negro race could be made into efficient workmen, the equal of whites as field hands under adequate supervision. They could become highly skillful in performing such jobs as cotton planting and cotton picking. They were also trained to be skillful mechanics. Such Negroes as were irresponsible or lazy could be effectively kept in line by proper supervision and discipline, and were so managed on the larger, well-managed plantations. The incentive of self-interest could be kept alive for slaves by the ordinary promises and rewards of the plantation system. Slaves not only were satisfied by the rewards of the system but took pride in their master's prosperity. The production of a slave over a lifetime amounted to more than his direct costs. If all the direct costs were taken into account, and against these were reckoned the lifetime production of a slave, a substantial profit remained for the planter, provided the plantation soil was reasonably fertile. Slave upkeep amounted to little, since their living standards were very low. Also, the whole slave family—men, women, and children—could be employed in field work. This employability of slave families was in contrast with that of free families. Southern white women did not work in the fields. Southern social convention forbade it. As for the rising price of slaves and the declining price of cotton, these items were offset by improvements in plantation management and in methods of farming in the Gulf Plains, improvements which enormously increased slave productivity. In some periods, according to this school, the price of slaves was too high to permit profit, but this had always been a temporary phenomenon which had corrected itself.

Gray held that the profitableness of slave labor on good land was demonstrated by the fact that in the 1830's owners of well-run plantations in the Gulf Plains often made profits of 35 percent a year on their investment. Another very lucrative period for the Gulf Plains was the early 1850's. In South Carolina, on the other hand, bankruptcy was common among planters in the period of the 1820's, the 1830's, and 1840's. But that was the result, not of slave labor, but of worn-out soil, which could not compete with the virgin and cheap land of the Gulf Plains. In the North, in this same period, worn-out farms in New England and New York were similarly unable to compete with the fresh lands of the prairie province.

The linking of slavery to one-crop farming and its costs was also challenged by Gray. One-crop farming also prevailed in the northern free-labor system, and soil impoverishment was common in both sections, the result of a combination of forces unrelated to slavery—the insufficient attention to the seriousness of the problem, unwillingness to pay the costs of soil conservation, and the constant opening of new, virgin lands in the West, which discouraged efforts to preserve soil fertility.

According to the Gray school, slavery on rich land was not merely profitable but more so than free labor. The evidence for this was that on the rich land of the Gulf Plains, it was displacing free labor. Gray admitted that on marginal land slavery was unprofitable, as well as on small plantations, which did not have the superior organization and efficiency of the great plantations. Small plantations were likely to have the run-down appearance described by Frederick L. Olmsted in his reports of his travels in the South.

A totally different question is whether, from the point of view of the South as a whole, slavery was profitable. Here the verdict of scholars is virtually unanimous that slavery was a disadvantageous form of labor. One of its evils was that it tied up the capital of southern society in labor, to the neglect of other investment opportunities. Manufacturing languished; so did transportation improvement—the building of railroads especially. The great benefits of easy access to market were lost. The lack of railroads was attributed by some writers to the superior profitability of commercial agriculture. But in the North commercial agriculture and railroad construction went forward together. Nearly all parts of the South suffered from lack of improved transportation, but areas at a distance from water routes particularly languished. Without the great incentive of easy access to market for surpluses, they maintained an agriculture that was self-sufficing, easygoing, and careless.

Slavery was also responsible for the southern shortage of labor, which was chronic despite the great increase in the number of slaves. Foreign immigrants coming in large numbers to the United States were reluctant to go to the South, preferring to settle where they would not be in competition with slave labor.

Another liability of the slave system was its inelasticity—the difficulty faced by a planter in transferring such labor, along with his own household and farm equipment, from worn-out lands to the virgin soils of the Southwest. A more flexible form of migration of slaves was by way of the domestic slave trade, in which field hands were sold by seaboard and border-state planters to traders who then sold them to planters in the Gulf Plains. Sales of slaves to strangers was, however, frowned upon by many planters, and this was another illustration of the inelasticity of the system.

In the North the owners of worn-out fields had a wider choice than in the South. They transferred in New England and in New York from wheat to sheep when the competition of the prairies became overpowering, or they sold their lands and moved to the cities or to the West.

Finally, slavery was disastrous to the poor-white farmers and to the artisan class in the South. Its harm to these classes is graphically described by Hinton R. Helper in his book *The Impending Crisis*.

One of the most significant effects of slavery in the South was the unification of its sections, which occurred between 1820 and 1860. The initial joining was of the two seaboard sections—the tidewater and the Piedmont—after slavery had expanded from the one section into and across the other. The two were then able to compose the quarrels that had divided them since the colonial period. They adjusted their differences in conventions meeting in the 1830's and as late as the 1850's. They made peace especially on the controversial issue of the apportionment of representation in the state legislatures. The peace usually consisted of agreement on two principles: periodic reapportionment, and reapportionment that took into account both population and property values. Other agreements were reached by concessions that were usually victories for the Piedmont. They included liberalization of the suffrage, greater state support for internal improvements by using state credit, more support of public education, and a judiciary more responsible to the will of the people.

Most of the southern seaboard states worked out agreements of this kind, reflecting a greater willingness on the part of the tidewater to trust the Piedmont once slavery had crossed the Piedmont. But one among them, South Carolina, made no adjustments of this sort. In that state, as a result of the influence of Calhoun, the old order was retained virtually unchanged.

A similar unification was achieved between the southern watershed of the Ohio and the Gulf Plains. It was a product principally of trade passing up and down the Ohio and the Mississippi, in which food and farm stock moved south and sugar and molasses moved north. Another unification was that of the southern Atlantic seaboard and the Gulf Plains states. This was effected in part, as in the earlier history of the tidewater and Piedmont, by the movement of planters with slaves from the one province to the other; in part, by the rise in the Gulf states of a new plantation society that recruited its work force largely from the domestic slave trade, while tied to the older South in its economic, social, and legal institutions.

Among the forces uniting the southern sections, improvements in transportation were important, especially the building of such railroads as could be financed, and the harnessing of steam to river navigation. Another powerful force for unification was the bitter abolitionist assault on the slavery system, which drew Southerners together in self-defense.

A predilection to turn southern unification against the North became established at the same time. Propaganda was spread to prove that the South was being exploited in its economy by the North. The alleged exploitation seemed especially manifest in the raising and marketing of southern agricultural staples. The planter normally relied on borrowed capital since his own was likely to be tied up in his plantation and slaves and in expanding his acreage. He had no surplus to rely on while the crop was growing.

Financing of the production and marketing of cotton was done by an intermediary known as a "cotton factor," living in an export center such as New Orleans or Mobile. The supplies needed for the growing season were purchased and transported to the plantation by the factor. At harvest time the entire crop would be sent to him for sale. From the proceeds of the sale the factor would deduct his advances, the interest on them, the costs of inspection, other commissions, and his own charges, and remit what remained to the planter.

The merchants in New Orleans or Mobile who purchased cotton were usually agents of a business house in New York, Boston, or Philadelphia. Such a house, in turn, maintained connections with British or continental firms. In this matter cotton exports to England and the Continent were financed. The great British houses were Baring Brothers and the Browns.

The charges by cotton factors were always high, because they might not recover the amounts they had advanced if the price of cotton fell disastrously low, as it did in the late 1830's and early 1840's. The charges and interest rates were, however, regarded by Southerners as excessive and constituting northern exploitation of the South.

Even greater scope for exploitation of the South lay, so Southerners came to believe, in the shipping of cotton to northern manufacturing centers. Such commerce was virtually restricted to northern vessels, since the coastal trade was closed by law to foreigners and the South had little shipping of its own. Almost a third of southern cotton went to northern ports, especially to New England in the 1840's and 1850's. About two-thirds went to Europe, mostly to England, but even this was carried largely by northern vessels, whose freight charges were deemed high.

Of imports from overseas to the South, 70 percent were handled by shippers operating in and out of New York, Boston, or Philadelphia. Propagandists complained that these Northerners exacted enormous freight, insurance, and commission charges. Southerners were taught to believe that they were being exploited by Northerners in the imports they received as well as in their exports.

The protective tariff laws of the United States seemed to most Southerners yet another form of northern exploitation. The tariff forced southern planters to pay higher prices for the manufactures they needed than if foreign goods had been admitted free or under a low tariff.

Southern propagandists argued that in these ways the North kept the South in a state of economic vassalage, in a colonial relationship. The North was bleeding the South into a state of exhaustion. According to Robert Y. Hayne, Calhoun's South Carolina colleague in the Senate, the North gathered from the South, in the marketing of the cotton crop, 10 to 15 percent of the entire value of the crop.

Southern agitators began to demand emancipation from this economic vassalage. They did so from various forums—the commercial conventions that annually gathered in southern cities, in the press, and in Congress. They kept up the agitation particularly in the 1850's.

The means proposed to achieve emancipation were at first primarily economic. One was the stimulation of southern manufacturing by turning southern capital into textile and other industries. Another was the reduction of northern participation in southern trade, by encouraging greater involvement of the South in its own coastal trade and in commercial ties with the outside world. These goals were to be achieved through improvement of the navigation of the Mississippi by cutting through the bar at its mouth, and by the construction of a canal across the Isthmus of Panama, which would permit direct trade between southern ports and the west coast of South America. Another objective was a reduction of importation of food and farm stock into the South from the Ohio Valley, to be achieved by greater diversification of southern crops.

Diversification of southern crops would require increasing the labor supply, which, in turn, would necessitate reopening the African slave trade. The demand for the resumption of that trade grew in volume markedly in the 1850's. It was voiced at the annual southern commercial conventions and in the press of the Gulf states. A further indication of the pressure for more slave labor was the growing laxity in enforcement of the congressional act of 1808 prohibiting the importation of slaves and a resulting increase in the number of blacks illicitly brought into southern ports from Africa and from Cuba. In 1860 Stephen A. Douglas was reported to have declared that in the preceding year 15,000 Africans had been illicitly brought into the United States, a greater annual total than had ever been imported legally into the South.

The agitation to free the South from northern domination had little tangible result. In the field of manufacturing, some advance was made in the 1850's, but nothing compared with the great progress made in the North. The South was too much handicapped by lack of capital and trained labor. The demand for tariff reductions was almost an anachronism, for the tariffs of 1846 and 1857 were already so low as almost to amount to free trade. Moreover, some southern interests wanted protective tariffs—the Louisiana sugar planters, for instance, and the hemp growers of Kentucky and Missouri.

New York's domination of the southern import and export trade continued, chiefly because of that city's special advantages. New York could import in large quantities because it was the import center for much of the nation. It received goods by the shipload from Europe and distributed them by job lots to the South in coasting vessels. Also, New York enjoyed particularly advantageous freight rates because return cargoes could always be counted on out of that port. At New Orleans, by contrast, return cargoes were uncertain except in the rush season from November to May when cotton was moving to market. The navigation over the bar at the mouth of the Mississippi was not improved until the late 1870's when the jetties were completed, and a canal across the Isthmus was not built until the 20th century. The agitation for reopening the African slave trade was not successful for political reasons, and was regarded even in the South as the proposal of extremists.

The chief result of the southern agitation for economic emancipation from the North was to produce in southern minds the conviction that the South was being gouged, that it was paying tribute to the North. The middleman functions performed by northern cities, to the mutual advantage of both sections, were made to appear to the South as extortions. The South began to believe that the only way to escape economic vassalage was to win political independence.

For the South to feel that it was in a state of economic colonialism—of vassalage to the North—and to resent it was very natural. The same feeling was entertained by the Middle West against the East in that period, and later by the plains states. In a nation where different sections are at different levels of economic maturity such resentment is normal.

What is strange in the case of southern attitudes was that they were turned exclusively against northern cities. Against British shippers engaged in trade with the South there was hardly any feeling at all, though Liverpool and London followed the same practices and made the same charges and profits as New York and Philadelphia.

Thus a momentous chain of developments followed the westward advance of slavery across the South: first a southern sectional unification, then efforts for southern self-sufficiency and economic independence, and finally, when the clash over slavery had reached its climax in 1860 and 1861, political independence.

Internal Commerce
and Internal Improvements

THE WATERWAYS OF NATURE contributed both growth and direction to the life of the sectional societies rising west of the Appalachian Mountains after the War of 1812. They carried off the surpluses of production and brought back the means by which more surpluses could be produced. The widespread tributaries and the main stream of the Mississippi channeled the exchanges southward and northward. The Great Lakes system gave an east-west direction to the exchanges of the societies developing at that latitude.

The craft used for the exports to the South were rafts and flatboats. They were themselves articles of commerce, broken up at their destination and sold for lumber. Their crews, released at New Orleans, made their way home as best they could. Some returned by keelboat. Others walked home through the country of the not too hostile Choctaw and Chickasaw. Sometimes crewmen sailed from New Orleans to Philadelphia, and from there footed it over the mountains. Occasionally an enterprising returnee would purchase a horse and wagon in Philadelphia, load it with dry goods, for which the city was a center, and drive to Pittsburgh, where the dry goods, horse, and wagon were sold.

In 1812 the first steamboat appeared on Mississippi waters, initiating a revolution in upriver commerce. Downriver commerce continued by raft and flatboat. As late as the mid-1840's 4000 flatboats plied the river with a tonnage nearly half that of the 1200 steamboats on these waters.

On the Great Lakes, connection with the seaboard was possible by way of the Mohawk route and the Hudson. But for a heavy commerce this was not feasible because between Lake Erie and the Hudson the water connection was broken. To surmount this obstacle a costly internal improvement was necessary. In one respect the lake route was superior to that of the Mississippi. The lakes were deep and wide, and craft on them could make use of the wind by tacking, which was less possible on rivers.

As the interior matured, reservoirs of surplus became the mainstays of commerce. Those of the decade 1850–60 were, for the most part, agricultural. In the North they were zones of wheat and corn. In the South they were cotton and sugar. Basins of non-agricultural surplus developed also in individual states. In western Pennsylvania and western New York lumber was a principal export. It was also increasing in volume in the northern Great Lakes region, especially in northern Michigan and Wisconsin. Mining created freight for the carriers—coal in southern Ohio and Indiana and lead in the Driftless region of Wisconsin, Illinois, and Iowa. St. Louis was an export center for furs trapped in the Rocky Mountains.

The movement of internal trade flowed largely in reciprocating circles. Food from the Ohio Valley went to the South. In the South it was transmuted into cotton and sugar. Cotton was sent to New England and abroad. In New England it was turned into textiles, which were shipped West. Wheat and meat were delivered from the West to the East. Manufactured goods were carried by coasting vessels to the South; molasses, sugar, and coffee went from New Orleans to the upper Ohio and the upper Mississippi.

Beside these two great circles of internal commerce there was a triangular trade which developed in the 1820's and 1830's. This was a seasonal and partly foreign trade based on the rise and fall of the water level on the Mississippi. In the late summer and early autumn of each year the water level on the Mississippi was always low, especially on the upper river, so low that upper-river navigation almost stopped. Food reserves in New Orleans fell off and prices moved up. Relief was brought by eastern coasting vessels, which had picked up food at seasonal prices in New York, Philadelphia, or Baltimore and carried it to New Orleans for sale at a Yankee profit.

In January, February, and March the water level was high and food came down the river in quantity by flatboat and raft, producing a glut in New Orleans and a sharp drop in prices. This was another opportunity for the Yankee ship captains who had been doing odd jobs of shipping in the Gulf. The food was acquired at bottom prices and carried to the West Indies, where it was exchanged for molasses and sugar, which was carried to the New England seaboard. The molasses was distributed to interior New England as sweetener in place of sugar, or was converted into rum, for which there was always a wide market.

In this triangular trade several sections of the Union found reciprocal profit. The eastern seaboard and the Middle West won a market for surplus food, the lower Mississippi basin gained seasonal regulation in the price of food, and New England, chiefly Boston, received annually 13 to 14 million gallons of molasses. These regulatory functions continued until railroads brought new patterns of food distribution.

Turnpike transportation gave outlets to interior areas not served by water routes. Road building was at its height in the period 1800–40. It was done chiefly by private corporations under state charter and was expected to pay for itself in tolls, though this proved disappointing. A National Road was built by the federal government in the years 1811–18, from Cumberland on the Potomac to Wheeling on the Ohio, and was extended in sections westward, reaching Vandalia, Illinois, in 1852. It attracted an enormous traffic, but its construction and maintenance raised constitutional issues, and it was never completed as a National Road to the Mississippi.

Much of the eastward traffic on such roads consisted of herds of cattle and hogs hoofing it to market. The herds were formed in the West by experienced buyers and sent on drives of 60 days or more to the East in charge of mounted drovers. Feed and rest were provided at noon and again at the end of the day. Overnight stations, including taverns, were available in the 1830's and 1840's on all the principal droving roads. Some of them did a big business, handling as many as 150,000 steers and hogs a year. For the cattle the long drive of two months or more was a grueling experience. Steers were expected to lose 150 to 200 pounds of weight on the march.

The roads on which droving was done were likely to be unpleasant for travelers. They were blocked by incessant droves of cattle and swine, often a thousand head or more, moving to market, and were littered with filth. The National Road in the 1830's had an evil reputation of that kind.

A famous figure in the business was Daniel Drew of New York. He began his career as a drover and rose in it to become a buyer as well. He ingeniously increased the weight of steers by making salt readily available to them at feeding time. This produced thirst, which was slaked just before weighing in. He accumulated sufficient capital to build a cattle yard accommodating 1500 steers in a locality now part of New York City. He later became a director of the Erie Railroad, where he profited from stock watering.

At the yards steers were selectively marketed. Four-year-olds went at once to the block. Three-year-olds were sold to farmers for further corn fattening in areas west of the Hudson in New York and in New Jersey. In Pennsylvania fattening areas lay on the outskirts of Philadelphia, in Chester County; in Virginia they were in the region around Petersburg.

Hogs were marched to market less successfully than steers. Their loss of flesh was greater and the quality of the flesh deteriorated. The long-legged, razorback southern varieties, accustomed to ranging the forests for mast, deteriorated least in droving. Hogs of improved breeds, of short legs and massive body, had to be marketed otherwise. They went to market in barrels as salted or pickled pork.

By 1850 meat packing had become centered in the Old Northwest. Ohio led in corn production and in the marketing of hogs. Cincinnati was the Porkopolis of the West, favored by its strategic location on the Ohio and proximity to the valleys of the Scioto and Miami. It had connection with the South and Northeast by river and canal. It also had convenient access to salt for packing, in neighboring saline springs. By 1860 Illinois had displaced Ohio as the nation's leading corn producer, and Chicago, with outlets to the South, and to the East by canal, lake, and rail, had supplanted Cincinnati as the nation's primary center of meat export.

By the mid-1850's railroads had been built between the upper Mississippi and the eastern seaboard. Northwestern exporters were now able to dispatch cattle cars at least part of the way to the eastern market. This mode of marketing was more humane than droving, though cattle were sent in narrow cars and kept as much as three days without food or water. Public outcry finally induced the railroads to institute a system of detraining cattle at halfway points for water, food, and rest. The chief market for fresh beef was the northeastern states; the best market for packed pork lay in the South. Much of the pork reaching New Orleans was destined for the West Indies or for the northeastern seaboard.

The volume of trade between the interior and the seaboard reached large proportions between the close of the War of 1812 and the opening of the Civil War. It was greater than the entire foreign commerce of the United States. This was a measure of the spectacular growth of the interior provinces in those years and, also, of the maturing of the older sections of the seaboard.

The volume of trade was accompanied by an expansion of its mechanisms and by increased pressure on Congress for tariff legislation. Protection from undue foreign competition was demanded by the farming and extractive industries that were the sources of the trade. The banking practices of the states were made more flexible, and the currency was expanded. Henry Clay devised his "American System" to add to the national self-sufficiency and to reduce dependence on Europe for markets and for manufactures.

The Appalachian Mountain system constituted a massive obstacle to the growth of this internal commerce. It had dominated entrance into, and egress from, the interior throughout the colonial period. As already noted, openings through the ranges, cut by the upper tributaries of streams, had long been in use by Indians in portages to rivers flowing in the opposite direction, and these had been used by traders and explorers. They indicated where internal improvements might be constructed that would permit freight to be moved across the barrier in either direction.

A number of particularly promising sites of this sort existed in the latitudes of the middle Atlantic states. In New York a level valley lay between Lake Erie and the Hudson River. A canal joining this pair of waters would connect the whole chain of the Great Lakes with the ocean. It would be relatively uncomplicated to build, and the water needed for the canal would be provided by the Mohawk River, close at hand. In Pennsylvania streams flowing to Philadelphia could be connected with those flowing into the Ohio, and a junction made with the projected Erie Canal by means of an auxiliary canal from the upper Susquehanna. In Maryland a pairing of eastern and western waters was also feasible. The Potomac, which flows into Chesapeake Bay, runs close, in its upper reaches, to the Monongahela, a tributary of the Ohio.

Some formidable problems had to be overcome, however, in linking waters flowing in opposite directions. In New York the gap between Lake Erie and the Hudson River was of considerable length, and tools of excavation were pre-modern. In Pennsylvania linkage had to be established across successive ranges of mountains. In Maryland, where some of the ranges had been cut by the upper waters of the Potomac, others farther west had not been cut.

In New York, De Witt Clinton, mayor of New York City, led those urging the feasibility of constructing the Erie Canal. For years prior to the War of 1812 he had held before the New York public the vista of a vast interior tributary to the metropolis on the seaboard. The outbreak of the war deferred the project, but after its close the agitation was renewed with increased fervor. A year after the end of the war the plan was approved by the state legislature, and in 1817 construction began. By 1825 the canal had been completed, a distance of 363 miles from Buffalo to Albany. Its costs were financed by state bonds to the amount of about $7 million. It proved an immediate and sensational success, reducing the cost of shipping grain between Buffalo and New York City from $100 to $15 a ton, and travel time from 20 days to 8. The canal paid for itself in tolls in less than nine years. Its income in the first year of operation was approximately a million dollars. It became so crowded with traffic that within ten years it had to be enlarged and deepened.

In Philadelphia entrepreneurs were stirred by this great success to attempt improved connection with the interior. The city and the state were persuaded to undertake the construction of the Pennsylvania Canal and Portage Railway, an extraordinary combination of canal, railroad, and inclined plane, to link Philadelphia with the upper Ohio at Pittsburgh, surmounting the Appalachian barrier. The system was begun the year after the completion of the Erie Canal and was completed in 1834 at a cost of $53 million. It plunged the state government into virtual bankruptcy. It proved a failure as a carrier of traffic. Just prior to the Civil War it was sold to the Pennsylvania Railroad and junked.

In Maryland two enterprises competed to join Baltimore to the West. One was a canal—the Chesapeake and Ohio; the other was a railroad—the Baltimore and Ohio. The canal enterprise had state support; the railroad obtained the backing of the city of Baltimore. The federal government gave a million dollars to the project and President Adams turned the first shovelful of earth. Work on both the canal and the railroad began in 1824. Difficulties were encountered from the outset. The first was a legal contest for control of the narrow Potomac Valley in the interior, which ran on until 1832, when a compromise was reached. Construction difficulties were encountered; then came the panics of 1837 and 1839, and work halted in 1842. The canal was never completed through the mountains, but the railroad crossed them and in 1853 reached Wheeling, which became an important element in the growth of Baltimore.

Boston also aspired to the western trade. In the years 1830–42 the Boston and Albany Railroad was built by Boston capital through the Berkshires to meet the Erie Canal at Albany and thus divert at least part of the canal trade to Boston.

In Charleston, South Carolina, a railroad, to be built to Cincinnati on the Ohio, was planned in the same period. It was approved by Calhoun and was constructed as far northwestward as Hamburg in the state. Progress was halted there, and when it was renewed later its terminus was changed to Memphis, in southwestern Tennessee, a reflection of growing southern sectionalism.

States north of the Ohio also sought to redirect nature's travel courses. Ohio built two canals to open the East and the South to its commerce. One was the Ohio and Erie Canal, which tied the Ohio River at Marietta and Portsmouth to Lake Erie at Cleveland, and eventually to the Pennsylvania Canal and Portage system. The other was the Miami and Erie Canal, which connected the Ohio at Cincinnati with Lake Erie at Toledo. Indiana built the Wabash and Erie Canal connecting the Ohio at Evansville with Lake Erie at Toledo. These waterways were built across country that had been leveled in earlier geologic history by successive invasions of the glaciers, which eased the problem of constructing canals.

In Illinois a canal was built in the years 1836–48, which La Salle would have welcomed for his great voyage down the Mississippi. It was the Illinois and Michigan Canal from Chicago on Lake Michigan to La Salle on the Illinois River. It cut across the wheat region of the Rock River valley and the corn and hog belt of southern Illinois. It also gave access to the timber of northern Wisconsin and northern Michigan, which made lumber available to the West and the South. It is noteworthy, also, that the National Road and its extensions, connecting Maryland with St. Louis, served as a unifier and sustainer of these canals of the Old Northwest.

Railroads accelerated the reordering of the commerce of the Old Northwest. They were at first considered merely links between segments of canals or feeders of canals. Compared with floating carriers they seemed, and were, inefficient. But they underwent a rapid transformation from the horse-drawn to the steam-driven stage and were destined to supplant canals in most inland commerce. By the 1850's railroads were being built in the United States at a cost of about $100 million a year—a prodigious investment for that day. A large part went into construction north of the Ohio. By 1853 Chicago had been reached from New York City and, soon afterward, the Mississippi was reached and crossed. The magnets drawing railroads, as well as canals, were the reservoirs of surplus. The capitalists financing railroad construction recognized that a sufficient number of these must be tapped if the lines were to be prosperous.

These competing internal improvements, taken together, constituted an economic and social revolution. They reversed the plan of nature. The society of the upper Ohio and the upper Mississippi, which nature had linked to New Orleans, was turned increasingly to the East and to New York City. Sectional allegiances were reordered, and this was reflected in the politics of the Union.

A constitutional uncertainty beclouded the issue of federal aid to internal improvements. No express power was given Congress by the framers of the Constitution on that subject. The matter was little discussed as long as the national debt remained to be paid. Occasionally Congress voted aid for road building with a minimum of debate. In the Jefferson administration it authorized, in admitting Ohio to statehood, the setting aside of 5 percent of the proceeds of the sale of public land in that state for the construction of a road that would connect the Potomac and Ohio rivers. As already mentioned, construction began in 1811 and by 1818 the road had reached Wheeling. In 1825 additional construction to Zanesville, Ohio, was approved and thereafter further authorization through Ohio to Indiana and into Illinois. After reaching Vandalia, Illinois, in 1852, the road was extended without federal aid to St. Louis. Grants of land for canal construction were given by the federal government to states of the Northwest, one to Indiana in 1827 to aid in constructing the Wabash and Erie Canal and, on the same day, another to Illinois for the Illinois and Michigan Canal.

The successors of Jefferson remained skeptical as to the power of Congress in the matter of federal aid to internal improvements. Madison, who had been a member of the constitutional convention, believed no power had been conferred on Congress to give such aid. One of his last official acts was to veto, on constitutional grounds, a congressional measure which would have provided funds for the construction of roads, canals, and improvements of navigation on watercourses.

Monroe held like views. In his first annual message to Congress he confessed he faced a dilemma. He recognized that great advantages would flow from easy intercourse between the states, which roads and canals would afford. "Never did a country of such vast extent offer equal inducements to improvements of this kind, nor ever were consequences of such magnitude involved in them." The consequences he shrank from were violations of the Constitution. To the disappointment of those favoring federal aid to internal improvements, he denied that the Constitution conferred an express power of that kind, and recommended an amendment to the Constitution conferring such a power. The recommendation was not favorably received. Two members of Monroe's cabinet—John Quincy Adams, Secretary of State, and John C. Calhoun, Secretary of War, believed Congress already had the power. Adams was a firm believer in federal aid to internal improvements, and Calhoun, in the preceding

Congress, had obtained passage of a bill directing that the bonus from the Second National Bank, together with all future dividends from it, be paid into a fund for internal improvements—the very bill Madison had vetoed. Henry Clay, the Speaker of the House, went so far as to publicly express disgust with Monroe's ambivalent views on the issue. In 1818 William Lowndes of South Carolina brought resolutions into the House to the effect that Congress had the power to finance construction of roads, canals, and improvements in watercourses. But the House, by narrow margins, voted all of them down.

In January 1824, William Archer of Virginia offered a bill in the House authorizing surveys of whatever roads and canals the President deemed of importance for commercial, military, or postal purposes. He intended the surveys to become the basis for a program of internal improvements. The chief outcome of this Survey Bill was a debate revealing the attitudes of the sections on the issue.

As a section New England was divided. Its rural inhabitants did not relish the competition of cheap western farm products and were not eager to encourage more by voting for federal aid to internal improvements. But the commercial and manufacturing interests desired not only more cheap food but closer connection with western markets.

The middle Atlantic states contained the most promising routes for linkage with the interior. Their commercial elements were eager to enlarge the volume of western surpluses already being handled by them and, in return, to supply the interior with imported goods. They profited from state internal improvement projects and had warmly supported the early federal ventures such as the National Road.

The southern Atlantic states were opposed to federal aid to internal improvements. Separated by the almost impassable barrier of the southern Appalachians from the interior, they were reluctant to support a program that would benefit only other sections of the Union. They came to believe that such a program would only add to their burdens and that it was contrary to the Constitution. A notable exception to this belief was John C. Calhoun. His support of federal aid to internal improvements may have been inspired by a hope to win western support for his presidential aspirations. Also, Charleston, his political base, had under way the construction of a railroad to the Ohio River at Cincinnati.

The West was united in favor of federal aid to internal improvements. It hoped to overcome by means of such improvements the marketing handicaps imposed by its location. Henry Clay was the personification of the program. He believed the Union was destined to extend to the Pacific and thought its permanence depended on the ease of communication. One of the cardinal principles of his "American System" was federal aid to internal improvements.

These differences between and within the sections did not appear in the vote on the Survey Bill. By a wide margin both houses approved the measure. But the vote meant little, for the bill proposed nothing more than the gathering of information. As enacted in April 1824, it authorized merely the making of surveys, plans, and estimates regarding such roads and canals as the President might deem "of national importance" from a commercial, military, or postal point of view. The key term in the act was "of national importance." The sum of only $30,000 was voted for the survey, which indicated the significance attached to it.

A Board of Engineers for Internal Improvements was organized to implement the act. Its staff was headed by officers borrowed from bureaus of the War Department. It had a life of eight years. In the Adams administration its reports were made the occasion for repeated and unsuccessful recommendations to Congress to undertake projects chosen from its lists. In the Jackson administration the board was allowed to disappear.

In the era of indecision President Jackson undertook a fresh review of the issue in his first annual message to Congress. The public debt, he pointed out, would soon be extinguished, and a surplus of revenue would then accumulate in the Treasury. If such funds were to be used for the improvement of inland navigation or for highways in the states, everyone in the Union would be benefited. But this would raise questions of constitutionality and expediency. Jackson recommended therefore a constitutional amendment which would provide for the apportionment of the surplus among the states according to their representation in Congress, to be used as they chose. This was an ambivalent policy, harking back to Madison and Monroe.

A year and a half later Jackson took a firmer stand, acting on a measure by Congress, the Maysville Road bill, that would have authorized federal purchase of stock in a Kentucky company incorporated to rebuild a run-down road from Zanesville, Ohio, to Maysville, on the south side of the river, and to Lexington at the center of the state. The road was intended to form a link with the National Road and be part of a main highway to the East from Kentucky. It was to link up, also, with a road to Mobile on the Gulf via Florence in Alabama. It had been listed in reports of the Bureau of Engineers.

Jackson chose to ignore these plans. He deemed the road a local affair—a project wholly within a state—and for that reason ineligible for federal aid. What was more, he foresaw a scramble for federal aid from other applicants if this one succeeded. Congress would become the center of a contest by road promoters and land speculators to feed at the public trough. The duty of Congress was to seek retrenchment, to hasten the extinction of the federal debt. An attempt in the House to override the veto failed and the principle became established of denying federal aid to any internal improvement within a state or even between states.

In 1850 a new phase appeared in the evolution of federal aid to internal improvements. It coincided with the beginning of railroad dominance in overland transportation. Railroads had by then outstripped canals in performance. They had proved cheaper to build in whatever terrain, less costly to keep in repair, more effective as carriers of general freight. For long-distance hauling they were certainly superior to turnpikes. The constitutional issue of federal aid to internal improvements had softened. In 1850 Whigs were in control of both Congress and the Executive. They were the traditional friends of federal aid to internal improvements, whether in states or territories.

On September 20, 1850, a Whig majority in Congress adopted a bill conferring on the states of Illinois, Mississippi, and Alabama a vast grant of federal land, which the states were to donate to a railroad company for construction of a line from north central Illinois to Mobile. The grant was to consist of every alternate section of land in a six-mile strip on either side of the track. Sections already alienated were to be compensated by in-lieu lands chosen elsewhere in the strip. The alternate sections, retained by the federal government, were to carry a price not less than double the minimum charges for federal lands. Purchasers of these would be ready to pay the enhanced price, since they lay in proximity to a railroad. The government, by receiving the better price, would recoup the cost of its donation to the states for the railroad. Branch lines were to go from the main stem in central Illinois to Galena on the Mississippi River and to Chicago. At or near Chicago, a connection would be established with the approaching Michigan Central Railroad, which, in turn, was linked to the New York Central.

The Illinois Central grant reflected the contradictions registered in the earlier history of federal aid to internal improvements. The most powerful sponsor of the grant in Congress was an Illinois Democrat—Stephen A. Douglas—who had large real estate interests in Chicago. But the President signing the measure was a Whig—Millard Fillmore. By virtue of the act the nation became a partner on a large scale in internal improvement schemes. For twenty-one years thereafter Congress was plied with requests of similar nature, which were normally granted. A reflection of the agitation for the Illinois Central grant was the yet more grandiose plan of Douglas and his associates for a railroad to the Pacific.

The larger significance of these internal improvements was the realignment in trade and in outlook, to which they contributed. The commerce of the Northwest was turned to the Northeast. Buffalo became the turntable of the process. It had been little more than a country town before the Erie Canal was completed. By 1845 it surpassed New Orleans as a forwarder of the commerce of the Northwest, and every year thereafter it increased the lead. In the same proportions New Orleans lost more of the up-country trade and more of the grip she had held on the destinies of that section. Just after the War of 1812 New Orleans had drawn 80 percent of the commerce of the up-country. By 1860 what was left was 23 percent.

This loss created dismay among the merchants and spokesmen of the Queen City. It seemed a reversal of nature's mandate and led to an increased emphasis on projects of a southern cast—greater direct trade with the outside world and greater southern self-sufficiency. This occurred when the spread of slavery was transforming local southern regionalism into militant southern unification. In both North and South, unification within each section had become a peril to the unity of the whole.

The Tariff
as a Sectional Issue

THE PRIMARY SOURCE of federal revenues until the outbreak of the Civil War was duties levied on imports. The percentage varied from year to year, but in 1830, in terms of millions of dollars, it was 21 out of 24; in 1860, 53 out of 60. The revenue was sufficient for the ordinary needs of government in peacetime, though not in wartime. It was easy to collect, and reliance on it reflected also a preference for indirect over direct taxation. One of the values of such taxation was that it gave incidental protection to American industry, and to other interests, against foreign competition.

Incidental protection seemed not enough to Alexander Hamilton, Secretary of the Treasury under George Washington. He wished American industry to have avowed protection against the established industries of Europe. In a notable report of December 1791 he proposed that military and other essential products be afforded protection as a defensive matter. The report is a landmark in the history of protective-tariff philosophy, and also of the doctrine of the implied powers of Congress, but it did not achieve these ends. The laissez faire philosophy of the English economist Adam Smith was the prevailing sentiment of the day. Not until 1816 was a tariff measure providing more than incidental protection adopted by Congress.

European wars in the wake of the French Revolution occurred during this quarter-century. The American responses to the wars were the Embargo Act, the Non-Intercourse Act, and the War of 1812. These in turn stimulated the growth of American manufacturing, especially in New England and in the middle Atlantic states. The growth spurred a demand for protection of American industries against foreign competition. Protectionism became a sectional and political issue of increasing scope and bitterness. Tariff acts came from Congress in feverish succession.

The succession is exhibited on the accompanying chart of the measures adopted from 1816 to 1842. It depicts the votes cast on each measure in the House of Representatives arranged in sectional groupings. A plus sign indicates bills raising rates; a minus sign, those lowering rates.

TARIFF VOTES—HOUSE OF REPRESENTATIVES						
	+	+	+	−	−	+
	1816	*1824*	*1828*	*1832*	*1833*	*1842*
New England	17–10	15–23	16–23	17–17	10–28	26–7
Middle Atlantic	42–5	57–9	56–6	44–18	15–47	50–8
Southeast	16–35	4–56	4–48	31–24	57–1	8–41
Southwest	9–4	14–14	12–17	23–6	27–2	6–32
Northwest	4–0	17–0	17–0	17–0	10–7	13–11

The first column exhibits the vote on the tariff of 1816. The act was essentially a defense against dumping by British exporters, who sought quickly to recover their American markets after the war. Rates were raised by it only moderately—the average was not much over 25 percent. This was evidence of the strength of low-tariff sentiment in the nation. Congress expected that American industry would, in three years, become competitive with the British, and a proviso was attached to the act that all duties were to fall to a level of 20 percent in 1819.

The New England vote of 17–10 in favor of the measure was beyond the normal protectionist strength of the section at this time. It registered a reaction against British dumping. The prevailing temper of the commercial and shipping interests in the section was for tariffs for revenue only. Ship builders had like interests. They wanted the raw materials of their craft to enter the country from abroad unhampered—hemp for cordage, flax for sailcloth, and iron for ship's irons. Distillers wished to import, free of duty, West Indian molasses—the raw material of rum. Daniel Webster, representing these interests in 1816, opposed protection. He considered such tariffs contrary to the Constitution.

The middle Atlantic seaboard was a haven of protectionism in 1816. It contained two powerful groups demanding such help. Farmers were still the dominant interest in the section and they accepted as gospel the thesis of Alexander Hamilton and Henry Clay that if infant industries were nursed to maturity by favorable tariffs, a home market would be established for the surpluses of American agriculture. Farmers throughout the nation were suffering at the time. Their European markets, which had been so profitable during the Napoleonic wars, had collapsed with the return of peace. Even more ardent for a protective tariff than the farmers were the industrialists, especially the iron and textile manufacturers of Pennsylvania and New Jersey. The vote of the section for the tariff of 1816 was overwhelming.

The southern Atlantic states were strongly opposed to protectionist measures. Predominantly agricultural, they anticipated no major industrial development. Slave labor was more profitably employed in normal times in the fields than in factories. The section was influenced by the Jeffersonian concept that manufacturing and commerce produced a less wholesome society than farming. The evidence was the poverty and degradation of the working classes in England. Southern leaders made an exception of elementary industry, such as the spinning of yarn for homespun fabrics, but wished nothing more elaborate. They believed protective tariffs only increased the prices of the goods they imported and restricted the market for their surpluses by lessening

European sales in the United States. The chart as a whole exhibits a uniform southern opposition to protective tariffs except for the postwar measure of 1816. Supporters of that tariff included two prominent South Carolinians, John C. Calhoun and William Lowndes. Calhoun was then in his nationalist phase and voted for the bill as a defense measure.

In the Southwest sentiment on the protective tariff was divided. The section was becoming a producer of cotton, and views of cotton growers reflected those of its eastern counterpart. But protection was favored by other interests in the section. Louisiana was the center of a rapidly growing sugar industry that wanted protection against the Cuban product. The bill of 1816 gave ample protection, 3 cents a pound on brown sugar, 4 cents on white clayed or powdered sugar, and, on other types, 10 to 12 cents a pound. Kentucky and Missouri were growers of hemp and flax, for which they desired protection against European producers. Kentucky was the center of Bourbon whiskey production and wished to take over the markets for New England rum through higher duties on Cuban molasses. The molasses schedule in every tariff debate was a battleground of conflicting sectional interests. A temporary support was given to protection in 1816, but the basic statement before long proved otherwise.

The Northwest was one of the most consistently high-protectionist areas of the Union. This was by reason of its surplus of food. The section thought well of Clay's home-market argument. It wanted industry to develop in the West and in the East to create a home market for western wheat and meat. In Ohio a strongly protectionist special interest was sheep and wool. The vote of the Northwest was unanimous for every increase and against every decrease of tariff levels until the compromise tariff of 1833.

The tariff act of 1824—the next on the chart—was a mixture of incompatibles, as often occurred in such legislation. It gave increased protection to finished goods, but at the same time raised the rates on the raw materials used in their manufacture. Thus it accorded woolen fabrics high rates against foreign fabrics, but at the same time, in response to the wishes of New York, Ohio, and Pennsylvania, increased rates on foreign raw wool. So also with the ship-building industry. It was protected against ships built and owned in countries lacking reciprocity agreements with the United States, by a levy of tonnage duties on such vessels entering American ports, and by imposts on the goods they carried. But at the same time the raw materials needed in ship building were made more expensive by duties on foreign hemp, flax, and iron. Hemp and flax were raised in Kentucky and Missouri, and iron was produced in Pennsylvania. Mixing of protections in this way was politically expedient, but frustrating to industry. It is necessary to bear this in mind in examining the congressional voting on the measure.

The vote on the 1824 measure shows New England and the Southwest divided. The middle Atlantic states and the Northwest were overwhelmingly in favor of the measure; the Southeast was overwhelmingly against it. Planters in the Southeast had no faith in the home-market argument. Cotton planters, in particular, rejected it. Not more than a quarter of their surplus was sold in the United States; three-quarters went abroad, and that proportion was unlikely to change in view of the great extension of cotton production into the Gulf region. Protectionism would discourage the sale of European goods in the American market and raise their prices. Protectionism was thus an apple of discord between the sections and the states of the Union.

Constitutional objections were raised in the debate on the 1824 measure in Congress. The argument was that the powers to raise revenue and regulate trade conferred by the Constitution on Congress could not be stretched by implication to authorize protection to manufacturers or to other selected interests. John Randolph of Virginia presented that argument strikingly: "If, under a power to regulate trade, you prevent exportation; if with the most approved spring lancets, you draw the last drop of blood from our veins; if *secundum artem,* you draw the last shilling from our pockets, what are the checks of the Constitution to us? A fig for the Constitution! When the scorpion's sting is probing to the quick, shall we stop to chop logic? . . . There is no magic in this word *union.*" This emphasis was ominous for future peace.

The tariff of 1828, the third on the chart, was the product of a protracted and bitter political conflict that harked back to the presidential election of 1824, when the candidates were Andrew Jackson, John Quincy Adams, Henry Clay, and William H. Crawford. Jackson had scored a plurality of the popular and electoral votes, but not a majority of either. The contest was carried into the House, where the Adams and Clay forces united to choose Adams President. Clay was appointed Secretary of State. The union was normal, for the two men saw alike on the tariff and on the issue of federal aid to internal improvements. The cry of "bargain and corruption" was, however, at once raised, the echoes of which reverberated in the election campaign of 1828, when Adams and Jackson were again candidates.

In Congress, where the tariff issue was under discussion early in 1828, the Jackson forces were in control. They favored the producers of raw materials in the West and in the middle Atlantic states, rather than the manufacturers of finished goods in New England. Wool, widely produced in the West, was favored rather than the fabrics produced in New England, for which low-cost wool was desired. Hemp and flax, the raw materials for cordage, sailcloth, and cotton bagging, were in the same category. Hemp and flax were produced in Kentucky and in Missouri, but a better quality at lower prices could be imported from Russia. West Indian molasses, the raw material for the production of rum, had for years borne a duty of 5 cents a gallon to please Louisiana sugar planters. The duty on it was doubled, which distressed New England, but pleased producers of whiskey in Pennsylvania and Kentucky whose raw material was grain. Pig iron and bar iron, produced in Pennsylvania, were favored in the bill, though ship builders in New England needed the better and cheaper British irons.

A protectionist device for fabrics, known as the "minimum principle" of valuation, had been urged on Congress for woolens by a convention held at Harrisburg, Pennsylvania. It had been applied earlier to cotton textiles. The Harrisburg proposal was that all imported woolens costing, at the point of origin, between 40 cents and $2.50 a square yard, be valued on entering the United States as though costing $2.50 and be taxed accordingly; all goods costing between $2.50 and $4, be assessed as though costing $4 a yard; and so on. If Congress had adopted the Harrisburg proposal as drawn up, New England textile interests would have rejoiced. But the schedule, as decided by Congress, added a new level of woolens costing 33⅓ cents or less at the point of origin and taxed these at a low rate. This was designed to annoy New England manufacturers, the bulk of whose fabrics—those for slaves and the poor—were in the lower price range. An added evil of the minimum-value principle was that it invited frauds at the customs.

Every effort to remove the deformities of the bill was defeated by the Jacksonians controlling Congress. They were determined to frame a bill that would be rejected by the votes of New England and the South, and the defeat of which would, in the coming election, be ascribed to the Adams administration. A Jackson victory would thus be assured. One participant in the plan, George McDuffie, of South Carolina, later said of it: "We determined to put such ingredients in the chalice as would poison the monster, and commend it to his own lips." Another opponent, John Randolph, commented while the bill was making its way through Congress: "It referred to manufactures of no sort or kind except the manufacture of a President of the United States."

The scheme misfired. Enough New Englanders, including Daniel Webster, a recruit to protectionism, voted for the bill to pass it. Many manufacturers felt that even a tariff of "abominations" was better than none. The vote in the House was 105–94; in the Senate it was 26–21; and the measure was signed by Adams (May 19, 1828).

Calhoun did not vote on the tariff measure of 1828. As Vice-President and presiding officer of the Senate, he was without a vote. He had views regarding protectionism that he preferred to withhold. He desired re-election to the vice-presidency in the election. Anonymously he prepared for the South Carolina legislature, however, the "South Carolina Exposition," which embodied the doctrine of nullification. The tariff just enacted, he wrote, was unconstitutional and destructive to the liberty of the South. The states, which had created the national government, were the ultimate judges of its powers and authority. A state that considered a federal act unconstitutional might forbid enforcement within its own borders. If supported by three-fourths of the states in this decision, the law would become null and void. This was the answer of the cotton South to northern industrialists, and it came from the pen of a former nationalist.

The cotton South was suffering at the time from a heavy decline in the price of its staple. The average of upland middlings in 1816 had been near 30 cents a pound. By 1828 it had fallen to about 10 cents, where it long remained. At the same time the cost of slaves was rising as a result of the surge of settlement into the Gulf Plains. To cotton planters the protective tariff, which raised the price of manufactured goods, seemed to be the prime source of their distress. In South Carolina, agitation for state action grew.

As a result of the presidential election Jackson became President in March 1829. Calhoun remained Vice-President. As a member of the new administration he advised his South Carolina friends to take no new action regarding nullification. He hoped the Democratic-controlled Congress would bring relief from the Tariff of Abominations.

In the new administration action was deferred until 1832. Then it came at the instance of leaders of the opposition. Early in 1832 Clay in the Senate and Adams in the House proposed a new tariff. Adams had been elected to Congress, following his term as President, and had been named chairman of the Committee on Manufactures. His views on the tariff were moderate and the report he presented for his committee became, with amendments, the tariff act of 1832, which reduced the level of duties from the previous average of 41 percent to 33 percent. It placed imported wool, costing less than 8 cents a pound at the point of origin (the kind used for cheap clothing), on the free list. It also put flax for sailcloth on the free list, and reduced the duty on hemp and on iron. Most important, it abolished the system of minimum valuations, the frauds of which had become a scandal. The measure, scheduled to go into effect on March 3, 1833, was a genuine reform.

But to the radically discontented southern elements it seemed a defeat of reform. They had hoped Congress in 1828 and in 1832 would free them entirely from the oppressions of the tariff system. Now they sought relief outside of Congress. In November 1832 a special convention was summoned in South Carolina, which adopted a nullification ordinance declaring the tariffs of 1828 and 1832 ''null, void, and no law, nor binding upon this state, its officers, or citizens.'' If the federal government were to attempt to enforce the law in the state, secession would follow. This was no mere revolutionary ranting. The state prepared for military action by land and by sea under the direction of Governor Robert Y. Hayne. But war was more than the rest of the South was ready to accept. The state found itself alone.

Jackson's reply was a reminder that disunion by armed force is treason. A war vessel was sent to escort revenue cutters to Charleston harbor; the federal forts in the harbor were reinforced; and a vigorous proclamation was issued denouncing the nullification design. In January 1833 Jackson asked Congress to enact a law granting full power to the Administration to use the Army and Navy to enforce revenue collection in South Carolina. At the same time, however, he let it be known that he thought the 1832 tariff rates should be lowered.

In response to his recommendations a paired program was put through Congress. A ''Force Bill'' was adopted which was to go into effect just before the tariff act of 1832. Bills were also brought into the two houses of Congress to reduce the 1832 tariff rates. The Senate bill, introduced by Clay, was designed to preserve the principle of protection, and at the same time make concessions to southern opposition. It provided that all duties in the 1832 act which exceeded 20 percent should be reduced by increments, each alternate year, until 1840; then on January 1 and July 1, 1842, half the remainder over 20 percent should be removed on each date, so that on July 1, 1842, only a uniform 20 percent should remain. Calhoun, who had resigned the vice-presidency in the crisis and had become a senator, gave the bill his approval. This measure—the Compromise Tariff of 1833—was adopted by both houses of Congress on March 2, the day before the tariff of 1832 and the Force Bill would have become law.

In South Carolina the nullification convention was recalled on March 11. It repealed the nullification ordinance and the crisis passed. At the same time it passed another ordinance, nullifying the no longer needed Force Act. Thus each side felt it had had its way. The Compromise of 1833 maintained sectional peace on the tariff issue until 1842.

The Public Lands, 1800 – 62

THE FEDERAL GOVERNMENT became the owner of an immense public domain between the close of the Revolutionary War and 1853. Land in the area to the Mississippi River, amounting to approximately 233 million acres, was turned over to Congress during the Confederation period by the original states with western claims. Between 1803 and 1853 the public lands grew to approximately 1,413,333,000 acres, the result of treaties of acquisition with France, Spain, and Great Britain; of war and acquisition treaties with Mexico; and a purchase from the state of Texas.

This great acquisition had a political significance comparable to its extent. It served as a bond of union between the states. It provided revenue to the federal government second only to the amount derived from import duties. It was a major factor in the nation's cultural and economic institutions. It was also a source of discord between the sections. Disputes grew out of proposals before Congress for the disposal of the land to the public. Often the solutions to such disputes consisted of balancing off land-disposal terms with those in the areas of the tariff, internal improvements, and the distribution of Treasury funds to the states.

The seaboard states that had ceded their western claims had a special interest in the terms proposed for the disposal of the lands. They were interested especially in the price at which the lands would be sold. A low price would stimulate sales and draw migrants from worn-out lands in the East to virgin lands in the West. The West would soon have a surplus of food and other raw materials to sell in the East. The result would be a decline in eastern commodities and land values. Similar effects would follow any relaxation of other terms of land disposal. Yet the seaboard states realized that advantages for them would result from ample revenues derived from the sale of public lands. The revenues would hasten the extinction of the federal debt and create a Treasury surplus which could be distributed to the states. The states that had ceded their claims would thus derive some return on their gift.

In New England the prevailing view was that the federal government's disposal policy should be one that would least disturb its rural and industrial economy. This was especially the view in rural New England, which keenly felt the competition of cheap and fertile western lands. But some New England farmers, who had hopes of migrating to the West, favored liberalization of the federal land laws.

Industrialists in New England normally opposed liberalization of the land laws. Their attitude was a reflection, at least in part, of a wish to have always a sufficient labor reserve in factory centers and the smaller towns. They felt that an ample labor supply would be harder to retain if pioneering opportunities in the West became too attractive. Also, wages in the cities would rise if workers left for the West.

The views of factory workers resembled those of farmers in unprosperous areas. The western lands were regarded by them as a haven of refuge from exploitation. Even some factory owners found merit in liberalizing the federal land laws. They regarded a growing West as a market for their product. Some industrialists with strong antislavery views saw the Northwest as an ally in the fight against slavery expansion.

In the middle Atlantic and southern seaboard states the same diversity of opinion was found. In both sections agriculture was the dominant interest, though in Pennsylvania and in New Jersey industry was on the rise, and the views on land policy in these states resembled those in the factory areas of New England. In the southern seaboard the planter class—the cotton and tobacco growers, in particular—suffered from the competition of cheap western lands, and were loath to intensify it by liberalization of federal land policy.

The section that most uniformly wished liberalization of land laws was the trans-Appalachian West. This was especially true in the years of the great migration after the War of 1812, when the Allegheny uplands, the prairies, and the Gulf Plains were being occupied. Westerners believed that fiscal considerations should not alone determine policy. They urged that social objectives should prevail—the aim of establishing in the West communities of landowning farmers. Westerners felt that the money derived from the sale of public lands should be no more than what was necessary to defray the costs of administering them.

Congress began to discharge the obligations of ownership with the Land Ordinance of 1785. As described in an earlier chapter, this set forth the basic principles of land disposal—survey prior to sale, rectangular laying out of townships and sections, sales at public auctions, and the orderly recording of titles. It also set a minimum price per acre at which bidding should begin, and the minimum size of tracts the government would sell. The ordinance was re-enacted after the adoption of the Constitution.

In 1796 and in 1800 laws were adopted by Congress to meet the needs of settlers. The act of 1800, which William Henry Harrison, delegate of the Northwest Territory, had pressed on Congress, reduced the minimum size that could be bought from 640 to 320 acres. More important, it established a system of installment payments, which met one of the chief demands of settlers. It provided for a down payment of one-fourth the purchase price, and remittance of the remaining three-fourths over a period of four years. The minimum price, however, remained high—it was $2 an acre. Better terms, especially longer credit, could be had from land-speculating companies. In western New York, Pennsylvania, and other states large purchases of state lands had been made by speculators at bargain prices.

An increase in the sale of federal land occurred in the years following the War of 1812. In the decade prior to the war the annual average of sales had been only 272,000 acres, but in one year (1817) the sales were 995,000 acres; in the next year, 1,303,000 acres. This increase reflected a combination of forces. One was the credit system of the act of 1800. Another was the defeat of the northwestern Indians at the Battle of the Thames, which made settlement safe north of the Ohio; and the crushing of the Creeks at the Battle of Horseshoe Bend, which opened the Southwest. A third was the ease with which money could be borrowed in a period of unregulated state banking. In the same period Congress adopted military bounty acts under which veterans of the War of 1812 were given a total of 4,475,000 acres.

This upsurge of land disposal came to an abrupt end in the Panic of 1819. The panic brought the nation to economic prostration. Banking in the states collapsed. The Bank of the United States, in the effort to save itself by foreclosures, spread disaster. Bankruptcy prostrated the cities. Farm products fell in price to the point where producing them hardly paid for the labor. Installments due the government on land purchases were in arrears more than $22 million in 1820.

Corrective legislation was obtained from Congress in the Land Act of 1820. This abolished the credit system, which had lured pioneers into purchasing more land than they could pay for. Cash sales were to be required in the future. Purchases could be made at a public auction, or after an auction at "private sale." At the public auction land previously announced to be for sale would be sold to the highest bidder, the bidding to start at no less than $1.25 an acre. Lands not sold at public auction were "offered" lands and could be bought at any time thereafter at the local land office for $1.25 an acre. By way of compensation for the cancellation of credit, several concessions were made. One was the lowering of the minimum price from $2 to $1.25 per acre. Another was the reduction of the minimum tract purchasable from 320 acres to 80 acres. Other concessions came in the Relief Act of 1821, permitting relinquishment of land not yet paid for under the credit system, the application to the retained land of any payments made, and the benefit of the reduced price on payments still due.

The wide range of interests and problems touched by land policy was evident whenever the issue was raised in Congress. An illustration of this is the famous debate in the Senate in 1829–30, which culminated in the Webster-Hayne exchanges. Senator Samuel A. Foot of Connecticut precipitated the debate with a resolution calling for an investigation to determine whether the land-surveying office should be closed and sales limited to the area already surveyed. He believed enough public land was already surveyed and available for any reasonable needs of settlement. He pointed out that 72 million acres were already surveyed and for sale in the West, while only 1 million acres a year were currently sold.

This New England proposal brought an instant western reply. Senator Thomas H. Benton of Missouri pointed out that of the 72 million acres on the market, much was mountain and wasteland. To withhold new land from the public until all this poor land had been sold was comparable to the policy of a father who would not permit his children to have a second roast chicken until all the bones and feathers of the first had been consumed.

Benton denounced the Foot resolution as an example of New England hostility to the West. He traced this hostility from the beginning. In 1786 New England had supported the Jay-Gardoqui proposal to close the Mississippi River to the West. In 1803 New England had objected to the acquisition of Louisiana. In 1812 it had objected to admitting into the Union a state carved out of that territory for fear of the precedent that would be established. According to Benton the Foot resolution was a new example of the determination of New England factory owners to hold the laboring classes forever in a condition of serfdom.

Benton thought he saw an opportunity in the Foot resolution to break up a political alliance formed between New England and the West in 1825, whereby a New Englander, John Quincy Adams, had become President and a Westerner, Henry Clay, had become Secretary of State and heir-apparent. He suggested that a more natural alliance could be formed between the West and the South, one to fight off the Foot resolution.

This invitation was accepted by Senator Robert Y. Hayne of South Carolina, acting in place of Calhoun, then Vice-President. Hayne welcomed the idea of an alliance between the South and the West to defeat the Foot resolution. He wanted a permanent coalition and referred ironically to the Adams-Clay combination (already called the ''bargain and corruption'' alliance) as the ''happy union'' of 1825. With a view of a partnership of South and West, he proposed a policy which he felt both sections would welcome: that all federal land within state boundaries should be turned over to the states, not at once, but as soon as the debt of the federal government had been extinguished, which was not far in the future. He complained that while the federal government held those lands they were a source of danger to the South, of immoral bargains and logrolling agreements whereby New England would gain western support for a high protective tariff in return for making concessions to the West on land policy.

Hayne argued that the real purpose of the Foot resolution was to perpetuate the high tariff policy. If the Surveyor General's office were to be closed down, land revenues would be reduced and higher tariff rates would become necessary. He launched a bitter attack on the high tariff as an instrument whereby New England manufacturers exploited both the South and the West—the South especially. The South, with only a third of the nation's population, was obliged to pay two-thirds of the revenue collected by the federal government. Hayne thought the tariff system not only oppressive but unconstitutional, and he declared the remedy for its oppressions was nullification.

The speech brought Daniel Webster, the orator of New England, into the debate. He spoke not merely as a New Englander but as a defender of the protective-tariff system and of American nationalism. He had come to the conclusion that the Foot resolution was a tactical error—that it was driving the West into the arms of the South. He opened his speech, therefore, with the suggestion of an amendment to the Foot resolution that would have neutralized it, providing merely for an inquiry to determine whether a slowdown or a speedup of surveying public land should be ordered. Ultimately he got the Foot resolution withdrawn altogether. Webster took special pains to refute the charge that New England had been inveterately hostile to the West. New England, he declared, had been consistently the friend of the West and had made great contributions to its development. She had contributed the main principles of the Land Ordinance of 1785 and the Northwest Ordinance of 1787. She had supported the policy of congressional aid to internal improvements, in contrast to the South. She had also supported the West in the effort to restrict the spread of slavery. Webster extolled the antislavery provisions of the Northwest Ordinance of

1787, framed, he said, by Nathan Dane of Massachusetts. In a burst of eloquence Webster compared Dane to Solon, the lawgiver of the Greeks.

To this speech Hayne made a sarcastic reply. He ironically challenged the accuracy of Webster's history. Nathan Dane—the Solon—the benefactor of the people of the West! The Nathan Dane known to the South was the New Englander who had been an active member of the Hartford Convention, where he had favored an amendment to the Constitution which would have denied new western communities admission to the Union as states except by a two-thirds vote of both houses of Congress.

Hayne wished to know why the South had been made the target of Webster, when it was a Westerner, Benton, who had initiated the criticism of New England. "Has the gentleman's distempered fancy been disturbed by gloomy forebodings of new alliances to be formed?"

Webster, in his famous reply, shifted ground. He realized he was not secure in regard to New England's past attitude toward the West, especially on land policy. As a clever lawyer he concentrated on the South Carolina doctrine of nullification and the nature of the Union. The debate went off on that tangent and reached its climax in the dramatic appeal of Webster to nationalism and unionism as against the localism and separatism of South Carolina.

The Webster-Hayne debate is an illustration of the kind of sectional clashing that took place in Congress between the close of the War of 1812 and the Civil War. It is an example of the maneuvering of the Northeast on the one hand, and the southern Atlantic section on the other, to obtain an alliance with the West, and the West playing off these eastern sections against each other, in order to get what it wanted in Congress.

High on the list of western desires regarding land law in the 1820's and 1830's was the enactment of legislation that would benefit squatters. Squatters were intruders on the public land—settlers without legal right to the land they were denuding of timber and cultivating. Congressional legislation early in the century had set penalties for intrusion. But such laws had seldom been enforced, for squatting was widely defended on the ground that it was a benefit to the community and nation that the wilderness was being occupied. Yet the squatter labored always under the danger that when the public land sale took place his "claim"—the land which he had cleared with sweat and toil and from which he was now taking harvests—would be auctioned off to the highest bidder.

Western members of Congress regularly brought petitions from their constituents for legislation permitting a squatter to buy at the local land office a parcel of 40, 80, or 160 acres embracing his claim, for $1.25 an acre at any time after the land was surveyed up to the holding of an announced auction. This privilege of "buying before" the auction was called "pre-emption." Such legislation would enable the actual settler to forestall the speculator, who might otherwise acquire not only his claim but also all his improvements.

In response to such petitions, Congress had from time to time enacted pre-emption measures applicable to selected areas where squatters had already established themselves. In 1830 it enacted a measure giving such rights to squatters generally, except on certain types of land, such as town sites and salt-spring areas.

This general, retrospective pre-emption measure was re-enacted later in the 1830's. But defenders of squatters wanted more. They wanted a law not just for the established squatter, but one that would give pre-emption rights prospectively—to any settler who would in the future settle anywhere on surveyed land. Also they wanted a law not limited in time but open-ended.

All these desires—a permanent pre-emption law, both retrospective and prospective, plus a guarantee that the minimum price would not be raised—were satisfied in an act of September 4, 1841. This legislation, "to appropriate the proceeds of the public land and to grant pre-emption rights," included a significant tariff concession to the South. The act is an illustration of how public land policy became intertwined with other economic issues and how the sections were won to supporting the package because there was something in it for each of them. The debates preceding enactment illustrate, as forcefully as did the Benton-Webster-Hayne debate, the rivalry of East, West, and South in the second quarter of the 19th century.

One part of the package was "distribution," an objective long sought by Henry Clay. The act provided that, after deducting certain costs of administration, the proceeds of the sale of public land should be divided among the states and territories according to their "respective federal representative population," the amount to each state and territory to be used as each legislature should direct.

This provision was desired by both eastern and western Whigs, partly because it was an indirect way of keeping the tariff high and partly because the funds to be used by the states would enable them to liquidate debts incurred in constructing internal improvements. Especially helpful for western internal improvements was the provision that the states and territories within whose borders public land lay would receive an extra 10 percent of the proceeds, together with total grants of public land up to 500,000 acres.

The important tariff concession to the South came in the form of a proviso: ". . . if at any time during the existence of this act, there shall be an imposition of duties on imports inconsistent with the provision of the Act of March 2, 1833, and beyond the rate of duty fixed in that act, to wit, 20% on the value of such imports . . . then the distribution provided in this act shall be suspended . . ." The low tariff proviso was necessary to win the votes of the southern Whigs in the Senate. That aspect, along with the distribution features, explains why the act had the approval of such unlikely recruits to a liberalization of the land laws as Henry Clay and John C. Calhoun and their followers.

Because of an impending Treasury deficit in 1842, the tariff was raised by law above the 20 percent *ad valorem* level, and the distribution to states and territories of proceeds from public land sales was brought to an end after one apportionment. But other features of the act remained: the grants of land to states and territories for internal improvements, and the long-sought multiple pre-emption features.

The law of 1841 retained one restriction. Pre-emption was still limited to surveyed land. But the desires of squatters to make claims prior to surveys was gradually met. In 1853 unsurveyed land in California was opened to present and future settlers on a pre-emption basis. Later, unsurveyed land in Oregon and in the territories of Washington, Kansas, Nebraska, and Minnesota was similarly opened. Such a wide extension of the right of pre-emption amounted to an undermining of the auction system.

Another western demand was "graduation," a lowering of the price of offered land (land not sold at auction and still on the market). Such land was available at government land offices to any buyer at the uniform price of $1.25 an acre. Those urging graduation felt that the price of offered land should not be uniform since not all of it was of equal value. An assessment of all offered land on the basis of quality would be prohibitive in cost. Therefore it was suggested that a sliding scale of price be established, based on the length of time the land had been on the market unsold.

The chief advocate of the plan was Senator Benton. He had been pressing it in Congress for thirty years. His 1828 plan was favored by Jackson, Van Buren, and Polk. Popular support for it came from the Southwest, and especially from Missouri. A cogent challenge to its premise was made years later by the Commissioner of the Land Office, John Wilson. He pointed out that for years the practice had been to survey and bring into the market each year 10 million acres of land, though only 1 to 3 million acres would have supplied the demand. "It would be absurd," he declared, "to suppose that there was not . . . very much as good land remaining as any that had been sold." The graduation plan, according to its critics, would hold out a standing invitation to squatters to enter into agreements to hold off buying until the price had fallen to the level they desired. The answer of Benton to his critics was that the number of squatters on the public domain would be lowered if graduation were adopted, and that those buying at reduced prices could be required to sign affidavits that they had never entered into agreements to hold off buying.

In 1854 a graduation act was finally passed. It provided that all public land (except mineral land or reserved land) that remained unsold after being up for sale from ten to fifteen years should be priced at $1 an acre; if unsold for fifteen to twenty years, at 75 cents an acre; if unsold for twenty to twenty-five years, at 50 cents an acre; if unsold for twenty-five to thirty years, at 25 cents an acre; and any land unsold for thirty years or more, at 12½ cents (one bit) an acre.

Under the act any settler on land that had declined in price to the level specified in the law had the first right to buy the land at that price, if he qualified under the pre-emption laws. If he already owned or occupied 160 acres acquired under federal land laws, he was limited to 160 acres more. Otherwise he might buy as much as 320 acres.

A rush of bargain hunters to the public lands followed the adoption of the act. The total acreage sold at the lowered prices during the life of the act was 25,676,000 acres, of which more than half went for 12½ cents an acre. Of the total acreage sold, 22,244,000 lay in the Southwest, with Missouri, Alabama, and Arkansas accounting for 18,338,000 acres. By contrast the sales in the non-slave states accounted for only 3,432,000 acres, chiefly in Michigan, Illinois, and Wisconsin. Most northern investors preferred to buy first-choice lands.

Because the act had been loosely drafted, the 320-acre limitation was not enforced. As a result, much of the cheaper land (an undeterminable amount) went to speculators, mostly local operators in the Southwest. When the act was passed the assumption was that it would be permanent, but it remained on the statute books for only eight years, partly as a result of the widespread frauds practiced under it. The law's brief life contrasted with the continuity and expansion in scope of the pre-emption acts.

Among western demands for liberalizing the land laws the most basic was for a "free homestead" or "donation" law. This had a background reaching back to the colonial period, when pioneers were offered donations as inducements to take and hold frontier areas exposed to Indian, French, or Spanish attack. In the 19th century donation reappeared in the philosophy of the reformer George H. Evans, who believed that everyone had an inalienable right to such gifts of nature as air, water, and soil, and consequently to a free homestead of 160 acres of wilderness land. In the 1830's organized labor in the East supported the doctrine, and Horace Greeley of the New York *Tribune* added his blessing.

In the mid-1840's, however, opposition to homestead legislation developed in the South as a result of the issue of slavery expansion that arose during the Mexican War. At that time the Wilmot proviso, a proposed amendment to a House appropriation bill, would have forbidden slavery or involuntary servitude in any territory acquired in the war. The proviso was approved in the House, and rejected by the Senate. But the vehemence of northern demonstrations for its adoption alarmed southern leaders, who concluded that the North was determined to exclude slavery from all territory acquired thereafter, and that homestead legislation would be the means to that end. Thus they sought to unite the South in opposition to homestead proposals.

In 1852 and again in 1854 a homestead measure was approved in the House. Had either measure been agreed to by the Senate, it would have been vetoed by President Pierce. The Graduation Act was what the South wanted and obtained. In the Buchanan administration a homestead bill passed both houses in compromise form, but was vetoed by the President. Only after the election of Lincoln and the secession of the southern states was homestead legislation achieved.

The Homestead Act of 1862 offered any head of family or person who had attained the age of twenty-one, whether a citizen or an alien who had filed an intention of becoming one, a quarter-section of land—160 acres. The recipient paid a small fee and agreed to live on the homestead or cultivate it for five years. The act fulfilled dreams reformers had long cherished and was more generous than the measure Buchanan had vetoed. It replaced the Graduation Act and supplemented the other modes of federal land disposal of the time—cash sales at auctions or later at land offices, pre-emption sales at land offices, military warrants or scrip, and grants to states for various purposes.

The Homestead Act constituted a landmark in American frontier history. It was the triumph of the doctrine that the public lands were to be used to shape economic and social institutions in the American democracy. Yet cash sales were not repealed. The homesteader or pre-emptioner was limited to 160 acres, but the man of wealth continued to have the privilege of buying unlimited quantities of public land, either at an auction or following an auction, at a district land office.

A brief review is now in order of the impact of public land disposal on the national economy. The accompanying graph (54) exhibits annual sales and gifts from 1800 to 1934. The lands disposed of were almost altogether western and indicate the speed of western growth. The figures overemphasize the growth, for much land passed into the hands of speculators. The line is in terms of millions of acres. It reveals alternations of peaks and valleys. The peaks show economic prosperity; the valleys show depressions. Three peaks rise in the period 1800–60, the first in the years

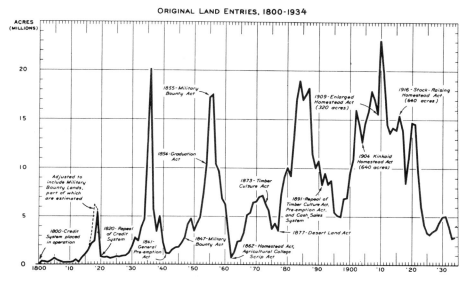

ORIGINAL LAND ENTRIES, 1800-1934

54. Public Land Disposal (from Robbins)

following the War of 1812, the second in the presidency of Jackson, the third in the mid-1850's.

In the first peak, that of the years 1817–18, land disposal rose to the annual rate of about 6 million acres. This was a response to forces earlier indicated, chiefly the defeat of Indian tribes, North and South, in the War of 1812, which opened vast areas to settlement. It was due, also, to the credit system in land purchases adopted by Congress in 1800. Other forces were the ease with which money could be borrowed at state banks and the military bounty lands granted by the federal government to veterans of the War of 1812. The end of this upsurge came with the Panic of 1819. A decade of stagnation followed during which land entries remained at a level of about a million acres a year.

A new peak rose in the Jackson administration, one of the highest in American history. By 1836 it had attained a height of 20 million acres. It was fueled by the prosperity in Jackson's second administration and by a currency inflation on the part of state banks after the restraining influence of the Second Bank of the United States had been removed in 1833. A third force was the removal of the southern Indians from the rich cotton and sugar lands of the Gulf Plains. A fourth was speculation in the public lands, which became a veritable craze in Jackson's second administration.

The profits of speculation in public lands were unusually promising in this period because of the acceptance of the currency of state banks at the land offices. A speculator with a supply of such currency, supplemented by soldiers' bounty warrants, which could be bought at low rates, would purchase lands as heavily at a public auction as his funds permitted. He would obtain a loan on the security of these lands from a state bank, and with this acquire more land. The operation would be repeated as often as possible. The pyramided purchases would be held a few years, while settlement was coming in. Then they would be sold at a price several times what had been paid to the government.

Contributing to this operation was the deposit of Treasury funds in certain state banks after Jackson had broken with the Second Bank of the United States in 1833. These funds encouraged the recipient state banks to maintain an easy loan policy. The loans were made in the form of notes of these banks. The notes of any bank rested on its capital, and on the specie reserves it kept for the redemption of its notes. In most states specie reserves were required to be equal to a third of a bank's outstanding notes. Such currency was accepted by the land offices and sent to the Treasury of the United States. The Treasury returned it to the banks as government deposits, thus encouraging the making of further loans. A complete circle of speculation was thus established.

It was an evil circle. It encouraged the speculator to acquire land at the low price intended by the government for the benefit of the settler. It promoted overexpansion of loans by state banks. It brought to the Treasury the currency of these banks, which, in a time of economic crisis, might become worthless in the hands of the federal government.

The evil of the situation was understood by Jackson, and the remedy applied to it was the Specie Circular of July 11, 1836, ordering the land offices to accept nothing in the future in payment for public land except gold and silver coin. By that order the bubble of speculation and inflation was punctured. The order was an important factor in precipitating the Panic of 1837, which abruptly halted speculation in land and leveled the peak of its disposal.

The third peak in land disposal came in the years 1852–56. It reached its tip in 1856 with almost 18 million acres disposed of. The forces responsible for it included an immense national prosperity, produced, at least in part, by the discovery of gold in California and the outbreak of the Crimean War in Europe. Another factor was the adoption by Congress of the Graduation Act. A third was the great rise in immigration to the United States. Other elements included land grants to railroads and other internal improvements.

Finally there were the military bounty acts adopted by Congress in 1847 and 1855. These granted to veterans of American wars bounties in the form of land scrip. That of 1847 was a reward to veterans of the Mexican War. That of 1855 was a retroactive grant to veterans of all United States wars since 1790. It gave Treasury scrip for 160 acres to any person who had served as much as fourteen days in any foreign or Indian war since 1790. The gift was not only to soldiers, and sailors, but to militiamen and even wagoners in the service of the state or federal governments. If such veterans had already received gifts of land, but not to the full extent of 160 acres, the deficiency was to be made up. The rights of any deceased veteran passed to his widow or minor children and the scrip was transferable. The act purported to be a measure of delayed gratitude to patriots of American wars and was pressed on Congress as such. In reality it was a job put through Congress by speculators, who anticipated buying the scrip cheap in the active scrip market of that period. Congress authorized such scrip to the amount of more than 65 million acres.

Land disposal in the decade 1847–57 exceeded that of any previous ten years in American history. Besides the amount of land passing directly to settlers from the government, much was sold to speculators or given to states for internal improvement companies, and from them went ultimately to settlers. The great rise in land sales of the middle fifties was ended by the Panic of 1857, which was devastating in the West, and the collapse went even further in 1861 as a result of the secession of the southern states and the onset of the Civil War. The annual disposal fell for a time below the million-acre level.

In these fluctuations the valleys shown on the graph have a further historical interest. They mark periods of great depression when Congress normally liberalized land laws. Nearly all the great liberalizations of land policy came at such times. In 1800, after the speculative bubble of the middle 1790's had burst, Congress adopted the Harrison Act, establishing the credit system for all purchasers of government land. Up to that time only the large purchasers had been permitted to pay in installments. Similarly, after the Panic of 1819 came the liberalizations in the Land Act of 1820, as to price and minimum size of tract. In 1821 came the assistance of the Relief Act to those in debt to the government under the terms of its credit sales. In 1841, after the Panic of 1837, came the Pre-emption Act, giving to present and future squatters the privilege of purchasing a 160-acre claim at $1.25 an acre. Again, the Homestead Law of 1862 was adopted by Congress in the period of economic collapse following the outbreak of the Civil War.

An undeclared economic policy was evident in these major acts liberalizing land policy. The laws were meant to be a form of "priming the pump." They were expected to stimulate the settlement of the frontier and thus rejuvenate a depressed economy. That expectation was realized, as the graph makes clear. The public lands thus served not merely to meet the financial and institutional needs of the nation, but to keep the economy in vigorous health.

Physiography
of the Far West

WHILE THESE PROBLEMS of sectional politics were drawing public attention to Washington, adventurers were moving into the Far Southwest, beyond the national domain. They were moving into the intermountain plateaus of that country and into the provinces of the Pacific coast. To reach them they had to cross immense open spaces and overcome obstacles of a sort absent east of the Mississippi. The open spaces and the territory to be reached are indicated on the accompanying map of the physiographic regions of the United States (55).

The first of the regions beyond the prairie province is the Great Plains. This is one of the mightiest provinces of the continent. It extends from the Rio Grande north to the Canadian border, and in Canada north to the sub-Arctic. Westward it stretches from the great bend of the Missouri to the base of the Rocky Mountains. It is really not plains at all. It is a plateau that tilts upward from the east to the west and attains an altitude at the base of the Rocky Mountains higher in some places than the highest peaks of the Appalachians. Much of the western part of the province is semi-arid; some is virtually a desert.

West of the Great Plains lies the province of the Rocky Mountains. This is the backbone of the continent. It is a gigantic and overpowering mass. Its front ranges rise like a jagged wall from the Great Plains. Its chief early significance was as a massive obstacle to communication between the East and the Pacific slope.

In the Rockies were the so-called mountain parks. These are high mountain meadows, often of considerable size. The most notable in the southern Rockies are North, Middle, and South parks and the San Luis Valley. In the northern Rockies are such lesser meadows as the valley of Jackson's Lake and the Grand Teton Basin. The parks are well watered. They are the sources of some of the major western streams. Jackson's Lake is the source of the Snake; North Park contains the source of the North Platte; South Park holds the source of the Arkansas; and the San Luis Valley, the source of the Rio Grande.

In the parks flourished rich grasses which played an important part in the development of the West. They attracted herds of game, which in turn brought hunters and trappers. Later the grasses fostered a cattle-growing industry in the mountains, which in turn provided food for gold-mining camps. A succession of economic stages occurred in these parks—first hunting and trapping, then grazing, then mining. Today they are the playgrounds of the nation.

West of the Rockies are three intermountain plateaus. The first, the Colorado Plateau, consists of numerous plateaus lying at different altitudes and separated from each other by steep cliffs. Tremendous canyons and gorges, carved by the Colorado River and its tributaries, crisscross the whole area. One of them is the Grand Canyon of the Colorado—thirteen miles wide at one point and a mile deep. The whole province is a country of rugged grandeur—a tourist's paradise.

The significance of the Colorado Plateau was that its gorges presented a barrier to emigrant wagon travel even greater than the Rocky Mountains. Through the Rockies a wagon route to the Pacific West was found at South Pass. But through the Colorado Plateau province were only the narrow and precarious mule-pack trails used by fur traders and by a few indomitable Santa Fe merchants.

A second intermountain plateau province is the Enclosed, or Great Basin, lying west of the Colorado Plateau and extending westward to the Sierra Nevadas. It is a land-locked basin that was to become the home of the Mormons. (A description of it is part of the chapter on the Mormon migration.)

North of the Enclosed Basin, between the northern Rockies and the Cascades, lies the third intermountain province—the Columbia Plateau. This is geologically an immense bed of lava, 200,000 square miles of it, of a depth varying from a third to a half mile. No other lava bed of such magnitude exists anywhere in the world except the Deccan Plateau of southern India. It was the product of 50 successive outpourings of lava from the earth's interior. The flows came from great crevasses in the earth and from volcanic peaks. The Cascades were volcanic peaks that literally blew their tops off in the violence of their eruptions. Such peaks as Mount Rainier, Mount Adams, and Mount Baker are all truncated volcanoes. No part of this province is free of lava except the mountain peaks rising above it. The profile of the flows is strikingly revealed in the gorges cut through them by such rivers as the Columbia and the Snake. The gorge of the Columbia, with its black basalt walls, is an especially revealing picture of the violent early geologic history of the area. The soil of the province is composed of disintegrated lava and is especially good for wheat and for fruit production.

The climate of the province is a major handicap. It is semi-arid. The province pays the price of lying in the climatic shadow of high mountains. The winds sweeping in from the Pacific are wrung dry of their moisture in crossing the Cascades. A little rain gets to the Spokane area in eastern Washington, which has become a major wheat region under modern methods of dry farming. The Columbia Basin irrigation project has been developed in southeastern Washington. But as a whole the province is heavily handicapped by lack of rainfall, and to the early pioneers it seemed quite hopeless.

The most western of the physiographic regions of the United States is the Pacific coast province, which on the map has the appearance of a giant letter "H." One arm of the "H" consists of the Cascades and the Sierra Nevadas. The other arm is the

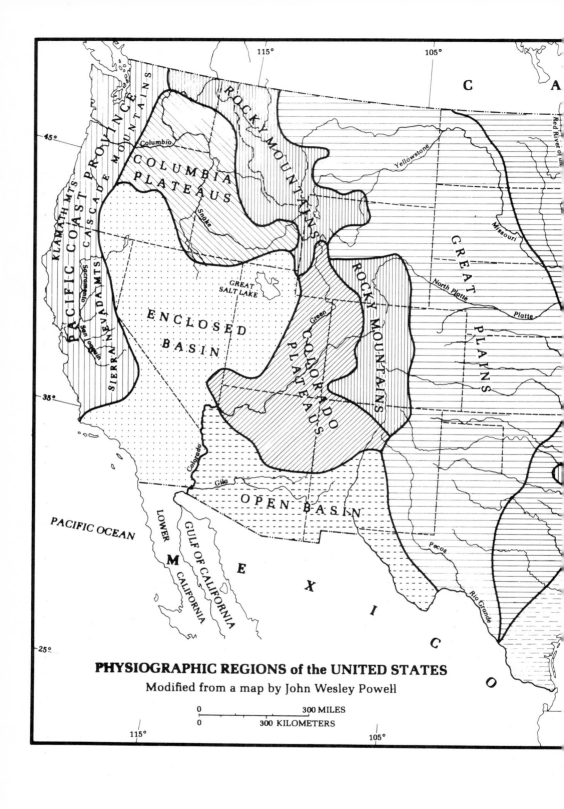

PHYSIOGRAPHIC REGIONS of the UNITED STATES
Modified from a map by John Wesley Powell

0   300 MILES
0   300 KILOMETERS

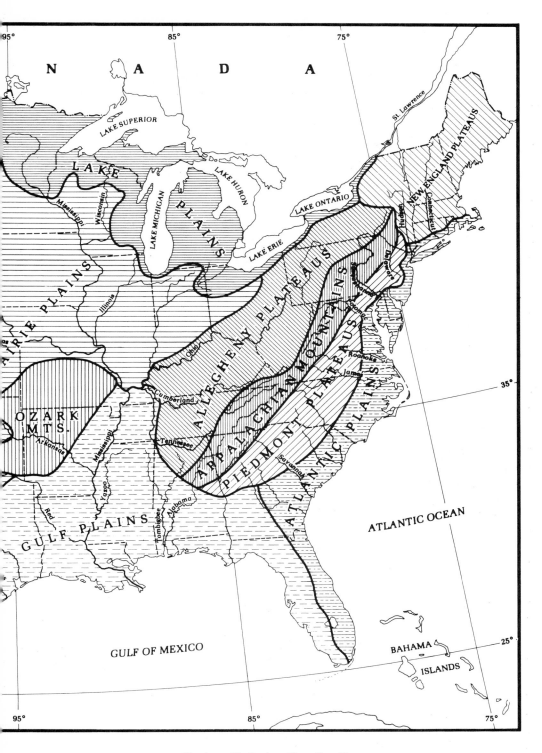

55. Physiographic Regions (from Powell)

coastal range of the Pacific. The bridge of the "H" is the mass of the Klamath Mountains.

In the arms of the "H" lie a succession of fertile valleys. The northernmost is the Puget Sound trough, which contains excellent soil. But much of the region was covered by huge Douglas fir, the roots of which were a killing job to remove.

South of the Puget Sound trough is the valley of the Willamette, a wonderfully attractive region. From an agricultural point of view it was the prize of the Pacific Northwest. Its soil is deep and fertile; its climate is ideal. It gets an abundance of rainfall and is not too heavily forested. The region had easy access to market by way of the Willamette and Columbia rivers. In the late 1830's and early 1840's the valley was a major pioneer attraction drawing thousands to the Pacific Northwest. It was the region that generated the so-called Oregon fever in the East.

South of the Willamette is the Sacramento Valley. This was also attractive to settlers, especially its southern portion. Hardly less alluring was the San Joaquin Valley, the southern counterpart of the Sacramento. These valleys were the magnets which drew American pioneers to the Pacific West and ultimately brought the vast area into the Union.

A characteristic of the far western provinces is their great size. Compared with the eastern seaboard provinces, they are of immense extent. On the accompanying map is shown a comparison of an entire eastern province with a single state in a western province. New England could be tucked into a corner of Texas (Map 56). Pennsylvania, which is considered a big state in the East, fits into the Texas Panhandle.

Nature in the Far West is on a vast scale. It was done up, as Ralph Waldo Emerson once said, "in big packages." The Rocky Mountains and the Sierra Nevadas are huge masses, the Great Plains are immense expanses, like the steppes of Russia; the canyons are awe-inspiring affairs such as the Grand Canyon. The rivers, such as the Missouri and the Columbia, are mighty. Even vegetation is on a vast scale—the giant Sequoia and the Douglas fir, for instance.

This vastness of nature seemed overpowering to many immigrants from the East. It seemed to dwarf and overwhelm mankind. The effect of it on some of the migrants is illustrated in a story told of a Connecticut Yankee who had taken up residence in the Pacific West, intending to retire there. After a few months he was overcome by homesickness and decided to return to New England. He was given a farewell dinner by his friends and invited to tell his impressions of the Far West. He complied by relating the story of creation.

When God made the United States He began in the Far West. With His trowel He piled up great mountain masses, one on top of the other; He carved out gigantic gorges and dug the channels of majestic streams. At the end of a day's labor He sat back and surveyed His work. A frown of dissatisfaction came over His face and He said, "Gosh, I've overdone it." Then He set to work on the Great Plains. There, with sweeping strokes of His trowel, He laid out vast spaces of level ground. At the end of the day's labor, He leaned back and surveyed His work. He shook His head and said, "That's even worse." Finally He came to New England. Here He threw aside His trowel, and with His fingertips delicately and tenderly molded the rolling hills, the intervales, the rocks and rills. At the end of a day's labor, He leaned back; a look of supreme contentment came upon His face, and He said, "This is God's country."

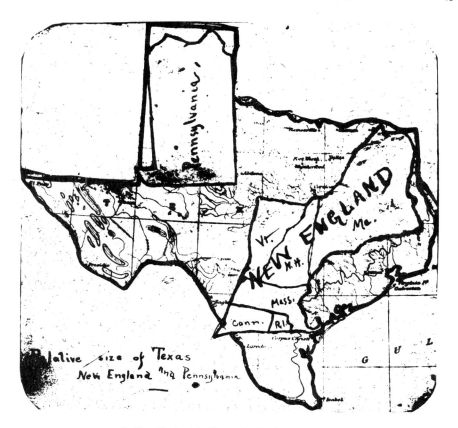

56. New England in Texas (by Frederick Merk)

Another characteristic of certain of the far western provinces is the domination of climate over their economy. This is especially true of the Great Plains and the three intermountain plateaus, which are all under the spell of water scarcity. The average annual precipitation in the United States is shown on the next map (57). The precipitation includes rainfall and snowfall. The areas of scarcity of rainfall and snowfall are the ones shown in the lighter shadings. They are the areas of the western Great Plains and the intermountain plateaus. Those areas get less than the minimum of precipitation needed for agriculture of the ordinary type. The minimum of precipitation needed for crops raised by ordinary methods is about 20 inches a year, and the greater part should fall in the growing season. In the East every section gets more than this minimum. In the western Great Plains and in the intermountain plateaus most of the land gets less than this minimum.

The line dividing the region of insufficient from that of sufficient rainfall is known to climatologists as the line of semi-aridity. It is the most significant line in the economic life of the nation. It runs from the northeastern corner of North Dakota in a

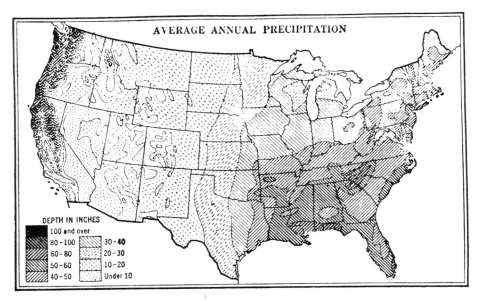

57. Annual Precipitation (from Kirkland)

sweeping arc to the mouth of the Rio Grande. It is not a fixed line but one drawn from Weather Bureau averages.

The scarcity of rainfall on the Great Plains and in the intermountain plateaus is a consequence partly of their interior location. It is also the result of the location of mountains and the direction of the prevailing winds. The effect on climate of the presence or absence of mountains is well illustrated by the record of the Pacific Northwest. In an early geologic age, before the Cascade Mountains had been thrust up, winds moved freely over the Columbia Plateau from the Pacific and brought an abundance of moisture. A lush vegetation flourished in the plateau. Evidence of this is a remarkable forest, now petrified in lava, in central Washington. This is the Ginkgo Forest in Ginkgo State Park. When the Cascades rose they intercepted the winds from the Pacific and wrung them dry. The rain has since fallen in torrents on the west slopes of the Cascades, tumbling down the slopes facing the Pacific in lovely cascades that gave the ranges their name. But the lands to the east—once the beneficiary of those rains—became a desert or semi-desert until the advent of irrigation.

Similarly in southern California, the winds from the Pacific hit the western slopes of the coastal ranges and the Sierra Nevadas, where a tremendous precipitation occurs. Then the winds, as they pass over southern California and the intermountain plateaus, pick up moisture rather than bring it, and deposit their collection on the western slopes of the Wasatch and the Rockies. The Rockies in the same way cast their climatic shadow over the Great Plains. The most arid portions of the Great Plains are those just east of the mountains.

In earlier American history the southwestern Great Plains and intermountain plateaus were regarded as desert areas, and were so described in early atlases. In 1855 Congress authorized the expenditure of $30,000 to buy camels and dromedaries for use on the deserts of the southern Great Plains. Seventy-five of various breeds of camels were bought by the War Department during the secretaryship of Jefferson Davis. They were imported from Tunis and Smyrna and were experimented with by the Army in the 1850's and 1860's on the western plains of Texas. Unfortunately, from the point of view of color in western history, that interesting experiment was abandoned with the advent of railroads, and the surviving camels were sold to circuses.

Another characteristic of the weather of the Great Plains is its variations or oscillations of rainfall. Over a period of five or six years, the annual rainfall may be fairly good and agriculture will flourish. Then will follow a cycle of five or six years of drought, worse even than normal, which re-establishes the low rainfall averages. These cyclical variations have been traps to settlers. In times of more than average rainfall, pioneers were lured out beyond the line of safety on the Plains. In drought periods, they had to abandon farms that had been built up at great pains. Some parts of the Great Plains have been settled and then unsettled three or four times.

During the 1930's depopulation of large proportions occurred as a result of droughts and duststorms. Then during World War II, and after, rains were good on the whole. Farmers flourished, and a land boom got under way on the Plains. In 1956 and in 1964 Kansas, Colorado, and the Southwest again suffered from drought and duststorms.

The effects of scarcity of rainfall on the Great Plains and intermountain plateaus are revealed on the next map, which shows improved land in farms in the United States in 1920 (58). Each black dot represents 25,000 acres of improved land. In the humid eastern half of the United States, a large percentage of land was in improved farms: in Iowa, 80 percent; in Illinois, 76 percent. But in the semi-arid West—and particularly in the region of the intermountain plateaus—the percentage of land in

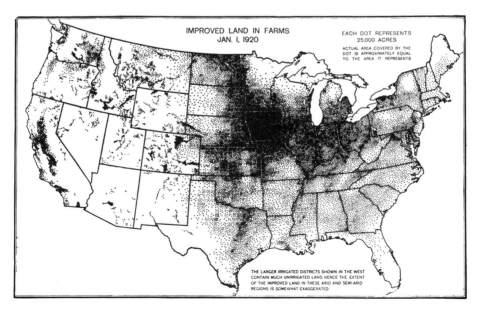

58. Improved Land in Farms, 1920 (from the *Yearbook of Agriculture*, 1921)

improved farms was very low. The states with low percentages are virtually white on the map. In Nevada, which relied heavily on gambling and divorce for its livelihood, the percentage of improved farm land was less than 1 percent; in Arizona, 1 percent; in New Mexico, 2 percent; in Utah, 3 percent. In 1920 the non-improved land in the semi-arid West consisted of 66 percent grazing land and 16 percent desert. The grazing land was not very rewarding.

In the humid East, the land that appears white on the map was often usable. It was forest or good pastureland. In the northern Great Lakes area the white regions were cut-over land, reforested or being reforested. In the Florida swamp area there was much land being reclaimed by drainage. But in the semi-arid region the whiteness on the map meant no use or almost no use in 1920.

On the Great Plains high winds are a serious climatic handicap. In the winter they come roaring down from the Arctic in the form of blizzards that, in the open-range stage, were destructive to cattle. In the summer hot winds come up from Mexico or the staked plains of Texas—winds that reach a temperature of 100 degrees or more and burn up the growing crops that lie in their path. These winds not only burn up crops, but produce disastrous duststorms.

Other climatological characteristics, especially of the High Plains and inter-mountain plateaus, are the purity and rarity of the atmosphere. These characteristics, associated always with high altitudes, produce unusual visibility on the western plains. The Rocky Mountains become visible at a distance of 100 miles or more. This phenomenon was of real use to the earlier travelers on the Great Plains. The atmosphere was so pure that Indians, and later the whites, used it for curing meat. They would simply cut up the meat of buffalo they had killed into slabs and hang them up to dry in the sun. The slabs dried sweet and wholesome. They did not spoil, as would have happened in a humid climate.

The dryness and rarity of the air are an important factor in agriculture. They are relied on by farmers to keep down certain diseases of plants. However, some insect pests, such as locusts and grasshoppers, originate in areas of semi-aridity.

In the matter of forest growth, the Great Plains were, in nature, treeless, or nearly so. The only trees were those lining the banks of streams. One cause of this was the insufficiency of precipitation, which in years of great drought was fatal to trees. The nature of the soil was another impediment to forest growth. In the westernmost part of the Plains the earth is often a clay, which packs hard and does not allow rain to be easily absorbed. Such rain as falls is held near the surface, where it quickly evaporates. Because of the imperviousness of the soil 75 percent of the rain that does fall in those sections is lost; only 25 percent ever gets as much as a foot or two into the ground. A third explanation is the high winds on the Great Plains—the blizzards of winter and the scorching winds of summer. Young growth cannot survive such an environment.

The treelessness of the Plains was an important factor in determining the order of succession of economic stages in the life of the province. Because of the lack of timber the range cattle industry, which needed little lumber at the outset, came first; then later, the settlers. Only after railroads had tied the Plains to the timber country of the northern Great Lakes region could a farming society become established in the section. Other large areas of treelessness in the Far West are the intermountain plateaus, the Central Valley of California, and the desert area south of the Enclosed Basin.

Forested areas do exist, however, in the Far West. There is timber in plenty in areas of good soil and high precipitation—on the western slopes of the Rockies and the Wasatch, and especially in the mountains of the Pacific Northwest and northern California. The Douglas fir and pine of the Pacific Northwest became the basis of a great lumber industry when the pine of the Great Lakes region had been exhausted.

Native grasses were of major importance in the evolution of the society of the Great Plains and the Far West. They were in large part a reflection of the moisture available to them. Prairie grasses grew tall east of the line of semi-aridity in the eastern Dakotas, Nebraska, Kansas, and Oklahoma. In part of Texas they grew as high as a horse. Their base was a thick, continuous sod. The grasses provided food for buffalo and later for settlers' livestock. The sod provided building material for houses and became an excellent soil when plowed under.

The prevailing grass of the Great Plains was a short variety, several inches in height and rising from shallow roots. It was a continuous variety but gave way in dry areas to bunch grass. The varieties of short grass were grama, buffalo, and curly. They were the food of buffalo and later of cattle. Mesquite grass was a pasture variety found scattered in the drier parts of the Southwest.

In the intermountain plateaus a still lower form of vegetation was, and is, dominant—the sagebrush. It survives in semi-arid regions because it has inner protective qualities—a relatively scant foliage, so that it does not throw off much of its interior moisture in the sun; also it has a pale green, almost a white foliage, which is an important protection. A dark green foliage would absorb too much heat and dry up the plant. Sagebrush has another quality enabling it to survive in the intermountain plateaus—it thrives in an alkali-tainted soil.

But it is not a very useful plant. It is nibbled by cattle a little when the plant has new growth, but they are sickened by too much of it. Its chief use to pioneers was as firewood in crossing the intermountain plateaus, if no tree growth was available. In some cases, where nothing was available for fires, dried buffalo dung was used in cooking.

On the desert of the Far Southwest still lower forms of plant growth were dominant, especially the mesquite, creosote, and greasewood shrubs. The mesquite carries beanlike pods that give food to livestock. These desert shrubs all adjust themselves to the sun's rays by having scant and pale foliage, and a resinous gum in their branches that prevents too much evaporation. They are all adjusted to an alkali soil.

The native animals of greatest use to man in the Far West were the buffalo, the wild horses of the Plains and intermountain plateaus, and the beaver of the mountains. The buffalo roamed the Great Plains in uncounted millions, moving south in the winter and north in the summer. They were a major food resource of the Plains Indians, keeping them alive the larger part of the year. Buffalo were hunted by the Indians with the aid of trained ponies. The mounted Indians would ride alongside a stampeding herd, firing arrows at close range down into the backs of cows, one after another. The shooting would go on for hours before the carcasses were gathered. Cows were preferred to bulls, which were likely to provide tough meat.

An Indian with his bow and arrow was exceedingly effective in a buffalo hunt, more effective than a white man with a rifle. An Indian could fire his arrows in quick succession until his quiver was empty. A white man with a rifle had to reload, an awkward exercise while galloping on a pony. Repeating rifles did not come into general use on the Great Plains until after the Civil War. An Indian could put an amazing force behind his arrow. Francis Parkman saw arrows discharged with such power by galloping Indians that the whole arrow, flint, shaft, and feather would all disappear inside the buffalo.

Buffalo were of equal value to white men. Pioneers crossing the Plains made use of the carcasses in the manufacture of dried and jerked buffalo beef. A carcass would be cut into thin slices and hung up to dry in the sun. If the hunters were in a hurry, the drying was hastened by the building of a fire. Meat cured with the aid of a fire was known as jerked beef. On the Canadian Plains the carcasses were converted into pemmican, which was made from dried slabs of buffalo meat. The slabs were first pounded to a pulp, which would then be packed into bags made of buffalo hide. Over the pulp was poured the melted tallow of the buffalo, and the whole would be allowed to harden. One bag of pemmican was one buffalo without his legs.

Pemmican was a compact and concentrated food. It was widely used in the far-flung transportation system of the Hudson's Bay Company. For express canoes shuttling between the Pacific shore and Hudson Bay, bags of pemmican, stowed in the canoes, was a major food reliance. Pemmican was later manufactured from reindeer meat for Arctic exploration.

Other conspicuous animal occupants of the Plains and intermountain plateaus were wild horses or mustangs. Millions of them roamed the Plains. They were a vital element in Indian economy. They were essential, also, in the mountain fur trade, for both white and Indian traders. Mustangs were wild descendants of Andalusian horses brought by Spanish settlers to Middle America. They had degenerated in size, weighing not more than 600 pounds, but they had endurance and speed. Though of great importance in the early stages of occupation, they came to be regarded as a nuisance. After the Plains had been taken over by the cattle industry, wild horses were pests because they ate grasses needed for cattle. Also, they lured away the horses of cowboys. In the 1920's, when they still numbered a million on the public domain, especially in Montana, Wyoming, and Nevada, the Department of the Interior started a campaign to exterminate them. The program was intensified in the 1950's and 1960's after Congress had established the Grazing Service to protect the native grasses on the public domain. The process was pressed by airplane, trap corrals, and roundups, the meat being converted into dog food. Eventually the public became aroused over the prospect of extinction of a species linking the present with the old Spanish American frontier, and in 1971 Congress prohibited the killing of wild horses on the public land. It directed the Departments of Agriculture and the Interior to preserve the remaining mustangs (about 8000) on ranges where they could be scientifically studied and be observed by tourists.

In the mountains the animal of greatest significance was the beaver, the staple of the mountain fur trade. Its fur had been sought ever since the discovery of North America, and had been a large factor in the Anglo-French wars for control of the interior.

Beaver fur was used chiefly in the manufacture of men's hats. It began to be put to this use commercially in the century following the discovery of America. From the colonial period onward high hats made of beaver fur were fashionable for men's winter wear in both Europe and America. Such was the market for beaver until the 1840's. Other furs were taken in the mountains, but beaver was much the most important.

The trapping of beaver was of major significance in the exploration of the Far West. It took American trappers from St. Louis and British trappers from Fort Vancouver into every mountain stream and pass of the Rockies, long before any official explorers, except Lewis and Clark. What the search for gold and silver was to exploration of the Spanish Southwest, the quest for beaver was to the Far Northwest. The trade was also important in the diplomacy of the Far West, and especially in the diplomacy of the Oregon Country. Conditioned by such factors of nature as these, the flow of population and trade into and across the trans-Mississippi West was begun.

Trans-Mississippi Trade

OF THE VAST WILDERNESS extending from the Great Plains to the Pacific coast, portions were claimed in the era of the War of 1812 by three powers—the United States, Great Britain, and Spain. The United States claimed the entire basin of the Columbia River by virtue of the discovery of the mouth of the river by Robert Gray (1792), by the explorations of the Lewis and Clark expedition (1804–06), and by John Jacob Astor's trading post, Astoria, built in 1811 near the river's mouth. Great Britain claimed the same area on the basis of the voyages of Drake, Cook, Vancouver, and Broughton, and by the overland explorations of Alexander Mackenzie. Spain held the Texas country and the region westward to the shores of the Pacific as provinces of New Spain. They had been acquired by overseas and land explorations and mission activities among the Indians of the area.

The principal attraction in this continental domain was its wealth of furs, which commanded high prices in the world markets. They were cheaply trapped by Indians or footloose whites, their transport costs were low, and their merchandising could be left to corporations that combined zeal for profit with imperialistic aspirations. The lure of furs had for centuries fueled the rivalries of empire in North America.

Each of the contenders for that trade had a western center for its operations. That of the United States was St. Louis, which was admirably situated for the mountain trade. It lay near the mouth of the Missouri River, the stream draining the richest of the Rocky Mountain fur preserves, and had long been the base for exploitation of those preserves. It had been founded by the French in 1764, partly for that purpose.

The British fur-trade center was Fort Vancouver, located on the lower Columbia River, opposite the mouth of the Willamette. It was as strategically placed as St. Louis. It commanded the trade of the whole Columbia Valley, including the valley of the Snake, the great southern tributary of the Columbia, and the valley of the Willamette. It had been built by the Hudson's Bay Company in 1824.

The third center was Taos, lying a hundred miles north of Santa Fe, in territory of Spain's successor—the Mexican Republic. It was a supply and trade base for mountain trappers in the Southwest, its supplies provided by St. Louis via Santa Fe. Its trapping parties consisted in large part of Americans, who operated with, or without, Mexican licenses. Some of them pushed north far enough to come into touch with Hudson's Bay Company trappers. Taos was not as strategically located as St. Louis or Fort Vancouver, and its trade was of smaller proportions.

Old and new concepts were united in the mountain trade. The old were those of eastern origin. Trading posts of this derivation were a combination of store and fort. The person in charge was a merchant to whom the Indians brought the furs they had trapped and from whom they received trade goods in exchange. Examples of such stores in the East were the Northwest Posts on the Great Lakes. They appeared in the early posts established on the upper waters of the Missouri by the famous St. Louis merchants Augustin Chouteau and Manuel Lisa.

The post technique contained a number of weaknesses. The Indians, who did the trapping, were not always as skillful or dependable as whites. The notion that Indians were invariably the best trappers is a fiction of the romanticists. The maintenance of the posts also entailed risks. They were filled with trade goods which tempted the cupidity of the Indians. Or, if they were protected by soldiers, they might arouse Indian apprehension that they represented a taking possession of the Indian country. The posts were likely to be overwhelmed by the Indians and destroyed.

A new technique—the brigade technique—was therefore instituted in the early 1820's. It was developed by American entrepreneurs in St. Louis and by British field directors at Fort Vancouver. In this procedure posts in the heart of the Indian country were for the most part dispensed with. The old complete dependence on Indians to do the trapping was abandoned. Instead, the whites did their own trapping in large brigades, moving through the Indian country.

The manner in which this system was made to work is illustrated by the operations of William H. Ashley of St. Louis and his successors, the Rocky Mountain Fur Company. It was experimented with by Ashley in 1823 and came into general use by 1825. A party of 100 or more men, with traps and other supplies, was sent from St. Louis to the mountains. On reaching the mountains it divided into several brigades, each going its own way in search of beaver. Each brigade trapped for a season, which extended from autumn to the succeeding June or July. The summer was the natural end of the season—furs not being then in the best condition.

In July or August a rendezvous of the several brigades was held at a prearranged place of meeting. The trappers of each brigade would bring their season's catch and settle accounts with the company. If a trapper was working for wages, he would collect his pay. The normal pay in this dangerous work was about $130 for the season. If the trapper was on his own—if he was what was known as a "free trapper"—he would turn in his furs at a prearranged rate.

To the rendezvous fresh supplies would be sent each year from St. Louis. Also, fresh men would come. Any trapper who had been a year in the mountains and wanted to remain another year would take a new outfit of traps and equipment. Any trapper who wanted to leave the mountains and return to civilization would go back with the caravan that took the season's catch to St. Louis.

Trappers usually stayed a number of years in the mountains. Usually they had to, for at the rendezvous the earnings of the year, and enough more to create a debt to the company, would be drunk up, gambled, and caroused away. The proprietors of the Rocky Mountain Fur Company saw to it that enough whiskey was sent to the rendez-vous to make it likely that this would happen.

The rendezvous usually attracted friendly Indians who joined in the festivities. The Snake Indians were the most common guests. The daughters of the Snakes would come too and find favor with the trappers. They would be purchased from their guardians with trapper presents. By the time of the next rendezvous, the maidens would themselves have presents of offspring to make to the trappers who had pur-chased them.

Trappers were free and easy about establishing such relationships. Usually they had women and children among a number of friendly tribes. They were equally casual about breaking off such relations. Milton Sublette, a partner in the Rocky Mountain Fur Company, in the course of his wanderings as a trapper acquired a Snake maiden whose name was the Lamb of the Mountain. He kept the Lamb contentedly as long as he remained in the mountain trade. When he retired to St. Louis, he bestowed her as a gift on his good friend Joseph Meek, by whom she became the mother of numerous children.

The mountain rendezvous were held normally in the mountain parks near South Pass. A favorite place for them was Pierre's Hole in the Teton Basin. Another was the country of the upper tributaries of the Green River. The rendezvous country was the meeting ground of the three rival fur-trading frontiers—the American, reaching out from St. Louis; the British, reaching out from Fort Vancouver; and the one reaching out from Taos in Mexican territory, led by Americans with Mexican licenses and with Mexicans in their trapping parties. Trapping and trading parties, thus representing three nationalities, sometimes came together at a rendezvous. If they were well dis-posed toward each other, they would exchange supplies, tobacco, and furs, and the rendezvous would take on the aspect of an international fair. The classic account of such a mountain rendezvous is to be found in Washington Irving's *Captain Bonne-ville*.

If, however, the leaders of trapping parties were disposed to overreach each other, or a meeting occurred in an area where trapping by any was out of bounds, episodes occurred in which all the venom of territorial rivalries rose to the surface. An instance was a hostile encounter which occurred in the valley of the Bear River in present-day Utah. The Bear Valley was Mexican soil, but boundary lines were not drawn and, even if they had been, would not have been observed by the mountain men. A Hudson's Bay Company party, under the command of Peter Skene Ogden, appeared there in the spring of 1825. Its trappers were partly "engagés," partly "freemen," ex-servants of the company, and Indians equipped by the company. The freemen were sullen because of years of exploitation by the company. A party of Americans—Ashley trappers headed by Johnson Gardner—appeared in the area and contacted the freemen. Gardner offered them a price for their furs eight times that which they had been receiving. The freemen and Gardner's party joined, moved on Ogden's camp, and made off with the freemen's furs, horses, and equipment. Gard-ner raised the American flag and denounced Ogden as an intruder on American soil. A battle in the wilderness was narrowly averted, which might have escalated into an Anglo-American conflict.

The brigade technique was superior to the post technique in a variety of respects. It offered greater safety from Indian surprise. A vigilant brigade of 30 to 35 trappers could hold off any ordinary Indian attack. The danger was lessened by the fact that the brigades were steadily on the move.

The means of transportation of the brigades were strings of mustangs or ponies bought from Indians. The animals were useful not merely for transport but as food if trappers were in danger of dying of starvation in a desert country. The mountain trapper leading his string of ponies is a distinct western type. Its spirit has been admirably caught by Frederic Remington in a famous painting, "Mountain Trapper."

The contribution of the Rocky Mountain fur trade was greater than the exploitation of the economic resources of a vast area. It included opening to the world knowledge of the geography of the region. The trappers were the discoverers of most of the geographic secrets of the Far West. Especially notable were those employed by the Rocky Mountain Fur Company and the Hudson's Bay Company. Some of the most important individual explorers were William H. Ashley, Jedediah Smith, and Jim Bridger of the Rocky Mountain Fur Company, and Peter Skene Ogden of the Hudson's Bay Company.

In the late 1830's and in the 1840's Captain John Frémont of the United States Army traveled over much of the Rocky Mountain West. He described his explorations in a series of reports, written with his wife's help, in a pleasing style. His journals were reprinted and distributed by the United States as government documents. They were widely read and used by many prospective migrants to the Far West. They became a kind of guide to the West. They won for Frémont a national reputation as a pathfinder, and this helped make him the Republican presidential nominee in 1856. But wherever he went in his expeditions he had with him mountain men who, as trappers, had explored the country a whole generation earlier. Frémont was merely the popularizer of the achievements of the mountain men rather than an explorer in his own right.

The mountain trade was significant in another respect. It was a cover for territorial rivalries of nations whose companies competed for the trade. Territorial domination was the ultimate goal of this trade, just as it had been of the eastern fur-trade rivalries in the colonial period. The region fought over in this rivalry was a vast one. Part of it was the area later known as the Oregon Country, extending from California to Alaska and from the Rocky Mountains to the sea. But the Oregon Country was only a fraction of the whole area at stake. All the California area and the vast intermountain plateaus—the equivalent of half of Europe—was in contest.

The California and southern intermountain plateau areas were, to be sure, the possessions of Spain, and later of Mexico, and were universally recognized as such. But they were held by so feeble and ineffective a grasp that the only question regarding them was whether the United States or England, or, in the case of California, Russia, would take them. The United States finally gave the answer by seizing them in 1846–48. Its armies took California and all the Southwest in the Mexican War. The United States also acquired the Oregon Country up to the 49th parallel at about the same time. The total territory thus obtained was 800,000 square miles. In all modern history there have been no rivalries or seizures comparable to these in magnitude except the rivalries of the European powers in Africa and in China.

The mountain trade was significant in another respect. It led to agricultural settlement of the Far West by Americans. The trappers who survived the dangers of their calling seldom returned to their Eastern homes. They had become unfitted by the wild freedom of their lives for civilized living. They were ordinarily tied to the wilderness by an Indian squaw and a brood of children. When they were too old to be effective trappers any longer they settled in some far western locality, especially in the Willamette Valley of the Oregon Country or the Central Valley of California. These choice regions were turned to farming by ex-mountain men, who thus initiated the process of American pioneer occupation. Finally, the trade was significant in the growth of St. Louis, which became the greatest primary fur market in the United States and one of the largest in the world.

While the mountain trade was developing, one of a very different type was unfolding in the Southwest. It was the Santa Fe trade, by which that Mexican community was supplied with goods from St. Louis. Santa Fe was the distributing center for the province of New Mexico and other parts of northern Mexico, and was also the political capital of the province. It was one of the oldest white settlements in North America. The date of its founding is usually given as 1609.

Santa Fe was initially an outpost of the Mexican port of Vera Cruz, whence came all its imports. These were carried by annual pack-mule train over a mountain trail 15,000 miles long. The volume was not large. Only the most valuable merchandise could bear the great costs of pack-mule transportation from Vera Cruz to Santa Fe.

Until 1821 trade with Santa Fe was a Spanish monopoly. Under traditional Spanish mercantilism, nationals of other countries, including the United States, were excluded from participating in the commerce of the empire. This exclusiveness was protected by the discouraging distance of Santa Fe from the settlements on the American frontier. Despite these deterrents attempts were made by Americans to break into the trade during the Spanish regime, but all ended in failure.

A new era in the history of the trade opened in 1821 as a result of the success of the Mexican revolt against Spain. As soon as independence was achieved intercourse was opened to Americans, subject only to normal Mexican tariffs. Also, by 1821, the American frontier settlements had drawn nearer Santa Fe. They had moved up the Missouri River to its big bend, where Independence is now. They had also moved up the Arkansas River. They were within 800 miles of Santa Fe, and that 800 miles covered level, open plains, which could easily be negotiated by wagons.

As soon as word of the success of the Mexican Revolution reached the ears of American traders on the frontier, two expeditions set out for Santa Fe—the Becknell expedition from the Missouri border, and the Glenn-Fowler expedition from the Arkansas border. This was the beginning of a commerce that soon became large, amounting in some years to almost half a million dollars. The trade continued without interruption until it was temporarily halted by Santa Anna in 1843, in violation of a commercial treaty with the United States—an act of arbitrary power that led to pressure for war with Mexico.

The route used in the trade was the famous Santa Fe Trail, which ran from Independence across what is now Kansas to Fort Dodge on the Arkansas River. From there traders either followed the Arkansas to Bent's Fort on the upper Arkansas and thence south to Santa Fe, or took a shortcut, the Cimarron Cutoff, across desert country, to the Cimarron River, then southwest along the Cimarron into New Mexico.

The trail was a dangerous road to travel. It was infested by marauding Indians, particularly by the Pawnee and the Comanche, the most accomplished horsemen and the most inveterate robbers of the Plains. If the traders had moved in small parties, they would have been at the mercy of those Indians. They therefore adopted, as the trade grew in volume, the caravan mode of travel. They gathered early in the springtime at Independence. Each trader might possess several wagons, sometimes a half dozen, driven by hired muleteers. The drivers would move together, without much organization, to Council Grove. Beyond that point the Indian danger became serious and a caravan would be organized.

A caravan might consist of as many as 100 wagons, each drawn by eight horses or mules, so that the draft animals would number 800 to 1000 head. The traders would choose a captain selected for experience and character. He would divide the wagons into four columns, which would move side by side across the plain. Each column would have a lieutenant in command, and there would be scouts ahead and at the rear to watch for Indians.

At night the columns would be formed into a hollow square. The two outer ones would turn in, and meet at right angles. The two inner ones would spread out and close the square. The wagons would interlock their wheels so as to form a corral. Inside the corral the horses and mules would sleep. They would be tethered as an additional safeguard against a stampede caused by Indians. It was vital to prevent a night stampede, which would render the caravan helpless. Here was a Kentucky station on wheels. It was impregnable against any ordinary attack by Indians.

This mode of travel was followed until Santa Fe came in sight. Then the caravan would break up. Each trader would whip up his teams, trying to beat his fellow travelers to the city. The Mexican customs officials would be bribed to be lenient in their tariffs and the sale of merchandise would begin.

For the muleteers and bull whackers, the arrival at Santa Fe was the signal for a barbaric debauch—the reaction to the abstention and monotony of the march across the Plains—succession of fandangos, graced by the maidens of Santa Fe, and sprees until all the earnings of the march had been blown in.

The goods brought to Santa Fe in this trade were predominantly textiles—cottons, calicoes, velvets—also cutlery and firearms. The return freight was silver—minted dollars and bullion from the Mexican mines—furs trapped in the mountains of the Southwest, mules, and horses.

The best description of this trade is Josiah Gregg's *Commerce of the Prairies,* a classic of western literature. Its author was a cultured Easterner, a physician, who went to the Great Plains for his health and engaged in the Santa Fe trade. He recovered his health, but in the meantime had been caught by the fascination of the Plains, the sense of limitless space, the stimulation of the high altitude, and the romance of the Plains life. He was spoiled for civilization, as he wrote back to eastern friends. He came to feel that he could not return to civilization, that it hemmed in a man and crushed his soul. He remained in the Far West and lost his life there.

The Santa Fe Trail was extended by an offshoot to California known as the Spanish Trail. This went north and northwest by a wide detour around the impassable gorges of the Colorado Plateau and turned southwestward in the Enclosed Basin, following water holes in the desert, to a termination in Los Angeles. On this trail a trade by mule-pack train was opened in 1829 by a Mexican, Antonio Armijo, and was continued by Americans bearing Mexican licenses. The goods so brought to Los Angeles consisted of silver from northern Mexico and woolen blankets woven in New Mexico. To Santa Fe in return came horses and mules from California, and furs trapped in the southern mountains. These swelled the volume of imports into St. Louis.

The significance of this far-flung commerce was nationwide. The Santa Fe trade was the school in which the frontier learned the arts of caravan travel over long distances. Pioneers found out how to make the even more arduous caravan journeys, in covered wagons, to Oregon, California, and Utah.

The silver brought to Independence and to St. Louis was an important element in the Missouri economy. Minted silver dollars had wide circulation in Missouri. They preserved the state from the worst of frontier paper-money heresies, and help to explain Thomas H. Benton's hard-money views. He was so sturdy an exponent of such views in Congress that he was known throughout the country as "Old Bullion." The bullion of the trade had another importance. It induced Congress in 1835 to establish in New Orleans a branch of the national mint, the first in the West. Of no less economic significance was the flow of mules in the trade, which started Missouri on its career as a mule breeding and exporting state.

Another result of the trade was that it turned the attention of the American people to the Spanish Southwest. Their imagination was caught by the picturesque, exotic civilization of the Far Southwest. The American frontier learned also of the weakness of the Mexican grip on its northern provinces and learned as well to dislike the uncertainty and corruptness of Mexican officialdom. All these were factors in bringing on the Mexican War.

The trade was significant also in terms of American military expansion. At Fort Leavenworth, opposite the starting point of the Santa Fe Trail, Colonel Stephen W. Kearny began collecting a frontier army at the onset of the Mexican War, and in the summer of 1846, as brigadier general, he moved down the trail to Santa Fe and captured the city. Soon thereafter, along another traders' trail, he crossed from the Rio Grande to the Gila, and followed that stream to southern California, where, after a costly battle at San Pasquale, he seized San Diego. Here was the course of empire taking a familiar pattern—economic penetration, followed by territorial possession.

The Mississippi Valley Frontier and Its Outlets to the Far West

THE POPULATION DRAWN to Texas and the Far West in the 1830's and 1840's was prevailingly southern in origin. It was drawn from that portion of the trans-Appalachian West bounded at the north by the National Road and at the south by the Gulf of Mexico. Specifically the recruiting ground included the southern half of the Ohio Valley, the whole of the Cumberland and Tennessee valleys, and, on the west side of the Mississippi, the valleys of the lower Missouri and the lower Arkansas. In the Gulf area it included Alabama, Mississippi, and Louisiana. On the census maps of 1830 and 1840 the recruiting ground assumes the appearance of a massive spearpoint, thrust into the interior from the base of the Appalachians and carried to the western limit of Missouri, where it was blunted against a serried row of Indian reservations.

Unoccupied or sparsely settled land was to be found in the valleys of the Ohio, Missouri, and Mississippi. In northern Illinois and Indiana prairies were open to settlement but they were large and were avoided by Southerners. Wisconsin, Iowa, and Minnesota lay mostly beyond the zone of southern expansionist forces and were left to Northerners and European emigrants. Missouri and Arkansas contained vacant land, but it was not choice. The Ozark Plateau was particularly rough country. In the Gulf Plains the best lands were taken. Great areas were unsettled because they were subject to overflow, or were not well suited to sugar or cotton production. In Texas and the Far West lay beautiful lands that were to be had virtually free.

In the recruiting ground for pioneers bound for Texas and the Far West there was a considerable element of turbulent characters, believers in direct action and quick to violence. Outlaws and criminals were also there. They were a small minority. The bulk of the population was self-respecting and hard-working. But turbulence was common, especially in the river societies of the 1830's and 1840's. The evidence for it is to be found in travelers' accounts and in newspaper reports of the river towns. An observation on the Ohio River society, written in 1817 by Morris Birkbeck, an

Englishman who traveled down the Ohio and made a settlement in Illinois, is revealing:

> There are about two thousand people regularly employed as boatmen on the Ohio, and they are proverbially ferocious and abandoned in their habits, though with many exceptions, as I have good grounds for believing. People who settle along the line of this grand navigation, generally possess or acquire similar habits; and thus, profligacy of manners seems inseparable from the population on the banks of these great rivers. It is remarked, indeed, everywhere, that inland navigators are worse than sailors.

The banks of the Mississippi from north to south were a line of disorder from the lead-mine region of Wisconsin down to the river's mouth. The lead mines in Wisconsin, Iowa, and also in Missouri were areas of an excitable population. Most of the miners were Southerners. Those in the Driftless region had come by way of the Mississippi from Missouri or Kentucky. They were a speculating, restless, and adventurous type. Also present were foreigners, predominantly Cornish miners and Irish.

In this society the southern code of dueling honor prevailed, but the duels were of the frontier sort, fought with bowie knives rather than with pistols. Even the ex-governor of Wisconsin Territory, Henry Dodge, who lived in the lead-mine region in the early 1840's, was reputed always to carry a bowie knife around with him. He was rebuked by the Milwaukee press in 1841 for bringing a bowie knife to a Milwaukee hotel and leaving it in a fit of forgetfulness under his pillow. Street brawls with clubs and shillelaghs were a common occurrence in the lead-mining towns.

The turbulence of the southern elements in the lead-mine regions was in contrast to the relative orderliness and peacefulness of the New England and German folk in the lakeshore counties of Wisconsin. The contrast is pointed out with self-righteousness by the editors of the lakeshore newspapers. They chided the lead-mine regions for disorders and a false southern code of chivalry.

In Illinois—in the three Rock River counties of Boone, Ogle, and Winnebago—a sort of guerrilla war went on in the early 1840's, according to the Milwaukee press, between two evenly balanced elements, one of them an organized gang of horse thieves, counterfeiters, and outlaws; the other a body of vigilantes, who were lynching or mobbing in protection of their lives and property. The lakeshore press charged that the administration of justice in some Illinois counties was dominated by criminals.

In Jackson County, Iowa, along the banks of the Mississippi, occupied largely by pioneers of southern extraction, a similar situation existed. In this county a gang of horse thieves and criminals was operating, which, with its adherents, was resisting the efforts of vigilantes to expel them. A local war took place between them in the early 1840's, known as the Bellevue War, which culminated in a pitched battle. In these communities conditions prevailed much like those later in the gold-mining camps of California and Montana.

On the Missouri-Arkansas border, and especially in parts of the highland region of the Ozark Plateau, there was a broken-down element of poor whites who had lost out in the competition for the good lands of the Missouri Valley. Brawls were common there of a kind characteristic of the poor whites in the lower South. The rules of fair fighting were all off. The chief object was to get the opponent down and, with fingernails, to gouge out one or both of his eyes. Measuring the length of the eye strings of the opponent was the objective. Some toughs were said to let their finger-nails grow long for this purpose.

In the river towns of the Mississippi, from one end of the river to the other, there was a large element of keelboatmen and flatboatmen, given to drunkenness and low morality, and taking pride in being tough. The type was described by Mark Twain as half horse, half alligator. It was exemplified in the legendary hero Mike Fink, King of the Keelboatmen. Other types in the river towns were steamboat roustabouts and deckhands, and various categories of floating transportation labor. On the steamboats was a brotherhood of gamblers and confidence men. Mark Twain caught the spirit of this river society in his *Life on the Mississippi*.

On the lower Mississippi the tradition was still affectionately nursed of river pirates in the bayou country and robber gangs on the Natchez Trace. In the early 1840's a German traveler, Friedrich Gerstäcker, made a pilgrimage to the lower river towns and picked up the folklore of this society, which he published in the form of a series of romantic works, *Pirates of the Mississippi* (1848), *Regulators of Arkansas* (1845), and *Mississippi River Pictures*.

In the mid-1840's Charles Dickens visited the United States and traveled in the Mississippi Valley. He was struck by the disorder and the violence of this society. In his *Notes on America,* he cited page after page of newspaper reports of crimes of violence in the Mississippi Valley. These crimes he attributed to the slavery system. Actually they were a frontier characteristic, of which the 1840 frontier was an exaggerated example.

The method used by Dickens of piling up cases of disorder produced an over-drawn picture. It understated the normal and overstated the abnormal. The normal on the Mississippi Valley frontier was the dull work of clearing the forest. The pioneer sought relief in hunting and fishing, in occasional revivalist meetings, or in bottled spirits. But tolerance of disorder, impatience with restraint, and a reliance on self-help were part of life. Also, there was a higher percentage of toughs there than was usual on western frontiers.

If the prevalence of this disorder is to be understood the geography of the region must be emphasized. The chief rivers—the Ohio, Missouri, and Mississippi—kept in constant circulation on the steamboats a large element of floaters—gamblers, card sharks, light-fingered gentry, and counterfeiters—the flotsam and jetsam of transportation life. Into St. Louis came the half-wild mountain trappers; into Arkansas and Missouri came the coarse muleteers and bull whackers of the Santa Fe trade. The hill areas of Arkansas contained poor-white "trash" and outlaws. Up against the row of Indian reservations on the western borders of Missouri and Arkansas were those who preyed on the weaknesses of the Indians—traders, whiskey dealers, and other dregs of society.

The economic disorganization of the period was a factor in producing restless-ness and disorder. The years following the Panic of 1837 to the mid-1840's were a time of economic collapse, bankruptcy, depressed prices, and widespread distress. Society in the West was unhappy, tense, eager for a change. All these forces joined in producing disorder and in sending the discontented to Texas, to Oregon, and to California.

The Far West had its own elements of confusion to add to the volatility brought to it from the Mississippi Valley frontier—the conflicts of sovereignty within the area, the mysteries of a strange and unexplored geography, and the dangers from the aborigines. To all these were added the disorders of the wilderness vocations—the wild freedom of the trapper's life, and the excitements of convoying trading caravans across deserts, around gorges, and through mountains.

As colonizers, the adventurers from the Mississippi Valley frontier were well qualified to subdue and acquire a wilderness, especially one that was feebly held. They moved at an early date into Texas, where they led the way in defying Mexican authority and precipitating the revolution in 1835. Once the revolution began, organized companies from the Mississippi Valley went to the area of battle, in violation of American neutrality laws. They joined the Texans to overpower and destroy the invading Mexican army at the battle of San Jacinto and to win for Texas a *de facto* independence. Texan leaders dreamed of seizing other northern provinces of Mexico and extending the dominion of Texas to the Pacific. In Congress their cause was pressed by American expansionists. In the spring of 1842 Henry Wise of Virginia, an intimate of President Tyler, urged this program in a glowing speech that reflected the sentiment of many Southerners. He observed:

> While she [Texas] was, as a state, weak and almost powerless in resisting invasion, she was herself irresistible as an invading and a conquering power. She had but a sparse population, and neither men nor money of her own to raise and equip an army for her own defense; but let her once raise the flag of foreign conquest—let her once proclaim a crusade against the rich States to the south of her, and in a moment volunteers would flock to her standard in crowds from all the States in the great valley of the Mississippi—men of enterprise and hardy valor before whom no Mexican troops could stand for an hour. They would leave their own towns, arm themselves, and travel on their own costs, and would come up in thousands to plant the lone star of the Texian banner on the proud ramparts of the Mexican capital. They would drive Santa Anna to the South, and the boundless wealth of captured towns, and rifled churches, and a lazy, vicious, and luxurious priesthood, would soon enable Texas to pay her soldiery and redeem her State debt, and push her victorious arms to the very shores of the Pacific.

Migrants to the Oregon Country from the Mississippi Valley faced a power not as easily dispossessed as Mexico, Great Britain and her agent, the Hudson's Bay Company. They did succeed, however, in arousing fears in the directorate of the company for the safety of the stores housed in its base on the Columbia River. This led to a shift of base to the safety of Vancouver Island, with consequences that were to be significant in the settlement of the Oregon question. Migrants of the same type, flowing into the inner valley of California, precipitated the Bear Flag revolt in 1846, which was a preliminary to the acquisition of California. The colonization of Utah was indirectly the work of frontiersmen in Missouri and in Illinois, who brutally attacked Mormons in their midst and forced them to move. The Mormon flight in 1846–47 to the Great Basin was the beginning of another far western state.

In this period came the Mexican War, precipitated by a Tennessean, President James K. Polk. The war was acclaimed by Mississippi Valley elements, who volunteered in it with enthusiasm. They knew the weakness of Mexico's hold on the northern provinces. Ever eager for a fight, they saw in the war an opportunity to "sack the Halls of the Montezumas." During the war an "Army of the West" was recruited at Fort Leavenworth on the Missouri, which descended on Santa Fe and seized it.

Later, in the mid-1850's, such elements were an important factor in producing the frontier episode known as "Bleeding Kansas." After the Kansas-Nebraska Act had been passed by Congress in 1854, "border ruffians" from Missouri moved over that state's boundary into Kansas, and stuffed the ballot boxes in the territorial elections in order to capture Kansas for slavery. They sacked the New England town of Lawrence, and helped to precipitate the civil war in Kansas which was the prelude to the greater bloodbath of the Civil War.

Coinciding with the restlessness and turbulence of the Mississippi Valley society in the 1840's was the flowering of the doctrine of Manifest Destiny. The doctrine was that the destiny of the United States was to expand sooner or later over the continent of North America. It was trumpeted by the penny press of the eastern seaboard and had a vogue among the Democracy of the larger cities. It was echoed on the hustings and in Congress by dough-face Democrats and by Mississippi Valley expansionists. It was repudiated by Whigs and reached only partial realization. In the scattered episodes of the 1830's and 1840's, alluded to here, it takes on the coherence of a pattern.

In the colonization of the Far West transportation routes were factors of great significance, more so than they had ever been east of the Mississippi. In the East the advance of the frontier had been by short stages—New England to New York, New York to Ohio, Ohio to Wisconsin, and so on. The same short stages were true of westward migration in the Old South.

But in the Far West the advance was of different sort. The region just west of the Missouri and Arkansas borders was closed to settlement by rows of Indian reservations and, beyond, by the factor of semi-aridity. Texas was relatively near, and wonderfully rich lands were obtainable there at bargain prices. But it lay in the latitudes of slavery and most Northerners preferred to avoid it. In the Pacific West lay lands of incomparable attractiveness and easily obtained, but at a forbidding distance across a wilderness of mountains, semi-arid plains, and deserts. Migration to them was feasible only because through this maze ran easily followed trails, particularly the Oregon and California trails.

The Oregon Trail had its starting point at Independence, at the great bend of the Missouri. This was the outfitting center for the journey across the continent, the jumping-off place of the pioneer. From Independence the route ran up the Missouri, the Platte, the North Platte, and the Sweetwater to South Pass, thence by the valley of the Bear to the Snake River, and along the route of the Snake and Columbia to the Pacific coast. The California Trail was an offshoot from the Oregon Trail.

The Oregon Trail was an excellent route. It was the shortest, the most direct road to the Pacific. The grades on it were easy, especially those between Independence and South Pass. They could be negotiated by wagons and the way was well known. It was the route the fur traders had used and was relatively safe from Indians. No large caravan on it was ever attacked by Indians. Only small parties of stragglers found it dangerous. The essentials for travel were available. Water was always near at hand and forage for draft animals was easily available. Grass could be depended on from the beginning of May, when migrants set out from Independence, until the wintertime. Food for the pioneers was also to be found, especially in the buffalo country. Firewood for cooking was usually available even in the sagebrush country. Where no firewood was to be found, dried-up buffalo dung, the so called "buffalo chips," could be used.

Compared with this trail the Missouri River route, which had been explored by the Lewis and Clark expedition, was quite inferior. It was circuitous and much longer than the Oregon Trail. It could not be taken by wagons. Neither could it be advantageously used by river craft. Its channel was difficult. It could be ascended only by going against the current—by keelboating—and its water level was unpredictable. The river was jealously guarded by hostile Indians who sought to blackmail or pillage travelers. At its headwaters lay the ferocious, implacable Blackfoot.

The Oregon Trail offered the traveler an ideal passageway through the Rocky Mountains—South Pass. It not only provided a low pass over the Continental Divide, but the grades to and from it were easy. The opening is so wide that travelers using it hardly realized they were traversing a pass.

South Pass became the hub of transportation in the Far West. It was the center to which and from which all the natural highways radiated. The Missouri, the Platte, the Arkansas, the Rio Grande, the Colorado, and the Snake all have their headwaters near it. What Cumberland Gap was to the East, South Pass was to the Far West.

Discovery of the pass was a cumulative achievement of fur traders. In 1811 Robert Stuart, of John Jacob Astor's Astoria on the lower Columbia, led an overland party east to report to Astor the loss at sea of an essential supply ship. He took a shortcut from the upper waters of the Snake to those of the North Platte by way of South Pass. Whether his course in the pass was that later taken by wagons is unclear. His achievement was described at the time in the Missouri and the national press. But the fact that he had found a route practical for wagons through the Rockies was not reported. The existence of the pass was all but forgotten until its rediscovery in 1824 by a party of Ashley trappers under the command of Jedediah Smith. Immediately the pass became vital to fur traders. In its vicinity their annual rendezvous were held and its potential for wagon transit became apparent. In the early 1830's fur traders took the first wagons over the pass. This was crucial knowledge for the overland movement of agricultural settlers to the fertile valleys of Oregon and California.

Migration to the provinces of the Pacific was a major exertion, even after the Oregon Trail had become the accepted road. It meant travel in the blistering sun and duststorms of the Plains and through the inhospitable Enclosed Basin or the Columbia Plateau—travel without rest for five months. The caravans often approached the Willamette in a state of utter exhaustion and had to be rescued by relief parties sent out by the Hudson's Bay Company.

The significance of the Oregon and California trails in American history is twofold. They were the "paths of empire" in the nation's formative years, opening the provinces of the Pacific West to occupation by American pioneers and to acquisition by the United States. Later they served as arteries between the Pacific coast and the Mississippi Valley, through which the life currents of travel and trade flowed until the advent of railroads.

Texas

BETWEEN THE WESTERN boundary of the Louisiana Purchase and the Pacific Ocean lay two stretches of territory that were either part of a foreign state or of undetermined nationality: Texas and the Oregon Country. Texas was southwest of the Louisiana Purchase and was part of New Spain. It was claimed by some American expansionists to be part of the Louisiana Purchase, but its rivers flowed directly into the Gulf of Mexico and not into the Mississippi.

Geographically Texas was a composite of portions of three major provinces — the Gulf Plains, the Prairie Plains, and the Great Plains. The Gulf Plains portion was partly attractive to pioneers and partly less so. The less attractive was the northern part, a piney woods region which pioneers avoided. Some of the southern part was semi-arid, though later irrigated. But most of it was, and is, good grazing land, the location of a great Texas cattle industry. One of the great oil fields of the world was discovered there in the 20th century and became the foundation of a rich petroleum and chemical industry. But of this possibility the pioneers were completely unaware.

On the western side of Texas is the Great Plains portion. This is a land of semi-aridity that becomes more and more marked in the westernmost Plains, until actual desert conditions are reached in southwestern Texas. This area was once described by a humorist as having more streams and less water, more cows and less milk, where you can look farther and see less than in any other part of the world. This would have been less flippant if its author had suspected that West Texas would also be found to be a center of great oil fields, and that irrigation would make it a producer of cotton.

The third zone lies between these two. It is the prairie section of Texas. It is a southward extension of the prairie province and its soil is of comparable richness. It is similar to the Black Belt of Alabama in the texture and fertility of its land. Locally it is known as the Black Prairie of the Black Waxy. It was intermittently timbered. Its

265

timber was sufficient for houses and barns, and yet not so heavy as to be an encumbrance. For either farming or grazing the area was ideal.

Early in the 19th century Texas was an almost unbroken wilderness. It contained only three outposts of Spanish civilization, with a total population of not over 3000 or 4000. These settlements were maintained with difficulty against the raids of marauding Indians. One of the settlements lay in the valley of the Neches, near the Sabine River. It consisted of six clusters of population that had gathered around Spanish missions early in the 18th century (1716–17). Another settlement was Goliad on the Texas coast near the site of La Salle's destroyed colony (1685). A third, at San Antonio de Bexar, was a remnant of a mission founded in 1718.

All these settlements were remote from Mexico City, the center of Spanish authority. All were dissatisfied with Spanish rule and supported rebellion in the era of the disintegration of Spanish authority in the New World. Their mood was an invitation to American adventurers to add the region to the United States.

Between 1800 and 1821 several attempts were made to revolutionize these settlements. The first was by Philip Nolan, who flits across Texan history at the end of the 18th century. He was a hunter of mustangs, corralling them for export to the United States. He was a correspondent of Thomas Jefferson, who had a scientific curiosity about wild horses and the plains over which they roamed. In 1800 Nolan led a small force into Texas ostensibly for the purpose of capturing wild horses. To the Spanish he seemed to have filibustering in view. They had been alerted to his coming by one of his men. His force was intercepted at the Red River. He was killed and the rest of his men were captured and sent to prison.

Another American expedition that may have been headed for Texas was the famous one of Aaron Burr in 1805–06. Whether Texas was actually in his mind is not known, but the Spanish authorities in Texas thought it was, and came across the Sabine River into what is now Louisiana in the expectation of meeting and fighting the invader. Zebulon Pike's expedition to the Southwest in 1806, which was under the orders of James Wilkinson, is believed by some historians to have had some connection with the Aaron Burr project, though none has ever been determined.

The most ambitious attempt on Texas was the Gutierrez-Magee expedition of 1811. Gutierrez was a Mexican revolutionary; Magee an ex-lieutenant in the American Army. The expedition consisted of about 3000 men, partly American frontiersmen from the Mississippi Valley society, partly Mexicans and Indians. For a time it was successful, penetrating as far west as San Antonio and capturing a Spanish general and his army. But it was torn by internal dissensions and broke apart over the issue of the execution of the captured general. After the execution the Americans withdrew in disgust and the Mexican contingent soon after was disastrously defeated and dispersed.

In 1819 the last of these invasions occurred—that of James Long. It represented, in part, a protest against the Adams-Onís Treaty of 1819, in which the United States yielded its claim to Texas as a part of the Louisiana Purchase, in return for the cession by Spain of Florida and its rights in the Oregon Country. The treaty was denounced by American expansionists as an unconstitutional and unpatriotic surrender of American rights to Texas. The Long expedition was an attempt to rectify that error. In the course of the expedition the town of Nacogdoches was captured. A republic was organized, and an alliance was made with the famous Gulf pirate Jean Lafitte, whose headquarters were on Galveston Island. But ultimately the expedition was defeated and sent flying back across the American boundary.

In 1821 a new era opened in Mexican-American relations with the achievement of Mexican independence from Spain in a war in which Mexico had the sympathy of the American public. Opportunities of settlement and trade were extended by the new republic to foreigners, and filibustering lost some of its old attraction. In particular Mexico offered land in generous tracts to foreigners, virtually free, in three successive colonization laws of the years 1823 to 1825. Under an 1823 law empresarios were given contracts if they agreed to bring at least 200 families into Mexico within a specified period and to settle them. A designated tract of land would be reserved for the operations of each empresario.

The empresario was authorized to grant land to settlers varying in amount according to the use each expected to make of it. If the use was to be farming, the grant could be a *labor* of arable land (177 acres). If the use was to be the grazing of cattle, the amount could be at least a *sitio* of grazing land (4428 acres). The intent of the law was to draw a distinction between farming and grazing land. But in the Texas prairies virtually all land was good for farming. Most colonists decided to be grazers.

Other attractions than land were held out to immigrants. One was exemption from civil and ecclesiastical taxation for six years, and only a half liability for a further six years. Another lure was tariff privileges. Each immigrant family entering Mexico could bring free of duty all tools needed for its own use and merchandise to the value of $2000. The only requirements imposed on immigrants were those of religion and character. Immigrants had to be, or become, Roman Catholics. They also had to become citizens of Mexico within three years after the acceptance of land.

An empresario who entered into a colonizing contract was to receive for his services two *labors* and fifteen *sitios* of land (66,774 acres) for each 200 families he brought into Mexico and located. These were his premium lands. He might also be allowed to sign up for three such contracts and, if he fulfilled their terms, he would receive three times the premium lands. As a safeguard against building up great estates, the empresario was required to sell two-thirds of his premium lands in twenty years.

The conception of this system was in part the work of two Americans, Moses Austin, of Connecticut origins, and his son, Stephen F. Austin. Both were respected in Mexican government circles. The elder Austin had once been a lead miner, who had spent his youth in Virginia lead mines. Then he had moved to Missouri, where he made a fortune in the Missouri mines, which he lost in the Panic of 1819. In 1820 he learned of opportunities to acquire Texas land, and applied to the Spanish authorities at San Antonio for a grant. They were favorable to his request and he was awaiting a validation of the grant when the Mexican Revolution of 1821 intervened. He died soon thereafter and the confirmation was made to his son, Stephen. It was Stephen who assisted the new Mexican authorities in formulating the provisions of the colonization law of 1823, while waiting for validation of his grant.

In August 1824, after a federalist form of government had been established in Mexico, a new colonization law was passed by the Mexican Congress. In it the details of colonization were entrusted to the states, while the central government retained control of important aspects of colonization. Two clauses offered inducements to colonists: one, a guarantee by the federal government of contracts between empresarios and the families they introduced; the other, an exemption of foreigners from all taxes for a period of four years. But restrictions on empresarios and settlers were more numerous. No more than eleven square leagues were to go to one person. No land was to be transferred by a colonist to a religious order and none to nonresidents of Mexico. Foreigners were not to settle within twenty leagues of an international boundary or within ten leagues of the coast. Finally, the federal government could forbid individuals of a particular nation to enter Mexico. A month earlier, July 13, 1824, the federal government forbade the introduction of slaves into Mexico. These provisions indicated fears and suspicions arising in the Mexican Congress.

In 1825 the state of Coahuila-Texas passed a colonization law, as states were permitted to do. It established an empresario system much like the one outlined in the law of 1823. It welcomed foreign immigrants of good character, who would become Mexican citizens and Roman Catholics. Settlers were expected to pay a small fee to the state for their land. An empresario was permitted as many as eight contracts, each to bring in 100 families within six years. The empresario might indicate the "grant" area he desired, from which he and his colonists would select their lands, but the actual location would be set by the state. An empresario could obtain somewhat more premium land than the federal law of 1823 had allowed, but he had to sell, after twelve years, all but eleven square leagues. Settlers could acquire a square league of partly arable and partly grazing land. The law included anti-speculation provisions, which proved difficult to administer. A special inducement to empresarios and to colonists was exemption from state and local taxes for a period of ten years. Regarding the introduction of slaves, new settlers were ordered "to subject themselves to the laws that are now, and shall be hereafter established on this subject."

The colonization system was expected to yield important benefits to Mexico. It would develop Texas and other portions of the republic and enrich Mexico; the new settlements would serve as a buffer, protecting the southern states from the raids of Indians of the Great Plains; and communities of superior quality would be established. The self-interest of each empresario would lead to the establishment of desirable communities. The value of an empresario's own premium lands would be dependent on the character of the community he built.

Empresario contracts proved immediately popular to speculators. They were applied for in such numbers that by the end of the 1820's almost all the best land of Texas was reserved for empresario operations. The size and locations of the areas reserved are shown on the map (59). Note the location of the 1823 grant to Austin, embracing the valleys of the Colorado (of Texas) and the Brazos, and Austin's later reservations under the law of Coahuila-Texas.

All reservations for empresarios were deliberately made oversize, in order that ample choice of land might be open to settlers and to the empresario for his premium lands. At the end of the time limit of any contract, whatever land had not been selected by the empresario, or his immigrant families, reverted to the government. The heavy black line, drawn on the map, embraces the area where empresario contracts were either wholly or partially fulfilled. The area of the Black Prairie is altogether within the heavy line. It has been estimated that empresario contracts were made for attracting over 5000 families, and that approximately 2900 families were brought in under

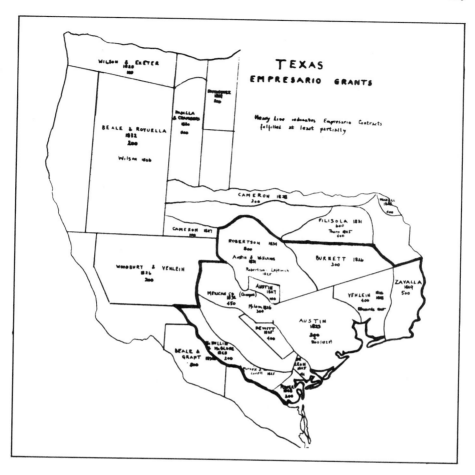

59. Empresario Contracts (based on Barker)

the system. Some grants were made directly to individuals by state authorities. But because the latter were at first only Spanish-speaking, American immigrants preferred to settle through the agency of the empresarios, who took care of obtaining titles for them. In addition, squatters came in considerable numbers.

The Mexican expectation was that a diversity of nationalities would be attracted to Texas—that native Mexicans, Europeans, and Americans would all come. That expectation is reflected in the names of the empresarios to whom grants were given. The map shows the names Felisola, Zavala, DeWitt, Vehlein, McMullin, and McGloine. A vague idea seems to have been entertained that the Americans coming would be chiefly from Louisiana and would be of French or Spanish Catholic extraction. Mexico did not expect that Anglo-Americans would form the one great element that would appear in Texas.

But no elements other than Americans came in substantial numbers. Mexicans were not of pioneering stock. They were reluctant to run the risks and Indian dangers of the Texas frontier, and they lacked the means and the enterprise to undertake the journey north. In 1830 not more than 4000 native Mexicans were settled in Texas, and they were chiefly in, or near, the settlements dating from the 18th century.

Europeans likewise showed little interest. Germans came, but not on a large scale. They appeared only after the Texas Revolution. A few Irish came. McMullin and McGloine had a contract to bring 400 families to San Patricio. But the Irish they brought were from New York City or New Orleans, rather than from the homeland. Europeans arriving in the New World in those years preferred to settle in the United States.

The Anglo-Americans who went to Texas were attracted by the prospect of beautiful agricultural lands virtually free. In the United States the minimum cost of public lands was $1.25 an acre. More specifically, the American migrants were mostly from the Mississippi Valley, from the restless frontier society described in the previous chapter. A few came from the Atlantic seaboard of the South, and a few from the northern states. But the bulk were from the Mississippi Valley. Their number cannot be given with precision. No reliable Mexican statistics for the period exist. The best estimate is that, in 1830, of the 25,000 or 30,000 persons of various nationalities in Texas, there were 4000 native Mexicans and the rest were chiefly Americans.

That great preponderance of Americans produced growing alarm in Mexico. Texas was developing into an American state. The alarm was heightened by various episodes. An empresario, Hayden Edwards, whose settlement lay near the Louisiana border, became involved in 1826 in a dispute with the authorities of the state of Coahuila-Texas. He was a man of violent temper and erratic judgment, and became so aggressive that his empresario contract was canceled. Thereupon he started a revolution, proclaimed the Republic of Fredonia, and tried to make an alliance with the wild Indians in Texas. He was promptly defeated by Mexican troops with the aid of Austin, and expelled from Texas. But the revolt highlighted the dangers of American colonization.

Mexican fears were also aroused because of the persistence with which the United States government tried to buy Texas. In 1825, 1827, and 1829, informal or formal proposals of purchase were made. In 1829, under Jackson, the proposal was formal. When it was not favorably acted on, the American minister in Mexico City, Anthony Butler, suggested bribing the Mexican authorities. The British minister in Mexico City added his fears to those of the Mexicans by repeated warnings of the dangers of American colonization.

The result was that the Mexican government in 1828 sent a fact-finding commission to Texas. After a year's investigation the Terán commission reported that Americans were not only an overwhelming majority in Texas, but evaded or ignored the requirements of the colonization laws. They ignored the slavery restrictions, and the limitation regarding the location of foreign-born settlers along the coasts and boundaries of Texas. Virtually all ignored the religious requirements of the laws.

The Mexican Congress, in alarm, reversed its policy with regard to Americans. On April 6, 1830, it adopted a law prohibiting any further American colonization, and forbade the further introduction of slaves into any part of Mexico. Special incentives were given as a means of creating a counterweight to the Americans. Native Mexicans were offered free transport, free tools, and free provisions over a period of years, if they would migrate to Texas. Also, Mexican convicts serving sentences in the Army were encouraged to settle in Texas on expiration of their sentences. In an attempt to tie Texas more closely to the southern provinces the law opened the coastal trade to non-Mexican shipping, since Mexico had little shipping of its own. In order to make sure of proper obedience to Mexican laws, Mexican garrisons were ordered to be established in Texas near the American settlements. The law was intended not only to end further American colonization of Texas but to serve as a rein on Americans already there.

But the law proved a failure. It ran into resistance and broke down. The Americans were hard to discourage once they had their foot in the door. The Mexican Treasury lacked enforcement money and the Administration was feeble and inept.

The flow of Americans into Texas continued after 1830 almost as if no restrictions had been imposed. The influx was tolerated for a time; in fact, certain trusted empresarios, such as Austin and DeWitt, were given virtually an exemption from the restrictions by special interpretations. The effort at countercolonization by native Mexicans failed, partly because native Mexicans were not interested in pioneering. The attempt to tie Texas to the southern provinces of Mexico by means of a coastal trade failed. The commerce that did develop tied Texas instead to New Orleans. The garrisons were equally ineffective. Though some were enlarged and new ones were added, the total number of soldiers stationed in Texas was never more than a few hundred. The Treasury could support no more. Finally, the restrictions of the law as to slavery proved virtually unenforceable.

The most important result of the law was a growing friction between the Americans already in Texas and the Mexican government over old issues, and over new ones arising from the law of 1830.

One old source of discord was the status of Texas in the Mexican federation. Texas and adjacent Coahuila had been joined as one state in the Constitution of 1824. This had been a matter of administrative convenience and antedated any flow of American settlers to Texas. In the joint state the legislature was controlled by Coahuila, whose population was much larger than that of Texas. Coahuila had ten delegates in the legislature, Texas only two. The legislature was ineffective, and regarded as corrupt in matters of land administration. The Texans therefore demanded, as their number grew, separation from Coahuila and did it with increasing energy. Their insistence on separate statehood was characteristic of American frontier history and failure to attain it aroused characteristic irritation.

Another issue was religion. The Texans were obliged to become Catholics as a condition of receiving land. They never took that obligation seriously, not even Stephen F. Austin, who was otherwise law-abiding. The Mexican government did not press the issue aggressively but under Mexican law all marriages had to be performed by Catholic priests, and children born to marriages performed by other than Catholic priests had no legal rights of inheritance. That was a steady source of irritation.

The tariff was a further item of friction. Texans had been exempt from Mexican tariffs under the colonization law of 1824. This exemption had expired in 1830, after which Texans had to pay the same duties on imports that Mexicans paid. On some commodities they were prohibitively high, made so in the hope of developing manufacturing in Mexico. The issue never became explosive, however, because duties were evaded by wholesale smuggling at Galveston and elsewhere. The Mexican government was handicapped by its lack of a navy.

Mexican garrisons near Texan settlements were another irritant. Many of the troops were the scum of society. Some were convicts serving out a sentence in the Army. Their officers, however, were usually well behaved and tactful. Even the troops were not an unmitigated evil. They provided the Texans with local markets for their surplus.

A major source of friction was slavery, which Texan settlers considered essential to their future. Mexican leaders wished to eradicate it. Under Spain, Mexico had had a long history of Negro slavery, but by 1800 the number of slaves had declined to approximately 10,000. Many of the revolutionary ieaders of 1810 and 1813, imbued with the radicalism of the French Revolution, had urged complete abolition of slavery. Some of them were mestizos. Antislavery sentiment was also present among adherents of the more conservative Iturbide revolution of 1821.

The Congress that framed the Colonization Law of 1823 following the overthrow of Iturbide also reflected this sentiment. A committee formulating the law proposed a clause abolishing slavery and forbidding the slave trade, news of which reached Austin, who was then in Mexico City. Austin had grown up in Virginia and had absorbed the planter view that labor in such heat as that of the Texas summer could not be performed effectively except by Negroes. He believed that desirable immigrants could not be attracted to Texas if slavery were prohibited. He pressed that view and a compromise was adopted in the colonization law. Migrants to Mexico were permitted to bring their slaves with them, but the buying or selling of slaves in Mexico was forbidden. Also, children born to slaves in Mexico were to be free at the age of fourteen. The law was reminiscent of the earlier gradual emancipation legislation of states of the North Atlantic seaboard in the United States.

On July 13, 1824, the Mexican Congress, while drawing up a constitution for the new federal republic, passed a law forever prohibiting the introduction of slaves into Mexico for purposes of sale. Any slaves so brought would become free upon touching Mexican soil. Persons engaged in such trade would be severely punished, and property so used would be confiscated. As this was interpreted, however, it did not prevent masters bringing in their own slaves for their own use.

In March 1827, the constitution adopted by the state of Coahuila-Texas stiffened the national law. The further importation of slaves "under any pretext" was prohibited, and henceforth no one born in the state should be a slave. A law passed later that year implemented the constitutional provisions. A census of all slaves was to be taken, giving name, age, and sex. A register should also be kept of all children born of slave parents, and of the deaths of all slaves. Slaves of masters dying without heirs were to be immediately free. When a master died having heirs, even of the nearest kinship, 10 percent of his slaves must be freed. The free children born of slaves were to be educated in the public schools. Local officials were to be heavily fined for failure to carry out these provisions. Most significant was a provision that persons introducing slaves into the state were to be subjected to the severe penalties of the national law of July 13, 1824.

But the state law was evaded. Slaves were imported as indentured servants by Americans entering Texas. Contracts of indenture were signed on the American side of the boundary. In them the slaves were promised freedom as soon as they had worked out their value in wages. The value, however, was set so high, and the wages so low, that freedom would never be achieved. In 1828 this practice was legalized by the Coahuila-Texas legislature.

In 1829 a decree was promulgated by President Vicente Guerrero, a radical reformer, wherein slavery was abolished altogether in Mexico. It was issued under emergency powers granted him during an abortive Spanish invasion of Mexico, designed to restore the monarchy. The decree never went into effect in Coahuila-Texas. Before its publication there, the Coahuila-Texas authorities, at Austin's urging, sent Guerrero a petition to exempt that state from its operation on the ground of its injustice to the settlers there, and their need for slave labor. Guerrero granted this request.

Shortly afterward, a more conservative regime took over in Mexico City, the one that favored the law of April 6, 1830, forbidding further American immigration. That law also contained an important article with respect to slavery:

> No change will be made with respect to the colonies already established, nor with respect to the slaves which they now contain, but the general government, and that of each particular state, shall exact, under the strictest responsibilities, the observance of the colonization laws and the prevention of the further introduction of slaves.

The explicitness of this legislation regarding the further introduction of slaves was an indirect method of discouraging American immigration into Texas. A further step in this direction was taken in 1832 by the Coahuila-Texas legislature, when it forbade indenture contracts running for a period of longer than ten years.

This wavering obstruction to the spread of slavery in Texas is comparable with the American record of the Confederation period. The Northwest Ordinance of 1787 closed a portion of the federal territory to slavery. But in the seaboard states slavery was tolerated, partly because it seemed to be dying out. In Mexico slavery rapidly declined in the era following the revolt against Spain, though peonage was common. Even in Texas, in 1830, the number of slaves was not large, probably not more than 1000. Texans were chiefly grazers and had no overriding need for slaves. Moreover, they lacked the means of acquiring them.

They did have, however, visions of cotton plantations in the future, and the restrictive measures relating to slavery of the Mexican Congress and of the Coahuila-Texas legislature were resented. These efforts to block the flow of American settlers into the province by forbidding the importation of slaves were not merely futile, they were countereffective, for they annoyed Americans already in Texas and produced a friction that was to eventuate in revolution and independence.

The first major uprising occurred in 1832. It was set off by an incident in Galveston, where the most important of the Mexican garrisons was stationed. The officer in charge was Colonel John Bradburn, an ex-American and a petty tyrant. He made an arbitrary arrest of several Texans, whose friends used force to obtain their release. Before the fighting was over the garrison had yielded and evacuated the post.

Parallel to this uprising was one in Mexico City, one of its constantly recurring revolutions. It appeared to be a revolt against overcentralization of power on the part of the regime that had enacted the restrictive Texan policy, and its goal was ostensibly the restoration of federalism, of state autonomy, as required in the Constitution of

1824. Actually the revolt was a bid for power by the Mexican general Antonio López de Santa Anna. The two uprisings succeeded together. In 1833 Santa Anna was raised to power as President of Mexico. Then Austin was sent to Santa Anna with the demands of the Texans: the repeal of that part of the Mexican law of 1830 prohibiting further settlement of Texas by Americans; exemption of Texas from Mexican tariffs for a further period of years; and the separation of Texas from Coahuila.

Santa Anna granted the first. He made promises as to the second. He denied the third—the separate statehood request. His refusal, and the fact that he threw off the mask of federalism and maintained the centralized form of government added to the Texan grievances.

Austin remained in Mexico City on his mission until 1834. Then he started home with only part of the Texan demands satisfied. On the way he was seized by the Mexican police. The offense for which he was arrested was a letter he had written a friend in San Antonio that had been intercepted, suggesting that if consent for separate statehood was not given by the Mexican authorities the separation should take place anyhow. For that transgression he was held until the middle of 1835 in Mexico City, part of the time in prison.

In the meantime an incident occurred that set off the final Texan revolt of 1835. It was a practical joke, played by a Texan on a customs officer at Galveston, which indicated the disorderly character of the Texans and the contempt they felt for Mexican authority. Under Mexican law all exports had to be inspected and an export tax had to be paid. The practical joker, Andrew Briscoe, filled a box with sawdust and marked it for export. He collected a crowd to watch the customs officer open the box. When it was opened and found to contain only sawdust, the crowd hooted the officer. Such a trick would probably not be appreciated by any customs officer. The Mexican tried to arrest Briscoe and a fight followed. Military support was called for. When the Texans learned that a military force was on the way, they revolted. Austin, who reached home at just that moment, threw his influence in favor of resistance, and by the autumn of 1835 the revolution was in full swing.

It is evident that the traditional view of the Texan Revolution—that it was the result of cruelty and tyranny by the Mexican government—is unfounded. That view is the product of propaganda spread by Texans during the revolt to justify the uprising. The Mexican administration of Texas had been weak and vacillating, the central government of Mexico had been disorderly, and the provincial government of Coahuila-Texas had been corrupt in matters of land disposal. But Texan historians are now agreed that the Mexican government had not been cruel or oppressive. The Texan revolt was the result primarily of the initial Mexican error of admitting into the rich prairies of Texas a race of aggressive and unruly American frontiersmen who were contemptuous of Mexico and of Mexican authority. Mexico had repeated the old Latin mistake of admitting Gauls into the empire.

In the United States the uprising was universally applauded. Nearly all Americans wished it to succeed, a reflection of the ties of kinship between Texans and Americans, and of a very effective propaganda campaign carried on in the American press. One of its themes was that even the people of southern Mexico regarded Santa Anna as a tyrant and would, under Texan leadership, overthrow him. Horror stories were spread. Santa Anna was pictured as a butcher who had ordered the execution as traitors of several hundred Texan prisoners captured at Goliad. The charge was also made that the Indians of Texas were being incited by Mexican agents to rise against the Texans.

Against these horrors was contrasted the heroism of the Texans, especially of the defenders of the Alamo, who had perished to a man in the defense of San Antonio. Religious propaganda was, also, spread. The Texans were Protestants, as were most Americans. The Mexicans were Catholics. The revolution was described as a struggle to halt and reverse the northward spread of Roman Catholicism. Texan offers of land bounties to all who would enlist in its forces were given wide publicity. Men enlisting and serving six months would receive an entire square mile of Texas land. Those serving a year would receive two square miles.

Of the newspapers spreading such propaganda the most influential were those of New Orleans and New York. They were important because they kept special correspondents in Texas who wrote feature articles on the revolution. No elaborate system of news collection then existed, and large metropolitan papers regularly stationed correspondents in the trouble spots of the world to write feature articles, which were simply copied by lesser journals. They shaped public opinion throughout the United States. The New Orleans journals were of especial importance because of their proximity to Texas. Of the five in New Orleans, four ardently supported the Texan cause.

The result of this propaganda was a flow of American volunteers to the Texan revolutionaries, which increased throughout the war. In the larger American cities public meetings of support were called, money was raised, and volunteer companies were organized. In the Gulf states, and in those bordering the Ohio and Mississippi, companies of volunteers left with equipment and supplies and pledges of further help. In the autumn of 1835 the Mexican minister in Washington wrote the American Secretary of State that no less than twelve vessels were about to sail from New York and New Orleans with military stores and men for Texas. A considerable portion of the Texan forces consisted of such adventurers.

The military history of the Texan uprising is no part of this survey and may be dismissed with a summary. The Texan army, under the command of Sam Houston, adopted a policy of retreat toward the United States border in the face of Santa Anna's advancing Mexican army. Houston learned on two occasions that the Mexican army had been divided, but took advantage of neither opportunity. He finally turned to attack only after his troops had threatened to mutiny if he did not make a stand.

The ensuing battle of San Jacinto, on April 21, 1836, is one of the strangest of the world's important battles. The Mexican troops were in the habit of an afternoon rest. Generals, troops, and sentries indulged the custom in the midst of campaigning. Houston was aware of this, and took advantage of it in a midafternoon surprise attack. The Mexican troops woke to find the enemy among them and went into a panic. In a few minutes the battle was over. The casualties tell the story. On the Texan side there were two killed; on the Mexican side, 630 killed, 208 wounded, 730 prisoners. The battle was a massacre of fleeing troops. Santa Anna was found after the battle hiding in the tall Texas grass. If he had been recognized he would have been killed. When he was brought to headquarters and was identified, his life was saved by Houston to be put to Texan use. As a prisoner of war Santa Anna signed the Treaty of Velasco of 1836, in which he agreed to the independence of Texas. The treaty was immediately repudiated by the Mexican Congress on the ground of having been made under duress by a prisoner of war and was never ratified. Theoretically the war continued for years, but only by threats, proclamations, occasional raids, and a brief naval encounter. Mexico was financially too weak and disorganized to enter a genuine campaign of reconquest.

With independence virtually achieved the Texans faced the future. Four choices were open to them. One was to go forward as an independent state, retaining its old boundaries, and so circumscribed, being no more than a buffer between Mexico and the United States. The second was to create a larger independent state by a campaign of conquest against Mexico. Expansion seemed particularly feasible against the lightly populated provinces extending westward from the Rio Grande. These provinces, including California, could be easily overrun. If they could be acquired Texas would be a power comparable in size and prospects to the United States, a transcontinental state, with frontage on two oceans. Such a power could, with dignity and safety, stand alone.

A program of expansion was approved in Texas as soon as independence had been won. In initial form it was a declaration by the Texan Congress, in December 1836, that the territory of Texas extended to the Rio Grande. This meant a doubling of the territory of old Texas. It constituted a claim to parts of five other Mexican provinces lying to the west and northwest of Texas, including the city of Santa Fe, which for two centuries had been the capital of the province of New Mexico. None of the area claimed was then in the possession of Texas troops.

But this was only the beginning of Texan ambitions. The full scope of Texan dreams, as set forth at different times by its legislature, embraced half the territory of Mexico (Map 60). It included northern Coahuila and all of Chihuahua, Sonora, New Mexico, and the two Californias.

Texan expansionists professed to believe that these western and northern provinces would not have to be conquered, that their sparse population would willingly enter into a new Texan-led confederation. They were only tenuously held by Mexico, and Texans believed they could easily be induced to enter a new alignment in which Texas would be the leader.

Expansion by conquest was believed possible. After San Jacinto the Texans had a supreme contempt for Mexican military power. If conquest became necessary, military assistance could be expected from the United States, from the restless spirits of the Mississippi Valley frontier looking for excitement and believing Mexico to be filled with tempting plunder. In the New Orleans press the eagerness of the Mississippi Valley frontiersmen to join any Texan force that might undertake a crusade of expansion against Mexico was proclaimed over and over. It was most vividly described in Congress by Henry A. Wise of Virginia in the spring of 1842 in the speech described *ante* p. 262.

A more distinguished American who encouraged Texan expansion was Andrew Jackson. Early in 1837, while still President, he secretly recommended to William H. Wharton, the Texan agent in Washington, that Texas claim everything to the Pacific. As Wharton reported:

> General Jackson says that Texas must claim the Californias on the Pacific in order to paralyze the opposition of the North and East to annexation; that the fishing [whaling] interest of the North and East wish a harbour on the Pacific; that this claim of the

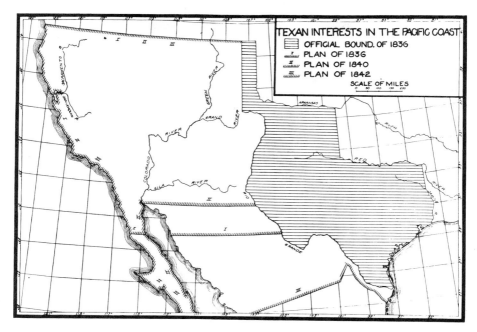

60. Texan Expansionism (from Binkley)

Californias will give it to them and will diminish their opposition to annexation. He is very earnest and anxious on this point of claiming the Californias and says we must not consent to less. This is in strict confidence. Glory to God in the highest.

Among expansionists in Texas one of the most ardent was the second President of the Texan Republic, Mirabeau B. Lamar. In 1838 Lamar made expansionism the dominant note of his inaugural address, and in 1841 he set in motion the famous Lamar Expedition as a first step toward a realization of this goal.

In the Lamar Expedition, military and commercial objectives were united in a curious fashion. A military objective was the capture of Santa Fe, which was expected to fall easily and without serious fighting. Its garrison consisted of only a handful of Mexican troops, and its civilian population was believed to be willing to come under Texan protection. The force that was to take Santa Fe included a considerable contingent of merchants, 40 of whom went with the soldiers carrying merchandise to the value of $200,000. The commercial objective was to turn the Santa Fe trade away from Missouri and Arkansas to Galveston Bay.

The expedition was not well managed, and it ended in disaster. The hardships of the journey to Santa Fe were not adequately prepared for. The expedition was captured by the Mexican garrison outside the gates of Santa Fe without the firing of a shot, and its members were sent in irons to Mexico City. The Texan Congress, on hearing the fate of the expedition, voted in 1842, as a gesture of defiance, to carry Texan boundaries to the Pacific.

In 1843 the Charles Warfield Expedition was commissioned by the Texan government to capture Santa Fe. The troops consisted partly of American mountain trappers who had assembled on the upper Arkansas. It captured Mora, a village near Santa Fe, but was then compelled to retreat. In 1843 the Snively Expedition set out from Texas to turn the Santa Fe trade to Texas. But Mexican troops were able to force its members to cross the boundary into the United States, where it was disarmed. Texan dreams of expansion thus failed. They were carried out only at a later stage by the armies of the United States during the Mexican War.

Two other choices were open to the Texas Republic. One was annexation to the United States. The other was independence with diplomatic ties to England and France. These mutually exclusive choices were under discussion by the nations concerned throughout the late 1830's and early 1840's.

The Movement
for Annexation and the
Defeat of the Treaty

AMONG THE PROSPECTS opened to the Texans by their victory at San Jacinto the most attractive was annexation to the United States. This would mean reunion with the land of their birth and, more important, security for the future. Shortly after the battle of San Jacinto the provisional Texas government ordered a plebiscite on the issue. The response was all but unanimous for annexation. An informal offer was made soon after to the American government.

It was promptly declined by President Jackson. He believed the Texan declaration of independence had been a rash and premature act. He thought an immediate conversion of it into annexation would be a violation of the obligations of the Untied States to Mexico. Besides, it would precipitate a clash over the extension of slavery in the United States. He dearly desired that Martin Van Buren be elected in the forthcoming presidential campaign, and he feared this would be imperiled by a clash over slavery. He refused even to recognize the independence of Texas until the last day of his administration.

On August 4, 1837, Memucan Hunt, the Texan minister in Washington, formally proposed annexation to John Forsyth, Van Buren's Secretary of State. He defended, in so doing, the revolt of Texas against Mexico and he outlined the benefits of annexation to the United States. He warned that Texas must turn to Europe if annexation should fail. His proposal was promptly declined. Forsyth referred in his letter to the treaty obligations of the United States to Mexico and he questioned that the Constitution conferred authority on the federal government to annex Texas. The slavery issue was not referred to. It was a domestic problem not proper to include in such a communication.

The proposed annexation raised for the United States two related problems. One was slavery, the other was its extension. Most Northerners were willing to leave the first problem where the framers of the Constitution had left it—with the states. Southern moderates took a like stand. They considered slavery an evil the British had

279

foisted on the American colonies. An attempt to remedy it by repatriation of the blacks to Africa had failed. Emancipation without repatriation would be a remedy worse than the disease. This apologetic view of slavery was held in the South until the early 1830's.

But during the 1830's a new philosophy emerged in the South that slavery was not an evil but a positive good, had the sanction of the Bible, was of benefit to the blacks in health, morals, and spirit, and was indispensable to southern democracy. These views emanated from the intellectual centers of the South, especially from Virginia and South Carolina. They were a reflection of the growing profitability of slavery and, also, of the shock produced by the Nat Turner insurrection.

In the Van Buren administration issues other than annexation kept the Administration occupied, especially those of recovery from the Panic of 1837. Congress was torn by conflicts over banking, currency, the independent Treasury, and land reform. An old diplomatic issue—the northeastern boundary dispute—flared up and taxed the energies of statesmen to preserve peace.

In the 1840 presidential campaign the Whig candidate was the war hero William H. Harrison. Clay was passed over—he had been a loser too often. John Tyler, whose constitutional views of strict construction were the opposite of Clay's, was nominated for Vice-President. In the "frolic campaign" the Whigs overwhelmingly defeated Van Buren, and Harrison became President. For Secretary of State he chose Daniel Webster, who had committed himself against the annexation of Texas. A month after the inauguration Harrison died and Tyler entered the White House.

Tyler adhered to his strict construction views as President. He broke with the Whig directorate almost at once. The Cabinet resigned—except for Webster—and denounced its leader. Tyler became that rare phenomenon in American politics—a President without a party. He saw no prospect of succeeding in domestic affairs. He turned to foreign affairs, where executive authority was greater, and where the rewards of success were likely to be higher. Webster had a plan to settle the longstanding Northeastern Boundary controversy with Great Britain by a negotiation based on the principle of an exchange of equivalents. Previous attempts had proceeded on the principle of finding the boundary in that quarter, as delineated in the Treaty of 1783. Negotiations based on that principle had proved fruitless for more than half a century. Arbitration had been tried and had failed. Maine insisted on discovering the treaty line, and rested its case on the doctrine of states' rights. Webster proposed to remove that obstacle by reversing public opinion in Maine. He had in mind relying on propaganda financed by undercover use of federal funds that Congress had voted for international affairs. The scheme was approved by Tyler, though it contravened his states' rights principles, and was successfully implemented. The Maine authorities and public were brought to acquiesce in a negotiation based on the principle of exchange of equivalents. A treaty embodying this was obtained from Lord Ashburton, the British negotiator, which was signed on August 9, 1842, and ratified eleven days later. It was acclaimed in the United States and, even in Maine, as a masterstroke of diplomacy.

This success was a spur to Tyler's ambitions. Other opportunities were open in foreign affairs—the annexation of Texas and a settlement of the Oregon dispute with England. The acquisition of California beckoned also. A scheme for acquiring California from Mexico, with British approval, had been under discussion in the Ashburton negotiation as part of a settlement of the Oregon question. If such dreams of expansion could be converted into reality a national hero would emerge. The temper of the period was expansionist and its tide might carry the statesman riding it into a term of his own in the White House.

On January 23, 1843, a striking letter on the Texas issue appeared in *The Madisonian,* the Washington organ of the President. Its author was Thomas W. Gilmer, an intimate of Tyler, a former governor of Virginia, and a present member of its delegation in Congress. He was a believer in the new creed of the beneficence of slavery and also in the doctrine of Manifest Destiny as applied to Mexican territories in the Southwest. He had a special interest in Texas as a speculator in its lands. He developed in his letter the view that the annexation of Texas would be of special benefit to the northern states of the Union. It would open to the northern Atlantic states a rich market for their manufactures; and to the northwestern states an unlimited market for their agricultural surpluses. It would confer on the southern states less in terms of economic advantage. Indeed, it would erect in the Union a rival to their cotton and sugar planters. But, if admitted as a state, Texas would offer the South security for its institutions. If not admitted, Texas would establish connections with European states which would be fatal to the security of the South and the nation. The slavery issue might be an obstacle to annexation, but that problem had been left by the Constitution to the states. The South wished it to remain there. If it were not left there, the Union would be imperiled.

The letter was recognized at once as a major pronouncement on the Texas issue. The attention of Andrew Jackson was called to it and he warmly approved it in a letter written for immediate publication, but which was withheld until interest in the issue had been further developed.

Daniel Webster resigned as Secretary of State in mid-1843. His presence in the Cabinet had become an embarrassment to Tyler as the annexation issue emerged. He had declared as early as 1837 his insurmountable objection to the annexation of Texas, which, he had pointed out, would become a slaveholding state. He was unwilling to do anything that would extend slavery or increase the number of the slave states in the Union. He would abide by the Constitution, which left the slavery issue to the states, but he could not agree to add to the union a slaveholding country large enough for half a dozen new states. Moreover, he believed a self-governing country, with institutions and treaties of its own, could not be admitted constitutionally to the Union.

Tyler chose, as Webster's successor, Abel P. Upshur, who was a devotee of strict construction and an exponent of the southern doctrine of the beneficence of Negro slavery. In 1839 he had contributed to the *Southern Literary Messenger* a widely read article lauding the writings of the chief southern proslavery exponents, and he added that slavery was the foundation of southern democracy. His appointment was an omen of the coming drive for the annexation of Texas.

Another omen was the sending of Duff Green, a confidant of President Tyler, as executive agent to London in the spring of 1843. Green had aided Tyler to win the vice-presidential nomination on the Whig ticket in 1840. He carried a personal letter from the President to Edward Everett, the American minister in London.

The letter outlined the aims of the Administration. These were to gather information in London in preparation for a negotiation to be held in Washington. The subjects of the negotiation were to be a reciprocal tariff reduction and, tied into it, an adjustment of territorial issues. A settlement was to be made of the Oregon dispute by a deal combining it with the acquisition of the part of California containing the harbor of San Francisco. Texas was referred to in the letter only incidentally. The whole plan was nebulous and unrealistic. Control of Congress and of the British Parliament was held at the time by protectionists. In 1841 Tyler had sent Green to England and to France on a similar vague mission. Green had then busied himself, in collaboration with Lewis Cass, the American minister in Paris, to defeat ratification by the Chamber of Deputies of the Quintuple Treaty to suppress the maritime slave trade, a treaty which Guizot, the French Premier, had approved.

The chief outcome of Green's 1843 mission, like that of 1841, proved to be related to slavery. It was the discovery of a British "plot" to abolitionize Texas, at the center of which was Lord Aberdeen, the British Secretary for Foreign Affairs. He was alleged to have promised a delegation of British and American abolitionists a government guarantee of interest on a loan to Texas, the principal of which was to be devoted to abolitionizing Texas.

This startling intelligence reached Upshur near the end of July 1843. The tidings from Green also went to Calhoun and to the President at about the same time. Upshur accepted their truth without verification and sent off a warning at once to the American chargé in Texas to be on his guard. Green was not named as the source but was referred to as a "man of great intelligence, and well versed in public affairs."

Upshur sought advice as to further action from Calhoun, the mentor of southern proslavery extremists. At the same time he expressed his own views. The British, he wrote, were determined to abolish slavery not only in Texas but in the United States and throughout the continent, which would be a disaster. As a protective move Texas must be annexed. This would be a matter not merely of safety but of southern rights, and the cause would unite the South as one man. The prospect of annexation would be greeted in the North with a burst of repugnance. But the North needed only to be persuaded that annexation would be of economic benefit to itself to be converted. A hint was thrown out to Calhoun that he take the lead in a campaign of propaganda on behalf of annexation.

Calhoun's reply was in full agreement with Upshur's analysis. In addition, he outlined a program to achieve it. The British should be confronted, the other powers of Europe should be converted, and the North should be won by propaganda to accept annexation. Propaganda should precede the opening of a negotiation with Texas. Upshur should himself lead the propaganda from the State Department with anonymous articles. Cuba should be kept in mind. An agreement should be considered with France whereby Spanish possession of the island, with its slave institutions, would be guaranteed against British interference. The Oregon and Texas questions should be joined in the propaganda campaign as a means of winning western support. Calhoun ruled himself out as the leader of the campaign, on the ground that it would be considered a bid for the presidency.

New "evidence" that the British were intent on abolitionizing Texas reached the American government soon after the revelation of the loan plot. On August 18, 1843, Lord Aberdeen was questioned in the House of Lords as to what the government was doing regarding the trade in slaves to Texas and the interminable war between Mexico and Texas. Aberdeen made no direct reply, but did say that the government was using its good offices to end the war and that an armistice had been arranged. He added what he thought the world knew, that the British government hoped to see slavery abolished in Texas and everywhere else in the world, and would continue to use its good offices to obtain actual peace between Mexico and Texas.

The American government learned of the exchange from British press reports several weeks later. It found support in them for Duff Green's news of July. Prompt action was necessary to meet the threat. Tyler at once authorized Upshur to open a negotiation with the Texan government. On September 18, 1843, the word was passed to Isaac Van Zandt, the Texas minister in Washington.

Ten days later Upshur sent two dispatches to Edward Everett, ordering an inquiry into the truth of the charges against the British. One dispatch was official, the other confidential. Both found proof of evil British designs in Aberdeen's Parliament statement. Those designs were described as disastrous to the United States if carried to success. The emancipated Negroes would inundate the North, where their presence would mean economic and social chaos. Those remaining in the South would demand social and political equality. War and the extermination of the Negroes would follow, as would war between the North and the South. The British would succeed in dominating the Gulf of Mexico. They would set up in the New World their favorite concept of the ''balance of power.''

Everett was directed to find the evidence for this plot. He was to apply directly to Lord Aberdeen, and, also, to make inquiry of the Texan chargé in London, Ashbel Smith. He was likewise to examine the published proceedings of abolition societies in London for evidence. In neither dispatch was notice taken of Duff Green's report that the British government had agreed to guarantee the interest on a loan to Texas to finance abolition. That report had lost credibility since no loan of the sort had surfaced on the London money market. But the doctrine of British selfishness in seeking abolition, which Green had been distributing to Tyler, Upshur, and Calhoun, was visible throughout the confidential report.

Upshur's dispatches reached Everett while Aberdeen was absent from London. On his return an interview was obtained. Everett was on terms of personal friendship with Aberdeen, which permitted questioning with entire frankness. His questions were centered on the alleged loan offer to Texas, though the matter had not been mentioned in Upshur's dispatches. Aberdeen assured Everett that his government had never proposed to Texas the abolition of slavery as part of any treaty, that it had never considered a loan to Texas with the abolition of slavery as a condition, and that the British connection with the slavery issue in Texas has consisted merely of advice to Mexico to recognize Texas in the hope that the abolition of slavery might be part of a peace agreement. This reply Everett wrote out and had Aberdeen confirm before mailing it to Washington.

Ashbel Smith, the Texan chargé, was also consulted by Everett. He had not been present at the conference at which Aberdeen was alleged to have promised his government's aid to Texas to abolish slavery. He had learned of it only from an abolitionist, Stephen Pearl Andrews, who attended the conference. Smith had not considered it necessary to say this in his first report to the Texas government, written when he was suspicious of British intentions. But a month later, after a conference with Aberdeen, Smith reported Aberdeen as saying to the group that ''he was not prepared to say whether the British government would consent hereafter to make such compensation to Texas as would enable the slaveholders to abolish slavery.'' Smith afterward charged Upshur with having prepared the way for a treaty of annexation "by charging on the British government the machinations and plots of anti-slavery fanatics for interfering with Southern institutions."

Everett's report of the testimony he had gathered constituted a negation of the Duff Green letter and of the charges Upshur wished to fasten on the British ministry. It undermined the thesis of a British plot in Texas that Upshur was readying for submission to the Senate in documents which would accompany a treaty of annexation. Everett sent with his dispatch a private letter in which he expressed the opinion that the present British ministry was less committed to antislavery causes than had been its predecessor in office, or the British public.

The Texan minister in Washington, Isaac Van Zandt, favored annexation. His government, however, had informed him that it intended to take no action in the matter, that it would, instead, await "events now in progress," and that he was to inform the American government of this. Van Zandt had passed this word orally to both the President and to Upshur, and had declined Upshur's invitation to enter an annexation negotiation. The "events now in progress" that were referred to were negotiations between the Mexican government and Texas for an armistice and an ultimate peace, which the British were encouraging. If Texas were to open annexation discussions with the American government, those negotiations would come to an end.

To his government Van Zandt wrote that his declination had served only to fire Upshur with renewed zeal for annexation. It had been followed by a series of conferences at which the Secretary of State had pressed the values of annexation to both parties, and his hope that the Texan government would have a change of heart. Van Zandt would make only one concession—a private suggestion that Texas might agree to a negotiation if the American government would definitely propose annexation and give strong assurance that the resulting treaty would win Senate ratification. This, Upshur felt, he could not agree to, and, indeed, did not think it proper to consider unless Van Zandt possessed authority to negotiate. On this indecisive note the conference came to an end.

A month later Upshur again raised the question of negotiations. He assured Van Zandt that though a favorable reception by all branches of the American government could not be given, the President would press the issue in the strongest terms. This persistence, however, brought no reward. No powers were sent to Van Zandt. The Texan government had no fear of British interference with its form of labor. The Texan Secretary of State noted that the issue was never so much as alluded to by the British representative in Texas, other than to disclaim any intention of interference. What the Texans really feared was a reopening by Mexico of hostilities in the event of attempted annexation to the United States and a resulting withdrawal of British good offices for peace. But Upshur and Tyler persisted in believing that what was called for was more urgent proposals to Texas. The American government had become the suitor of Texas, as was later pointed out in anger by the Whig press, when the public learned that for months an annexation treaty had been secretly in negotiation in Washington.

The courtship of Texas, begun on September 18, 1843, was pressed by Upshur in repeated conferences with Van Zandt and also directly on January 16, 1844, in an ardent dispatch designed for Houston's eyes, though nominally addressed to

William S. Murphy, the American chargé in Texas. Houston was told that earlier American failures to respond to Texan overtures had been due to a misunderstanding of the issue. Annexation was now favored even in the North to a great extent, and its popularity was daily increasing. A treaty to effect it would command a clear constitutional majority of two-thirds of the Senate for ratification. Reliance on England by Texas would be fatal.

On the day after this dispatch went off an informal question was posed to Upshur by Van Zandt—whether the United States would agree to station army forces along the Texas border and navy forces in the Gulf at the request of Texas, for protection from a Mexican invasion during the interval between the signing of an annexation treaty and its ratification. The question went to the heart of Texan hesitation about entering an American negotiation, and also to the heart of the American constitutional principle of the separation of powers. Congress alone has the power to declare war. The President is, however, commander in chief of the Army and Navy. What was involved in the question was whether the President could set the stage for a war with Mexico by assembling army and navy power along the borders of its revolted province, over which it still claimed sovereignty.

Upshur's answer was only verbal. But it enabled Van Zandt to write home that the moment a treaty of annexation was signed the United States would assemble army and navy forces on the borders of Texas and in the Gulf of Mexico ready to act as circumstances might require, and that the American government would say to Mexico she must not disturb or molest Texas.

In Texas the populace overwhelmingly desired annexation. They preferred the security and prosperity associated with reunion to the homeland to visions of expansion to the Pacific which dazzled some of their leaders. That sentiment was especially evident in the Texas Congress which assembled early in December 1843.

To this sentiment Houston bowed. He reversed the stand he had been taking. In a secret message he recommended to the Congress the opening of an annexation negotiation. Without awaiting an answer he sent authorization to Van Zandt to open a negotiation at once. He directed that the principal topics in the negotiation be the status of Texas in the Union, the Texan debt, and the ownership of Texan public land. The Texan Congress promptly gave its approval, and a second plenipotentiary, General J. Pinckney Henderson, an outstanding advocate of annexation, was sent to Washington to act with Van Zandt.

The negotiations for a treaty thereafter moved rapidly. They were nearing completion before the arrival of Henderson, but were interrupted by a tragic accident. On February 28, 1844, Upshur attended a reception on the warship *Princeton* on an excursion down the Potomac River. The party included the President, Upshur, Gilmer, and Senator Benton. Part of the entertainment was an exhibition of the ship's firing power. On the third discharge of her great gun, the breech exploded. Upshur and Gilmer and others were killed; Benton and the ship's commander were wounded. The President escaped harm. The annexation treaty had been virtually completed at the time and a prompt ratification of it seemed ahead.

A likely successor to Upshur was Calhoun. He was known to be eager for Texas; he had been Upshur's counselor on the issue, and was at the moment in retirement from the Senate. He was given the appointment. A tale was later told by Henry Wise that the President had been hesitant about naming Calhoun but had been tricked into doing so, a view no longer credited. Calhoun was confirmed, and brought the negotiation to a successful conclusion.

The treaty so framed, and signed on April 12, provided that Texas be admitted as a territory subject to the same constitutional provisions as other territories. It was to cede all its public land to the United States. Its boundaries were not specified. All valid real estate titles in Texas were to be held valid by the United States. The public debt of Texas, to an extent not greater than $10 million, was to be assumed by the United States.

Van Zandt and Henderson felt that the treaty was favorable to Texas, though not as favorable as they had wished. If they had dealt only with the President and the Cabinet, they wrote, it would have been much more favorable. But the views of the leading parties had to be taken into account, which meant avoiding the very liberal terms southern politicians would have granted, and also the restrictions the antislavery North would have imposed. What the Senate would ratify was kept constantly in mind.

Between the signing of the treaty and its transmission to the Senate an interval of ten days occurred. The time was needed for Calhoun to prepare new documents as background material for the Senate. One document, addressed to Richard Pakenham, the British minister in Washington, was in essence a reply to a message from Aberdeen of the previous December relative to British policy toward Texas. Aberdeen had firmly denied any British intention to interfere with slavery in Texas or in the United States, though Great Britain wished slavery to be done away with everywhere and would rejoice if a Mexican recognition of Texas should be accompanied by a Texan engagement eventually to abolish slavery. Britain would, however, merely give counsel. With regard to slavery in the United States it "would resort to no measures, secret or open, tending to disturb their tranquility." Aberdeen wished this message sent, for the record, to the State Department. It had been sent to Upshur by Pakenham two days before Upshur's death.

Aberdeen's message was resurrected by Calhoun and used as the basis for a reply that included a lengthy defense of slavery, a declaration that, if Great Britain should succeed in accomplishing in the United States, what she avows to be her desire . . . throughout the world, she would involve in the greatest calamity the whole country, and especially the race which it is the avowed object of her exertions to benefit." Calhoun informed Pakenham, further, that the American government had concluded an annexation treaty with Texas as the most effectual, if not the only, means of averting the threatened dangers.

The second new document framed for the Senate was a copy of an instruction to Benjamin E. Green, the American chargé in Mexico City. Green (son of Duff Green) was directed to assure the Mexicans that the American government had been forced to conclude the annexation treaty as a defense against British policy in Texas, which, if successful, would have been extremely dangerous to the United States. In negotiating the treaty every precaution had been taken to render the treaty as unobjectionable to Mexico as possible. This applied to the boundary of Texas, which had been left without specification in order that the line could be discussed and settled later according to the rights and security of the two countries.

The Tyler administration expected that the treaty and the Senate deliberations on it would remain an executive secret. The public would learn of the treaty only after it had been ratified. This expectation was unrealistic, for the public had learned that an annexation negotiation was under way and the antislavery press of the North was on edge to know of its outcome. Five days after the treaty reached the Senate it was leaked to the press by an antislavery Democrat from Ohio, Senator Benjamin Tappan. On the same day letters from Henry Clay and Martin Van Buren appeared in the press declaring their opposition to an immediate annexation. These events were manifestations of public concern regarding both immediate annexation and the undercover mode of attempting its effectuation.

An even more vigorous manifestation was Senator Benton's. On May 13 he proposed that the Senate summon for examination Duff Green, ''believed to be the author'' of the ''private letter'' which had prompted the annexation proceedings—a motion the Senate approved. Several days later Benton opened a three-day speech in which, with full quotations from the testimony of Aberdeen, Everett, and Ashbel Smith, he tore to shreds the tale of the British plot to abolitionize Texas. He assailed the omission of a Texas boundary from the treaty. Inasmuch as Texas claimed the Rio Grande as the boundary, ratification of the treaty would mean assuming a dispute with Mexico 2000 miles in length and probably a war. Benton ridiculed Calhoun's notion that the boundary had been left undefined to permit a fair and full discussion later with Mexico. He asked, ''Would we take 2000 miles of the Canadas in the same way? I presume not. And why not? Because Great Britain is powerful and Mexico weak.'' In closing he offered a motion that his speech be made public, which the Whig Senate gleefully adopted and soon afterward expanded to include all speeches and proceedings occurring on the same subject. These were political sensations, for Benton was a leading Democrat and a well-known expansionist.

In the meantime the President replied to the Senate resolution requesting the ''private letter'' of Duff Green on the British plot. He forwarded a written assurance from Calhoun that no communication answering the Senate's description could be found in the State Department files. A follow-up request went to the President for copies of all Green's 1843 correspondence relating to the annexation of Texas. To this the President replied by transmitting Calhoun's answer that there was ''no communication whatever, either to or from Mr. Green in relation to the annexation of Texas, to be found in the files of this department.'' This was not a falsification, strictly speaking, since no Green communications of the sort were in the department files. Yet Green in 1843 was serving as executive agent of the President, was being paid from the President's secret fund, and in this period had written numerous personal letters relating to the annexation of Texas to the President, to Upshur, and to Calhoun. More remarkable still, Green had revealed to the press that he was the author of the July letter to Upshur which had triggered the discussions with Texas.

In the Senate debate on the treaty ten speeches were delivered sufficiently important to win full printing in the *Congressional Globe*. One was Benton's; six were from Democrats urging ratification of the treaty; three were from southern Whigs opposing it. The speeches by administration supporters emphasized the theses developed in the documents accompanying the treaty—the British menace, the security of southern institutions, and the economic advantages to the North of annexation. The Whig speakers emphasized the underhandedness of the negotiation, the unconstitutionality of annexation, and the divisiveness of the issue. Senator Archer of

Virginia, the chairman of the Foreign Relations Committee, who closed the debate, described the opening of the negotiation as "revolting," and the whole of it as revealing a fixed purpose to fasten on the British government the false imputation of interfering with slavery in Texas.

The vote on ratification was taken on June 8, immediately after this speech. The count was an overwhelming rejection by a margin of 35–16. It was a commentary on the assurance of the Administration to Van Zandt, six months before, that a "clear constitutional majority of two thirds are in favor of the measure."

On June 10, two days after the rejection, the President asked the lower house of Congress to take over the issue. He declared that Congress was as competent to annex territory as the Senate. He had thought the treaty mode the more suitable, but if Congress should prefer some other method he was prepared to yield his prompt and active cooperation. He pointed out that annexation involved interests that were nationwide, and would especially benefit the North. At the same time it would afford protection to an exposed frontier, and place the whole country in a condition of security and repose. Some objections had been raised to the treaty, Tyler admitted, especially the failure to specify the boundary. He had thought this question needed to be raised only after annexation. To have it dealt with sooner would have been offensive to Mexico and insulting to Texas. He emphasized a matter on which all sections of the Union would agree: resistance to European interference in American affairs. He observed that we leave to "European powers exclusive control over matters affecting their continent and the relations of their different states" and "claim a similar exemption from such interference on their part."

The transfer of the annexation issue to Congress was clever strategy. It brought the issue to a body where a mere majority would give victory. Also, it moved the issue into the presidential campaign of 1844, which was under way. The national nominating conventions had met already in May.

In the Whig convention Clay was named the party candidate by a unanimous vote, despite the stand he had taken on the Texas issue. In the Tyler convention, which contained a large number of officeholders, the President was nominated without contest. In the Democratic convention Van Buren was defeated by erecting the two-thirds rule against him. In the resulting confusion James K. Polk, a southern slaveholder and expansionist, won the nomination.

In the ensuing campaign expansion was the central issue—the immediate annexation of Texas and the reoccupation of all Oregon. A balance of sections was intended to be so achieved—the annexation issue attracting the South, the Oregon reoccupation attracting the Northwest especially. The propaganda distributed in the campaign was designed therefore for sectional audiences.

Among the propagandists the most effective was Robert J. Walker, a Northerner, who had become a Mississippi planter and senator. He was an outstanding advocate of the doctrine of Manifest Destiny. In a pamphlet entitled *Letter Relative to the Annexation of Texas,* he addressed himself especially to northern Democrats with expansionist leanings but with qualms about extending the area of slavery. He argued that the slaves from the worn-out areas of the South would be drawn gradually to the virgin soil of Texas, which in time would also become worn out. Planters would be faced with the alternatives of bankruptcy or freeing their slaves. The slaves would be freed and would move across the Rio Grande into Mexico and Central America. An annexed Texas would be a safety valve drawing off slavery and the race problem to Central America. But the valve would not work if Texas remained unannexed and were abolitionized by the British. The emancipated Negroes would in that case overflow the North, carrying ruin with them, or would remain in the South producing race war and extermination. Reprintings of Walker's *Letter,* subsidized by a "Texas fund" to which rich Southerners subscribed, were distributed by the million in the North.

In the South, Whig followers of Clay needed to be converted. With this in view an anonymous pamphlet was published under the auspices of the Democratic Association of Washington. Its argument was that Clay was the candidate of northern abolitionists, pledged to destroy slavery, and that any southern Whig desiring to preserve the institution must support the candidate of the Democrats. The pamphlet was discovered to be Walker's and was reprinted in the North by the Whigs in four large editions to illustrate the hollowness of the earlier *Letter.*

Clay shifted ground in the campaign. In one of his "Alabama Letters" he wrote that if annexation could be achieved without dishonor, without war, and with the common consent of the Union, he would be glad to see it. To northern Whigs this retreat seemed a betrayal, and in the crucial states of New York and Michigan it brought party disaster.

A clear mandate did not emerge from the November balloting. Polk, Clay, and an avowed abolitionist, James G. Birney, divided the vote, Tyler having withdrawn in discouragement. If Clay had held a solid Whig vote he would have won a popular majority of 24,119, in a total vote of 2,698,605. More significantly he would have carried the states of New York and Michigan, winning an electoral majority of 146–129. As it was, Polk won an electoral majority of 170–105, which was cited as evidence of the wishes of the American people. Tyler took this line. In his annual message to Congress on December 3, 1844, he observed: "A controlling majority of the people and a large majority of the States have declared in favor of immediate annexation. Instructions have thus come up to both branches of Congress from their respective constituents in terms the most emphatic."

As background the President reviewed the treaty that had been defeated in the Senate. He defended its omission of a boundary for Texas, ascribing it, as he had in June, to consideration for the feelings of Mexico and Texas. He offered the assurance that if Texas were annexed a most liberal settlement with Mexico would follow. An accompaniment of the message was an extensive body of documents covering the developments of the summer. Among the documents was an important dispatch from Calhoun to William R. King, the American minister to France.

King was an Alabama Democrat devoted to slavery and to annexation of Texas. He had been appointed to France in the spring of 1844, and had been received at a welcoming dinner, attended by King Louis Philippe, on July 4, 1844. After the failure of the Texas treaty the French government had joined the British in a temporary agreement of opposition to a renewal of annexation attempts. But the French monarch in an amiable after-dinner conversation assured King that his government would take no steps "in the slightest degree hostile, or which could give the United States just cause of complaint." This was reported by King to Calhoun in triumph.

Calhoun doubted the genuineness of the assurance. He was aware of an Anglo-French collaboration to maintain the independence of Texas. He undertook to produce a rift in the collaboration. On August 12, after consultation with the President, he sent minister King a carefully phrased dispatch.

Calhoun maintained that a prime objective of British diplomacy was to produce the abolition of slavery not only in Texas but in the United States and throughout North America. A sum of $250 million had already been devoted by the British government to this end in the West Indies and elsewhere, which had produced only a disastrous failure. The government could not reverse its course and had decided to destroy slavery everywhere else in the world in order to reduce all competitors to the low British level of effectiveness. This was the argument Duff Green had been pressing.

The dispatch was intended to reach the opposition to the Guizot ministry in the French Chambers, especially two elements in it—one, the faction denouncing the ministry for subservience to the British government; the other, the representatives of the French West Indies slaveholding planters, who were fearful that France might in the near future follow the British example of emancipating the slaves in its colonies. These groups were those to whom Calhoun indirectly addressed the following section of his dispatch:

> It is little short of mockery to talk of philanthropy, with the examples before us of the effects of abolishing negro slavery in her own colonies, in St. Domingo, and the Northern States of our Union, where statistical facts, not to be shaken, prove that the freed negro, after the experience of sixty years, is in a far worse condition than in the other States, where he has been left in his former condition. No: the effect of what is called abolition, where the number is few, is not to raise the inferior race to the condition of the freemen, but to deprive the negro of the guardian care of his owner, subject to all the depression and oppression belonging to his inferior condition. But on the other hand, where the number is great, and bears a large proportion to the whole population, it would be still worse. It would be to substitute for the existing relation a deadly strife between the two races, to end in the subjection, expulsion, or extirpation of one or the other: and such would be the case over the greater part of this continent where negro slavery exists.

This revealing dispatch was included by Tyler without comment in the documents sent to Congress on December 3, 1844. It appeared at once in the American, British, and French press. Its effect in Europe was everything the President and Calhoun could have desired. The assurance, reported in it, from Louis Philippe to the American minister angered the British, who denounced it as evidence of French duplicity in the Texas collaboration. Guizot made a harried effort to pacify Aberdeen, at the same time assuring the American minister that the French government was committed to the policy mentioned by the monarch. Guizot confirmed this in a confidential letter, which King at once sent to a London journal for publication, with the result of a renewal of charges and countercharges. In the Chamber of Deputies, in the meantime, the opposition assailed Guizot for subservience to the British, with the result that Anglo-French collaboration in Texas came to an end. The rift in France between parties widened and eventuated in the Revolution of 1848, in which Louis Philippe abdicated the throne, Guizot fled as a refugee to England, and slavery in the French West Indies was abolished.

Calhoun's dispatch to King is a revelation of the proslavery extremism of the Tyler junto. Especially is this true of Calhoun's sweeping assertion: "It is little short of mockery to talk of philanthropy, with the examples before us of the effects of abolishing negro slavery in her own colonies, in St. Domingo, and the Northern States of our Union, where statistical facts, not to be shaken, prove that the freed negro, after the experience of sixty years, is in a far worse condition than in the other States, where he has been left in his former condition." Calhoun would have been more truthful had he written that the "statistical facts," drawn from the census of 1840, had been for years under fire in Congress and in the press.

The census had reported social statistics in 1840 for the first time and included information with regard to the incidence of insanity in the population. In the northern states it had reported one free Negro insane out of every 162, which was ten times the rate found among Negroes in the slave states. The rate among free Negroes in the New England states was especially alarming, one out of every 14 in Maine, one out of every 28 in New Hampshire, one out of every 43 in Massachusetts. By contrast the rate among Negroes, slave and free, in the southern states was one out of 1309 in Virginia, one out of 2447 in South Carolina, and one out of 4310 in Louisiana.

A notable specialist in the field of insanity and its geographical incidence, Dr. Edward Jarvis, of Concord, Massachusetts, interested himself in these statistics and found them grossly in error. On the basis of an examination of the returns from all the northern states he found repeated instances of Negro insanity more numerous in localities than their total Negro population. He described his findings in three articles in medical journals. In the spring of 1844 he enlisted the help of the American Statistical Association. A committee was established to prepare a report, of which Jarvis was made chairman. The report, in the form of a memorial presented to Congress, was that the census should be disowned by Congress.

Of the three Jarvis articles one came to the attention of John Quincy Adams. Its author probably had sent it. It became the basis for a resolution submitted by Adams to the House on February 26, 1844: "*Resolved,* that the Secretary of State [Upshur] be directed to inform this House whether any gross errors have been discovered in the printed Sixth Census . . . as corrected at the Department of State in 1841, and, if so, how those errors originated, what they are, and what, if any measures have been taken to rectify them." In the transmission of the resolution there occurred a blunder. The date "1841" became "1843." Upshur was spared the embarrassment of answering the inquiry by death. The problem fell into the lap of Calhoun. He did not raise a question as to the incorrect date in the House resolution. Instead he made full use of the error in his reply. He wrote that no work bearing the date "1843" had been received. As for the work of 1841, there had been no gross or material errors discovered in the printed copy.

Calhoun's letter was summarized to the House by the Speaker and only the closing sentence was entered on the *House Journal.* Adams, who had insisted on seeing Calhoun's letter, moved the next day to amend the *Journal,* but was defeated. He arranged a confrontation with Calhoun at the State Department and pressed the issue of the letter. He recorded later in his diary that Calhoun "writhed like a trodden rattlesnake on the exposure of his false report . . . that no material errors have been discovered in the printed census of 1840, and finally said that where there were so many errors they balanced one another, and led to the same conclusion as if they were all correct.''

These statistics had been exploited by Upshur in his dispatches to Everett in 1843, they had been used by Walker in his *Letter Relative to the Annexation of Texas,* and in more detail by Calhoun in his letter to Pakenham which had appeared in the press. The renewed use of them by Calhoun in his 1844 dispatch to King was further evidence of the weight attached to them by the Tyler junto. But such tactics disgusted southern Whigs and Van Buren Democrats in the North. George Bancroft wrote Van Buren after Calhoun's letter to Pakenham appeared in the press: ''What can be more sad than for a man to serve under John Tyler? What: Unless it be to found an argument in defense of slavery on fictitious statistics, and address it to a British minister!''

The exploitation of fictitious statistics was not a work of which those engaged in it were proud, and as little as possible of it was left in their personal correspondence. A like silence marks the biographies of the Tyler junto, though the issue resounded for years in the halls of Congress and in the press. But the Whigs no sooner won control of the federal government than they moved to reform the census. Early in the Zachary Taylor administration Jarvis and his mentor, Samuel Shattuck, were called to Washington as consultants to prepare for the census of 1850,and that survey set new standards for the gathering and analyzing of social statistics. As for Jarvis, in 1852 he was honored by being chosen president of the American Statistical Association, an office he held for the remainder of his active career.

Annexation Achieved

A MARKED CHANGE in Tyler's Texas strategy appeared in his annual message of December 3, 1844, to Congress. It consisted of an unequivocal recommendation of a joint resolution of Congress to accomplish annexation. In the preceding spring, after the rejection by the Senate of the annexation treaty, a recommendation of that sort had been foreshadowed in the message to Congress, in which the President declared that the power of Congress is "fully competent in some other form of proceeding to accomplish everything that a formal ratification of the treaty could have accomplished."

The response from expansionists in Congress was abundant. From the Senate came seven resolutions; from the House, ten. Most of the resolutions were from Democrats; only two came from Whigs, one in each house. The first resolution offered was by Senator McDuffie of South Carolina, proposing a resurrection of the dead treaty in a new form. It was followed by one from Senator Benton, opposite in spirit, which proposed negotiations concerning the boundary of Texas between the United States, Mexico, and Texas. It specified that the line should run from a point on the Gulf of Mexico south of the Nueces, in a northwesterly direction to, and along, the highlands dividing the waters of the Rio Grande from those of the Mississippi, to the northern latitude of 42°. A state of Texas, not exceeding in dimension the largest American state, should be admitted to the Union; the remainder of the annexed area should become a territory. In the northern and northwestern part of this territory slavery was to be forever prohibited. The whole of the annexed country should be divided between slaveholding and non-slaveholding states as equally as possible.

Senator Haywood of North Carolina proposed a resolution annexing Texas as two territories, each of which could be ultimately divided into as many as two or three states, the principle of the Missouri Compromise of 1820 being applied to them. The public lands and the debt of Texas were to be taken over by the United States. The United States was to settle boundary disputes with foreign states.

On February 5 Benton offered a second measure in substitution for his first. It omitted much of the detail of the first. It provided for the admission of Texas, partly as a state and partly as a territory, on an equal footing with existing states and territories, the precise terms to be subsequently worked out. The terms were to be settled in a negotiation with Texas for which an appropriation was authorized. The measure was a response, in part, to voices reaching the senator from his Missouri constituents.

From Tennessee, the home of Jackson and Polk, came a Whig resolution, offered by Senator E. H. Foster. It proposed that the territory properly included within and rightfully belonging to the Republic of Texas be erected into a new state subject to the adjustment by the United States of all boundary questions arising with other governments. Additional states might be formed, with the consent of Texas, from its territory. Any organized south of the line of 36°30' were to be admitted with or without slavery as the people might desire. All mines, harbors, and means of defense were to be ceded to the United States. All public lands and public debts were to be retained by the state.

House resolutions for annexing Texas were similar. One by C. J. Ingersoll of Pennsylvania copied the pattern of McDuffie's Senate resolution in merely resurrecting the abortive annexation treaty of the preceding April. A new feature, appearing in some resolutions, was the concept that Texas had always been part of the Louisiana Purchase, and that annexation would really be reannexation. A resolution by J. E. Belser of Alabama contained the idea that, if any attempt were made by a foreign power (Mexico) to invade Texas during the pendency of an annexation proposition, the President of the United States would be directed to afford such military and naval protection to Texas as would be necessary. This would have sanctioned the protective arrangement Tyler had made with Texas on his own authority.

On January 13 Milton Brown of Tennessee submitted the one Whig proposal offered in the House, which was accepted as a substitute for that of Ingersoll. It authorized admitting Texas as a state, with all boundary questions to be settled by the United States. It also permitted the creation of new states of convenient size from the territory of Texas with her consent, and provided that those lying south of 36°30' were in the future to be admitted to the Union with or without slavery as their people should desire. Texas was to retain her public lands and the proceeds of the lands were to be used to extinguish her public debt. This resolution foreshadowed the one Congress was ultimately to accept.

Other proposals were brought before the two houses which added few new ideas, often old ones in new combinations, and principally demonstrated a wish to please constituents who were expansionists. Speeches defending the proposals were the principal business of the session. They once again subjected the public to annexation propaganda, initially spread by spokesmen of the Administration under cover, then by expansionists after the exposure of the treaty, and again on the hustings. In equal volume came answers from embattled Whigs and antislavery Democrats.

Two constitutional issues, not clearly visible before, rose to the surface to increase the complexities embedded in the joint resolutions. One dealt with the three-fifths provision of the Constitution (Article I, Section 2), that in determining a state's population for apportionment of representatives in Congress, three-fifths of the slaves, in addition to all free persons, should be counted. The other was whether the annexation of a foreign territory could be accomplished in any other way than by a treaty. The three-fifths clause had been described by William Ellery Channing as early as 1837 as a circumlocution shamefacedly employed in the Constitution by framers who could not bring themselves to pronounce the word "slave" in an instrument for the government of a free people. Its evil potentialities had become apparent in the North with the reopening of the Texas issue. If Texas were annexed with the understanding that it could be divided into an indefinite number of new states as soon as population warranted, not only would southern power multiply in the Senate, but also in the House, and in the electoral college. The policy of balancing the admission of slave and free states would likewise break down.

On March 3, 1843, the Massachusetts legislature adopted a resolution urging in strong terms the elimination of the three-fifths provision from the Constitution by amendment. It ordered copies of the resolution sent to the Massachusetts representatives in Congress, to the President, and to the governors of all the states. In December, John Quincy Adams offered the Massachusetts resolution to the House. Since it was a request by a legislature for an amendment of the Constitution, it could not be conveniently brushed aside under House rules. Adams moved that it be referred to a select committee of nine and his motion prevailed. The committee was named by the Speaker, with Adams prescriptively its chairman, but surrounded by colleagues who could be depended on to keep him shackled.

Six reports were written by the committee of nine. The first was by Thomas W. Gilmer, author of the seminal Texas letter in *The Madisonian,* and Armistead Burr, a Calhoun Democrat from South Carolina. It pronounced the Massachusetts amendment proposal destructive of the compact between the states: If agreed to, it would convert the Union into a consolidated despotism of numbers; the slaveholding states actually were underrepresented in Congress; to confer equality on them would require counting slaves on the basis of five-fifths, not three-fifths of their numbers. Concerning blacks, the authors continued, "the livery of nature proclaims them, whether bond or free, the inferiors of the white man."

To Adams these views were anathema. Though he was not yet ready to support his state's proposal, he considered the three-fifths clause repugnant to the vital principles of popular representation, to the self-evident truths proclaimed in the Declaration of Independence, and to the liberties of the people of the free states.

The practical operation of the three-fifths clause seemed to Adams as evil as its theory:

> The first consequence has been a secret, imperceptible, combined and never-ceasing struggle, to engross all the offices and depositories of power to themselves . . . At this day the President of the United States, the President of the Senate, the Speaker of the House of Representatives, and five, out of nine, of the Judges of the supreme judicial courts of the United States, are not only citizens of the slaveholding States, but individual slaveholders themselves. So are, and constantly have been, with scarcely an exception, all the members of both Houses of Congress from the slaveholding States; and so are, in immensely disproportionate numbers, the commanding officers of the army and navy; the officers of the customs; the registers and receivers of the land offices, and the post-masters throughout the slaveholding States.

One problem arising from domination by slaveholders of the lower House under the three-fifths clause was that they were encroaching on the right of petition, guaranteed in the Bill of Rights. That right was being increasingly relied upon by antislavery groups during the excitement produced by the annexation issue. Adams traced in his report the growing encroachments on the right. From 1789 to 1834 petitions for the abolition of slavery had regularly been received, referred to committees, and acted on. But with the emergence of the Texas issue when more petitions came to the House, the system of refusing them began, which developed into the 25th rule of the House. That rule was not only a violation of the Constitution but a suppression of freedom of debate in the House. It deprived the House of the power of deliberating upon subjects of vital importance to the Union, of mitigating the sufferings of the oppressed, even of regulating the traffic in slaves which the laws of Congress had declared piracy, punishable with death. The immediate object of these encroachments was the project secretly conceived by the Administration and now openly avowed, to annex Texas on behalf of the slave oligarchy of the South. The report was signed by another representative of the New England conscience, Joshua Giddings of Ohio.

Another report, sponsored by two Whig committee members, was that of J. R. Ingersoll of Pennsylvania and Garrett Davis of Kentucky. It contained a survey of the conditions leading to the adoption of the three-fifths compromise, and concluded that the compromise, having been essential to the formation of the Union, should be retained for the preservation of the Union.

Three of the committee's six reports were individually authored. One was by an Indiana Whig, S. C. Sample, who concluded that the Massachusetts proposal was a matter of expediency and that to go forward with it was inexpedient. Another was by a northern man with southern principles, Edmund Burke of New Hampshire, who concluded that the Massachusetts proposal was a naked proposal to subvert the Constitution and to dissolve the Union. The third individual report was that of a Maine Whig, F. H. Morse, who showed sympathy with the Massachusetts proposal without actually favoring it. He concurred with Adams that one of the great evils of slave representation in the House was the abridgment of the right of petition.

Despite this diversity of opinion a majority of the committee managed to agree that the Massachusetts resolves not be recommended, that the House instead be requested to accept the journal of the committee's proceedings, and that the committee be discharged. In the meantime further petitions to remove the three-fifths clause flowed into Congress—ten from Ohio, eight from New York, and more from elsewhere, in the months of January and February 1844, all evidence of a grass-roots uprising against annexation of Texas.

Early in April 1844, the House agreed to accept the recommendations of the majority of its committee and to print the reports. The state and local proposals to eliminate the three-fifths clause seemed to have been laid to rest. But they remained very much alive. Antislavery elements in the North had come to see that there was a connection between the three-fifths clause, the ability of the slavery elements to throttle opposition, and the drive for Texas. On December 3, 1844, on the reassembling of Congress, Adams moved the following resolution:

> Resolved, that the twenty-fifth standing rule for conducting business in this House, in the following words, ''No petition, memorial, resolution, or other paper praying the abolition of Slavery in the District of Columbia, or any State or Territory; or the slave-trade

between the States or Territories in which it Now Exists, shall be received by this House, or entertained in any way whatever,'' be, and the same is hereby rescinded.

A hostile motion to lay the resolution on the table failed, whereupon Adams called for the ayes and nays. The resulting vote, as he recorded in his diary in ecstasy, was favorable—''one hundred and eight to eighty. Blessed forever blessed, be the name of God!''

A constitutional issue even more divisive than the three-fifths clause was whether an extensive foreign territory may be legally added to the national domain. Jefferson had been tormented by the issue when the Louisiana Purchase treaty was thrust upon him. He considered obtaining an amendment to the Constitution to legalize acceptance of the treaty. But he was warned that the treaty might be cancelled by Napoleon, and since it quieted an emergency at the mouth of the Mississippi, he reconciled himself to a ratification, and that precedent established itself as the law.

However, there was a distinction between accepting by treaty an unorganized territory, such as Louisiana, and admitting by treaty a foreign state such as Texas, laden with its own treaty obligations and institutions. Such a distinction was drawn by John Forsyth, Van Buren's Secretary of State, and by Daniel Webster.

After the defeat of the annexation treaty Tyler adopted the view that Texas could be annexed under Article IV, Section 3, which reads: ''New States may be admitted by the Congress into this Union.'' Texas was surely a new state, and thus a legislative annexation would be legal. Indeed, it would be preferable, for it would require only a majority vote in the houses of Congress, whereas a treaty required a two-thirds vote of the Senate. Tyler was not troubled that legislative annexation abandoned the principle of strict construction of the Constitution, on which he had been adamant in domestic policy.

This reinterpretation of the Constitution was unpopular among northern anti-slavery Democrats. It evoked a correspondence between Albert Gallatin and David O. Field, an authority on the Constitution, in which Gallatin pronounced annexation by joint resolution a direct and undisguised usurpation of power, and a violation of the Constitution—a judgment with which Field agreed.

Among Whig statesmen, the new interpretation seemed even less sound. Rufus Choate, successor to Webster in the Senate and himself an eminent constitutional lawyer, excoriated it in a Senate speech. So did southern Whigs, among them two distinguished Virginians, William C. Rives and William S. Archer, and John Berrien, of Georgia, all members of the Senate Foreign Relations Committee. Rives in an eloquent speech asked: ''What would it profit us should we gain Texas, if thereby we lost our regard for that sacred instrument which was the bond of our national union, the pledge and palladium of our liberty and happiness?'' A House Whig, Robert C. Winthrop, quoted Calhoun as maintaining in a House speech on January 16, 1816: ''A treaty never can legitimately do that which can be done by law; and the reverse is also true.'' Yet Calhoun did approve the Tyler thesis that Congress could annex Texas by a joint resolution.

Another objection to annexation was speculation in the public debt of Texas. This was of undetermined size but was estimated to total $10 million. Part of it had been incurred during the revolution, but the bulk was an accumulation of expenditures during eight years of preparation for renewed fighting. It consisted of bonds, exchequer notes, and other forms of liability, but chiefly of land scrip, which entitled the holder to parcels of public land wherever such existed in Texas free of pre-existing claims. The scrip had been issued to soldiers, merchants, and others in payment of services. Many of the recipients did not wish to be settlers and since the scrip was negotiable it quickly passed into the hands of speculators at a minor fraction of its face value.

A part of the problem was uncertainty regarding the amount of public lands remaining in Texas. Great unoccupied areas had passed into private ownership, granted administratively by Coahuila-Texas during the Mexican era. Some had been distributed under the laws of Texas after the revolution.

In the annexation treaty the debt and the public-land questions had been dealt with together by transferring both to the United States. The expectation was that the debt would be extinguished from receipts of the sale of the public lands. This had raised the issue whether speculators with scrip, acquired at starkly depreciated rates, should be allowed to profiteer at the expense of the American government. The problem was comparable to that of the bonds and certificates of indebtedness of the old Continental Congress, which had passed into the hands of speculators who had reaped immense profits under the refunding program of Alexander Hamilton.

Another element in the drive for annexation was the activity of speculators who had made purchases of Texas land. They were ubiquitous in Texan affairs. Some of them—Gilmer, for example—had valid titles to land obtained by purchase. Others—John Woodward, for example—had claims from the Mexican era and of uncertain validity. Both types were protected in the abortive treaty of annexation. A provision in Article III read: "All titles and claims to real estate, which are valid under the laws of Texas, shall be held to be so by the United States." A rush of emigration into Texas was expected to follow annexation, and this would hoist land values.

The several categories of speculators in lands and in the public debt were organized, before and after the failure of the treaty, into an aggressive pressure group that operated in Washington in the shadow of the Capitol. They maintained the "Texas fund," which defrayed the costs of distributing pro-annexation propaganda addressed to the northern public, such as Walker's *Letter Relative to the Annexation of Texas*.

One of Benton's services to realism, after the annexation treaty had been defeated and the issue had become part of the 1844 campaign, was his exposure of the activities of this lobby. He devoted his energies to it, especially in a speech delivered at Boonville, Indiana, on July 17 and 18. Referring to Washington during the Senate deliberations on the annexation treaty, he declared:

> The city was a buzzard roost; the Presidential mansion and Department of State were buzzard roosts; defiled and polluted by the foul and voracious birds in the shape of land speculators and stock-jobbers, who saw their prey in the treaty and spared no effort to secure it. Their own work was to support the treaty and its friends—to assail its opponents—to abuse the Senators who were against it—to vilify them and lie upon them in speech and in writing—and to establish a committee, still sitting at Washington, to promote and protect their interest. The treaty assumed ten millions of debt and confirmed all the land claims under the law of Texas.

The speech was widely circulated in the press and in pamphlet form. It raised awkward questions concerning the private interests of annexationists. In Congress it necessitated a reshaping of the terms of the Joint Resolution. At the same time sectional and party alignments in Congress needed to be changed in view of the overwhelming defeat of the treaty.

Realignments occurred in the winter in the course of the debate on the Joint Resolution. The mode was suggested in the one Whig resolution offered in the House, that offered by Milton Brown of Tennessee on January 13, 1845, which made concessions, or the appearance of concessions, on a number of major issues. To avoid speculation and the unloading on the nation of the Texas debt and its security in Texas public lands, Brown proposed that both be left in the possession of Texas. To deflect the issue of slavery extension, Brown proposed what seemed a slavery limitation in the area to be acquired from Texas. The Missouri Compromise was to be extended across Texas. By implication there was to be no slavery north of that line. South of the line, states carved in the future from Texan territory were to have a choice of becoming free or slave. This was local self-determination, widely popular in the West. Whether Texas had a legitimate claim to territory north of the Missouri Compromise line was very doubtful, but the impression created by the resolution was one of compromise.

Another controversial issue, on which an appearance of concession was made, was the boundary between Texas and Mexico. The resolution called for the annexation of "territory properly included within and rightfully belonging to the republic of Texas." A further specification was that the new Texas state be "subject to the adjustment by this government [United States] of any questions of boundary that may arise with other governments." This left the boundary issue in a convenient state of vagueness.

Finally, the controversial matter of constitutionality—the issue whether a treaty was required, or a congressional resolution would do—was dealt with soothingly by silence. The resolution simply took for granted the constitutionality of a congressional annexation.

The Brown resolution had the usefulness of a decoy. Coming from a southern Whig, it might attract other southern Whigs who were hesitating, and likewise northern Democrats who were on the fence. It might do this in the House, and more importantly, in the closely divided Senate.

A transplant was therefore effected in the House. The moribund joint resolution of C. J. Ingersoll, the northern Democrat, which had merely given a legislative title to the dead treaty, was decapitated, and its title was grafted onto the Brown resolution. It passed by a comfortable margin on January 25, which promised success for a like strategy in the Senate.

In the Senate the initial reception of the Brown resolution was far from cordial. The measure was referred to the Foreign Relations Committee, headed by Archer. The report of the committee was a lengthy denunciation of the resolution on the score of unconstitutionality and a recommendation that it be rejected.

To overcome this recommendation required the conversion of Benton and his Democratic followers. His shift alone might swing the vote. He had seemed irreconcilably opposed to immediate annexation. In the minds of antislavery voters he had been carried to great heights by the flow of his oratory. Yet his constituents in Missouri did want Texas. He had heard from them in a message of instruction from the Missouri legislature adopted on January 3, 1845. He had also heard indirectly from Andrew Jackson. Benton believed he should not ignore the opinions of these friends. Some descent from the heights was prudent, especially if the path down could be smoothed. The path down had become smoothed by the Brown resolution.

Benton's downward movement began on February 5, 1845. It took the form of a greatly simplified resolution, which provided that Texas be annexed with "suitable extent and boundaries" as soon as the terms could be agreed to by Texas and the United States. A sum of $100,000 was to be appropriated to defray the expenses of a newly negotiated treaty with Texas or an agreement on the terms of a legislative admission to the Union. Andrew Jackson was immensely cheered by this resolution. He saw in it evidence that the senator was headed right.

The final step taken by Benton came on February 27, 1845, during the Senate's consideration of Brown's resolution. An amendment to it was proposed by Robert J. Walker, in the form of a set of resolutions strikingly like Benton's of February 5. Under the amendment the President (Polk was in Walker's mind) was authorized to offer Texas the choice of a new treaty or an agreement of legislative admission of Texas to the Union—all in the exact language of Benton. To head off the amendment Archer proposed another—simply to substitute the negative report of his committee for the House measure. The Archer amendment was rejected and Walker's was accepted. The vote was an omen—it was 27–25.

A New Jersey Whig, Jacob W. Miller, now moved yet another amendment to the House measure. He proposed to strike out everything after the word "resolved," and to replace it by Benton's early proposal of June 10. He explained that the speech Benton had made in introducing that proposal "had made a strong impression upon him, and he hoped the senator would not destroy his own child." To which Benton made the laconic reply, "I'll kill it stone dead." Cheers rang through the chamber, which could only with difficulty be suppressed. For the senator had announced, in these few words, his return to the fold, and this gave assurance that the Joint Resolution would pass. When the final vote on the Walker amendment was taken immediately afterward, it was again upheld, 27–25. The amended Senate measure had now to go back to the House for approval. It was approved there by a bigger margin than before. "Thus," the *Congressional Globe* recorded, "the joint resolution for annexing Texas to the United States is finally passed, and awaits only the signature of the President to become law."

The triumph of the Joint Resolution in the Senate was thus the outcome of effective maneuvering to close party ranks. The egregious errors of the Tyler junto had been recognized and corrected. Every Democrat in the Senate, including those who had joined the Whigs in rejecting the treaty nine months before, toed the party line on February 27.

Outside Congress the same process was at work. Francis P. Blair, of the Washington *Globe,* who had savagely assailed the treaty, warmly supported the Joint Resolution. So did William Cullen Bryant, of the New York *Evening Post,* and other Democratic editors of lesser importance. They were attracted to annexation by the allurements that had moved Benton. They wanted Texas. They represented the spirit of Manifest Destiny. Some Democrats had no deep aversion to the expansion of slavery. Others may have been drugged by Walker into believing that an annexed Texas would one day end slavery and the race issue. Democrats in general hated Tyler, but had hope and respect for Polk. The new President was, it was true, a major slaveholder, but he was sound on the tariff and on strict construction of the Constitution. He could be trusted to choose wisely between annexation by a joint resolution or by a new negotiation. For all these reasons it was desirable to take a stand beside the slave oligarchy of the South.

The Joint Resolution, as signed by Tyler on March 1, was a cluster of provisions framed either to exclude divisive issues or to substitute obfuscation for clarity in regard to the issue of the extension of slavery. Article II, Part 2, relegated to Texas the issues of the public lands, the debt, and their interrelated speculation, which, in the treaty, had enraged Benton. Part 3 of Article II blandly assured what Brown's resolution had merely implied—that, in any state carved out of Texas north of the Missouri Compromise line, slavery would be excluded, while south of the line slavery might be permitted if the people desired it. The unreality of Texan claims north of the Compromise line was dealt with by silence. Two articles kept the issue of the Texas boundary carefully clouded. Article I provided that "territory properly included within, and rightfully belonging to the Republic of Texas" could be admitted into the Union as a state. But Article II, Part 1, left the issue dangling, by providing that annexation would be subject to the "adjustment by this government [United States] of all questions of boundary that may arise with other governments." The issue of constitutionality was also dodged. By Article III the Chief Executive (which one, incoming or outgoing, was not disclosed) was left to decide whether annexation should be under the Joint Resolution or by a new treaty to be negotiated.

The effectiveness of these tactics in closing Democratic ranks on the Joint Resolution was highlighted by the divisions opened in the ranks of the Whigs. A crucial trio of southern Whigs, two of whom had voted to reject the Tyler treaty of annexation, cast their lot with the Democrats in the Senate vote in favor of the Joint Resolution. It was a rupture of party solidarity symptomatic of what was happening to Whigs. They were increasingly torn by the sectional conflict over slavery which had led Clay astray in the presidential campaign of 1844. Even as to expansion they were not of one mind, and some were attracted by the profits an annexed Texas would bring. Whig divisions were deep and more enduring than those of the Democrats, as was to become evident in the disintegration of the party in the not distant future.

The triumph of the Joint Resolution was acclaimed by Democrats and lamented by Whigs. John Quincy Adams, who felt numbed by what had happened, wrote in his diary on February 28:

> The day passes, and leaves scarcely a distinct trace upon the memory of anything, and precisely because, among numberless other objects of comparative insignificance, the heaviest calamity that ever befel myself and my country was this day consummated.

The implementation of the Joint Resolution could have been left by Tyler to the incoming President, as the strategists who had maneuvered it through Congress intended, and as courtesy would have suggested. But Tyler dearly desired credit for the work he had done. He consulted Calhoun, who also wished immediate action, and Tyler convinced himself that safety required speed. If a new negotiation were to be opened the British would at once get into it and the great end would be defeated. A courier was dispatched to Texas just before Polk became President, with the invitation to come into the Union.

In the meantime, shortly before the close of the Tyler administration, an episode in Texas affairs came into public notice that was embarrassing. It involved Duff Green, whose earlier services in London had proved so useful. On September 12, 1844, he was given an assignment as consul at Galveston, Texas, and was handed an ordinary printed instruction by Calhoun. His job carried no salary, consuls being expected to draw their sustenance from fees they collected. He was directed, however, to proceed on the quiet to Mexico City as a courier to deliver dispatches to the American minister there. The mission appears to have been a cover for other services. Later in life Green wrote of the mission:

> At his [Calhoun's] request I went to Mexico to aid in conducting the negotiation for the acquisition of Texas, New Mexico, and California, and upon handing me his letter of instructions, he remarked: "If you succeed in this negotiation our commerce in the Pacific will, in a few years, be greatly more valuable than that in the Atlantic."

During a preliminary stay at Galveston, en route to Vera Cruz, Green sent political news to Calhoun. The most important item was a conversation with General Thomas J. Green, whose hospitality he was enjoying and from whom he had obtained enticing vistas of opportunities west of the Rio Grande. One of them was a valley west of the Rio Grande 50 miles wide and of unsurpassed fertility. Another was water and inland communication all the way from the Rio Grande to the navigable waters of the Gulf of California. Green journeyed as soon as possible to Mexico City, where he wrote letters to Calhoun reporting the likelihood of a British negotiation with Mexico for California. As for any hope of American acquisition of Texas or California by purchase from Mexico, Green was very pessimistic. Any Mexican party agreeing to the sale of Texas or California to the United States would be driven from office and its leaders would probably be shot.

Frustrated in his Mexican mission, Green returned to Galveston, where he met frustration again. Consul's fees were meager and the life was dull. He therefore appointed a vice-consul to his post and hastened to the Texan capital, where he formed a land company, for which he hoped to obtain a charter from the legislature. The company was to have rights to acquire and sell real estate, manage railroad and trust companies, and exercise a perpetual monopoly of all navigable streams in Texas. At the same time Green formed the "Del Norte Company," which was to procure the "conquest and occupancy, in behalf of Texas, of the Californias and the northern provinces of Mexico" with an army organized in Texas and reinforced by some 60,000 Indians, who were to be brought to Texas from the United States.

In quest of charters for the companies, Green called on the Texan President, Anson Jones. To win his favor he held out to Jones an offer of stock in the projected land company. This angered Jones, who had to check a temptation to shoot Green on the spot, as the British chargé in Texas reported to Aberdeen. In the stormy exchange which followed Green warned President Jones that his administration was suspected in Texas of being opposed to annexation, which rendered its tenure insecure. Jones replied that Green's own tenure was insecure—that his consular status would be revoked. Green wrote a public letter in reply, charging the President with opposing annexation and being too much under the influence of Charles Elliot, the British chargé. The matter was now so unpleasant that Jones referred it to the Cabinet, and the American chargé, Andrew J. Donelson, was notified that Green would be expelled.

But expulsion would irritate annexationists in both countries. Green was no ordinary consul. He was a confidant of Tyler and of Calhoun. He epitomized the annexation cause. Yet to ignore the matter was not feasible either, since Green's letter had appeared in the press. All that was feasible was to lower the affair's crisis potential and to this end Donelson turned all his diplomatic talents.

He wrote the Texan Acting Secretary of State a soothing letter in which he showed that Green had no official status whatsoever in making proposals to President Jones. Green had given up his consular status in delegating it to his deputy. He had not intended to show the slightest disrespect to the President, and the objectionable conduct imputed to him had no higher importance than what belonged to his private character. Green's public letter was left unexplained, but Green himself later offered the explanation that it had been written under the apprehension that the President was seeking a quarrel. Publication was the editor's fault—he had printed it prematurely.

In London, to which the news had traveled, the affair created a stir in cabinet circles. Peel wrote Aberdeen, when it seemed that Green might be expelled, that the expulsion might be made a "pretext with the U.S. for direct hostility against Texas—and annexation by that means instead of by amicable arrangement."

The repercussions of the Green affair were loudest in the United States, especially among Whigs. A New Jersey Whig, Senator W. S. Dayton, a foe of annexation on slavery grounds, brought into the Senate a pointed series of questions in the form of a resolution, which was sent to Tyler:

> Resolved, That the President be requested to communicate to the Senate, if in his opinion not inconsistent with the public interest, whether Mr. Duff Green does now hold, or has lately held, any diplomatic or official station near the government of Texas; and if so, what, when appointed, at what salary, and with what instructions.

The President's answer came in the form of a letter from Calhoun:

> The Secretary of State, to whom has been referred the resolution of the Senate of the 4th instant . . . has the honor to state, in reply thereto, that Mr. Duff Green was appointed consul of the United States at the port of Galveston, in Texas, on the 12th day of September, 1844, and received from this department his ordinary printed instructions as such, and none other; that no salary attaches to the appointment; and that he neither holds, nor has held, any diplomatic or official station near the Government of Texas.

This letter was read in the Senate, referred to the Committee on Foreign Relations, and ordered to be printed. It was characteristic of Calhoun's letters composed under pressure. It contained scarcely a word of untruth, but was filled with truth of the kind that concealed the truth. Dayton did not press the matter further and Green's exploit produced no further eruptions in Congress.

To Polk, Tyler's haste in dispatching to Texas the invitation of Congress to enter the Union seemed uncalled for. He thought that *he* should have had the decision as between the alternative modes of annexation which the Joint Resolution had offered. He was no less eager for Texas than Tyler, no less a slaveholder, and no less on guard against British interference. Indeed, he was pledged to the "re-annexation of Texas at the earliest practical period." He decided to undo Tyler's last-minute action. He wished advice from his Cabinet, and the Cabinet had not yet been named. So he countermanded Tyler's message to Texas and held off his own decision as to the mode of annexation until the Cabinet had been assembled. Then, on March 10, 1845, he accepted the Cabinet's advice, reactivated Tyler's offer of immediate entrance by Texas into the Union, and thereafter ran things as he desired.

In Texas the Cabinet was aware of the terms of the Joint Resolution before the document itself arrived. Its leaders, Anson Jones, Ashbel Smith, and Ebenezer Allen, were dissatisfied with the terms. So was Houston, who was still a power in Texas though no longer in office. He wished that Texas be admitted to the Union as a territory rather than as a state, a territory divisible, as its population grew, into as many states as the United States would think proper. On April 9, 1845, he wrote Andrew J. Donelson unofficially that he desired the alternative of a new negotiation to set the terms of entrance which had been included by Congress in the Joint Resolution. He thought the terms in the Joint Resolution illiberal. He also took exception to the manner of legislative annexation proposed: "The terms are dictated, and the conditions are absolute. They are of a character not to have been expected by anyone who regarded annexation as a compact between two nations, where each had substantive and acknowledged sovereignty, and independence."

Such a reaction in Texas to the Joint Resolution, even though unofficial, was not surprising. It was a predictable reaction to an instrument framed to win a majority vote in a narrowly divided Congress. The victory won in converting a treaty into a legislative act ricocheted. An opposition to acceptance of the terms of the Joint Resolution developed in Texas sufficient to induce Polk to embark on a program of interference in Texan internal affairs, far more real than any charged by American expansionists to have come from the British.

With Mexican prompting, an alternative to the American offer was suggested to the Texan leaders by Charles Elliot and Alphonse de Saligny, the British and French chargés in Texas. It was that Mexico be brought to acknowledge Texan independence, that Texas agree not to accept annexation to the United States, and that a negotiation be opened between Texas and Mexico to set the terms for their separation. One of the terms would be the boundary separating them. If this could not be settled, the question should be referred to an umpire. Time was needed to carry this proposal to Mexico City, to obtain a decision on it, and to return to Texas. An estimate of 90 days was suggested, and President Jones agreed to a corresponding date for a special meeting of the Texas legislature. If the mission proved successful the legislature would have a choice between peaceful independence and annexation to the United States.

The scheme was advantageous to Texas and it cost little. If it succeeded two alternatives would be before the Texas legislature, each of which could, perhaps, be improved by competition between the American and Mexican bidders. If the Mexican government should remain stubbornly hostile and the American Congress ungenerous, the status quo could be retained. The cost of the venture was no more than a 90-day delay in submitting the American offer of annexation to the Texas legislature.

To carry out the mission, speed and secrecy were essential. The answer to the American invitation could not be too long withheld. Secrecy was required so that no charges could be brought of acting under British inspiration and huckstering for terms. The messenger carrying the plan to Mexico City had to be a person of standing, who could present it authoritatively to the Mexican leaders. The obvious man for the job was Charles Elliot, the intimate of President Jones, who, on an earlier occasion, had volunteered such a service as a go-between. Yet he was apprehensive of the secrecy of such a mission. Pressed by Jones, he agreed, against his better judgment, to go secretly. He went by water to Vera Cruz and thence overland to Mexico City.

In Mexico his mission prospered. The Mexican hand had been forced by the American annexation offer to Texas. The government agreed to make peace, with the understanding that Texas retain its independence and that the terms of separation be worked out. What the Texan government wanted it got. Yet time had been consumed in Mexico. The return to Texas took time. Elliot had the misfortune to be recognized on the way to Mexico City wearing a big white hat and his mission was guessed. News of it was rushed to the American press. The affair of the "Man in the White Hat" became a political sensation in the United States. It became the subject of an urgent dispatch from Secretary of State Buchanan to the American chargé in Texas that was similarly exploited in the expansionist press.

On June 3, 1845, Elliot was back in the Texan capital with the eagerly awaited news of the agreement obtained from the Mexican government. On the next day Jones issued a proclamation informing the public that, through the good offices of the British government, he had obtained peace with Mexico and that Texas now had a free choice between peaceful independence and annexation. But his only reward for his pains was the accusation that he was a British stool pigeon.

As for Elliot, his yielding to the pressure of President Jones to go on a secret mission to Mexico City had been a grievous error. Secrecy in itself was not the error. In diplomacy it was normal. It had been the staple of Tyler's negotiations with Texas. What was wrong with it was that it had been detected. Just as Tyler's treaty had been exposed by Tappan and Benton, so the mission of Elliot, detected, had backfired. As soon as Aberdeen received word of the mission he wrote Peel in anxiety: "The only part of the transaction which I do not much like, is the journey of Capt. Elliot to Mexico at the request of President Jones, and his attempt at concealment. This cannot succeed, and it will make English agency appear too active, and too hostile to the United States." Peel agreed, and Aberdeen sent Elliot a reproof in which he drew a distinction between the aims of British policy and the mode used by Elliot in attaining them. Elliot was warned not to compromise his government again by clandestine operations.

In Texas two aspirations for the future had been in conflict. The people of Texas desired annexation to the United States. For the most part they were Americans, whose flow into Texas had been in progress for twenty years in response to the invitations of the empresarios. It had expanded to an actual flood in the forties, reflecting hope of annexation to the United States. The settlers valued annexation for the security it would bring from future Mexican harassment and for the likelihood that their land values would rise. They were content with the terms of the congressional resolution and ready to unite their destiny with that of the old homeland.

On the other hand, the Texan leaders included ambitious men who had visions of greatness for a Texas that would maintain its independence; would expand over the provinces of northern Mexico; would reach the Pacific in California, and become a transcontinental power rivaling the United States. Houston dreamed of acquiring even the Oregon Country. These expansionists held out for the new negotiation permitted under the Joint Resolution in the hope of obtaining from the United States at least better terms. They chose not to consider seriously Donelson's suggestion that improved terms would be offered by Congress in an ultimate act of incorporation, if the offer of immediate annexation were accepted. Their tactic was to stall with regard to summoning the Texan Congress, the tactic earlier adopted for awaiting the news from Mexico.

In this critical period Polk sent more than a mere offer of annexation. He sent agents to help the Texans make up their minds. Among them was Charles A. Wickliffe, former governor of Kentucky and Postmaster General in the Tyler administration. He had directions "to oppose the machinations and influence of Great Britain and France." He was to use, on proper occasions, arguments best adapted to convince the authorities and people of Texas that reunion with the United States would promote their best interests and those of their posterity. An unnamed half of this assignment was to counteract the machinations and influence of the Texan leaders. Another of the visitors was Archibald Yell, a member of Congress and former governor of Arkansas. Another was Captain Robert F. Stockton of the United States Navy, charged with guarding the Texan coast. His assignment was light, and he had time to come inland to counteract British influence. Finally, there was Andrew J. Donelson—the American chargé in Texas and nephew of Andrew Jackson—who combined skill with tact and became a major force in the Texas councils.

If Ashbel Smith is to be believed, the American visitors, including Donelson, went up and down the settlements of Texas holding out promises of American aid if annexation were consummated. "Under the fostering protection of the United States it was gloriously prophesied, with spread eagle magniloquence, that capital would flow into Texas in ocean streams to develop and utilize our incalculable resources. Employment, wealth, prosperity would reign in this land. Here, in the West, lay the inexhaustible Orient." According to Ebenezer Allen, the Texan Attorney General, the visitors instigated the calling of public meetings to whip up enthusiasm for annexation and held out to Texan politicians expectations of obtaining federal office if it took place.

For Houston a shift was necessary from positions he had held. He had become aware in April 1845 of strong winds blowing for annexation and had decided it was best to sail before them. He was intrigued by suggestions that he might someday be chosen President of the United States. In any case, he was likely to become a senator soon. He was anxious to please Andrew Jackson, whose eagerness for annexation was touching and who was approaching death. He let Donelson know of his conversion, to the latter's joy, and early in May he arranged for a visit to the Hermitage. On May 29, while in New Orleans awaiting passage up the river, he made a significant speech, which disclosed that inwardly he had always favored annexation. He opened with a "statement of facts." Then he concluded:

> He would leave to the public to infer whether he was opposed to, or in favor of, annexation. It was true, he said, that he had coquetted a little with G. Britain, and made the

United States as jealous of that power as he possibly could; and had it not been, he said, for the eagerness of the Texan congress in passing and sending this country [in 1844] a declaration that nine-tenths of the people were in favor of the measure, he would have so operated on the fears of the American Senate . . . as to have secured the ratification of the treaty last spring.

The hero of San Jacinto recovered in this way his old rapport with the people of Texas. He made evident to them that, though he had seemed at odds with their wishes for a time, it was only because he had been cleverer than they in effecting what they wanted. The speech prepared the way for his election as one of the state's two original senators. But Jones was left holding the bag. He thought the speech infamous, false, and disgraceful, though at the time he kept his peace.

On June 18, during Houston's absence, the Texan Congress met. It rejected out of hand the Mexican peace proposal, and unanimously approved the offer of annexation to the United States. A specially summoned convention did the same on July 4, by a virtually unanimous vote. The convention remained in session to frame a state constitution for presentation to Congress. It completed its work on August 27, 1845.

On December 2, 1845, President Polk, in his first annual message to Congress, presented the state and its constitution in a glowing speech of welcome. He declared:

> This accession to our territory has been a bloodless achievement. No arm of force has been raised to produce the result. The sword has had no part in the victory. We have not sought to extend our territorial possessions by conquest, or our republican institutions over a reluctant people. It was the deliberate homage of each people to the great principle of our federative union. If we consider the extent of territory involved in the annexation, its prospective influence on America, the means by which it has been accomplished, springing purely from the choice of the people themselves to share the blessings of our union, the history of the world may be challenged to furnish a parallel. The jurisdiction of the United States, which at the formation of the Federal Constitution was bounded by the St. Mary's on the Atlantic, has passed the capes of Florida and been peacefully extended to the Del Norte [Rio Grande]. In contemplating the grandeur of this event it is not to be forgotten that the result was achieved in despite of the diplomatic interference of European monarchies. Even France, the country which had been our ancient ally . . . most unexpectedly, and to our unfeigned regret, took part in an effort to prevent annexation and to impose on Texas, as a condition of the recognition of her independence by Mexico, that she would never join herself to the United States. We may rejoice that the tranquil and pervading influence of the American principle of self-government was sufficient to defeat the purposes of British and French interference, and that the almost unanimous voice of the people of Texas has given to that interference a peaceful and effective rebuke.

Polk's declaration that the jurisdiction of the United States had been peacefully extended to the Del Norte was a deception. If the river named had been the Nueces the declaration would have passed muster. But the Texan claim to the Del Norte was woefully flimsy, and in any case, an international boundary is not established unilaterally. The emphasis on the peacefulness of the extension and the casualness of the reference to the Del Norte had the desired effect. Not even such distrustful journals as the *National Intelligencer* and the New York *Tribune* were roused to challenge what was in fact an arrogant assertion, portentous for the peace of the future.

In Texas, on February 14, 1846, Anson Jones presided over the ceremony of the transfer of his state's sovereignty to the United States. Before an audience of legislators and citizens he delivered a valedictory with this brief peroration:

> The lone star of Texas, which ten years since arose amid clouds over fields of carnage, and obscurely shone for a while, has culminated, and, following an inscrutable destiny, has passed on and become fixed forever in that glorious constellation which all freemen and lovers of freedom in the world must reverence and adore—the American Union . . . The final act in this great drama is now performed. The republic of Texas is no more.

In the silence following the peroration the President lowered the flag of the republic. As it came down, the pole which had been carrying it broke in two. For a moment, before the banner of the Union was raised, the Lone Star flag shrouded the retiring President. Thirteen years later, deeply depressed over the misunderstanding of his efforts for Texas, which had reappeared in his defeat for election to the United States Senate, he took his own life.

A traditional view of the acquisition of Texas is that it was the achievement of the westward movement. This accords with early developments in Texas history and has therefore been easy to accept. American emigrants did move into Texas in the 1820's and 1830's, where they could obtain excellent land virtually free. In 1835 they revolted against Mexican authority and won a *de facto* independence. But an interval of ten years separated this development from the admission of the Republic of Texas into the Union. During seven of these years annexation was a dormant issue because of northern objection to the extension of slavery. Then the course of history was changed by new forces: the emergence in the South of the doctrine that slavery was a beneficent form of labor—that it was necessary to the southern economy, to southern democracy, and to the well-being of the slaves—a way of life threatened by international abolitionism.

At the same time there developed in the Northwest and in eastern urban centers the doctrine of Manifest Destiny, which could be brought to the support of slavery expansion. In the field of government a series of accidents occurred—the advent to the presidency of John Tyler, the clash of Tyler with the chiefs of the party, who had supported him for the vice-presidency but who repudiated him as President, and the consequent search by Tyler for an issue that would build for him a party of his own. The annexation of Texas became the catalyst of these forces and of this ambition. An undercover propaganda campaign produced a treaty of annexation, which was overwhelmingly rejected by the Senate. A presidential election followed, in which the cause of expansionism won by a narrow margin. A lame-duck Congress, by an even narrower margin, adopted a joint resolution of annexation in the final hours of a dying administration. This strange succession of events and developments, not the simple westward movement of pioneers, brought about the annexation of Texas. It brought about also sectional bitterness that intensified with the events of the succeeding decade and a half, culminating in 1861 in the disaster of the Civil War.

35

The Oregon Question

THE OREGON COUNTRY at the time of the acquisition of Louisiana was a vast wilderness adjoining the United States at the northwest. It extended from the Continental Divide to the shores of the Pacific and from New Spain to Alaska. In geographical terms it comprised the drainage basin of the Columbia River and of its great southern affluent, the Snake. Its square mileage of territory was approximately one and a half times as great as that of the original thirteen states after they had ceded their western claims to Congress. To American expansionists it had special attractions. If acquired, it would round out American boundaries and, not less important, would give the nation frontage on the Pacific. It was the only frontage on the Pacific to which the United States had any undisputed claim prior to the Mexican War.

The province first appeared on the national horizon in the presidency of George Washington. Its chief exportable asset was furs. The trade in the furs was part of a world-circling commerce that drew its ingredients not only from the Pacific Northwest but from the Hawaiian Islands and the Orient. The commerce was of especial interest to Massachusetts and New York.

When a Boston mariner prepared for a voyage in this commerce his first step was to gather a cargo of trade goods at India Wharf. The cargo would consist of an abundant supply of rum, blankets, guns, trinkets, and beads that would attract the Indians of the Northwest coast. It would include, also, quantities of ginseng, a wild root found in the forests of New England and the eastern seaboard. Ginseng was valued by the people of China, who manufactured from it a medicinal drink.

With a cargo of such goods a ship captain would sail for the Pacific by way of Cape Horn. In the Pacific he would head for the Hawaiian Islands, propelled by favorable trade winds. There he would take aboard food and fresh water; also sandalwood, a fragrant lumber, prized in China. For the sailors the great attraction in the Hawaiian Islands was the Hawaiian maidens, whose ideas of modesty and virtue were the same as those of the sailors.

After a generation of this trade the Hawaiian people were in need of missionaries. In 1819 missionary activity began, with headquarters in Boston. The missionaries and their descendants became political powers in the islands. S. B. Dole, the leader of the revolutionary movement which overthrew the native monarchy and made Hawaii a republic seeking annexation to the United States, was the son of a New England missionary.

From the Hawaiian Islands the traders would sail to the Northwest coast. They would ply up and down the coast, making exchanges with Indian traders found at the ports—blankets, guns, beads, and rum, for furs. The coastal fur principally sought was the sea otter, which brought high prices in China. It was caught in the coastal waters in an ingenious hunting operation. The Indians, in their kayaks, would find a sea otter asleep on the surface of the water and would quietly form a circle around him. Then, with a loud shout, they would dash on him. The otter would wake up and dive. The kayaks would then swiftly spread out and wait until the otter rose to the surface. Then they would noisily dash on him a second time and force him down. That operation would be repeated again and again, until the otter was so exhausted he could not quickly submerge. Then the Indians would get in range of him as silently as they could and shoot him with their arrows. The Indian whose arrow struck the otter nearest the ear was the one that got the fur. Other furs were bought also, especially beaver, which were the staple of the trade. They were trapped in the interior of the Oregon Country and brought down by way of the rivers to the coast.

With a full cargo the traders would sail for Canton. There the furs, sandalwood, and ginseng were exchanged for silks and teas and chinaware. The return to the Western world would be by way of European markets, or back to the Atlantic seaboard of the United States via Cape Horn. The trade was romantic and profitable and was the foundation of many a Boston and New York fortune.

It was also historically significant. For it was in the course of this trade that a New England mariner, Captain Robert Gray, in 1792, discovered the mouth of the Columbia River, giving to the United States its first claim to the Oregon Country. This claim was strengthened by the overland explorations of the Lewis and Clark expedition during the Jefferson administration. In 1811 John Jacob Astor, a merchant of New York, built Astoria for carrying on the trade. The post was located strategically near the mouth of the Columbia River, so as to command the trade of the whole basin and, likewise, the coastal commerce. A series of disasters dogged the enterprise, and during the War of 1812 Astor's associates, under threat of a naval seizure, sold the post to the British-Canadian North West Company. But the founding of Astoria was the basis of a strengthened United States claim.

Originally four powers had claims to the Oregon Country—Spain, Great Britain, Russia, and the United States. The Spanish and British were the earliest, dating from the 16th century, and the Russian, from the early 18th century. British claims were strengthened at the end of the 18th century by the coastal explorations of Captain George Vancouver, the overland explorations of Alexander Mackenzie and others; an agreement arrived at with Spain, and by erection of fur-trading posts on the coast and in the interior. Russian claims extended along the coast from the Bering Sea to California, strengthened by trading posts. In 1819–21 Spain eliminated herself by ceding to the United States all her rights north of the 42nd parallel. In 1824–25 Russia relinquished her rights south of 54° 40′ in separate treaties with the British and the

United States. Thereafter the two contenders were the United States and Great Britain.

These two endeavored three times in London and twice in Washington in the period 1818–45 to negotiate a partition of the Oregon Country, each time without success. In the early negotiations the American government repeatedly proposed the 49th parallel as the line of partition from the Rocky Mountains to the Pacific Ocean. The British government repeatedly offered the line of the 49th parallel from the Rockies to its intersection with the Columbia River, and then, the river to the sea. These offers greatly reduced the area genuinely in dispute, narrowing it to the triangular area between the Columbia River and the 49th parallel. That region was the real bone of contention throughout the later stages of the controversy.

It was of special importance to the government and people of the United States. It contained a succession of excellent harbors, from the Strait of Juan de Fuca down into Puget Sound. Those harbors were the only usable ones on the whole Pacific shore to which the United States, prior to the Mexican War, could lay claim. A harbor lay, to be sure, at the mouth of the Columbia River, but it was a bar harbor, dangerous to enter or to leave. Also, its river connection with the interior was so broken by waterfalls and rapids as to be unusable for a heavy commerce.

In Great Britain, on the other hand, the illusion was nursed that the Columbia was indispensable to the future of western British America, that it was the St. Lawrence of the West. If navigation on it was to be safeguarded, the northern bank of the river on which the triangle rested must remain British. The British fur-trading interests in the Oregon Country saw no need to dispel this illusion. The triangle constituted thus that bane of international relations—the crossing of commercial rivalries and ambitions.

Since the two governments could not agree upon a line of partition the best recourse seemed to be a convention of joint occupation. One was concluded on October 20, 1818, designed for a period of ten years. Under its terms the whole Oregon Country was declared open to the activity of the traders and settlers of both countries. At the outset the convention proved of benefit chiefly to the British. A powerful British fur-trading organization was already established in the region, the North West Company, which had purchased Astoria from the partners of Astor in the course of the War of 1812. In 1821 it and the still more powerful Hudson's Bay Company entered a merger at the request of the British government to end a trade war. The merged organization took the name and held the charter of the Hudson's Bay Company.

The new company was a colossal affair, one of the world's greatest corporations. It had possession, under its 1670 charter, of the major part of what is now Canada. It obtained, also, from the British government in 1821, as a reward for the merger, a monopoly of all rights of British trade in the Oregon Country,

The head of the company in Canada was George Simpson. He was a Scotchman of remarkable administrative talent and energy. In the summer of 1824 he made a canoe voyage from the company's headquarters at York Fort on Hudson Bay to the Oregon Country. This was followed by a crowded year of reorganization of the company's trade, which had become demoralized as a consequence of the trade war. He was determined, also, to drive the Americans out of that country. Expulsion by force was out of the question because of the Convention of Joint Occupation. But Simpson achieved the result by instituting a system of cutthroat competition. Whenever an American vessel appeared on the coast a Hudson's Bay Company vessel would draw alongside and offer the Indians twice as much for their furs as the American could afford. In the interior, when an American trading or trapping party appeared a party of the company would arrive and outbid it. The Hudson's Bay Company, with its giant resources, could take temporary losses to achieve a long-run gain. The American traders, chiefly small operators, had to give up the fight and withdraw.

Special tactics were followed in special areas. One area was the extensive wilderness between the Rockies, the Spanish line, and the Columbia. It was almost certain, in view of its location, to become American in any partition of the Oregon Country. Simpson's program therefore was to have it stripped bare of its furs as rapidly as possible. As a denuded area it would serve to insulate the area north of the Columbia from American trappers operating out of St. Louis.

As a further assurance for the future Simpson also erected a new British head-quarters on the north side of the Columbia, opposite the Willamette's confluence with it. The new base was named Fort Vancouver to associate that side of the river with the explorations of Vancouver. The site would permit company surveillance of any future settlement by Americans in the valley of the Willamette. The buildings of the old Astoria post, which had been acquired by purchase during the War of 1812, were, on the other hand, dismantled.

Simpson's principal interest was, however, to restore to a profitable basis the trade of the triangle, which had become demoralized during the trade war, by eliminating the extravagance, laxity, and disorganization that had become established and to replace this with economy, energy, and discipline. Of equal importance was to extend the trade of the company northward into the valley of the Fraser and the upper waters of the Columbia. This would require a large investment of capital and labor and would, in turn, call for assurance from the government that the Columbia River—the central transportation route to the interior—would stay open to the British for the indefinite future. Negotiations to that end had been held in 1818 and in 1823–24, but had failed. An early renewal of them was therefore imperative.

On Simpson's return to the East his next order of business was a voyage to London to report progress to the directorate of the company and to press his recom-mendations. The principal recommendation, adopted at once, was that the company propose to the Foreign Office a new negotiation with the American government to partition the Oregon Country. Simpson suggested a desirable partition line—the 49th parallel from the Continental Divide to the point where the Lewis and Clark expedi-tion had crossed the mountains, then a drop to the Snake, and thence the line of the Snake and the Columbia to the sea. This line was far less favorable to the United States than one that had been proposed to the American government in the negotiation of 1823–24, and which the American negotiator had rejected out of hand.

In accordance with Simpson's recommendation the London governor of the company addressed a letter, late in 1825, to George Canning at the Foreign Office. He reported what the company had done and what it proposed to do in the Oregon Country. He wrote of the company's contemplated expansion northward from the Columbia and behind the mouth of the Fraser. For this expansion the Columbia River would be necessary. The river was the highway by which the country behind the mouth of the Fraser was provisioned. The governor called attention to a recently published American map, on which a boundary line had been drawn from the Rocky Mountains to the water's edge along the 49th parallel. He thought the American government might make improper use of the map in the future. He proposed a line that would be fair to the United States and necessary to the company. The line was the one Simpson had suggested. The governor suggested, in conclusion, that Simpson was in town and would be happy to attend any appointment the Foreign Secretary would be pleased to make.

The British cabinet in this period was the same Tory body that had been in office during the two earlier negotiations. It had held power since the War of 1812. It was an inharmonious body, held together by the tact of its leader, Lord Liverpool. It consisted of a nucleus of ultra Tories, a group of moderate conservatives, of whom Liverpool was one, and an element of Canningites, chiefly Canning and William Huskisson. The high Tories disliked and distrusted Canning, whom they considered an adventurer, a man of talents, without character. So great was their aversion to him that later, when Liverpool was obliged to resign because of ill health and Canning was invited by the King to form a new cabinet, they refused to serve under him, and Canning was obliged to accept alliance with the Whigs. Canning was an intense nationalist and imperialist. He was described by the London *Times,* which was his devoted admirer, "as an eloquent expounder and advocate of that policy which fixed a lever on every foreign soil whereby to raise the British empire to honour and prosperity." The Oregon Country would raise the empire to honor and prosperity, Canning believed, and, in the Hudson's Bay Company, he discerned a lever with which to do it.

In compliance with the suggestion offered by the governor of the company Canning directed Henry U. Addington, Undersecretary for Foreign Affairs, to obtain from Simpson a memorandum on the potentialities of the Oregon Country. Addington drew up a questionnaire for Simpson to answer. Its inquiries, and the answers Simpson gave to them, are equally revealing. A first set related to the agricultural possibilities of the Columbia Valley. The answer given by Simpson was a glowing picture of the lower Columbia as the seat of a future agricultural settlement. The soil of the lowlands was described as alluvial and rich, and, where well located, as at Fort Vancouver, capable of producing large quantities of grain and pasturing numerous herds of cattle and hogs. The climate was described as delightfully temperate, with little or no frost or snow.

A second series of questions related to the fur potentialities of the Columbia Valley. The answer of Simpson was that the hunting grounds immediately on the northern bank of the river were nearly exhausted of furs, but that the backcountry was still productive, and that in all the small rivers and lakes beaver were found. He estimated that the gross value of the furs taken was between £30,000 and £40,000, divided about equally between the northern and the southern parts of the Columbia Valley. This was a total less than the gross of many a Lancashire textile establishment. Simpson prefaced this testimony by the observation that the trade of the Columbia as a whole was still in its infancy, which was, however, an opinion of doubtful accuracy.

A third series followed concerning the country's outlets to the sea. The Columbia and the Fraser were particularly inquired about, and a comparison of the two as outlets was requested. This series went to the heart of the Oregon problem. If the

Fraser was navigable it was a possible alternative to the Columbia as an outlet, and it lay wholly north of the 49th parallel. Simpson affirmed in answer that the Columbia was the only navigable river he knew between the interior and the coast. It was the only certain outlet for the trade west of the mountains, comprising thirteen of the company's trading establishments. As for the Fraser, it was impassable. Its banks, in stretches of its course, formed precipices where the towing line could not be used, and its current was so impetuous as to render navigation in certain seasons out of the question. Simpson concluded his testimony with the round statement that in his opinion "if the navigation of the Columbia is not free to the Hudson's Bay Company, and that the territory to the Northward of it is not secured to them, they must abandon and curtail their trade in some parts, and probably be constrained to relinquish it on the West side of the Rocky Mountains altogether."

Canning had an even more compelling reason for wishing to reopen the Oregon negotiation. He was disturbed by an agitation going on in Washington for a military occupation by the United States of the mouth of the Columbia. Initially this had been the work of a few zealots in Congress, but it had become of graver character. In December 1824 President Monroe had formally recommended to Congress that a military post be established at the mouth of the Columbia, "or at some other point in that quarter within our acknowledged limits." Within sixteen days a committee headed by John Floyd introduced a bill authorizing the establishment not merely of the post but of the territory of Oregon including all the country west of the Rocky Mountains and north of the 42nd parallel, with no restriction of northern boundary. The bill passed the House by an overwhelming majority and obtained a disquietingly large vote in the Senate. In December 1825 President Adams repeated Monroe's recommendation and added the suggestion that provision be made for a public vessel to explore the whole Northwest coast of the continent. The message led to no actual legislation, but produced an aggressive House committee report—the first of two by the so-called Baylies Committee.

These proceedings had been reported home regularly by British ministers in Washington. In March 1826, at the suggestion of Canning, they had been summarized by Addington, who had been an observer of some of them at close range while he was minister in Washington in 1824–25. Addington suggested to Canning publication of a series of parliamentary papers exhibiting the claims of England to the Oregon Country. This would be an antidote to the agitation in Congress and a warning to the American government against aggressive measures. It did not seem adequate to Canning, who issued instead an invitation to the American government to join the British government in a general negotiation to be held in London.

The suggestion was eagerly accepted by the American government. It seemed to open the way not only to a settlement of the Oregon question, but of other stubborn issues as well. Albert Gallatin was persuaded to accept appointment as the American plenipotentiary. His instructions were prepared under the eye of President Adams, who was more familiar with the problems of the negotiation than Henry Clay, the Secretary of State. The President was insistent that the line of the 49th parallel from the Rocky Mountains to the sea be the limit of American concession on the Oregon issue. Gallatin was displeased with these instructions. He had asked freedom to concede to the British the drainage basin of Juan de Fuca Strait, part of which he had informally offered in a negotiation in 1818. He believed no partition agreement could be reached unless the old American insistence on the 49th parallel be relaxed. But Adams was adamant. He believed that "one inch of ground [below the 49th parallel] yielded on the North-West coast . . . would be certain to meet the reprobation of the Senate."

Public opinion in the United States was in accord with Adams's in one respect—resistance to British encroachment on territory held, or claimed, by the United States. Resistance to it had been the impelling force of American policy on the northern border ever since American independence—first in the effort to clear the British out of the Northwest Posts, then in the determination to keep the British from access to the upper waters of the Mississippi, and again to recover Astoria. The fight for the line of the 49th parallel in the Oregon Country was merely the projection to the Pacific of an old, embittered clash.

American public opinion was not equally united on the issue of extending American sovereignty to the Pacific. The Pacific lay at a forbidding distance west of the Mississippi. The travel time of the Lewis and Clark expedition from St. Louis to the Pacific had been eighteen months. The sea voyage from the eastern seaboard by way of Cape Horn took six to eight months, depending on the weather. Between the western settlements in Missouri and the Pacific coast extended vast barrens, so it was believed. In the report of the Stephen Long expedition of 1819–20, the 500-mile stretch westward to the base of the Rockies between parallels 39° and 49° was described as unfit for habitation by a people dependent on agriculture. West of this waste as far as the Cascades was a desert of sand and alkali.

For the crossing of these barrens only primitive means of travel were available—the horse, the ox, the canoe. No one of right mind dreamed of railroads ascending the heights of the Rockies or the Cascades. Not until 1829 was the first crude locomotive put in service in the United States. The use of steam in ocean transport was a development of the future.

The society formed in the Oregon Country was expected to consist of migrants from the United States. Its government would, of course, be colonial. Yet to Americans a colonial government, maintained over a people of their own kin, seemed repugnant. It would be an entrance to imperialism. If attempted it would subvert the liberties of the Republic. The expectation and wish of thoughtful Americans was that the society formed west of the Rockies would follow the course taken by the American colonies in 1776, or by the Latin American colonies of Spain—it would become independent.

Such a destiny was predicted and desired by Thomas Jefferson, who gave wide currency to the prediction. Among his disciples, who expected that an independent Pacific republic would rise west of the mountains, were Gallatin, Monroe, Crawford, Clay, Benton, and probably Madison. The most vocal exponent of the concept in Congress and in the press was Benton. He declared in Congress on March 1, 1825:

> Westward, we can speak without reserve, and the ridge of the Rocky Mountains may be named without offence, as presenting a convenient, natural and everlasting boundary. Along the back of this ridge, the Western limit of the republic should be drawn, and the statue of the fabled god Terminus, should be raised upon its highest peak, never to be thrown down. In planting the seed of a new power on the coast of the Pacific ocean, it

should be well understood that when strong enough to take care of itself, the new Government should separate from the mother Empire as the child separates from the parent at the age of manhood.

Parallel to the question whether the territory west of the mountains could be held, or should be held, was another: Was it worth holding? Debate on this question was proceeding in the press and in Congress from the time of the restoration of Astoria to the conclusion of the Oregon Treaty in 1846. The opinions ran the gamut from the rhapsodies of Benton and Floyd, according to whom the country was a Garden of Eden, to the strident judgment, expressed in a New York journal, that the country was fit only for the seat of a penal colony. The debate is hardly worth reporting. It was a display, for the most part, of ignorance and factionalism.

Debate was also going on in Congress and in the press over individual stakes of Oregon diplomacy, especially over the most important of all the stakes, the Columbia River. In this debate Benton, Floyd, and their followers gave free rein to imagination. They pictured the Columbia as forming, together with the Missouri, a channel of communication between the Orient and the Mississippi River, and as connecting the Pacific coast with St. Louis. Furs from the Oregon Country would flow to China. In return, teas, silks, nankeens, and spices would move to St. Louis, which would become the Venice of the New World. A modern Tyre would rise at the mouth of the Columbia.

Realists sought to bring these flights of fancy to earth by adverting to such geographic facts as the bar outside the mouth of the Columbia, the waterfalls obstructing navigation higher up the river, and the mountains separating the heads of navigation of the Columbia and the Missouri. They also referred to marauding Indians that would be encountered. A deep-water harbor that could become a naval station for the United States in the Pacific was also mentioned among the stakes of Oregon diplomacy. Such a harbor existed at Port Discovery, at the entrance to Puget Sound, which William Sturgis, a prominent Boston fur trader, reported in the Boston press in 1822. President Monroe likewise had in mind a naval station in Juan de Fuca Strait.

The chief consideration in the mind of Adams in instructing Gallatin to permit no deviation from the line of 49° was containment of the British. The line of 49° was the demarcation east of the mountains; it should not be departed from west of the mountains. Adams believed that the North American continent—indeed, even the South American continent—should be closed to future European colonization. The noncolonization doctrine had been introduced by him into Monroe's famous message of December 2, 1823, to Congress. It had been earlier set forth by him in an instruction to Richard Rush on the Oregon issue on July 12, 1823.

The enunciation of such a concept had seemed premature at the time. It seemed so to Albert Gallatin as late as 1846. To Calhoun it seemed impolitic, unclear in formulation, "broader than the fact"—which was a manner of saying that it was extreme—and that it exhibited precipitancy and want of due reflection. It had appeared in Monroe's 1823 message without cabinet deliberation.

Canning had been enraged by it. In 1826 his anger was further roused by the growing agitation in Congress for the military occupation of the mouth of the Columbia. The non-colonization doctrine and the congressional agitation seemed to him parts of a policy of American aggression.

As soon as the British cabinet began discussion of the Oregon issue a division appeared in its ranks, caused by a suggestion of Liverpool that the old American proposal of the 49th parallel be given consideration. How the members divided and how close the division was, cannot be ascertained. All that is known is that Liverpool, who usually stood with Canning, was ranged on one side, and that Canning was on the other. The division was evidently close, for it remained long unresolved and eventually had to be compromised. In the meantime Canning carried on a persistent propaganda within the cabinet to turn Liverpool and his abettors away from any thought of concessions to the United States.

Canning's initial step was to direct Addington to prepare a memorandum evaluating the claims of Britain and the United States in the Oregon Country. The memorandum, presented on May 10, 1826, was less an evaluation than a partisan defense of British claims. Addington was a protégé of Canning and was vindicating the position his chief had taken in earlier negotiations, and wished to take again. The memorandum was distributed to the cabinet by Canning with a covering letter in which he outdid Addington. He declared, in closing, that he did not know how to contemplate surrendering England's claims.

Liverpool was unconvinced. He wished further information concerning the value of the Hudson's Bay Company's transmountain trade. He also wanted to know whether the partition line at the 49th parallel, proposed by the Americans in the negotiation of 1823–24, would leave the British an outlet to the sea by way of Nootka or other ports, and whether such an outlet would be any less advantageous than that of the Columbia River.

Canning was aware that the meagerness of trade in the disputed Oregon area, revealed in Simpson's replies to Addington, would come before the cabinet. He did what he could, before complying with Liverpool's request, to lessen the impact of the Simpson statistics. He wrote to Liverpool: "But it is not from what our trade is now, that the question is to be estimated. It is when China shall be open to English as well as American commerce that the real value of settlements on the northwest coast of America will become apparent."

On July 7, 1826, a fortnight after this exchange, Canning submitted to Liverpool and to the cabinet the information desired. It consisted of the letter of the governor of the Hudson's Bay Company of the preceding December; also of the replies of Simpson to Addington's questionnaire. In a long covering letter Canning anxiously desired Liverpool to bear in mind:

> That the trade between the Eastern and Western Hemispheres, direct across the Pacific, is the trade of the world most susceptible of rapid augmentation and improvement . . . We cannot yet enter into this trade, on account of the monopoly of the E.I.Cy. [East Indian Company] But ten years hence that monopoly will cease; and though at that period neither you nor I shall be where we are to answer for our deeds, I should not like to leave my name affixed to an instrument by which England would have foregone the advantages of an immense direct intercourse between China and what may be, if we resolve not to yield them up, her boundless establishments on the N.W. Coast of America.

The second report of the Baylies Committee of the House of Representatives reached Canning in the week following this correspondence. It contained a slashing attack on the British claims to the Oregon Country. It charged Britain with inordinate imperialist ambitions, and uttered a half defiance of her. It infuriated Canning. He refused to be persuaded that committee reports of Congress do not emanate from the Executive. He made the document the occasion for pressing to adoption an order in council closing the British West Indies to American vessels. A more immediate use was to send it to Liverpool with a note that after such a report "it is impossible to suppose that we can tide over the Columbia, or make to ourselves the illusion that there is any other alternative than either to maintain our claims or to yield them with our eyes wide open." Liverpool was momentarily silenced, and Canning was able, in drawing up the instructions for the negotiation with Gallatin, to state that the government had not changed its position on the Oregon issue since 1824, when it had stood immovable at the Columbia River.

The plenipotentiaries chosen to deal with Gallatin were Huskisson and Addington. Huskisson was selected for his expertness in the commercial phases of the negotiation, Addington for his knowledge of the boundary problem. He was the voice of Canning. On all topics, as Gallatin later observed, he was "extremely difficult."

The conference opened on November 15, 1826. The Oregon issue was placed promptly at the head of its agenda. The British plenipotentiaries called for a report on a proposal their government had made in 1824 that the boundary be drawn at the 49th parallel from the Rockies to the Columbia and thence follow the Columbia to the sea. Gallatin reported that his government had declined this proposal. He presented a counterproposal—the old American offer of the 49th parallel to the sea, with the concession that the nagivation of the Columbia from the point of intersection to the sea be perpetually free to British subjects. This the cabinet rejected. The British inquired whether Gallatin was authorized to deviate from the 49th parallel as a boundary. Gallatin replied that he must adhere to it as a basis, but that a deviation from it at the south would be entertained, provided it was compensated by an equivalent variation north of the parallel. This led to a proposal to concede a quadrilateral of territory adjoining Juan de Fuca Strait—roughly the Olympic Peninsula—which would have given the United States a portion of the deep-water harbors inside the Strait, especially Port Discovery, earlier described by Vancouver as especially good. The offer doubtless was a cabinet compromise of Liverpool's and Canning's views—an attempt to meet the American requirement of a deep-water harbor inside the Strait without loosening the British hold on the lower Columbia.

As a bid for agreement the offer was woefully inadequate. It was the proposal of an enclave for an American naval station—an isolated tract of land hemmed in on every side by British territory, or by water dominated by the British Navy. Gallatin at once rejected it, declaring that even to take it for reference to his government would be inconsistent with his instructions.

As a rejected offer it now became a recording problem. The British wished to exclude all reference to it from the minutes of the conference. They wished it to be regarded as having been informally made. Gallatin would have agreed to this, but was further asked to accept a positive statement in the protocol that no new offer had been made. He resisted this as contrary to the truth. The British finally relented and agreed that the offer should be recorded as made, though with a reservation that it was not to be regarded as prejudicing their position in the future.

The offer did exactly that. Its very presence on the protocol, notwithstanding the reservation, formed a precedent of concession north of the Columbia. Canning had warned Liverpool that the cabinet must maintain its position immovably at the Columbia, that retreat would be but the first symptom of weakness. In agreeing to the enclave offer Canning had, however, himself betrayed a symptom of weakness, and this was destined to prepare the way for a later American advance to the line of the 49th parallel.

After Gallatin's refusal even to refer the enclave proposal to his government, the conference recognized that it could reach no agreement to partition the Oregon Country. It turned, instead, to the more modest undertaking of renewing the Convention of Joint Occupation of 1818, which was due to expire in two more years.

A complication appeared at once in the form of a British proposal to insert an interpretive stipulation into the convention. The stipulation was that neither party, during the life of the convention, would "assume or exercise any right of exclusive sovereignty or dominion over any part of said country, nor form therein any establishment in support or furtherance of any such claim." The meaning of the stipulation was spelled out to Gallatin. It would forbid the erection of any military post in the Oregon Country. Gallatin's initial understanding was that the prohibition would apply only to a post at the mouth of the Columbia. But later it became clear that it would apply to a military post anywhere in the disputed country. Also forbidden would be the establishment over the Oregon Country of any distinct territorial government by either power.

This stipulation was Canning's idea. Probably he had it in mind in proposing an Oregon negotiation to the American government. It is unlikely that he expected a boundary agreement, opposed as he was to offering the concessions an agreement would have required. He could, however, have hoped to obtain the stipulation as part of the renewal of the convention. It would satisfy immediate purposes, giving the Hudson's Bay Company time to firm up its grip on the region north of the Columbia. It would be the British answer to congressional agitation for a military post at the mouth of the Columbia and an American territorial government over the whole Oregon Country.

A plausible argument was offered for the plan by the British plenipotentiaries. They held that the stipulation merely clarified the intent of the convention to suspend the right of exercising sovereignty in the Oregon Country. No nation had sovereignty there, they maintained. They connected with the stipulation the question of the term for which the convention should be renewed. The term favored by Canning was fifteen or twenty or even twenty-five years instead of ten, if agreement on the stipulation could be reached. The lengthened term would fit well into the plans of the Hudson's Bay Company.

Gallatin met the proposal as required by his instructions, referring it to his government. He had been directed to refer any British proposal involving a substantial change in the convention. He was authorized only to agree to a simple renewal for ten years. He sent the proposal home in December 1826. The reply from his government came the following March. It was a rejection of the proposal in unequivocal terms. The delivery of the reply was delayed to the end of May owing to a cabinet crisis in England, caused by Liverpool's illness and retirement.

Canning still hoped the stipulation might be vendible if offered in a new dress. On June 19 Gallatin was told that a simple renewal for ten years would be acceptable if a declaration were permitted to appear in the protocol that both parties were restricted "from exercising, or assuming to themselves the right to exercise, any exclusive sovereignty or jurisdiction" over the territory mentioned in that article. Gallatin rejected the proposal, pointing out that to admit it into the protocol would be tantamount to inserting into the convention a stipulation which the American government had already given notice it could not accept.

At this stage Gallatin was in a position to expound the American view of the meaning of the convention. As one of its authors he had the knowledge for an authoritative exposition of it, but had remained silent while awaiting the President's verdict on the projected stipulation. The convention, Gallatin now held, was what it appeared on its face to be—a commerce agreement, and nothing more. Its intent was to keep the Oregon Country open to trade and settlement by nationals of both parties. The issue of sovereignty was left where it had been. Neither party was precluded from exercising sovereignty so long as no interference occurred with the freedom of commerce and settlement of the other. Gallatin was stating facts of history. He had been asked during the 1818 negotiation to agree to a declaration in the convention that neither party would exercise sovereign authority in the Oregon Country and had refused. The convention had been kept silent on the sovereignty issue deliberately.

As for the erection of a military post, Gallatin held it was not forbidden to either party. A military post would be no infraction unless it interfered with the freedom of trade and settlement of the other party. The erection of a military post by the United States might become necessary for protecting American traders and settlers against Indians and lawless whites, or for the defense of the Indians themselves against aggression. Such post as Congress and the President merely contemplated, the British already had in the stockaded forts and the powerful organization of the Hudson's Bay Company.

A territorial government established by either party would, like a military post, be no infraction in itself of the convention. It would be an infraction only if it obstructed the freedom of trade and settlement which the convention assured. The United States might deem it necessary to form a territorial government in the Oregon Country as a means of maintaining order in a remote wilderness inhabited by savages and licentious traders. It would in that case be doing only what the British government had already done.

The British government had admitted the Hudson's Bay Company into the Oregon Country and had given that company a monopoly there of British rights of trade. A powerful incorporated company, operating to the exclusion of private British traders, was in itself a territorial government. Through such agency Britain had long governed extensive and populous regions in the Orient. Experience in North America had shown that where private British traders competed with each other for the peltry of savages, disorders and bloodshed resulted. When, however, there was an exclusive company, its agents governed. All were kept in order and restrained from committing outrages on each other and on the Indians.

Nothing was wanting, then, to a complete system of government but courts of law for the trial of criminal and civil cases. Such courts the British Parliament in 1821 had established. A criminal and civil jurisdiction had been initiated for certain parts of British North America and for the Oregon Country in the same act which authorized the monopoly given the Hudson's Bay Company. Courts presided over by justices of the peace had been created. Capital and other high offenses, and civil suits above a certain amount, had been placed under the jurisdiction of courts in Upper Canada. No provision had been made exempting citizens of the United States in the Oregon Country from this jurisdiction. The United States might have reason to complain of the act as an infraction of the right of sovereignty in the Oregon Country which was claimed by the United States. If no such complaint had been made, it was probably because the act had not been literally enforced.

Gallatin pointed out that the American government could not create an incorporated monopoly in the Oregon Country. Incorporated monopolies were incompatible with the genius of American democratic institutions. The American mode of control in a wilderness area was the territorial form of government. The United States might consider it necessary to establish such a form of government in the Oregon Country as a means of preserving peace and order, but it had never actually exercised sovereignty or jurisdiction there. By this exposition Gallatin justified his government's rejection of the British proposal of a stipulation, and his own rejection of the British project of a declaration in the protocol.

It was clear by now that the campaign of the British to write their own interpretation into the convention would not succeed. In the course of the debate one position after another had been taken by them only to be abandoned. An end to it had now clearly come. Renewal of the convention, unchanged, or no convention, had become the choice. The British protested to Gallatin that a convention of joint occupation, renewed without definition and known to mean opposite things to the signatories, would be hardly better than no convention at all. Inwardly they felt it would be somewhat better and would place a moral restraint on American aggression. The undefined convention had served British purposes well enough in the past. It had been a factor in preserving peace and had permitted British fur companies to maintain their domination of that country. It would be likely to have greater utility in the future. A reorganized and reinvigorated Hudson's Bay Company was at the beginning of a new program of expansion.

On July 21 the British plenipotentiaries made their final move. They informed Gallatin that they would accept a simple renewal of the convention, though, in view of the rejection of the stipulation, only on a short-term basis. This Gallatin readily approved and he also suggested the form—renewal for an indefinite period, subject to the condition that it could be terminated on a twelve-month notice by either party. This was acceptable to the British. On August 6, 1827, the convention, so framed, was engrossed and signed. Its renewal had been a labor of eight months.

Between the first negotiation in London in 1818 and the first in Washington in 1842, a quarter of a century passed. This was an era of revolutionary changes in the world's modes of transportation. In 1829 the first locomotive was set going on American tracks. By 1840 locomotives operated on 2800 miles of rail tracks in the United States. Imagination outraced construction. It carried railroads of the future to the shores of the Pacific. In the 1840's Congress was being besieged by the American public to give aid to the construction of a railroad from the Great Lakes to the Pacific. Concepts of national growth expanded with the new modes of travel and communication. The Jeffersonian concept, that prohibitions of distance and mountains precluded an extension of the government of the Union to the trans-Rocky Mountain area, was discarded. Instead the concept of Manifest Destiny—that the American Republic would yet acquire continental proportions—became an article of faith among American expansionists.

Dreams of connection by rail altered the character and location of specific stakes of Oregon diplomacy. They gave new value to the harbors inside the Straits. Prior to the railroad age the Straits harbors seemed hopelessly circumscribed by lack of natural connection with the interior, such as was enjoyed by the harbor at the mouth of the Columbia. The Straits were cut off from the interior by range after range of mountains. Their only river connection, the Fraser, was utterly unnavigable. Now the harbors were viewed as connected with the interior by the railroads of the future. What nature had denied, man would provide. The intrinsic excellence of those harbors—their deep waters, their capaciousness, their inland position, safety from the winds and sands of the ocean, and convenient lanes to the sea—received more notice than ever before. Those harbors became the major commercial prizes of the Oregon Country.

The Columbia River harbor declined by comparison. It did so in the estimation of the American and British governments alike. Its perilous entrance and its broken interior course were given increasing notice in public discussion in both countries. The report of the Charles Wilkes Exploring Expedition, which described the loss of one of its vessels on the bar, and lauded the beauties of the harbors at the Straits, enforced the contrast. It became clear that the Straits harbors were the only safe ones on the entire Pacific shore to which the United States had any claim.

But the area in which those harbors lay—the whole region from the Straits southward to the north bank of the lower Columbia—was a British sphere. It reflected the triumph of the cutthroat tactics of a giant monopoly, and the defeat and withdrawal of a divided American competition. It was British in trade, farming, and grazing. The inhabitants were British—servants of the Hudson's Bay Company and of the Puget Sound Agricultural Company. British claims to it had been maintained for a quarter-century. They must be surrendered if the United States were to reach the safe harbors on the Pacific it was demanding.

A new negotiation on the Oregon issue—the first in the Washington series—was held in 1842. It was held by newly established governments in both countries. In England the Peel government came into office in 1841, with Aberdeen as its Secretary for Foreign Affairs. In the United States the Tyler government became established in the same year as successor to that of Harrison, with Daniel Webster as Secretary of State. The two governments were eager to clear away an accumulation of issues that had dogged their relations for years. The most stubborn were the northeastern boundary dispute, the Oregon dispute, and the old controversy over the British practice of search at sea in peacetime—a controversy revived as a result of Britain's efforts to suppress the African slave trade.

A special mission to deal with these problems and others subsidiary to them was proposed by the British government at the end of 1841. Washington was selected as its seat, and Lord Ashburton, formerly head of an internationally known banking house and popular in the United States, was named as its head. This plan was gladly approved and the work of preparing instructions for the negotiation got under way in London.

The ministry was handicapped by lack of time. It wished the negotiation to begin promptly to avoid the effect of a quarrel between Tyler and his party. Aberdeen and Ashburton had little knowledge of the Oregon problem. Their special competence was that of the northeastern boundary. The Oregon portion of the Ashburton instruction was left, therefore, to be drawn by the career staff of the Foreign Office, which was leaderless at the time, having recently lost its veteran head. Aberdeen was obliged to fill the post with an emergency appointment. The person chosen was Henry U. Addington, minister to the United States in 1824–25 and Undersecretary for Foreign Affairs with Canning.

In drawing up the Oregon instruction Addington relied heavily on his earlier experience. As a first offer to the Americans he chose the Columbia River line suggested by Simpson in 1825. Canning had earlier offered a more favorable line which the Americans had promptly rejected. Yet this was the line Addington directed Ashburton to begin with. The second offer Addington authorized was the 49th parallel to the Columbia and the river to the sea, which had thrice been refused by the United States in previous negotiations. It was nevertheless made Ashburton's final recourse. More remarkable still, Ashburton was given no authority to repeat the enclave offer of 1826, to which reference was made nowhere in the instruction. Neither Aberdeen nor Ashburton knew that it had once been offered the United States.

The negotiation with Webster under these circumstances ran onto shoals promptly. At the outset Ashburton informed Webster of the limits of his instructions. Mystified, Webster took refuge in a misty proposal. He intimated a plan under which Mexico might be induced to cede territory to the United States sufficient to include the port of San Francisco. The United States would accept an Oregon partition line at the Columbia. The plan, as later amplified by Webster, is now known among historians as the ''tri-partite'' plan. It derailed the Oregon portion of the negotiation, which was not thereafter resumed. Ashburton could doubtless have obtained a liberalization of his instructions had he realized in time their restrictive character and the vagueness and difficulty of Webster's response to them. But he realized this only when his mission had virtually come to an end. He had found the Northeast phases of the negotiation strenuous. He was tortured by the heat and humidity of the Washington summer and was eager to return home. He did not recognize the signs of a coming Anglo-American storm gathering in the Oregon Country.

One of the signs was an increased flow of American settlers to the Oregon Country. The earliest of them were broken-down trappers, who settled with their half-breed families in the valley of the Willamette. They formed the nucleus of a growing pioneer force. None of them had any love for the Hudson's Bay Company. After the Panic of 1837 they were reinforced by footloose spirits from Missouri and other parts of the Middle West, who moved to Oregon to retrieve lost fortunes. In the early 1840's organized caravans began to arrive in the Willamette. By 1843 American settlers in that lovely valley numbered several thousand. In Congress agitation for the ''reoccupation'' of the Oregon Country was muted while the Webster-Ashburton negotiation was proceeding, in order that noises coming from the Far West should not disturb the progress of peacemaking on the Northeast issue. But in the Senate, Lewis F. Linn was not silenced. He continued to press a measure designed to encourage migration to Oregon by such means as the promise of generous donations of land, providing military protection to migrants on the way, or in the area, and by establishing in the Oregon Country an extension of the civil and criminal jurisdiction of the courts of Iowa Territory.

Ashburton's failure to make a clean sweep of Anglo-American controversies was a disappointment to Aberdeen and Peel. They did not fully realize their own contribution to the failure. In 1843 Aberdeen moved toward a new negotiation in Washington, in response to the urging of Edward Everett and the news of the passage in the Senate of Linn's bill. He appointed a new minister to Washington—Richard Pakenham—who had won his spurs as minister to Mexico, and had been called to London to receive his instructions.

In drawing the instructions Everett was consulted. From Everett, Aberdeen learned with astonishment of the enclave offer made by Canning to Gallatin in 1826. He had to have it verified by a reference to the published record of the 1826 negotiation, which Everett sent him. In chagrin he consulted Addington, who insisted he had no recollection of such an offer ever having been made. When this was reported to Everett the latter was "staggered," as he wrote home. Addington was the plenipotentiary who had submitted the enclave offer to Gallatin.

Aberdeen took a direct hand thereafter in drawing Pakenham's instructions. He repeated every concession made in previous negotiations to the United States, including the enclave offer. He proposed to convert any harbors on the coast between the 49th parallel and the Columbia River into free ports. He had no authority to go further in formal instructions, and he believed the cabinet would oppose anything more. He directed Pakenham to propose arbitration, if the negotiation should not prosper.

Candidly Aberdeen told Pakenham on the latter's departure for Washington that he was not very sanguine of an agreement on the basis of these instructions. Should such apprehensions prove well founded, Pakenham was told to draw from the American negotiator a proposal that the 49th parallel to the water's edge be the boundary, with the proviso that all Oregon harbors south of it, including the one at the Columbia's mouth, be free ports to Great Britain. The American negotiator might be given reason to hope that such a proposal would be viewed by the British cabinet with favor. But Pakenham was warned that the cabinet would need to be won over.

In Washington the chief interest of the Tyler government at the time of Pakenham's arrival was the annexation of Texas. This and the Oregon issue were being joined by Democratic politicians in preparation for the oncoming presidential election of 1844. The Whigs, on the other hand, considered the immediate annexation of Texas and the claim to "All Oregon" to be not only extravagant but a menace to peace.

In this climate of opinion Calhoun, who became Secretary of State in 1844, moved gingerly in the Oregon negotiation. He had served in the Senate as a brake on aggressive American proposals. He now made clear that any British proposal short of the 49th parallel would run into trouble in the Senate. Also, he declined, on the same ground, Pakenham's pleas for an arbitration. He could not be drawn into suggesting American terms of a settlement, which Pakenham had been directed to extract. The negotiation hardly more than drifted as the Tyler administration moved to its close.

A decided change came with the election of Polk to the presidency. He was committed, or at least he seemed to be, to an "All Oregon" program. He had pledged himself to it in a public letter prior to the Democratic nominating convention of May

1844. Even more, he seemed committed by the party's platform, which declared that no portion of the Oregon Country was to be "ceded" to England or to any other power. On entering the White House he declared in his Inaugural Address that American title to the country of the Oregon was "clear and unquestionable." He won applause, thus, from American expansionists.

Yet several months after the Inaugural he proposed to Pakenham that the Oregon Country be divided by the old American proposal—the line of the 49th parallel. He withheld one offer his predecessors had made—British rights to navigate the Columbia south of 49°. The overture seemed to Pakenham so far short of his government's requirements that he immediately rejected it. He did not even take it for reference to his government. Polk, in reply, ordered the tender withdrawn and refused to resubmit it when Pakenham requested resubmission on orders from Aberdeen. The negotiation came to an end.

Polk carried the problem now to Congress. In his first annual message he reported what had happened. He explained his compromise offer as having been made out of deference to his predecessors. He assured Congress he would not make it again. He would make no offer to the British. He recommended that Congress adopt a resolution serving "notice" on the British of termination of the Convention of Joint Occupation. He declared that when the convention had expired, after notice, "we shall have reached a period when the national rights in Oregon must either be abandoned or firmly maintained. That they can not be abandoned without a sacrifice of both national honor and interest is too clear to admit of doubt."

The tone of the message was belligerent. It cheered such Democrats as believed that the British had no rights in Oregon, were mere intruders there, and were, by their presence, violating the principles announced by Monroe in 1823 against new colonization of America by European states. In Congress the "notice" debate, in which such views were persistently aired by Democrats, ran to nearly the end of April 1846.

Polk encouraged such views as far as he could. He calculated that a show of belligerence, combined with the notice which would follow, would bring the British to terms. He believed in tactics of pressure in diplomacy. Yet, in correspondence with Louis McLane, his minister in London, he remained moderate in his objectives. He wished merely that the British government repeat the offer he had submitted and which had been rudely declined—the old proposal of the line of 49°. But he let McLane know that if the British were to submit such a proposal, while retaining a right to the free navigation of the Columbia south of 49°, it would not be entertained. He thought free navigation had been improvidently proposed by his predecessors in the hope of a settlement. In general he differed from his predecessors less in the matter of his goals than in the manner of reaching them.

The implementation of his ideas was attended by difficulties. One was that Congress remained uncertain whether all this belligerence was really meant, or was just a pose. Congress could not be enlightened since even a confidential word would leak out, the British would get wind of it, and the act would be spoiled. Yet Whigs in Congress, wishing a peaceful settlement, were reluctant to vote on the notice without knowing whether it meant peace or war.

Congress was Democratic in both houses. But its Democrats were divided on the Oregon issue. A small, but vocal minority, chiefly from the Middle West, was attracted by the lure of "All Oregon." But the great majority wished a peaceful settlement and thought one based on partition at the 49th parallel was attainable. This feeling was especially strong among cotton Democrats in the South. They were not interested in vast territorial additions to the North, and they wished British markets to remain open for their surplus. An Alabama congressman, Edmund S. Dargan, voiced this feeling in the House in a speech and in a resolution that attracted national attention. He declared the Anglo-American differences to be still open to honorable negotiation and compromise. He proposed: "That the line [49°] separating the British provinces of Canada from the United States should be extended due west to the coast . . . and from thence, through the centre of the Straits of Fuca to the Pacific ocean." He would have attached this idea to the resolution of notice. In form and rationalizations, the Dargan proposal was reminiscent of a Gallatin offer to the British of 1818. In the Senate similar sentiment was expressed by Calhoun.

Whigs were a minority, but a strong one, in both houses. They were nearly unanimous in wishing a settlement of the Oregon dispute on the basis of a partition at the line of 49°. They opposed arming Polk with a pressure device against the British in view of the belligerence of his tone. They and southern Democrats of like feeling were the real center of authority in the American government on the Oregon issue.

As the debate dragged on into the spring of 1846 these elements came to regard the notice resolution in a new light. They came to believe that it might, if couched in conciliatory terms, seem to the British government an opportunity to reopen negotiations on the closed issue. They had learned from reading British newspapers, from observing the parliamentary debates, and from the conciliatory views on the Oregon issue of opposition leaders, that it might actually be welcomed in London. They were hopeful that a notice would be followed by a British proposal of real concession to the United States. Consequently the form of notice became an important issue in the Senate discussion. Under the leadership of a southern Whig, Senator John J. Crittenden, a form that was conciliatory was adopted, despite the agonized opposition of William Allen of Ohio, the chairman of the Foreign Relations Committee, who was the leader of the "All Oregon" element. A conference committee of the two houses, from which Allen was pointedly excluded, also agreed to a form that was conciliatory. This was overwhelmingly adopted by both houses and was sent by Polk to London.

In London the cabinet readily accepted the notice as an invitation to submit a new British offer. It framed an offer under the leadership of Aberdeen, with discreet outside guidance from McLane, that was highly conciliatory. The offer was to partition the Oregon Country by a line that would follow the 49th parallel from the Rocky Mountains to the water's edge, then go out to sea via the Strait of Juan de Fuca, leaving Vancouver Island to the British. With regard to the Columbia River, navigation rights on it south of the 49th parallel would be reserved to the Hudson's Bay Company, though not generally to British subjects. Protection would also be given to the posts and lands the company actually possessed south of the line.

This offer reached Polk on June 6. It did not meet all his requirements, but it satisfied the essential ones. By then the Mexican War was under way. Polk thought the offer worthy of being submitted to the Senate for previous advice. He hesitated to do this on his own responsibility, however, for it meant betraying his 54° 40′ followers. He believed he should have unanimous cabinet approval even for referring it to the Senate. His Secretary of State, James Buchanan, who had suddenly exhibited

54° 40′ symptoms, was bludgeoned into changing his mind, and the offer went to the Senate. It was approved there at once, without change. It was formalized into a treaty by Buchanan and Pakenham and was ratified by the Senate on June 18 with more than the needed two-thirds majority. The treaty was basically the proposal Gallatin had made in London twenty-eight years before.

It was a product of forces released partly in the Oregon Country and partly in the politics and diplomacy of the United States and Great Britain. The nature and the effectiveness of those forces have led to a wide diversity of opinions among historians. For a long time the American pioneers in Oregon were credited with having determined the outcome. They were said to have stamped their impress on the outcome by the simple act of taking possession of the area in dispute. Possession, according to this view, was nine-tenths of the law. However, this explanation ignored the location of the pioneers, which was the valley of the Willamette, lying on the south side of the Columbia. The settlers on the north side, the area which was the core of the dispute, were British subjects numbering a thousand—servants of the Hudson's Bay Company and of its subsidiary, the Puget Sound Agricultural Company, and their families. Only a handful of Americans were on the north side. If possession had been nine-tenths of the law this crucial area would have become British in the treaty.

One contribution, however, the American pioneers did make. Among them were a considerable number of lawless characters, who hated the Hudson's Bay Company and aroused fear in George Simpson for the safety of the trade goods stored at Fort Vancouver. This had led him to order a shift of base of the company from Fort Vancouver to Fort Victoria, at the tip of Vancouver Island. The transfer was reported to Lord Aberdeen and was exploited by him as showing that the lower Columbia was no longer as vital to the Hudson's Bay Company's trade as it once had been, and that a partition line along the 49th parallel to the water's edge could be agreed to without disaster to British imperial interests.

Another force credited with having contributed to the peaceful settlement was British sea power, which was overwhelming in its superiority to other navies of the world, and was markedly so during the Oregon crisis. Because of it Polk is said to have backed down in the belligerence of his instructions to the American minister in London early in 1846. But this thesis is unsupported in the instructions then sent to the American minister, which remained as they had been.

An opposite thesis has been offered to prove that the British government was alarmed by French naval construction in this period and agreed to concessions on the Oregon issue to ward off the danger of a collision with the combined navies of France and the United States. But a revealing letter from Peel to Lord Ellenborough, First Lord of the Admiralty, dated March 17, 1846, is a sufficient answer to this thesis. Peel wrote that all prospect of hostilities with France had passed and that further naval appropriations were unneeded.

Still another thesis brought into the Oregon equation is the British food crisis of 1845–46. In the autumn of 1845 the harvest of potatoes in Ireland was tragically reduced by the rot, and the wheat harvest in England was deficient. A famine scare developed that was exploited by the portion of the British press demanding repeal of the Corn Laws, the protective duties on imports of grain. The scare is alleged to have produced in England a sense of dependence on the United States for food, and a consequent readiness in the government to come to terms on the Oregon issue. This hypothesis has long since collapsed.

But a realignment of British political parties in the winter of 1845—46 did contribute vitally to the solution of the Oregon problem. A cabinet crisis developed over the famine alarm, followed by the resignation of Peel. Lord John Russell, the Whig leader, who was in favor of lower duties on grain, was invited to form a Whig cabinet. He failed, as a result of dissension within the Whig party over the nomination of Lord Palmerston to the Foreign Office. Peel was recalled. He reorganized his cabinet, retaining Aberdeen as Foreign Minister, and, with the support of Russell, proceeded to the abolition of the Corn Laws. Peelites and Whigs, neither strong enough to effect repeal alone, were thus brought, in the winter of 1845–46, into a temporary alliance against the embittered protectionists of the Conservative party. The compact, formed for domestic affairs, extended to foreign affairs. It rendered possible framing a British treaty of renunciation. It assured Peel and Aberdeen of Whig support—at least until the Corn Laws had been repealed—if such a treaty were offered to the American government.

During the cabinet crisis British Whigs had themselves been won to a policy of Oregon concession. Their failure to form a government had resulted from Lord Palmerston's belligerent tone while his party was out of office. His belligerence had produced the impression that the Whigs were controlled by a war faction. It was necessary for the party leaders to erase that impression if they were to be successful in taking over the government on Peel's impending fall. Russell, therefore, in two speeches advocated a settlement of the Oregon problem by concession. In these speeches he made the free-trade issue a bridge, over which to transport himself and the Whig party from earlier belligerence on the Oregon issue to the new policy of peace. In response to an appeal from Edward Everett, the former American minister at the Court of St. James's, Russell assured Aberdeen privately that he would make no objection to the surrender by the ministry of the lower valley of the Columbia. He bound his Whig associates by such a pledge, for they could not, without a party rift, publicly attack what he had privately approved.

These developments rendered an Oregon treaty, based on extensive concession, politically safe. Aberdeen was able to offer such a treaty as he had been ready to negotiate already at the end of 1843. Delay was occasioned by the difficulty of reopening a negotiation, which Polk had chosen to slam shut in December 1845. Aberdeen was willing to regard as a peaceful reopening the notice from the American government announcing its decision to terminate the Convention of Joint Occupation at the end of a year. The result was a draft of a treaty which, on arrival in Washington, was accepted by the Senate without any alteration. Sir Robert Peel, in his valedictory to Parliament at the end of June 1846, was able to announce triumphantly that the menacing Oregon controversy had been brought to a close.

In this triumph the basic force was the will to preserve peace, which was effectively marshaled in both countries in the critical final months of the controversy. In England the leader in the work was Aberdeen, who had quietly slipped into Conservative and Whig journals propaganda for a treaty of concession. Highly effective, also, was the open agitation of the Anti-Corn Law League, which carried on a crusade for peace as part of its crusade for free trade in food.

In the United States the peace forces were more widely distributed. They were the cotton growers of the South, who relied on British consumers of their surplus for prosperity, the business and transportation elements in the nation who needed British capital to help rejuvenate an economy not yet recovered from the paralysis of the early 1840's, and above all, those of common sense who considered the polemic in Congress that the British were intruders in the Oregon Country to be the ravings of lunacy. The triumph of such forces and methods on opposite sides of the Atlantic was hardly less significant than the treaty itself.

The treaty, ratified on June 15, 1846, by the Senate and proclaimed by Peel soon afterward, divided about equally between the two claimants an area of approximately a half million square miles. It gave to each claimant, in addition, effective outlets to the Pacific, the first to be formally recognized. It provided the United States and Canada with windows to the Orient, and interests, immediate and future, in the affairs of the Pacific world. Not least, it completed a transcontinental boundary that the United States and Canada have lived with in harmony for more than a century and a quarter.

The Mormons

IN THE EARLY 1840's a major physiographic province of the Far West, a possession of a foreign state, lay in the path of American expansion. It was the Enclosed Basin, part of a northern province of Mexico. Known also as the Great Basin, it was a high plateau, hemmed in by mountain ranges. On the east side lay the Wasatch Range, a spur of the Rocky Mountains, and the rugged Colorado plateaus. On the west side was the steep wall of the Sierra Nevadas. To the north was the country of the Columbia Plateau and to the south lay an area of desert.

The Enclosed Basin is well named. It is a basin in a literal sense. It is a container from which no water ever gets out to the sea. Any waters falling into it, or any rivers flowing into it, end up in lakes that have no outlet and are in consequence exceedingly salt. Great Salt Lake, which is the largest of these, is estimated to contain 400 million tons of salt. It is in many respects comparable to the Dead Sea in the Middle East. There are a few freshwater lakes in the province, such as Bear Lake and Utah Lake, but they are fresh only because they have outlets to other lakes which are salt. In some cases the streams flowing within the province do not even reach lakes. They simply disappear in the sand, or flow into sinks, such as Humboldt Sink or Carson Sink, where the water evaporates or seeps underground.

From the point of view of pioneers the province was unpromising country, chiefly because of its arid climate. The province is one of the most arid in the United States. The prevailing winds from the Pacific have been wrung dry in crossing the coastal ranges and the Sierra Nevadas. Instead of bringing moisture they pick up such as is in the Basin, and deposit it later on the slopes of the Wasatch Range. The annual precipitation of the greater part of this province is less than ten inches, and the most favored portions get only fifteen inches. That lack of rainfall is the curse of the whole region, but also, in a sense, its salvation. Inasmuch as the region has no drainage to the sea, if even a slight increase in rainfall were to occur, saline lakes would form in all the low-lying areas and much of the province would be drowned out.

In the glacial period, when rainfall was more abundant than it is now, a large part of the Enclosed Basin was underwater. The greater part of northern Utah was then covered by an immense lake, 1000 feet deep, of which the Great Salt Lake of today is only a small residue. That lake had beaches still to be seen on the mountainsides of Utah 1000 feet above Great Salt Lake. Another huge lake extended over much of what is now northwestern Nevada and southern Oregon, of which Pyramid Lake is the present vestige. If there should ever occur an even moderate increase in rainfall in the Great Basin, the old salt lakes would reappear.

The soil of the Great Basin is, in large part, infertile and tainted with alkali, as is often the case with semi-arid regions. The excess of alkali is not washed out by rains and the subsoil in many places is even more alkaline than the surface. Alkalinity is a problem in irrigation farming. Soaking the land periodically with water is necessary. If this is done unskillfully, the subsoil alkali rises to the surface. Some of the fields of the Enclosed Basin are so impregnated with alkali that they must be put through a washing process.

Adjoining the Enclosed Basin at the south is an actual desert, known by different names in different localities. The Mohave Desert lies east of Los Angeles; the Colorado Desert, west of Yuma; the Arizona Desert, east of Yuma. All this is part of one vast waste of 60,000 or 70,000 square miles. In many localities the soil is a shifting sand, unstable because it lacks plant roots to hold it down. Brilliantly colored in parts, as in the famous Painted Desert of Arizona, it is a region of fascination, a land of mirages, of sunrises and sunsets with a luminous beauty, and with nights that sparkle and shine with the brilliance of the starlight. But to the pioneers traveling through it, this desert was a death trap to be avoided.

Part of the desert in southeastern California is Death Valley. To the pioneers, who first encountered it, Death Valley was a ghastly sink of soda and alkali, 250 feet below sea level, and stifling in the summer. It took its name from the disaster of a party of Forty-niners, who left a reliable trail to take a deceptive cutoff to the mines, became lost, and nearly all perished.

The unattractiveness of the Enclosed Basin to pioneers was also due to the fact that it contained little timber. There were forests in the Wasatch Range and in the Sierra Nevadas, but the timber was hard to get out of the mountain canyons, and transportation costs were a major deterrent to its use.

The agricultural bleakness of the Enclosed Basin is revealed by statistics of its agricultural production in 1920 and a half-century later. In Nevada less than 1 percent of the surface was improved farm land in 1920; in 1972 it was about 3 percent. In Utah the percentages in 1920 and 1972 were 3 and 5½ percent. The principal agricultural use of Nevada land in 1972 was grazing—176,000 sheep and 49,000 head of cattle.

In all this immense, inhospitable region there was only one strip of land that had promise for farming—the narrow zone lying at the western base of the Wasatch Range, where streams of water could be caught just before they emerged from the canyons, and could be turned without great expenditure of capital onto the fields below for irrigation. This strip could, with relative ease, be reclaimed from aridity and converted into an oasis in the desert.

The people destined to settle this land were not the Southerners then flowing into Texas, California, and Oregon. They were a northern element consisting partly of New Englanders, partly of second-generation New Englanders from western New

York and Ohio, and only a few Southerners. They were a people of a particular religious outlook—the Mormons—the followers of the Mormon prophet, Joseph Smith.

Joseph Smith was himself a New Englander, born in Vermont in 1805. At the age of ten he was taken by his parents to western New York, a normal destination of New England migration. The family settled in Palmyra in the Burnt Over area, where a series of religious experiences befell the youth. He became the vehicle of the central miracle of Mormonism. He was shown by Moroni, a messenger of the Lord, the location of a stone casket, buried in a hill near Palmyra, a casket that contained a set of golden plates, on which were inscribed ancient hieroglyphics not decipherable by the ordinary human eye. But the casket also contained a pair of magic lenses, by the use of which the hieroglyphics could be translated into English and given their true meaning. These plates and their rendition into the *Book of Mormon* constitute the foundation of Mormonism. By 1829 the translation had been completed, with the aid of various amanuenses, and by 1830 it had been published by a Palmyra press.

The *Book of Mormon* has been the subject of a heated controversy ever since it appeared. By Mormons it is regarded as a revealed work, a miracle that is intrinsically no more difficult to accept than others underlying Christianity, such as the revealed Scriptures, the virgin birth of Christ, and the resurrection. Mormons believe the only difference between the Mormon miracle and the early Christian miracles is nineteen centuries of time. The reality of the golden plates was attested to by the affidavits of eleven people other than Joseph Smith, men who swore they had seen the plates. At least some of these men had reputations for veracity.

A less exalted view of the *Book of Mormon* has been held by secular historians who consider the golden plates and the *Book of Mormon* self-deceptions on the part of Joseph Smith. According to this view, he was a paranoid personality who had delusions of grandeur, and who in lucid moments supported the position in which he had placed himself by whatever devices came to his mind. The contention that he was a neurotic is buttressed by some historians with evidence that in his New England ancestral background there was a record of the hearing of supernatural voices and the seeing of visions.

The *Book of Mormon* is in part an account of God's dealings with the ancient inhabitants of North America. It is prefaced by a book that is in the realm of history. The history is as follows. When the Israelites were stricken with the confusion of tongues at the Tower of Babel, one of their tribes moved to America, where it was ultimately destroyed. But a second tribe—the tribe of Lehi—arrived in 600 B.C. in boats, and became firmly established. Later this tribe broke into two factions—the Nephites and the Lamanites. The Nephites were white—they were God's chosen people. The resurrected Christ preached to them in A.D. 37. The Lamanites were dark and were the ancestors of the American Indian. The Nephites fell from grace and were destroyed by the Lamanites at the great Battle of Cumorah, A.D. 384, fought in the hills around Palmyra. The Nephite prophet, Mormon, perished in the battle, but among the few survivors was his son, Moroni. About A.D. 420 the resurrected Christ appeared to Moroni and again made manifest his true teachings, the gospel of Mormonism. This was recorded by Moroni on golden plates, as his father had recorded the earlier history. The plates were buried by Moroni in the hill at Palmyra, together with the means of deciphering them. They remained safely hidden until they were made known to God's chosen servant, Joseph Smith.

This account of the golden plates and the *Book of Mormon* was received with incredulity by the non-Mormon world. It was in general ridiculed. The *Book of Mormon* was represented by some critics to be a crude plagiarization of a manuscript written by an obscure New York novelist, Solomon Spaulding. According to the critics, Spaulding in the 1820's composed a fanciful account of the peopling of the New World, which had circulated in manuscript form among acquaintances in western New York. It had never been printed and ultimately disappeared. It was said to have come into the hands of Joseph Smith, who simply appropriated it for the historical framework of his *Book of Mormon.*

That agnostic explanation of the historical chapters of the *Book of Mormon* is now discredited. There is no reliable evidence to substantiate it. A later romance by Spaulding was found in manuscript form in the Hawaiian Islands. Its style bore no resemblance to the narrative in the *Book of Mormon.*

Four revealed books are holy to Mormons: the Christian Bible, including the Old and New Testaments; the *Book of Mormon,* including its historical account and reinterpretations of portions of the Christian Bible; the *Book of Doctrine and Covenants,* which consists of additional revelations to Joseph Smith—prophecies, promises, and precepts—and contains the moral code of Mormonism. It contains the commands to Joseph Smith regarding community living and communism among the Mormons. Its communistic commands have sometimes been attributed to one of Joseph Smith's lieutenants, Sidney Rigdon, but they probably do not stem from any single individual. They were ideas widely entertained in the period of the 1820's and 1830's in the United States.

The fourth revealed book is the *Pearl of Great Price,* which contains a body of later revelations to Joseph Smith and an account of the visions connected with the finding of the golden plates and their translation and publication. The Mormons at one time believed in continuous divine revelation. Brigham Young, by gift of revelation, made important additions to Mormon doctrine, but finally stamped out private revelations.

On the basis of the *Book of Mormon,* a church was organized in 1830, later taking the name of the Church of Jesus Christ of the Latter-Day Saints. In structure it was hierarchical, consisting of two priestly orders, the Order of Aaron and the Order of Melchizedek, the first revealed to Joseph Smith by John the Baptist, the second by Peter and the other disciples. By virtue of priesthood in the second of these orders, Joseph Smith acquired the power of the laying on of hands, and he went about in western New York and in western Pennsylvania performing miracles of various kinds, casting devils out of those possessed, curing the sick and the lame.

Converts were gained rapidly, particularly in rural New England and in areas in the West settled by New Englanders. A considerable percentage of Utah Mormons trace their ancestry to these areas. The speed with which the Church grew in membership was due largely to the magnetic personality of Joseph Smith, who had gifts of spiritual leadership. Revelations and visions and miracles have come to many persons, but more substantial qualities are required to build a great and successful church.

The headquarters of the Church for a time was Fayette in western New York. Later it was moved to the Western Reserve in Ohio, where on the outskirts of Cleveland the town of Kirtland was built, comprising a temple and a community, including tannery, sawmill, and gristmill. The plan of settlement was in the traditional manner of a New England town.

But the building of the temple led to debt, and the debt brought trouble. Smith was commanded in a revelation to pay the debt by organizing a bank and issuing paper money. He founded the Kirtland Safety Society Bank, of which he was an officer, and sanctioned the emission of paper money. The bank was without a charter, and for an uncharted bank to issue paper money was, under Ohio law, illegal. When the bank failed in 1838, Joseph Smith was indicted and, to avoid arrest, fled to Missouri.

Missouri contained several established Mormon colonies in the early 1830's, the largest of which was at the big bend of the Missouri, just west of Independence. Joseph Smith declared that this settlement would be the gathering place, the Zion, where the Saints and converted Indians would meet the Lord in 1841. Mormonism included the doctrine of the second coming of Christ—the second advent. Some devout Mormons still regard Independence as the ultimate seat of the Church—the New Jerusalem.

But when Joseph Smith arrived in Missouri in 1838, the Mormons had already been expelled from the Independence region and from other localities by rowdy frontiersmen. They were on the eve of a general expulsion from Missouri. They were disliked for a variety of reasons. Their gospel was distasteful to the religious; their Yankee origin was a firebrand to Missourians; and they were converting Indians and inviting them into the fold. To frontiersmen Indians were anathema. As a result of such irritants, in the winter of 1838–39, the Mormons were once again set upon and driven out of the state. Fifteen thousand men, women, and children were expelled from their homes in the dead of winter, with the loss of most of their belongings. This was one of the most disgraceful instances of religious intolerance and persecution in American history.

The refugees established themselves at Nauvoo, Illinois, on the Mississippi River. They were granted a local charter by the Illinois legislature, under the terms of which they enjoyed a large measure of local self-rule. Abraham Lincoln, a member of the legislature at the time, voted for the granting of the charter.

For four years the Mormons prospered at Nauvoo and spread over the surrounding country. By 1844 they were 20,000 to 30,000 strong. They built a new temple and a university; Joseph Smith was courted by local Illinois politicians and in 1844 announced himself a candidate for the presidency of the United States. He and the Mormons were at the height of their prosperity in the East.

But they were, also, at the end of their peace. Peace was shattered as a result of a revelation made to Joseph Smith in 1843, which permitted and encouraged polygamy. It was communicated by him to the Church membership promptly, though it was not avowed publicly until many years later. It led within the Church to an immediate clash. Several Mormons, who controlled the Nauvoo newspaper, publicly attacked the Prophet on grounds of immorality. His defenders replied by destroying the Nauvoo printing press, whose owners fled to the neighboring city of Carthage, where they swore out a warrant for Joseph Smith's arrest. He and his brother, Hiram, voluntarily submitted to arrest and were lodged in jail at Carthage, guarded by the local militia. In 1844, with the connivance of the guard, they were murdered. The Prophet suffered martyrdom.

Various contenders for his mantle appeared. One was Sidney Rigdon, a chief counselor of Smith. Another was James J. Strang, who had found copper plates by revelation in Wisconsin, and had established a Zion on an island in Lake Michigan. The principal contender, however, was Brigham Young, who was in Boston at the time of the assassination, electioneering for Smith. Young hurried back to Nauvoo and succeeded in having himself chosen to the headship of the Church.

Brigham Young was a real leader. He did not have the spiritual qualities of Joseph Smith, or at least not to the same degree, but he was superior to him in every other respect. He was a genius as an organizer, a modern captain of industry, a man of powerful body, of dominating personality, of strong, forceful character. He has been aptly named the Moses of the Mormons.

A leader of that type was needed in 1844. For after Joseph Smith's assassination the Illinois mob spirit swiftly grew, and it was obvious the Mormons would have to move again. This was recognized by Brigham Young at once and he entered into an agreement with the leaders of the frontiersmen that the Mormons would move if they were given until the spring of 1846 to dispose of their belongings. The agreement was broken by the mobs and the Mormons were set upon and driven from their homes with the same brutal spoliations as had marked their expulsion from Missouri.

These repeated expulsions were evidence to Brigham Young that Mormonism could not work out its mission within the borders of the United States, certainly not within the settled borders. A new migration must be made. In the *Book of Mormon* was a prophecy of a resting place for the Lord's people in the Far West. To the Far West Brigham Young decided to lead his flock. This required more than ordinary courage. It called for a plunge into the little-known Far West. The Oregon Country and California were well known, but they were closed to the Mormons by reason of the fact that a population of turbulent Mississippi Valley frontiersmen was flowing into them—the very people from whom the Mormons were fleeing.

The choice of the valley of Great Salt Lake by Brigham Young as the abiding place of his flock is no longer a question obscured by legend. According to recent historians, both Mormon and non-Mormon, Brigham Young was already canvassing the problem of the location of the coming settlement while at Nauvoo in 1845–46. He became acquainted with John C. Frémont's *Report of Exploring Expeditions to the Rocky Mountains in 1842, and to Oregon and North California in 1843–44,* which had been published as a government document in 1845. Accompanying the *Report* was a map depicting the Wasatch Range, and just west of it the valley of Great Salt Lake and the Bear River. Of the latter Frémont wrote: "the bottoms [are] extensive, water [is] excellent, timber sufficient, soil good and well adapted to grains and grasses . . . mountain sides covered with nutritious grasses called bunch grass . . . its quantity will sustain any amount of cattle."

Young relied, also, on reports of missionaries and mountain trappers, whom he met in 1846–47 at Winter Quarters, the Mormon assembling place just outside Omaha, where food, seed, and stores for building a future settlement were being gathered. He consulted there the Jesuit missionary Pierre Jean De Smet, who knew the Bear River Valley from having stopped there on his journeys east and west. It seems certain that Young's choice of Salt Lake Valley as the future home of the Mormons was made on the basis of knowledge received from such sources.

Early in April 1847, as soon as fodder for draft animals was green on the prairies, Brigham Young left Winter Quarters with an advance party of volunteers, to scout the route and prepare the way for later companies of Mormons. They stopped at Jim Bridger's post, where they received a discouraging report as to the potentiality of Salt Lake Valley for growing corn, but were not dissuaded, and soon the first settlement was made, to be followed by mass migrations through 1847 and 1848.

The selection of the valley of Great Salt Lake as the home of the Mormons, if not by revelation, was the nearest thing to it. It was a stroke of genius. A better refuge could hardly have been found anywhere in the Far West. The desert could be converted by irrigation into an oasis. On every side protection was provided—the protection of isolation—a vast waste of desert and mountain, a safeguard for the future against the danger of being encircled by close, intrusive neighbors.

Moreover, for the creation of a theocracy, the region was ideal. In this desert, irrigation water, flowing from the canyons of the Wasatch Range, was the source of life. It could be taken possession of by the Church community simply by occupying the mouths of canyons at points before the streams emerged and diverting their waters. The Church community by that simple expedient could take control of the destiny of every person living in the settlements. Also, the valley had salt—that essential of life—close at hand in Great Salt Lake.

To the Mormon enemies as well as to the faithful the significance of this location seemed clear. It was commented on in vitriolic terms by a San Francisco clergyman in 1857 in a sermon to his congregation, which serves as an example of the loathing of this branch of Christianity by other Christian Churches in the United States:

> There is Utah, reeking in its corruption by its lake of salt, with nothing to save it. It is the pandemonium of tyranny, sensuality, and deviltry, where hell holds jubilee on earth in the name of God and the saints. But it is walled in like a pit, within its own mountains and deserts, with no natural outlet to the sea. Thank God for that, that he has shut that abomination within that great basin, where its impurities settle and stagnate, and where all its streams of death, like its rivers, fall back upon itself. Yet its accumulations have forced one passage southward and westward to the sea, and begun at San Bernardino to poison the shore. Its miasma, too, has sometimes crept up our mountain sides and settled down through our mountain passes upon the western slope, like the breath of the pestilence. For its evils are most powerful within itself, and Sodom, in its worst state, was never more fit for the fire.

In this outburst three ideas stand out: first, that the Mormon community is fit for the fire; second, that in the Enclosed Basin it is walled in as in the pit of hell; and third, that any cleansing fire of the outside world will for that reason be difficult to apply.

The reclamation of the valley began where Salt Lake City now stands. A town was laid out much as a New England town of the 17th century would have been. A common was set aside for a future temple and tabernacle. Streets were laid off, though much more regularly and much wider than in a New England community. The land of the town was then divided into ten-acre lots. Some of these near the center of the city were subdivided into house lots containing an acre and a quarter, enough for a house and a garden, and given to business and professional men. Artisans were allowed five acres. Farmers received one or two lots—ten or twenty acres—depending on the size of their families. On the outskirts, the lots to farmers were also ten to twenty acres.

The conquest of the soil and the creation of a society was more difficult than in eastern frontier communities. The topography, climate, and isolation were all strange and created new problems. Life for a time was a struggle for bare survival. In most areas of semi-aridity locusts are a periodic problem. A plague of them settled on the valley in the second year and threatened to destroy the entire crop. However, a flock of gulls from Great Salt Lake came to the rescue. It devoured the pests, so that part of the harvest was saved. The intervention of the gulls was attributed to divine favor. An interesting monument in Temple Square in Salt Lake City was later erected to commemorate the intervention.

In 1849 came the turning point in Mormon fortunes. It was the result of their successful adaptation to irrigation farming, and of the discovery of gold in California. In the summer of 1849 gold seekers began to arrive on their way to California and Salt Lake City became a halfway house to the Pacific. The Mormons were able to dispose of their surplus food to the Forty-niners at high prices, and to buy for almost nothing equipment the gold seekers were not able to transport further. But the gold rush also created problems, for some of the Mormons were tempted to join the gold rush. The whole of Brigham Young's great authority was needed to hold the colony intact. He told his followers that gold was good only to pave streets with.

As soon as the first settlement had been made secure, the Mormons spread rapidly over the whole belt of land along the base of the Wasatch Range. New settlements called "stakes" were planted in succession under the direction of the Church and in the traditional manner of New England town planting.

First, an exploring party would be sent out to find a suitable site for a new settlement. When a site had been found, certain Mormons would be chosen by the Church to make the settlement. The persons selected would include men of experience in the laying out of new settlements, and others with knowledge of blacksmithing, carpentry, and milling in the right proportions. Mormons so chosen to build up a new stake felt honored. They sold their property and prepared to migrate. In a few cases the hesitant were ordered to go.

The location of the new stake was always where a mountain stream emerged from a canyon and an irrigation canal could be constructed. A village was laid out there by the Church authorities. A lot was reserved for the Church. Each head of a family got a village lot big enough for a residence, a garden, and an orchard. The farm lands adjacent to the village were divided into lots, of which each Church member got one, with lots left over for latecomers. Lots contained five to ten acres of land. Commons were set apart to which settlers could bring cattle and oxen, and where town herdsmen looked after cattle during the day. The whole process is in accord with New England town planting tradition.

Land distribution took into account the needs of each family. Speculation was discouraged. The normal total allotment of land to each family was twenty to thirty acres. The reason for so small a holding was not scarcity of land, but scarcity of water. The leaders felt that only as much land should be held by a family as could be cultivated without waste of water.

The Mormon settlements were at first squatter communities on Mexican land. Until the close of the war with Mexico in 1848 the region was Mexican. In 1849 the squatter state of Deseret was organized by the Mormons, but was never recognized by the federal government. In 1850 Utah Territory, including present-day Nevada, was organized by Congress under the Compromise of 1850. The man appointed to be governor of the territory was Brigham Young. The elected territorial legislature authorized by the act was controlled by the Mormons. In 1852 it enacted a law authorizing the filing of land claims in the county courts of the territory. Claims were nothing more than squatters' claims, since the land in the territory belonged to the federal government. In 1869, after the passage of the Homestead Act, a federal land office was opened in Salt Lake City, and for the first time actual title to land could be obtained. But special arrangements had to be made. According to the Homestead Act a settler was given 160 acres. But in the cultivated valleys of Utah five or more families would already be established on any 160-acre tract. A method had to be devised to obtain title from the government without disturbing families already established on the soil. This was done under the leadership of the Church. One settler would perfect title to a 160-acre tract and then he would divide the land under Church direction among the families that were established on it.

Irrigation water was the source of life in the Enclosed Basin, as was instantly recognized by the Mormons. They were the first Anglo-Saxons in the New World to practice irrigation. The swiftness with which they turned to a type of agriculture of which Anglo-Saxons had previously no experience, is a tribute to the administrative genius of their leaders, who directed every phase of irrigation development. In a newly formed farm community a bishop would call a meeting of the settlers, over which he would preside. The meeting would appoint a committee led by the bishop to supervise the work of constructing a canal.

The principle applied in construction was that each settler would contribute work in proportion to the quantity of land assigned to him and the amount of water he expected to use. The construction of Utah's irrigation canals was the greatest cooperative enterprise in American history, and one of the most important achievements of Mormonism. In 1958 more than two-thirds of Utah's irrigated land was watered by cooperative canals.

Another Mormon achievement was the development of a code of law regulating the distribution of irrigation water. This is one of the enduring contributions of the Church to the settlement of the West. In the eastern parts of the United States and in England the use of the water of streams was governed by a legal system known as the "riparian code," a part of the common law. Under it the uses which could be made by abutters of a stream were carefully restricted. Those permitted were the so-called "natural uses," such as the domestic ones of drinking, cooking, and washing. If other uses were to be made of the water—the "artificial uses," such as milling, manufacturing, or mining—a special permit had to be obtained from the legislature.

If a miller who was a riparian wished to turn aside the water of a stream in order to make it pass over his mill wheel and produce power, he had to get a permit to do so. He knew that he was responsible for returning the water to the stream before the land of the next riparian owner was reached, and returning it unchanged in quantity or quality. Thus each riparian, in exercising his right to use the river's flow, also had an obligation not to alter the amount or the quality of the flow with respect to other riparians. The thrust of riparian law was that riparians had a right to use the water of a river, but not to use it up.

Such a doctrine, applied to the arid West, would have made irrigation impossible. Irrigation requires using the water of a stream, so completely in some cases that the flow may be reduced to a mere trickle. In answer to this need the Mormons worked out a new water code for the arid West known as "prior appropriation." This embraced two main principles. The water in a stream could be appropriated and used by riparians for irrigation, without returning an equal flow into the stream. Irrigation took rank with drinking and washing as a "natural" use in the eyes of the law. Also, persons other than riparians in the stream's basin could use the water.

The other main principle established in the new code was that a legal right to a stream's water was created by virtue of priority of appropriation. Early users acquired rights to water as against later comers for all future time. If, for example, early comers made a settlement on the lower part of a stream, and thus acquired prior rights to water, any later comers locating higher up the stream were obliged, in time of shortage, to let enough water pass down the stream to satisfy the full rights of the first appropriators.

These two principles became incorporated in the water law of all the states of the semi-arid West. They were written also into federal law by Congress in 1866. In recent years several semi-arid western states have modified their prior appropriation code by recognizing the doctrine of "reasonable beneficial use," which is a combination of the doctrine of prior appropriation and the older concept of riparian obligations.

In addition to developing legal principles the Mormons worked out the practical rules of water distribution. They established the precept that a settler on an irrigation canal might take water only in proportion to the amount of labor he had contributed to the building of the canal or the amount of stock he held in a canal company.

The Mormons also worked out regulations covering the time when users could draw water from an irrigation canal. It was essential to have a carefully worked out schedule. Otherwise during the day farmers might try to get more water than was available, while during the night the water would run to waste. In each community a water master was appointed who designated the days in the month and the hours in the day or night when each person could draw water, and saw to it that no person had his water gate open at any other time. Usually the times when a man might have his water gate open were a week apart. Every phase of farm life was thus dominated by the Church leaders. It was the Church organization that directed the location of new settlements, the cooperative building of the canals, and the working out of the practical rules of water distribution.

Such voluntary cooperation had always been emphasized as doctrine by the Church. But the imperious needs of irrigation farming and the facts of physiography in the Enclosed Basin made cooperation the law of survival. Brigham Young never showed his genius more strikingly than when he chose as the home of Mormonism a desert where control of water by the Church community gave control of life.

The Church also gave leadership in the field of trade. That was done particularly after 1869, when the Union Pacific reached Utah. Its completion brought to Utah a great many non-Mormons who went into business. They seemed a threat to the unity of Mormonism and the authority of the Church.

The answer given to this challenge was the organization in 1868–69 of Zion's Cooperative Mercantile Institute. ZCMI was a cooperative store, with headquarters in Salt Lake City and branches throughout Utah. At the head of it was Brigham Young, and to this day the president is the president of the Church. Brigham Young urged every Mormon family in Utah to buy shares in the branches of ZCMI. The response was immediate and membership in the branches was widespread.

The result of the creation of ZCMI was the concentration of Utah trade in Mormon hands. In the smaller Mormon cities and villages non-Mormon traders were put out of business. Trading with them was regarded as disloyal to the Church, and in 1869 a vote was adopted by the General Conference to cut off from Church membership anyone who traded with gentiles. Even in the larger cities the number of gentile traders fell off. In 1883 ZCMI was estimated to be handling 33⅓ percent or more of all the goods imported into Utah.

Church leadership was also given in manufacturing to some extent. Brigham Young wished his people to engage in cooperative industry in connection with ZCMI, and his wish was to a large degree realized. There were cooperatives in printing, mining, and iron manufacturing. In 1870 a boot-and-shoe factory was established in connection with ZCMI, and in 1871 a woolen mill on a cooperative basis at Provo, the wool being provided by Mormon sheepmen who belonged to the cooperative.

One of the most successful forms of cooperative enterprises was organized in the beet-sugar industry. It was initiated in 1879 when Zion's Cooperative Board of Trade was established as a means of stimulating the raising and refining of sugar beets in Utah. The head of the organization was the president of the Church. In 1891 the Utah Sugar Company was organized. It was initiated at Lehi and consisted of farmers who raised sugar beets under expert guidance. It included a refinery, where extraction of the sugar was expertly done. This company became the biggest beet-sugar producer in the United States. The Utah-Idaho Sugar Company in the 1970's was still a major factor in American sugar production. Most of its stock is owned by the Mormon Church.

Thus in trade, in manufacturing, and in agriculture Mormonism meant cooperation under Church leadership. Mormonism was an experiment in cooperation and in social planning, one of the most successful large-scale examples of it in American history, prior to the rural electrification cooperatives of the New Deal era. These constructive economic achievements were for a long time obscured by what was spectacular or unusual in Mormonism, such as the golden plates and the doctrine of polygamy.

For a time the Mormon leaders were ambitious for something beyond economic cooperation. They undertook to establish a system of communism for Mormon society. The origin of this interest was a revelation to Joseph Smith at Kirtland in 1831. A communistic society—the United Order of Enoch—was revealed, which had flourished under the Nephites, the ancient inhabitants of America. The society had flourished while the Nephites were in God's good grace, and it had brought them prosperity. However, when the people fell from grace through selfishness, the society had disintegrated and that had been one of the factors in the downfall of the community and its destruction by the Lamanites.

At the time of this revelation, communist societies were numerous in the eastern part of the United States. The Rappist society, the New Harmony Colony of Robert

Owen, the phalanxes of the Fourierists, and many others were in the public eye. Sidney Rigdon, a leading disciple of Joseph Smith, was especially interested in communism and is believed to have been the real voice that Joseph Smith heard in his revelation. But Joseph Smith was well acquainted with the history of early Christianity and knew of the experiments with communistic forms of living among the early Christians. In response to his vision the United Order of Enoch was set up at Kirtland and later spread to the Mormon communities in Missouri.

It was on a purely voluntary basis. No compulsion was used on any Mormon to join it. If a Mormon joined he gave all his property to the Church. He got back a so-called stewardship of part of the property he had given. The property returned was enough to permit him to support himself and his family. A Mormon might give not only his property but his surplus income. Each Mormon joining the Order decided the proportion that he would give and that he would take back in the form of a stewardship. If a member of the Order ever wished to withdraw he could do so. But he got back only that part of his property which he still held in stewardship.

The property and income acquired by the Church in this way were used to support the poor and to maintain the Church leaders. The system differed from other contemporary forms of communism in that every member supported his own family through his retained income and his stewardship of property.

The prospect of distributions of property was attractive to the poor, and helps to explain their flocking into the Mormon Church. It explains especially the crowding into Missouri stakes where gifts of property were believed to be easier to obtain. Men of wealth in the Mormon Church were reluctant, however, in most cases, to enter the United Order and in its early form it did not last long. In Missouri it was dissolved when the Mormon settlements were broken up in 1834. At Kirtland the experiment dragged on until 1837, when it was wiped out by the panic of that year. When the United Order collapsed, an alternative method was established for the care of the poor and maintenance of the Church leaders. This was the system of tithing, established in 1838, whereby a tenth of the annual income of every Mormon was paid to the Church for these purposes.

The chief significance of the United Order in its first form is that it later became the basis for a second and modified form. The Second United Order was set up by Brigham Young in 1874, after his people had become established in Utah, and was pressed forward with his characteristic energy. It was a village form of communism, organized under Church leadership. Like the First United Order, it was on a voluntary basis. Its purposes were to be largely economic. Brigham Young believed a higher efficiency would be achieved under a communistic form of society than would ever be achieved under a society of individual enterprise. A communistic form would permit a more effective division of labor. One part of the community would do the work of the fields; another, the work of the household, providing a community table; another, as nurses, would look after the children. The saved labor would be employed in developing new forms of farming, such as sugar-beet cultivation, fruit growing, or dairying. Or the saved labor might be turned to manufacturing, with resulting diversification of production.

All this was directed toward an increase in Mormon self-sufficiency. The Mormon community would be less dependent on the outside world. Also the Mormon poor could be put to useful work and would be less a drain on the Church resources.

The result would be greater unity in the Mormon community, which was the passion of the Church leaders.

In response to this appeal many southern Utah villages entered the Second United Order. In that part of the territory, society was still almost exclusively rural, and the rural areas there, like those of colonial New England, were apt to be especially under the influence of the priesthood. In northern Utah, where some urbanization had taken place as a result of the coming of the railroad, and where the grip of the Church was less firm, communities were less likely to be attracted to the Second United Order. Wealthy Mormons and even some of the hierarchy in northern Utah looked with disfavor on this communistic experiment. When a village voted to join the Second United Order, individuals in it could, if they wished, stay out. However, social pressures might be applied to a hesitant individual where a village was very enthusiastic.

Several different types of organization were tried by villages entering the Order. The most common was the St. George type, so called from the name of the village where it was initiated. In this type a person entering the United Order gave it part or all of his property as he chose. An appraisal was made of the value of the property given, which was entered on the books to the member's credit in capital stock. The property given might be a farm, a dairy, a tannery, a lumberyard, a woolen factory, or a boot-and-shoe shop. A member might put into the Order also part or all of his daily labor. He received credit for this on the books at a rate of pay determined by an appraiser's committee. Members of the Order and their families took meals at a common table, which were charged against them on the books. Control of each local was in the hands of a board of managers chosen by the membership. At the end of five years an inventory was taken and each member was given a dividend, on the property and on the labor he had put in. That dividend was entered to his credit. All dividends were reinvested in the Order. If a member withdrew from the Order he received back only half the property and half the normal dividend. That was a discouragement to withdrawing and was an added hold of the Church on the individual.

A few localities—those most under the influence of the Church—adopted a more thoroughgoing variety of communism. This was the Orderville form, named after the community where it was initiated. In it each person who joined put all his property and all his labor into the Order. Members worked and ate together as one big family. Each member received the same labor credit regardless of his skill or trade. At the end of each year all credits and withdrawals were canceled on the books and the members began again on an equal footing. The Orderville society was not only the most thorough, but the most successful and enduring of all the societies of the United Order. It ran prosperously from 1875 to 1882, and thereafter somewhat less harmoniously for three years longer.

By 1885, however, all the branches of the Second United Order had disintegrated. Communism could not be made to work. The "heavenly principle" was too great a strain even for the devotion that the Mormon Church called forth. Idle and inefficient members fared as well as the industrious and competent. Some members did not take as good care of the property of the United Order as they would have of their own. Where members put into the Order only part of their property, there were disputes regarding the amount of labor to be devoted to what was held out. There were also disputes over labor credits given in accord with skill.

Non-Mormons in Utah fought the United Order and did their best to discredit it since it emphasized Mormon unity and self-sufficiency, which meant a reduction of trade. In 1877, Brigham Young, who was the most deeply interested in the Order, died, and his successor, John Taylor, did not struggle to keep it alive. After it had completely disintegrated in 1885, the Mormon Church never again undertook to put communism into practice.

The preoccupation of the Mormon leaders with the worldly affairs of their flock was characteristic of the Church from the beginning. Mormonism aimed not only at a new heaven but also at a new earth. This was especially characteristic of Brigham Young, whose sermons were to a very large extent devoted to mundane affairs. In this respect Mormonism was characteristic of American life and particularly well suited to the frontier. The earthy character of Brigham Young's leadership is illustrated in a story told of him by a Utah Mormon, who was a devoted disciple with a sense of humor. Brigham Young ordered a can of red paint from Omaha. His writing was not very legible and the word "can" was misread as "car." A carload of red paint was dispatched and created dismay when it arrived. A correspondence with the Omaha company followed, and it soon was clear that to return the carload would cost more than the value of the paint. A compromise was arranged under which the Church president kept the paint at a big reduction in price. Soon after, he announced a revelation, that barns painted red were pleasing in the sight of the Lord. After that the paint ceased to be a source of economic embarrassment.

Church direction extended to the social as well as to the economic life of the Mormon community. An outstanding illustration of social direction was polygamy. Polygamy was not originally a part of Mormonism—in fact, it seemed to be forbidden in the *Book of Mormon,* but the way was left open for the introduction of it at a later time. The language of the *Book of Mormon* was:

> There shall not any man have save it be one wife, and concubines he shall have none, for I, the Lord God, delighteth in the chastity of women. . . . But if I will, saith the Lord of Hosts, raise up seed unto me, I will command my people, otherwise they shall hearken unto these things.

In 1843 a revelation authorizing polygamy was made to Joseph Smith. There are charges that the leaders of Mormonism had been practicing it earlier. Joseph Smith is believed to have had 28 wives. Polygamy was given its theological rationalization by Brigham Young in the only important contribution he made to Church doctrine. According to him, God was plural. There were many Gods; and they were arranged in a hierarchy. In this hierarchy the primeval Adam is the highest God. Jesus Christ, Mahomet, and Joseph Smith were Gods of lower level. All faithful members of the Church were deified on death and formed yet another class of Gods. A main function of Gods was the propagation of human souls. Souls were always being propagated and waiting to enter human bodies. Some souls had been waiting to be incarnated for thousands of years. Souls that did not find bodies of believers were in danger of entering the bodies of unbelievers. Mormon polygamy was therefore desirable, because it brought bodies of potential believers into the world to receive these waiting souls. The glory of Mormons in heaven was therefore in proportion to the number of their wives and children. Brigham Young had wives variously numbered up to 27 and 56 children.

Among Mormons a woman, unprovided with a husband, on death found the gates of heaven closed. It was common for Mormons, therefore, to marry women even of advanced age to help them get past the gates. Some of Brigham Young's marriages were of this type. Marriages by proxy to the dead were also performed as a means of assuring salvation to women no longer living.

While polygamy was encouraged, it was also controlled by the Church. Ordinarily plural marriages were approved only where a man was able to support several families. Polygamy was practiced by not more than 10 percent of the marriageable men in Utah. In 1882 a Mormon count set the figure at 5 percent, but this was an understatement. The men who practiced polygamy were in general the more successful and more prosperous. There was accordingly a crude eugenics in Mormon polygamy, and the studies that have been made of the children of polygamous marriages show achievements fully equal to those of the children of monogamous marriages.

The doctrine of polygamy was kept under cover by the Church from 1843 until 1852, when it was officially avowed. It then led to dissension among Mormons, especially those outside Utah. In 1853, at a conference in Wisconsin, the so-called Reorganization was set up. By 1860 several other groups of dissenters had coalesced with the Reorganization, and a son of Joseph Smith (Joseph Smith III) was named its president. This group maintained that polygamy had never been revealed to Joseph Smith; that it had never been sanctioned by him; that it had been foreign to all his teaching, and had been foisted on the Church after the Prophet's death by Brigham Young, an interloper. This Reorganized Church, later known as the Josephite Branch, was in 1970 ranked second in membership to the Utah Church, though a distant second.

In 1855 sanction was given polygamy in Utah by a law, not altogether explicit, enacted by the territorial legislature. It was brought to the attention of Congress in 1862 and was annulled by an act declaring polygamy in any territory of the United States a crime. The Utah law and the congressional act were fought over for years in the Utah territorial courts. They were finally carried to the United States Supreme Court in the case of *Reynolds v. United States* (1878). Reynolds was a prominent Mormon, once a secretary to Brigham Young. He had been convicted of polygamy under the congressional act of 1862 in the Utah territorial courts, and sentenced to jail. He appealed the conviction to the United States Supreme Court, arguing that the congressional act making polygamy criminal was an unconstitutional measure. He cited the Bill of Rights of the Constitution, the first article of which provides: "Congress shall make no law respecting an establishment of religion, or prohibiting the free exercise thereof." He argued that because of this provision Congress was barred from enacting a law making polygamy criminal in the territories. Polygamy was an integral part of the Mormon faith and to penalize it was a prohibition of the Mormon religion.

The Supreme Court ruled in the case that, while Congress was barred by the Bill of Rights from interfering with the free exercise of religion in the domain of doctrine and thought, it had unrestricted right to interfere if religion broke over into overt acts that were contrary to good order and morality. This ruling rested on principles established in other spheres of law, and has since been the accepted law of the federal and state courts of the United States.

In 1882 Congress adopted the Edmunds Act, which renewed the earlier ban on polygamy and added more stringent sanctions. This was followed by the seizure of the Church properties in Utah and holding them in trust, pending submission by the Church. Many Church leaders went into hiding. In 1890, after a bitter struggle and great suffering caused by the breaking up of families that had been established in good faith, the Mormon Church surrendered, and polygamy was renounced by President Wilford Woodruff. In 1896, when Utah was admitted as a state into the Union, polygamy was repudiated in the state constitution. Since 1896 polygamy has disappeared and occasional efforts of zealots to reinstate it have been frowned upon by the Church.

Not only marriage but the moral code of Mormonism was carefully safeguarded by the Church. The sex standards among Utah Mormons have been the strictest and highest found in any state in the United States. Sex laxity was not condoned by the Church. It was a deadly sin. Drunkenness is practically nonexistent among Mormons. The use of alcohol is forbidden in a commandment that was revealed to Joseph Smith in 1833 and that is contained in the *Book of Doctrine and Covenants*:

> Inasmuch as any man drinketh wine as strong drink among you, behold it is not good nor meet in the sight of your father. And again, tobacco is not for the body, neither for the belly, and it is not good for man. And again hot drinks are not good for the body or belly.

The use of meat at certain seasons was also restricted among devout Mormons. The rule in regard to the drinking of hot coffee and hot tea had been relaxed, but that against the drinking of alcohol and the use of tobacco was still maintained in the 1970's. A Mormon who persists in violations is denied the right to enter a Mormon temple.

The Church has been from the outset an earnest proselytizer, reflecting the New England background of Mormonism. Its success was marked among the humbler classes, particularly in European countries such as England, Wales, and Scandinavia. Prior to World War II successful proselytizing was going on in Hawaii and Japan.

Missionaries are often university graduates. They go on two-year terms which may be renewed. They serve without compensation and are not provided even their living expenses. They receive only transportation home at the end of their service. They support themselves or are supported by relatives. Such service calls for real devotion. One of the higher ordinances is the giving to the Church of all talents and means asked for by it.

In earlier years converts were urged to migrate to Utah. In 1849, to help converts to come from the eastern parts of the United States, or from Europe, a revolving loan fund, the Perpetual Emigration Fund, was organized by the Church. This was used to help defray costs of transportation, farm implements, seed, and stock. Persons who borrowed from the fund agreed to repay the loans either in money or in labor. The Perpetual Emigration Fund was continued until 1887, when it was broken up by federal authorities in the campaign against polygamy. In the 20th century, with restrictions on immigration to the United States, Mormon converts often remained in their own countries, or, if they came to the United States, settled outside Utah. In 1970 Mormons were one of the largest religious groups in the United States (2,186,000 members) and total world membership was nearly 3 million.

In every field of activity Mormon society was a Church society. In agriculture, in trade, in family life, in moral and religious life, it was a theocracy, the 19th century equivalent of the theocracy in colonial Massachusetts. Brigham Young was a 19th century counterpart of John Winthrop of the Massachusetts Bay Company.

The Mormon theocracy was superbly successful. It achieved in the inhospitable Enclosed Basin a high degree of social and religious unity, coherence, and material prosperity. How is this success to be explained? The answer lies partly in the martyrdom of the Prophet, Joseph Smith. In Mormonism as elsewhere in Christianity, the blood of the martyr was the seed of the Church. Another element in the answer is the peculiarity of some of the features of Mormonism, especially the miracle of the golden plates and the doctrine of polygamy, which gave to the Mormon flock a sense of being a people apart—a chosen few—and made for unity and coherence among them. On the other hand, the doctrine of polygamy was a liability in that it eventuated in a split in the Church and produced later struggles with the federal government.

An important element was the effectiveness of the government of the Church. This consisted of two hierarchical priesthoods, those of Aaron and of Melchizedek. The priesthood of Aaron included the lower officers of the Church, who were concerned with temporal affairs, especially with social work. The highest rank in this order was the bishops. The priesthood of Melchizedek comprised the upper officers, concerned chiefly with the spiritual government of the Church and its missionary activity. In the 1970's it consists of the president of the Church, who is the ranking officer, his counselors—the twelve apostles—who are a traveling high council, and the seventy elders, who direct the missionary and propaganda work.

Among the elements accounting for the coherence and success of the Church one of the most important was the physiography of the Enclosed Basin. A province so inhospitable could be subdued only by effort that was planned, united, and devoted. Such effort a Church organization of the Mormon type was supremely well equipped to give, and it was this combination of physiography and of religion that transformed the Enclosed Basin from a barren wilderness into a prosperous farming society.

California

Upper California, in the 1840's, was a province of Mexico with a history similar to that of Texas. It consists of three zones paralleling the Pacific Ocean. One is a coastal range of mountains; another is the beautiful inner valley; and to the east of it, the mighty Sierra Nevada range, flanked at the south by the Mohave Desert.

The coastal range is a rough country, for the most part unsuited to farming, and useful principally for grazing. It contained at intervals, however, lovely little side valleys and coves in which the climate was ideal and in which farming and grazing on a small scale were possible. In these side valleys civilization first gained a foothold in California. In them the Spanish missions were established to Christianize and civilize the Indians.

One of the side valleys was of more than ordinary agricultural attractiveness. It lay between the coastal range and the San Bernardino Mountains, the region now dominated by the city of Los Angeles. It was a beautiful valley, with sufficient land of good quality for farming and grazing, and with a climate that was ideal until it was mixed by civilization with smog. The area lacked sufficient rainfall, but some rain and snow fell, owing to the location of the valley between mountains. Also, at Los Angeles, there were springs and artesian wells fed by snows from the mountains. Here one of the earliest of the missions, San Gabriel, was established in 1771, and here a cattle industry developed on a large enough scale to attract trade in an early day.

Nowadays this valley is a great citrus grove, except where it has been industrialized. It is the home of oranges, lemons, and grapefruit, and also of walnuts, peaches, and vegetables. Vegetables are grown ten months of the year. Adjacent to the area is the date kingdom of the United States. But these developments are a result of irrigation in the 20th century.

The coastal range contains a major geographical asset—the harbor of San Francisco. One of its major virtues is its interior location. It is almost land-locked, which gives it safety from the winds, swells, and sands of the Pacific Ocean. It is not obstructed by a sandbar and has a safe entrance—the Golden Gate—which is kept scoured by the tremendous force of the tides sweeping back and forth through it. It is commodious—the whole of San Francisco Bay—and its waters are deep.

The value of this harbor is increased by the fact that it is the only good harbor on the whole stretch of coastline from southern California to the Strait of Juan de Fuca. Other harbors on that coast are open. They front directly on the ocean, and bars are formed there by the action of the winds and tides.

Because San Francisco is so excellent a harbor, and because it is the only good one on so long a stretch of coast, it was one of the commercial prizes of the province. It was declared by Daniel Webster in a private letter to be worth twenty times as much to the United States as the whole of Texas. That was an exaggeration. But the value of the harbor and the American eagerness to acquire it were primary factors in producing the Mexican War.

Between the coastal range and the Sierra Nevadas lies the great inner valley— the Central Valley of California. This is one of the agricultural treasures of the Pacific coast. Its soil is excellent, its climate is good, and it enjoys warm winters and hot summers. The northern part of the valley—the Sacramento—has fair amounts of rainfall, almost enough for ordinary farming. Its rainfall deficiencies are easily met by irrigation. Snow collects on the northern Sierra Nevadas to an average height of 35 feet a year, and often as high as 50 feet. The runoff of that snow, impounded by small irrigation dams, was used by pioneers for farming.

The southern part of the valley—the San Joaquin—has less rainfall. It suffers from the fact that it lies in the climatic shadow of the coastal range. It receives no snowfall either. It seemed for years to be fit for not much more than grazing. Then the pumping of underground waters was resorted to until they proved insufficient. Now the valley receives the surplus water from the mountains of northern California through the canals of the Central Valley project. The forest growth in the inner valley made it attractive to American pioneers. It had no burdensome stand to clear away. But the slopes of the Sierra Nevadas, which catch rainfall or snowfall all year, were a valuable timber area.

The first step toward civilized life in California was taken by a religious institution, the Spanish mission, which moved into California from a base in Mexico. Not only in California but in all the Spanish borderlands of the United States, the mission was one of the earliest carriers of civilization. Missions rank among the great frontier institutions shaping history in what is now the United States. In the Spanish borderlands of the South and Southwest, they were the symbol of frontier advance, as was the fur-trade post of the French advance and the log cabin of the Anglo-American.

Missions in the Spanish borderlands were semi-official institutions, given government support in various forms. They obtained the use of public lands for grazing and farming, though not title to the lands. They had presidios located near them for protection from foreign or Indian encroachment. Each mission also had the protection of a squad of guards drawn from a nearby presidio. California missions received financial support from the so-called Pious Fund, which had been established by Mexican and Spanish Catholics toward the end of the 17th century.

Since missions were costly to the Spanish government new ones were reluctantly undertaken at times when the government was in financial stress. One such period was the middle of the 18th century, when the Spanish treasury was chronically bankrupt.

Funds were not devoted then to such purposes unless the advance of some rival power threatened the safety of Spanish territorial possessions. In the case of California consent was given to creating new missions only after the threat of the Russian advance down the Northwest coast had developed. Then, in 1769, the San Diego mission was established, the first Spanish mission in Upper California. Others were later built at Monterey, Los Angeles, and elsewhere in rapid succession.

A California mission was normally a three-unit affair. The central unit was a cluster consisting of a chapel, the homes of the mission fathers, and the workshops and storehouses. A second unit, lying near the first, was the Indian village, where lived the neophytes, those Indians who had been persuaded to accept baptism. They were regarded as having consented to undergo a period of instruction. Having committed themselves, they were not free to leave the mission until the instruction had been completed. The third unit was the headquarters of a small military garrison, of a half dozen or dozen soldiers, who were thought necessary to keep the neophytes in order and to bring back any runaways. The garrison also provided escorts for the missionaries when they traveled.

The missions were great industrial schools. They offered the men training in the best methods in agriculture and herding, and the industrial arts of blacksmithing, tanning, and weaving. Women were given training in cooking, sewing, and spinning. Some of the teaching was done by Indians who had been trained in the older mission establishments of Spanish America.

The California missions were intended to be temporary. The theory under which they were established was that no long period of time would be necessary to complete the work of Christianizing and civilizing the Indians of any locality. As soon as the work in one locality had been completed the fathers would move on to a new frontier. The Indians, who had become civilized, would be given the buildings, the improved lands, and the herds of cattle they had helped to raise. Secular clergy would be called in to replace the mission fathers as spiritual guides. The mission, in short, would be secularized. Such was the theory of the missions and it was attractive: The Indians were to be won to Christianity, trained in the practical arts, and raised to the position of loyal subjects of the Spanish Crown.

The number of missions in Upper California was considerable—21 at the height of their prosperity. They occupied all the side valleys of the Upper California coast, and were all of the Franciscan Order. The number of Indians undergoing training was 21,000 souls in the period just preceding secularization, which was about one-fourth of the total number of California Indians and half of those within reach.

The missions were, in general, self-supporting. Their properties in the form of buildings, herds of cattle, and stores of grain were large. The cattle multiplied with little care. Each spring they would be gathered in a big roundup. Newborn calves would be branded; grown steers would be slaughtered. The meat would be salted down; the hides and tallow would be exported. Hides and tallow were the first important California exports. Tallow, the fat of slaughtered cattle, was melted to eliminate fibrous matter, then hardened, and used for candles and soap.

Other units of civilization besides the missions existed in California. There were a few incorporated towns or pueblos, a few private ranches and presidios. But the missions were the most important units of civilization.

A controversy regarding the missions and their status developed in Spain in the latter half of the 18th century. It was part of a larger controversy occurring in Spain and in Latin America between the clericals and the anticlericals. The clericals were in general the conservatives, who regarded the Church and missionary orders as bulwarks not only of Christianity but of law and society in Spain and in the empire. They believed these orders should be supported by the government and given a free rein. The anticlericals had been influenced by the rationalism in religion of the 18th century and by the radicalism in politics of revolutionary France. They wished to loosen the grip of the Church and the mission orders on the life of Spain and of the empire. Throughout the closing years of the 18th century and the early years of the 19th, these two points of view were in clash in Spain and in America.

The specific issue fought over in America was how long the missionaries should be allowed to keep Indians in training before the property of their establishments should be distributed. In other words, how many years of training should precede secularization. The clericals, and the missionary orders themselves, favored a long period of training, and felt that a premature secularization would be disastrous. They were willing to leave to the friars the decision as to the timing of secularization.

On the other hand, among anticlericals the feeling was that the training period should be brief, that the timing of secularization ought to be decided by the civil authorities and that if it was left to the missionary orders, the determining factor would be reluctance to give up property and power.

A complication in the issue arose from the fact that in Middle America, where the missionizing of the Indians began, the neophytes had been relatively advanced in their level of civilization. They had been much more advanced than those of California at the time of contact. The training time needed there had been relatively brief—only about ten years. This had set a kind of standard.

The cultural level of the California Indians was low, and, if they were secularized prematurely, they would be likely to squander the property they had received, or lose it to white land sharks. Premature secularization would leave the Indians worse off than they had been before.

Another complication was that, to many Mexico City politicians who were of the anticlerical party, secularization was attractive for the opportunity it would offer to obtain the spoils that would attend a distribution of mission property to Indians.

In 1813 a secularization law was pushed through the Spanish Cortes, or Parliament, which was to apply generally to all the missions in Spanish America, including those in California. It provided that all missions which had been in existence for ten years or more should be secularized. In the process of secularization each Indian in the mission should receive lands sufficient for his needs. He should also receive his share of the other properties of the mission. Any undistributed lands should revert to the Crown. The secularized Indians were to be organized into self-governing pueblos, under the spiritual guidance of secular clergy. The mission fathers were to move on to new frontiers. This law, however, never went into effect. Its implementation was halted by revolts against Spanish authority, which in 1813 were already under way in large parts of Latin America.

In 1821, with the independence of Mexico established, the center of the secularization conflict was transferred to Mexico City. In the subsequent clashing there, the California friars were in an even weaker position than before. They had become discredited in the Mexican Republic by having remained loyal to Spain in the struggle for independence. They had been the Tories of that war, traitors to the Republic. They were subjected to a campaign of abusive propaganda by the anticlericals, who accused them of gross neglect of the Indians under their care and of actual mistreatment. Such charges were accepted at face value by Protestant commentators who wrote before the great work of Father Zephyrin Engelhardt, the historian of the missions, was published, and before the records of the missions, now at Santa Barbara, had been used by dispassionate scholars.

One of the charges against the friars was that they had reduced the Indians under their care to a state of slavery. An element of truth lay in the charge. For the Indians, having accepted baptism, were regarded as having agreed to a period of instruction, and were not free thereafter to return to their wandering life. Indians in the missions sometimes tired of the uplift ideas of the missionaries. They were irked by the requirements of regular labor and regular worship imposed on them. Indian habits of life were contrary to regularity or discipline of any kind, particularly regularity of labor. The missionaries found it necessary, in the case of recalcitrant Indians, to resort to coercion. That gave the whole system an unpleasant aspect of slavery. Indian training could easily be pictured by the enemies of the missionaries as a form of servitude. Corporal punishment was sometimes necessary as a last resort in the case of rebellious neophytes. Some mission fathers were more severe in their discipline than others. But the testimony of impartial travelers in California is that heavy physical punishment was quite unusual, that on the whole the missionaries were patient and indulgent with the Indians, and were beloved by the Indians. But such corporal punishments as were inflicted could be distorted by the anticlericals into charges of systematic brutality.

One of the most serious charges against the missionaries was that the health of the Indians was broken by overwork and neglect, and that the mortality rate among them was excessively high. This accusation also had some basis in fact. The mortality rate among the mission Indians was unquestionably high. But the cause of it was not overwork or neglect. The California Indians were unclean in their habits. Indians up and down the Pacific coast allowed filth to accumulate about their villages. Village sites were overrun with vermin. When one site became intolerable, Indians simply moved to another.

Coastal Indians, even in their free wandering life, were periodically visited by fearful epidemics of fever, smallpox, and other diseases. The records of fur traders and explorers contain accounts of the decimation of whole areas by epidemics. Gathering such natives into mission villages increased the dangers of epidemics. The missionaries did their best to keep the huts and bodies of the Indians clean. Still, in the absence of the germ knowledge of disease, the death rate was very high. In the period before Pasteur the death rate from contagious disease was high everywhere, disastrously high in American cities. But the high mortality rate among the mission Indians gave plausibility to charges of neglect.

One of the items of friction between the civil authorities and the missionaries was payment for the food supplied to soldiers in the presidios. The cost of the food was supposed to be borne by the Mexican government. The missionaries, who were called upon to do the providing, received government drafts in payment, but these were hardly ever honored. At the end of the mission period unhonored drafts, amounting to half a million dollars, were held by the California missionaries.

The character of the troops was another source of contention. The troops used were the offscourings of Mexican jails. They corrupted the Indian women and men faster than the friars could uplift them.

In 1833, after a long controversy, the Mexican Congress, under the leadership of Santa Anna, who was an anticlerical, passed a law providing for the secularization of the California missions. That law was amplified in 1834 into a concrete plan of gradual secularization. Ten of the 21 missions were to be secularized first—the remainder later. Commissioners were to be appointed by the California authorities, who were to direct the distribution of the mission property.

Under this plan every Indian adult or family in a mission was given an allotment of land from the area used by the mission. The allotment was made under restrictions as to sale, as a protection to the Indians. Any land undistributed was to revert to the government, and to be used for incoming settlers. The movable property of the missions was also to be secularized. Some was to go to the Indians. The rest was to be held by the commissioners and gradually sold, with the proceeds to be used for religious and educational purposes.

Until secular clergy could be provided, the Indians were to remain under the spiritual guidance of the friars. Civil jurisdiction was conferred on the government commissioners. Ultimately the natives were to be organized into regular pueblos and to be so governed. This scheme of secularization was put into effect, and by 1835, 15 of the 21 missions had been secularized.

The results were disastrous. Much of the property distributed to the Indians passed into the hands of whites. The Indians became laborers serving rancheros, or they scattered to the mountains. Only a few remained to work their lands under the care of the mission fathers. Mission herds were slaughtered off, often merely for hides and tallow—the meat was wasted. This squandering was attributed by the anticlericals to the mission fathers, who were charged with seeking to liquidate their property. The newer researches into the problem, however, indicate that the slaughtering was at the order of the Mexican commissioners appointed to carry out secularization.

In 1835 the Mexican government tried to put a halt to further secularization, but its orders were not carried out. In 1843 the governor in California ordered that whatever remained of the mission land and property be left under missionary care. This order was defeated by a local revolution in which the governor was expelled. In 1845 a measure was adopted by the California legislature that all remaining mission property should be leased or sold. This measure was at once carried out by the local authorities in spite of a last-minute revocation of it by the Mexican Congress. When the United States took over California, the legality of all the later sales and leases was tested in the United States courts and ultimately some of the chapels, with the lands immediately adjacent to them, were restored to the Franciscan Order.

The California mission program thus ended in failure. Its chief contribution was to leave attractive mission buildings to the future. But elsewhere in Latin America the missions were more successful, and millions of natives got what they knew of Spanish civilization directly or indirectly from the teachings of the friars.

The Bear Flag Revolt

IN THE SETTLEMENT of Upper California grants of land for colonization were a relatively late development. Few were made in the Spanish era—not more than 30, all told. In the Mexican period grants were authorized by the federal colonization law of August 18, 1824. The law was general in its terms; details were left to be worked out by local authorities. Empresarios were not employed in Upper California as they were in Texas. The governor made grants directly to settlers, with the approval of the Deputación, the legislative council. With the secularization of the missions grants became more numerous.

Grants were assumed to be for grazing purposes. Each was made on condition that the grantee put a specified number of cattle on the land. They were of a size that might vary from one square league (4438 acres) to eleven. The average size in the period 1833–48 was five square leagues (22,190 acres).

The boundaries assigned to grants were inexact. Sometimes they were oral. The terms of written grants were likely to be vague. No surveying of boundaries was required. There never was a surveyor employed by the government in California throughout the Mexican period. Even prescribed legal forms were carelessly administered. The confusion of land titles was so great that after the United States took over in 1848, a land commission was set up by Congress in 1851 to clear it away. The average length of time required to get the early grants cleared of confusion was seventeen years.

The portion of California first granted away under this system was the coastal region, the valleys and the coves that had hitherto been used, in part, by the missions. Later the interior valley was disposed of in the same manner. One of the best known of the interior valley grants was made in 1839–41 to a Swiss, John A. Sutter, the grant where gold was subsequently discovered in 1848. It was located in the Sacramento Valley. It was of maximum size—eleven square leagues. It was intended by Sutter to become the foundation for a kind of baronial estate, worked for him by tenants and laborers. The tenants and laborers, Sutter thought, would be imported from his native Switzerland; the grant was named New Helvetia.

Altogether, some 800 grants totaling more than 9 million acres were made by 1846, mostly in the coastal area, but a number were in the Sacramento Valley. They went chiefly to Mexicans. They were normally used for ranching and brought only a slight population. In 1845 there were probably not more than 7000 Mexican settlers in the whole of Upper California.

American interest in California began in the closing years of the 18th century. It was a fur-trade interest, directed at first to obtaining sea otter, whose fur was greatly desired in China, and later to the trapping of beaver in the interior, for the European market. The fur trade in California was never as important as that of the Oregon Country. In general, California furs were not as good, or as numerous, as those further north.

In 1822 a new American interest began, the hide and tallow trade. A distinctly Boston business, it was opened by a Boston ship, the *Sachem,* and a Boston firm, Bryant and Sturgis, was the most important company engaged in it. The trade was at first chiefly with the mission establishments. The Boston commodities brought to California were cutlery, finery, and Yankee notions. They were sold from shipboard, on vessels moored in the harbors. A ship would be rigged up like a department store as soon as it anchored. Then invitations were sent to prospective customers, the missionaries, rancheros, and California ladies, to come out to do their shopping. In payment for such goods, tallow was obtained from the great storage vats of the missions. It was shipped to Peru, where it was turned into candles for use in homes and in silver mines. The hides went to New England, where they were used in harness and shoe manufacturing. San Pedro, near the San Gabriel mission, and San Diego were shipping centers for this trade. The classic account of the trade is Richard Henry Dana's *Two Years Before the Mast.* Dana was a clerk in the employ of Bryant and Sturgis. He was a Harvard undergraduate whose health suffered from over-application, and who went to sea to recover.

After the secularization of the missions the hide and tallow trade was carried on chiefly with rancheros, and it continued to be primarily a New England interest. As it expanded, Yankee agents were employed by New England companies to remain the year round in California ports. In some cases they adopted Roman Catholicism and married California heiresses. A considerable merchant class, largely of New England origin, came thus to occupy the coastal towns. It was influential and worked quietly for the annexation of California to the United States. The American government kept a consul, Thomas Larkin, at Monterey, who, in 1845, was also made a confidential agent of the State Department.

In the inner valley of California lived Americans of a different type, frontiersmen, for the most part from the Mississippi Valley. The earliest of them were broken-down mountain trappers, who were reinforced by deserters from American trading vessels. In the early 1840's pioneers began to come from the Missouri, Arkansas, and Kentucky frontiers. Pioneers could buy lands in the interior valley from native Californians for ridiculously small sums. In 1837 Dr. John Marsh, a Harvard graduate, purchased a 15,000-acre ranch in the Sacramento Valley from a native Californian for $500.

A large-scale pioneer movement into the Sacramento Valley began in the early 1840's—about the same time as the movement into Oregon. The same forces were operating to move Mississippi Valley frontiersmen to this valley as were sending them to Oregon. One was the Panic of 1837 and the long depression that followed. Another was the agricultural attractiveness of the valley, which was widely advertised in the American press. A third was the excellence of the California climate— and especially the absence of malaria, the curse of most American frontier regions. But in California, so the story ran, "there was never a man who had malarial chills except one. He was from Missouri and carried the disease in his system. It was such a novelty to see a man shiver and shake with the chills of malaria that people traveled from a radius of 15 to 20 miles around to see it." Even in that early day Californians were immodest about their climate.

Another factor in this large-scale movement was the publicity of American land speculators in the Central Valley. John Marsh, for instance, who was eager to attract Americans to California, sent booster letters to newspapers in Missouri, Arkansas, and elsewhere, setting forth the favorable terms on which land could be obtained in California.

Sometimes this propaganda was false or misleading. In 1842 an article appeared in a St. Louis journal in which the assertion was made that Americans could obtain liberal land grants in California on the sole condition of taking an oath of allegiance to Mexico and adopting Roman Catholicism. The article ignored the fact that in 1842 the Mexican Congress enacted a law forbidding further land acquisition or settlement by foreigners in California except by special permission of the authorities in Mexico City. The St. Louis article was widely copied in newspapers of the Mississippi Valley, though it was denounced by the Mexican minister in Washington as false propaganda of land speculators.

The movement to the Sacramento Valley was stimulated by Captain John Sutter, whose initial immigration scheme for New Helvetia did not have much success. He kept an agent at Fort Hall on the Oregon Trail to deflect pioneers to California who had set out for Oregon. Sutter was hospitable to Americans, and his fort at the junction of the Sacramento and the American rivers became a center of American influence in the interior. Also, many Oregon settlers, dissatisfied with the Willamette Valley, came down to the valley of California. This was a manifestation of a fundamental pioneer trait, a conviction that the best and most attractive lands were those just a little further on.

Migration by caravan to California began in 1841, when the Bartleson-Bidwell party arrived from the Missouri frontier. Thereafter the caravans became steadily larger. By 1846 there were 500 to 800 Americans in California, and observers were predicting that California would go the way of Texas. The number of native Californians in the province was ten times that of the Americans, but they were disorganized, quarreling, and indolent, and no match for the Americans.

The administration of California was ineffective, partly because of the distance of the province from Mexico City, 1500 miles over mountains and deserts. Communication by sea was infrequent, since Mexico had virtually no merchant marine. The instruments of Mexican authority in the province were a governor and a *comandante-general,* neither able to enforce respect for law. When a governor was unpopular he was simply deposed by the people and sent home. Only as much of Mexican law was obeyed in California as the people wanted to accept. The province was for all practical purposes a self-governing republic.

It was, however, disorderly and chaotic, torn from end to end by sectional and personal rivalries. The governor's headquarters were in the south. Those of the *comandante-general* were on the northern frontier. These two, and their factions, were always at daggers points. Revolutions were frequent. There were four in the twelve years prior to 1846. None of them, however, involved much bloodshed. In the last the casualties were two horses killed on one side and a mule wounded on the other. Chaotic conditions of this sort were an invitation to outside aggression.

In the United States an increasing interest was taken in this derelict province in the early 1840's, stimulated by a number of developments. In 1844, by the Cushing Treaty, the China trade was opened more widely to the United States than ever before. In addition to Canton, the treaty made accessible four more ports, the "Treaty Ports." The China trade had always interested Americans. The likelihood of a large increase in it emphasized the need for a good harbor on the Pacific coast and drew attention increasingly to the harbor of San Francisco. At that time no harbors on the coast in Oregon had been acquired by the United States.

In the early 1840's numerous publications, some issued by the United States government, appeared, all enthusiastically describing California's beauties. In 1845 came Frémont's *Report,* including his California travels. In the preceding year appeared Lieutenant Charles Wilkes's *Narrative of the United States Exploring Expedition,* which had a wide reading. At about the same time came Dana's *Two Years Before the Mast,* Alfred Robinson's *Life in California,* Lanford W. Hastings's *Emigrants' Guide to Oregon and California,* and many others.

The interest of the American public was kept active in the 1840's by the fear that Great Britain was about to seize the province. The fear was groundless. The British government had no designs on California. It wished only to prevent California's falling into American hands. Still the Tyler and Polk administrations professed to fear English aggression. All this interest in California, both of the public and of the government, was reflected in American diplomacy.

In 1842 the American minister to Mexico was instructed by the Secretary of State, Daniel Webster, to obtain all of Upper California, if possible, or at least San Francisco, in exchange for the damage claims of American citizens against Mexico. In the same year the tri-partite arrangement was proposed by Webster to Lord Ashburton in the Webster-Ashburton negotiation. This was a proposal that the Oregon Country, which the United States and England were contesting with each other, should be divided by a line of boundary pleasing to the English, the line of the Columbia River to the sea, that would leave to Britain all the harbor waters inside the Strait of Juan de Fuca. Britain, in return, would take a position of benevolent neutrality toward a peaceful American acquisition of the portion of Upper California containing the harbor of San Francisco. Under the proposal Mexico would yield the area in exchange for the cancellation of the unpaid damage claims of American citizens. This suggestion was submitted by Ashburton to the British government. It was toyed with there for a time, but then rejected.

In 1842 the commander of an American squadron in the Pacific, Commodore

Thomas ap Catesby Jones, hearing a report that war had broken out between the United States and Mexico, seized the port of Monterey and hoisted the American flag. When the report proved to be false, he withdrew and apologized. But his act revealed the temper of American naval policy in the Pacific.

In 1845, Secretary of State Buchanan sent an extraordinary instruction to Thomas Larkin, the confidential agent at Monterey. Larkin was instructed to quietly let California leaders know that if California would set herself free from Mexico and apply to the United States for annexation, it would be welcomed. Larkin was ordered to win the goodwill of the California leaders as a means of converting them to the idea of annexation to the United States. The original of these instructions was sent by sea and ultimately reached Larkin. In the meantime a special courier, Lieutenant Archibald Gillespie of the Marine Corps, was sent to California by way of Mexico. He was given a copy of the instructions to be committed to memory and destroyed, which was done. Once out of Mexico on a vessel bound for Monterey, he wrote out the instructions from memory with exemplary accuracy and in this form in mid-April delivered them to Larkin.

In late 1845 John C. Frémont, a captain in the U.S. Army, in charge of an exploring party of 65 men, arrived in California. He obtained permission from the local California authorities to winter there. But his actions aroused their suspicions and in the spring he was ordered to leave. At first he defied the order and raised the American flag over his camp. Then he changed his mind and started northward toward the Oregon Country. On the way he was overtaken by Lieutenant Gillespie, who had come up from Monterey after delivering the State Department's instructions to Larkin. What message passed between Gillespie and Frémont was never revealed. It was not inquired about in the case of Gillespie, who soon died. It would not be divulged by Frémont. It was probably a mere repetition of the Larkin instructions. Personal letters were also delivered to Frémont, who was a son-in-law of Senator Benton. Later in life he hinted he had received a special message from Benton. But it is unlikely that the message conveyed any sanction from Benton for imperialistic adventures. Benton was opposed to acquiring Mexican territory by force, and Frémont's letters to his wife of that period indicated no encouragement of rash moves from Benton.

If the message delivered to Frémont was merely a repetition of the Larkin dispatch, Frémont put the wrong construction on it. He supposed that the American government desired a revolution in California by any means whatever. What Buchanan wanted was something more subtle—a revolution carried out by the natives of California with the United States merely smiling approval. Whatever the nature of the message, Frémont immediately turned back and established his force on a ridge not far from Sutter's settlement. His return, in defiance of Mexican authority, led to the belief on the part of the more volatile American pioneers in the interior valley that a revolt by them would be supported by the American government. A revolt was accordingly staged in mid-June 1846, before news of the outbreak of the Mexican War reached California. The Bear Flag Republic was proclaimed, and Sonoma, just north of San Francisco Bay, was seized. The revolt and the occupation of Sonoma were supported by Frémont's forces. This seizure of a Mexican city was later explained by Frémont as intended to prevent bloodshed. As a result of Frémont's actions, the strategy of Buchanan and probably of Polk with regard to California was defeated.

This strategy was to have a revolution by native Californians, secretly encouraged by Consul Larkin. Frémont's activity made the revolution a rising by Americans.

The result was that the native Californians were resentful and resisted the Bear Flag uprising, which seemed to them part of a conquest of California by Americans, led by a United States Army officer. When, in the Mexican War, which followed immediately, an American force under General Stephen W. Kearny marched into southern California from Santa Fe, it was met by a hostile force of native Californians, the battle of San Pasqual had to be fought, and California had to be taken by conquest.

Frémont was a man quite without judgment, as his whole subsequent career indicates. He quarreled violently with Kearny, who commanded operations in California during the war. He was court-martialed for insubordination. Fifteen years later, as commanding officer of the Missouri Department in the Civil War, he played politics with the emancipation issue and had to be relieved of his command by Lincoln. After the Civil War he became a railroad promoter, none too scrupulous or successful. In France he was indicted for the sale of railroad securities by means of misleading advertisements. His private affairs were badly managed. The Bear Flag revolt was merely an early instance of his blunderings.

One of the most scholarly accounts of the Bear Flag revolution is a history written by an eminent Harvard philosopher, Josiah Royce. This appears in his *History of California*. Royce did original work on the Bear Flag revolt, and his book is an American classic. He did his best to extract from Frémont, who was still alive when the book was written, a statement of the nature of the message which had passed from Lieutenant Gillespie to him, but Frémont refused to tell. That was a secret that remained to tantalize historians.

The Bear Flag revolt is another illustration of the influence of physiography on American history. The California valley, like the Texas prairie, was a magnet that irresistibly drew American pioneers from the Mississippi Valley frontier. Given the character of these pioneers and the weakness of Mexican administration in California, the revolt and seizure of the province at the first opportunity was almost inevitable.

The War with Mexico

ON THE MORNING of May 11, 1846, President Polk sent Congress a special message announcing war with Mexico. He declared in it that a large body of Mexican troops had crossed the boundary of the United States, had invaded American territory, and had shed American blood on American soil. He closed with the words: "War exists . . . by the act of Mexico herself." He asked Congress to meet a requirement of the Constitution by a formal declaration of a war that was in progress. This was the first instance in American history of a notice by a President to Congress that the nation was at war before a war declaration had been made by Congress.

The boundary crossed by the Mexican troops was the Rio Grande. If this was truly the boundary it had only recently become so, as recently as December 1845, when Texas was formally made a state of the Union. The Rio Grande had never, in earlier history, been the Texan boundary. The Spanish government had set the boundary in 1816 at the Nueces River, which runs 130 miles north and east of the Rio Grande, and the Mexican government had made no change. On all reliable maps of the period the Nueces appeared as the boundary and such sturdy Americans as Stephen F. Austin, Andrew Jackson, Thomas Hart Benton, Martin Van Buren, and John C. Calhoun had accepted it as such.

However, when the Mexican President, Santa Anna, was captured by the Texans after the battle of San Jacinto in 1836, he signed at Velasco an agreement that Texas might be permitted to extend to the Rio Grande. The agreement was at once repudiated by the Mexican Congress, the final treaty-making body under the Mexican Constitution. Later in the same year the Congress of Texas asserted a claim more extensive than that of the Velasco agreement. It declared that the boundary of Texas at the southwest and west was the Rio Grande from its mouth to its source and thence northward to latitude 42°. This meant an enormous expansion of Texas, more than twice its original size. It brought Santa Fe, the capital of the Mexican territory of New Mexico, within the confines of Texas. The claim had not been asserted with much confidence as originally made. It had been advanced for bargaining purposes. Insofar as it related to the region between the Nueces and the Rio Grande the land was occupied by Mexican ranchers, settlers, and troops. But Polk chose, after the annexation of Texas, to consider the claim valid. This was the basic issue in 1846 between the United States and Mexico.

In the background of the Mexican War were other grievances of the United States and Mexico against each other. An old grievance of the United States was the injuries American citizens had suffered in the recurring Mexican revolutions, and the Mexican government's failure to pay for supplies that American citizens had furnished on credit. In 1839 the Mexican government agreed to the submission of these claims to a mixed commission. Claims to the amount of about $8,500,000 were reviewed, of which about a quarter was found to be valid. The rest proved to be fraudulent or heavily padded. The Mexican government undertook to pay the valid claims in installments, but went bankrupt after three had been paid and defaulted on the remainder. The defaulted payments seemed to Polk a major grievance. Their total, as afterward set and assumed by the American government, was $3,250,000. By comparison American states and corporations were in default at this time on bonds held in England to a total estimated at $200 million, as critics of the war pointed out.

As described more fully below, another grievance of the Polk government was the refusal of the Mexican government to receive John Slidell, an American minister, who had gone to Mexico City at the invitation of the Mexican government.

Mexican grievances were more numerous and more substantial than those of the American government. One was the failure of American officials to effectively enforce the nation's neutrality obligations during the Texan uprising. American public sentiment had been overwhelmingly hostile to Mexico and favorable to Texas. It had been outraged by the extermination of a Texan force of 200 men, caught by a Mexican army in the Alamo at San Antonio, and by the execution, several weeks later, of the greater part of a force of 400 Texans at Goliad, who had surrendered on promise of life. As a result of this feeling, American adventurers flocked to the aid of the Texans in armed companies, organized as far northward as Cincinnati and Pittsburgh. They had marched as on parade to the Sabine, where they broke ranks and crossed as individuals. On the Texan side they re-formed and marched to the aid of Houston. Ostensibly they were peaceful immigrants. They did carry rifles, but pioneers to the West normally did so for defense against Indians. The fact that they were military formations was joyfully proclaimed in local newspapers. The only persons remaining ignorant of their military objectives were the federal authorities at the Sabine boundary. Other motives than sympathy for the Texans had lured American volunteers to the ranks of Houston. An important consideration was the land bounties offered by the Texan legislature to volunteers—a square mile of land for six months' service, two square miles for a year's service.

Under federal law Americans who enrolled in an armed expedition against a country with which the United States was at peace were subject to a heavy fine and imprisonment. The Army and the Navy were at the service of the President to carry out the law's provisions. But President Jackson, whose sympathies were with the Texans, had no heart for a vigorous enforcement of those laws. The State Department files for this period are filled with protests from the Mexican minister concerning the violation of American neutrality obligations by bodies of armed men moving to the aid of the Texans. The evidence offered was excerpts from local newspapers in the Southwest describing, in vivid detail, the departure of armed companies bound for Texas. The replies of the Secretary of State or of his assistant were always assurances, obtained from local district attorneys of the United States, that the companies were composed of peaceful emigrants.

Another Mexican grievance of the same period was the so-called Gaines affair. General E. P. Gaines, the commander of the American Army on the Sabine, was openly partisan to the Texans. On a rumor that an Indian war had broken out beyond the border he ordered a force of American troops to cross the boundary and to occupy the town of Nacogdoches in the summer and autumn of 1836. What he had in mind is still a mystery. The occupation was so indefensible that Gaines was finally disavowed and sent to a different frontier.

A third Mexican grievance was the Jones affair, the capture of the port of Monterey, California, in 1842. Though Commodore Jones evacuated it the next day, the episode was a legitimate grievance against the United States.

The heaviest Mexican grievance was the annexation of Texas. This was not in itself a valid grievance. Texas had maintained its independence for nine years and its decision as to its future was its own. Yet the notorious part Americans had played in winning their independence gave to annexation the appearance of dismemberment of Mexico by the United States.

The advent of the Mexican War is best traced in terms of chronology. On March 1, 1845, Congress adopted the Joint Resolution of Annexation of Texas. The Mexican minister in protest asked for, and received, his passports, and the American minister, at the request of Mexico, was recalled. On June 15, an order was sent to Brigadier General Zachary Taylor to have his army of several thousand men "on or near the Rio Grande" as soon as he should receive word of the result of the July 4 vote of the Texas people on annexation. The news of the vote came promptly. By August 1, Taylor had stationed his troops at Corpus Christi on the right bank of the Nueces near its mouth, just within the disputed area. Ostensibly he was there for defensive purposes in case Mexico reacted to annexation by military action.

The Mexican government, instead, made a diplomatic move. On October 15, its Foreign Office sent word to the American State Department that it was willing to receive a "commissioner" to settle the Texas affair. In November, the American government sent to Mexico City an "envoy extraordinary and minister plenipotentiary," John Slidell, a Southerner, later famous as a Confederate agent to England.

The instructions he carried are a revelation of Polk's ambitions and methods. He was to demand immediate payment of the American damage claims, though it was clear they could not be paid. He was to suggest that these claims be assumed by the United States in return for a boundary that would be the Rio Grande from its mouth to its source and thence due north to 42°. An additional payment of $5 million was to be offered for all of New Mexico. For California and the area eastward to the Rio Grande, Slidell could offer $25 million. "Money would be no object," Slidell was told, "compared with the value of the acquisition."

Slidell's departure on this mission was intended to be secret. But secrets were hard to keep in Polk's day. Rumors of the mission and half-informed guesses as to the instructions were soon circulating in the press and, more to the point, in the press of Mexico City.

When Slidell arrived in Mexico City in December 1845 the government refused to receive him. It was disposed to come to terms with its powerful neighbor, but fearful of doing so. The Mexican press believed that Slidell's instructions were to acquire vast stretches of Mexican territory other than Texas. The government was menaced by an army commanded by a rebellious general, Mariano Paredes, an extreme nationalist. It based its refusal on the valid ground that it had agreed to receive only a commissioner to settle the Texas issue. It may have nursed hopes, also, that the United States would become embroiled in a war with Great Britain by its grasping Oregon policy, which would reduce pressures on Mexico. Slidell withdrew, finally, in discouragement, but waited outside Mexico City for the impending revolution. The revolution did occur, bringing Paredes to power. But he was no more inclined than his predecessor to receive Slidell.

When Polk received word of these rebuffs he resorted, in January 1846, to tactics of pressure. He ordered the army of Zachary Taylor, held until then at Corpus Christi, to advance across the territory in dispute. This was a belligerent order, and was implemented in the same spirit. On arrival at the mouth of the Rio Grande, Taylor erected a fort there and emplaced cannon so as to command the public square of the Mexican port of Matamoros on the opposite side. He also sent naval units to blockade the city, so that food could not move by sea to the Mexican garrison. An explosive situation was created, out of which an incident soon developed. On April 24, a Mexican force crossed the Rio Grande well above its mouth. It encountered a reconnoitering party of 60 American dragoons and surrounded it. The dragoons undertook to fight their way out. They failed, with three killed, a number wounded, and the rest taken prisoner.

News of the affair reached Polk late on Saturday, May 9. Before its arrival he was already in a warlike frame of mind. Slidell had reached Washington the previous day and had described to the President in exasperation his luckless mission. He felt that the only recourse left to the American government for redressing the wrongs inflicted by Mexico on American citizens was to take matters into its own hands and to do it promptly. Polk agreed. At a cabinet meeting the next morning the President announced his intention of sending a war message to Congress on the succeeding Tuesday. He felt confident an aggression would be committed by the Mexicans at Matamoros. All the Cabinet except George Bancroft, Secretary of the Navy, agreed with Polk. Buchanan, in agreeing, indicated he would have felt better if a hostile act had already been committed. The President began writing the message. Late in the afternoon word arrived of the hostile Mexican act. The Cabinet was hastily reconvened and without demur agreed to an immediate war message. The President devoted the evening and the next day to the writing, with regrets that he must use the Sabbath that way. He combined the issues of the claims and the boundary, declaring he had not for a moment entertained the thought that the claims "should be postponed or separated from the settlement of the boundary question." The cup of forbearance had been exhausted before any clash on the border had occurred. Now Mexico "has passed the boundary of the United States, has invaded our territory, and shed American blood upon American soil." "War exists, and, notwithstanding all our efforts to avoid it, exists by the act of Mexico herself."

In Congress the message was heard with mixed feelings. It was cheered by expansionists and by all who had ears close to the ground. It evoked dismay in the opposition, among both Whigs and Democrats. Its thesis that an American boundary had been crossed, that American territory had been invaded, that American blood had been shed on American soil, became a battleground in itself. A dissident Whig, John J. Crittenden, pointed out at once that when the Joint Resolution to annex Texas had come before Congress, few persons had considered the Rio Grande the boundary. Another Kentucky Whig, Garrett Davis, declared forthrightly that all the area between the Nueces and the Rio Grande was Mexican soil. Others declared it was at least debatable soil.

A war bill came before the House with the President's message. Prepared on the Sabbath by the Committee on Military Affairs, it was destined to become a fighting issue in both houses. As initially submitted it was politically inoffensive, merely a bill "to authorize the President of the United States, under certain contingencies, therein named, to accept the services of volunteers, and for other purposes." But a Democrat obtained a new preamble, which was held to be necessary to give formal congressional recognition to a state of war. It read, in final form: "Whereas, by the act of the Republic of Mexico, a state of war exists between that Government and the United States." To dissident Whigs and Democrats, this seemed designed to confront them with the harsh dilemma of endorsing the President's thesis as to the origin of the war, or of voting to reject a supply bill, thus opening themselves to the charge of preventing the rescue of imperiled American troops.

A virtual gag on debate was imposed, especially in the House. A war-minded majority, "haughty and dominating," as described by the opposition, insisted on approving the bill the day it was presented, despite voluminous documents that came with the bill. They amounted, as printed ultimately in the congressional set, to 144 pages. Selections from them were read by the Clerk of the House, but a real examination of them in the course of debate was impossible.

In other ways debate was muzzled. Whigs, on rising to the floor, became invisible to the Speaker. To gain the floor Garrett Davis had to resort to a parliamentary trick. He asked to be heard on a point of personal privilege, which was that he wished to be excused from voting. Such a request could not be denied. On obtaining the floor he took longer than expected to state his reasons. One of the reasons was the preamble. It was "so bold a falsehood" as to defile, at the outset, the whole bill. Its purpose was to force Whigs against their will to build a shelter over the administration. Other reasons were the denial of a chance to study the documents and to state what was in them. Davis questioned whether General Taylor, strengthened by militia from Texas and adjoining states, was in any peril, and even if he were, his fate would be settled before Washington could get help to him. The Whigs were willing to vote men and supplies instantly if the majority would only agree to remove that preamble from the bill. More reasons would have flowed forth except that Stephen Douglas interrupted with a point of order, namely, that all those reasons were an attack on the preamble rather than an elucidation of a request to be excused. Davis was ordered to desist. Another member of the opposition, Thomas Bayly, a moderate Democrat from Virginia, also requested to be excused and to give reasons. His reasons resembled those of Davis.

To forestall more requests a vote was hastily taken. It showed an overwhelming majority for the bill, 174 ayes, 14 nays. Abstentions were numerous, of which 25 were northern, 10 southern. In party terms they were 22 Democrats, 13 Whigs.

In the Senate the House bill was debated for a day. Part of the preceding day had been devoted to the President's message. The debate turned on the truth of the message, the form given to the House bill, and the precipitance of those demanding a vote. The minority demanded an opportunity to study the documents before voting. Especially eloquent were three Whigs—John M. Clayton of Delaware, later to be Secretary of State, John J. Crittenden of Kentucky, successor to Henry Clay, and John M. Berrien of Georgia. Clayton thought the President, by his orders to Taylor, had committed acts of war without consulting Congress. Moreover, the implementation of his orders—the pointing of cannon at Matamoros and the blocking off of the river—were as much aggression, he thought, as pointing a pistol at another's breast. The Crittenden view was that the American government ought to foster republicanism in the New World through continuing friendly relations with sister republics to the south, and especially with our nearest neighbor, which in her troubles should be dealt with in especial compassion. All the Whig speakers urged striking from the House bill the false and offensive preamble. Among Democrats, Calhoun was especially impressive. Not normally emotional, he declared he would find it more impossible to vote that preamble than to plunge a dagger into his own heart. With characteristic penetration of mind he went beyond the question of who had been the aggressor (he made clear that it had been Polk) to the more basic issue—whether a local rencontre, a mere skirmish between parts of armies on the Rio Grande, constituted war. War, he insisted, required a declaration by Congress in both republics, and he would not make war on Mexico by making war on our Constitution.

The vote in the Senate on the war bill was as one-sided as it had been in the House. It was 40 ayes, 2 nays. The valorous nays were Clayton of Delaware and John Davis of Massachusetts. The vote concealed, as it had in the House, as much as it disclosed. Benton voted aye, though he had told the President the day before that he disagreed with the war message and with the order given Taylor to advance to the Rio Grande. John A. Dix, of New York, voted aye, and wrote Van Buren four days later that the war was "a violation of every just consideration of national dignity, duty, and policy." Crittenden and William Upham, a Vermont Whig, voted "aye, except the preamble." Calhoun, Berrien, and George Evans, of Maine, declined to vote. A few days after the vote Calhoun declared that not 10 percent of Congress would have agreed to the war bill if time had been given to examine the documents. Eleven senators were absent, including Webster, who was out of town.

In the press the same criticism was made of the war bill as had been made in Congress. The Boston *Whig* contained a letter from Charles Francis Adams, in which he pronounced the preamble to the war bill "one of the grossest national lies that was ever deliberately told." He singled out for special attack Robert C. Winthrop, Boston's representative in Congress, who had voted for the war bill. Charles Sumner assailed Winthrop with even greater bitterness. He declared that Winthrop's hands were covered with blood. In the New York *Tribune* Horace Greeley wrote sarcastically: "Grant the Father of Lies his premises, and he will prove himself a truth-teller and a saint by faultless logic . . . only assume premises enough, as Polk does, and you may prove that it is New Orleans which has just been threatened with a cannonade instead of Matamoros, and that it is the Mississippi which has been formally blockaded by a stranger fleet and army instead of the Rio del Norte." In Washington the

National Intelligencer, another of the nation's great Whig dailies, used similar language.

After the excitement at the war's opening the political parties settled down to fixed positions. Whigs, North and South, were highly critical of the war. Administration Democrats upheld the war. In both parties, however, there were variations of criticism and of support.

Conservative northern Whigs emphasized the fraud and aggressiveness of the war. They wished to avoid the added charge, made by the radicals, that the primary aim of the Administration was the extension of slavery. Such an accusation offended southern Whigs, who, though opposed to the war, were slaveholders and were sensitive about attacks on slavery. Moreover, conservative northern Whigs were not wholly persuaded that slavery extension was the primary aim of the Administration.

In Massachusetts, Whigs upholding the moderate view included such politicians as Webster and Winthrop and such wealthy businessmen as Abbott Lawrence and Nathan Appleton, who were connected with the cotton belt by business ties. They were known as the Cotton Whigs. In Boston and in the North as a whole the conservatives outnumbered the radicals.

The evidence from which northern Whig conservatives drew the conclusion that the war was not a crusade to extend slavery was partly the stand taken by southern Whigs. Nearly all Whig leaders in the South, though slaveholders, were strenuous opponents of the war. The northern conservatives were fearful that if, in denouncing the war, they made the charge that its purpose was to extend slavery, they would offend their southern allies, destroy the unity of the party, and imperil even the Union. They also recognized that among the most conspicuous war hawks in the nation were northern Democratic expansionists. Radical northern Whigs, who drew the slavery issue into their opposition to the war, relied for their evidence upon the crusade for the annexation of Texas on the part of southern proslavery extremists.

The Democrats were likewise divided. They had come into power on a platform emphasizing expansionism and had been responsible for the adoption of the Joint Resolution annexing Texas with an unclear boundary. Many of their leaders, moreover, subscribed to the doctrine, recently come into prominence, that it was the Manifest Destiny of the United States to expand over all the continent of North America. Among the leaders of that view were such party figures as Vice-President George M. Dallas, James Buchanan, Robert J. Walker, George Bancroft, Caleb Cushing, and Stephen A. Douglas. They had no strong objections to slavery extension—they were willing to postpone the solution of that problem to a future day. Yet the Democratic party embraced a large body of antislavery radicals, personified by David Wilmot, John P. Hale, and Preston King. It contained, also, old-fashioned Jeffersonians, personified by Albert Gallatin. And finally it included Calhoun and his following in the South.

In view of all this diversity in both parties the overwhelming vote by which war was declared against Mexico needs to be explained. The explanation is found in a momentary hysteria which Polk converted into a stampede. Horace Greeley explained the vote in an editorial in the New York *Tribune* as a normal public response to an attack on the flag. The editorial, entitled ''Our Country, Right or Wrong!'' ran: ''This is the spirit in which a portion of the Press, which admits that our treatment of

Mexico has been ruffianly and piratical, and that the invasion of her territory by Gen. Taylor is a flagrant outrage, now exhorts our People to rally in all their strength, to lavish their blood and treasure in the vindictive prosecution of War on Mexico. We protest against such counsel.''

The tactic of stampede to carry the country into war was precisely what the framers of the Constitution had sought to prevent. They had sought to do it by writing the principle of checks and balances into the war provisions. A war-minded President was to be controlled by vesting in Congress the powers to declare war and to provide supplies. The framers had faith in Congress because it represented diverse interests and because its minorities would keep a rein on majorities. All those precautions failed in the crisis of May 11 and 12, 1846, because Polk had stampeded Congress and because minorities did not function.

The minorities failed in both parties. The Whigs did not function because, in the opinion of Henry Clay, they feared that if they voted against the war declaration they would meet the fate which had overtaken their predecessors, the Federalists, who had destroyed themselves by opposition to the War of 1812. Hesitant Democrats were equally quiet because of the party's stand on annexation in the Tyler adminis- tration—which had eventuated in the war.

Once the war declaration was approved by Whigs the party was committed to further support of the war. Most Whigs regularly voted supplies and men for the fighting, though they still denounced the war as iniquitous and unconstitutional. Even John Quincy Adams did this. Toward the end of 1847 he wrote Albert Gallatin, who was a fellow objector to the war: ''The most remarkable circumstance of these transactions is that the war thus [unconstitutionally] made has been sanctioned by an overwhelming majority of both Houses . . . and is now sustained by similar majorities professing to disapprove its existence and pronouncing it unnecessary and unjust.'' Abraham Lincoln, who entered Congress in 1847 and registered his protest against the war, regularly voted supplies for it.

The defense for voting supplies was set forth in the House by such Whigs as Winthrop, and in the Senate, by Crittenden. Congress, they pointed out, cannot abandon armies it has called into the field. Soldiers at the front cannot question orders on moral grounds. To do so would be subversive of all discipline. A war, right or wrong, which Congress has voted must be upheld.

In the House a radical antislavery Whig, Joshua R. Giddings, from the Western Reserve of Ohio, challenged the worth of that reasoning. He cited the great British Whigs of the era of the American Revolution who announced in Parliament in 1776 their refusal to vote supplies for an unjust and oppressive war against America. Giddings proposed that similar means be used by American Whigs to force Polk out of Mexico. But Winthrop frowned on this revolutionary procedure and thought British precedent inapplicable in any case, for whereas in England the defeat of a supply measure brought down an administration and forced the creation of a new one, in the United States it would paralyze an administration which would still hang on.

As the war progressed Whig conservatives made further adjustments of expe- diency to its demands. While always denouncing Polk they not only voted supplies and men but lauded the gallantry of the front-line troops and the achievements of the generals leading them, especially the glory-covered Whig generals. On a number of occasions they voted resolutions of thanks to Generals Zachary Taylor and Winfield Scott.

These tactics were excellent politics and paid high dividends. In the congressional election of 1846, which came half a year after the war declaration, the Whig party reversed the Democratic control of the House, thus acquiring, in the next session of Congress, the control of the purse.

The loss of control of Congress in the midst of a highly successful war was to the Polk administration an unusual and humiliating experience. It was a clear reflection of the moral protest which had developed against the war. What was equally significant was that the Whigs gained strength in all sections of the nation except in the interior of the South, and there they stayed even.

The President sent his annual message to Congress on December 8, soon after this rebuke. In it he took a defensive stand, devoting two-thirds of the message to an elaboration of his earlier argument as to the origins of the war. He insisted that the boundary really was the Rio Grande and that the Mexican force, in crossing it, had invaded American soil and shed American blood. He deplored Whig charges that he had been the aggressor. He thought those who made such charges were giving "aid and comfort to the enemy," which was saying that they were traitors.

The Whigs greeted the message with a new explosion of wrath. In Congress a Whig from the President's own state called the message "an artful perversion of the truth . . . to make the people believe a lie." The challenge of lie was thrown at the President again and again in Congress and in the press. His suggestion that the Whig opposition was giving aid and comfort to the enemy was denounced as a "foul imputation" for purposes of intimidation, which would have the opposite effect of the one intended.

In April 1847 the Massachusetts legislature adopted a set of resolutions still more condemnatory. The resolutions lifted the slavery issue into prominence. They read:

> Resolved that the present war with Mexico . . . was unconstitutionally commenced by the order of the President to General Taylor to take military possession of territory in dispute . . . and that it is now waged by a powerful nation against a weak neighbor . . . at immense cost of treasure and life, for the dismemberment of Mexico, and for the conquest of . . . territory from which slavery has been . . . excluded with the triple object of extending slavery, of strengthening the slave power, and of obtaining the control of the Free States. . . . That such a war of conquest, so hateful in its objects, so wanton, unjust and unconstitutional in its origin and character, must be regarded as a war against freedom, against humanity, against justice, against the Union, . . . and against the Free States. . . .

These resolutions were approved by overwhelming majorities in both Massachusetts houses. They were based to a large extent on a report Charles Sumner had written for a committee of the legislature. Sumner took the radical stand that Congress should withhold supplies from the armed forces, but the state legislature refused to go that far.

The growing bitterness of the radicals against the war was evidenced in a startling speech delivered in the United States Senate on February 11, 1847, by Thomas Corwin, an Ohio Whig. He denounced the war as "flagrant," "a usurpation of authority," "a senseless quest for more room," a quest he would, if he were a Mexican, respond to with the words: "Have you not room in your own country to bury your dead men? If you come into mine we will greet you with bloody hands and welcome you to hospitable graves." He predicted that the war would generate a sectional clash over slavery and plunge the sister states of the Union into the bottomless gulf of civil conflict. The speech seemed traitorous to conservative Whigs and Democrats. But to such radical Whigs as Charles Francis Adams and Joshua Giddings it seemed admirable. They thought hopefully of Corwin as a presidential candidate in 1848.

In December 1847 the Congress chosen the preceding year convened in Washington and took the necessary measures to organize itself. In the election of a Whig speaker of the House, a contest developed between the conservative Whigs and the Conscience Whigs, which brought to the surface all the bitterness that had developed between them. Robert C. Winthrop was the leading conservative candidate, but on the first ballot he was short three votes of a majority necessary for election. The three holdouts were John G. Palfrey, Giddings, and Amos Tuck of New Hampshire, all of them radical antislavery men. They held out because Winthrop had shown halfheartedness in opposing the war and because, as speaker, he would appoint committees that would support war measures. In the end he won the speakership, but only after several conservative Whigs, who had been voting for other candidates, switched to him. One of the Whigs who voted for him from the beginning was John Quincy Adams. He voted so because of an old friendship with Winthrop's father. Afterward there was an embarrassing situation between the younger Adams and the elder, because the elder had abandoned his principles.

While the antiwar feeling in the North was intensifying, the American armies were battering down Mexican resistance. Taylor's force crossed the Rio Grande, seized Matamoros and Monterrey, and by the end of 1846 had taken possession of the capitals of three northeastern states of Mexico. Another force under Stephen W. Kearny took Santa Fe and pushed on to California. A column under Colonel Alexander W. Doniphan that had been detached from Kearny's force at Santa Fe descended the Rio Grande as far as El Paso, then continued south and captured Chihuahua. Kearny himself proceeded to California, where, in cooperation with Captain Robert F. Stockton of the Navy, he conquered southern California. The main American army under General Winfield Scott moved by sea to the vicinity of Vera Cruz, which it captured in March 1847, and where it prepared for the march to the heart of Mexico. These armies were winning spectacular victories against great odds. Not a single major engagement was lost.

The appetite of American expansionists was stimulated. The All Mexico movement and the related Manifest Destiny movement reached a climax during the second half of the war. Those ideas were especially attractive to the great urban centers of the northeastern seaboard, the city Democrats, in considerable part immigrants, the "unterrified Democracy" of New York City and Tammany Hall. The penny press of Philadelphia, Baltimore, and Boston also fed these ideas to its readers. In Boston, the Boston *Times* was the great expansionist teacher. In the interior, Illinois was an outstanding center of All Mexico feeling.

Southerners were hesitant about accepting the All Mexico program. Absorption would mean extending citizenship to colored and mixed races, which ran counter to all southern instincts. It clashed especially with the instincts of Calhoun, who was the voice of southern racism. His speeches in Congress were a bitter assault on the All Mexico movement on this ground. He felt that, if any Mexican territory were to be taken, it should be only the sparsely populated northern parts—California and New Mexico. Even these areas he hesitated to accept because he doubted they were suitable for slavery. He wanted no territory that would spawn free states.

Meanwhile, the great military successes produced fears of an opposite nature in the North. Antislavery radicals feared that acquisition of territory deep in Mexico would open an opportunity for a vast expansion of slavery, and they were determined to prevent that.

The President himself did not want a prolonged war. He wanted the fighting to go on only long enough to obtain a boundary that would be basically the one he had set forth in peacetime in his instructions to Slidell. After that mission had failed and Taylor had been instructed to move his army to the Rio Grande, but before hostilities had broken out, another mode of settling differences with Mexico presented itself to Polk. It had come from Santa Anna, who was then an exile in Cuba hoping to return to Mexico and recover his old power. An emissary recently in conversation with the exiled general brought to Polk on February 13, 1846, an alluring scheme.

The emissary was Colonel Alexander Atocha, a Spaniard who had served with Santa Anna in Mexico. The plan was one that would fill the Mexican treasury and perhaps Santa Anna's own coffers with American dollars. For the sum of $30 million, Santa Anna would, on his return to Mexico, recognize the American claim to the Rio Grande boundary and, in addition, cede all Mexican territory north of a line drawn from the Colorado of the West "down through the Bay of San Francisco to the sea."

Polk was suspicious of the offer and of its bearer, but he did not dismiss them from his mind. With the coming of the Mexican War he ordered the navy blockading the coast of Mexico to let Santa Anna slip through. The general was soon able to re-establish himself. He had the support of powerful elements in Mexico hostile to the Paredes government with whom he had been in communication during his exile. In mid-September, in alliance with this group, he overthrew the government and returned to power. But instead of moving to a peace negotiation he reorganized the Mexican resistance, and the only outcome for the United States of Polk's maneuver was more bitter fighting.

This story became known to the Whig opposition in Congress late in 1846 and was exposed. Polk's tactics were denounced as contemptible for a great state to use in fighting a weak one. A southern Whig summed up this sentiment in the House in the form of a rhetorical question: "Does history furnish an example of more abhorrent perfidy? Was any government through its chief magistrate ever more vilely prostituted?"

In the meantime, on August 4, 1846, when Santa Anna was back in Mexico but not yet returned to power, Polk sent the Senate a message asking confidential advice regarding an appropriation he desired for facilitating a peace negotiation with Mexico. The appropriation was to be made in veiled terms. The request was debated by the Senate in executive session and was approved.

Accordingly the President sent Congress on August 8 a message requesting an appropriation of $2 million to restore peace by adjustment of a boundary that would be satisfactory and convenient to both republics. He expressed the wish to offer a fair equivalent for a concession to be made by Mexico. But the Mexican government might find it inconvenient to wait for the whole sum stipulated while a treaty was before the Senate and an appropriation was being voted by Congress. It would therefore be important to place $2 million in the control of the Executive to be advanced to Mexico immediately on the signing of a treaty.

A bill was at once brought into the House to appropriate the $2 million desired by the President. The language of the bill was obscure, perhaps reflecting attempts at secrecy. The appropriation was described as being ''for the purpose of defraying any extraordinary expense which may be incurred in the intercourse between the United States and foreign nations.''

The bill came to the House two days before the scheduled adjournment of Congress for the session. No effective exploration of the critical problems raised by the bill was possible. However, the explosiveness of the issues was revealed in the discussion.

One critic of the bill was Charles H. Carroll, a New York Whig. He pointed out that the Mexican government was indebted to the American to the extent of some ten or twenty million for spoliations on American property. Was an advance of two million more needed ''unless it was to carry out the ambitious views of the Executive for the enlargement of our territory beyond its rightful bounds? . . . To Mr. C. it looked very much as if this money was wanted to purchase California and a large portion of Mexico to boot. . . . He was aware that we were now at the heel of the session; but why was it that this message was delayed to the last day? Was it to avoid discussion?''

The slavery issue was injected into the discussion. An antislavery Democrat from Pennsylvania, David Wilmot, offered as an amendment to the bill ''that neither slavery nor involuntary servitude shall ever exist in any part of said territory [acquired from Mexico], except for crime, whereof the party shall first be duly convicted.'' The amendment was made part of the bill after cursory discussion on the evening of the day the bill was submitted. Support for the amendment was almost exclusively northern and was intended to kill the bill in the final vote. But the bill safely passed soon after and was sent to the Senate. In the Senate a filibuster met the measure. Senator John Davis, an antislavery Whig of Massachusetts, succeeded in obtaining the floor and, once in possession, held it until the hour set for adjournment of the session had passed.

To the President the injection of the slavery issue into an attempt to obtain peace with Mexico seemed incomprehensible and disreputable. On August 10 he entered in his diary the following indignant paragraph, a summation of what he had been writing in the preceding six days:

> Late in the evening of Saturday, the 8th, I learned that after an excited debate in the House a bill passed that body, but with a mischievous & foolish amendment to the effect that no territory which might be acquired by treaty from Mexico should ever be a slave-holding country. What connection slavery had with making peace with Mexico it is difficult to conceive. This amendment was voted onto the Bill by the opponents of the measure, and when voted on, the original friends of the Bill voted against it, but it was passed by the Whigs and Northern Democrats, who had been opposed to making the appropriation. In this form it had gone to the Senate. Had there been time, there is but little doubt the Senate would have struck out the slavery proviso & that the House would

have concurred. Senator Davis, however, resorted to the disreputable expedient of speaking against time & thus prevented the Senate from acting upon it, until the hour of adjournment had arrived.

In March 1847, in the next session of Congress, a new bill to appropriate $3 million to facilitate a boundary negotiation was passed by both houses without the antislavery proviso and signed by the President. Thus Polk finally got his way. In April he sent an agent to Mexico to open negotiations with Santa Anna. The agent was Nicholas P. Trist, chief clerk of the State Department, who had been recommended by Buchanan.

Trist operated under the wing of the American Army while Scott was advancing on Mexico City. Late in August 1847 an armistice was arranged and an offer of peace was made by Santa Anna, which was not, however, very genuine. It proposed, among other things, that a buffer state—a kind of neutral zone—be erected in the disputed area between the Nueces River and the Rio Grande. This was a throwback to the old boundary dispute. Trist rejected it, but was incautious enough to send it, with the other proposals, for reference to his government. Polk was furious with his agent for showing weakness regarding the sensitive issue of the origins of the war. He canceled Trist's powers, rebuked him, and ordered him home.

By the time the orders reached Trist the armistice had collapsed. Mexico City had been taken, Santa Anna was in disgrace, a new government had been formed, and peace commissioners appointed. With the new commissioners, Trist, in defiance of his orders, but supported by Scott, negotiated the Treaty of Guadalupe Hidalgo of February 2, 1848. The treaty took from Mexico more than a third of her territory. It established a boundary following the Rio Grande from its mouth to the southern boundary of New Mexico; thence the line ran westward to the southwest corner of New Mexico; there it turned due north to the Gila River, following it to its junction with the Colorado, and thence to the Pacific by way of the existing boundary between Upper and Lower California. Mexico was to receive $15 million for consenting to the new boundaries and the United States was to assume the damage claims of its citizens against Mexico to the amount of $3,250,000. In terms of territory taken from Mexico, the treaty met the minimum of the instructions issued to Trist in April 1847. It did not exact from Mexico what might have been taken, considering the victories won in the ten months since the date of the instructions, and their cost in blood and treasure. In spite of this and of the irregularity of the negotiation, Trist believed the President would submit the treaty to the Senate for ratification. And he was right.

The treaty reached the President on February 19, 1848. He was infuriated by the manner of its negotiation and its terms. He had come to the conclusion that Trist was an "impudent and unqualified scoundrel." Yet the treaty conformed with the instructions, and, if it were rejected, Whigs would press the charge that the war had been begun, and was being continued, to acquire All Mexico. The public was eager for peace. The burgeoning debt alarmed conservatives, including Democrats, such as Calhoun and Gallatin. Congress held the purse strings. If the war were to be prolonged and further support for it were to be withheld, even California and New Mexico might be lost. Polk resolved to submit the treaty to the Senate. He called the Cabinet, but only to share a responsibility he preferred not to carry alone.

Polk told the Cabinet at once that he thought the treaty should go to the Senate.

He himself would have preferred more territory, perhaps to the Sierra Madre, but he doubted the Mexicans would ever have agreed. He had hardly concluded his remarks when Buchanan began objecting, especially to withdrawing from the Sierra Madre line. Walker took the same stand. Polk was particularly annoyed at Buchanan, pointing out that, at the opening of the war, Buchanan had proposed to inform foreign governments that the United States did not desire or intend to acquire any Mexican territory and that he had later approved the Trist instructions. Buchanan's reply was that a great deal of money and blood had been spent since the instructions were drawn and that now he was not satisfied with the treaty. During this exchange the Cabinet sat silent, only to vote afterward to send the treaty to the Senate.

In the Senate to which the treaty was submitted without presidential recommendation, the desire for peace was strong. But the senators differed as to the amount of territory to be required. Sam Houston thought all territory should be taken north of a line drawn from Tampico on the Gulf of Mexico to the head of the Gulf of California, with a deflection of the line so as to include all of Lower California. Jefferson Davis was more moderate. He proposed a line starting north of Tampico and proceeding northwestward on a course that would transfer all of Coahuila and a large part of Tamaulipas, Nuevo León, and Chihuahua to the United States. Ten of his colleagues supported this proposal. On the other hand, Whigs wanted no territory south of the Rio Grande though most of them would have accepted Upper California in exchange for the assumption by the United States of the damage claims of its citizens against Mexico. The financial provisions of the treaty aroused little controversy. Democratic senators agreed with the President that payments to Mexico were an evidence of American liberality. Whig senators considered them conscience money for the wrongs done Mexico.

Articles IX and X of the treaty proved unacceptable. Article IX dealt with religion in the ceded territory and called for statehood as soon as possible for California and New Mexico. It was objected to on the ground that it gave the Catholic Church a special status in the ceded area and that it usurped a function of Congress in its statehood provision. Article X was opposed because it might be construed to revive lapsed land claims in Texas. A substitute for Article IX was adopted and Article X was eliminated.

The treaty was otherwise approved by a vote of 38–14. The size of the affirmative vote reflected a universal demand for peace and also a wide tolerance for acquisitions that were thought unsuitable for slavery. The fourteen negative votes reflected dissatisfaction with the treaty on diverse grounds. Six were from expansionists who felt defrauded because the treaty did not take enough. Seven were from Whigs who thought the treaty took too much. Benton voted nay, probably because he agreed with the Whigs.

The vote, taken on March 10, 1848, was merely a stage in the peacemaking process. The treaty, with its amendments, had to be returned to Mexico for the approval of the Mexican Congress. Commissioners carried it to Mexico, where the amendments proved acceptable. Early in May the Mexican Congress assembled and by May 24 the two houses had overwhelmingly approved ratification.

The Mexican War and the treaty which closed it were momentous in their consequences. They enormously expanded the territory of the United States. They rounded out and completed American frontage on the Pacific, giving the United States the great harbor of San Francisco. They created a need for improved transportation to the Pacific coast and led to an agitation for a transcontinental railroad and for a canal in Central America to connect the two oceans. In 1850 the Clayton-Bulwer Treaty with Great Britain provided for the joint control of any canal that would be built in the future. Finally, the war and its acquisitions led in the United States to a furious sectional conflict over slavery extension that almost severed the Union.

The Issue of Slavery
in the New Territories and
the Compromise of 1850

THE VAST TERRITORY acquired in the Mexican War was more easily won than governed. Sectional contention regarding it began even before its acquisition, and continued for two years after the war closed. The contention came near to fulfilling the somber prediction of Thomas Corwin that the war would "light up the fires of internal war, and plunge the sister States of this Union into the bottomless gulf of civil strife."

In March 1847, when Polk's request for funds for peace negotiations came before Congress a second time, the House had again attached the Wilmot Proviso. The Senate had again eliminated it and the subsequent vote of the House to accept the bill without the proviso was a result of a shift of northern Democrats. In the meantime an embittered debate over the proviso took place in the House. This debate in historical perspective was more significant than Polk's success in obtaining the $3 million he had requested to initiate peace negotiations. It was a preview of an even more acrimonious controversy after the territory had been annexed to the United States.

Besides the question of the status of slavery in the vast area acquired west of the Rio Grande, there was the exaggerated claim of Texas to all that Mexico ceded east of that river. The question was how much of this should be accorded to the state of Texas and how much to the territory of New Mexico. If Congress accepted the claim of Texas to all of the cession east of the Rio Grande, it would mean a major extension of slavery. A large fraction of that territory had been part of New Mexico, and had been closed to slavery under Mexican law. Texas had land claims in the disputed area. But Santa Fe and its dependent area east of the Rio Grande had been conquered by United States forces in the war.

Another issue, unrelated to the Mexican cession, was the status of slavery in the District of Columbia. This was an old problem, heated to new intensity by the debate over the Wilmot Proviso. The northern public considered slavery in the national capital a disgrace and this sentiment was augmented by the use of the District as a depot for the collection of slaves to be sold either there or elsewhere in the South. Though sale of slaves at public auction was not permitted, petitions from the North to forbid any sales of slaves in the District, or even slavery itself there, flooded Congress. Southerners considered these a northern aggression. Washington was surrounded on all sides by slave states, and the drive on slavery in the District seemed the beginning of a drive on slavery even in the southern states.

Another problem was the return of fugitive slaves. In the North resistance was growing over the return of the fugitives to their masters. Individuals were giving asylum to runaways, and organizations offered underground escape to Canada. The old law of 1793 providing for the return of fugitive slaves no longer gave adequate protection to slave owners.

Over this cluster of issues the most dangerous sectional crisis in American history prior to the Civil War developed. The crisis went to the verge of breaking up the Union. A secession sentiment led by Calhoun developed in the South. The South Carolinian had come to believe, as a result of the northern drive for the Wilmot Proviso and the agitation for the abolition of slavery in the District of Columbia, that the South was no longer safe in the Union.

Early in 1849, before the close of the Polk administration, Calhoun wrote, as head of a self-constituted committee of fifteen southern delegates in Congress, an *Address,* which was designed to unite the South against northern aggression. The *Address* opened with an account of the compromises regarding slavery made by the framers of the Constitution, without which the instrument could not have been drawn or adopted. It then traced northern intrusions on the institution, pronounced by Calhoun "the greatest and most vital of all the institutions of the South." Especially dangerous had been the northern attempt to prevent the admission of Missouri as a slave state in 1819, and the condition had been attached to the admission, by an almost united northern vote against a southern minority, whereby all the territory of the Louisiana Purchase north of the line of 36° 30' had been closed to slavery. Even more serious was the northern determination to exclude slavery from the entire Mexican Cession, which had been won by the common sacrifices of all the states and especially by those of the South. Similarly menacing was the proposal, gaining strength in the North, to abolish slavery in the District of Columbia, and to prohibit what abolitionists called the internal slave trade. The object of all this would seem to be to render slaves worthless "by crowding them together where they are, and thus hasten the work of emancipation." The *Address* was an extremist southern reply to northern antislavery extremists.

Publication of the *Address* was opposed by the moderates on the Committee of Fifteen, by other moderates in the South, and by President Polk. Only 48 signatures to the *Address* could be obtained among 121 representatives of the slaveholding states who were asked to sign it. But the document was a symptom of fever in the South, and a warning of what lay ahead unless a compromise could be reached.

A compromise, or at least an avoidance of extreme declarations on the slavery issue, was desired by both the major political parties in the presidential campaign of 1848. Each party realized the divisiveness of the issue in its own ranks. The Democrats, meeting in the spring of 1848, chose Lewis Cass, "a northern man with southern principles," as their presidential candidate. Cass was the spokesman of the doctrine of congressional non-interference, which he had set forth in the so-called

Nicholson letter of December 29, 1847. He proposed in it that the issue of slavery in the territories be relegated to local decision. The Democratic convention made no pronouncement on the disruptive issue except to name Cass as its party leader.

The Whig party was equally discreet, and embarked on the campaign without a platform. It chose as its standard bearer a military hero, General Zachary Taylor, whose involvement in politics was indicated by the fact that he had never in his life voted in a presidential election. As a Louisiana planter and owner of 300 slaves, he was expected to be friendly to the South.

The one party that took a forthright stand on the issue of slavery in the territories and in the District of Columbia was the Free-Soil party. It declared in its platform for Free Soil, Free Speech, Free Labor, and Free Men. Free Soil meant closing the territories to slavery and, also, the grant of free homesteads for the landless, which would win the territories for free men. It also probably meant closing the District of Columbia to slavery. It did not mean interfering with slavery in the states of the Union, which the platform specifically disclaimed. The Free-Soil convention named as its candidate Martin Van Buren, whose record on the slavery issue was equivocal, but who had opposed the annexation of Texas and had undertaken not to veto any measure, if passed by Congress, forbidding slavery in the District of Columbia.

The victory in the election went, by a scant margin, to Taylor. The states which gave him their electoral vote were both northern and southern. Cass lost the big, normally Democratic states of New York and Pennsylvania, as a result of Democratic defections to the Free-Soil party. Van Buren obtained no electoral votes, but his popular vote was significantly five times that of the abolitionist, Birney, in 1844. In the two houses of Congress the Democrats won a majority.

The new Congress, which assembled on December 3, 1849, was an able body. The Senate was at the height of its glory. It contained the great trio of the older generation—Webster, Calhoun, and Clay—as well as a distinguished array of leaders of the new generation. The Congress reflected, however, the passions of the period. The session was one of the most disorderly and partisan in American history. The House needed a week to choose a doorkeeper, and was convulsed for three weeks over the choice of its Speaker. In the Senate the debates were marked by furious personal encounters, in one of which a pistol was pulled by a Southerner on Benton.

The central issue in both houses was constitutional—whether Congress had the power under the Constitution to close the territory acquired from Mexico to slavery. This question had arisen in 1819–20 over the bill conferring statehood on Missouri. Missouri had been admitted to the Union as a slave state, but balancing this was the closing of the remainder of the Louisiana Purchase above 36° 30′ to slavery, and the admission of Maine as a free state. The compromise had been achieved without a searching debate. The question of the constitutionality of excluding slavery from so large a part of the territory had bothered President Monroe, but he had smothered his doubts after consulting the Cabinet and James Madison, the father of the Constitution. The issue had never been carried to the Supreme Court, so that in 1849 it was still very much an open question.

The language of the Constitution was an obvious point of departure for any judgment on the issue in 1849. Unfortunately Article IV, Section 3, which dealt with the territories, could be variously interpreted. It reads: ''The Congress shall have power to dispose of and make all needful rules and regulations respecting the territory or other property belonging to the United States." The meaning of this sentence was unclear as to the powers it conferred on Congress.

Daniel Webster was the most eminent of the northern expounders of the meaning of the sentence. In the course of debate on the government to be established for the Mexican Cession he declared on February 24, 1849, that the words "all needful rules and regulations" in the sentence conferred on Congress not merely complete power, but almost absolute power over the territories. The only exception would be that fundamental human liberties could not be denied. Relying on a decision handed down by the Supreme Court in 1828 (*American Insurance Company v. Canter*), Webster maintained that Congress might withhold even jury trial and the writ of *habeas corpus*. Since Congress had as sweeping a power in the territories as was upheld in that case, it could close the territories to slavery.

Southern interpreters of the Constitution and particularly Calhoun gave Article IV, Section 3, no such commanding importance. Indeed, they regarded it as a mere grant of administrative authority, an authority to dispose of the public domain and other property of the United States. The word "territory" in the article seemed to relate only to public land. If the framers had intended legislative authority to be given in the article the terminology would have been altogether different. The terminology they used in conferring legislative power was shown in Article I, where Congress was given authority in the District of Columbia: "To exercise exclusive Legislation in all Cases whatsoever, over such District (not exceeding ten Miles square) as may . . . become the Seat of the Government of the United States, and to exercise like Authority over all Places purchased . . . for the erection of Forts, Magazines, arsenals, dock-yards, and other needful Buildings." A comparison of the terms used in this article with those used in Article IV, Section 3, was revealing. It showed that the framers, who took the greatest pains to be precise, intended the latter article to be only a grant of administrative power.

Then, where did the legislative power come from that Congress exercised over the territories—one that it undoubtedly had? This, Calhoun maintained, was derived from other powers, such as that to make treaties, or to admit new states, or power derived from the federal ownership of the territories. But Calhoun declared that this derived power was as limited as any other power of Congress. It was subject to all the ordinary limitations imposed by the Constitution on Congress.

Calhoun next turned to the issue of slavery in the territories. Slavery was a form of labor clearly recognized by the framers in the three-fifths provision of the Constitution, and elsewhere. When the Constitution was framed, slavery was legal in nearly every state of the Union. The territories belonged to the people of all the states, to the people of the southern as well as of the northern states. Since this was so, and since slavery was a legal form of labor and property, no right was possessed by Congress to shut the territories to the people of the southern states who wished to go into them with that form of property.

Calhoun's argument, set forth on June 27, 1848, in the course of debate on the bill to establish a territorial government in Oregon, was powerful. It seemed more firmly based than Webster's, and was in agreement with a view expressed in 1819 by James Madison—that no authority was given by the framers to exclude slavery from the territories. It was the view later adopted by the Supreme Court in the Dred Scott case as the correct interpretation of the Constitution.

Strong as this argument was, however, it contained a personal weakness in coming from Calhoun. It was out of accord with the position he had taken when he was a member of Monroe's cabinet in 1820 and the question arose of the exclusion of slavery from the Louisiana Purchase territory north of 36° 30'. Monroe had asked every member of the Cabinet to give him an opinion as to whether a measure excluding slavery from any of the territories would be constitutional. The Cabinet, including Calhoun, was unanimous that such a measure would be constitutional.

Calhoun may have written an opinion, as Monroe requested of each cabinet member. These opinions were deposited in the State Department files. But all that remains of them is the envelope in which they were once held. The opinions may have been lost through carelessness or they might have been removed by Calhoun, when he became Secretary of State in 1844.

Calhoun maintained in 1848 that he had never given a written opinion to Monroe on the Missouri Compromise. It is possible he neglected to comply with the President's request. But there is no question that orally he agreed in 1820 that the Missouri Compromise was constitutional. This does not in itself destroy the validity of the argument he advanced in 1848, and it must be remembered that it was a view widely held in the South.

A third constitutional doctrine regarding the power of Congress in the territories was set forth by Lewis Cass in the so-called Nicholson letter of December 1847. According to Cass, the extent of the power of Congress over the territories was a matter of doubt. The framers of the Constitution did not intend Article IV, Section 3, to be used as a grant of legislative powers. They intended it as a grant only for the disposition and management of public property. Congress could not rely on it to interfere in the internal policy of the territories. It could merely set up territorial governments, leaving all questions of internal policy, such as that of slavery, to the determination of the people of the territories. Cass maintained that as a practical matter the question of slavery in the Mexican Cession was already settled. It was determined by the nature of the country and the wishes of its inhabitants. This was the doctrine of congressional non-interference, of "popular sovereignty," a compromise doctrine, earlier conceived by others in the North, but fully developed by Cass. It attracted moderates in both sections.

To southern extremists of the Calhoun school, Cass's thesis seemed beneath contempt: its premise and its logic were awry. For if, as Cass maintained, legislative authority over the territories was not clearly vested in Congress by the Constitution, how could it get vested in a territorial government which was a creation of Congress?

The territorial problem was thrust on Taylor, immediately after he took office, as a result of the discovery of gold in California. In the gold rush 80,000 miners poured into the territory. Some kind of organized government was needed there to prevent anarchy. In this crisis Taylor formulated a program for Congress that was simple and statesmanlike. It was designed to halt angry argument over the authority of Congress in the territories. There was no doubt that any state had the right to decide for itself whether or not to permit slavery within its limits. If California could be organized as a state, and the rest of the Mexican Cession as the state of New Mexico, and these two would apply for admission as such to the Union, the dangerous and fruitless argument over the power of Congress in the territories could be sidetracked.

Taylor therefore sent a personal messenger to California to encourage the organization of a state, and he instructed the military officers in New Mexico to advance popular movements in the same direction. When Congress assembled in December 1849, he urged that there be no further debate on the territorial issue and that Congress merely wait until California and New Mexico applied for admission as states.

But Congress refused. The majorities in both houses were Democratic and thought they should decide issues of policy. The nation had been engaged for three years in angry debate over the Wilmot Proviso. Every northern legislature save one had adopted resolutions of one sort or another favoring it. The southern states were as united against it. The problem was no longer susceptible of so simple a solution as Taylor's.

The debate is a classic example of the sectionalism of American politics. Henry Clay spoke for the border states. He had just been returned to the Senate, after an absence of some years, by a unanimous vote of the Kentucky legislature. He was believed to be needed in Washington to preserve peace. He was privately favorable to the exclusion of slavery from the new territories, but he feared the effect on the permanence of the Union of an attempt to impose it.

On January 29, 1850, Clay proposed to the Senate a series of compromise solutions. California should be admitted as a state with her free-soil constitution. The remainder of the Mexican Cession should be divided into two territorial governments, Utah and New Mexico, without any restriction as to slavery, though recognizing that "slavery does not exist [there] by law and is not likely to be introduced." The question of slavery there should be left to the territorial courts, with the right of appeal to the United States Supreme Court. The Supreme Court would be given the ultimate duty of deciding that dangerous question. Texas should yield in her boundary dispute with New Mexico, in return for which her debt prior to annexation should be assumed by the United States. Congress should enact an effective fugitive slave law. In the District of Columbia the slave trade, but not slavery itself, should be abolished. These proposals, insofar as they related to the territory acquired from Mexico, were gathered in an "Omnibus Bill."

A week later Clay analyzed and amplified these proposals in a memorable speech. He urged that the proposals formed a middle ground, just to both sections of the nation, but chiefly good in that they would save the Union. He emphatically denied the right or the possibility of a peaceful secession. Dissolution of the Union and war, he declared, were identical. He ended with a glowing appeal to Congress to save the Union.

A month later Calhoun spoke for the cotton South. He was near the end of his life. He was so weak he had to be carried into the Senate chamber, and his speech was read for him. He urged the rejection of the Compromise. The South, he said, had already yielded too much to northern aggression. The South had yielded so much on territorial issues that the old balance in the Senate between the two sections, essential to southern safety, had been upset. The South should yield no more. She must stand uncompromisingly by her rights or be lost. Calhoun thought the Union was virtually beyond saving. The old bonds had snapped one by one. Even bonds of religion had snapped. As a result of northern aggression, all the Protestant denominations except the Episcopal Church had broken into North and South churches. Calhoun believed the Union could be maintained with safety to the South only by the restoration of the equilibrium between the South and the North which had once existed in Congress.

How was that old equilibrium to be restored? Calhoun did not say, but it was revealed after his death in his *Disquisition on Government*. It was to so amend the Constitution that two Presidents of the United States would be in office at the same time, one from the South and one from the North. Each, like a Roman tribune, was to have the power of veto over all congressional legislation. The speech was the voice of southern extremism.

For New York and Ohio, and especially for their population of New England origin, the chief spokesmen were William H. Seward and Salmon P. Chase, who were regarded as the voices of northern extremism. They urged rejection of the Compromise. The Compromise proposals, they said, conceded too much to the South. The two demanded the adoption of the Wilmot Proviso. In Seward's speech the revolutionary doctrine of the higher law was set forth, that, if the Constitution recognized slavery, there was a higher law that did not, the law of God, natural law, which superseded the Constitution. This was the doctrine which was later seized upon in the North to justify resistance to the fugitive slave law.

Stephen A. Douglas spoke for the Northwest, and urged the adoption of the Compromise measures. But he did so only as a means of quieting sectional discord. He had little faith, he said, in paper restrictions on slavery. He pointed out that in Illinois slavery, though illegal under the Northwest Ordinance of 1787, had nevertheless existed down to as late as 1840 in the form of indentured servitude. The issue of slavery in any region would be determined, Douglas argued, by such factors as physical geography, soil, and climate, and by the will of the inhabitants. He calculated that in the unorganized territory west of the Mississippi seventeen states would ultimately be created. Slavery would never take hold in any one of them, no matter what the laws of Congress, since the climate and soil of these areas would not support the slave crops, cotton and tobacco. Slavery in the territories, Douglas said, was a matter that ought to be settled locally by the people living there. Slavery should not be made the football of congressional politics. Douglas was restating the doctrine of congressional non-intervention. He later pretended that the doctrine had actually been embodied in the Compromise measures.

Of all the great orators in the debate, Webster was the only one who did not reflect the prevailing views of his section. He sacrificed those views and feelings in his eagerness to save the Union, especially in his great March 7 speech, which was the climax to the debate. He had made an investigation of the secession temper of the South by keeping in touch with southern Whigs in whom he had confidence. As a result, he took very seriously the secession threats which Seward, he thought, regarded too lightly. He felt that a compromise on the question of slavery in the territories was essential to preserving the Union. He argued that the Compromise measures were fair to the North and ought to be adopted. California would come into the Union as a free state. In the remainder of the Mexican Cession, slavery was in any case impossible.

This speech drew down on Webster's head the furious denunciation of New England. He was charged with selling out his section to the South in order to win for himself united Whig support for the presidential nomination in 1852. Whittier, in his poem "Ichabod," compared him to a fallen star. The judgment of historians is, however, that in advocating the Compromise measures he was actuated by the highest sense of duty.

The Compromise proposals were finally adopted by Congress in August and September 1850. Their enactment was partly the result of the strategy of dividing Clay's proposals into five separate bills, each of which commanded a different majority. Their adoption was partly the result of the death of President Taylor in the preceding July. Influenced by the northern wing of the Whig party, Taylor had been opposed to the Compromise. He believed it yielded too much to southern threats. He would have put the exorbitant boundary demands of Texas under restraint, forcibly if necessary. He would have met any southern move toward secession at the head of the United States Army. On Taylor's death Millard Fillmore, who approved the Compromise measures, became President, and his active aid in the form of distribution of patronage contributed to their adoption.

As a result of the adoption of the Compromise measures, the secession threat, which had worried Webster so much, gradually subsided. Conventions had been held in four southern states in the period following the crisis to consider the advisability of secession, but all voted to accept the Compromise and to take no further action. By the time of the 1852 presidential election public feeling on both sides of the Mason-Dixon line was near normal, and the popular vote in the election showed no storm clouds over the Union.

The crisis of 1850 was the price paid by the nation for overindulgence in territorial expansion. The nation's area, which for a quarter of a century had been 1,787,880 square miles, had been extended in the Polk administration by 1,204,740 square miles. The increase had been at the expense of Mexico except for the 285,580 square miles of the Oregon Country. The greater part of Texas was exceptionally well adapted to slavery and the area acquired in the Mexican War was deemed in the North suitable by latitude, if not otherwise, to slavery. The Wilmot Proviso was invoked by northern moralists to close the area to slavery. No one knew, at the time the proviso was introduced into Congress, how much of Mexico would be absorbed. Extreme expansionists were demanding all. The proviso was the northern answer—to close to slavery whatever area would be annexed. The reply of southern extremists was the movement for secession. That calamity was averted by the Compromise of 1850. This proved to be only a truce, but it gave the North eleven years in which to extend its agricultural, industrial, and transportation superiority over the South and to save the Union in the Civil War.

The Kansas-Nebraska Act
and Bleeding Kansas

THE SECTIONAL PEACE following the Compromise of 1850 was of short duration. It was broken in 1854 by a new clash of greater intensity than the first. Once again it was over the issue of the expansion of slavery into the western territories. But in 1854 it was over territory long in the possession of the nation, the Louisiana Purchase acquired from France in 1803. This recurrence of crises was symptomatic of a growing northern sensitivity over slavery expansion following the excitement of the South over the Wilmot Proviso.

The new disturbance was set off by two sensational developments. One was the publication in 1852 of Harriet Beecher Stowe's novel *Uncle Tom's Cabin*. The book was an emotional picture of Negro slavery at its worst. It had an enormous sale in the North. It accomplished what northern abolitionists had never succeeded in doing. It turned the northern masses against slavery. This was considered in the South evidence of increasing northern fanaticism.

Another sensation occurred in 1854—the adoption by Congress of the Kansas-Nebraska Act. This opened to slavery all the part of the Louisiana Purchase which had been closed to the institution by the Missouri Compromise of 1820. The part opened was popularly known as the Platte Country, a vast area, bounded at the south by the line of 36° 30′, at the north by the international boundary, at the east by the states of Missouri and Iowa, and the upper Missouri River, and at the west by the Continental Divide. It contained 485,000 square miles of territory.

The Platte Country was a region of wide differences of physical character. At the east it was a prairie region, an offshoot from the prairie province. Its soil in Kansas and Nebraska was wonderfully rich, and the climate was good. Normal precipitation was 30 to 40 inches of rainfall or snowfall a year, well distributed over the growing season. The western portion was part of the Great Plains. Its soil was less fertile, and it was an area of semi-aridity. It was treeless, whereas the prairie section contained timber along its streams sufficient for houses and barns. The eastern portion was a prize agricultural area, one of the most attractive in the world. Its virtues were well known in Missouri and Iowa. For more than a quarter-century it had been crossed and recrossed either by traders to Santa Fe or by mountain trappers and emigrants on the way to Oregon and California. In 1850 the census showed population pressure already developing upon the area, especially from Missouri. Vacant public land was still available in Missouri but it was rough—the upland country of the Ozark Plateau.

The Missouri public was eager to have territorial organization conferred by Congress on this country and to have land offices opened there. Senator Benton of Missouri was the spokesman in Congress of this demand. Even in Iowa there was pressure for such legislation, led by Senator Augustus C. Dodge. In the genesis of the Kansas-Nebraska Act an important element was thus pressure from the central portion of the frontier, which had been, throughout its history, running ahead of other sections in the speed of its settlement. In 1854 there were already many speculators who had crossed the line into the Platte Country.

An obstacle to opening this attractive region to settlers was a row of Indian reservations erected in Jackson's presidency that stood in almost solid array on the eastern boundary of the Platte Country. Most of the Indians there had treaties of special solemnity promising they would never be moved again. But such guarantees were never considered by the West an insuperable obstacle to white advance. New treaties could be made with the Indians, moving them away, and the land could be conferred on settlers who would make better use of the soil. As early as 1848 a proposal was made to Congress by the Commissioner of Indian Affairs that the Indians in the Kansas and Nebraska region be moved away—that some of the tribes be shifted southward and others northward, in order that the center area could be opened to white settlement.

In the spring of 1854, while the Kansas-Nebraska debate was going on, nine treaties of land cession were obtained from the Kansas and Nebraska tribes by the Commissioner of Indian Affairs, by which the Indians giving up their lands were pushed southward into the Indian Territory or northward into the Dakotas. These treaties, and others subsequently negotiated, removed from Kansas at least some of the tribes, though a considerable number of reservations remained.

A further important element in the genesis of the Kansas-Nebraska Act was the need for a railroad connection between the Middle West and the newly acquired territories on the Pacific coast, which could be used by the tens of thousands of pioneers moving across the plains and mountains to Oregon and California. With the discovery of gold in California the primitive wagon trails had become outmoded. The number of migrants moving to California and Oregon annually in the early 1850's was 50,000 to 60,000. A strategic factor also was part of the problem. A transcontinental railroad was necessary as a means of tying California to the rest of the Union, integrating this distant coast more closely and safely to the heartland of the nation.

Improvement in the means of reaching the west coast had been especially urgent in the mind of Douglas of Illinois. As early as 1844, while a member of the lower house of Congress, he had begun pressing it as a means of encouraging migration to the Oregon Country. For the same reason he was demanding territorial organization of the Platte Country. He remained active in these causes as senator and chairman of the Senate Committee on Territories.

If a railroad were to be built to the Pacific only one route could be selected, because of the cost of construction and the lack of immediate traffic. A choice had to be made between a northern, southern, and central route. A northern route had long been under discussion. It had been advocated by Asa Whitney, a prominent railroad promoter, as early as 1844. He would have built a railroad from the western tip of Lake Superior to the Pacific Ocean, roughly along the line occupied now by the Northern Pacific. Whitney urged federal aid in the form of a land grant and that idea had intrigued the American public. It had been recommended to Congress by sixteen of the states in the 1840's. But by 1854 it had lost support. The northern route had come to be regarded as too handicapped by severe winters and too distant from likely latitudes of settlement.

A southern line had many supporters, especially one running via New Orleans and the Gila Valley to Los Angeles, the route for which provision was being made in the Gadsden Purchase Treaty. Such a course was advocated especially by Jefferson Davis, who in 1853 was Secretary of War and in charge of the Pacific railroad surveys.

A central route was favored in the northern states. It was the route of the Oregon and California trails, and roughly the one taken later by the Union Pacific and Central Pacific railroads. It would have as its eastern terminus Omaha, with branch connections to Chicago and to St. Louis.

Douglas had political and personal interests in a central route. He would benefit from a St. Louis terminal, which would give satisfaction to his constituents in southern Illinois. He would benefit even more directly from a Chicago terminal, where he had large real estate holdings. The central route was also advocated by Benton.

Congressional legislation was needed to make any one of the routes available. A land grant would be needed to enable builders of the road to obtain loans to pay construction costs. Also, territorial organization of the Platte Country was required so that the land, through which the railroad would pass, could be opened to settlement. Settlers were indispensable to any railroad to provide traffic and to give value to a land grant.

But before the Platte Country could be given territorial organization the southern slavery interests in Congress had to be reconciled. They had to be persuaded not to block its opening. They were reluctant to permit the Platte Country, which was north of 36° 30′, to be organized on a free-soil basis. They resented the old Missouri Compromise restricting slavery north of that line, and demanded the repeal of that restriction before they would agree to give it territorial government.

These elements were led in Congress by Senator David R. Atchison of Missouri, an extremist on the slavery issue and for years an ardent disciple of Calhoun. He said in 1852 that he would see the Platte Country "sunk in hell before he would agree to organize it as free-soil territory."

But Atchison had to take account of the fact that the people of Missouri were eager to get the Platte Country opened to settlement. He was being attacked at home, especially by Benton, for keeping that country closed. He was forced to adopt the compromise that he would vote for the opening of the Platte Country if it were on the basis of "popular sovereignty." Atchison was a close friend of Douglas and spurred him to introduce a bill to organize the Platte Country on that basis—on the doctrine that the people of the territory should make the decision as to slavery. Douglas had long been an advocate of that doctrine. Later, in the Lincoln-Douglas debates, he said regarding it: "I care more for the principle of self-government, the right of the people to rule, than I do for all the negroes in Christendom." Though New England-born he had no great moral objection to slavery. He was himself a slave owner through his wife, who owned a plantation in the state of Mississippi, worked by 150 slaves.

Douglas was moved by presidential aspirations. He hoped that, by identifying himself conspicuously with the doctrine of popular sovereignty in the West, he might obtain the Democratic nomination for the presidency in 1856. A western Democrat, Lewis Cass, had won the party nomination in 1848 by enunciating the doctrine of congressional non-interference with slavery in the territories. Cass was 72 years of age in 1854, and thus out of the running. Douglas probably calculated that by associating himself prominently with the similar doctrine of popular sovereignty he would attract compromise sentiment on the issue of slavery both North and South. If he won the Democratic nomination he would probably win the presidency. For in 1854 the Whig party was in a state of virtual dissolution.

Douglas was charged on the floor of Congress with this personal ambition in introducing the Kansas-Nebraska bill. Congressman William Cullom, a Tennessee Whig, said of the bill: "This bill, Sir, should be on the private calendar, and the title of it should be so amended as to read, 'A bill to make great men out of small ones and to sacrifice the public peace and prosperity upon the altar of political ambition.'" This personal element in the genesis of the Kansas-Nebraska Act was seized upon later by New England historians, who made it the central explanation of the introduction of the bill.

In the bill as originally drawn in 1853, the Missouri Compromise was not openly repealed. The same kind of a provision was incorporated in the bill as had been contained in the Compromise of 1850—that the question of slavery in the Platte Country should be left to the territorial courts with the right of appeal to the Supreme Court. But in this form the bill did not satisfy southern extremists. They demanded an outright repeal of the Missouri Compromise. In response to these demands Senator Archibald Dixon of Kentucky moved, as an amendment to the bill, an outright repeal of the Missouri Compromise.

Douglas was on slippery ground. He had lost standing in the North by his first concealed concession to the South. In order to solidify southern approval he had to make further concessions. He accepted the Dixon amendment. Then he was pushed still further—he agreed that the Platte Country should be organized not into a single territory, but into two, Kansas and Nebraska. Both should be organized on the basis of popular sovereignty. But the tacit understanding was that Kansas was to become a slave territory and Nebraska a free one. The fugitive slave law was to apply to both territories. This was the final form of the bill, which was pushed through Congress by the Democrats, who controlled Congress, and was approved by President Franklin Pierce. The act specifically empowered the people of each territory to decide the issue of slavery within their borders.

The law opened to the possibility of slavery all the remaining unorganized territory of the United States—territory from which slavery had hitherto been excluded by an old and honored sectional compromise.

The law was greeted in the South with enthusiasm, though no demand for such legislation had existed there. It was represented in some southern circles to be a free-will concession to fairness by the North. In the North, on the other hand, the law was greeted by furious indignation and the greatest political excitement since the days of the American Revolution. It was considered a repudiation of a binding agreement made with the South of 1820. Douglas was denounced in the North as a traitor to his section. The press called attention to the fact that his middle name was Arnold. Douglas later said he could have traveled all the way from Boston to Chicago by the light of his burning effigies.

The law was momentous in its consequences. It was one of the most explosive of any of the laws ever passed by Congress. It completely destroyed the peace between the sections that had been made in 1850. It reopened wide the sectional conflict over slavery in the territories, only recently quieted. Now the conflict came up in the form which was to end in the Civil War.

It began with charges of bad faith made by each side against the other. The North charged that the South had rejected the bargain it had made in the Missouri Compromise of 1820, that it had repudiated a compact. Among New Englanders, and their children in the West, there was something peculiarly reprehensible about the repudiation of a compact. The religious concepts of New England Congregationalists rested on the foundation of a compact with God, and the revocation of a compact regarding a moral issue, such as slavery, seemed especially evil. This deep feeling rendered difficult any future agreements on the slavery issue and that was ominous for the peace of the Union.

The South, in turn, charged the North with bad faith because of the recent adoption by state legislatures of the so-called Personal Liberty Laws. These laws were ostensibly passed to protect free northern Negroes from being kidnapped and returned to slavery in the South. But their real purpose was to nullify the Fugitive Slave Act of 1850 by introducing such legal obstacles in the way of the return of fugitive slaves as to discourage Southerners from attempting their recovery. The laws were defended in the North in terms of personal liberty and, also, on the ground that the South had repudiated the Missouri Compromise.

An important consequence of the Kansas-Nebraska Act was that Abraham Lincoln was brought back into public life. He had been withdrawing from politics, but the Kansas-Nebraska Act roused him and made him the champion of the principle of resistance to any further extension of slavery in the territories. Another consequence was the shattering of the old national political parties—the Whig and Democratic parties. This was one of the most ominous consequences of the act. National parties had been strong and useful bonds of union, tying the different sections of the nation together. So long as national parties were intact, politicians were able to adopt compromises on the slavery issue. In both sections they were able to defend compromises on the grounds of party harmony, on keeping party members in other sections satisfied. In that way sectional differences had been softened and collisions had been avoided. With the breaking up of national parties those valuable conciliation forces disappeared, and the sections moved toward an appeal to arms.

The shattering of the old parties and formation of new ones is depicted on the diagram presented here.

The Whig party broke into three segments. It had already been cracked during the Mexican War over the issue of Wilmotism. Two new parties absorbed most of the Whig migrants. Beginning in 1854 a large portion of them in the Northwest joined the new Republican party, pledged to fight the extension of slavery into the territories,

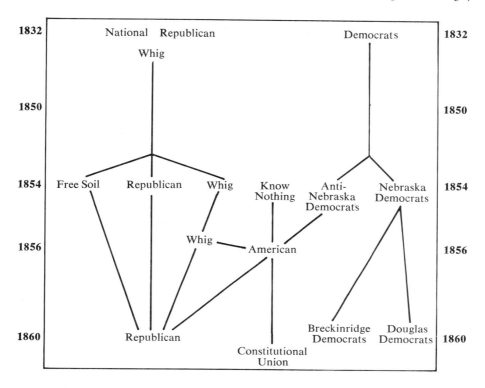

Kansas and Nebraska in particular. In 1854 a large fraction of the southern Whigs moved into a nativist party—the Know-Nothing or American party, as did some of the eastern Whigs. An insignificant fragment of the Whigs stayed loyal to the old party. It hung on a few years, like a ghost, after the party had died.

The Republican party sprang up in different portions of the North almost simultaneously with the adoption of the Kansas-Nebraska Act. It had many birthplaces. An animated rivalry has existed among local historians as to the locality that deserves the credit as the birthplace of the party. The truth is there was no single birthplace. The multiplicity of them is significant as a reflection of the widespread revolt in the North against the extension of slavery north of the Missouri Compromise line.

The Know-Nothing party, dating as such from 1854, had roots extending back to the nativism of the 1830's and 1840's. Increasing manifestations of nativism in the 1850's reflected fears arising from the great influx of Irish and Germans at that time. The fears were partly religious. The Irish and German immigrants were Catholics. They were believed to be undermining American Protestantism because of their allegiance to the Pope. Political anxieties were also potent. The Irish were feared in the large cities because they voted as a racial group under the influence of their own leaders. The Irish were feared, also, on economic grounds. They had a lower standard of living than the native-born and were believed to be taking work away from them. Many Irish had been assisted in migrating to the New World by the British government to get them off the poor relief. They were considered a charity problem unloaded by Britain on the United States. The Germans were unpopular because some of them were freethinkers in religion and others were Socialists in politics. They were disliked, also, because they observed the Sabbath after the continental fashion.

In the South, as well as in the North, objection was felt toward foreigners partly on religious and partly on economic grounds. In the southern cities, especially along the Gulf and in the Mississippi River towns, objection was taken to the Irish on the ground that in the job market they undercut the native elements.

Nativism was stimulated also by a desire, widespread among party leaders, to escape the disruptive issue of slavery by fastening upon an issue on which the North and the South could agree. Every member of the Know-Nothing party took an oath to support the Union. The party program was "America for the Americans." No person except a native-born American, and no Roman Catholic, was to be permitted to hold office in the United States. In land legislation there was to be discrimination against aliens. Also, the period required for naturalization was to be extended to 21 years.

In the Democratic party the Kansas-Nebraska Act was also divisive, though for a time not as shattering as among the Whigs. In the congressional election of 1854 the party became divided into Nebraska and Anti-Nebraska Democrats. Among the latter, a minority, the confirmed antislavery elements soon deserted to the Republicans. In the presidential campaign of 1856 the majority of Democrats (Nebraska Democrats) straddled the issue of slavery in the territories and did not split. Buchanan was named to head the ticket; John C. Breckinridge was nominated for the vice-presidency. Buchanan had privately disapproved the Kansas-Nebraska measure, but had happily been absent from Washington during its enactment as American minister to England. Breckinridge was an extremist on the slavery issue. The Democratic platform endorsed the doctrine of non-interference by Congress in the territories, and specifically approved the Kansas-Nebraska Act. It ignored the Ostend Manifesto, a pronouncement by Buchanan and two other American ministers at European capitals, favoring American acquisition of the Spanish slaveholding island of Cuba.

In 1856 the Know-Nothings (renamed the American party) and the remnant of Whigs avoided the slavery issue and separately nominated Millard Fillmore. The Republicans denounced the extension of slavery into the territories, urged the admission of Kansas as a free state, and named John C. Frémont, the romantic pathfinder of the West, as its presidential candidate. The newly formed Republican and American parties fell far below the Democratic party in the electoral vote—174 for Buchanan, 114 for Frémont, 8 for Fillmore. But, as the diagram shows, the ultimate effect of the Kansas-Nebraska Act on the Democratic party was its split in 1860 and defeat by the Republicans.

The House vote on the explosive Kansas-Nebraska Act is shown on the map (61). It foreshadowed the Republican vote in the presidential election of 1860. The nay vote on the map conforms almost exactly with the later area of Republican majorities. It is a storm cloud formed in Congress threatening the Union. The single nay vote in Louisiana was a Whig hero—Theodore Hunt—who made an excellent speech denouncing the Kansas-Nebraska measure as a breach of compact and deriding the argument that the bill was a free-will offering by the North.

The immediate practical outcome of the Kansas-Nebraska Act was a rush of population into Kansas. It was of major proportions. It brought a sufficient population

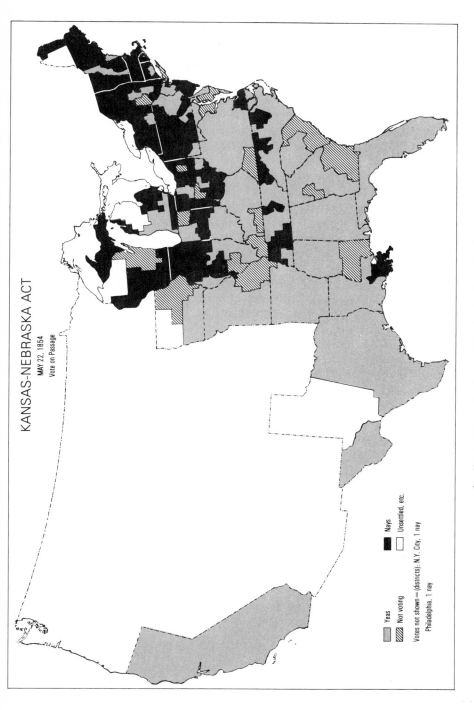

61. House Vote on the Kansas-Nebraska Act (from Paullin)

to Kansas in seven years to entitle the territory to statehood. The source of the population was for years a subject of historical controversy. Some historians emphasized the contribution of New Englanders. Deceived by the newspapers of the 1850's, they represented the flow as a crusade to save Kansas from slavery. But this was a myth. All the states in the latitude from New England to Iowa contributed only 16 percent of the Kansas population in 1860. New Englanders and New Yorkers were moving in those years into Michigan, Wisconsin, and Minnesota.

The principal sources of the Kansas population in 1860, according to the census of that year, were the valleys of the lower Ohio and lower Missouri, which are in the Kansas latitude. They provided 59.5 percent of the Kansas population. They had been providing a comparable proportion of migrants to that part of the West for years. Migrants had convenient means of access to Kansas by the waters of the Ohio and Missouri, and steamboat service on them was at its height in the 1850's. The Ohio Valley was thoroughly propagandized by local emigrant aid societies as to the beauties of the Kansas prairies. The lower South contributed even less than the North to the population of Kansas—only 13.5 percent. Migrants from the cotton South preferred to move to Louisiana and to Texas, where conditions were safer for holding slaves.

The motive of the rush was thus largely economic. The emigrants settled in the prize portion of Kansas—the fertile eastern section—in response to the normal pioneer desire to take advantage of the attractiveness of prairie soils. Not many moved for the political purpose of saving Kansas from slavery, though they preferred free labor to slave. A few, usually New Englanders, went as crusaders against slavery. Some were under the spell of Eli Thayer, the head of the New England Emigrant Aid Company. Thayer was a Massachusetts abolitionist who had a comprehensive plan to surround the cotton South by a cordon of free states. An initial phase of the plan was to be worked out in Kansas, which would be converted into a community of free men. From that center the whole Southwest would be abolitionized. Another zone of freedom would be formed in the border states of the Union from Virginia to Missouri where free labor would be demonstrated to be more profitable than slave. The demonstrations would occur in pilot projects of enterprising northern farmers, in parts of the border region, where slavery was of marginal profit. If all these could be carried to success, a cordon of freedom would surround the Deep South. Then slavery could be allowed quietly to burn itself out there.

To implement this plan Thayer worked at both ends. In Kansas he gave aid to antislavery migrants through the New England Emigrant Aid Company. The aid was in a variety of forms—economic and military. In western Virginia—in Wayne County of what is now West Virginia—he established a colony at a site named Ceredo, which was to be the first of several in the border states to demonstrate the superiority of free labor. The project got off to a good start. By 1858 it had a population of 500. Ultimately, however, it failed for economic reasons, and, with it, Thayer's scheme of redeeming the border region failed.

In the South a similar concept of winning Kansas by eastern action was entertained. The plan was described in a famous southern journal, the Charleston *Mercury*.

If the South secures Kansas, she will extend slavery into all the territory *south* of the fortieth parallel [of north latitude] to the Rio Grande, and this, of course, will secure for her pent-up institution of slavery an ample outlet, and restore her power in Congress. If the North secures Kansas, the power of the South in Congress will gradually be diminished, the [border] states of Missouri, Kentucky, Tennessee, Arkansas, and Texas together with the adjacent territories, will gradually become abolitionized, and the slave population confined to the States east of the Mississippi, will become valueless. All depends upon the action of the present moment.

None of these attempts, northern or southern, to artificially colonize Kansas succeeded. But efforts at such colonization did have one effect—they created anger, especially among Missourians. Missourians regarded the work of the New England Emigrant Aid Company as a nefarious attempt to establish an abolitionist state on their western border. They resented most the financial help given by the company to New Englanders to settle Kansas, which they considered a natural field for Missouri expansion. Southerners in general were indignant not merely because of the money provided by the company, but because of the source of the money. Among the large contributors were New England textile manufacturers who profited from the protective tariff, which, though lower than it had been, was still considered in the South an exploitation of consumers. The bitterness of Missourians was the greater because of the exaggeration of the effectiveness of the aid given by the Emigrant Aid Company. All this contributed to the later conflict in Kansas.

The principal effect of artificial colonization was that troublemakers moved into Kansas. The Northerners were crusaders for freedom, such as John Brown, higher-law men, religious fanatics, who took the Old Testament literally, who believed in the doctrine of blood atonement, an eye for an eye, and a tooth for a tooth. On the southern side, the troublemakers were Missouri border ruffians, the type that had already driven Northerners of the Mormon persuasion out of the state. With extremists of these types gathering in Kansas violence was almost inevitable.

A prolific source of turmoil was the lack of specification in the Kansas-Nebraska Act as to the size of population in each territory that would justify election of a legislature. The omission was first used to advantage by the Missourians, who reached Kansas earliest because they were nearest. An election was held on order of the governor in March 1855. The number of legal voters then in Kansas was 2905. The votes cast in the election were 6307, the excess representing Missourians who had crossed the border for the purpose. The legislature so chosen at once drew up a slave code. Neither the legislature nor the code was recognized by the free-staters in Kansas.

In October 1855, the free-staters, in an extralegal election, chose a constitutional convention. The convention, meeting in Topeka, named a "governor," framed a free-state constitution, and ordered an election in December—in which the free-staters ratified their constitution. Now Kansas had two governments: one consisting of a federally appointed governor, acting with a legal, though fraudulently chosen, legislature; the other consisting of an illegally chosen body which exercised the dual functions of a convention and legislature, and selected a "governor." Neither body sought to exert authority except over its own adherents. Early in 1856 the free-state legislature applied to Congress for the admission of Kansas as a state.

In Congress the House voted to admit Kansas as a state under the Topeka constitution. The Senate, under Democratic auspices, approved a comprehensive and fair-minded bill providing for a new census in Kansas and a new election for a constitutional convention, both under the supervision of a presidential commission. The measure was allowed to die in the House, where Republicans were willing to let developments in Kansas take their course.

The developments were increasing violence. Shootings had occurred in Kansas in the spring of 1856 in which a pro-southern sheriff was wounded. In retaliation, on May 21, the pro-southern militia, aided by border ruffians, stormed the New England settlement at Lawrence and sacked it.

Then John Brown swung into action. He calculated that five free-state men had been killed and that five slave-state men should die as atonement. He and his sons collected five slave-state men in their neighborhood indiscriminately and murdered them—not only murdering them, but mangling their bodies. The act was that of a maniac. A report of it by a relative of the victims was:

> I found my father and one brother lying dead in the road about 200 yards from the house. I saw my other brother lying dead on the ground about 150 yards from the house in the grass near a ravine. His fingers were cut off and his arms were cut off, his head was cut open; there was a hole in his breast. William's head was cut open and a hole was in his jaw, as though it was made by a knife. . . .

This retaliation, the Pottawatomie massacre, was repudiated with horror by the Kansas free-staters. But it led to a veritable civil war in the territory, in which in a few months 200 lives were lost and $2 million in property was destroyed. This was "Bleeding Kansas."

In the 1856 presidential campaign the Republicans made full use of the issue. In their platform they proposed, as the solution of the problem, that Kansas be immediately admitted as a state under the Topeka constitution. The Democratic platform, on the other hand, endorsed the Kansas-Nebraska Act, which had left the issue of slavery to territorial governments, without congressional interference, and subject only to the Constitution of the United States. On this platform the Democrats won the election and James Buchanan became President.

Shortly before Buchanan's victory Kansas held its annual election for the territorial legislature. The free-staters refused to participate in it. The legislature as a result was again proslavery. In 1857 it summoned a constitutional convention to meet at Lecompton in the latter part of the year. The convention framed a proslavery constitution and submitted it to the voters for ratification on spurious terms. The choice offered was: "for the constitution with slavery" or "for the constitution without slavery." In either case, the constitution, in which slave property already in Kansas was recognized and given protection, had to be accepted. Submission on these terms was denounced throughout the North as a fraud and as a mockery of squatter sovereignty. The vote, taken on December 21, 1857, was boycotted by the free-staters. The resulting count was: "for the constitution with slavery," 6226, of which 2720 were later shown to be fraudulent; "for the constitution without slavery," 560.

Two weeks later another referendum on the Lecompton constitution was taken, under the auspices of the territorial legislature, which in the election of October 1857 had passed under the control of free-staters. The vote on this occasion was: "for the constitution with slavery," 138; "for the constitution without slavery," 24; against the constitution, 10,226.

In the meantime, with its credibility damaged by the mode of its submission to the electorate and the response made to it, the Lecompton constitution had been sent to Congress. In February 1858, President Buchanan urged Congress to give its approval, and admit Kansas to the Union. He maintained that the Lecompton constitution was the choice of the Kansas electorate, and that the free-staters were in rebellion against the government. Buchanan was defied on the issue by Douglas, who insisted that the vote taken in Kansas on that constitution had made a mockery of the principle of popular sovereignty.

Ultimately, after a savage struggle, a compromise measure, the English bill, was adopted by Congress. This provided for a new vote on the Lecompton constitution. If Kansas would accept the constitution a reward would be given in the form of a generous land grant for educational purposes. If it should reject the constitution, its admission as a state would be indefinitely delayed.

In August 1858 the new vote was held. The result was a rejection of the Lecompton constitution, by a vote of 13,088 to 11,300. Kansas was unable to enter the Union as a state until after the opening of the Civil War.

The Kansas struggle was of special significance in the history of the westward movement in two respects. It gave a rigorous testing to the doctrine of popular sovereignty, which disclosed its inherent weaknesses. It brought the nation closer to the final catastrophe of the Civil War.

The Dred Scott Decision

THE CONFLICT BETWEEN the sections over the extension of slavery into the western territories was more than a moral, political, or economic issue. It was a constitutional issue, the question whether Congress, under the Constitution, had the authority to close the territories to slavery. That issue had been debated with great earnestness in the contest over the Wilmot Proviso. It was debated again in the fight over the Kansas-Nebraska Act. It had never been carried, except peripherally, to the Supreme Court, the final interpreter of the Constitution. In 1855, a year after the adoption of the Kansas-Nebraska Act, it reached the Supreme Court.

The case had a history reaching back to 1834. In that year, Dred Scott, a Missouri slave, was taken by his master, an army surgeon, to the free state of Illinois, where he served his master for several years. He was then taken to the free territory of Minnesota, where he served a time longer. Eventually he returned with his master to Missouri. In 1850 he was persuaded to bring a suit for his freedom in the state courts of Missouri. The thesis of his lawyer was that Scott had gained freedom by residence in the free state of Illinois and also in the free territory of Minnesota, but the suit was rejected.

Scott was then sold to a New Yorker named Sandford. A new suit was brought, this time in the federal courts. It was a contrived, a framed case to get a federal ruling on the right of Congress to exclude slavery from the territories. Sandford was an abolitionist who wanted a ruling that Congress had authority to exclude slavery from the territories. Officially the Supreme Court did not know this was a contrived case. That appeared nowhere on the face of the record.

The first question to be decided was whether the case could properly come before a federal court. This remained from beginning to end the central issue in the proceeding. A case may come to the federal courts only where the contestants are citizens of different states, or where some federal issue is involved. The lawyer for Dred Scott argued that this was a case of "diversity of citizenship"—that Scott was a citizen of Missouri bringing a suit against a citizen of New York.

The Supreme Court, speaking through the Chief Justice, Roger B. Taney, decided that Dred Scott was not a citizen. He could not be a citizen because he was a person of Negro blood. No person of Negro blood, if descended from those brought to this country as slaves, could ever become a citizen even if he became free. Citizenship, the Court held, was intended by the framers to be denied to Negroes, even to free Negroes. They were considered by the framers to be unfit for American citizenship. That they were regarded as an inferior race was shown by the fact that in most states they were ineligible, even if free, for militia service, were forbidden to intermarry with whites, and were made subject to slavery. Thus Dred Scott could not bring a suit into the federal courts on the ground of diversity of citizenship.

Here the case might have ended. But a new line of argument was developed by the Court to prove that Scott was not a citizen. If it could be shown that he was still a slave, he was clearly not a citizen. Therefore the question was canvassed by the Court: is Scott still a slave? The answer to the question was that, indeed, he was still a slave. He was not made free by residence in the free state of Illinois because from Illinois he voluntarily returned to Missouri. Once back in Missouri his status was fixed by the laws of Missouri, not by the laws of Illinois.

In support of this position the Court cited an 1851 federal case—*Strader v. Graham*. This was a case involving Kentucky slaves, part of a traveling minstrel show, who had been taken by their master across the Ohio River to put on a performance in the free state of Ohio. After the performance they had voluntarily returned to Kentucky. Somewhat later the question arose whether they had acquired freedom by their sojourn in a free state. The unanimous judgment of the Court was that they had not—that their sojourn in Ohio had operated merely as a temporary suspension of their slave status, that when they voluntarily returned to Kentucky their status was determined by Kentucky law. If these minstrels had refused to return to Kentucky from Ohio they could not have been forced to do so. They were not runaways or fugitives in Ohio and so were not covered by the Fugitive Slave Law. But they had voluntarily returned to a slave state and were therefore still slaves.

The next inquiry of the Court was whether Scott had been made free by virtue of his residence in Minnesota, a territory north of 36° 30'. The judgment of the Court was that he had not become free by virtue of such residence, because that territory had never been made free soil. The Missouri Compromise of 1820, which was intended to make the region north of 36° 30' free soil, was contrary to the Constitution.

The Court held that a territory could not be closed to slavery. There was no authority given to Congress in the Constitution to do so. The provision "to dispose of and make all needful rules and regulations respecting the territory or other property belonging to the United States" was a grant only of administrative power to Congress. It gave Congress nothing more than an authority to sell the public land and to fix the rules for doing so. Here the Court was taking over the argument of Calhoun.

This argument was pressed a step further by the Court. Whatever might be the meaning of the language in Article IV, Section 3, that section applied only to territory belonging to the United States at the time the Constitution was framed. It did not apply to territory later acquired, as the Louisiana Purchase. The framers were very exact in their language. If this section had been intended to apply to territory later acquired, it would have said so. When the Constitution referred to the treaties which were binding on the United States, it said "treaties made, or which shall be made, under the authority of the United States."

None of the territory west of the Mississippi River belonged to the United States when the Constitution was framed and none became part of the United States until 1803, when the Louisiana Purchase was made. Therefore Article IV, Section 3, whatever its meaning, did not apply to the Minnesota area, and conferred no authority at all there.

Then where did Congress get authority to legislate for that western region? The Court held that it was a derived power, from the powers to make treaties, to make war, to admit new states. This derived power Congress must exercise as a trustee acting for the people of all the states. As a trustee, Congress must legislate for the benefit of all of them, and it is also bound by the restrictions imposed by the Constitution, in particular by the Fifth Amendment, which forbade Congress to enact any legislation depriving persons of life, liberty, or property, without due process of law. Slaves were recognized as a legal form of property under the Constitution, and any congressional legislation which deprived persons of their slave property for simply taking slaves into a territory, was contrary to the due-process clause of the Constitution and void. Thus that part of the Missouri Compromise of 1820 barring slavery from the territory north of 36° 30' was never valid law and Dred Scott was not made free by residence in the territory of Minnesota.

An awkward fact which the Court had to face was that the Northwest Ordinance of 1787 had been passed by the Confederation Congress. It had closed the Northwest Territory to slavery. That act had been reaffirmed in 1789 by Congress under the Constitution. Many of the members of Congress so voting had been framers of the Constitution and presumably knew what the instrument was intended to do. None of these men had ever questioned Congress's right to reaffirm the Northwest Ordinance—to shut a territory to slavery.

In facing this problem the Court used Calhoun's argument that the Congress of the Confederation, which initially adopted the Northwest Ordinance, could exercise powers that belonged to states since it was then the representative of state sovereignties. The states, everyone admitted, could exclude slavery from their western territories. The states of 1787 had done so in Congress, and the Northwest Ordinance was therefore legal. Later, when Congress under the Constitution reaffirmed the Northwest Ordinance, it was only giving recognition to an act that an earlier government of the Union had adopted.

The crucial part of the decision in the Dred Scott case was the part that held invalid the exclusion of slavery north of 36° 30' by the Missouri Compromise. That aspect of the decision was at once made the target of northern critics. According to them it was not a necessary part of the decision. It was a mere collateral statement, a mere side remark of the Court, an *obiter dictum*. This line of attack was taken particularly in New England, and was also taken by Abraham Lincoln. It was adopted by New England historians in accounts of the decision. Subsequently this view was challenged. In the newer view the Missouri Compromise part of the decision was integral to the case. What the Court was doing was merely returning to the central issue of whether Dred Scott was a citizen. It was demonstrating, by a second line of argument, that Dred Scott could not be a citizen because he was still a slave, and that he was still a slave because he had not been freed by residence in Minnesota Territory, where the exclusion of slavery was invalid.

Another line of attack on the decision was that it was politically motivated. The record of the case was used to substantiate that thesis. When the decision was first written, it stopped short of canvassing the Missouri Compromise. It stopped at the first leg of the argument. Then it became known that Justice John McLean, a Republican who had political ambitions, was writing a dissenting opinion, and that he was canvassing the whole issue of the constitutionality of the Missouri Compromise, in an effort to uphold its validity. When that became known, the majority decision was rewritten, and in this form, as finally handed down in 1857, it covered the problem in its entirety, including the constitutionality of the Missouri Compromise. Chief Justice Taney, who wrote the majority opinion of the Court, came to be regarded by legal historians at a later time as one of the greatest justices of the Court.

Two of the nine justices wrote dissenting opinions, Benjamin R. Curtis and John McLean. The dissent of Curtis was particularly strong, abler than that of McLean. He analyzed the argument of the majority point by point. On the question whether Dred Scott was a citizen he challenged the majority. He argued that Scott was a citizen and had a right to bring a suit in the federal courts. According to Curtis, a Negro born within the United States and free, was *ipso facto* a citizen of the United States. Curtis argued that any free person born in the United States was a citizen of the United States, and of the state in which he resides. The fact that a Negro was formerly a slave or had ancestors who were slaves, was not, in itself, a bar to becoming a citizen of the United States.

According to Curtis, no barrier existed in the Constitution to the admission of free Negroes to citizenship. The framers, he wrote, regarded all free Negroes residing in the United States when the Constitution was formed as citizens; and all their living descendants were citizens. In five of the thirteen states, free Negroes were not merely citizens, they were voters, and actually voted on the ratification of the Constitution.

Taney answered this argument by admitting that free Negroes had a right to vote in some of the northern states, but he insisted that the right to vote was not proof of citizenship. Aliens were allowed to vote in many of the American states. On the other hand, women, who were citizens, did not have the vote.

Curtis next challenged the majority thesis that Dred Scott was still a slave. He maintained that Scott was freed by residence in the free state of Illinois, where even a temporary residence gave him permanent freedom. Freedom is not an impermanent, a transitory status that could be lost. It is indelible. It was fixed on Dred Scott as a status for the remainder of his life by residence in Illinois and was not divested when he returned to Missouri. Here, however, Curtis was flying in the face of the unanimous judgment of the Supreme Court in *Strader v. Graham*.

Curtis gave special emphasis to the issue whether Dred Scott was made free by residence in the territory of Minnesota. His judgment was that Scott had been made free by that residence. The Compromise of 1820, by which the area north of 36° 30′ was made free, was a law that Congress had the right to pass. Under the Constitution, Congress had the right to close the territories to slavery. Congress was given this right by Article IV, Section 3, which was a sweeping grant of legislative authority. Curtis was stating here the old Webster constitutional doctrine.

The public reaction to the Dred Scott decision was sectional. In the North the decision was received with indignation. The North felt that the Court majority had sold out to the South. The Curtis dissenting opinion was hailed in the North; it was felt to have demolished Taney's argument. But in the South the Court's decision was received with satisfaction. It seemed to completely vindicate the old southern position regarding the question of slavery in the territories.

The real meaning of the decision was that the western territories were all legally opened to slavery. The invalidation of the Missouri Compromise of 1820 was not in itself of any practical importance. That measure had already been repealed by the Kansas-Nebraska Act. But the principle had now been established that no western territory could ever again be closed to slavery by Congress.

A second consequence of the decision was that the Republican party was put outside the pale of the Constitution. For the party platform rested on the thesis that the territories could be closed to slavery. A third result of the decision was that Douglas's doctrine of squatter sovereignty was made legally untenable. For if Congress was without constitutional power to bar slavery from the territories, still less was a territorial legislature able to do so, which was a mere creature of Congress.

The final consequence of the decision was that the Supreme Court became discredited in the North, and was regarded as a protective shield for southern property interests in slaves. This loss of standing became evident in the Civil War and in the Reconstruction period. In the Civil War Lincoln was able to flout the opinions of the Court with impunity, especially in the famous case of *ex parte Merryman*. In the Reconstruction period the Court did not for years dare to take a vigorous stand against congressional measures of Reconstruction, some of which were patently unconstitutional.

Ultimately the Court's decision in the Dred Scott case was nullified. It was reversed by the Fourteenth Amendment to the Constitution, adopted soon after the close of the Civil War, which provided: "All persons born . . . in the United States, and subject to the jurisdiction thereof, are citizens of the United States and of the state in which they reside. . . . " By this amendment American citizenship was lifted above the racial level read into it by the Supreme Court in the Dred Scott case.

The West and Slavery,
1856 – 60

THE NEW POSTURE given by the Dred Scott decision to the status of slavery in the territories became the fighting ground of American politics for years thereafter. It was the central theme in the Lincoln-Douglas debates in the Illinois senatorial contest of 1858. The contenders in those debates were spokesmen of the two major political parties and of the two major population stocks in the state. Paradoxically, Lincoln, a Southerner, spoke for the New England stock inhabiting the northern part of the state; Stephen A. Douglas, a New England Yankee, born in Vermont, spoke for the Southerners inhabiting southern Illinois.

In the discussion Lincoln tried to put Douglas and his party in a logical box. He asked how, in the face of the Dred Scott decision, they could adhere any longer to the doctrine of squatter sovereignty. How could the doctrine and the Dred Scott decision be reconciled? "Can the people of a territory in any lawful way . . . exclude slavery from their limits prior to the formation of a state constitution?"

Douglas answered with a statement that came to be known as the Freeport doctrine. He argued that squatter sovereignty and the Dred Scott decision could be reconciled. The people of a territory could exclude slavery despite the Dred Scott decision by simply neglecting or refusing to provide police protection for the institution. Slavery could not exist in a territory without police protection, and the people of a territory therefore still possessed the power to decide the issue. They still had the substance of squatter sovereignty despite the Dred Scott decision. This doctrine was profitable to Douglas in his campaign for the Senate, but disastrous to him in the long run. It ruined him as a candidate for the presidency in 1860.

To the people of the South the Freeport doctrine seemed tricky and dishonest. It suggested a mode not merely of nullifying a Supreme Court decision, but of robbing them of legal rights the Court had declared were theirs. The South decided not to support the sponsor of such a doctrine as its presidential candidate in 1860.

In the eyes of antislavery Northerners also, Douglas was brought to destroy himself as a candidate. Lincoln led him to say again and again that he did not care whether slavery in the territories was voted up or down, so long as the people had the right to do the voting under the doctrine of popular sovereignty. Prior to the debates Douglas had won a considerable amount of goodwill among Republicans by his denunciation of the fraudulent submission of the Lecompton constitution to Kansas voters and by his break with President Buchanan over it. When he began his campaign for re-election to the Senate, many Republicans thought he ought to be encouraged. He was even regarded by some eastern Republicans as a possible future party leader. But after the revelation of his moral obtuseness on the slavery issue in the debates, he was ruled out as a Republican candidate. He stood exhibited as a man of easy virtue on the slavery question.

The presidential campaign of 1860 was another stage in the continuing clash over the issue of slavery in the territories. It was unusual in one important respect. Issues were defined and positions taken by the contesting parties with entire clarity. The usual ambiguity and vagueness of party platforms was, in this campaign, conspicuously absent.

The first of the nominating conventions to be held was that of the Democratic party. It met in the summer of 1860 at Charleston, in South Carolina. That meeting place was unfortunate. It set the stage for extremism on the slavery issue and prepared the way for the ultimate disruption of the convention and of the Democratic party. More than half the delegates there were Northerners, which was a reflection of the fact that the chief strength of the party lay in that populous section. The North was in control on the floor of the convention. But the South was able to control the crucial platform committee.

The platform committee made a valiant effort to find a compromise solution to the issue of slavery in the territories. It wrestled with this problem day after day. In the end it failed and a divided report was submitted. The majority report, reflecting the southern extremists, demanded that slavery be not merely permitted, but protected and guaranteed in the territories. Protection was declared ''the duty of the federal government in all its departments.'' This was a summary of a set of resolutions Jefferson Davis had submitted to the Senate on Febuary 2, 1860. It was the extremist reply to the Freeport doctrine.

The minority report was a reaffirmation of the 1856 party platform. It proposed leaving the issue to the territorial governments without congressional interference. On the convention floor this minority report was adopted. Thereupon the extremists, in a separate rump session, approved the majority report. This split prevented naming any candidate at Charleston. At an adjourned convention at Baltimore, attended by both factions, an attempt was made to unite the party. The effort failed when the credentials committee seated enough Douglas delegates to nominate him. To the Deep South, Douglas was anathema. The extremists, a second time, walked out, joined by border-state delegates. In their separate convention they again approved the principle that it was the duty of Congress to protect slavery in the territories, and named John C. Breckinridge as their standard bearer in the campaign. A hopelessly divided party thus entered the campaign.

The Republicans, on the other hand, went into the campaign as an amalgamated and united party. For six years they had been going through a process of unification. In that process they had absorbed the fragments of parties left by the explosion of 1854 and had welded them into an effective political machine.

The process by which the welding was achieved is worth study. It is the process by which new political parties are formed in the United States, and also the process by which parties once formed are kept intact. The chief welding element was the principle of opposition to the extension of slavery into the territories. That principle was kept as conspicuously before the public as possible. Bleeding Kansas was kept bleeding. All the proposals of Douglas and others in Congress to restore peace in Kansas by a fair ballot were voted down by the Republicans, who also exploited to the utmost the unpopularity of the Dred Scott decision.

Another welding element was a business depression hanging over the country after the Panic of 1857, a source of strength always to the party out of office. This one was attributed by the Republicans to the Democratic Tariff Act of 1857, a low-tariff measure, which was said to have been ruinous to American industry. A high-protective-tariff measure was demanded by the Republicans and the platform of 1860 contained a resounding declaration to that end. Here was a combination of ideas beloved of New Englanders—a crusading issue on the moral problem of slavery in the territories, combined with the profit issue of the protective tariff.

A technique used in the fusing process was for the different wings of the party to make concessions to each other on secondary matters, as a means of removing deterrents to uniting on the central issues. The concessions were mostly made by the eastern to the western wing.

One important eastern concession was on the issue of the public lands. Easterners had traditionally been hostile to liberalization of land law. They abandoned the hostility as a concession to the western wing. The platform of 1860 contained a plank favoring homestead legislation—free land for the landless—and in 1862 a Republican Congress gave the West the Homestead Law.

Concession was also made to the West in regard to the problem of anti-foreignism—nativism. On that problem concession was not easy to make. In the Northeast anti-foreignism was rampant, especially in Massachusetts. In 1859 the constitution of Massachusetts had been amended so as to make voting by naturalized immigrants more difficult. Not only naturalization, but a two-year residence after naturalization, and educational qualifications were required for voting—all aimed primarily at immigrants. The same attitude toward immigrants prevailed in other parts of the Northeast. When the Know-Nothing party became absorbed into the Republican party in the Northeast that feeling was absorbed too.

But to the western wing of the party the German vote was important. The Germans were promising material for Republicanism. They were bitterly opposed to the Kansas-Nebraska Act. They objected to admitting slavery into the western territories, but the Democratic party had otherwise appealed to them. Douglas, its spokesman in the Northwest, had denounced nativism, and had been consistently in favor of giving welcome to foreigners. In 1856 most Germans had voted the Democratic ticket. The eagerness of the western Republicans to win the German vote was reflected in Lincoln's attitude. He bought a German-language newspaper in Illinois and used it as an instrument of Republicanism, vigorously denouncing the Know-Nothings. The first concession by the East to the West on the nativism issue was to play it down. Then it began making direct appeals to immigrants for their support by emphasizing the slavery issue. The East thus gradually worked itself free of nativism.

By 1860 the Republican party was ready to repudiate nativism completely. The

1860 platform contained a plank popularly known as the Dutch Plank which read: "Resolved that the Republican party is opposed to any change in our naturalization laws, or any state legislation by which the rights of citizenship hitherto accorded to immigrants from foreign lands shall be abridged or impaired."

Similar adjustments were made by the Republicans on another secondary issue—Prohibition. On this issue New Englanders and second-generation New Englanders in the West had been moralistic. They had been greatly attracted in the mid-1850's by the Prohibition movement. They felt that rum and slavery were the twin children of Satan.

But to the western Germans the Prohibition movement was anathema. They wanted their beer and would enter no party that would deny it to them. That issue had to be adjusted. The Republicans decided to play down the question. It was carefully kept out of party conventions and platforms. The Prohibition movement itself gradually subsided. It practically disappeared during the Civil War, partly as a result of greater tolerance for beer-drinking Germans who were fighting in Union armies, partly because New Englanders themselves began to think that beer was not so bad after all, that it was a lighter and less harmful drink than rum.

Another secondary issue was Sabbath observance. In New England and among western New Englanders, the traditional mode of Sabbath observance was contemplation and prayer. To the Germans in the West, the way to spend the Sabbath was to enjoy band music and malt in their beer gardens. That issue was carefully kept out of Republican party conventions; it was never allowed to disturb party unity, though it continued to be a source of friction between New Englanders and Germans in the West until long after the Civil War.

Thus by bargains and concessions at party conventions, and by concealments on issues that might have been disruptive, the Republican party achieved cohesiveness. In 1860 the party was a coalition of two sections, an eastern and a western one, held together by concessions and forbearance.

The success of these tactics is best revealed in the election returns from 1854 to 1860, as shown on the maps. The first shows the congressional election of 1854 (62), the election immediately following the Kansas-Nebraska Act. It exhibits the shattering of old parties that the act brought about. Black is the area of the new Republican party. Notice that the center of Republicanism was the Old Northwest: Wisconsin, Michigan, northern Illinois, northern Indiana, and Ohio.* There was some scattering strength in New England. The gray is the area of the remaining Whig party. It was rapidly disappearing, a mere ghost of the old party. However, it still survived in New York, Vermont, Pennsylvania, and New Jersey. In the West it still lived in the Missouri Valley.

The white shows the Democratic areas. The party had lost strength in both North and South as a result of the Kansas-Nebraska Act. It had lost control of the House.

The Know-Nothing or American party, shown on the map in the striped areas, had in 1854 swept New England, where the native elements were in alarm over the Irish influx. In New England 23 Know-Nothings were elected to Congress out of a

*It should be remembered, with regard to the maps of congressional elections and of votes in the House of Representatives, that regions of sparse population cover more area on a map than regions of the same sized population where population is more dense. While the voting strength of congressional districts is equal everywhere, the area that districts cover differs.

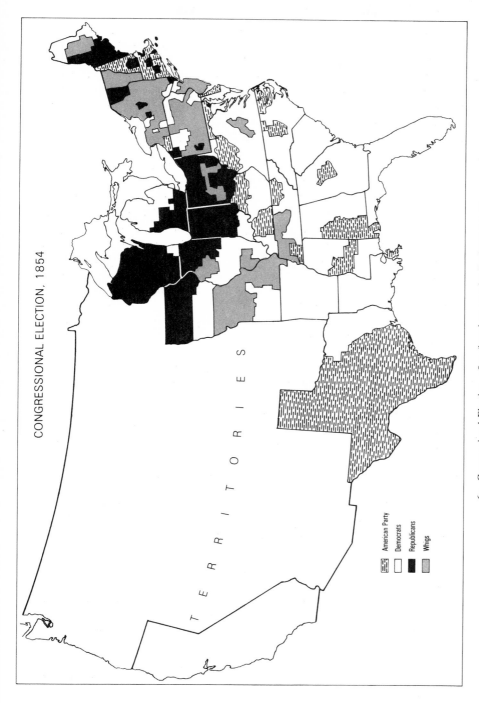

CONGRESSIONAL ELECTION, 1854

American Party
Democrats
Republicans
Whigs

TERRITORIES

62. Congressional Election, 1854 (based on map by Frederick Merk)

total of 29 congressmen. In Massachusetts the entire delegation to Congress was Know-Nothing and so was the state machinery. On the day after the election of 1854 the Whig editor of the *Lowell Courier,* who had been fighting the Know-Nothings, remarked mournfully, "We have met the enemy and we are theirs." In New York City the Know-Nothings also were strong. In the border areas Know-Nothings had great strength in Kentucky, western Virginia, Maryland, and Delaware. In the southern states they were also strong. The Know-Nothing upsurge was so spectacular that some commentators predicted they would capture the presidency in the next election.

On the next map (63) is shown the presidential election of 1856. The Republican party is shown in black. Its growth by the amalgamation process was well under way. It had grown swiftly, though not yet to sufficient size to win the presidency. John C. Frémont was the candidate. Northeastern Whigs had now, for the most part, disappeared into the new party. So had the northeastern Know-Nothings.

The Whig and American party areas are shown in stippled gray. Millard Fillmore was nominated by both parties. In the border states and in the rich lands of the Gulf Plains, the American party showed strength. As in the case of the southern Whigs, their program was intended to avert conflict between the North and the South. But they were a flash in the pan. After this election the party disintegrated. The northern wing moved into the Republican party. The southern wing disappeared, though some of its leaders later joined the Constitutional Union party.

On the map all white areas within the states (except portions marked "no returns") were won by Democrats. They were strong enough to win the presidency. They won all the South except Maryland, and also four northern states—New Jersey, Pennsylvania, Illinois, and Indiana. They also won control of Congress, so that they were able to carry out their program.

They enacted in 1857 a low-tariff measure, almost a free-trade measure, in response to southern demands. They put this through Congress by a line-up shown on the map (64). The black vote here was the opposition to a low tariff, a Republican vote, chiefly concentrated in the Northwest. New England, however, supported the measure, which seems illogical. Actually it is logical, for the 1857 measure, though reducing rates on woolen textiles, more than made up for the reduction by putting raw wool on the free list. What textile manufacturers were interested in was the differential, and the differential in this measure was big enough. But the sheep-growing interests of western Pennsylvania and southeastern Ohio were very unhappy with the bill. So were the Pennsylvania iron manufacturers. They lined up against the act. Because of their resentment, Pennsylvania abandoned its ancient allegiance to the Democratic party, it abandoned Buchanan, and it moved into the Republican ranks. The South voted solidly in favor of the Tariff Act of 1857.

The Panic of 1857 hit the nation soon after this act was passed and was followed by a depression that continued well into the Civil War. The real cause of it was excessive speculation and inflation. But the Republicans blamed it on the low rates of the new tariff. That was very effective propaganda, especially in Pennsylvania, where the iron industry was hard hit by the depression.

In the 1858 congressional election, which appears on the next map (65), Republican unification is achieved. The Republicans had gathered up all the fragments into which the Whig party in the North broke in 1854. They had also won the anti-

Nebraska Democrats. They had captured Pennsylvania—Buchanan's home state. The two big issues in Pennsylvania were the tariff and the Lecompton constitution of Kansas. This congressional vote was highly significant as a foreshadowing of the Republican triumph of 1860. After this vote Republican politicians were confident of the result two years later. Carl Schurz wrote, "If the Republican Party is wise enough in its politics to hold the ground we have gained, we are sure of the Presidential election in 1860.".

On map 66 the election of 1860 is depicted. Four parties are represented, the residual parties at the bottom of the diagram on page 387, resulting from the breakup of the Whig party after the Kansas-Nebraska Act and that of the Democratic party in the Charleston convention of 1860. The Republican party is the solid black. It shows the correctness of the Schurz prediction. The unification of the party has been completed. In the East the New England states and New York are solidly Republican. In the West the children of New England and New York have carried into the Republican column all the states north of the Ohio, together with Minnesota and Iowa. To this combination has been added the crucially important state of Pennsylvania, with its large electoral vote.

In the West, Republican strength was in the area of good soil north of the Shelbyville moraine, the region enriched by glaciation. Its population was predominantly of New England and New York extraction. The Germans in Wisconsin had been won over, or at least mostly so, in spite of their liking for Douglas. Those in the Belleville region of Illinois had likewise been converted. In Missouri they were in the process of conversion.

The compromise areas on this map are shown in various shadings of gray. The vertical lines show the area of the Douglas Democrats—the moderates among Democrats. The plain gray is the area of the moderates of the Constitutional Union party—the party of John Bell and Edward Everett. The Douglas Democrats are a shrunken party located chiefly in southern Illinois and in Missouri, with some scattering strength in Indiana, Ohio, and Wisconsin. The Constitutional Union party is strong in the border states of the Union, areas of trade with both the South and the North that feared the results of extremism in the North and the South. This party is also strong in the South, in old centers of Whig dominance, in the floodplain of the Mississippi, in the cotton area of central Georgia. It is weak in the Black Belt area of Alabama, where moderate sentiment has been swept away by the fire-eaters of the Yancey and Jefferson Davis type. A moderate party, the horizontally lined gray on the map, is the Fusion against Lincoln. It is centered in the commercial areas around New York City and Philadelphia, which had an important coastwise trade with the cotton South that would have suffered if the Union were dissolved. Its adherents were strong enough to divide the electoral vote of New Jersey between Lincoln and Douglas.

The white areas in the states (except portions marked "no returns") are those won by the Breckinridge Democrats, who accepted the doctrine that the federal government must not merely permit slavery in the territories, but also protect slavery there. They repudiated the Freeport doctrine of Douglas, whom they considered to be as reprehensible as the abolitionists. They represented diverse elements in southern society.

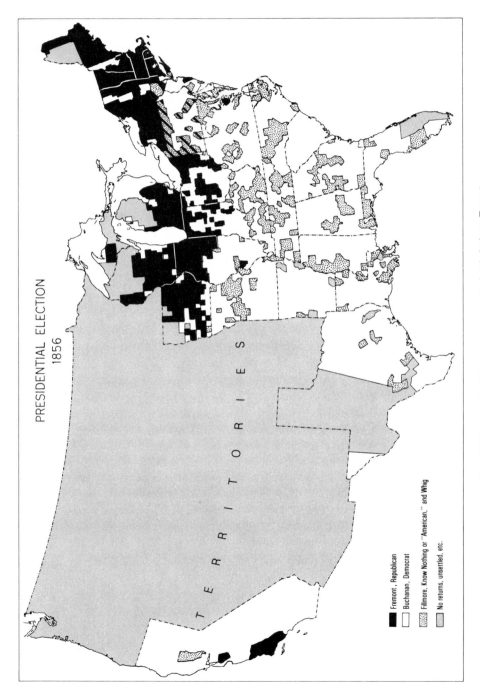

PRESIDENTIAL ELECTION
1856

T E R R I T O R I E S

Fremont, Republican
Buchanan, Democrat
Fillmore, Know Nothing or "American," and Whig
No returns, unsettled, etc.

63. Presidential Election, 1856 (based on map by Frederick Jackson Turner)

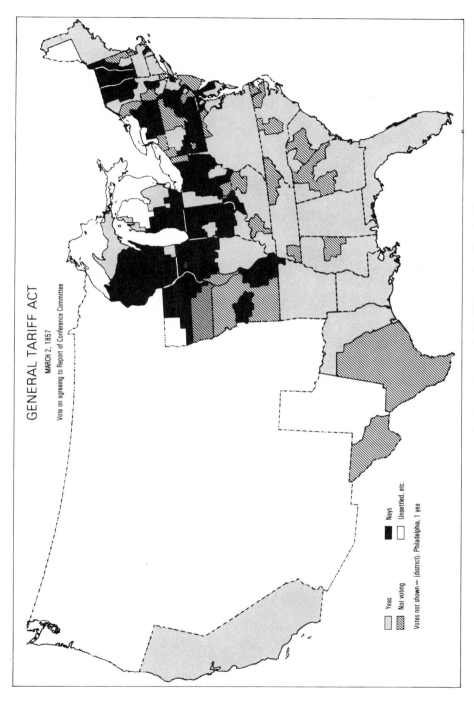

GENERAL TARIFF ACT

MARCH 2, 1857

Vote on agreeing to Report of Conference Committee

Yeas

Nays

Not voting

Unsettled, etc.

Votes not shown = (district): Philadelphia, 1 yea

64. House Vote on the Tariff Act, 1857 (from Paullin)

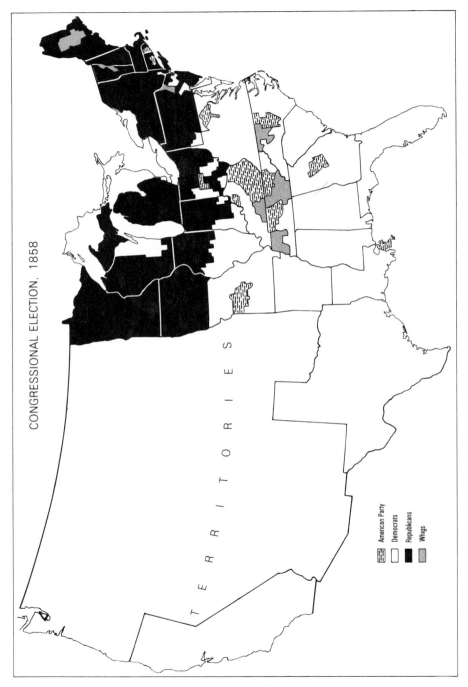

CONGRESSIONAL ELECTION, 1858

American Party
Democrats
Republicans
Whigs

65. Congressional Election, 1858 (based on map by Frederick Merk)

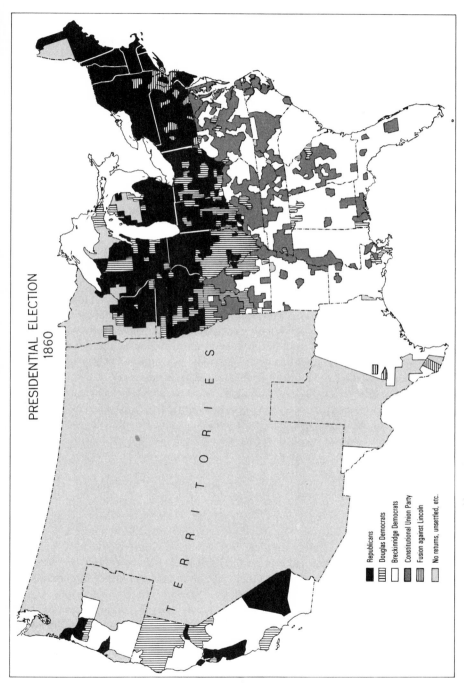

PRESIDENTIAL ELECTION
1860

T E R R I T O R I E S

Republicans
Douglas Democrats
Breckinridge Democrats
Constitutional Union Party
Fusion against Lincoln
No returns, unsettled, etc.

66. Presidential Election, 1860 (based on map by Frederick Jackson Turner)

In the Gulf Plains the overwhelming vote is for Breckinridge. The yeoman whites in the hill areas and the poor whites in the lowlands and swamps are for him. The yeoman whites wished the territories to be open to slavery because they hoped some day to become planters with slaves there. The poor whites hated the Negroes and wished the institution of slavery to be fully protected. The planter class is not united in its vote. In the Alabama Black Belt it has moved over to extremism, but elsewhere in the Gulf Plains, notably in the Mississippi floodplain and in central Georgia, both of which had once been Whig in politics, the planter class has moved into the Constitutional Union party.

Another large segment of southern society was the mountain whites, who occupied the higher upland portions of the Allegheny Plateau province in western Virginia, eastern Kentucky and Tennessee, and northern Alabama. They were to a large extent Scotch-Irish, backward and illiterate. Those in western Virginia, eastern Kentucky, and eastern Tennessee, though southern in outlook, were opposed to secession. Many of them voted for the Constitutional Union party, and when the war came, they cast their lot with the North and joined the Republican party.

In the 1860 election the Republicans won an electoral majority but not a majority of the popular votes. Lincoln had only 40 percent of that vote. His three opponents—Douglas, Breckinridge, and Bell—had a combined vote of almost a million more than his. The nation was a house divided in 1860.

From the point of view of peace the Republican victory was calamitous. The question of slavery in the northern territories was hardly more than academic. In none of those territories could slavery have won a secure hold. The slave crops—cotton, sugar, tobacco, and rice—could not be produced there. In Kansas there were two slaves in 1860. In 1855 the number had been 55, but their owners had nearly all found it prudent to depart for safer and more profitable locations. If the issue of slavery in the territories could have been handled by national parties it might have been brought to a nonviolent conclusion. But the emergence of sectional parties, North and South, rendered accommodation impossible. The formation of the Republican party was described by Rufus Choate as the maddest act of mad times—"the permanent formation and actual present triumph of a party which knows one half of America only to hate it."

Choate was in error in describing the election of 1860 as a " triumph of a party." A "triumph" would have given the Republicans control of the federal government and this was far from what the election gave. If the southern members elected to Congress had taken their seats the Senate would have remained Democratic and the House would have been narrowly divided. The Supreme Court would have been dominated by the majority that had written the Dred Scott decision. Only the presidency changed hands and Lincoln was a moderate on the slavery issue, though this was not recognized by southern extremists.

The answer the extremists gave to the election was an expression of resentment at the prospect of a government, one branch of which was controlled by a party almost entirely sectional. Not a single vote had been cast in the lower South for the Republicans and only a handful in the border states. So divisive a sectionalization had never been experienced in American history, and the lower South refused to accept it. In this sense the formation and partial success of the Republican party led to secession and the war that followed.

Sectionalism as a force in politics has been on the whole an influence for peace in the United States. It has taught Americans the arts of mutual concession, of tolerance, of neighborliness. But sectionalism broke down as a method of adjustment in the years just prior to the Civil War, and the war was the result.

Mining Advance Across the Cordilleran West

IN THE HALF DOZEN years preceding the Civil War the far western territories did more than embroil the East in the slavery issue. Their mountains, located in an area possessed by the United States since 1803 and in acquisitions of the years 1846–53, became the scene of a new frontier advance, that of miners, which turned the nation into one of the greatest producers of precious metals in the world.

Gold was found in the mountains of Colorado just before the Civil War. The first discoveries were in the Pike's Peak region in 1858 and in the region around Boulder and Denver the following year. The Fifty-niner rushes were on a big scale, rivaling those of the Forty-niners into California. They put nearly 100,000 persons in motion, and continued throughout the years of the Civil War. A squatter government, calling itself the state of Jefferson, applied to Congress in 1859 for admission to the Union. No action was taken by Congress, however, on account of the shifting miner population and the national absorption in the slavery controversy. Colorado was given not even territorial organization until 1861, and did not get statehood until 1876.

Nevada was another region attracting gold rushes. Gold was discovered at Virginia City in 1858 and also at Carson City along the old California Trail. At Virginia City the great Comstock lode was found in 1859, which was worked at first for gold but proved later to contain an immense body of silver. The population of Nevada rose in response to these discoveries to 30,000 and by 1861 was large enough to win separation from Utah as a territory. Three years later Nevada was given statehood, partly as a product of politics. The radical Republicans in Congress needed additional votes for Reconstruction purposes.

The Comstock lode proved fabulously rich. An immense quantity of silver and gold was taken out of it. Many great American fortunes were founded there—those of the Hearsts, the Millses, the Mackays, the Floods, and others. With the exhaustion of the lode in the 1880's a decline in Nevada mining set in until the early years of the 20th century, when fresh discoveries of gold, silver, and especially copper lifted the state to new prosperity.

Another gold field in the Far West opened just before the Civil War in Arizona, a discovery made at the old Mexican mining village of Tucson in 1860. Other finds occurred at Prescott (1862), which proved to be less important for gold than for copper. As a result of these rushes Arizona was separated in 1863 from New Mexico Territory.

In the Pacific Northwest the Rocky Mountains were also found to be rich in gold. In Idaho a field was discovered in the upper waters of the Snake in 1860. Discoveries at Idaho City proved fabulously rich. A billion dollars in gold and silver was ultimately taken from the Idaho mines, and in 1863 Idaho became a territory as a result of these developments.

In Montana gold was found at Bannock City in the upper tributaries of the Missouri. The first rushes occurred there in 1862 and continued throughout the Civil War. One with the greatest promise was made at Butte in 1864. Originally a gold find, it proved to be a mixture, principally of copper, but also of other ores. It was the richest hill on earth. It produced over two billion dollars' worth of copper, silver, gold, and zinc, and is still going strong. The mines are at least a mile deep—they contain 3000 miles of underground rails. Immense amounts of low-grade ore are in this area and are being exploited by open-pit mining. Montana was given territorial status because of its mining population in 1864. In Wyoming the region around South Pass was found to contain gold in 1867 and Wyoming obtained territorial status in 1868.

The type of mining used in the newer fields was that of California. It was placer mining—the washing of the sand and gravel found in the bed of streams for nuggets and gold dust. This method was based on the principle of gravity. When a pan full of sand and gravel with gold nuggets and gold dust was shaken gently in running water, the nuggets and dust, which are heavy, sank to the bottom of the pan, while the sand was flushed away by the water.

This process was so simple that placer mining was practiced by prehistoric men. The tools consisted of a shallow pan—a frying pan with the handle knocked off—a pick and a shovel. Some miners used a cradle or "long tom"—a box set on rockers like a baby's cradle which was rocked to and fro in running water. The gold sank to the bottom of the cradle, and was caught there.

Placer mining was well adapted to frontier conditions. Not only did it require no costly tools but no equipment for smelting or refining, since the gold came in virtually pure state. The process also dispensed with transportation of crude ore. The gold dust and nuggets were exported in bags—dust was often sent to market in goose quills.

A more complex form of mining followed placer mining, usually in the richer areas—the so-called lode mining. This was the exploitation of a vein of quartz containing gold. Lodes were usually the sources of the nuggets and gold dust found in the streams. Their discovery was the work of prospectors moving upstream in search of nuggets and their source.

As soon as a promising lode was discovered, machinery to deal with its quartz had to be brought in. It consisted of stamp mills to pulverize the quartz. After pulverization, whatever gold was present was extracted chemically. A quantity of mercury, which has a strong affinity for gold, was poured into the pulverized material and formed an amalgam. The amalgam was then put through a process for the recovery of the gold. Large quantities of mercury were used in this work. It was obtained from the New Almaden mine, discovered in 1845 south of San Francisco in the San Jose Valley, one of the three greatest mercury mines in the world.

Lode mining proved attractive to eastern capitalists. During the Civil War great quantities of adventure capital flowed to the Far West. The amount available for these purposes was surprisingly large. The eastern public was excited by the prospects of sudden and great wealth in the western fields. The extraordinary richness of the Comstock lode had fired popular imagination, and eastern newspapers during the war and after were filled with advertisements of gold-mining stocks, many of them in phony enterprises.

The land on which the Rocky Mountain mining rushes took place was the public domain. It was being trespassed on as had been the case in California. The miners acted under the frontier doctrine that any person had the right to enter the unoccupied federal land or land held only by Indians, and gather the products of the soil un-molested. Land seemed as free to exploit as the air or the water.

The policy of the federal government from an early day was that its mineral lands were in a separate category from its other lands and were reserved from sale. Lead was a necessity to the War Department. In 1807, in the Jefferson administration, a leasing law was passed for the lead lands in Missouri and in the Wisconsin portion of Indiana Territory. The law required miners who took lead from the public land in those territories to pay the federal government as rent a tenth of what they took. However, the law proved impossible of enforcement. Frontier individualism in the lead-mining regions of Missouri and Wisconsin was beyond restraint. In 1821 the Army Ordnance Department assumed enforcement of the law and, for a time, really collected some rents. Then Senator Benton swung into action on behalf of his constituents in Mis-souri. He brought into the Senate a measure for the repeal of the leasing law on the ground that the government ought not to stand in a landlord relationship to the frontier miners. The outcome of the agitation was that the system was abandoned by Congress in 1829 as applied to the mines in Missouri and a system of outright sale there was substituted.

In 1846 the same change was enacted with respect to the lead lands in Wisconsin, Illinois, Iowa, and Arkansas. The legislation provided that the lands be offered at auction at the minimum starting price of $5 an acre. Persons who held licenses to mine lead were given the right to buy at $5 an acre at private sale. The govern-ment's decision to sell rather than to lease its lead lands was a significant change. The change was confirmed the next year in acts for the sale of copper and lead lands at the minimum price of $5 an acre in two newly created land districts—northern Michi-gan and northern Wisconsin. Not until 1920 did the United States return to the policy of leasing its mineral resources.

In his annual message to Congress at the end of 1848, President Polk suggested that the recently adopted sale policy be extended to California, but his suggestion was not approved. No policy was adopted for the California mineral lands for nearly twenty years. In 1850 the selling of lead and copper lands in northern Michigan and northern Wisconsin was encouraged further by reducing the minimum price to $1.25 an acre.

In the absence of government policy the miners of California established their own. In every gold-mining district they set up at miners' camp meetings local regulations governing the use of land and water in their operations. A typical example of such regulations is the one drawn up by the miners' camp of the Jacksonville District in 1850:

1) Any miner coming into Jacksonville may stake out a claim to government land—a claim twelve feet in width and extending at right angles from the bed of the miner's creek back to the hill or mountain. No man or party of men is permitted to hold more than one claim at a time.

2) Any claim in condition to be worked must be steadily worked. It is considered abandoned and may be taken by someone else, if left unworked for longer than a week. This rule, however, is suspended in case of illness.

3) If a claim becomes unworkable because of a freshet or flood, the claimant retains his right to it if he leaves on it his pick, shovel, or crowbar.

4) No claim can be held by any person coming "direct from a foreign country."

Codes of this informal sort for both placer and lode mining were drawn up in hundreds of miners' camps in all the mining states and territories of the Far West. Though differing in detail, all were based on the principles that the public lands were free to be exploited by American citizens, that claims to the lands could be staked out in the order of first come, first served, and that the miner must develop his discovery in order to maintain his claim. Here were the principles of the pre-emption law applied to mining. In some places the miners' code was the only law. As time went on, the codes were incorporated in county, state, and territorial laws.

The rationalization for this exploitation of the minerals of the public domain in the Far West was that the government gave its tacit consent, that it wanted the lands worked and its resources brought forth. Congressional efforts in the 1850's and early 1860's to provide for the sale of these lands received little support. The miners' codes seemed to be working satisfactorily and the miners were content to be occupiers, rather than owners, at least in the era of placer mining.

But mere occupancy was obviously not suited to lode lands. For the mining of ores embedded in hard rock, heavy machinery had to be imported, shafts had to be sunk, waterworks had to be constructed. Private ownership of lode lands was therefore essential. It was what capitalists required before they would make large investments. In 1866 strong pressure from the lode miners of Nevada, combined with the initiative of the Secretary of the Treasury, produced the first congressional legislation for the sale of the government's far western mineral lands, and it was on terms the mining interests wanted.

The Mineral Land Act of 1866, and the two amendments to it of 1870 and 1872, may be considered as a unit. While purporting to establish a general policy for mineral lands, these acts were basically drawn up by, and for, miners and the mining interests of the mountainous areas west of the Great Plains. The lands dealt with were specified in 1866 as those bearing gold, silver, cinnabar (mercury), and copper. The act of 1872 extended this list to include tin, lead, and "other valuable" minerals.

Because these laws were designed to establish secure property rights and to provide federal revenue in the process, the acts provided for government surveys, for the marking of boundaries and recording of plats. Both placer and lode claims could be patented. The placers that miners especially wished to patent were "deep gravel" deposits, beds of ancient gold-bearing rivers that had been elevated by geologic change. These were being exploited by means of powerful streams of water applied through costly equipment. The price for placer land of any description was $2.50 an acre; for lode land, $5 an acre.

A claim that could be patented rested basically on conditions for occupancy that had long before been laid down in the miners' codes. One condition was that no claim could be made until a vein (a lode) was discovered on it. All claims of lode lands were, by custom, small and rectangular, along a lode. One of the changes in the federal legislation was to permit the rectangle to be larger than had been customary. Even so, a claim, in order to be patented, could be no more than 1500 feet by 600 feet. One or more individuals might patent a claim of this size. Placer claims could not be more than 40 acres nor less than 10.

The federal legislation specifically protected water rights. The first miner to divert a stream to his use was protected in his customary right of ''prior appropriation'' to continue this use, but after 1866 the right for others was subject to certain safeguards. The legislation also protected the rights of homesteaders, to the extent of 160 acres of agricultural land, if no minerals turned up on their land.

The freedom of the mineral prospector to roam freely over the public land was protected in Section 1 of the act of 1866, and was not altered in the amendments. The government's tacit consent to trespassing on its mineral land was now given statutory force, just as the trespassing of the pioneer farmer was given statutory force in the pre-emption acts. Normally a prospector would sell a claim, to which he had obtained title, to interested capitalists. Or a partnership would be formed to include the prospector. Claims, once patented, quickly passed to other owners. On the Comstock lode, for example, several claims amounting to twenty acres passed into the hands of the Consolidated Virginia and California Company. Approximately $100 was paid to the government to obtain the original patents. Ultimately the twenty acres produced $60 million.

The mining camps made rules not only for land use, but also for the government of their camps. When a mining rush into a remote area occurred, formal government was slow in getting started. Months or years passed in the process of getting a territory organized, a governor appointed, and a legislature elected. Territorial officials were often mediocre politicians, appointed as part of the spoils system in the federal government. During the Civil War the best talent in Washington was attracted into more important jobs. In the absence of formal government, informal government was instituted by the miners in their camp meetings.

An example of such government is that of the miners' camp ot the Jacksonville District. The officers were a magistrate (alcalde) and a sheriff, elected and holding office at the pleasure of the camp. In all civil cases, such as overlapping or disputed claims or jumping of claims, the trials were by juries of miners or magistrates. In criminal cases juries, usually of eight persons, served. Any person who stole a horse or mule or entered a tent and stole gold dust or other articles to a value of $100 or more, or who willfully committed murder, was on conviction to be hanged. Any person convicted of stealing tools or clothing or other articles to a value of less than $100 was to have his head and eyebrows shaved and to be ejected from the camp.

Such informal codes were for years the only means of preserving public order in the gold-mining regions of the Far West. They were illustrations of the frontier practice of setting up extralegal voluntary government to take the place of formal government. The miners' camps were the successors in the Far West to the Plymouth Compact, the Watauga Association, and the squatters' claims clubs of the East.

Their effectiveness in preserving order was no greater than the orderliness of the population that enforced them. That population was heterogeneous. It consisted of adventurers from the East, often Civil War draft dodgers and deserters. Aliens arrived from all over the world, usually the less substantial and more mercurial elements. Some types were excluded. Negro slaves were excluded in the pre-Civil War era from the California diggings, as were Chileans with peons. Mexicans were admitted on sufferance, Chinese were given a half tolerance—they would be excluded from new and rich discoveries but were allowed to work over the tailings in areas where the best gravel had been exploited. This population was like a swarm of grasshoppers, gathering thickly in an area where pay dirt was reputed to be rich. When word of a new gold discovery arrived, it would swarm to the new region.

The preservation of law and order in such a society was at best difficult. Not only were the miners a rough and transitory population, but many had had an apprenticeship in the wild California gold camps. Thrown together in an exhilarating mountain atmosphere, with plenty of bottled exhilaration available, it was likely to get out of hand. When crimes were detected, punishment was uncertain. A miners' camp meeting was prone to gusts of feeling, rage in some cases, maudlin sympathy in others. Since crime was not effectively dealt with, vigilante committees to cope with it had to be set up. That meant anarchy—the wild conditions recorded by Mark Twain and Bret Harte.

Such conditions were in contrast with the order and peace in the gold fields of British Columbia on the Canadian side of the border. These fields were discovered at about the same time as those on the American side. The population that flowed into them was largely American—the same type of rough miners that raised hell on the American side. But disorder in the British Columbia fields was conspicuously absent. The contrast is so marked that some explanation of it is necessary.

One of the elements in the explanation is that in British Columbia the Crown asserted the right to all precious metals in the soil. A license was required of every miner who took gold from public land. The license had to be renewed each year at a cost of £1 sterling. It was indispensable to a miner. In case of overlapping or jumping of claims, no miner without a license had any standing in the British Columbia provincial courts. The license became a means of exercising control and maintaining order in mining districts.

The government in British Columbia was almost wholly executive. A governor was appointed by the Crown as soon as the gold rushes began and was given full power. A handful of marines was stationed in the province to support him. A mining code was formulated, copied from that of New Zealand. Under it a gold commissioner was appointed for each mining field as soon as a discovery had been made. He was given all the local authority that on the American side was vested in the miners' camp. He had jurisdiction over civil cases, claims, titles, and contracts. He decided disputes, assessed fines and damages without jury trial, though a right of appeal existed, in certain cases, to the Supreme Court of British Columbia.

A very superior type of governor was appointed in British Columbia. The first appointee was James Douglas, who had been chief factor of the Hudson's Bay Company at Fort Victoria. He was a man of high character and ability and had been trained in a great administrative system. He had the advantage, also, that he knew British Columbia by heart.

This executive system of government had the merit that it was swift and elastic. Control was on the spot, in the person of the gold commissioner, almost as soon as miners arrived. Authority came simultaneously with population. Law and order were promptly established. Crime was swiftly dealt with in legal fashion. There never was a lynching or a vigilante committee because there never was need for one. Peace was as well maintained as in the older societies of the East.

On the American side of the line effective authority did not enter new finds simultaneously with population. It came late. The substitute for it—the miners' camp—though better than nothing, was not dependable. Self-help and direct action took the place of it. The habit of violence got established, and was hard later to eradicate.

The contrast between the Canadian and the American mining camps raises questions regarding the whole history of the American frontier. One question is whether the local democracy of the frontier—informal squatter government—was the best government for a frontier society, or whether better results would have been obtained from executive government on the frontier. But this raises the further question whether an executive form of government would have been feasible, whether it would have been admitted on an American frontier. It probably would not have been.

The result of the existence of disorder and violence on American frontiers for two centuries was that a kind of tolerance of them became established in American society. Tolerance of violence came to be an American habit. It appeared in the American tendency to relish Western films, to dramatize and even exalt violence in the national literature. It appeared in the tendency to treat criminal trials as a kind of public entertainment, and in the failure of the American people to deal more effectively than they have with crime. This, at least, was the thesis of Roscoe Pound in his book *The Spirit of the Common Law*.

A number of important consequences flowed from the advance of the miners over the Rocky Mountain West. One was a large increase in the gold and silver output of the United States. The increase occurred in spite of the fact that the California mines by 1860 were beginning to show signs of depletion. The overall increase was a shot in the arm to the economy of the North in the Civil War. It coincided with a great increase in gold production in Australia and New Zealand. It was part of a world increase in gold production. A second important consequence of the mining rushes was the parceling of the West into territories. This was completed in the 1860's, except for the division of the Dakota Country, which came later. Another outcome was the initiation of agriculture in the mountain parks and valleys of the Rockies. Agriculture was needed to supply the food markets which the mining camps created. A fourth consequence was the stimulus given to the construction of the transcontinental railroads. The growth of mining communities in the mountains gave to railroad entrepreneurs the traffic incentive to building across the mountains and to the Pacific. Finally, Indian problems in the Far West resulted. In the mining rushes the Indians of the Great Plains, whose reservations lay in the path of the miners, and the mountain Indians whose lands were overrun by the gold seekers, rose in protest and introduced new chapters in the old problem of the dispossession of the original holders of the soil.

Plains and Mountain Indians and the Dawes Act of 1887

A SUCCESSION OF SPORADIC Indian wars accompanied the advance of the miners across the Great Plains and into the Cordilleran West. The wars coincided in time with the years of the Civil War. They were attributed, in the East, to Confederate instigation. They seemed a replay of British incitement of Indians on American frontiers in the era of British occupation of the Northwest Posts and of Spanish incitement on the West Florida frontier. Actually they were of local origin.

The tribes in the path of the miners belonged to three major Indian groups. One was the northern Plains tribes, numbering about 83,000. It included about 30,000 of the great Sioux linguistic family, occupying the area from the Minnesota lakes to the Powder River valley in Montana. In the Minnesota country representatives of the Sioux were the Santee; in eastern South Dakota, they were the Yankton; in Montana, the Teton and the Oglala. Allied with them were the northern Cheyenne and Arapaho. Hostile to them were the Crow of southern Montana, who, though speaking a Sioux dialect, were traditional foes of the Teton Sioux and therefore friendly to the whites. A second major Indian group lay in the central Rockies and Colorado plateaus. Numbering about 65,000 souls, they included the southern Cheyenne and Arapaho in the Colorado region, and the Apache and Navaho in the Far Southwest. A third group lay in the southern Plains. It included the Five Civilized Tribes in the Indian Territory and such wild Indians as the Comanche, Kiowa, and Pawnee. Their total was about 75,000.

Prior to the Civil War these Indians had not been at war with the United States. Neither had they been at peace. They were likely to rob or destroy small parties of whites traveling across their country. But no general hostilities existed. With some of these tribes peace treaties had been concluded. In 1851 the Fort Laramie treaty had been made with the northern tribes, which permitted whites to travel along designated trails through their country and gave sanction to certain military posts in their midst. Under the terms of this treaty, annuity goods worth $50,000 were distributed among these Indians every year. A similar agreement had been made with the southern tribes in 1853, and annuity goods worth $18,000 had been divided among them.

With the opening of the Civil War sporadic Indian hostilities tormented the trans-Mississippi West. They began with a revolt of the Minnesota Sioux. The tribal reservation, dating from the treaty of Traverse des Sioux (1851), gave no easy access to good hunting grounds, and those Indians were often in a state of starvation. In the summer of 1862 the discontented in the tribe revolted and for two weeks ravaged southwestern Minnesota with raids that cost 450 lives. Especially ferocious was the New Ulm massacre. In terms of casualties the war was one of the costliest Indian uprisings in American history. It horrified the nation and federal troops were needed to restore peace.

In 1864 and 1865 the Teton Sioux, aided by the Cheyenne, rose in revolt and terrorized the ranches of the Montana and Dakota area. In the same year (1864) the southern Cheyenne and Arapaho in eastern Colorado went on the warpath, and as a result 500 of them, including women and children, were the victims of a brutal massacre by a Colorado militia led by Colonel John M. Chivington. Prior to the massacre they had sued for peace.

The Indian grievances erupting in these wars differed from locality to locality and from tribe to tribe. In the mountain areas they were the encroachments of miners on Indian lands. In other areas they were traffic overrunning hunting grounds either on the Plains or in the mountains, which scared off or destroyed game, leading to starvation. A common grievance was the failure of the government to provide annuity goods of the quality specified in treaties. The Indian Office, infested with corruption, was a factor causing this grievance. The charge that the revolts were instigated by Confederate agents was baseless propaganda.

The war of the Teton Sioux and Cheyenne in western Montana in 1866 is an illustration of the traffic problem. When gold was discovered there a demand went up for a guarded road across the lands of the Teton Sioux to the diggings. The route, later named the Bozeman Trail, would branch off from the Oregon Trail at Fort Laramie on the North Platte and run to Virginia City in Montana across the valleys of the Powder River and the Yellowstone.

In order to satisfy this demand the federal government negotiated a treaty with a fragment of the Sioux known as the "Laramie Loafers," permitting a road to be marked out and a series of forts to be built upon it. The treaty was repudiated by the main body of the western Sioux. The marking off of the road and construction of the forts created excitement among the Teton Sioux. It meant ruin of their best hunting lands—those in the Powder River valley. They rose and attacked the construction troops in a succession of desperate assaults. The fighting ran on for years.

A common denominator of these wars was the bewildering advance of civilization on the tribes from opposite directions—some miners westward, others eastward out of California—and ranchers taking lands in scattered, but attractive localities. Surveys for railroad lines and the building of the Union Pacific were other aspects of letting in the white flood.

Part of the problem lay in maladministration in the Indian Office. It was one of the most inefficient and corrupt bureaus in the federal government. One of its functions was to see that treaty goods—annuity goods—which the Indians were entitled to receive, were of the proper quality. They were contracted from private firms under the supervision of the Indian Office. They were often of the poorest quality—blankets of shoddy material, flour that was wormy, ammunition that was defective. Such frauds were passed off on the Indians because of corruption or inefficiency in the Indian Office. In the Grant presidency the administration of the Office was especially lax.

Jurisdiction over the Indians was divided. When the Indians were at peace, the civilian Indian Office was in charge. When the Indians went to war the War Department took over. The two departments were in constant dispute over questions of what was war and what was peace. In an earlier era the War Department had exclusive control of the Indians. After the Civil War many reformers wanted the military to regain exclusive control as a means of assuring honest administration. This ''transfer question'' was an issue which got into politics and complicated the problems of preserving peace.

Because of defective administration and the brutalities of retaliation against tribes that had gone on the warpath, much sympathy was felt in the East for the Indians. The East also objected to the cost of the Indian wars, which in 1865 reached $40 million. In response to this sentiment, Congress undertook to pacify the western tribes. It authorized two peace commissions to proceed to the West, one to go to the Sioux in the North, the other to the Cheyenne in Colorado. The commissions made peace with individual bands of Sioux and a temporary peace with the Colorado Cheyenne. But they failed to effect a general pacification.

In 1867 a new commission was sent out and did succeed in making peace during the next two years. It brought about a general pacification of the plains and mountain tribes. An agreement was made with the Montana Sioux in 1868, which was facilitated by the fact that the Army had agreed to abandon the Bozeman Trail and the forts guarding it. The Army was willing to make that concession because a steamboat route to the upper Missouri had been found feasible, and the Union Pacific railroad was approaching. The Sioux agreed, in return, to accept a South Dakota reservation, with rights to hunt as far west as the mountains. The Peace Commission of 1867 made peace with the southern Cheyenne and Arapaho of Colorado by providing them a new reservation in what is now Oklahoma.

In all these negotiations removal of the tribes from the main lines of travel across the Plains and mountains was the objective. But the difficulty was that new lines of travel were always needed as new gold discoveries were made or new routes to the Pacific coast were opened.

An important recommendation of the commission was that two large Indian districts on the Great Plains should be formed, into which all the Indians of the Plains should, if possible, be moved. The northern should comprise roughly what is now South Dakota; the southern, what is now Oklahoma. The recommendation of a northern district was not in the end adopted. What appears on contemporary maps as a district is merely the Sioux reservation. But the recommendation of a southern district was approved and all the region that is now Oklahoma was set aside for it. In order that lands might be made available for additional tribes in the southern district, cessions of land were extorted in 1866 from the Five Civilized Tribes already there. The cessions were taken on the ground of alleged disloyalty of those tribes during the Civil War.

The location of those tribes at the outbreak of the Civil War is shown on the map

(67). It was a hot spot in the war. It lay between the Confederate and Union armies in the West. The tribes had accommodated themselves to the problem by doing what people under pressure often do, giving allegiance to whatever army marched in on them. The impact of the fighting was chiefly the loss of cattle as the Union and Confederate armies moved back and forth across tribal lands. The Choctaw and Chickasaw had been slaveholders prior to the Civil War and were sympathetic on the whole to the Confederates. The Cherokee, Creeks, and Seminole were divided, each containing a northern and a southern faction. The Cherokee actually raised a military force that fought on the Union side.

The federal government took the position in 1866 that all these tribes had forfeited their treaty rights and reservations by their conduct during the war. Each was obliged to cede, or to sell, about half its territory to the government, though it was allowed to retain the better eastern half. The territory so acquired was assigned to new tribes brought in from the Great Plains and elsewhere. This concentration policy was carried out over a period of about twenty years. By 1887, 22 reservations were located in Indian territory. An Indian population was built up there of nearly 75,000 and, in addition, 6500 Negroes, who had been slaves of the Choctaw and Chickasaw.

The twenty-year period from 1867 to 1887, during which this consolidation was

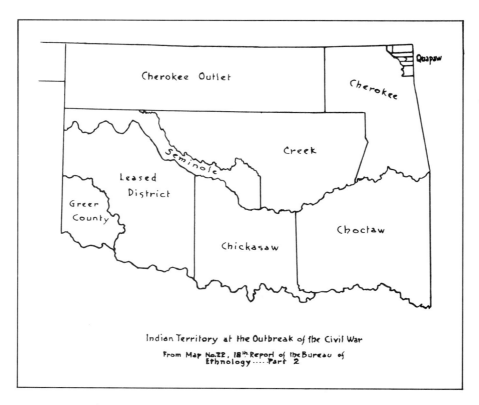

67. Five Civilized Tribes, 1861 (from the Dept. of the Interior)

taking place, is often referred to as the "reservation period" in Indian history. It is the period in which many of the big tribes of the Plains and elsewhere were assigned their ultimate homes in the Indian Territory, comparable to what went on in the era of Jackson. During this period the military aspect of the Indian problem gradually became less important. The power of resistance of the Indians had been broken. Outbreaks still occurred as a result of frontier encroachments on reservations and tribal restlessness. But they were usually not much more than enlarged police problems. In wearing down the Indian power of resistance, a number of forces proved especially effective. One was the extermination of the buffalo on the Plains in the 1860's and 1870's. Another was the construction of the transcontinental railroads. A third was the rising tide of white occupation of the Plains.

The reservation policy involved feeding the Indians to a certain extent. It meant doling out rations periodically to supplement the food the Indians could gather themselves by hunting or farming. The giving of rations was intended to be temporary. It was based on the theory that the Indians could be tided over to the time when they would have been taught to be self-supporting farmers. Training was to be by government teachers. As soon as agriculture had become well established, the periodic distribution of rations would cease. The justification offered for the rationing system was that it was a cheap method of keeping the Indians quiet so that they would not molest the frontier, that it was cheaper to feed the Indians than to fight them.

The feeding system proved, however, to be more than a temporary expedient. It was continued decade after decade. One reason was that the Indians of the Far West did not take kindly to farming. Many of them, unlike those of the sedentary eastern tribes, had little farming tradition. They had been primarily hunters and warriors. Another discouragement was that the training program of the government was not effectively carried out. The teachers sent to the reservations were underpaid, so that those employed were normally only persons who had failed at everything else. Also the Indians looked upon rations as something coming to them in return for the lands they had given up. The ration system tended to become permanent and its effect was to pauperize the Indian.

In 1874 Congress undertook to force able-bodied Indians to work as a condition of getting rations, either on a tribal project or for themselves. Luxuries such as sugar, coffee, and tea in particular were to be obtained only by work. But even such a modest program could not be effectively enforced. The Great Plains Indians became dependents when they ceased to be hunters.

The manner of distribution of rations was defective. As a matter of economy food was sent in big lots and at long intervals. The Indians would use up in a few weeks of gorging and feasting supplies intended to last for months. Then they would starve. In 1875 Congress had to provide that the rations be distributed weekly.

There were defects in the manner of distribution. On ration day each band of Indians would gather at its rationing station. The Indian agent would turn loose, at a signal, half-wild cattle, which the Indians on their ponies would chase and shoot down in the manner of buffalo hunting. Then the carcasses would be relieved of their entrails by the women and a feast would take place of the sort that traditionally followed buffalo hunts. The raw entrails would be devoured like stick candy. Bucks, squaws, children, and dogs would all pitch in, fists full of raw entrails. Then the solid meat on the four quarters would be divided to be carried home. Morbid tourists came long distances to behold such spectacles. A civilized distribution of rations, at stations conveniently located, did not come until relatively late.

These defects of Indian administration called forth little sustained protest from the American public in the years immediately following the pacification of the Indians. In the 1870's a more compelling problem was at the center of the stage—that of the Negro in the South. The plight of the red man did not press itself on humanitarians because that of the black man seemed so much more urgent. Some public interest was aroused, after the Indian wars on the Great Plains, by exposures of graft in the Indian Office in the Grant administration, but not enough to achieve important results.

In the 1880's came greater public interest with the publication in 1881 of Helen Hunt Jackson's *Century of Dishonor*. This was a highly emotional picture of Indian wrongs. Theodore Roosevelt once said of it that not a sentence in it could be trusted without verification. But the book did create much public interest as a kind of *Uncle Tom's Cabin* of the Indian question. In 1883 the annual Mohonk Conference was initiated. This was an annual conference at Lake Mohonk, New York, of organizations staffed by government officials and representatives of organizations interested in the Indians, to consider Indian problems and formulate policies. But in spite of conferences and discussions, reform of Indian administration moved slowly.

One important reform had already been made, however, one concerning the treaty method of dealing with Indians, which had uniformly worked out to the disadvantage of the Indian. In treaty negotiations Indians had no real equality of bargaining power with the federal government. Even if negotiations were equitably carried on, the full implications of the agreements were seldom understood by the Indians. They were, moreover, seldom an effective restraint on the advancing white frontier; they served only as a restriction on the Indians. The whole concept of treaty making with Indians was unrealistic and false. The theory was that the Indian tribe was comparable to a nation, that Indian leaders had the knowledge and the intelligence to understand treaty implications and the organization to carry them out. Reformers demanded that the treaty system be abolished and that Indians be treated as wards of the nation, entitled to protection and civilization.

In 1871 Congress had ended the system of formal Senate-ratified treaties, replacing it by informal agreements made by the Indian Office with tribes, under congressional supervision. The agreements were comparable to contracts made by the government with whites. The episode precipitating the legislation was a scandalous purchase by railroad interests of Osage land—about 8 million acres in Kansas—a purchase ultimately declared illegal by the courts. This scandal did not directly involve treaty making, but it set off that reform.

Another reform demanded by humanitarians was the abolition of tribalism, especially of tribal government. Such government seemed to reformers an obstacle to uplifting the Indians. Under it hereditary chiefs were a controlling force in a tribe. They were usually resistant to change, especially to measures to uplift Indians. They wanted the Indians to remain as they were. In many cases the chiefs were corrupt half-breeds or squaw men (white men married into a tribe), who were ready to sell out the interests of the tribe to predatory whites.

Attempts were made by the government in the 1870's and 1880's to supplant tribal chiefs by representative Indian councils, but with little progress. In 1885 Congress took from the tribes jurisdiction in cases of murder committed by one Indian against another. It was vested in the federal courts.

But the aspect of tribalism that most troubled humanitarians was tribal owner-ship of the land of reservations. It seemed evil in two ways. One was that it lacked the incentive to improve farms and methods of farming. The incentive of self-interest, which was so effective with whites, was absent when lands were held as tribal property. Another evil was that, under the system of tribal land ownership, chiefs could make leasing arrangements with cattlemen. Leases were often corrupt, the chiefs being bribed to agree, on behalf of the tribe, to inadequate rents. These consequences of tribal ownership were especially prevalent in the Indian Territory. The Cherokee chiefs, for instance, leased 6 million acres of land in the Cherokee Outlet to the Cherokee Strip Livestock Association for an annual rental of about 1½ cents an acre. The Cheyenne and Arapaho leased all their western lands at the same rate.

Proposals to abolish tribal ownership of reservations were therefore urged by reformers in the decade of the 1870's and in the 1880's by Carl Schurz, the great reform Secretary of the Interior. These proposals came regularly before Congress. In 1887 a major piece of Indian legislation was finally adopted, the Dawes Act, or Lands in Severalty Act.

The Dawes Act provided that whenever the President considered an Indian tribe sufficiently civilized to become farmers and its reservation good enough to be culti-vated, a distribution of its land should be made to the Indians of that tribe in severalty. In the distribution every Indian who was the head of a family in the tribe was to receive 160 acres. Adults without family and orphans were to have 80 acres, and all other Indians of the tribe, 40 acres. Each Indian was to have the right to make his own selection of land for his farm. The choice had to be exercised within four years after the President had authorized the distribution. If any Indian failed to make his own selection, it could be made for him by the government.

Every Indian receiving an allotment got what was known as a "trust" title. This was not a full right to land. Full title was retained by the government on behalf of the Indian for at least 25 years. During the period no sale could be made by the Indian of the land nor could a mortgage be put on it. If, at the end of the 25-year period, an Indian was still considered unqualified to take final title, the trust period could be extended. Citizenship was to be conferred on all Indians obtaining a trust title. The surplus land in a reservation after the allotments had been made was to be bought by the federal government and thrown open to white settlement. The money paid for the land was to be held in trust for the tribe by the government. Eventually it was to be used for educating and civilizing the Indians of the tribe. The Five Civilized Tribes of Oklahoma were exempted from the operation of the Dawes Act. They insisted on being excluded from it. In 1906, however, after many years of negotiation, they agreed to divide their land in severalty by themselves and to sell their surplus land to the federal government.

The Dawes Act was regarded as a great reform act at the time it was enacted. It was pushed by eastern humanitarians. Its author, Senator Henry L. Dawes of Mas-sachusetts, had long been interested in Indian advancement. The measure also had considerable western support, though not always on humanitarian grounds. It was in part based on the expectation of surplus Indian land being turned over to white settlement.

Some opposition was made to the measure in the West, chiefly by big cattlemen holding leases in Indian reservations, which would have to be given up. Also, some hard-boiled Westerners thought the Dawes measure too liberal to the Indian. They wanted simply to move the Indians off the reservations and let them shift for themselves. The opinion widely held by disinterested persons was that the act was a great measure of Indian emancipation, that it would usher in a new era in the history of the relations of the two races in the West.

Technical defects in the law soon appeared. One was that citizenship automatically passed to any allottee to whom a trust title to land was given. Citizenship was used chiefly to buy whiskey. Indians had been protected, in theory, from whiskey dealers while they were noncitizens. This situation was altered in 1906 by the Burke Act, amending the Dawes Act. Future allottees were not to become citizens during the trust period but only after land had passed in final title.

Another defect in the Dawes Act was that all Indians, competent as well as incompetent, were dealt with alike. Every Indian had to wait 25 years for full title. The long wait, it was argued, was a discouragement to competent Indians. This was altered in another section of the Burke Act. Allottees who were judged competent could be granted final title to their lands at any time—at once or later.

The outcome of the Dawes Act and its amendments is illustrated on the next maps. The map of 1875 exhibits the extent of the reservations before the act was passed (68). The map of 1930 reveals what remained then of the reservations (69). The only considerable reservations remaining are those in the semi-arid grazing country of the Southwest: the Navaho, Hopi, Apache, and other reservations.

For many years after its adoption the central principle and general purpose of the Dawes Act went unchallenged. As late as 1909 the measure was described by a historian of the West, Frederick L. Paxson, as an Indian emancipation act.

Challenges were made, however, to its administration as soon as distributions in severalty began, and these became more insistent when Indians on a wide scale received final title to the land. The right of an Indian to make his own selection of land was often exercised ignorantly and carelessly, on the basis of such unimportant considerations as proximity to a berry patch or to firewood, rather than the quality of the soil. Where an Indian failed to make his own selection the choice was left to a government agent and was made mechanically. Under the act, leasing by an Indian of his land during the trust period was permitted and became common, especially to cattlemen. It enabled the Indian to live in relative idleness. He did not develop as a farmer.

But the greatest error was the premature granting of final title to land under the Burke Act of 1906. Thereafter final title could be given whenever an Indian was adjudged competent. The judge of competence was the Indian Office. A test of competence was drawn up by it for Congress in 1908. It was intended to apply only to the Five Civilized Tribes, but was later used generally. It was woefully lax. Any Indian of the Five Civilized Tribes was considered competent who was more than half white or half Negro. Full-blood Indians were considered competent if they had a record of primary-school attendance for several years.

These loose tests were applied with particular recklessness in the presidency of Woodrow Wilson. His Commissioner of Indian Affairs, Cato Sells, was wholly without experience in Indian matters. Under him final title was given with appalling speed. No effort was made to ascertain whether the recipient had developed enough responsibility to hold final title to the land. In the Harding and Hoover administrations this reckless policy was reversed. Under Hoover the Indian Office followed a conservative policy. But that was too late. The damage had been done.

The Indians who got final title promptly lost the land. Eighty percent of them lost their land almost at once. The amount of reservation land belonging to Indians in the United States just before the Dawes Act was passed was 137 million acres. Of this amount 90 million was lost. In 1933, when Franklin D. Roosevelt became President, only 50 million was left to the tribes, including land still held tribally though assigned in trust to individuals. Of the land left to the tribes as such, about half was desert or semi-desert, such as the Navaho and Hopi reservations in the Far Southwest. In 1933 it was estimated that of the 325,000 Indians in the United States 100,000 were landless, off-reservation laborers, and another 100,000 had only fragments of poor land left. The American Indian, as a result of the operation of the Dawes and Burke acts, met the fate the California mission Indians had suffered as a result of premature secularization.

One mode by which lands passed out of the hands of Indians was by direct sale to white land sharks, the money received being spent for an automobile or some other luxury. In many cases Indians were secretly assisted in obtaining full title to land by white lawyers in order that they might be fleeced immediately afterward. Thus, subtle methods were used to accomplish the separation of the Indian from his land, which, in an earlier day, had been achieved by the strong-arm methods of the frontier.

Another mode of loss of land was tax delinquency and forfeiture to state or local governments. The payment of taxes was something unfamiliar to Indians. As long as an Indian's land had been held in trust by the federal government, it had been exempt from all taxes, local, state, and federal. For this reason the more intelligent and responsible Indians wanted the trust period to be indefinitely extended.

A third factor contributing to the loss of land was Indian inheritance legislation of Congress. Under the Burke Act and subsequent legislation the land of a deceased Indian, if held in trust, was to revert to the United States and be sold, and the money obtained from it distributed to his heirs.

Besides land, other tribal assets of the Indians were disbursed, especially the tribal trust funds. These were held in the name of certain tribes in the Treasury Department. Some had been acquired in payment of lands ceded to the federal government in the early part of the century. Another source of trust funds was the payments made by the government for surplus land after allotments had been made under the Dawes Act. Some of the trust funds were greatly enriched by the discovery of oil or coal on tribal reservations late in the 19th and early in the 20th century. Oil and coal were found in abundance on the Oklahoma reservations. In 1898 the Curtis Act was passed by Congress on behalf of these Indians, under which underground rights to oil and minerals were reserved to the Indians even if surface rights were sold. Under the lands of the Osage Indians great pools of oil were discovered, while coal was found under the Choctaw and Chickasaw reservations. Royalties paid into tribal

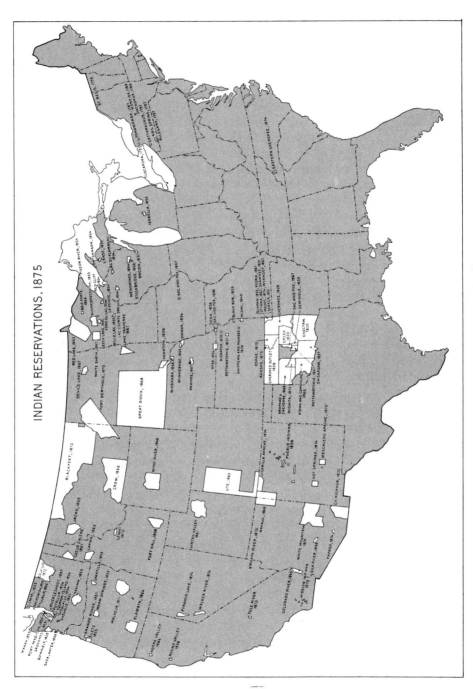

68. Indian Reservations, 1875 (from Paullin)

69. Indian Reservations, 1930 (from Paullin)

trust funds by companies formed to exploit these resources amounted to many millions. Royalties of $240 million were paid into the Osage tribal fund down to the 1930's.

The intention of the federal government was that the tribal trust funds should be used to educate and civilize the Indians of the lucky tribes. That was definitely stated in the Dawes Act. But in 1907 a new policy was adopted by Congress. It was to pay to any Indian found competent by the Indian Office his pro rata share of the tribal funds. That policy was reaffirmed in repeated acts by Congress in the era of Cato Sells. Under this legislation some $500 million, the greater part of the trust funds, was ultimately distributed. In one year members of the Osage tribe received a total of $17,065,000, which was at once squandered. The justification given in the Indian Office for such dispersion of the tribal funds was that they were an evil influence in that they kept alive the tribal consciousness and stood in the way of individualizing the Indians and absorbing them into the mass of American citizens. Also, they kept the Indians expecting to get something from the government and therefore less willing to work for a living. The Indian Office felt that responsibility would be developed by the Indian only if his property was turned over to him. If his property was then dissipated, at least he would be obliged to work for a living.

Most of the money distributed to the Indians was squandered in drink, riotous living, gambling, expensive luxuries, or it was lost to swindlers. It was estimated that seven out of ten of the adults in the Osage tribe became alcoholics.

A notorious mode of dispersion of the property of the Oklahoma Indians was the so-called guardianship system. This was established by Congress in 1908 for the purpose of protecting the property of orphaned children in the Five Civilized Tribes. Under it the property of such children was put under the supervision of the local probate courts in Oklahoma. In 1912 the property not only of orphans but of incompetent and insane members of the Osage tribe was put under the care of the same courts. White lawyers were appointed by the judges to look after the property of court wards. Many of these lawyers used the guardianships as a means of enriching themselves. They absorbed the property of their wards by extortionate fees and commissions, by purchases at inflated prices, and by other devices. The Oklahoma guardianship system was ultimately exposed and became a national scandal. The Oklahoma Supreme Court in 1914 undertook to intervene for the protection of the Indians, but was blocked by the state legislature. Ultimately Congress had to withdraw the care of Indian estates from the Oklahoma courts and restore the responsibility to the Indian Office. The net result of the policy initiated in the Dawes Act, and its implementations, was that by the 1930's two-thirds of the Indians in the United States were virtually without property, and a large part of them were thrown on the public for support.

Agriculture in the Middle West and the Granger and Greenback Movements

IN THE ERA OF THE Civil War a swift advance of farming occurred across the prairie province and into the Great Plains. In 1860 the outer edge of civilization in the Middle West was in northwestern Iowa, western Minnesota, northern Wisconsin, and northern Michigan. A decade later the frontier lay at the edge of the Great Plains, in Kansas, Nebraska, and the Dakotas. It had advanced despite the strains and fatalities of the war in the South, an indication of the material strength of the North. In the same decade scattered settlements were forming in the gold-mining areas of the Cordilleran West.

By 1880 the Red River valley of the North had been occupied, largely by Scandinavians. Western Kansas and western Nebraska were rapidly filling and Colorado had become a state of the Union, with a society partly miners, partly farmers. A white society surrounded the Indian Territory, which was one of the forces evoking the Dawes Act of 1887.

This rapid spread of population meant that the Middle West between 1860 and 1880 became an enormous grain-growing community. The grain was partly corn. Corn production maps for 1839, 1849, and 1859 have shown that the Ohio Valley was then its main center. The corn kingdom was also the empire of hogs and pork production. In 1859 Cincinnati and Chicago were rivals for primacy in meat packing in the United States. By 1869 Iowa and northern Missouri were coming into their own (Map 70). Chicago was now unrivaled as the world's greatest meat-packing center. It had far surpassed Cincinnati. By 1879 corn had swept like a tornado over Illinois, Iowa, northern Missouri, Kansas, and Nebraska (Map 71). This is the period when lyrics were written by Kansas poets on the beauties and virtues of the hog. A new rival to Chicago as a meat-packing center was rising in Omaha.

Wheat was also established in the Middle West in these years as a great staple crop. The variety was spring wheat, which had its location in 1859 north of the corn

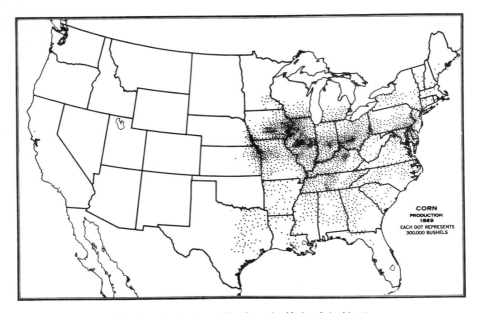

70. Corn Production, 1869 (from the National Archives)

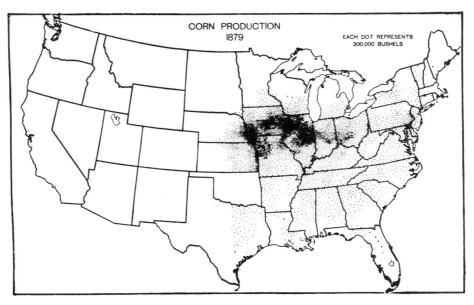

71. Corn Production, 1879 (from the National Archives)

belt. The valleys of the Rock River, in Illinois, and of the Fox, in Wisconsin, stand out. Iowa and Minnesota were beginning to appear as wheat producers. The Middle West was the breadbasket of the nation. In 1869 the most striking concentration was in northwestern Wisconsin and Minnesota (Map 72). By 1879 new advances were across Minnesota's Red River valley, the coming center of the wheat empire. Wisconsin had thinned out as a wheat state, and also northern Illinois (Map 73). Dairying was taking its place. That readjustment, though constructive, was painful, and these areas were centers of political discontent.

The Middle West was also a great wool producer in the years 1860 to 1880. Map 42 (page 178) shows Ohio in 1860 as the chief wool-producing center of the Union. New England had been almost cleaned out. Twenty years later Ohio was still the premier wool state, but the Far West, led by California, had become a close competitor (Map 74). In the twenty years 1860–80 the Middle West thus held primacy in American agriculture. It dominated the agriculture not only of the United States but of the world. How did it acquire and hold that position?

One of the factors was the development and widespread use of agricultural machinery. The machine age of agriculture may be said to have reached the Middle West in the years immediately preceding the Civil War and during the war. Among the many varieties of machines prominent in this development the most important was a recently developed combination of reaper and binder. This united the functions of cutting the ripe wheat in the fields and binding it. The bundles of bound wheat were left in the field to season before they were threshed.

Another great improvement was a plow made of chilled steel, which was put on the market in 1868. This was a light and tough instrument, admirably suited to breaking the prairie sod. Other agricultural machines came in quick succession, machines for drilling seeds into the ground, corn planters, corn huskers, and scores of others. They produced a revolution in farming comparable in extent and in significance to the Industrial Revolution, which was transforming the urban production of the United States in the same years. Its effect was to neutralize the high labor costs of the West, which had previously been one of the chief handicaps in competing in the food markets of the world.

Another factor in the rise to dominance of middle western agriculture was the extraordinarily favorable land legislation of the federal government. In 1862 the Homestead Law was passed by Congress, which gave to settlers 160 acres of fertile land free. At the same time especially well-located land could be bought from states and from railroad companies at favorable rates. A major factor in the growth of the section was the free immigration policy of the United States. This brought great numbers of hard-working foreign farmers to the United States.

Highly important was the expansion of railroads across the Middle West. Railroads made their way to the section after 1850. They had been of only minor importance earlier. By 1860 the middle western network was well outlined (Map 75). It was beginning to have a nucleus at Chicago. St. Louis was also developing as a railroad center. Between Chicago and St. Louis there existed in 1860 a keen rivalry for control of the trade of the trans-Mississippi country. It was comparable to the rivalry which had existed earlier between the cities of the Atlantic seaboard for command of the Ohio Valley trade. Railroad expansion was significant not only in economic history but in the military history of the United States. It was one of the decisive factors in the

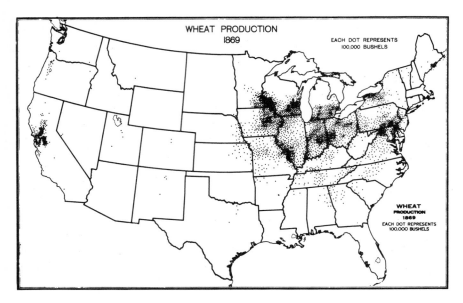

72. Wheat Production, 1869 (from the National Archives)

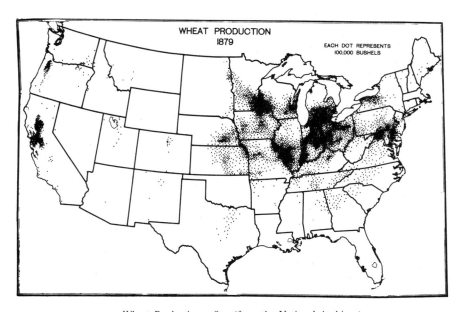

73. Wheat Production, 1879 (from the National Archives)

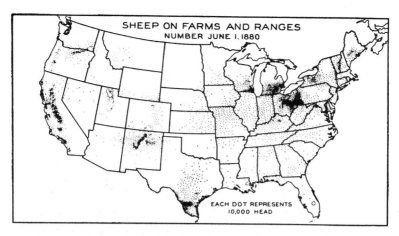

74. Sheep on Farms and Ranches, 1880 (from the *Yearbook of Agriculture,* 1923)

outcome of the Civil War. That war was the first conflict in history in which railroads played a decisive part.

By 1870 railroads had crossed the Minnesota wheat belt and the Iowa and Missouri corn belt (Map 76). They were moving into the Great Plains. The single thread of the Union Pacific stands out on the map—also the Kansas Pacific, a branch of the Union Pacific.

Railroads were not only expanding their net; they were becoming more efficient by improving their roadbed, laying steel rails in place of iron, and building bigger locomotives and freight cars. They thus achieved the ability to compete successfully with lake and canal carriers. They had already captured from the lake and canal carriers the profitable passenger and express business by the late 1850's. In the 1860's they took over much of the wheat transportation and even the carrying of corn and lumber.

In reply to this competition the lake and canal companies added to their efficiency. They constructed larger vessels, powered by steam instead of sail. They induced the federal government to deepen lake harbors. The Erie Canal was enlarged by New York State. Similarly, improvements were made in ocean carriers. All this represented a revolution in grain transportation.

At the same time a revolution was occurring in the methods of grain handling in the transfer centers of the West. Prior to about 1855 the handling of grain in such centers had been primitive. Wheat was shipped in bags. On reaching a transfer center it was shifted on the shoulders of Irish roustabouts from an incoming carrier to an outgoing one. Storage facilities were primitive. Wheat was stored in ordinary warehouses, with bags stacked one on another. Inspection was cumbersome. A buyer wishing to inspect a parcel of wheat had to open individual bags. The whole process of shipment, storage and inspection was clumsy and costly.

In the late 1850's and early 1860's a new system of transfer and storage of grain was developed in Chicago and Milwaukee. It was the elevator system. Grain elevators were specialized structures for the handling and storing of grain, and for that

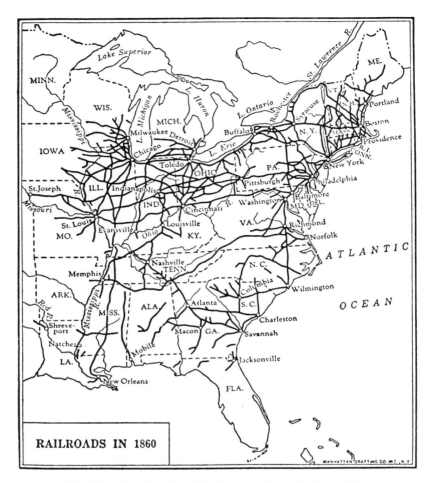

75. Railroads in Operation, 1860 (from *Scribner's Statistical Atlas*)

purpose alone. They were on a big scale. Some of them had a capacity of millions of bushels. The Armour elevator in Chicago could hold 5 million.

Internally, elevators consisted of a series of tall, perpendicular bins into which grain of predetermined grade was hoisted by buckets on endless belts, after the manner of snow loaders. Carloads of grain could thus be elevated into a bin in a few minutes. As grain arrived at an elevator it was weighed, and its quality was determined by an inspector who was a grain specialist. An elevator receipt was handed the owner specifying the weight and grade of his grain. The grain then lost its identity as a parcel. In country elevators the weighing and grading of grain was done by the elevator owner. In the big grain centers the inspector was an appointee of the Chamber of Commerce. Once elevated in a terminal elevator, the grain was handled in mass. All the economies of mass handling became possible. Wheat could be spouted from an elevator bin into a lake vessel for the journey eastward at the rate of 8000 to 10,000 bushels a minute.

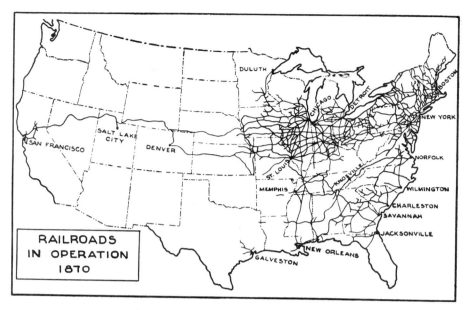

76. Railroads in Operation, 1870 (from Brown)

The advantages of the new system can be judged from a comparison of the old and the new charges for the handling of wheat. Under the old system the charge had been about 6 cents a bushel. The new cost, including the hoisting of the wheat, storing it for 15 days, and loading it onto a lake vessel, was, during the Civil War years, 2 cents a bushel. If grain was stored through the winter in Chicago, the total charge was 4 cents a bushel.

The elevator system made possible a new form of commercial credit. Elevator receipts were used as such. In Illinois they were designated commercial paper by the legislature in 1867 and this expedient was adopted by other middle western states. The result was that an owner of grain could borrow money on it while it was on the way to market.

Another institution—part of the marketing of grain—was developed in the 1860's in the Middle West, the so-called futures trading. This was of special use to flour millers operating on a large scale. A miller entered a contract for flour he was to deliver, well in advance of the actual grinding. His occupation required planning for continuity of work. He had to have, at the outset, time to prepare wheat for the grinding, to clean and dry the grain, and to mix hard and soft varieties in proper proportions.

Purchase and storing of the full amount of grain to fulfill a contract would not be economical at the time of its signing, as a large investment of capital and a heavy cost in storage would be required. Furthermore, it would entail a major financial risk, since wheat prices are subject to constant fluctuations in response to world conditions in agriculture and international relations. In the main producing countries wheat can prove seriously short, or war break out or end, any one of which would be promptly reflected in the wheat exchanges of Chicago or New York.

The press carries the highest and lowest bids for wheat each business day. Bids may be for wheat at the present price, to be delivered at once; or they may be for "futures," wheat to be delivered on a future day at an estimated price. As a protection for his future needs, the miller, as soon as he has made his flour contract, orders his broker to buy wheat futures to the full amount of the wheat he expects to need for the contract. He pays the broker a fee of a tenth of 1 percent of the estimated price for the futures he buys.

As soon as work begins on his contract the miller buys cash wheat, and, at the same time, orders his broker to sell an equal amount of his futures. Any loss or gain in the price of his purchases that might have resulted from market changes is offset by equal loss or gain from the sale of his futures. If the price of wheat has fallen he will have gained in his cash purchase. If the price has risen, the loss he would otherwise have suffered on his cash purchases is covered by the sale of the futures. The operation is repeated as batch after batch of wheat is used. What has been achieved is the elimination of the risk of a disastrous rise in the price of the wheat he must use. He has insured the one profit in which he is interested—the profit of a manufacturer. Futures trading is a form of industrial insurance. It leaves the risk of loss to the speculator, who is skilled in the business.

Trading in futures became normal not only for grain but for derivatives of grain, such as pork. It became so extensive during the Civil War that, at its close, a body of rules regulating it was drawn up by the Chicago Board of Trade. Similar modes of operation were later extended to textile manufacturing to eliminate the risks of cotton price fluctuations, and to the processing of other agricultural commodities. Trading in futures became an outstanding characteristic of American economic life, the outcome of the fact that, in the grain elevators of Chicago and Milwaukee, methods of storing and grading grain were worked out in the period of the 1850's and 1860's.

The new methods, whether of transportation or marketing grain, were of major advantage to the farmers of the Middle West. They made possible effective competition with foreign growers in the grain markets of Great Britain and of continental Europe. They permitted moving the increasing surpluses of the United States to those markets, just when the surpluses had become too large to be absorbed on the American side of the Atlantic Ocean.

But improvements in the modes of transporting and marketing grain in the era of the Civil War proved a mixed blessing to grain producers in the Middle West. On wheat, moving from the upper Mississippi to the lake ports of Chicago and Milwaukee, the freight rate rose in the war years from 10 cents to 35 a bushel. This was a joint river and rail rate applied to through traffic from the upper river to La Crosse, and thence by rail to Chicago or Milwaukee. The 1865 rate was extraordinary not only as compared with the rate at the opening of the war, but also in comparison with the rate eastward from lake ports to the Atlantic seaboard. In 1865 the river and rail rate—a distance of 300 miles—was three and a half times what it had been in 1861. The lake rate to the Erie Canal, a distance of 1000 miles, was 5 cents a bushel less, about what it had been in 1861.

Explanation for the high western rate was in part the nature of the western freight. In the region west of Lake Michigan one-crop agriculture prevailed; wheat and corn and not much else were shipped by the farmers. The harvest went to market in a rush in the autumn or in the spring. During the remainder of the year there was relatively little traffic. Even in the busy shipping season, traffic was heavy only one way—from the river to the lakeshore; on the return trip, freight cars went half filled, or empty. A more important factor, however, was monopoly. In the period following the close of the Civil War, a single great monopoly of transportation lines was established in the region west of Chicago and Milwaukee, including almost every railroad running west out of Chicago or Milwaukee, as well as the steamboat lines operating on the upper river.

Another factor was the absence west of Lake Michigan of effective water competition. This was a result of the Civil War, at least in part. Prior to the Civil War, water competition had existed in that region in the form of river steamboats. If freight charges on railroads between river and lake got unduly high, independent steamboats carried the grain to St. Louis or New Orleans. But during the Civil War the downriver trade to St. Louis and New Orleans ceased, and it was not resumed after the war on any considerable scale, because the river was too roundabout a route for grain destined for Europe. Also, the river route was objected to on the ground that grain was likely to heat and spoil in shipment through the Gulf of Mexico. The river ceased to have its old rate-regulating influence. By contrast, in the region from Lake Michigan eastward to the seaboard water competition never completely lapsed. The lake and canal route remained for years an effective competitor to the trunk-line railroads that ran between Chicago and New York or Philadelphia, though rate discriminations were practiced by railroads both as between communities and as between individual shippers.

Land monopolization by railroads was yet another grievance. Land grants had been given by the federal government to railroads, either directly or via states, to the extent of 155 million acres in the years 1850 to 1871, and further grants had been made by the states to the extent of 49 million acres. Federal grants west of Lake Michigan had been especially lavish. Railroads received only the alternate sections on opposite sides of their track, but the total amount of land so given was five times the size of the state of Pennsylvania. The single grant to the Northern Pacific was almost equal to the whole of New England.

Most of the grants were in the farming or potential farming areas of the Middle West, though some of the most enormous were in the Plains and Far West. Since railroads were given every alternate section for a distance of five or ten miles on either side of their track (twenty miles in the territories), they controlled half the land within easy hauling distance of their lines. In the area of a railroad grant, not even the government sections lying within the limits of the grant could be made available for settlement until the railroad had chosen its lands. This meant that wide strips of land were virtually closed to settlement.

Another source of irritation was the attitude taken by railroad managements toward the public. It was that such transportation was a private business, which did not require conciliating the public. The attitude of many railroad employees was: "Damn the public. If you don't like the railroad, use a wheelbarrow." When damages to freight resulted from careless shipment and lawsuits followed, the practice of railroads was to wear down litigants by protracted litigation in the courts.

The domination of state governments by railroad corporations was another western grievance. It was a national as well as a sectional problem, a result partly of the distribution of free travel passes to legislators and to members of the press. In some cases it was obtained by outright bribery. It was resented in spite of a recognition of the need for this new form of public transportation. Westerners were suspicious of the giant capitalism the large railroad corporations represented—the mightiest aggregations of private capital the world had seen up to that time. The Middle West was determined that the state should remain the master, that it should not become the servant of the railroads in its own household.

Such resentments were extended to elevator companies, which were regarded by the public as part of railroad systems. Usually those in the larger cities were under railroad influence. The chief complaints made against them were their increasing storage and transfer charges, which were felt to be excessive, and the belief that owners lined their pockets with undue profits.

Complaints were also made that the elevator operators were engaged in dishonest weighing and grading of grain, though these were supposedly under the eyes of impartial appointees of boards of trade or chambers of commerce. Elevator influence was believed to control inspectors. In some country elevators the owners were themselves dealers in grain and were popularly believed to be engaged in the business of mixing grades.

A hypothetical example of mixing grades will illustrate the process and the objections to it. A farmer brings to a country elevator 1000 bushels of high-grade wheat; the kernels are plump, the weight is 60 pounds to a bushel, the grain is free of dirt and seeds of weeds. It is No. 1 wheat and paid for as such by the elevator owner— wheat that weighs 56 to 60 pounds to the bushel. Another parcel comes to the elevator—2000 bushels—of less high quality, weighing only 55 pounds to the bushel. It is No. 2 wheat and paid for as such. The owner of the elevator now mixes the two lots.

1000 bushels at 60 pounds	=	60,000 pounds
2000 bushels at 55 pounds	=	110,000 pounds
3000 bushels weighs		170,000 pounds

The elevator owner has brought the mixture to an average of 56 pounds to the bushel —in other words, No. 1 wheat—but for two-thirds of it he paid only the price of No. 2 wheat. He has enriched himself at the expense of the farmer supplying the wheat. Farmers do not normally have facilities for mixing wheat in quantity. The miller is also defrauded.

Such grievances against railroads and elevator owners were accentuated in the older parts of Illinois and Wisconsin by crop difficulties in the years after the Civil War. In the older parts of these states soil exhaustion was beginning to affect harvests, likewise diseases incident to one-crop agriculture. The painful process of readjustment to a new type of agriculture was under way. These difficulties, and also the great slump in farm prices that followed the Panic of 1873, added to the bitterness against the railroads and grain elevators.

In the fight to bring railroad and elevator companies under public control, the instruments used by the western farmers and shippers were the Granges, state and local branches of a national organization known as the Grange, or Patrons of Husbandry. Formed in 1867, the Granges were in the beginning nonpolitical in character. They became political as the fight progressed. They became the instruments for bringing pressure on legislatures to subject railroad and elevator companies to effective regulation. The uprising came to be known as the Granger movement.

As a result of Granger pressure, the legislatures of Wisconsin, Illinois, Iowa, and Minnesota—all states west of Lake Michigan—adopted measures in the 1870's to bring the railroads and elevator companies under control. Legislation of three types was adopted, some states choosing one type, some another. One was maximum-rate laws, which fixed detailed rates that the railroad and elevator companies were permitted to charge. A second type was mandatory-commission laws, which established boards with power to fix the level of rates and services. These commissions were the most common form of regulation undertaken. They provided an elastic form of regulation—more flexible than maximum-rate laws. A third type was supervisory commissions, possessing recommendatory rather than mandatory powers. They could not fix rates, they could only summon witnesses and gather evidence and make recommendations. They depended on public opinion to get their recommendations adopted. This type was copied from Massachusetts, where it had been initiated by Charles Francis Adams in 1869.

All three types of regulation proved in the end to be failures. State authorities did not have the intimate statistical and technical knowledge of railroads sufficient for regulatory purposes. Railroading was a relatively new science, and most men competent in the field were likely to be in the employ of railroads. Also, the companies warded off the enforcement of the regulatory laws by prolonged litigation in the courts or, in the period after the Panic of 1873, escaped regulation by going into bankruptcy. In many cases they were practically bankrupt before the Granger Laws were enacted, chiefly on account of overbuilding and bad management. But they managed to put the onus of their collapse on state regulation. State regulation was thus discredited. Most commissions passed under railroad influence, or became moribund. Effective state regulation of railroads was not achieved until the days of the elder Robert La Follette.

But the Granger movement was no exercise in futility. It achieved important long-term results in formulating the law and the principles regulating railroad and elevator companies, and their relationship to the public. It called forth the notable Granger decisions of the Supreme Court handed down in 1877.

These decisions were reached in eight cases that crowded into the Supreme Court. The Court did what it often does in such circumstances—it heard argument on all of them before deciding any. The most important of the decisions were two in railroad cases and one in an elevator case. The railroad cases were *Peik v. Chicago & Northwestern Railway,* 94 U.S. 165, and *Chicago, Burlington & Quincy Railroad v. Iowa,* 94 U.S. 155. The elevator decision was *Munn v. Illinois,* 94 U.S. 113.

In all the railroad cases the chief arguments made by the corporation lawyers were rejected by the Court. Their principal thesis was that railroading was a private business which the state had no right to regulate. A like argument was made regarding elevator companies.

Another contention was that the railroad corporations were protected by charters, granted by earlier state legislatures, which conferred on them the right to fix their own charges and services. These charters would be impaired if the right to fix charges were transferred by legislation to public authority. Such a transfer would be unconstitutional, violating the provision of the Constitution which forbade the states to impair the obligations of a contract.

A third contention of the railroad lawyers was that the rates established by state laws and commissions were so low as to leave no adequate margin of profit. The rates were alleged to be confiscatory, and took away the incentive for railroad investment by rendering it profitless. Such rates violated the Fourteenth Amendment, which forbade states to take property without due process of law. A fourth contention was that, on commodities moving from one state to another, rates fixed by state authority would be an interference with interstate commerce and therefore conflict with the provision of the Constitution which leaves the regulation of interstate commerce to Congress.

All these contentions the Supreme Court rejected. It upheld the authority of the state governments to regulate railroads and elevator companies at every point. The Court held that railroads were a form of property clothed with a public interest and therefore subject to public regulation. Railroads were comparable to toll roads and ferries, which from time immemorial had been subject to public regulation. The Court also held that state authorities were not precluded from regulating railroads and elevator companies by provisions in their charters which allowed them to set their own rates and service. Those charters were in every case given subject to the provisions in all the western state constitutions that charters may be altered or repealed by succeeding legislatures. The Court further held that even if the level of rates established under legislative authority was so low as to preclude a profit, the remedy lay with the state legislature, and with the legislature alone. The Court concluded that, on commodities moving in interstate commerce, the states had the right to regulate charges on that portion of the haul lying within their own boundaries. They had a right to do this as long as Congress had not itself regulated interstate traffic.

These decisions were landmarks in American corporation history. They reasserted clearly and specifically the principle of the public right to control great corporations whose business is clothed with a public interest.

In two important respects the Granger rulings were later modified. In 1886, in the Wabash case, the Supreme Court ruled that on commodities moving in interstate commerce a state government is not free to regulate charges on the portion of the haul lying within its own boundaries; that state regulation in such a case interfered with the flow of interstate commerce even in the absence of congressional legislation. That decision led Congress in 1887 to adopt the Interstate Commerce Act. In 1898, in *Smyth v. Ames,* the Supreme Court ruled that if a state fixes a rate that is so low as to be confiscatory, it deprived railroads of their property without due process of law and violated the Fourteenth Amendment. The Court ruled that the federal courts would determine whether the state had set the rate too low. These modifications of the Granger decisions were important, but the essential principle remained, that railroad and elevator companies were subject to public control.

The Granger movement made other contributions. It stimulated the process of gathering public information regarding the techniques of railroad operation. The obligation was placed on railroad companies to submit detailed annual reports of their businesses, which contained data valuable for regulation. Also, in 1874, as a result of the Granger excitement, a special committee of the United States Senate made a highly valuable report, *Transportation Routes to the Seaboard,* containing invaluable technical information used when effective regulation began. Another result of the Granger resentment was that railroad companies were brought to a realization of their dependence on public goodwill. In the popular magazines of the late 1870's and 1880's, stories appeared of elderly ladies taking trips across the continent, assisted all the way by polite railroad conductors.

Yet another consequence of the movement was a series of experiments undertaken by local Granges in cooperative buying, which were designed to eliminate middlemen. They proved unsuccessful, but provided the experience that paved the way for success later, when two-thirds of the farm families of the United States belonged to some kind of cooperative. Finally, the Granger movement afforded an opportunity to western farmers to get together in local gatherings for social purposes, which meant a brightening of farm life.

In the Granger movement sectionalism had a striking manifestation. In the Middle West public control of railroads and grain elevators was considered indispensable and a matter of self-preservation. But in New England and in the Northeast, where stockholders and bondholders of the railroads were concentrated, compulsory regulation of railroads was regarded as an interference with vested rights, a confiscation of property, and an immoral repudiation of contracts.

Contemporaneous with Grangerism was a currency issue, an outgrowth of the Civil War. It had its inception in the need of the federal government for more money than could be raised by taxation or by loans through bonds. Early in the war the government was obliged to discontinue payments in specie, and set the printing presses to work. The Treasury Department emitted fiat or paper money—the famous "greenbacks," so named from their color. The printing began early in 1862 in spite of doubts as to its constitutionality. Under the Legal Tender Act of February 1862, an issue of $150 million was authorized. This was followed four months later by another authorization of the same amount, and by two more of $100 million and $50 million, in January and March 1863. By June 1864, a total of $450 million had been authorized, of which $431 million was outstanding. This currency was non-interest-bearing, unsupported by specie, and depended for redemption on the future financial strength of the federal government. It was made receivable at face value, and was legal tender for all debts except duties on imports and interest on the public debt, which had to be paid in coin.

The reliance of the government on this paper was fiercely resisted at first in conservative financial circles. It was denounced in the eastern cities and by the banking community in general. But objection to it subsided with subsequent authorizations. The war needs of the government seemed too great and too urgent to be met otherwise.

Depreciation in the greenbacks began as soon as they appeared. In April 1862 a dollar of this paper was worth 98 cents in gold. A year later it had fallen to 66 cents, and by July 1864 it had dropped to the low point of 39 cents. This decline reflected the large quantity issued, the lack of security behind it, the heavy dependence on the good faith and financial strength of the government, and the discouragement of the North over the slow progress of its armies. The Union victories at Vicksburg and Gettysburg, which marked the turning point in the war, permitted a cessation of new authorizations, but did not at once halt deterioration in the value of greenbacks. The halt came only a year later, when the ultimate triumph of the North had become evident. By the close of the war, the value of the greenbacks was 67 cents in gold. One of the consequences of the depreciation was that the cost of living in the North had almost doubled by the end of the war.

The main reliance of the federal government during the war was on long-term, tax-exempt bonds. The first to be issued in 1861 were the so-called 7/30's which could be redeemed in seven years and had to be redeemed in thirty. The largest and most controversial issue was the 5/20's of 1861, which bore interest at the rate of 6 percent, and specified that this must be paid in gold, but there was no indication as to whether the principal was to be paid in gold, which led to later controversy. The bonds could be purchased with greenbacks at face value, and by the end of the war more than $800 million of them had been sold. The war loans lacked uniformity. Some were 60-day loans, others were 10/40's. Some bore compound interest, others simple interest.

A third element in wartime financing was bank notes, issued by the national banks set up under the National Currency acts of 1863 and 1864. National banks could issue bank notes equal in amount to 90 percent of the value of federal bonds they deposited with the Treasurer of the United States as security. The amount of national bank notes was originally limited to $300 million but, after the war, this was increased. It was the intent of the acts to create an expanded market for federal bonds. In the meantime, in 1865, Congress enacted a prohibitive tax on state bank notes.

These were the chief methods of federal financing in the Civil War. While they served a primary purpose in permitting the government to keep taxes at a level the public could bear, the issuing of greenbacks was a dangerous remedy for the ills of the time. It was a departure from sound fiscal policy and was heavily paid for. One of the penalties was the most severe inflation in the national economy since the era of the American Revolution. And this let loose heresies in financial thinking and practice that plagued the nation for decades after the close of the war.

As soon as the war ended the eastern financial centers demanded a return to standard financial principles. In response, the House of Representatives on December 18, 1865, by a vote of 144-6, adopted a resolution that the currency be contracted, with a view to early resumption of specie payments. In the following April, Congress passed the Contraction Act which ordered a gradual withdrawing of Treasury notes, whether bearing interest or not, in exchange for federal bonds. A limitation was fixed on the rate of contraction of not more than $10 million in six months nor more than $4 million in any one month. The law applied to greenbacks as well as to treasury notes. Under this authorization, the Secretary of the Treasury reduced the amount of greenbacks from $431 million to $399 million by October 1866. Then a business depression set in, and in February 1868 the Contraction Act was repealed.

In the 1868 presidential campaign the greenback problem became a major issue. It became united with a program for redemption of the 5/20 bonds. Western Democrats, especially in Ohio, demanded that the principal of the bonds be paid off in greenbacks. The act under which those bonds had been authorized stated specifically that the interest on them was to be paid in coin, but made no like provision for redeeming the principal. This led the Democratic convention to write into the platform a plank declaring that government debts should be redeemed in greenbacks, unless the act of issue specifically stated that they be redeemed in coin. The declaration was known as the "Pendleton plan," from the name of its principal sponsor,

G. H. Pendleton, the governor of Ohio. It was defended on the ground that the bonds had been purchased with depreciated greenbacks and that a currency good enough for the plow holder was good enough for the bond holder.

The Republicans won and Ulysses S. Grant, a military hero and a conservative in financial matters, became President. In March 1869 Congress pledged the faith of the United States "as soon as possible" to redeem all United States notes and all interest-bearing obligations in coin, except where the law authorizing the issue has expressly provided that the "same shall be paid in lawful money [greenbacks] or other currency than gold or silver." The next year Congress authorized a fund to facilitate the discharge of the 5/20 bonds in coin at face value. Debt-ridden western farmers were angered by this legislation, for it permitted wealthy Easterners, who had acquired 5/20 bonds with depreciated greenbacks, to reap an unearned increment. Congress and the Grant administration persisted in this hard-money favoritism, until a depression set in following the Panic of 1873. Then Congress responded to the public feeling that a more plentiful money supply would restore prosperity, and voted an increase in the quantity of greenbacks in circulation to $400 million. The measure was vetoed by Grant.

The veto triggered the formation of the Greenback party—a combination of middle western farmers, small businessmen, and labor intellectuals. Its objective at first was the expansion of greenbacks, which was favored also by many middle western Democrats. Partly the result of the Administration's rejection of greenback expansion, and partly the result of its corruption, the Republicans met defeat in the congressional election of 1874.

In the lame-duck session of 1875 the Republican Congress adopted the Resumption Act, which provided that specie payments be resumed on January 1, 1879. The Secretary of the Treasury was authorized to use for the purpose any surplus in the Treasury. He was, also, to sell bonds for "coin," which then meant gold. Thus greenbacks would be redeemable in gold, dollar for dollar, and their quantity was to be reduced to $300 million.

The adoption of the act altered the focus of the Greenback movement. Its focus became repeal of the Resumption Act before it could go into effect. In a special session of Congress, prior to the presidential election, the House adopted a repeal measure by a vote of 106–86. The majority consisted of Democrats, who controlled the House, aided by Greenbackers and their sympathizers. In sectional terms the majority consisted principally of Westerners and Southerners. The Senate took no action and the bill failed.

In the presidential election of 1876 the Greenback party ran its own candidates pledged to repeal the Resumption Act and to expand the volume of greenbacks. The ticket drew only a small vote. But the new Congress that met in December 1877 was under Democratic control and included sympathizers with the objectives of Greenbackism. It passed bills for the repeal of the Resumption Act, for expansion of the volume of the greenbacks, and for an unlimited coinage of silver. In the Senate alternatives were worked out early in 1878 that blunted the proposal to repeal the Resumption Act. In both houses supporters of repeal were persuaded to join the silver advocates in adopting the Bland-Allison Act, which authorized a limited coinage of silver dollars. President Rutherford B. Hayes, though a hard-money man, signed it, and soon afterward signed a measure providing for an increase in the volume of greenbacks that would circulate after the resumption began. Thus the drive of the Greenbackers to repeal the Resumption Act was "stopped at the silver line," but the silverites and Greenbackers had won concessions.

The congressional elections of 1878 reflected continuing Greenback strength. Its labor contingent became more active, and it was renamed the Greenback-Labor party. With labor reforms added to its program and coalition with Democrats in some states, the party polled a million votes in the 1878 election. In 1879 approximately fifteen Congressmen of the third party and others pledged to its program entered the House. Here, under the leadership of James B. Weaver, they formed a bloc, consisting of representatives of every section of the country, but especially of the agricultural middle western states of Ohio, Indiana, Wisconsin, Michigan, Iowa, and Minnesota. The Greenback party disintegrated after the Resumption Act went into effect in 1879. Its representatives turned increasingly to silver as a solution of the nation's economic problems. To the end of the century inflation of the currency in this form remained an issue that divided the sections of the nation.

Industrialization of the Great Lakes Region

WHILE THE NORTH CENTRAL section of the nation resounded to the noisy politics of Grangerism and Greenbackism, the Great Lakes country converted itself almost unnoticed from a frontier society into one of the world's great industrialized societies. It made the change in the years between the Civil War and the close of the 19th century. Three industries—flour milling, lumbering, and iron and steel making— were conspicuous in this development. For all of them the Great Lakes basin contained essential raw materials and favorable transportation facilities.

Especially favored was the flour-milling industry. It lay in one of the world's most extensive wheat areas—Wisconsin, Minnesota, and the Dakotas. It was served by the convenient transport facilities of the Great Lakes and a rapidly expanding railroad net. It profited from a notable technological development which transformed the methods of flour milling.

An account of this development requires a description of the internal structure of the wheat kernel. This consists of four parts, an outer shell or husk, a layer of gluten cells, a starchy inner core, and a germ or embryo. The outer shell is the protection which the growing grain wraps around itself against the weather. It becomes bran in the grinding. The gluten cells next to it are the protein part of the wheat. United with yeast added by the housewife, they make dough. Without the yeast the dough would be merely a sticky paste. The starchy interior of the kernel is the largest part of the grain. It is interlaced with thread-like impurities. Finally, the germ, the embryo of the kernel, is the element that begins new life when the grain is planted in the ground. It is an oily substance and becomes a problem when the grain is ground into flour.

All these ingredients of the grain were ground into flour in the process known as low milling or flat milling. The process was simple and of ancient origin. The grain was ground between two revolving stones. The top stone ran low over the nether so that almost its whole weight rested on the wheat kernels in grinding. The surfaces of the two stones were grooved so as to provide a maximum crushing and grinding effect in their revolutions.

The product of such milling was whole-wheat flour, excellent except for two defects. It did not keep well. It was likely to get wormy as a result of the fact that the shredded bran in it attracted moisture from the air. Also, it was likely to turn rancid as a result of the presence in it of the crushed oily germ. Sifting the meal was sometimes done, on specially made bolting cloths, to eliminate the bran and the oily germ.

The sifting produced a flour with somewhat better keeping qualities than the whole-wheat variety, but it was not a complete success. The reason was that, in grinding, the ingredients of the wheat had been so scrambled and crushed into each other that not even a sifting could separate them. Splintered particles of bran remained in the finished product, as well as the juices and particles of the oily germ. The keeping qualities of the flour were never very good.

This flour had an even more serious defect. It was deficient in gluten. The gluten cells, which are the hardest part of the grain, were never completely pulverized in a single grinding. They remained coarse and were likely to be sifted out of the flour and to be thrown away as roughage. The resulting flour lacked the rising strength necessary for bread.

With one variety of wheat, the spring wheat of the North, the low-milling process was especially unsatisfactory. One reason was that the husk of northern spring wheat is thin and fragile. It is a growth of mild weather. It splintered in the grinding, and the splinters could not be completely removed in the sifting. This impaired the keeping quality of the flour. Also, northern spring wheat is very hard by reason of the large amount of gluten it contains. To grind it the stones had to be run at great speed and under great pressure. The resulting flour was a little burned—a little brown. It did not look as white as housewives liked.

Winter wheat, grown in the Missouri and Ohio valleys in the wintertime, was much better for low milling. Its husk was thick and tough, and in grinding did not splinter easily. It flattened out and could be completely eliminated in the sifting process. Also, it was a soft wheat because of the low percentage of gluten in its make-up. This permitted it to be ground without resort to great pressures or high speed of the stones. The resulting flour was white and attractive and had good keeping qualities. The superiority of the southern winter wheat was reflected in its market price, which was always higher than that of northern spring wheats of a comparable grade. The superiority of the southern wheats was also reflected in the location of flour milling. At the time of the Civil War, St. Louis was the greatest flour producer in the Union, and lay in the center of the winter-wheat belt.

In 1871 a new mode of milling was developed—the high milling and gradual reduction process. Its basic principle was a gradual pulverization of grain by a series of grindings rather than by a single grinding. In the first grinding the stones were set far apart—the upper stone high over the lower. The purpose of that operation was merely to crack the grain. The cracked grain was sent to the sieves and the bran and oily germ were separated out.

A second cracking was given the meal on a pair of stones set slightly closer together than the first. The meal was then given a second cleansing by sifting and bolting; then a third cracking, with stones set still closer together, and a third cleansing. All together, five or six alternate crackings and cleansings were applied, the result of which was that all the impurities, external and internal, of the grain were removed. Pulverization took place only at the very end. This process produced a flour that was exceedingly white and pure, and had almost indefinite keeping qualities. Also, it retained all the gluten of the wheat. A complete pulverization of the gluten was made possible by the gradual reduction process.

In this process two valuable parts of the wheat could not be saved, the bran and the oily germ, which went into the waste. They were an unfortunate loss, for bran contains valuable minerals, and the oily germ valuable vitamins. But they had to be discarded because they detracted from the keeping quality of the flour. Nowadays in the manufacture of flour, the loss of these parts is compensated by substitutions. Flour is enriched by the addition of riboflavin, niacin, and thiamine to take the place of the bran and the oily germ. In some states, especially the southern, enrichment of flour in this way is required by law as a means of combating pellagra.

The new process was perfected in Minneapolis. The Washburn A mill, the greatest in the world, was constructed there in 1873 on the basis of this technology. It was kept modernized by later improvements. In place of stones for milling, rollers were used, first porcelain, then chilled steel. The rollers were an importation from Hungary, where flour milling was an advanced art.

As a result of the new process, a reversal occurred in the relative value of the different wheats in the United States. The most valued wheat became northern spring. It was preferred because, being harder, it did not crumble in the early crackings. It permitted a more thorough purification process with less loss of flour. Also, having a higher gluten content, which could now be effectively pulverized, it produced a stronger and a richer flour. The result was that Minneapolis, Superior, and Duluth, in the northern spring-wheat area, quickly supplanted St. Louis as the milling centers of the United States. Minneapolis became the greatest flour-milling center in the world.

Another industry in the Great Lakes region, erected on the basis of an important natural resource, was lumbering. The northern parts of Michigan, Wisconsin, and Minnesota contained the finest stand of white pine to be found anywhere in the world. Of equal importance was the convenient access of this resource to the Great Lakes waterway. Most importantly, the Mississippi River, and the railroads fanning westward from it, gave the pineries access to the rich markets of the prairies and the treeless Great Plains.

In this industry, standing timber was reduced to lumber in a number of operations, each normally performed by its own agencies. The initial operation was the locating and acquiring of promising stands of timber, usually from the public domain. Timber "cruisers" or "explorers," wizards of forest lore, were sent into the wilderness on the heels of government surveyors, to make selections of choice stands. On their advice the stands were purchased. The gathering of the timber was let out to logging contractors, who hewed out the pine at a stipulated price per 1000 feet, and had it hauled to the banks of neighboring streams. The logs were left banked until the floodwaters of spring rose high enough to carry them to sawmill yards. The acreage logged was often greater than the acreage paid for. Commonly, it was a "big forty," jocularly so called, which embraced a wide margin of adjacent public land. Federal and state lands were not guarded with much care against intrusion. The forty, stripped of its lumber, was later sold to incoming settlers.

The reduction of logs to lumber was the next stage in the process. It achieved an enormous acceleration during and after the Civil War. Rotary, or circular saws took the place of the old-fashioned up-and-down "muley," with a cutting capacity ten times as great. The "double rotary" was developed, consisting of two saws, running one above the other, which doubled the speed. These advances called out greater speeds in all the other operations of the mill. The log carriage, conveyor of the logs to the saws, was accelerated by making it steam-fed. The steam "nigger" was introduced to transfer logs more quickly from the mill pond to the saws. Live rolls, driven by chains, were developed to move sawed boards to the place of transport. The sawmill of 1870 bore slight resemblance to that of a decade earlier. The great mills of the 1870's were capable of turning out lumber at the rate of 100,000 to 200,000 feet in a twelve-hour day, compared with 50,000 feet in 1860.

Concentration of the functions of milling became marked in the industry in the 1870's. A conspicuous example was Knapp, Stout & Company of Menominee, Wisconsin, on a branch of the Chippewa, which was said to be one of the greatest lumber corporations in the world. In 1873 the firm owned 115,000 acres of pineland on the Chippewa and Menominee rivers, from which it manufactured that year 55 million feet of lumber, 20 million shingles, and 20 million laths and pickets. It maintained a foundry, a machine shop, a grain warehouse of 40,000-bushel capacity, and a gristmill, where its yearly requirements of flour were ground. The company owned six large farms containing 6000 to 7000 acres of improved land, upon which were raised its supplies of wheat and pork. It conducted general merchandise stores and large lumberyards at strategic points on the west bank of the Mississippi. Twelve hundred men were on its payroll throughout the year.

But more commonly the sawmilling function was divided. Sawmill owners on the banks of the Mississippi or on the shores of Lake Michigan bought the timber they used from loggers and converted it into lumber while it was already partway to market. This meant that millers operating within the pineries had to pay higher prices for their logs and met increased competition for the western markets. It led to clashes within the industry.

The most spectacular of the clashes occurred in the late 1860's on the Chippewa River in Wisconsin and was known as the Beef Slough War. The Chippewa divides, near its junction with the Mississippi, into two channels. One of them, Beef Slough, was not generally navigable. It formed an admirable harbor for sorting and rafting logs destined for downriver mills. To forestall its use for such purposes, an association of upper Chippewa millmen bought the land at the entrance to the Slough and in 1866 obtained from the state legislature a charter granting log-storing privileges there, which they intended not to use but to close to others. Early in 1867 prominent state loggers, with interests in sawmills on the Mississippi, organized the Beef Slough Log Driving Company and applied to the legislature for a charter to erect within Beef Slough the booms and piers necessary for their work. The bill was defeated. Thereupon the upper-river millmen sent a crew of some hundreds of their employees down the river to close the entrance with rafts of slabs. The logging company obtained a court injunction to stop the closing, but was not quick enough to prevent its completion. The next step was more effective. The logging company prevailed upon friendly local authorities to condemn the land at the obstruction for a public highway, and then tore out the offending slabs. A pitched battle between the opposing forces was narrowly averted and became merely a wordy war of rivermen's English.

In 1869 the logging company again sought a charter from the Wisconsin legislature, but its bill was decisively defeated. A few days later, just before adjournment, an innocent-appearing measure was brought into the Senate, providing for the incorporation of the Portage City Gas Light Company. The bill was pushed through the legislature with the rush that attends the close of sessions, and was signed by the governor a few hours before adjournment.

Several days later the discovery was made that hidden near the close of the law was the provision: "In all cases where any franchise or privilege has been, or shall be granted, by law to several persons, the grant shall be deemed several as well as joint, so that one or more may accept and exercise the franchise alone." The logging company had won its fight, for one of its members was a Chippewa millman who in 1866 had been included among the incorporators in the charter intended not to be used. To his new associates he assigned the rights and privileges that the joker in the Portage City bill had given him. The public chuckled over the sly maneuver, while the two belligerents prepared for a renewal of hostilities.

Within a few months the season for the log drive from the pineries was at hand. The Beef Slough Logging Company served notice on the Chippewa River millmen to allow any logs bearing the Beef Slough mark to pass unmolested. This the millmen were not only unwilling but unable to do, for only two of them had the necessary sorting facilities. Moreover, they were unwilling to agree upon a system of log exchanges such as had heretofore governed operations on the river. Here was a deadlock in which force again proved to be the only arbiter. The Beef Slough log drivers, numbering 75 rough fellows, were not loath, on their way down from the pineries, to cut open whatever sawmill reservoirs they found containing logs marked Beef Slough, taking not only their own logs, but large quantities of others. Lower down the river was waiting the opposing army of the upriver sawmill owners, numbering some 200 equally rough and determined men, led by a county sheriff. As the two forces approached each other the danger of a bloody clash increased. An open battle was, however, averted. The upriver sawmill army was too overwhelming to be resisted, and the leaders of the drive were obliged to submit to arrest. An armed truce was effected and the Beef Slough log drivers continued on their way.

For several years after 1868 the contentions on the Chippewa River continued. In 1870 the Beef Slough Logging Company contrived to obtain from the Wisconsin legislature a confirmation and extension of its newly acquired charter rights, but its stormy life soon brought it to bankruptcy. At the close of 1870 its river improvements were leased to an association of Mississippi River sawmill owners, among whom the leading spirit was Frederick Weyerhaeuser, who was destined to become the lumber king of America. Early in 1871 this association organized the Mississippi Logging Company, which soon became part of the greatest lumber syndicate of its time.

In the meantime the growth of the log traffic on the Mississippi surpassed even the gloomiest predictions of the Chippewa sawmill owners. The quantity of logs received and rafted at Beef Slough increased from 12 million feet in 1868 to 274,367,900 feet in 1873. On the neighboring Black River the traffic rose from 6 million feet in 1864 to 195,398,830 feet in 1873. "In a few years, " complained the sawmill owners of Black River Falls in a remonstrance to the legislature, "the wealthiest portion of the pineries will present nothing but a vast and gloomy wilderness of pine stumps."

The mode of moving logs to mills was transformed during the 1860's. The old mode was to leave the problem to nature. The timber, as felled in the winter, was hauled by sleigh to a nearby river and banked up, as already described, along the shore. It was to be floated with the spring rise of water to the mill to which it had been sold. But this entailed risks. The rise of water in the spring might be insufficient to float the logs, which would leave the mill unsupplied till the next year. Or a surging mass of logs might produce a logjam that could be untangled only at the risk of life and limb of the attending redshirts. In any case, it would leave stranded a considerable quantity of logs.

In the mid-1860's log rafts came into vogue on rivers tributary to the Mississippi. They were constructed by augering holes in both ends of the logs and binding them together with pins to long stout poles. This was, however, costly of lumber lost in the borings and of labor in the construction. It was superseded by the "brailed" raft, in which logs were surrounded and held in place by a "boom," or chain of logs and a network of ropes skillfully arranged.

More important was rafting of sawed lumber. The boards, coming from the saws, were piled, twelve to twenty courses deep, and fastened stoutly together in cribs. Six or more cribs were fastened end to end to form a "string" or "rapids piece." Where rivers ran quietly, from two to four "pieces" (the number varying with the streams) were coupled side by side to form a river raft. With its top loaded with bundles of shingles and lath, and equipped with ponderous sweeps, fore and aft, this moved down stream, even over waterfalls, usually with success, but sometimes to its sorrow. Sometimes a raft was halted, to be divided into its parts, to pass an obstruction and then was recoupled.

Further consolidation occurred on arrival in the Mississippi. Eight to eighteen strings were combined into a single great hulk with sweeps at either end, known as a Mississippi River "fleet," on which were erected the cabins of the crew. The size of Mississippi rafts became progressively larger as the industry grew. Before 1860 a raft was considered large that contained more than 500,000 feet of lumber. By 1870 rafts covering three to four acres of surface and from two to two and a half million feet of sawed lumber were moving down the river.

In 1864 an innovation in raft locomotion appeared that transformed the process. It consisted of towing or, more correctly, pushing rafts to market by steamboats specially designed. Lumber so transported arrived at its destination in half the time earlier required and at a cost of shipment reduced in proportion. Eventually "bow-boats" took over the function. They proved so successful that, by 1873, 73 were operating on the upper river.

By comparison the pineries tributary to Lake Michigan employed, for shipping sawed lumber to market, a considerable fleet of vessels, nearly all of the sailing type. Many of the craft were worn-out sailing vessels, too leaky for grain or merchandise transport, but still useful as lumber carriers. During the early 1860's an innovation appeared that had possibilities. Worn-out sailing vessels were stripped of their rigging and left in charge of steam tugs to be hauled back and forth. They became steamers for all practical purposes. A further development was the displacement of tugs by vessels known as steam barges, which not only were able to drag "hookers" but were themselves laden with cargoes. In the early 1870's it was possible to see steam barges, with four or more laden tows, in tandem, plowing their way to market. Before many years the old schooner fleet was powered not by sails but by steam.

Chicago was the chief distributor of the lumber of the pinery districts of north-eastern Wisconsin and northern Michigan. It was the greatest lumber market in the world. Already by the end of the 1860's it had five lumber-carrying railroads and the canal between Lake Michigan and the Illinois River, transporting pine to the western and southwestern prairies and plains. It provided the lumber entering the homes, barns, and fences of incoming pioneers. Other lake ports such as Milwaukee, Oshkosh, and Green Bay, employing rail and canal facilities, supplemented this distribution.

The rise of the Great Lakes states to eminence after the Civil War in the produc-tion and distribution of lumber becomes evident from an examination of census statistics. According to the 1870 census, three northern states, Michigan, Pennsyl-vania, and New York, led all others in the Union in the value of their lumber products. By 1890 the leading states were Michigan, Wisconsin, Pennsylvania, and Minnesota, three from the Great Lakes region. In terms of millions of dollars of forest products, they yielded, respectively, $83.1, $60.9, $29.0, and $25.0.

Another industry that developed to giant proportions in the Great Lakes area after the Civil War was iron and steel. A magnificent natural resource was again the foundation—the iron-ore deposits that lie along the southern and western shores of Lake Superior. They were the Menominee and Marquette in Michigan; Gogebic in Wisconsin; Cuyuna, Mesabi, and Vermilion in Minnesota. The greatest of all of them was the Mesabi, a field 100 miles long and from two to ten miles wide stretching across the northeastern corner of Minnesota. It contained two principal varieties of iron. One was "soft ore," a red hematite that could be scooped up like gravel by power shovels. It was rich in mineral content, 50 to 60 percent. A second was taconite, a lean ore embedded in exceptionally hard rock, which contained only 25 to 30 percent of iron. The quantity of soft ore was estimated at 2 billion tons, the taconite at 60 to 80 billion tons.

All these fields were discovered in the period between 1850 and 1900. Those in northern Michigan and Wisconsin were found first and their ore was used for arma-ment for the Union Army in the Civil War. Some fields in Minnesota were discovered in the 1860's, but the tremendous potentialities of the Mesabi Range were made known only in 1890. When its potentialities were revealed it quickly surpassed all the others in importance. For nearly half a century it produced annually from 55 to 65 percent of all the iron ore mined in the United States.

The development of an iron and steel industry on a large scale is possible ordinarily only if the ore is in close proximity to coal, as in Germany or in parts of Russia. In the United States the Lake Superior fields were separated from Pennsyl-vania and Ohio coal by a distance of 1000 miles. But that distance was virtually wiped out by the Great Lakes waterway and by the remarkable methods of moving ore to it and shipping ore on it.

The 20th century method of moving ore to this waterway is illustrated in the operations between the great Mahoning mine at Hibbing, Minnesota, and the ore ports of Lake Superior. Ore was scooped up by great power shovels and loaded into freight cars. Five bites of the shovel filled a car in a few minutes. Trains of such cars were then hauled to Superior, the great ore port on Lake Superior. They were run onto high ore docks extending half a mile into the waters of the lake. The ore was dumped into huge pockets, which the docks provided. When ore vessels came up, the ore flowed by gravity from the pockets into the holds of the boats. An ore boat carrying 10,000 tons could be loaded in a few hours.

The ore docks were railroad properties. At Superior the Great Northern maintained four such docks, where boats to the number of 28 or 29 could be loaded in a single day. The boats were the property of the mining companies or their agents in the East. The ore was shipped to Erie in Pennsylvania or to some other lake port. Vessels were unloaded by clamshell buckets in a few hours. On the return trip the cargo was often coal from Pennsylvania or Ohio, transported to the lakeshore in freight cars, which were picked up bodily by huge derricks, and their content dumped into the returning ore boats. As a result of these efficiencies and the immensity of the resources, the Lake Superior region became the greatest ore producer in the entire world.

Not only ore mining but the manufacture of steel became centered in the Great Lakes area. The lake ports all the way from Erie to Detroit, and from Chicago to Gary, became steel manufactories, especially of machinery and automobiles. They became the rendezvous where iron ore from the Lake Superior fields met coal from Pennsylvania, Ohio, Illinois, and West Virginia, with the result that the Middle West became one of the major workshops of the world.

The passages between the Great Lakes became essential outlets of commerce. One of them in particular was important—the Sault Ste. Marie Canal, or the "Soo" Canal, completed in 1855, and later enlarged, connecting Lake Superior with the lower lakes. It became more important than any other canal located in the United States.

The lands containing the Lake Superior ore deposits were initially government-owned. They had high value not only for their ore bodies but in many cases for their superb covering of pine forest. These valuable lands passed out of the possession of the federal government and into the hands of capitalists at nominal prices.

In accounting for this development it is necessary to interweave the history of mineral-land legislation for the Lake Superior region and that for the Far West. The iron mining in northern Michigan during the Civil War had been done on land that had been surveyed in the usual subdivisions. After the war, when evidence of valuable iron-ore deposits in Minnesota became known, Congress ordered surveys of land there, but these went forward slowly. In the meantime the laws of 1866 and 1872 relative to mineral lands in the Far West were enacted. The first established the price of $5 an acre for gold, silver, mercury, and copper lands, and ordered that these lands be surveyed in small tracts and limited to one patentee. The act of May 10, 1872, increased the list of lands subject to these provisions to include those containing lead, tin, and "other valuable minerals."

Entrepreneurs interested in the Lake Superior iron lands feared that these laws might be construed to apply to iron lands. In 1873 Senator Zachariah Chandler of Michigan introduced an innocent-looking measure in Congress specifically exempting iron and coal lands in Michigan, Wisconsin, and Minnesota from the requirements of the act of May 10, 1872. His measure further provided that the mineral lands of the three states should be "free and open to exploration and purchase, according to the legal subdivisions, thereof, as before the passage of said act." The measure was adopted with virtually no discussion in both houses of Congress and signed by President Grant on February 18, 1873. It was the earliest congressional legislation relating specifically to iron-ore lands. It meant that the mineral lands in the three states could be obtained on the same terms as non-mineral lands. They would be surveyed as agricultural land and, after being offered at auction, could be bought in any quantity for $1.25 an acre. Entries could also be made under the Pre-emption and Homestead laws.

The Pre-emption Law permitted a settler to purchase 160 acres of government land prior to public auction at $1.25 an acre. In the Homestead Law, a settler was allowed to shorten the period for obtaining title to his 160 acres by commuting to the pre-emptioner's right to purchase at $1.25 an acre. In the decade 1882–92 mining and timber capitalists acquired valuable land at $1.25 an acre in the Duluth Land District by employing individuals to make pre-emption and homestead entries, which were at once sold to their employers. The government lost in the process the higher prices that bidding at auction would have brought. In this decade—embracing the Vermilion boom of 1887 and the Mesabi boom of 1891—annual homestead entries on iron land ranged from 50 to 92 percent of all homestead entries in the district. Pre-emptioners and homesteaders falsely signed affidavits that they had not acted for others.

In 1891 the Pre-emption Law was repealed by Congress to stop the frauds practiced under it. The Homestead Law survived. It was believed that the five-year period of tenure before a homesteader could obtain title would be a deterrent to the fraudulent use of such entries. But the 1891 legislation permitted a homesteader to commute his entry to a cash purchase after fourteen months and proof of residence. This was longer than the residence requirement under the Pre-emption Law, but it was not long enough to discourage fraud. One result was that employees of mining and timber interests continued to make entries for the purpose of commuting to cash and transferring them. In 1904 a public-land investigative report stated:

> It is common knowledge in the city of Duluth, Minnesota, that in 1892, 1893, and 1894 persons desiring to commute would take an ordinary dry goods box, make it resemble a small house with doors, windows, and a shingled roof. This box would be 14 by 16 inches, or larger, and would be taken by the entryman to his claim. On the day of commutation proof he would appear at the local office, swear that he had upon his claim a good board house, 14 by 16 with shingled roof etc. The proof on its face would appear excellent and was readily passed by the local officers.

Lands obtained in these fraudulent ways were often worth millions.

Zachariah Chandler, the author of the nefarious legislation of 1873, was a New Englander by birth—a native of New Hampshire. He exhibited the New England combination of crusading fervor on moral issues and economic realism. He was a crusader against slavery and one of the founders of the Republican party in Michigan. After the Civil War he served as a leader of the radical Reconstructionists in Congress. He became the Republican party boss in Michigan. He was one of the richest men in the state. In the Grant administration he was named Secretary of the Interior, and presided over the parceling out of the public domain.

Two active Duluth speculators in iron lands were the brothers Alfred and Leonidas Merritt. By methods such as are here described, they acquired some 17,000 acres of mineral-bearing lands in Minnesota, especially in the Mesabi Range. They proceeded to develop them on a grand scale, opening mines, building railroads, and acquiring ore boats on the lakes. The money they needed was in large part borrowed from John D. Rockefeller. In the Panic of 1893 they went bankrupt. Nearly all their property passed to Rockefeller, who presently sold it at a handsome profit to Andrew Carnegie. In 1901, when the United States Steel Company was organized, all this property went into the new corporation at inflated values.

In other Minnesota areas capitalists were able to amass big holdings of iron lands. In the Vermilion Range, considered at one time more promising even than the Mesabi, Charlemagne Tower, a Philadelphia lawyer and capitalist, acquired through fraudulent entries under the Pre-emption and Homestead laws more than 20,000 acres of such lands. These he sold, after some development, to a syndicate of the Rockefellers for $6,400,000.

A consequence of the industrialization of the Great Lakes province was the transformation of the portion of the West tributary to it. The rise of the flour-milling industry in Minneapolis, Superior, and Duluth gave new growth and prosperity to the wheat area of the Red River valley. The lumbering development of northern Wisconsin and Minnesota, and along the upper Mississippi, provided the means for building the homes and barns of the Great Plains society. And the rise of a rich urban market in the Great Lakes region created a new demand for the surplus food of the Middle West and the Great Plains. National self-sufficiency was in these ways fostered to a degree never before achieved.

Great Plains and Cattlemen

IN THE ERA OF THE industrialization of the Great Lakes region, a major rural counterpart developed on the Great Plains. It was a sectionwide cattle industry. The province was well designed by nature for that industry—a natural grassland of vast dimensions. The grasses were of excellent varieties. On the eastern Plains grew the tall prairie grasses which so astonished the early Spanish explorers. On the western Plains were the short grasses of various species—the noncontinuous grasses—buffalo, grama, and curly.

These had long provided the buffalo with fodder; they were doing so when the big brother of the buffalo—a now extinct huge species—roamed the Plains. They did so not only in the summer but in the winter. If buffalo grass is not eaten off in the summer, it becomes a natural hay, curing itself on the stem. It enabled the buffalo and, later, cattle to remain alive on the Plains almost uncared for in the winter.

The southern Plains—those of Texas—were well adapted to breeding cattle. Their winters are usually mild. No destructive blizzards, such as often roared across the northern Plains, occurred there. On the Texas Plains cows, heavy with calf, would come through the winter strong enough to deliver their calves safely in the springtime. Cows would normally have twelve calves in a lifetime.

The northern Plains were less good for breeding. After a hard winter cows were often so weak that, if the spring was cold and wet, they would perish at calving time. On the northern Plains cows normally lived to have only six calves.

But the northern Plains compensated for this handicap in affording especially good feed. They produced a richer and more succulent grass than the hot southern regions, and for that reason raised bigger and fatter steers. They provided even in the winter some fodder that was good, grasses that had been cured on the stem. The snowfall was not, in normal years, heavy enough to cover all the forage. Cattle could paw through the snow to the grass underneath. Blizzards were sometimes destructive, but from ordinary storms cattle found shelter in ravines and in gullies. So the dictum was that the southern Plains were the best breeding grounds; the northern, the best feeding grounds.

Texas was the region where the industry on a large scale began. It had the climatic advantages already mentioned, and also a land policy favorable to cattlemen. Texas never ceded its public domain to the federal government. It established its own land policy, which was favorable to grazers. Grazing lands could be bought from the state for 50 cents an acre. Also great tracts could be acquired at little cost from Mexicans whose title dated back to the Mexican regime. Cattle ranches of 50,000 to 100,000 acres were common. One, in the brush country south of the Nueces River—the famous King Ranch—contained over a million acres. Its founder, Richard King, started out in 1853 by buying land cheaply from a Mexican, and kept on adding more land and more cattle. He had over 100,000 cattle at one time on the ranch. On his death the ranch passed to his heirs and in 1955 was still intact in the hands of his descendants.

Another ranch, established in the middle 1870's, contained more than 3 million acres. It was the famous XIT Ranch in the Texas Panhandle, whose owners were a syndicate of Chicago capitalists. They acquired the land from Texas as payment for erecting a new state capitol building. They stocked the ranch with high-quality cattle. Ultimately, when the value of the land had gone up sufficiently, they broke up the ranch and sold the land at a big profit.

The exporting of cattle from Texas began even before the Civil War. Steers were driven overland to New Orleans or to Memphis. Later, after the Civil War, when railroads had been built, connections were made with the corn belt of the Middle West, which became a market for what were known as feeders. Feeders were cattle fattened on corn a few months before going to market. A third great outlet was the northern Plains, to which went stockers—stock to be fed on grass.

The northern Plains were reached by the so-called long drive. This was an important and a characteristic aspect of the cattle industry. A herd of 2000 or 2500 steers would be collected in Texas by an owner or a cattle buyer. It would be put in charge of a gang of a dozen cowboys, who would drive the cattle northward along the well-known cattle trails.

The drive was a job for experts. If entrusted to amateurs the cattle lost too much weight on the way. The cattle were moved slowly during the day with opportunities to rest and even to graze a little. Rests were taken if possible near water holes. At night the herd would be gathered in a compact mass, and a detail of cowboys would ride around it all night playing to the animals on harmonicas or singing cowboy lullabies. The cattle rested better when they heard the sound of the human voice. Cattle well cared for lost little weight; they might actually get fatter on the drive. Night stampedes were a special danger to guard against. Stampedes might be started by Indians who wanted to be paid for gathering the herd together again. The cowboy method of stopping a stampeding herd was to get the cattle running in a circle.

The trails used for the long drive are shown on the map (77). All crossed the Indian Territory. For the privilege of traversing tribal lands and taking grass in the process, a small payment to the tribe was made. The payment usually took the form of a few head of cattle—the poorest and weakest steers in the herd. The trails tended to shift westward as the eastern part of the Plains became occupied by settlers.

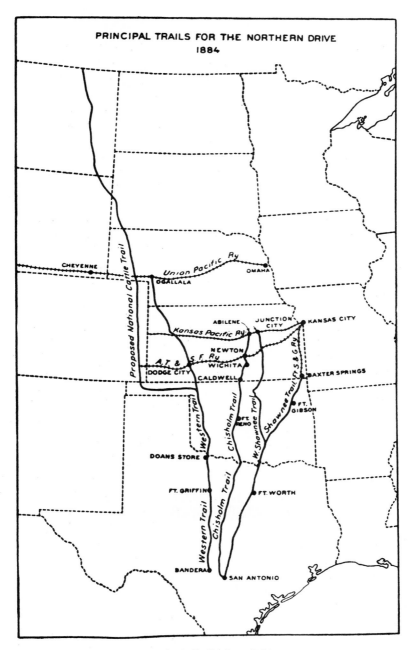

PRINCIPAL TRAILS FOR THE NORTHERN DRIVE
1884

CHEYENNE

Proposed National Cattle Trail

Union Pacific Ry.

OGALLALA

OMAHA

ABILENE

JUNCTION CITY

KANSAS CITY

Kansas Pacific Ry.

NEWTON

A. T. & S. F. Ry.

WICHITA

DODGE CITY

CALDWELL

BAXTER SPRINGS

Western Trail

Chisholm Trail

FT. RENO

W. Shawnee Trail

Shawnee Trail (M.T. S & Ry.)

FT. GIBSON

DOANS STORE

FT. GRIFFIN

Chisholm Trail

FT. WORTH

Western Trail

BANDERA

SAN ANTONIO

77. Cattle Trails (from Dale)

On reaching a railroad the owner or his cowboy representative had two alternatives. They could sell the herd for shipment to the corn belt or continue northward.
They were likely to adopt the first if the price of beef was favorable. They were likely
to adopt the second, and drive on to the northern ranges of the Dakotas, Wyoming,
or Montana, if, at the time of reaching a railroad, the price of beef was not favorable. The cattle in such a case would be sold to a northern cattleman for stocking
purposes. The cities located where the cattle trails intersected the railroads were
known as cow towns. Wichita, Abilene, Dodge City, and Ogallala were ripsnorting
places when the cowboys arrived.

The long drive had an important but short history. The history began in 1866,
after the close of the Civil War, when the first long drive from Texas occurred. By
1870 almost half a million head of cattle were being exported annually from Texas,
mostly by the long drive.

By the early 1880's the long drive was meeting resistance from the states of the
central Plains. This took the form of state quarantine laws against Texas cattle being
driven or shipped through. An early law was that of Kansas. Soon after, Nebraska and
Colorado followed suit. By the late 1880's the long drive had ceased to be a factor in
the Great Plains industry.

The objection of northern cattlemen to the long drive was a result, in part, of
improvements in their own techniques. They steadily improved the breed of their
herds. They kept cows in better state for calving, by winter shelter and by a little
winter feed. Northern beef was in any case much superior to that of the southern
longhorns. The long drive was resisted also because Texas cattle brought the dreaded
Texas fever, which was common along the Mexican border. It had long been a
problem there, though not a disastrous one, because Texas cattle had developed some
resistance to it. But carried to northern herds by the long drive, it produced widespread epidemics. Infected animals developed hemolytic anemia as well as fever,
with a mortality rate in hot weather approaching 90 percent.

In 1890 Drs. Theobald Smith and F. L. Kilborne discovered that the fever was
caused by a microorganism introduced into the bloodstream of cattle by the bite of a
cattle tick. The discovery led to the development of methods of destroying the ticks by
immersing or spraying cattle with a disinfectant. As a result, Texas fever was virtually
eliminated from the United States. This discovery was a medical landmark, because it
first demonstrated that disease in animals or man can be transmitted by an insect
vector. This in turn led to the later discovery by Drs. Walter Reed, Patrick Manson,
and others that bites of infected mosquitoes may carry diseases such as yellow fever or
malaria. A campaign for the destruction of mosquitoes in the South followed, which
has all but eliminated these diseases from the United States.

In the meantime the rash of quarantine laws by the states north of Texas led the
representatives of that state in Congress to stage a fight for a federal right-of-way
through the territories—a kind of corridor three miles wide to the international
border. But the project was fought off and defeated by the supporters of the northern
cattlemen.

The next illustration shows a comparison of the cattle industry of the Far West in
1860 and in 1880 (78). Each dot represents 2000 head. In 1860 the great concentration
is eastern Texas. The Plains are virtually untouched. Some development is shown in
the upper waters of the Rio Grande and in the valley of Great Salt Lake. The interior

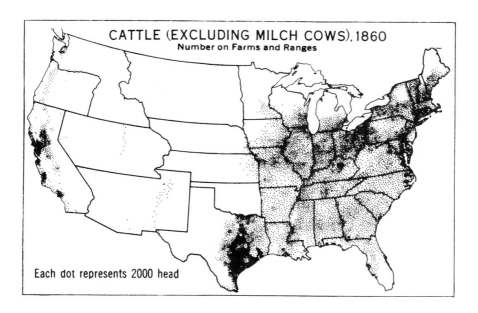

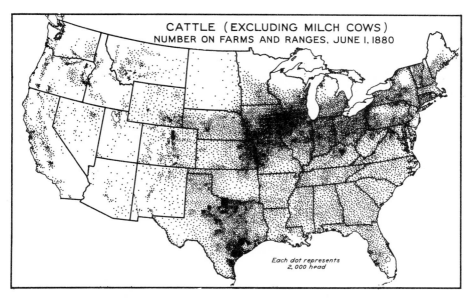

78. Cattle Industry, 1860, 1880 (from Paullin and the National Archives)

valley of California and the Willamette Valley in Oregon are big centers. By 1880 the Great Plains have come into their own. They are the cattle kingdom of the United States.

The land on which the Great Plains industry was nurtured north of Texas belonged to the federal government. It was exploited by the cattlemen without any return to the government. In Texas a grazing fee was collected from cattlemen who used state land. But on the federal domain a grazing fee was not even attempted.

The established system rested upon "range rights." Such "rights," like the claims of miners on gold-bearing streams, were taken out on a basis of first come, first served. Each cattleman assumed them in accordance with the number of cattle in his herd. Some big cattle companies took range rights extending over several hundred thousand acres. If an interloper undertook to encroach on an established right there was shooting. Appropriated rights were separated from each other usually by some natural dividing line such as the divide between two streams. A cattleman might occupy half the watershed of a minor stream.

Every cattleman tried to keep his herd as much as possible on his own range right and to exclude his neighbor's cattle. One of the chief duties of cowboys was to ride the "line," keeping the cattle of a neighboring ranchman away and the cattle of the boss at home. But in spite of all efforts, the cattle in an area inevitably intermingled. A periodic separation of them into their respective herds had to be undertaken. This was one of the functions of the institution known as the roundup, a community affair supervised by the local cattlemen's association. It was confined to a definite area, usually the drainage basin of a stream. It took place in the springtime. On an agreed date the cowboys in a roundup district would ride down the streams, driving all cattle ahead of them to a roundup point.

When all the cattle of the area had been collected the separation of the animals into their respective herds began. It was easy because each animal carried a brand on its flank. Newborn calves trotted along at their mothers' heels. When the separation had been completed all newborn calves were branded. Male calves were converted into steers by castration. Then the herds were taken back, each to its own feeding ground.

A second roundup was held in the autumn for the purpose of picking out the marketable steers in each herd. It was known as the "beef roundup." The steers thus chosen from each herd were shipped by their owner east to the corn belt or to a market, while the remainder were driven back to the feeding ground. The roundup costs were borne by members of the local association on the basis of the number of calves branded or yearling steers marketed. The organization in charge of the roundup—the local cattlemen's association—was a distinctive frontier institution, the equivalent of the miners' camp of the mountains.

On the northern Plains such associations were organized in the early 1870's. Theodore Roosevelt helped to establish one in North Dakota in the mid-1880's. Besides the supervision of the roundup, the local associations arranged for the protection of the members' range rights against interlopers. If an established range right was invaded by a newcomer, he was dealt with by the association. The members were also protected against Indians, wolves, and cattle thieves. For ferreting out thieves the associations employed detectives.

The local associations also tried to keep the breed of cattle in a district high, by making sure that each member maintained in his herd bulls of high pedigree. The quality of a herd can be bred up with surprising speed if the bulls are of good pedigree. English Herefords were brought in by English investors, and Black Angus by Scotch investors. From the Oregon Country stock of good quality began to be imported in the 1870's. The local associations brought pressure on railroad companies to give favorable freight rates and services in the shipment of cattle. Territorial associations had the function of coordinating the activities of the local associations and also of guarding against cattle thieves by keeping inspectors at cow towns to watch for stolen or misbranded cattle. State associations were also involved in lobbying activities. The National Cattle Growers' Association, organized in 1884, worked in Congress for legislation favorable to the cattle industry.

The golden age of the range cattle industry was the period from 1869—the date of the completion of the Union Pacific—to the middle of the 1880's. These dozen or fifteen years were a period of prosperity. The prosperity varied from year to year, depending on the price of beef in the eastern markets, the weather on the Plains, and other factors. In the early 1880's the profits of cattlemen were likely to be 20 to 30 percent on the capital investment. The result was that capital flowed to the Great Plains in quantity from the East and from England and Scotland. Europeans are estimated to have had interests in 20 million acres of range rights in the 1880's. Men who had made their pile in gold mining often retired to the cattle country.

The decline of the open-range industry was as swift as its rise. It occurred in the late 1880's and early 1890's. The principal reasons were the collapse of beef prices due to overproduction, overgrazing of the range, and the disastrous winter of 1886–87, when snow on the northern Plains was unusually deep and 40 to 50 percent of the cattle there died of starvation. Another factor was the depredations of cattle thieves—the so-called rustlers. Finally, the movement of pioneer farmers into the best parts of the range finished the era. It was the homesteaders, in the last analysis, who brought the open-range industry to destruction by forcing cattle farther and farther into areas of aridity.

The increasing scarcity of good range was reflected in the systematic engrossing by cattle outfits of what was left of the open range. One form was the building of fences around range rights on the public domain. The advantages derived were the discouragement of interlopers, the reduction of labor costs by reducing the number of cowboys needed, the assurance of high-grade herds by exclusion of low-grade bulls, and better protection for "winter range," an important aspect of the year-round pasturage of cattle. In the heat of summer cattle would not graze farther away than three or four miles from the source of water. Winter range could be farther from water, for cattle quenched their thirst from snow on the ground. If part of the range was to be reserved for winter pasturing it had to be closed off, and the answer was fencing. Fencing was inexpensive as the result of the development of superior barbed wire in 1874.

Complaints against fencing of the public domain were sent constantly to Washington by postal riders and by prospective settlers. In the administration of Grover Cleveland, Congress passed the Enclosure Act of 1885, but the law was not effective, for it contained no adequate enforcement machinery. Cleveland sent federal marshals riding over the Plains to cut the fences, but as soon as the marshals had turned away the wires went back.

A sham of legality for fencing came into general use. Extensive land grants had been made to railroads during the Civil War and its aftermath, to encourage building across the Great Plains. The Union Pacific received in 1862 every alternate section of land on each side of its track. These lands the railroads were willing to sell cheap to cattlemen. The cattlemen were often big operators who were able to buy land by the hundred thousand acres. What they bought they extended by a mode of fencing that had the semblance of legality.

An illustration of this practice is revealed in a case brought before a Circuit Court of Appeals in 1895—the case of *Camfield et al. v. United States.* The case originated in a fence constructed early in 1893 in Colorado on sections purchased from the Union Pacific. It was so built as to enclose 20,000 acres of government land. The legality of the fencing was challenged by a federal district attorney and, in the district court, Camfield was ordered to remove it. The case was carried to the Circuit Court of Appeals.

In the course of the proceeding the diagram here appended became part of the court record, as printed in the *Federal Reporter,* volume 66. The fence as depicted by the dotted line was throughout on private odd-numbered sections that had been purchased from the railroad. Appellants admitted that it enclosed all of the even-numbered public-land sections in two townships. They averred, however, that they were building reservoirs for irrigating lands owned by them, and that these would benefit not only their land but much other land in the vicinity. The court made short shrift of the argument of the appellants, and rejected their appeal. But as late as 1905 illegal fences were still up in some localities on the Plains.

Other forms of seizure appeared as cattlemen were forced farther and farther into semi-arid land. One was appropriation of water by monopolizing river frontage and water holes, which, in a semi-arid region, gave control of all the adjacent backcountry. Titles to riverfront areas were obtained by manipulation of the land laws. A favorite device was the use of dummy entries for homesteads or pre-emptions, filed by cowboy employees of the cattlemen. Another was recourse to the Timber Culture Act of 1873, which permitted a settler to buy 160 acres of public land, over and above a free homestead, at the minimum price of $1.25 an acre, on agreement to plant a fourth of it to trees. Such lands were purchased by cattlemen in the name of their cowboys. A few acorns would be scattered over them and the law was thus satisfied. Recourse was also found in the Desert Land Act of 1877, which permitted a settler to buy 640 acres of public land at the minimum price of $1.25 an acre on condition of irrigating a portion of it. That opened the way to many frauds. It has been estimated that 95 percent of titles obtained under the Desert Land Act were fraudulently obtained by or for corporations.

A further indication of the growing scarcity of good range in the late 1880's was the increase in range wars. These were sometimes between cattlemen of different groups fighting each other—established cattlemen against newcomers—or more often were between cattlemen and sheepmen. Cattlemen objected to the intrusion of sheepmen, for sheep were likely to ruin the range by grazing practically down to the roots of the grass. Also, sheep left a manure that was obnoxious to cattle, which preferred not to graze over land where sheep had been.

The era of the open range extended over approximately thirty years. By its nature it was transitory. It was marked by relatively inefficient and wasteful methods. It led to overgrazing of the range and production of cattle likely to be of poor quality. It led to loss of cattle through lack of care and to conflict and violence.

A new and better era opened in the 1890's with the advent of range ranching. This was a time in which the open range, the public domain, was relied on only for

6	5	4	3	2	1
7	8	9	10	11	12
18	17	16	15	14	13
19	20	21	22	23	24
30	29	28	27	26	25
31	32	33	34	35	36

The diagram of an enclosed township illustrates the ingenuity brought to bear in the seizing of public resources on the Great Plains.

summer and autumn feed. Winter feed was produced by the cattleman on land acquired from the government, or rented from an owner, which was the ''ranch.'' It might be land that could be irrigated and that produced alfalfa.

Range ranching had been practiced by some cattlemen almost from the beginning. The practice had always been to own the half section or section of land on which the headquarters of the boss and the cowboys were built, and on this some hay had usually been raised. Sheepmen had always been range ranchers, since sheep could not be left through a winter to shift for themselves. Range ranching had its most rapid growth after the disastrous winter of 1886–87. By the early years of the 20th century, it had completely superseded the earlier form of the industry in most parts of the Great Plains.

In the 20th century the industry gradually became more scientific and stabilized. Increased attention was given to breeding up herds and producing better-quality beef.

Pedigreed cattle were imported, especially the white-faced Herefords from England that came to dominate the Great Plains and the Black Angus from Scotland. Later, Brahman cattle from India were brought to the Gulf Plains, where they did well, both as beef and as dairy cattle. They proved immune to heat, to the cattle tick, and to fevers. In the new era water was more energetically exploited. More wells were drilled and reservoirs were built to hold spring rains. Winter feeding was increasingly done, and the feed was more scientifically balanced. More winter shelter was provided. The grade of beef produced was far superior to that of the old Texas longhorns, which virtually disappeared. They became almost an extinct species. Then the federal government interested itself in maintaining the species as a kind of museum piece, and now some hundreds are protected in wildlife refuges.

In the second half of the 20th century the bleak agricultural possibilities of the southwestern Great Plains were transformed by river-basin developments which brought waters for irrigation to western Kansas, eastern Colorado, and the panhandle portions of Texas and Oklahoma. Those areas became major producers of alfalfa and sorghum, which were the feed for cattle there, as were corn and silage on the northern prairies.

In the meantime the open-range and range-ranching phases of the Great Plains economy had served American consumers well. They had added a new province to the occupied portions of the nation. They had contributed abundant quantities of beef to the market at reduced prices, so that meat came within the reach of workers in the cities. It made Omaha a rival of Chicago as the largest livestock market and meat-packing center of the world. It added color and picturesqueness to western life and Westerns to the national literature. It gave at least one classic to this literature, Owen Wister's *The Virginian,* which is a brilliant picture of the industry in its heyday. It prepared the way for a new phase of Great Plains development—that of the settler, detested by the cattlemen.

Farmers on the Great Plains

A MASSIVE FLOW OF FARMERS moved into the Great Plains in the wake of the cattleman's advance. In 1880 it was at the line separating the prairie province from the Plains in Texas, Kansas, and Nebraska. Ten years later it had reached the heart of the Great Plains in these states. The Indian Territory had become nearly surrounded. By 1890 the frontier line was at the Colorado border. Pioneers along the edges of the Indian Territory had their eyes on a local area at its center known as Oklahoma District, which appears on the map shaped like a Greek column (79). The region had been ceded to the federal government at the close of the Civil War by the Seminole and Creek tribes. It had never been used for the location of other tribes and was unoccupied. It was a beautiful region of rich soil.

In 1880 a demand arose in Kansas that the region be opened to settlement. It was pressed by an irresponsible militia captain, David L. Payne, head of an association organized to force the federal government to open the district to settlement. The members were known as "boomers" because of their enthusiastic promotion of the beauties of the region. Each year the boomers marched into the district to stake out homesteads and each year were marched out again by federal cavalry. That went on from 1880 to 1884, when Payne died, and his place was taken by an associate.

In 1885 President Cleveland issued an order that in 1889 Oklahoma District would be opened to settlement. The area was laid out into sections by surveyors. On the day designated in 1889 a crowd of 20,000 people gathered at the borders of the district. The crowd included many land speculators who had their eyes on a locality that was expected to become the chief city of the new settlement—the area that is now Guthrie.

At noon that day bugles were sounded and the crowds streamed into Oklahoma District. A picturesque rush took place of men on horseback, in buggies, and on bicycles, featured in the film *Cimarron*. Within twelve hours the Guthrie region contained 5000 to 10,000 people. Many of the newcomers were not merely boomers;

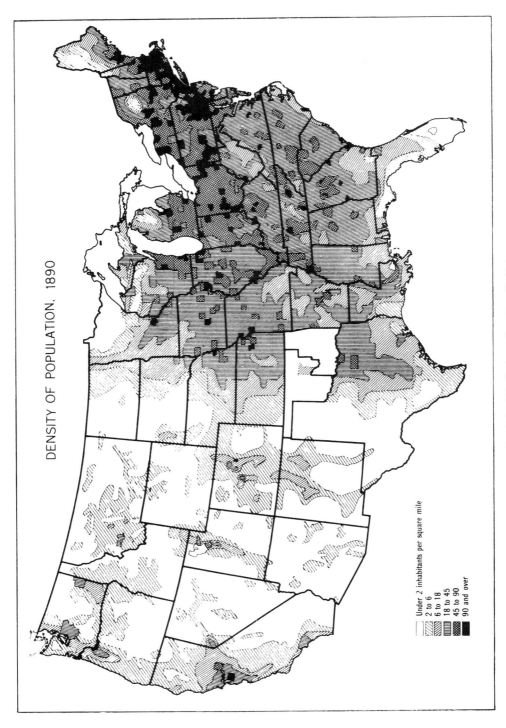

DENSITY OF POPULATION. 1890

Under 2 inhabitants per square mile
2 to 6
6 to 18
18 to 45
45 to 90
90 and over

79. Population Distribution, 1890 (from Paullin)

they were "sooners," who had sneaked past the guards and had hidden out near Guthrie. By the end of the year Oklahoma District contained 60,000 persons. The name Oklahoma was later extended by the federal government to the whole western half of the Indian Territory.

After 1890 that half of Oklahoma was opened gradually to settlement, as Indian reservations were divided in severalty under the Dawes Act, and the surplus lands acquired by the government were made available to whites. Each reservation, as it was opened, was overrun by rushes similar to that into the region around Guthrie.

At first the lands were given free under the Homestead Law. Later the government made a charge of $1.25 an acre to recover the price of purchase of the land from the Indians. Even at that price the land was a bargain and was eagerly sought. The confusion created by this process was so great and led so often to litigation or to shootings that the practice was eventually adopted of registering applicants for the lands in the order of application, and deciding between the applicants by lottery.

In 1890 the frontier line was no longer a simple, single line. In the region of western Kansas and Nebraska, settlers had moved so far out into the Great Plains that they had coalesced with the population of Colorado. Settlement had moved into the area of semi-aridity. The broken, irregular frontier line represents in part the search for water by cattlemen and homesteaders.

In this advance wheat was one of the migrants. Its earlier stages have been geographically depicted. By 1879 the crop had moved across Minnesota, with a finger pointing toward the fertile Red River and James River valleys. In Kansas and Nebraska wheat was the major crop (Map 73, page 434). By 1889 the Red River valley had become the center of the wheat kingdom (Map 80). This valley, and the eastern part of the Dakotas, was now an area of so-called bonanza farms, operated on a huge scale and highly mechanized, as for example the great Dalrymple farm in the Red River valley, a 25,000-acre estate, all in wheat. The wheat in the north was spring; that in Kansas and southern Nebraska was winter-grown. Wisconsin and Illinois had made their shift from wheat to dairying and to diversified farming. They were now prosperous, and on currency issues, especially that of free silver, less radical than they had once been.

By 1899 the Red River valley was the major wheat area of the United States (Map 81). If the map were extended into Canada, the Manitoba wheat belt, with its center at Winnipeg, would be revealed. The Red River valley and the eastern Dakotas were the nation's main bread reliance, with Kansas and Nebraska close seconds.

Not only wheat but corn moved into the eastern part of the Great Plains in these years. In 1899 Kansas and Nebraska were important corn as well as wheat areas (Map 82). They were engaged in fattening steers imported from the Great Plains, and also hogs. Omaha and Kansas City were important slaughtering centers.

By 1909 Kansas, Nebraska, Iowa, and Illinois were still centers of the corn and hog kingdom (Map 83). The corn belt had become relatively stationary. Seventy percent of the corn produced here was consumed on the farms where it was raised. West of the corn belt, in the region of semi-aridity, were winter wheat and range ranching.

The years 1870–1900 were a period of enormous agricultural growth in the United States. In those years 430 million acres of land were settled, which was more

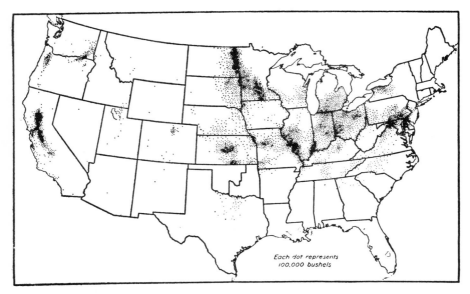

80. Wheat Production, 1889 (from the *Yearbook of Agriculture*, 1933)

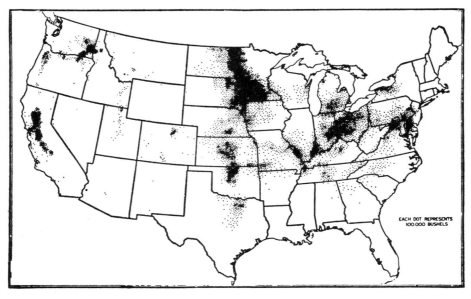

81. Wheat Production, 1899 (from the *Yearbook of Agriculture*, 1933)

than had been occupied in all preceding American history. A considerable part of this expansion took place in the Great Plains.

This enormous expansion was the product of a combination of forces. One was the Homestead Law of 1862. Another was the realization on the part of informed people that the era of well-watered, free land was drawing to a close. A warning had

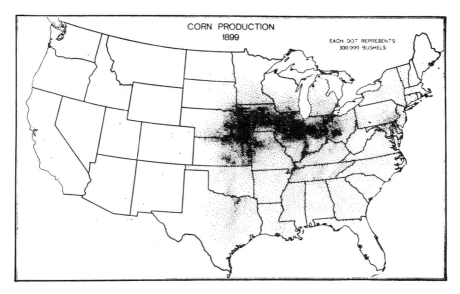

82. Corn Production, 1899 (from the *Yearbook of Agriculture,* 1921)

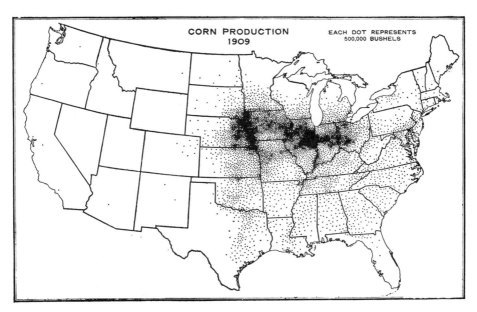

83. Corn Production, 1909 (from the *Yearbook of Agriculture,* 1915)

been given in 1880 by the Director of the Census that the era of free land was closing. The swift expansion across the Great Plains was thus, in part, a rush of American farmers to partake of Uncle Sam's bounty in areas that were well watered. A third factor was the sale of land by states at attractive prices. School lands, university lands, and other state lands were put on the market in competition with homesteads.

The chief factor, however, in this swift colonization was the railroad companies of the Great Plains. All of them were eager to transport settlers to the province, to get it colonized as a matter of developing traffic. The land-grant railroads had their own areas to sell. But they also aggressively advertised the free homestead lands of the federal government. The main objective was to build up settlement as a means of creating freight to carry. The prices at which railroad lands were sold varied according to location and soil, from $5 to $20 or more an acre, with easy credit terms. Many settlers preferred railroad lands that were favorably located to free homesteads. Railroad companies, especially those possessing land grants, were colonizers of the Great Plains on a big scale. They carried forward on a vast scale the work that had been done on a lesser scale by colonizing companies on the seaboard in the colonial period.

The Great Plains were advertised with extraordinary enthusiasm. The Northern Pacific Railroad kept 800 agents in various European countries distributing literature and assisting emigrants. Literature was spread in every important European language. Western railroads had agents in New York City to receive immigrants; they offered special immigrant rates to the West, and they gave new arrivals advice as to settlement and as to the best methods of farming.

The railroad colonization of the Great Plains helps to account for the origin of the colonists. Into Dakota and into Montana Scandinavian immigrants were brought by the Northern Pacific; into the Kansas region of the Arkansas River valley, 60,000 German Mennonites from Russia were brought by the Atchison, Topeka, and Santa Fe. The settlement of the Great Plains, at the north and center, may almost be said to have been a railroad colonization. This railroad enterprise is one of the most important aspects of the history of the West since the Civil War, and the reason the story is not more emphasized in summary accounts is that the story has thus far been told only for individual railroads.

Railroads were not always scrupulous in their colonization methods. They permitted their New York agents to use dubious means of enticing immigrants coming off steamboats to settle on their lands. Some were said to have stolen trainloads of immigrants from each other.

High-pressure salesmanship was used in disposing of lands to prospective settlers. Rapturous tales were told of what the land would grow. The climate of the Plains was misrepresented. Jay Cooke, the financier of the Northern Pacific, in order to counteract the impression that the region of the Northern Pacific was a harshly cold country, had weather maps printed in the 1870's on which the isotherm lines were twisted so as to represent the area served by the line as a region of warm winters. The Northern Pacific was thereafter jocularly referred to by newspapers as Jay Cooke's Banana Belt.

Lack of rainfall was known to be a crucial problem on the western Plains. The whole region is a country of semi-aridity and of climatic cycles. A series of wet years occurs when the annual rainfall is somewhat more than 20 inches; then a dry series will follow—years of terrific drought, when the country burns up. It so happened that the five years prior to 1887 were a wet series on the Great Plains, when the Kansas, Nebraska, and South Dakota Plains had fairly abundant rainfall. The average in those years was 21.63 inches, and half that rain fell helpfully in the growing season. The propagandists of the railroads, as a result, either denied the old assertion that the

Plains were a region of semi-aridity, or contended that the climate was changing—that rainfall was increasing. They advanced various theories to explain the change. Plowing of the sod was said to produce rain; "rain follows the plow." The stringing of telegraph wires was also said to produce rain. A theory was developed that the noise of civilization—clanging of locomotives, etc.—led to rain. These theories were repeated even by state officials.

The scientists of the federal government were not allowed to counteract such propaganda. In the reports of the Geological Survey, Major John Wesley Powell was obliged, at the insistence of western congressmen who were acting at the behest of railroad lobbies, to strike out, in his account of the Great Plains, every reference to "semi-aridity" and substitute the word "semi-humidity."

The flow of settlement was stimulated in the mid-1880's by another factor—the easy-credit conditions in the United States. Investment capital was plentiful in the East; it was seeking profitable mortgage outlets. Such outlets existed in mortgages on Great Plains farms at 8 or 10 percent interest. In Massachusetts alone, the amount of capital invested in western farm mortgages in the 1880's amounted to 8 or 10 million dollars annually.

The rush of settlement to the Great Plains had significant results. One was an immense addition to the production of food in the United States. This occurred at a time when great increases were being made in other countries—in Canada, South America, and Australia. Agricultural overproduction became a worldwide phenomenon. With it went steadily sagging farm prices. The twenty years 1877–97 were a period of ruinously low prices for farm produce, of intense distress for farmers, not only for those in the United States but for farmers elsewhere in the world.

In England grain growers were almost put out of business. Land values on English farms faded away; the farmers sank gradually from a yeoman to a tenant status. Britain's dependence on the outside world for grain became steadily greater. On the continent of Europe the importation of American food came to be regarded as a kind of hostile Yankee invasion. Government protection was demanded against it, protection against American meat in particular. Quarantine barriers were set up in one European country after another. In six countries—France, Germany, Austria, Italy, Spain, and Denmark—they were erected against American pork. In the 1880's these barriers became a major problem for American diplomacy and remained so for a quarter of a century.

To justify the barriers European governments maintained that American pork carried a parasite that caused the disease trichinosis. If the parasite penetrated the intestinal tract of human beings, it was fatal. The charge that American pork was thus infected was widely accepted in Europe in countries where people had the habit of eating chopped meat uncooked. This charge was largely without foundation. American hogs were almost completely free of trichinosis. One disease that did sometimes afflict American hogs was hog cholera, but this was not so terrifying to Europeans because pork so infected was not fatal when eaten. Another charge leveled against American meat in Europe was that unsanitary conditions prevailed in meat-packing establishments, that rules of cleanliness were not enforced, that proper inspection was lacking.

An effective answer to all charges would have been the creation of a federal meat-inspection service at the great American packing centers. But this was blocked by the packing interests. In 1890 a law was passed by Congress for federal inspection of pork destined for European markets, but the inspection was not adequate. During the Spanish-American War, when the American press was filled with charges that so-called embalmed beef was sold to the Army and fed to American soldiers, and in 1905, when Upton Sinclair published his novel *The Jungle,* which gave an ugly picture of conditions in Chicago packing houses, European feeling against American meats flared up again, and several countries passed quarantine laws. It was not until 1906, when an adequate inspection service under the charge of the Department of Agriculture was provided by Congress, that an end was put to European quarantines against American meats.

In the agricultural depression of the late 1880's and early 1890's farmers throughout the United States were in distress. On the Atlantic seaboard many gave up grain growing. Those possessing good soil escaped ruin by developing the arts of high farming. They engaged in truck farming, fruit growing, dairying, and producing quality foods. In New England farmers in the poorer hill country had no such means of survival and abandonment of farms became a notable development. Even in the Middle West producers of grain and meat were in trouble in spite of having favorable harvests. In the black years 1877–97 they despaired of seeing wheat rise again to the level of a dollar a bushel.

In the late 1880's a major reversal of the climatic cycle occurred, which added its woes to the troubles of the farmers on the Great Plains. A dry cycle of greater than normal intensity began in 1887 and continued with only occasional relief for nearly a decade. In this period Kansas, Colorado, Nebraska, and South Dakota had one crop failure after another. The colonization boom on the Great Plains collapsed. A disaster of major proportions overwhelmed the region. Ordinarily, in a period of crop failures, prices of grain and meat rise. Good prices compensate somewhat for poor crops. But in the period of the 1890's prices remained ruinously low because the middle western prairies and foreign countries were producing abundant crops. On the Plains, even when the drought occasionally relented and substantial crops were harvested, farmers made little profit.

In western Kansas, Nebraska, South Dakota, and in Colorado, farmers were flattened out. A third to a half of them were ruined. In western Kansas and Nebraska 100,000 people are believed to have given up their homes, whole communities were abandoned, and ghost cities existed in which hardly a soul remained.

The magnitude of the disaster was the result partly of the fact that a large proportion of the farmers there were inexperienced in the arts of dry-land farming, men who knew nothing of the techniques which enable farmers today to survive in western Kansas, Nebraska, and in Colorado. They have knowledge of dry-land farming and drought-resistant grains. In good years they lay by a surplus against the bad. But the earlier pioneers knew little of this. Many of them were not even experienced frontiersmen. They were Easterners or Europeans brought out by rail to the Plains— greenhorns at pioneering thrown up against the most difficult form of American agriculture.

The extent of the Plains disaster is revealed by a comparison of population maps—that of 1890, earlier shown (Map 79, page 468), with that of 1900, shown here (84). The contraction of settlement there is obvious. Even the settlers who managed to stay on their farms were able to do so only by mortgaging all their

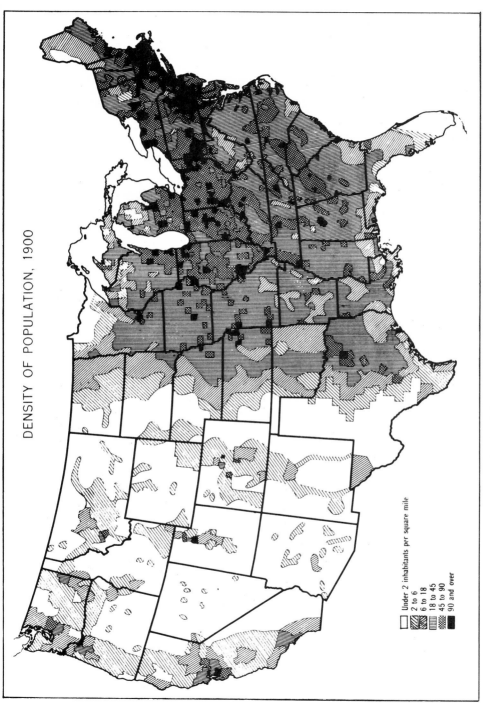

DENSITY OF POPULATION, 1900

Under 2 inhabitants per square mile
2 to 6
6 to 18
18 to 45
45 to 90
90 and over

84. Population Distribution, 1900 (from Paullin)

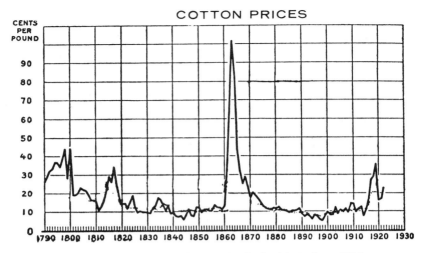

85. Cotton Prices Graph (from the *Yearbook of Agriculture*, 1921)

belongings. Throughout the late 1880's and the early 1890's the region was sinking deeper and deeper into debt. The Plains were an area of acute distress.

The cotton South was another such area. Its distress was the result in part of a vast overproduction of cotton, resulting from the advance of the crop across Texas and Oklahoma, which coincided with cotton expansion elsewhere in the world. The price of the fiber in the world markets sagged ruinously. In the United States it fell to the lowest level of American history, 5½ cents a pound.

The diagram exhibits this sag of prices (85). The peak on it is the Civil War price of cotton, 53 cents a pound. After the close of the war the price remained for a long time in the neighborhood of 10 cents a pound. In 1890 prices began a precipitous decline to a level of 5½ or 6 cents a pound. This drop meant debt. In the older cotton areas, where soil fertility had become depleted, it meant increasing debt and the descent of many farmers into the ranks of tenancy.

The Great Plains and the cotton South were thus areas of acute distress. They became areas of a political disturbance alarming to the nation in the late 1880's and the 1890's, the disturbance known as Populism.

Populism

SYMPTOMS OF ACUTE DISTRESS appeared on the northern Great Plains and in the South in the late 1880's. They took the form of farmers' alliances, a new kind of political machinery. A National Farmers' Alliance was organized in the northern Plains; in the South its prototype was the Farmers' Alliance and Industrial Union. A Negro branch was affiliated with the southern body—the Colored Farmers' Alliance. The Alliances consisted of local societies, initially formed for social and educational purposes, and cooperating in loose state and sectional bodies. In the late 1880's all of them became politically oriented. Largest in membership was the southern Alliance, containing more than a million members.

In 1890 these Alliances entered state and congressional contests and showed surprising strength in them. They won full or partial control of twelve state legislatures and six governorships. Eight members of the northern Alliance were elected to Congress, where they were joined by allies in the Democratic party who were committed to vote for agrarian measures. Only one avowed Populist, Thomas E. Watson of Georgia, was chosen to Congress. Southern preference was to win control of the Bourbon-dominated Democratic party. Southerners feared that if they abandoned the traditional one-party system of the South, they would endanger the treasured principle of white supremacy.

In 1891–92 the northern Alliance decided to enter the presidential campaign of 1892 as a third party, the Populist party. Its nominating convention gathered in the summer of 1892 at Omaha, Nebraska, the center of the Populist uprising. The Omaha platform opened with a dismal picture of a nation dragged by evil forces to the brink of destruction. Business was prostrate; homes were covered with mortgages; labor in the cities was impoverished; the nation's lands were concentrated in the hands of capitalists. "We breed two great classes," so the jeremiad concluded, "tramps and millionaires."

The platform framed to meet these dangers was directed primarily to the evils undermining rural life. But it included urban evils and defects in the modes of registering the public will. Special emphasis was on reform of the nation's currency. Two planks demanded such reforms. One was a major increase in the quantity of the national paper currency, together with changes that would make it more usable. The second was a huge increase in the quantity of silver and gold coin. The quantity theory of money dominated both planks.

Of the paper currency, greenbacks to the amount of $347 million were then in circulation. They had been at this low level partly to prevent inflation and partly because they could not be used to pay interest on national bonds or duties on imports. The platform called for the removal of these limitations. A common form of paper money was national bank notes. Their quantity in circulation was declining because the national debt, on which they rested, was steadily declining. They were regarded by the debtor elements with suspicion as bankers' emissions and not related sufficiently to the seasonal needs of the farm economy.

To fill this need the platform proposed the "sub-treasury" plan, a program of government-owned and operated elevators and warehouses, one in every county where annual farm commodities were produced to a value of $500,000 or more. To such an elevator or warehouse a farmer would take his grain, cotton, or other non-perishable commodities and borrow on them treasury notes up to 80 percent of their current market value. This would enable him to hold his commodity off the market for a year in the hope of improved prices. On the sale of the produce the government would recover its loan, plus interest at 2 percent and a low storage charge. In the meantime federal currency, amounting to $550 million, would be added to the insufficient currency of the nation. The plan resembled federal programs of storage of farm crops and loans of a later day.

A primary demand of the Omaha platform was the expansion of the nation's silver coinage. The free and unlimited coinage of silver at the ratio of 16 to 1 was to be maintained. This was attractive to other elements in the nation besides farmers. It had a strong appeal to eastern labor and to western silver-mine owners. For that reason it outlived the Populist third party movement and its analysis is for the moment deferred.

Another plank in the platform dealt with the public land. No further distribution of the public land to foreigners was to be permitted. Also, all lands which had been conferred on railroads that had not yet been disposed of by them and were in excess of their actual needs "should be reclaimed by the government and held for actual settlers only."

In regard to control of the agencies of transportation the Populists were successors to the Grangers and outdid them. The Omaha platform called for government ownership and operation of railroads and the nationalization of telegraph and telephone companies. The platform was suspicious of banks and called for postal savings banks for the safe deposit of the people's earnings. It demanded, also, a graduated income tax.

In addition to these actual demands the platform expressed Populist sentiments in a set of resolutions. It proposed that paupers, criminals, and contract labor be excluded from immigration to the United States. It recommended adoption of the Australian secret ballot. It proposed amendments to the Constitution limiting the President and Vice-President to a single term in office, and requiring senators to be chosen by direct vote of the people instead of by state legislatures. The platform was a thoroughgoing program of reform, an *omnium gatherum* of reform ideas. It was considered in the East the work of wild-eyed socialists. The nominee of the party for the presidency, on the other hand, was a moderate reformer—James B. Weaver of Iowa—a former Republican, a Civil War general, a Granger, and the Greenback candidate for the presidency in 1880.

In the balloting the party drew a surprisingly large vote, more than a million. The chief areas of the party's strength, as shown on the map (86), were Kansas, Colorado, Nevada, and Idaho, which were carried, and Nebraska, nearly so. These states were normally Republican and their defection meant the loss of the election. Grover Cleveland, a Democrat, was brought a second time into the White House. In the South the Populist vote was meager. But, as in the congressional election of 1890, many of the Democrats sent to Congress were Populists in sympathy.

The Populist upsurge was short-lived. Though the party showed even greater strength in the congressional election of 1894, it rapidly disintegrated thereafter. The reasons were, in part, that the men elected to state office by the party proved a disappointment to the public. Most of them were political amateurs who committed blunders. More important, the silver plank of the platform, which had the widest attraction to the distressed of the nation, was appropriated by the Democrats. "Free silver at 16 to 1" became, and remained for years, the central issue of American politics.

The issue had its origin in the nation's minting system, adopted in 1792, when the mint was established. On the recommendation of the Secretary of the Treasury, Alexander Hamilton, the system provided a bimetallic coinage. This was designed to meet the constant fluctuation in the value of silver and gold, the metals used in the world's coinage. Silver dollars were to be minted of the same size and weight as Spanish silver dollars, which were in wide circulation in the United States. They were to have a content of 371¼ grains of pure silver. Gold was then fifteen times as valuable commercially as silver, and the ratio of 15 to 1 was fixed, as between the two metals. This bimetallic system proved awkward to maintain because of the frequent changes in the quantity of the two metals mined. But precious metals of either kind were scarce in the United States and Hamilton believed the two would stabilize each other in the minting system.

Shortly after the adoption of the Mint Act the commercial value of gold rose as compared with silver. The ten-dollar gold piece came to have a value of $10.45 as measured in silver. The result was that gold pieces disappeared from circulation. They were melted down or exported.

In 1834 Congress adopted a new coinage act. The weight of the silver dollar was retained at 371¼ grains of pure silver, but the weight of gold coins was reduced. A ratio was established of 16 to 1. But again the commercial ratio between the two metals changed. This time the value of silver rose. More than a dollar's worth of silver went into the dollar at a ratio of 16 to 1. Relatively few dollars were coined and these were soon exported. The silver dollar disappeared from circulation. For a quarter of a century the American public saw silver dollars only in the hands of coin collectors.

In view of this situation, Congress, in 1873, dropped the silver dollar from the minting list. The public gave little notice to the change since the silver dollar had been so long out of circulation.

Then once again a turn occurred in the gyration of the metals, resulting from the

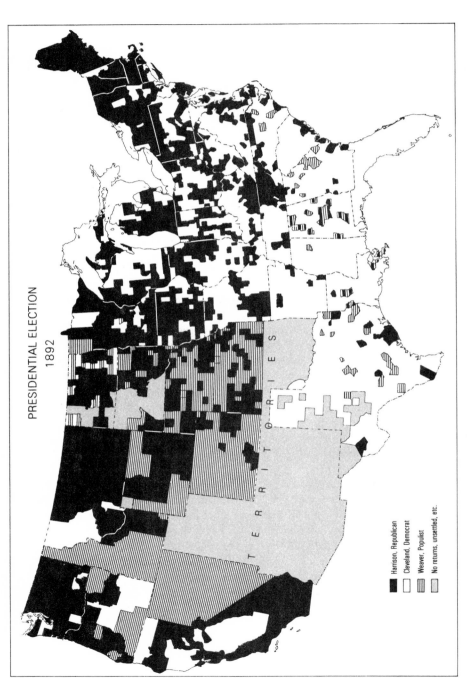

PRESIDENTIAL ELECTION
1892

TERRITORIES

Harrison, Republican
Cleveland, Democrat
Weaver, Populist
No returns, unsettled, etc.

86. Presidential Election, 1892 (from Paullin)

flood of silver coming from the Comstock lode and other great finds, and from improved methods of refining the ore. It resulted, also, from demonetizing silver in other countries of the world. The record of the commercial ratio between the metals is indicated below, and also the bullion value of the silver dollar.

	1860	1870	1873	1878	1890	1893	1895
Ratio	$\frac{15.29}{1}$	$\frac{15.57}{1}$	$\frac{15.72}{1}$	$\frac{17.94}{1}$	$\frac{19.77}{1}$	$\frac{26.49}{1}$	$\frac{31.57}{1}$
Bullion value of silver dollar				$.89	$.80	$.60	$.50

Coinciding with this decline in the value of silver and partly as a result of it, a demand arose in the United States for the remonetization of silver. That demand was supported in Congress by a number of interests. One was the silver miners, who wanted it used in coinage again in order that a government market for it would be re-established and augment its price. The silver-mining interests of the West were a powerful element in Congress. A second element demanding remonetization was the western farmers, who accepted the theory that more money would bring higher prices for farm products and better times. A third interest demanding remonetization was the nation's debtors, who believed that with more abundant coinage and better times debts would more easily be paid.

In response to these inflationary pressures Congress passed the Bland-Allison Act of 1878, which directed the Treasury to buy silver at commercial prices in the open market to an amount not less than $2 million a month, nor more than $4 million a month. The metal was to be coined into dollars at the ratio of 16 to 1. A dollar at this ratio in 1878 contained only 89 cents' worth of silver and was a cheap dollar.

The Bland-Allison Act remained on the statute books from 1878 to 1890. In this period $308 million worth of metal was bought by the government at the commercial price and converted into $378 million in silver dollars. The government made a profit of $70 million by minting a cheap dollar.

But the West was not satisfied, and demanded still further inflation. Accordingly, in 1890 Congress adopted the Sherman Silver Purchase Act, which directed the Treasury to buy, in the open market, at the regular commercial prices, 4,500,000 ounces of silver each month, nearly all the silver produced in the United States, and to pay for it in treasury notes of full legal-tender character, which would be redeemable in either gold or silver coin at the option of the government.

As long as the act was in effect the Treasury interpreted it to mean that its notes should always be redeemable in gold or its equivalent. What the Treasury in the last analysis was doing, therefore, was to buy silver and pay for it in gold. In order to pay in gold, the Treasury had to dip into its gold reserve. Actually this was the amount of surplus in the Treasury at any particular moment, but at the time of the resumption of specie payments for greenbacks in 1879, it had been set at $100 million. A tradition had become established in business circles that this sum was the minimum of safety for maintaining the credit moneys of the United States. Normally it had amounted to a good deal more than this. In 1890, when the Sherman Silver Purchase Act was passed, the amount was $300 million. It had gradually declined in amount, however, as a result of the extravagance of Congress and of the purchases under the Sherman Silver Purchase Act. When Cleveland came into office in 1893 the amount had sunk below the traditional $100 million mark.

This dwindling of the gold reserve alarmed the business interests in the East. If the gold reserve should become exhausted, the Treasury could no longer redeem either the greenbacks or treasury notes of 1890 in gold. The attempt to maintain parity would have to be abandoned and the country would be thrown on a silver standard. Debts would be payable in silver dollars, worth only 60 cents. That prospect was one of the forces producing the Panic of 1893—one of the greatest economic crises in the history of the United States up to that time.

In this emergency Cleveland undertook an immediate repeal of the Sherman Silver Purchase Act. He called Congress into special session for the purpose. The repeal proved to be politically difficult, for it was resisted by the distressed West and by the inflationist element elsewhere in the country. But Cleveland was a man of iron determination, and Congress was clubbed into repeal.

As a result of repeal the financial panic was ended. But so was the unity of the Democratic party. The party became broken into two wings—an eastern "gold" wing, headed by the President, and a western "silver" wing, catering to the distressed farmers, debtors, and silver-mine owners.

In 1896, in the Democratic national convention, Cleveland and the eastern gold wing were repudiated. The Populist silver plank of 1892 was approved—free and unlimited coinage of silver at the ratio of 16 to 1. The convention nominated as its standard bearer William Jennings Bryan—the silver-tongued orator of the West.

In the Republican convention, after a good deal of hesitation, the gold standard was inferentially approved, and William McKinley, whose record on the issue was equivocal, was made the nominee of the party.

In the ensuing campaign the central issue was currency inflation. The campaigning was a battle of the standards—gold versus silver. The Republicans staged a national program of education to illustrate the perils of currency inflation. They also resorted to buying of votes. The campaign manager, Mark Hanna, poured money liberally into doubtful states. The outcome was a Republican triumph and the election of McKinley.

After the election a turn occurred in the business cycle. It was a normal effect of economic factors. The world demand for food had caught up with the supply, as a result partly of industrialization and of short harvests in Europe. Prices of American farm produce rose to the point where farmers could survive. The discovery of gold in the Klondike in 1898, an expanded output of the great gold fields of South Africa, and the development of the new process of cyanide-refining of gold combined to meet the needs for an expanded gold currency in the United States. The advent of the Spanish-American War initiated large-scale government spending, which further stimulated the business recovery.

Farmer unrest subsided. Farmer allegiance to the old parties, temporarily deflected, returned to normal patterns. Credit was given the Republican party for having brought back the full dinner pail. The view that prosperity depended on an adequate tariff protection of American industry, which McKinley had stressed in the campaign, gained favor, and in 1897 the ultra-protective Dingley Tariff Act was adopted by Congress. The monetary issue fell by the wayside.

In 1900 the Republican Congress adopted the Gold Standard Act, an evidence of the subsidence of inflationism. The act declared gold to be the standard of American coinage. A gold reserve was set up to the amount of $150 million in the United States Treasury. It was declared to be for the one and only purpose of protecting the credit moneys of the United States. All the credit moneys were to be redeemable in gold. Silver coinage was retained and continued to be a legal tender, but the amount coined was not to be increased. The government made no pretense thereafter of putting a dollar's worth of silver into a silver dollar, and the only reason the coin continued to circulate at par was that it could at any time be exchanged for gold. Just prior to World War II the bullion value of the silver dollar was 30 cents and that of the subsidiary silver coinage was in like proportion.

The Populist movement marked the end of an era in American history. For almost three centuries, from the founding of Jamestown to 1890, public land had been available in the well-watered portion of the national domain. The frontier had been open; it had been an escape for the restless in the settled East. After 1890 public land was still to be had. But it was land that could be subdued only by techniques not yet well understood, and by application of capital not possessed by the average pioneer.

This profound change was reflected in the Populist platform of 1892. It appeared in a call for aid from the federal government—a weakening of the frontier faith in individualism. Faith in individualism had never been unlimited. The frontiersman had always been ready to accept help from the federal government, but had been loath to agree to regulation. He had been reconciled to accepting state regulation, as became clear in the Granger excitement. In the Populist era he invoked federal protection against exploitation by railroads, banks, trusts, and monopolies and even proposed government ownership of warehouses, elevators, railroads, and telegraph and telephone companies. All this marked a transition from the old frontier individualism to the concept of the welfare state.

Dry Farming

A NEW ADVANCE OF FARMING into the semi-arid Great Plains occurred in the years after 1900. It quickly reversed the shrinkage in farming that the ten-year dry cycle beginning in 1887 had brought about. The map illustrates the recovery by 1930 (87). Notice that by 1930 the Texas Plains had been occupied except for the actual desert portion in the westernmost angle of the state. The Oklahoma Panhandle had been taken up. Western Kansas, Nebraska, and the Dakotas were reoccupied. A greatly increased population had gone into the next tier of states to the west. The Populist losses had been recovered, and new areas of semi-aridity had been conquered.

This advance, expressed in terms of the expansion of farm acreage, is exhibited on the map (88). Each dot represents 5000 acres of land. The advance is the more remarkable in view of a considerable contraction of farm acreage in the humid region east of the Mississippi. The process of substitution of dry-land for humid farming continued in the next decade.

Dry-land farming meant specifically a migration of crops. The crop featuring it was wheat of the winter and spring varieties. In 1889 the center of winter-wheat growing west of the Mississippi lay in the Red River valley of the North, in western Minnesota, and in central Kansas, as already shown on map 80 (page 000). By 1929 it had moved to western Kansas and to the panhandles of Oklahoma and Texas.

This advance was a major argicultural achievement. It meant a triumph of man over the forces of nature. It was accomplished by means of a technique known as dry farming—a mode of growing crops with a minimum use of water. Dry farming consisted of a combination of principles and practices differing from region to region. In every case it involved an adjustment to local climatic and soil conditions. The techniques were partly of American origin, partly importations from foreign lands.

An important feature of dry farming is the selection of grains that are drought-resistant and economical in their use of water. This means, at the outset, wheats.

DENSITY OF POPULATION, 1930

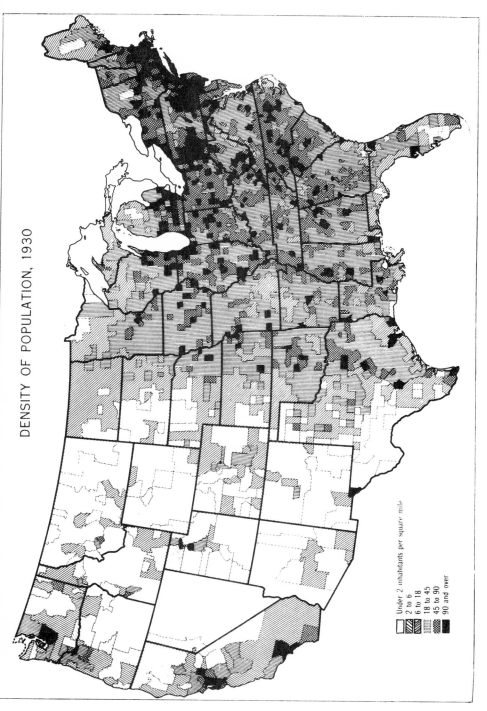

Under 2 inhabitants per square mile
2 to 6
6 to 18
18 to 45
45 to 90
90 and over

87. Population Distribution, 1930 (from Paullin)

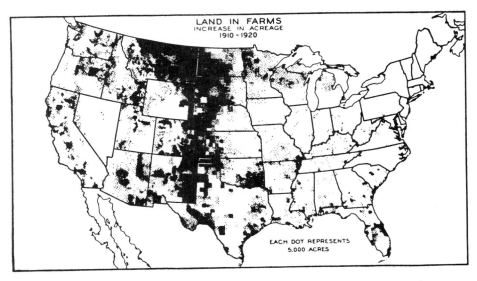

88. Increase in Land in Farms, 1910–20 (from the *Yearbook of Agriculture*, 1923)

Wheats of every type are economical in their use of water; all are to some extent drought-resistant. But some are much more so than others, and an important element in the spread of dry farming was the importation, or breeding, of especially drought-resistant varieties.

On the chart are listed the varieties of drought-resistant grains most important on the Plains. There are scores of other varieties, but these are the most significant.

Winter Wheat
  Turkey Red   Tenmarq
  Red Kharkov Pawnee
  Kanred   Comanche
         Wichita

Spring Wheat
  Marquis
  Kubanka (durum)

Sorghum Corn (Kafir, Milo)

Barley

The Turkey Red variety was brought to Kansas in the early 1870's by Mennonites of German origin who migrated there from a semi-arid part of southeastern Russia—the Crimean area. It proved a great success in Kansas, and later spread over all the semi-arid parts of the southern and central Plains. It is still one of the most widely produced wheats in the United States. Closely related to it is the Red Kharkov wheat, found in southeastern Russia toward the end of the 19th century by Mark Carleton, an expert of the Department of Agriculture. Another variety related to

Turkey Red is Kanred wheat, which was developed by cross-breeding in the Kansas Agricultural Experiment Station from varieties found in the Crimea in 1906. Another important type developed in the period was Tenmarq. Others were the Pawnee, Comanche, and Wichita, known to farmers as the "papooses" from their Indian names. They were developed at Kansas State College in the early 1940's and helped to account for the great wheat harvests produced in the West during the war years.

These seven varieties are all grown in the winter. They tolerate cold as well as drought and survive all except intensely cold weather. Wheat breeding is directed to producing hybrids that resist not only drought, but diseases, insects, and harsh climate, and have positive qualities, such as high yield, a short growing season, and desirable milling qualities.

On the southern Plains the planting is done in the early autumn, just after the autumn rains. The rains come ordinarily in September and help the seed to germinate. The plant gets well set in the ground before winter arrives. Growth continues through the winter, sometimes under a slight cover of snow. In the early spring the plant makes its chief development, while the ground is wet from melted snow and rains. Thus the plant reaches maturity during the moistest part of the year and is ready to harvest before the worst of the summer heat and drought arrive.

The southern Plains are adapted to winter-wheat cultivation because the season is relatively mild and the dangers of winter killing are slight. Texas, Oklahoma, Kansas, and Colorado are the center of that crop in the United States (Map 89). Winter-wheat cultivation became much more important on the Plains than that of the spring wheats. Kansas City, in the center of the winter-wheat area, was by the mid-20th century the greatest flour-milling center in the United States, far surpassing Minneapolis.

Spring wheat is the variety grown on the northern Plains (Map 90). It dominates the northern Plains as winter wheat does the southern. It is the only wheat that can be grown there. In the Dakotas and Montana, with their bitter winters, other crops would be wiped out. The wheat is planted in the spring, grows through the spring and summer, and comes to maturity in late August. It sometimes suffers in the summer droughts. But in general it benefits from the fact that when rains do come in the summer the moisture does not instantly evaporate, as it is likely to do in the southern Plains.

The varieties of spring wheat most popular in the North are Marquis and Kubanka. The first was developed in Canada toward the end of the 19th century. It is a hybrid, one strain of which came from India, the other from Russia. The second, Kubanka, is a durum wheat, found in Turkistan in Russia toward the close of the 19th century. It proved valuable not only on account of its resistance to drought but also because of its excellence for macaroni manufacture. It is rich in gluten. Its center of production is the Dakotas.

All wheats grown on the Great Plains are hard, whether they are winter or spring varieties. They are made so by the semi-aridity of the climate. The durum varieties are especially hard, and were long objected to for that reason by the millers. They could not be effectively ground until steel rollers were brought into use. The hard wheats are, however, the best bread makers. The soft wheats, grown in the humid East and South, are used chiefly for the baking of crackers and biscuits. Their milling center is

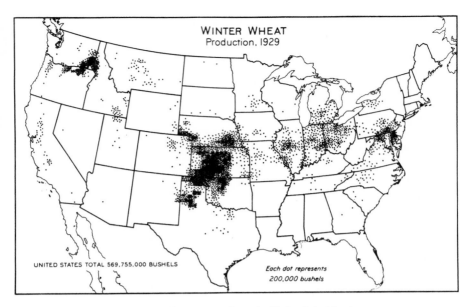

89. Winter Wheat, 1929 (from the National Archives)

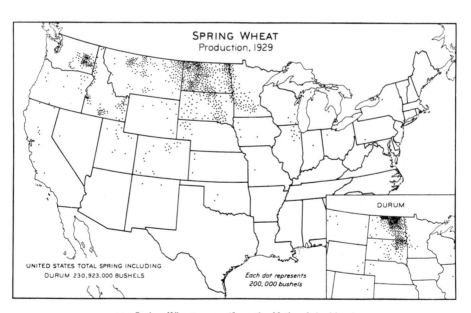

90. Spring Wheat, 1929 (from the National Archives)

Buffalo. The better varieties are often mixed with hard wheats to achieve uniformity in making flour. The poorer varieties, raised east of the Mississippi, are used a good deal for poultry and livestock feed.

Other grains than wheats are grown by dry farmers on the Plains. Sorghum corn is produced in more than 80 varieties. One is Kafir corn, which was found in the

Liberia section of Africa and brought to the United States in 1876. In the 1880's its value as a drought-resistant crop was recognized and it was introduced to the Great Plains. One of its excellent qualities is that, in periods of exceptional drought, when it gets not even a minimum of water, it does not wilt. It merely suspends growth, which is resumed when rain falls.

On the southern Plains, sorghum reaches full maturity as a result of the long growing season. It produces grain that is fed to cattle. It occupies the same place in parts of the southern Plains that Indian corn does in the North. On the northern Plains sorghum does not ordinarily reach full maturity, because the growing season is too short. There it is used for silage. A popular form of sorghum raised in arid parts of the Plains is Milo.

The grain sorghums of the Plains are not to be confused with the saccharine sorghums of the East. These were raised in the 1850's and 1860's for syrup. But they could not be grown on the Plains. The location of the grain sorghums of the West is shown on the next map in terms of the year 1939 (91). The center of the crop is western Texas and Oklahoma.

Barley is another crop able to survive on little water and is popular in the semi-arid region. Alfalfa and soybeans are also widely grown, especially in irrigated regions. Alfalfa was imported from Chile. It was brought first into California during the gold rush and from there spread to the Plains.

Dry farming includes other principles than the use of drought-resistant plants. All are directed to the end of conserving the water in the soil and carrying over as much of a reserve of it as possible from one growing season to another. An important principle is fallowing in alternate years. This is especially important in cycles of drought. It permits the building up of reserves of moisture in the subsoil. But fallowing is safe only on hard soils. On sandy soils it may result in blowing. In order to reduce this danger farmers resort to what is known as strip fallowing. One narrow strip will carry grain. Alongside will be a fallow strip protected somewhat against the wind by the strip that carries grain. This is a pattern of farming seen throughout the semi-arid West.

Another principle is careful weed eradication, since weeds mean a waste of water. Another practice is prompt turning over of the soil if flash rains occur before planting, so that the water will not evaporate. Where Milo is grown the seed is drilled in and planted deep, and the rows are widely spread so that the drain on water will not be too great.

The early exponents of dry farming recommended other principles, some of which proved to be not well based, and which were later abandoned. An exponent of dry farming in the 1890's who was not always sound in his ideas was a publisher, Hardy W. Campbell. A more scientific approach came in 1906, when the Bureau of Dry Land Agriculture was established in the Department of Agriculture. Also, experiment stations were established in dry-land areas which did valuable scientific research in dry farming.

In the conquest of semi-arid land an important factor was the legislation of Congress. In 1909 Congress adopted the Enlarged Homestead Act, which provided for 320-acre homesteads in certain semi-arid western states. In 1916, during World War I, the Stock Raising Homestead Act was passed, which increased to 640 acres the size of homesteads in certain dry areas. Under these laws, and under the old Home-

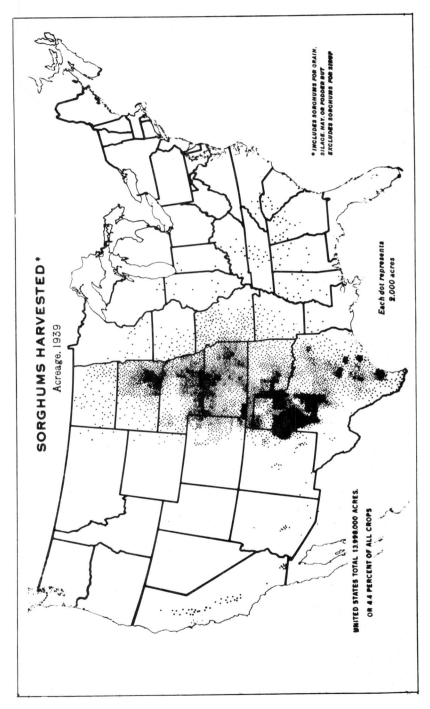

91. Grain Sorghum, 1939 (from the National Archives)

stead Law, an immense amount of land was put under the plow. The number of home-steads taken up between 1900 and 1920 was one and a half times as great as the number from 1870 to 1900. A factor in the conquest of the semi-arid West was the high price of wheat and meat prevailing prior to World War I and, even more, during and after World War II.

One of the most important of the forces in the conquest of the Plains was the mechanization of farm operations which occurred there in the first quarter of the new century. It was favored by the level terrain of the Plains and by the relative cheapness of land, which encouraged acquisition of big holdings.

In the mechanization of Plains farming the gasoline-powered tractor, which replaced the steam tractor, was a major advance. The old tractor, the road-roller type, powered by coal, was slow, hard to turn around, and so heavy that it injured the land. It was expensive to run because of the cost of hauling coal and water to it. The new machine was light, easy to turn around, and cheap to run. It was more economical to operate than a horse. It could do everything a horse could, as the Ford agents boasted, except make manure come out of its exhaust. By 1930 there were 275,000 gasoline tractors operating on the Great Plains. It was essentially a creation of World War I, the joint contribution of Henry Ford and Henry G. Ferguson, and it was known as the Fordson. Almost as important as tractors in mechanizing the agriculture of the Plains were ordinary auto trucks and automobiles. They solved many transportation prob-lems. They were already, prior to World War I, important equipment of the Plains, and they became even more important during the wars and after.

A dramatic addition to the mechanization of Plains agriculture was the combine. It served to unite two functions, reaping the standing grain and simultaneously thresh-ing it. It carried the threshed wheat in a container until a quantity had accumulated and emptied it into a truck that came alongside. An early form of the combine used on the Plains in the first quarter of the 20th century was unwieldy. Drawn by teams of horses or mules and attended by many workers, it was expensive to operate. The new combine, which came into general use after 1930, was light, cheap, and swift in operation. It could reap, thresh, and spout to attending trucks the wheat of 50 acres in a day. The activating force in all this farm mechanization was the shortage of labor during World War I. This did for the Great Plains what the labor shortages of the Civil War did for the prairies. In these ways the climatic handicap of the Great Plains was neutralized and a vast new farm section was added to the agricultural area of the United States.

In some important respects the province proved superior for agriculture, even to the humid eastern sections. Because the terrain is more level than that of the prairies, a higher degree of mechanization was possible. Also, as a result of its relatively low land values, bigger farms could be created, with their greater mechanization. In 1965 it was estimated that a man with a tractor, a combine, and a family could operate a farm of 4000 acres on the Great Plains. Elsewhere in the United States a man with a family and help at harvest time could operate a farm of only 160 or 320 acres.

A third advantage of this section was the relative immunity it enjoyed from certain wheat diseases. The semi-aridity of the Plains holds some diseases in check that flourish in the East. However, in the mid-1950's a virulent new variety of stem rust, labeled Race 15 B, raged in the northern durum-wheat area, and went nearly out of control. It destroyed from half to two-thirds of the annual crop. It was finally checked by eradicating barberry bushes that served as hosts to the spores and by developing strains of durum resistant to it.

A further advantage possessed by the Great Plains is the low cost of its harvesting. This is the result of the fact that wheat can be harvested there in a single operation. The grain can be left standing on the stalk until it is completely ripe and dry. Little danger exists of heavy autumn rains that would knock the crop down and get it tangled up. When the dry wheat is harvested it goes in a single combining operation from the field to the elevator.

By contrast, grain in the humid prairies cannot be left standing in the field until all stalks have become ripe, dry, and seasoned. Heavy rainstorms are a constant danger, which would knock the wheat down and leave it a tangled mass. The grain must be cut while the backward stalks are still half green and wet. Then the wheat must be tied in bundles and left in the field for full ripening and seasoning. The harvesting has to be done in two operations, cutting and later threshing, and this is more expensive than combining.

The harvesting advantage of the Great Plains is evident in the steady decline that has occurred in its need for harvest labor. In the early part of the 20th century the Great Plains had to import a large amount of harvest labor. The need was advertised in the big eastern newspapers. Transient workers were offered high wages if they would come out to the Plains. Many responded—hoboes, misfits of one sort or another, and college students. They traveled to the wheat fields hiding in railroad freight cars. They were tolerated by railroad trainmen because of the traffic in grain that was expected to follow the harvest. The work would begin in the early summer in Texas, where the winter wheat would be harvested. The gangs would work their way northward, as the season advanced, into the spring-wheat areas. They would end up late in the autumn in the Canadian wheat fields. Then some of the men would move into the lumber camps of the Pacific Northwest. The hoboes would hole up in the flophouses of middle western cities. College students would return to classrooms to rest up. With the invention of the newer combines this pattern of harvesting changed. The need for labor in harvesting wheat was cut by more than half. A fleet of combines manned by relatively few technicians moved northward, and transient labor was dispensed with.

Some urban individuals established a special pattern of farming in the dust-bowl area. They would hold a factory job for the greater part of the year. In the autumn or the spring they would pack a suitcase and motor out to land they had bought at a low price. With a tractor and gang plows they would prepare and seed the land. During the growing season they would be at their city job. In the spring or autumn they would return to their land and, with the aid of a hired combine gang, would harvest the crop. They were known as "suitcase farmers." In some cases they were big operators. This unorthodox mode of farming has persisted in the dry-land areas of western Kansas and eastern Colorado and in the panhandle areas of Oklahoma and Texas, even though it has been a perennial dust-bowl hazard to other farmers in that region.

The advantages offered by the Great Plains in the production of grain became evident in the period of the great agricultural depression of the late 1920's and early 1930's. Wheat growers there suffered less than those of the humid prairies, at least when drought and duststorms relented.

The cotton crop as well as the wheat crop established itself on the semi-arid Plains in the first quarter of the 20th century, especially in Texas and Oklahoma. The first map shows the location of the cotton plant in 1889 (92). The next shows it in 1929 (93). In 1929 the crop was established securely in the western parts of Texas and in western Oklahoma. The dots appearing on the map in New Mexico, Arizona, and California should, for the present, be ignored. They represent cotton grown by irrigation, which is a technique different from dry farming.

This cotton migration westward was the result of factors similar to those operating in the case of wheat. Cotton, like wheat, adjusts well to lack of water. It needs relatively little, especially in the later stages of its growth. It does need plenty of sunshine in its ripening stages and this it gets on the Plains. Also, insect pests and diseases, which afflict cotton in the humid parts of the South, are less a problem in western Texas and western Oklahoma. The boll weevil, for instance, which crossed the Rio Grande from Mexico in the early 1890's and produced havoc in the lower

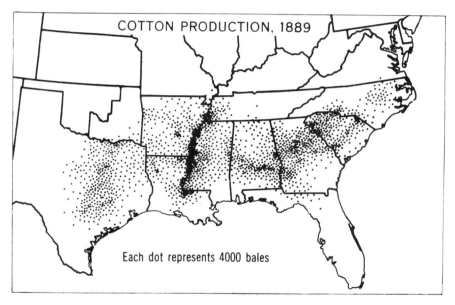

92. Cotton Crop, 1889 (from Paullin)

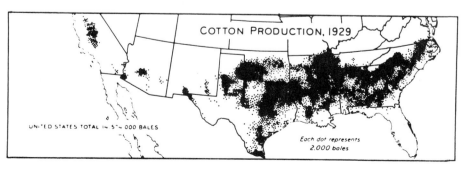

93. Cotton Crop, 1929 (from the National Archives)

South in the early years of the 20th century, troubled the semi-arid Plains relatively little. It found the Plains too dry in the summer, and too cold in the winter, for survival.

Another advantage cotton found on the Plains was the high mechanization possible on that level land, especially in planting and harvesting. Harvesting was increasingly done there by mechanical means, especially by stripper harvesters and mechanical pickers, which greatly reduced costs. For these reasons fiber, as well as wheats, has moved westward into the semi-arid Plains. And regions that the Populists considered hopeless in the 1890's were successfully farmed.

But the extension of crop production to the Plains had some adverse results. One of the gravest was the problem of duststorms which swept from the "dust bowl" region of Texas and Oklahoma northward over the Great Plains in the "dirty thirties" and later. They were a threat to the very permanence of agriculture in the province. They raised in dramatic form the issue of soil conservation in the nation, which became a major problem of national politics.

Mining Techniques of the Twentieth Century

A NEW PHENOMENON appeared in the development of the West in the closing decades of the 19th century and the opening ones of the 20th. It was the use of marginal resources that had not been profitable to exploit earlier. A resource of that kind, already discussed, was the dry-land soils of the Great Plains. Another was lean copper, lead, gold, and iron ore, found in the West in vast quantity. The exploitation of such low-grade deposits became possible as a result of the application to them of new techniques appearing in the mining industry in rapid succession. They appeared in such number that they can be described only by example. An important example is froth flotation.

Froth flotation was applied first in the copper industry. It was used for ores which were lean but in great quantity. Most western copper ores contain less than 1 percent of copper; 99 percent or more is rock and dirt. Froth flotation performed the work of extracting the mineral particles in this ore and concentrating them so cheaply and effectively as to make the mining operation profitable.

In western copper mines the ore was scooped up by power shovels in an open-pit mine. It was sent by rail to a nearby plant to be ground up. It was pulverized in a mixture of water and acid, and became what mining men call "pulp." In the grinding the particles of copper in the pulp became oxidized. They underwent a change comparable to rusting in iron.

While the grinding proceeded a small quantity of pine oil was poured into the pulp. The oil had an affinity for the oxidized particles of copper. As the oil spread through the pulp it formed a film around the copper particles. It coated all of them. It did not coat the pulverized rock and dirt particles. Then an agitation of the pulp was set up. It was done by machinery designed for the purpose, which was the whipping of air bubbles through every part of the pulp.

The air bubbles, as they shot through the pulp, came in contact with the oil-coated copper particles. They attached themselves to the particles and lifted them to

495

the surface. They formed a froth at the surface which was a copper concentrate. The concentrate held together long enough to be skimmed off and sent to the smelter.

Ordinarily air bubbles rising in a liquid burst as soon as they hit the surface. Anyone who has watched the air bubbles in ginger ale will have noticed that phenomenon. But no such bursting occurred in the oiled pulp because the air bubbles had been coated by the oil in the pulp. They had been strengthened by the oil, just as air bubbles made of soapy water by children are strengthened by the oil of the soap.

This is the froth flotation process. It was based on a principle the reverse of the principle of gravity, which, as applied to placer mining, has been described as carrying the heavy gold particles to the bottom of the miner's pan, while the sand at the top is flushed away by the moving water. In froth flotation the air bubbles lifted the tiny copper particles to the surface and left the pulverized rock behind.

This process has made possible a profitable working of lean copper mines throughout the West and throughout the world. Mines that had been unprofitable to work were revived by the process. Before 1900 copper mines had been unprofitable to work unless their ores contained 6 to 8 percent of mineral. The subsequent average for the whole country became less than 2 percent.

One of the states of the Far West containing immense deposits of very lean copper resources was Utah. At Bingham, outside Salt Lake City, was the greatest single deposit of copper ore known in the world, the property of the Kennecott Copper Corporation. Illustration 94 is a photograph of the mine pit. The copper-bearing rock in the mine, after blasting, was scooped up by power shovels into railroad cars and sent off to the mill to be ground. Illustration 95 shows one side of the mine. It shows the terraces, the height of which can be gauged by the height of the power poles. Notice the railroad tracks on the terraces and the giant power shovels that scoop up the

94. Copper Mine, Bingham Canyon, Utah

95. Giant Terraces of the Bingham Canyon Mine

blasted rock to be sent to the mills for grinding. The copper content of this material is less than 1 percent of the whole. More than 99 percent is waste matter. By froth flotation virtually all the copper in that material is extracted. In the process of exploiting the ore immense quantities of material must be moved. The amount moved was many times the amount moved to dig the Panama Canal. The debris was dumped in mountain canyons.

In Arizona a similar body of lean ore—the Morenci mine—was made profitable to exploit by flotation. The mine lies in the upper Gila Valley. It is a Phelps Dodge property. It is an old mine that had been abandoned after its richer veins had been exhausted. In 1941 it was resurrected as an open-pit mine by removing an overlying mountaintop of rock and dirt.

A useful gauge in measuring the contribution of froth flotation to the copper production of the nation is the smelter output of the United States in the century extending from 1860 to 1954. The record for the leading states is presented in summary form at the top of the next page.

From 1860 to 1880 Michigan was the leading copper producer in the Union. The Michigan mines were principally the Calumet and Hecla in the Keweenaw Peninsula, the mines in which the fortunes of the Agassiz family were invested and multiplied. The copper found in these mines was virtually pure.

In 1890, as the Michigan mines became depleted, Montana took the lead. Its great producer was Butte Hill, where for fifteen years a third or more of the world's annual production of copper was obtained. The Butte mines were in large part the property of the Anaconda Copper Company. They were underground. Their ores were of high grade—4 percent to 6 percent copper. By 1954, however, they were

UNITED STATES SMELTER PRODUCTION OF COPPER
MILLIONS OF POUNDS

	Michigan	*Montana*	*Arizona*	*Utah*	*Total United States*
1860	12				16
1880	51				60
1890	100	112	34		260
1900	142	270	116	19	606
1929	185	300	230	326	2002
1932	64	97	201	96	544
1937	85	281	580	404	1669
1940	91	258	574	497	1818
1943	90	276	794	651	2184
1954	46	119	757	422	1672

more than a mile deep and the ore was costly to bring to the surface. At that time extensive bodies of lean ore at Butte were beginning to be worked. They have been worked increasingly as open pit mines, and the mineral is extracted by froth flotation.

In the years after 1910 Arizona and Utah took the lead as copper producers. They did so largely as a result of the exploitation of very lean ores by froth flotation. Arizona became the greatest producer, with Utah running second. The United States, as a whole, produced in 1954 a third of the world's output of copper. Its greatest production years up to that time came in the crisis of World War II (1943).

Since 1954 the continued lead of Arizona is revealed in these statistics from the *Minerals Yearbook,* for 1973, published by the Department of the Interior.

MINE PRODUCTION OF PRIMARY COPPER

	Millions of Short Tons				
	1951–55	*1960*	*1965*	*1970*	*1973*
Arizona	407	539	703	918	931
Michigan	29	56	72	68	72
Montana	68	92	115	120	133
Nevada	65	77	71	107	96
New Mexico	70	67	99	166	208
Utah	254	218	259	296	258
Other States	30	30	32	45	29
United States	923	1080	1352	1720	1727

In these figures the migration westward of the copper industry is revealed, a migration that followed the successful application of froth flotation to lean ores.

Froth flotation is used not only for copper but for other minerals. One of its most important applications is to lead-zinc ores, which are usually mixed in western mines. In Missouri and Idaho, and likewise in Wisconsin, Illinois, and Iowa, this intermixture prevailed and constituted an embarrassment to the miners. It raised problems in refining. The most valuable constituent of the commingled ore was lead. But unless the zinc that came with it could be completely eradicated, the lead was of reduced commercial value. If lead is used to make a lead pipe and there are even traces of zinc in it, the pipe will presently be full of holes. An early method of getting rid of zinc in the mixed ore was to burn it out in the refining process. This was costly and did not always do a complete job of eradication. Moreover, the zinc was destroyed. So lead ore, heavily impregnated with zinc, was hardly worth mining.

Under the flotation process the separation of the lead and zinc was made easy. It was also done cheaply, and in the process the zinc was saved. A first step was to grind the mixed ore into a pulp. During the grinding, oxidation occurred on the surface of the particles of lead. A little oil was poured into the pulp. A film of oil was spread over the oxidized lead particles. Then air bubbles were whipped through the pulp by agitation. The bubbles attached themselves to the lead particles and raised them to the surface to be skimmed off. In the residue of the pulp were the zinc particles. These were not so easily coated with oil and for that reason had not been lifted up. But now an acid was added to the pulp and the zinc particles were coated. The pulp was again agitated and the zinc particles were lifted up and skimmed off, leaving only the waste pulp. The separation of the lead and zinc was complete and the zinc was saved.

Froth flotation transformed the lead and zinc industry of the United States. It made Missouri and Idaho, where the principal mines are located, the chief producers of primary lead in the Union, with a total of 85 percent. Together with Utah and Colorado, they produced, in 1970, 97 percent of the nation's primary lead. The lead producers are, also, major zinc producers. In 1970 the western mines produced 211,709 tons of the nation's zinc.

Froth flotation has been used also to make lean gold ores profitable to exploit. The same principles of separation are employed, with differences in the agents used for dressing and collection of ores in the pulp. Froth flotation has made profitable the working of lean ores in gold mines throughout the world, and this helps to account for the enormous increase in gold production that occurred just prior to World War II.

The history of the evolution of froth flotation remains to be written. It is unwritten, partly because to do it well would require the knowledge of the historian, the metallurgist, and the patent lawyer. The knowledge of a patent lawyer would be particularly necessary. The history is a record of lawsuits from beginning to end over patent rights and patent claims.

An early American patent was that issued in 1885 to Carrie J. Everson, the sister of an ore assayer in Denver. The popular tradition regarding it is that Miss Everson, in washing grimy ore sacks shipped to her brother's office, noticed that when soap bubbles rose to the surface of her tub, they were covered with tiny specks of shiny mineral. This led her to investigate the reason for the phenomenon and to discover the essential principles of froth flotation. She worked out certain apparatus and methods, but they were never commercially successful.

In 1903–04 the first effective process was developed in Australia by C. V. Potter and G. D. Delprat. In 1906 another, using different materials and different apparatus, was developed by an English concern—Minerals Separation, Ltd., and was patented. This was brought to the United States in 1912, but it was contested and became the center of prolonged litigation. The process is still being improved. New agents for dressing mineral particles, to make them receptive to filming over, have been found, and a whole science of ore dressing has developed. New collection agents have been found and improved frothing agents to give stability to air bubbles. Since 1912 hundreds of patents have been issued, some of a general sort, others for improvements relating to particular ores.

The process of upgrading lean ores was extended in the same era to the iron and steel industry of the Great Lakes area. The high-grade ores of the Mesabi Range, which had once seemed inexhaustible, were by the end of the century showing signs of depletion. There were, however, at lower levels in the same field vast deposits of lean ore known as taconite. These were estimated to contain three or four times the quantity of the soft ores, as much as 60 to 80 billion tons. But the exploitation of them presented problems. Their iron content was a fraction only of the ore requirement of blast furnaces, which was 51 percent. Taconite ores contained only 25 to 30 percent. Also, they were embedded in rock that was hard as flint. They were described despairingly in the press as "the meanest ore on earth."

Providentially new technology arrived by which those enormous resources were made usable. The problem of blasting them from their beds was met by jet-flame drills. Ordinary drills cut through such rock at a rate of a foot an hour and were soon worn out in the process. The jet-flame drill, relying on high heat as preparation, burned a hole through taconite at the rate of 20 to 30 feet an hour. The holes, so cut in series, were filled with explosives and fired. The released rock was sent first to a stamp mill and then to grinders to be pulverized in water. It became a pulp, a mud of crushed rock and iron particles. The iron particles were magnetic.

In order to meet the blast furnace requirement of iron ore of at least 51 percent another technique was developed that took advantage of the magnetic qualities of the pulverized iron. The pulp was passed through highly magnetized electric rollers. The iron particles clung to the rollers and were drawn off. The residue of the pulp was given a finer grinding to free the remaining iron particles of their silica coating, and was again run through the rollers. The concentrate so obtained was 60 to 63 percent iron. The water in the pulp was drained off for re-use.

The damp concentrate could not be fed into a blast furnace. Its fine particles, in the heat of the furnace, would be blown out at the top, or produce other complications. They were therefore subjected to a process of agglomeration. This called for mixing into the pulp a clay substance known as bentonite. The mixture was sent to a revolving drum to be shaped into pellets of the size of a walnut. A coating of coal dust was spread over the pellets and the combination was baked to harden it for shipment. It was a richer concentrate than was necessary for the blast furnace and could be mixed, if desired, with ore of a lower iron content.

In some cases the damp pulp was converted to sheet form. It was laid over an ore sheet of coarser texture and lower iron content, and the two were baked and then broken to size. This was known as sintering. The process was altogether automated, which reduced costs. The net result of these techniques was "beneficiated ore" which was competitive in cost with the richer natural ore for the blast furnace.

This technological advance was a response partly to the needs of war. The highest demand for steel occurs when war adds its requirements to those of peace. This was especially true of World Wars I and II. When the Korean War began in 1950 there were again shortages of steel.

In that year three major mining groups undertook to exploit the taconite ores of the Mesabi Range, using the technology just described. One was the Reserve Mining Company, a subsidiary of the National Steel Corporation; another was the Oliver Mining Company, a subsidiary of United States Steel; a third was the Erie Mining Company, in which Bethlehem Steel had an interest. By the Reserve Mining Company a contract was signed to erect a $75 million taconite-processing plant at Silver Bay on Lake Superior. This plant, and one erected by the Erie Mining Company, became the principal taconite-pellet producers in the nation. In 1964 the state of Minnesota adopted legislation giving tax incentives to taconite producers, which attracted other companies into the field. By the early 1970's there were seven such plants, and the capacity of these Minnesota producers was 41 million tons of taconite pellets, compared with 17.5 million tons of natural ores.

Some of the iron ores of the Lake Superior region—those of upper Michigan, for example—do not have magnetic properties. They were dealt with by the process of heavy-media separation, resting on principles long used in the coal industry. The ore from the mine was sent to a cylindrical vat containing a slush of sand and water kept in a whirl. Into this whirling mass of heavy media the crushed iron ore was dumped. The ore sank; the less heavy silica and dirt rose to the surface and was skimmed off. Another process of separation used was flotation, but, for the iron industry, it was found to be expensive.

In 1972 the Lake Superior region produced 64,174,000 tons of agglomerates, concentrates, and natural ores, as compared with 14,113,000 for the rest of the nation. As a result of the technological advances in ore production, the iron and steel industry, like the copper industry, had moved westward. The geographic center of iron and steel production in the United States had moved to the Great Lakes country.

Foreign ore contributed to the nation's high rank as an iron and steel producer. In 1972 Venezuela and Canada were the chief of these contributors. Venezuela sent to American ports, primarily to those on the Atlantic seaboard, 10,826,000 tons of high-grade ore. Canada contributed 18,168,000 tons of rich Labrador ore, which went mostly to the Great Lakes ports after the opening of the St. Lawrence Seaway in 1959.

The new developments in mining and in beneficiating ores were indications of a maturing economy. As the rich ore resources of the interior, which had once seemed inexhaustible, were depleted, the leaner ones were brought into play and the dangers of exhaustion were deferred through the development of the new technology.

The search for fuel minerals in the 20th century has received the public attention that the search for ores claimed in the 19th. Like the ores, the fuel minerals are non-replaceable. The threatened depletion of one of them—petroleum—is as marked a historical development as was its discovery at Titusville, Pennsylvania, in 1859 with the opening of a gusher there. For years petroleum production was an eastern industry. Then, in the early 20th century, great fields were found in the West—in California and in Oklahoma. The golden age of oil discovery in the United States came in the decade of the 1920's, culminating in 1930 with the discovery of the East Texas field, the richest at that time in the world. In 1948 the annual output of the United States was 2 million barrels. By 1973 it was estimated to be 3361 million barrels.

Petroleum is a compound substance. It consists of elements which, in the order of volatility, or explosiveness, are gasoline, kerosene, fuel oil, and lubricating oils.

At the base of petroleum are paraffin and asphalt. The technique used to separate petroleum into its components was at first simple heating. The petroleum was heated in a still to the point where gasoline, its most volatile component, was vaporized off. The gasoline was originally considered an undesirable product. For ordinary use its explosiveness was a handicap. It was sold, if sold at all, only as a cleansing fluid. In many cases it was discarded—allowed to run to waste.

Kerosene was the next of the components vaporized. It passed, as vapor, into another chamber and was there condensed. This was the product every refiner wanted. It was the product used in lamps. It made a brighter light than candles and did not explode unless the refiner had mixed back into it too much of the gasoline.

Next the fuel oils, known as residuary oils, were vaporized off. They were used in industry and in transportation as a substitute for coal. They were used, also, as heating for houses. Finally, only the paraffin and asphalt base remained. Paraffin was a substitute for wax; asphalt was used as a paving material.

Early in the 20th century a revolutionary technological change occurred, which reversed the order of value of these elements: The internal-combustion engine was perfected and became the motor of automobiles and trucks. In the motor of an automobile, gasoline was the ideal fuel just because of its explosiveness, its volatility. The object of the refiner now was to get the highest percentage of gasoline out of crude petroleum—to squeeze out every ounce of it. That purpose was still more intensified when the airplane was perfected and a high octane rating of gasoline was essential.

In 1913 the "cracking" method was discovered by which the percentage of gasoline extracted from crude petroleum could be yet more increased. If petroleum is kept under high pressure while heated, vaporization is delayed. Vaporization can be held off until a temperature of 700 degrees Fahrenheit is reached. At that heat the molecules of gasoline thrown off are almost three times as great per unit of crude petroleum as were thrown off under the old heating method. Molecules of gasoline were literally cracked off the crude petroleum.

The inventor of the process, William Burton, was a chemical engineer of the Standard Oil Company of Indiana. He discovered no new principle. He merely put together old and familiar principles into a commercially profitable combination. The cracking process not only increased the percentage of gasoline obtained from petroleum, but improved it in terms of anti-knock quality.

Other improvements in extracting gasoline from crude petroleum followed. One of the most important was the "catalytic cracking" process or the "cat cracker," as it is called. This was developed by the research staff of the Standard Oil Company of New Jersey. It employed a chemical catalyst to crack gasoline from petroleum under lower pressure and less heat. It made possible not only the recovery of more gasoline from the crude base, but gasoline of a higher octane rating than before.

New methods of locating oil fields and of draining old wells were developed. The search for oil had been limited at the outset to inland locations, to such as geologists considered promising. Later attention turned to areas under water, to offshore lands, especially those of Louisiana, Texas, and California. Drilling was, moreover, carried to new depths, to as much as two miles underwater. Such drilling was costly, three times as costly as drilling on dry land. But some of the major oil fields were thus located.

Offshore drilling raised a major constitutional issue—whether the federal government or the states had title to the tideland resources out to the three-mile limit. This was already in controversy in the Truman administration. The President believed title lay in the federal government. At his direction a suit was brought in the federal courts to test the issue. In June 1947, the Supreme Court decided, in the case of *United States v. California,* that title lay in the federal government.

The economic and political issue remained, however, wide open. In the next five years scores of bills were brought into Congress to transfer to the states the right to exploit these resources. Truman vetoed two such bills in 1946 and 1952. The issue was carried into the presidential election of 1952. During the campaign the Democratic nominee, Adlai E. Stevenson, opposed a cession of federal rights, though he was not averse to an equitable division with the states of the profits of exploitation of the offshore lands, a compromise Truman had suggested. The Republican candidate, Dwight D. Eisenhower, was vehement in demanding cession of the offshore rights to the states. In a speech at New Orleans, on October 13, he denounced as a "shoddy deal" the Stevenson proposal to share with the states the revenues from exploiting the offshore lands, and deplored federal "encroachments upon the rights and affairs of states." He promised that, if elected, he would approve "the legislation twice passed by Congress and twice vetoed, to give title to the coastal properties to the states." He may have been influenced by the knowledge that the electoral votes of the three states most immediately involved in the issue numbered 66.

In the ensuing Congress the Submerged Lands Act of 1953 was passed by overwhelming majorities and signed by Eisenhower. It conferred the tidelands resources, to the three-mile limit, on the states. The majorities voting thus were composed of northern Republicans and southern Democrats responding to the call of a powerful lobby of oil interests. The frontier, West and South, thus moved out to sea.

One of the most abundant and undeveloped sources of crude oil in the United States is oil shale. This occurs in special abundance in Colorado, Utah, and Wyoming, in an area of about 16,000 square miles. The deposits appear in seams of marlstone which contain the fossil remains of the life of ancient lake beds. Like coal, the seams are of various thicknesses and lie at various depths below the surface. They rose, in the process of mountain lifting, to the slopes of the Continental Divide. About 80 percent of the richer grades are in Colorado, 15 percent in Utah, and 5 percent in Wyoming. They have been estimated by the Geological Survey to contain more than 1.1 trillion barrels of shale oil, which is more than the known oil reserves of the rest of the world. Eighty percent of them are still in the public domain. The remainder, in private possession, are less promising.

Shale oils were already being produced in America and in Europe long before the discovery of crude oil in Pennsylvania. They are still widely produced in Europe. During the recent energy crisis they appeared to some commentators to be the road to deliverance. They were known to constitute problems of conversion into usable oil. But these seemed, in an age of technological miracles, not beyond overcoming.

One method of conversion, already in use, was conventional mining, followed by surface processing. The crushed rock was heated in retorts at a temperature of 800° to 1000° F. Its organic matter (kerogen) was converted thus into crude oil and gas, which were then upgraded to make them usable in a refinery. The spent shale remained a major environmental problem, which called for expensive land reclamation and revegetation, and a major use of water, which is not in superabundance in Colorado, Wyoming, and Utah. Experimentation was carried on by the Bureau of Mines in the years 1950–55 in three pilot plants, but was then discontinued. It was also pressed by major oil companies. It seemed, however, unprofitable while world prices of crude oil remained low.

In situ processing of the seams, which would leave the spent shale in place, is considered feasible. High electric voltage would be used to fracture the marlstone. Into the fractures liquid explosives would be introduced which would be followed by detonation. The crumbled material would be heated underground and the resulting oil and gas would be drawn off to refineries. But this is a prospect only for the future.

Coal is a more immediate and tractable source of energy than shale. The reserves of it in the United States are immense. They are reported to amount to about 193 billion tons, which is more than a fourth of those of the entire world. They contain four times the energy stored in all the oil fields of the Arab states. The coal reserves east of the Mississippi are in West Virginia, Kentucky, and in the southern parts of Ohio, Indiana, and Illinois. They are also in the Birmingham region of the South. Eastern reserves in deep mines are eight times those in mines near the surface. But the cost of deep mining is much higher than that of strip mining. The eastern coal is, moreover, impregnated heavily with sulphur, and the smoke it throws off in combustion is an environmental problem. It is a factor in producing the smog afflicting urban America.

Coal from mines close to the surface is cheaply extracted. In the eastern states such coal often occurs in seams conveniently one above the other. The removal of the overlay in such areas is effected by mammoth power shovels at little immediate cost. The overlay, consisting of soil, rock, and trees, is simply pushed downhill. This is done on the contour of the slopes and leaves behind parallel ridges of rubble, popularly known as ''spoil banks.'' Fragmented coal is also left behind, the sulphur of which is carried by rains into river systems, polluting the water, poisoning water life, and rendering any revegetation a long and difficult process.

In the western states known coal reserves are partly in deep, partly in surface mines. Colorado has coal mines of both types in large quantity. New Mexico is also well provided, and so, in the north, are Wyoming, Montana, and North Dakota. The predominant type is surface mines, and these have, as yet, been little exploited. In the United States as a whole the western states contain 83 percent of the strippable reserves, totaling about 45 billion tons, and the seams are often 12 times as thick as those in the eastern states, which adds to their unit value.

Western coal, whether from deep or surface mines, is superior to eastern in respect to quality. It is low in sulphur content. Also, the terrain containing it is relatively flat, and the cost of mining it, compared with that in eastern deep mines, is in the ratio of 1 to 3.

A significant difference between the western and eastern reserves of strippable coal is that those in the West are principally in federal or Indian lands. Eighty percent are so located. This means that their exploitation lies within the control of the federal government. The authority of the federal government is exercised under the Minerals Leasing Act of February 1920, adopted in the administration of Woodrow Wilson. This was legislation to promote the mining of coal, phosphates, oil, oil shale, gas, and sodium on the public domain. It provided that leases could be obtained by private operators for a term of 20 years by payment of annual royalties and rentals. The royalties were to be 5 percent of the annual take, plus a surface rental of $1 an acre. The lessee was to have preferential rights to other lands prospected by him on a royalty basis of not less than 12½ percent. Similar provisions were made for other nonmetallic minerals named in the act. The act was a resurrection of a leasing system initially adopted by Congress in 1807 for the public lead lands of Missouri and those of the Galena area of Iowa, Illinois, and Wisconsin.

In February 1973 the Secretary of the Interior declared a moratorium on the leasing of government coal lands in the West. He acted to forestall such spoliation of the lands in the West as had occurred in the eastern states. The moratorium was to give time for a study of the background of eastern state regulation, which would permit warding off the rise of a new Appalachia in the West. The coal-mining industry was in a downswing. Oil was increasingly the fuel of power plants producing electricity east of the Mississippi. Costs of deep-mined coal were rising as a result of federal legislation. In 1969 Congress had passed an act raising standards of safety and health for miners, which lifted costs and lowered productivity. In the next year Congress adopted the Clean Air Act, which established air-pollution standards that closed the market to much of the output of deep mines that had a high sulphur content. Hundreds of deep mines closed down. In 1971 for the first time strip-mined coal exceeded the deep-mined variety in output.

In March 1973 a congressman from West Virginia, a state devastated by strip mining, brought a bill into the House which would have phased out strip mining altogether in the United States eighteen months after enactment. He obtained as co-sponsors of his bill 84 other House members. He gave the number of deep mines closed since 1969 as 563, mostly for other reasons than depletion of their coal.

On September 21, 1973, a measure of greater moderation, S.425, was reported to the Senate. It proposed a federal-state program to regulate strip mining and promised federal assistance to restore stripped land to approximately its original contour, with high walls, spoil piles, and depressions eliminated. Where reclamation was not feasible strip mining was to be prohibited. The Secretary of the Interior was to be directed to prepare programs for states that had failed to submit or enforce an acceptable plan. An appropriation of $100 million was proposed to acquire and reclaim land that had been torn by strip mining. The costs of federal control and reclamation were estimated by the committee to add only 60 cents a ton to the costs of mining without controls. The bill was opposed by President Richard Nixon as an interference with coal production. He preferred an industry-supported bill that would increase coal production.

Early in 1974 an alternative measure similar to a Senate proposal was introduced into the House by Morris K. Udall. It would have authorized $200 million, drawn from the annual revenues of the outer continental shelf oil leases, to be used for reclaiming land that had been stripped and abandoned. The measure won House approval in August 1974 by a vote of 291–81. In December a fusion with the Senate bill was worked out, which the two houses adopted. It met a pocket veto from President Gerald Ford, who maintained that it would diminish coal production and increase unemployment.

A new measure, in slightly amended form, afterward worked its way through the two houses. It was adopted in the Senate by voice vote, and in the House, on May 8, 1975, by a vote of 293–15. It was vetoed, once again, by the President.

In the meantime a sensational oil discovery on the north slope of Alaska near Prudhoe Bay had been made in 1968. It was thought to be one of the greatest petroleum accumulations in the world. The governor of Alaska estimated that it might prove to hold 40 billion barrels of oil, nearly as much as the proven reserves of all the rest of North America. The discovery was the work of prominent American corporations, Atlantic Richfield and Humble Oil, the latter an affiliate of Standard Oil of New Jersey.

The site of the discovery was state territory. It had been donated to Alaska by the federal government. Sale of oil leases on it opened in the autumn of 1969. According to the press, oil companies stampeded to purchase "like thirsty cattle that smelled water." Bonuses were paid for drilling rights amounting to $900 million. The state finances were in clover. Subsequent estimates of the size of the field were more modest than the early ones. They were a fourth of those first proclaimed.

The discovery was not without problems. One was the remoteness of the field from a market. Another was the severity of the climate. An experimental voyage by an icebreaking tanker, financed by the Standard Oil Company at a cost of $35 million, via the Northwest Passage to the field proved unsuccessful. The only viable alternative was a pipeline and the route chosen, after much debate, was All American—from the field to an all-weather port at Valdez, on Prince William Sound. Congressional approval was given after an exhaustive inquiry into the dangers of disrupting the environment along the route. The Trans-Alaska Pipeline Act of November 16, 1973, provided for a four-foot diameter pipe, to be constructed mostly aboveground by a consortium of oil companies.

A common denominator of modern production and marketing of energy in the older states and in the new is the deterioration of the environment. In the older states the deterioration resulted from strip mining of coal in the effort to supplement depleted oil resources. In Alaska it is the damage that would be caused by a massive pipeline carrying hot oil over a frozen tundra to market. In the effort to avoid this damage, the aboveground pipeline was authorized. But the possibility of damage of another sort remains. Alaska has an ancient history of great earthquakes. The rupture of the line by such an upheaval would send a devastating flood of oil over a wide terrain.

Deterioration of land and water is a risk introduced by the new technology. The risk has appeared in varied forms in different areas. On the semi-arid Plains it accompanied the dry-farming technique in the form of duststorms. In the area of irrigation water applied to arid soil became saline to the point of withering the crops of farmers lower down the streams. The over-use of ground water produced in some regions subsidence of the land. In the East strip mining of coal led to the devastation of wide areas. In the case of the exploitation of taconite ore the techniques employed ended with the dumping of waste into Lake Superior to the hazard of other users of the water. These are the penalties of applying new technology to old problems, and they carry their warnings to the future.

Early Irrigation and the Colorado River Projects

THE CONVERSION OF THE DESERT of the Enclosed Basin into an oasis by the Mormons was an achievement ahead of its day. It was rendered possible by the devotion and the effective organization of a religious community. The example set by it was slow to be copied. In the humid East farmers relied on nature to provide the water required by their crops. When the American frontier reached the line of semi-aridity the arts of dry farming were developed which redeemed vast stretches of the Great Plains. But the perils of such farming were made painfully evident in the drought era of the late 1880's and drew renewed attention to the virtues of irrigation farming.

An explanation of the slow pace of irrigation advance is the primitiveness of the early projects. They were mere diversion dams that turned small streams from their beds into irrigation canals. Storage dams to hold back the floodwaters of spring for later use did not exist. The spring waters ran to waste, which meant shortages in the summer. Not until the late 1880's were storage dams attempted.

The beginnings of irrigation in the Far West other than Indian date back to the Spanish in California. The art was practiced in the mission lands adjacent to Los Angeles. This inspired the cooperative efforts of the Mormons in Utah. A cooperative society, under the inspiration of Horace Greeley, got under way on the upper waters of the South Platte in Colorado (Union Colony) in 1870. But irrigation spread slowly. In 1880 only an estimated million acres of land were thus farmed in the United States, and ten years later only 3,631,000 acres.

The belated advance is reflected in census statistics. Prior to 1889 the census gathered no accurate statistics of acreage under irrigation. In the era 1889–1919 a more rapid gain occurred. This was the period when dry farming also was spreading in the United States. In the decade after 1919 only a few hundred thousand acres were put under irrigation, a reflection of the agricultural depression that struck the nation after World War I.

On the table below appear the types of irrigation enterprises listed in the decade 1919 to 1929. They are listed in the order of their importance.

Types of Enterprise	Acres Irrigated	
	1919	*1929*
	19,191,716	19,547,544
Individual and partnership enterprises	6,848,807	6,410,571
Cooperative association	6,581,400	6,771,334
Irrigation district	1,822,887	3,452,275
Commercial companies	1,822,001	1,230,763
Carey Act	573,929	86,772
U.S. Bureau of Reclamation	1,254,569	1,485,028
U.S. Bureau of Indian Affairs	284,551	331,840
State	5,620	11,489
City and other	47,952	267,462

The most important type, in terms of the amount of land irrigated, was that of individual and partnership enterprises. It was more than a third of the total irrigated. The enterprises were likely to be on a small scale, often a few acres, the water for which was pumped by a windmill. Cooperative associations were introduced by the Mormons. They were associations in which water rights were held by members in proportion to the land each irrigated—a share of stock for each acre—the costs of irrigation being assessed in that proportion. These two types—individual and partnership, and cooperative associations—account for the greater part of the irrigated land in the West in 1919 and in 1929.

Irrigation districts were a third and rapidly growing type. They were semi-public in character. They made contracts with the Federal Reclamation Service for the water distributed to farmers. They had federal and, also, state powers since they operated under state charters. They had power to force all landholders in a given district to join and share costs. They had power to levy the costs and to issue bonds for irrigation purposes. They were favored by the federal government. Their members could borrow money on attractive terms from the federal government under the Farm Loan acts. They did not normally engage in construction of irrigation works. They were distributing agents merely. They took over a plant for irrigation built by some other agency. They were run by boards of directors elected by the members.

Commercial companies were a fourth type of enterprise. They were usually building organizations. They built works to be sold, together with the land that was to be improved. In other words they were a stage in the formation of an irrigation district. Prior to the 1890's commercial companies occasionally were distributors as well as builders, selling water to farmers from the works they had built. They had a reputation in the West for being grasping and unscrupulous. Often they contracted to supply water they could not deliver in the dry part of the summer. And their rates were exorbitant. They usually ended in failure.

Prior to 1902 the federal government remained an inactive partner in the sphere of irrigation. It gave encouragement, chiefly in the form of land grants, but left the work of construction to others. In 1877 the Desert Land Act was passed, which offered a 640-acre tract of land at the price of $1.25 an acre to anyone who would reclaim an eighth of it by irrigation within three years. The act was extensively used by speculators for obtaining water sites. In 1894 the Carey Act was adopted, under which a million acres of federal land was given to any state in the semi-arid West that would agree to reclaim it by irrigation.

In spite of this helpful legislation the states took little advantage of the opportunity. The reason was the great agricultural depression following the Panic of 1893 and the financial collapse of most of the commercially built irrigation projects. At the opening of the 20th century it was evident that if the arid land of the West was to be reclaimed, the federal government would have to do it (Map 96).

In 1902 this challenge was accepted by Congress. The Newlands Reclamation Act was adopted by Congress and approved by Theodore Roosevelt, under which the federal government became an active builder of irrigation works. Under the act a Reclamation Fund was established in the United States Treasury to receive all moneys the government collected from the sale of public land in the sixteen states of the arid and semi-arid West. The fund was also to receive any special appropriations voted by Congress for irrigation purposes. After 1915 immense sums were voted by Congress into that fund.

The act provided that all public land in the arid and semi-arid West lying in the path of prospective irrigation improvements should be withdrawn provisionally from homesteading. This was to forestall grabbing by speculators. Once a project was completed the land would be open again to homesteading. The maximum size of homesteads was to be 160 acres. No charge was made for the land. But the costs of building and operating the irrigation works were to be borne by the persons who used the water. The costs were to be assessed per acre. They were to be repaid to the government in ten annual installments. No interest was to be charged, however, on installments overdue to the government. Until full repayment had been made, final title to the land was not to pass to the settlers.

If an extensive private landholding lay in the path of a federal project, a limit was put on the amount of water the owner could take from the project. He could draw water only for the irrigation of 160 acres. This was a crucial provision of the law. The settlers on a federal project could organize themselves into an irrigation district and take title to the works as soon as a majority of them had completed their payments to the government. Only the storage dam and its care would be retained by the government. Under this act and subsequent legislation irrigation works were built on a considerable scale. By 1929 more than 100 federal projects had been constructed, irrigating about 1,500,000 acres.

The total of irrigated land reclaimed by all the agencies up to 1929 was unimpressive compared with the amount reclaimed by dry farming. More than two-thirds of it lay in California, Colorado, Idaho, and Utah. The remainder of the irrigated areas was so small and so diffused as to leave little impression on a map published by the Census Bureau in 1929.

The federal projects were in general financial failures. They had been intended by the government to be self-liquidating, to repay the government the money invested

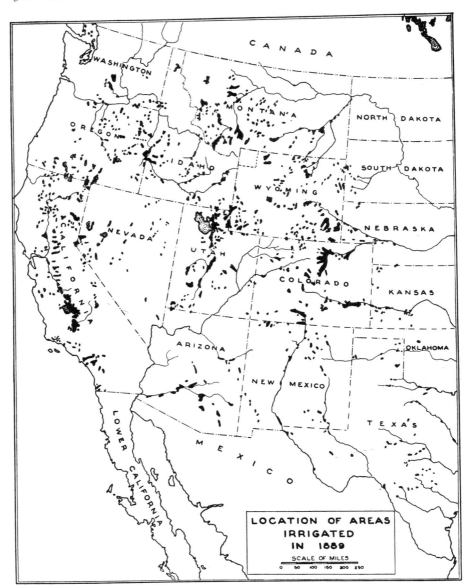

96. Early Irrigation (from Brown)

in them. On virtually none did the settlers succeed in doing so. The requirement of the Newlands Act that payment be made in ten annual installments of the per-acre costs of construction proved unenforceable.

Congress was obliged to pass relief measures—one after another—extending the time for paying the installments or cutting down the amount due. In 1914 an Extension Act was passed by which the time for paying the installments was lengthened from ten years to twenty years. Further leniency acts were passed in each of the years from 1921 to 1924. The effect of this relief legislation was that the federal government carried interest charges on the capital invested in irrigation works much longer than the act of 1902 contemplated. The amount of interest charges so carried was in 1929 already $70 million.

The reason for this failure of the federal projects was partly the high cost of building. The federal projects were the elaborate ones, projects that private enterprise would not undertake. The earlier simple works that cost not more than $15 or $20 per acre of land had already been built by private enterprise. The federal projects had been built at a rate of from $43 to $162 an acre, with an average of $85. Land so costly to reclaim did not produce return enough to repay the investment.

Some of the federal projects were not well located. By one of the provisions of the Newlands Act each state in the semi-arid West was entitled to receive irrigation construction proportionate to the amount of money received by the Treasury from the sale of federal lands within that state's boundaries. This was a typical pork-barrel provision. It meant that irrigation projects were not always located to the best advantage. That provision was finally repealed in 1910.

Another reason for the failure of the federal projects was that no careful selections were made of the settlers allowed to take up the irrigated land. Any citizen could take up an irrigation homestead, and many took advantage of this who were incompetent or were mere adventurers. Incompetence might mean either a lack of farming experience or of necessary capital to succeed in irrigation farming. An irrigation farmer should start with not less than $4000 or $5000 of his own capital. Many of the settlers had practically nothing. Another reason for failure was that settlers had no incentives to meet annual payments due the government. They had no interest to pay on deferred installments. They were tempted to put off payments as long as possible. Finally, the Great Depression in agriculture, which followed World War I, hit irrigation farmers quite as hard as it did others.

In 1923 a fact-finding committee was appointed to learn what was wrong with the federal program. In 1924 a report was made by the committee, which is a landmark in the history of the federal reclamation program. It contained a number of specific recommendations. One was that the attempt to collect full construction costs on the less successful projects be abandoned, and that a large amount of those costs be simply written off as loss. It was estimated at the time that $27,691,000 would probably have to be written off at the outset. The committee suggested that a crop payment plan should be established, with each settler paying the government annually 5 percent of his average crop income as an installment payment. Before any new irrigation project was undertaken a thorough investigation of its economic possibilities should be made. Before land on a new irrigation project was distributed to settlers it should be made ready for immediate cultivation. The land should be leveled off and the subsidiary irrigation ditches should be built by the government. Settlers on new projects should be selected on the basis of experience, character, and the possession of a minimum amount of capital. Also, financial aid in the form of federal credit should be made available to irrigation settlers.

Some of these proposals were at once adopted by Congress. A crop payment plan was enacted in 1924, the amount of annual payments being 5 percent of the average return of the land. The Reclamation Service adopted a program of more careful scrutiny of new projects. A requirement was established that settlers applying for irrigation homesteads must have at least $2000 in capital or equipment. In 1926 construction costs on existing projects were written down $10,900,000, and provision was made for the extension of credit by the Federal Farm Loan banks to irrigation farmers.

But in spite of this assistance farmers on federal projects were still in trouble. In 1926 the crop repayment plan had to be abandoned. A new annual repayment plan was adopted, spreading out the installments over 40 years. In the years 1931–33 moratoria had to be declared on all payments to the government. Ultimately, in 1939, Congress passed a Comprehensive Reclamation Project Act including provision for an initial 10-year period in which no payments were required, followed by 40 years of repayment on a gradual scale.

During the Coolidge administration this long-drawn failure of the federal irrigation projects led to a heated debate, in which two departments of the government became engaged. On the one side, the Department of Agriculture demanded an end to all new reclamation projects. On the other side, the Department of the Interior demanded that new ventures not only be undertaken but on a grander scale than ever before.

The argument advanced by the Department of Agriculture was that too much land was already under cultivation in the United States—that too much food was already being produced; that a federal program of retiring land from cultivation would make more sense than adding millions of new acres.

The reply of the Interior Department was that the only kind of land of which too much was in cultivation was poor land, which ought to be retired. Of good land there was not enough in cultivation. Also, that the only kind of food which was in oversupply was the staple grains, which were not produced on irrigated land. The kind of food produced on irrigated land was specialized, such as dairy products, vegetables, and fruit, and of those foods there was no oversupply in the United States. The Interior Department also maintained that considerations other than financial should influence the government in its reclamation policy, that social considerations should be the primary ones, such as the creation of a society of independent farmers in the arid region. In the humid region the aim of the government had been social, as exemplified in the Homestead Law, and this should continue to be the aim in the arid part of the United States.

During this heated debate a situation in the Far Southwest came into national prominence which ended the argument and started the federal government on a new era in reclamation history. That situation was the plight of the Imperial Valley in southern California.

The Imperial Valley lies in the lower basin of the Colorado River. It had once been the northern end of the Gulf of California. For centuries it had received the immense silt deposits of the Colorado River until the bed became a delta higher than sea level, resembling the delta on the lower reaches of the Mississippi River. At critical stretches along the lower river about 70 miles of levees had been built to ward off floods. But levee building hardly kept pace with the silt deposits of the river. The height of the levees had to be raised at intervals as the bed of the river rose, until raising was no longer feasible. The limit of engineering tolerance had been reached. In a high flood the levees were likely to break and a disaster would follow. In a flood in

1906 the levees did break at a point, and for a time the entire flow of the river overran the Imperial Valley (the Salton Sea). Only by a desperate outburst of energy and the expenditure of millions of dollars was the river restored to its channel. The valley needed assurance that floodwaters could be kept back.

The agricultural potentialities of the valley were, on the other hand, immense. The soil is unsurpassed for fertility and the temperatures are tropical. Specialty crops such as garden produce and fruits are grown there twelve months of the year. The region has no rainfall and could have used more irrigation water than it was able to obtain from the river. Its promise and its problem interested a powerful figure in the Coolidge administration—Herbert Hoover, the Secretary of Commerce and a skilled engineer. It led him to obtain from Congress in 1928 approval of the Boulder Canyon Project Act, authorizing the Colorado River Project, which was put under construction in his own presidency and was completed in 1936. Its central unit was Boulder Dam, later renamed Hoover Dam. This structure was located near the great bend of the Colorado, where it would receive and hold the waters of the whole upper basin of the river. The dam, pictured in the next illustration (97), is a massive structure, rising more than 700 feet above the bedrock of the river. It is high enough to hold back the entire flow of the Colorado for two years. It created a lake 150 miles in length, named for Elwood Mead, the far-sighted irrigation engineer who headed the Bureau of Reclamation when Boulder Dam was built.

The dam eliminated the flood danger to the Imperial Valley and gave full protection against future spring rises of the river. But it was much more than an impounder of floodwaters. It reserved water for the municipal needs of Los Angeles and 24 other cities and areas in southern California. For years these cities had been contending with the problems of water shortage. They had tapped every water resource within their reach and were in urgent need of more. Los Angeles had gone 250 miles to the Sierra Nevadas for water. But even with that supply it did not have sufficient water for its expanding needs beyond 1940.

Hoover Dam assured these rapidly growing cities of their municipal water for the foreseeable future. The impounded water was released and brought to them, as needed, by a route from the dam down the channel of the river to a diversion dam on the lower river—Parker Dam. As much as was needed for the California cities was turned at Parker Dam into a giant aqueduct that extends to Riverside in southern California, with branches to other cities. The aqueduct is partly an open canal, partly a covered pressure line that runs under and over mountains, and crosses deserts. It is serviced by a series of pumping stations which keep the water flowing to Riverside. The cost of the diversion dam, the aqueduct, and the pumping stations, amounting to $230 million, was financed by the cities themselves. It was done by organizing the cities, through state legislation, into a Metropolitan Water District with the power to issue bonds. These were sold to the public in California. None of this cost was borne by the federal government. A considerable fraction of the annual flow of the Colorado River, about one-fifteenth, was reserved for the Metropolitan Water District.

The third and most directly profitable purpose of the Hoover Dam was the production of electric power. The dam was designed to produce enough power to supply the whole Southwest. The plan of the engineers was that, when all this power

97. Hoover Dam (from the Dept. of the Interior)

was in use, other dams would be built, and the river's energy would be used at successive points for power generation. In 1951 a new dam—Davis Dam—was brought to completion.

Power generation at Hoover Dam raised a major question of policy for the federal administration. Was the power and its distribution to be a public or a private enterprise? The answer of Hoover was that it was to be neither, but rather a partnership. The dam and the power plant were to be publicly built. They were to be leased to private or semi-private agencies. The two agencies selected for the purpose were the Edison Company of Southern California and the city of Los Angeles. They were to have leases running for 50 years. They were to operate the power plant and market the power produced there. They would pay the federal government an annual rent of 1.63 mills for every kilowatt-hour of electricity generated. The contracts between the federal government and these two agencies were already signed before any construction on the dam or powerhouses began. Hoover did not propose to admit creeping socialism into the federal household. That concept of "partnership" in power between the federal government and private agencies became the regular Republican party gospel thereafter.

The marketing arrangement for the power was that the two agencies—the Edison Company and Los Angeles—would take for their own purposes or for commercial sale 64 percent of all the power generated at the dam. The Metropolitan Water District of Southern California would take the remaining 36 percent for the pumping of the water along the aqueduct. Under this contract one of the agencies—the city of Los Angeles—was obligated to offer power to any municipality or state in the lower Colorado basin which desired it, at terms set forth in the contract.

During World War II the power at Hoover Dam became an important defense asset. It became the foundation for a great airplane industry in southern California and, also, for a great magnesium plant at Las Vegas in Nevada.

The federal government, by virtue of its leases to private and semi-private agencies, will recover its total investment of money spent on Hoover Dam and the power plant, plus interest at the rate of 4 percent a year, when the 50-year contracts expire. Thus, in the last analysis, the whole cost of Hoover Dam is being paid by the power users of southern California. What the federal government did was merely to advance as a loan the capital needed for construction.

A major purpose of the project was irrigation. The water of the river, after having been tapped for its power, was to be used in farming. This was not the most urgent objective of the dam, but it was the one that gave rise to the greatest controversy. Rights to water for irrigation long continued to be a subject of controversy.

The most immediate need for irrigation water was in the Imperial Valley. Even before Hoover Dam was built this valley was taking irrigation water from the Colorado River. It needed more. Only half its acreage was under irrigation. Another half (450,000 acres) of equally rich land could be made productive if more water could be obtained.

But other states than California had the future in mind, especially those in the upper river basin. None of them had California's immediate need of water, but they needed to safeguard the future. Under the doctrine of prior appropriation, rights to irrigation waters became established in the first users. From Utah this doctrine had spread to almost every western state where irrigation was practiced. It had become interstate law as well, under a Supreme Court decision in 1922 in the well-known case of *Wyoming v. Colorado*. Therefore an agreement regarding future rights was essential to the upper-river states.

Accordingly, in 1922 a conference of representatives of the seven basin states was called by the federal government and held at Santa Fe. It reached an agreement whereby the doctrine of prior appropriation, as between states using Colorado River water, was abrogated. Each state was assured that no forfeiture of rights to water would result from delay in making use of the water.

Rights to the river's water for the future were worked out. The first step was to estimate the average annual flow of the river. Some years, when snow or rain was heavy in the mountains, the flow was 25 million acre-feet; in other years it would be as little as 9 million acre-feet. The conference made an estimate, based on records of flow over an extended period, that the average would be 15 million acre-feet, with a possibility of 16 million. Of the 15 million the conference gave rights to half to the upper states, Colorado, Utah, Wyoming, and New Mexico. To the lower states, Arizona, California, and Nevada, it gave rights to the other half. If the flow should average more than 15 million acre-feet, the lower states would get the surplus 1 million. This agreement was promptly ratified by six of the seven basin states, and was endorsed by Congress in the Boulder Canyon Act. It was rejected, however, by Arizona. Arizona was apprehensive that California would promptly grab the lion's share of the water allocated to the lower-river states.

Arizona had a large tract of excellent land in the central part of the state—the region around Phoenix. That land could be made highly productive if it could get water. But the cost of bringing water to it from the river would be enormous—somewhere between 1 and 2 billion dollars. Water would have to be pumped up from the Colorado, a height of 1000 feet, and a whole series of projects would have to be constructed to receive and distribute it. Only the federal government could finance such an enterprise, and Arizona feared that, before Congress could be induced to do it, California would have absorbed the greater part of the rights allocated to the lower states.

In spite of Arizona's refusal to ratify the Colorado River Compact, Congress had finally passed the law ordering the Boulder Dam to be built. In the act Congress tried to placate Arizona by writing into the law that California could never take, of the 7,500,000 acre-feet available for the lower states, more than 4,400,000, plus half of any surpluses. That stipulation was agreed to by California in 1929. Not until 1944 did Arizona ratify the compact. At the same time it agreed to limit itself to 2,800,000 acre-feet of Colorado River water, plus all of the Gila waters and half of any Colorado River surplus.

In the meantime construction went forward of works to bring water to the Imperial Valley. Imperial Dam was built above the mouth of the Gila to turn irrigation water into a new All American canal replacing an older canal to the valley running partly through Mexican territory. The dam and the canal were completed in 1941.

The costs of Imperial Dam and the All American canal were to be assessed against the Imperial Valley. Its two irrigation districts were to make contracts with the Federal Reclamation Service for the water they were entitled to distribute. They were to collect annual per-acre assessments from the growers in the two districts. The assessments would be for the cost of delivering the water, plus the obligation to reimburse the federal government over a period of 40 years for the cost of constructing the new dam and the All American canal. The assessments were not to include the cost of the water or of its storage at Boulder Dam. The water was free, in recognition of the fact that rights to it had become established in the lower-river region, and specifically in the Imperial Valley, before the Colorado River project was undertaken. Prior use gave prior right to users in the Imperial Valley.

The states of the upper Colorado Basin did not succeed in apportioning their rights until 1948. In the compact of that year, Colorado acquired somewhat more than half of the upper-basin rights, since more than half of the river's waters originated there. The compact stated that, of the 7,500,000 acre-feet annually allotted to the upper basin under the 1922 compact, 51.75 percent was to be available to Colorado,

11.25 percent to New Mexico, 23 percent to Utah, and 14 percent to Wyoming. Congress endorsed the action of these states in legislation of April 6, 1949. Included in the compact was the statement that the term ''upper basin'' comprised ''all parts of said states located outside the drainage area of the Colorado River system which are now or shall hereafter be beneficially served by waters diverted from the Colorado system above Lee Ferry.'' The reason for this clause went back a decade or more.

The Continental Divide cuts Colorado into an eastern and a western half. In both halves irrigation was under way well before the Santa Fe conference. In the eastern half—on the Great Plains—lay most of the good soil. Its farmers were obtaining water from the upper reaches of the South Platte and the Arkansas, but the waters so acquired were scant. On the western side the waters of the upper Colorado were abundant. If those waters could be diverted eastward, through the mountains, they would solve the problems not only of agriculture, but of city development. The financing of such a diversion was possible only by the federal government.

In 1937 Congress gave its support to a specific plan to divert water across the Continental Divide—the Colorado–Big Thompson project. It was one of the most ambitious diversion projects ever attempted. It called for lifting water up from the upper Colorado 186 feet into a reservoir. From the reservoir a tunnel thirteen miles long had to be cut through the rock of the Continental Divide. Water from the reservoir would flow by gravity down the tunnel into a reservoir built east of the mountains, from which it would be delivered as needed into the Big Thompson, a tributary of the South Platte. The water would be supplementary to that already in use. It would add annually 310,000 acre-feet to that available to farmers on the Big Thompson and the South Platte, which would insure them against drought in the height of the summer. The land so protected would be 615,000 acres. Power would be generated by the water, before it flowed to the land, to the annual amount of 900 million kilowatt-hours.

By 1949 the project had involved an expenditure of $160 million, which, in a sense, was a loan to be repaid to the government in the future. Of the total, $100 million was allocated to irrigation. It was to be repaid by users, organized in an irrigation district, over a period of 50 years. The remaining $60 million was to be repaid by power users. By 1949 two reservoirs on the western side and the thirteen-mile-long tunnel had been completed. The remainder of the project was completed six years later, with acclaim in the United States and elsewhere (Map 98).

In 1956, when water from the Colorado was beginning to irrigate the Great Plains, Congress enacted the Colorado River Storage Project Act. Its purposes were to store water for the upper-basin states so each could be assured of the quantities they had agreed upon, to store water to ensure the lower-basin states their share as agreed upon, and to alleviate the problem of silt in Lake Mead above Hoover Dam. The act was a significant step in protecting the entire Colorado River basin, and especially the lower states, against years of water shortage.

The act authorized construction of four key storage dams, Glen Canyon on the main stem near the Arizona-Utah border and three on tributaries of the Colorado (Map 99). The latter were Navajo on the San Juan, Flaming Gorge on the Green on the Utah-Wyoming border, and Blue Mesa within a canyon of the Gunnison River. A number of ''participating projects'' were also authorized—smaller dams chiefly to provide power and irrigation water. The initial plan had included two dams, Echo

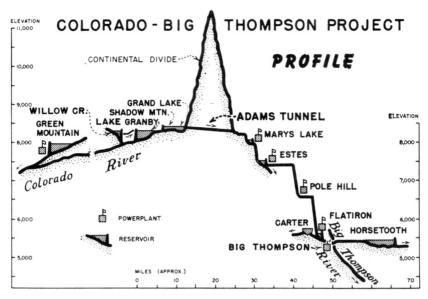

98. Colorado–Big Thompson Trans–Mountain Diversion (from the Dept. of the Interior)

Park and Split Mountain, that would have been built in Dinosaur National Monument. Protests by conservationists forced their elimination.

Glen Canyon, in storing water in Lake Powell, held back some 6 million tons of silt that had annually been entering Lake Mead. Navajo was a relatively low, earth-filled dam. One purpose of its reservoir was to irrigate 110,630 acres of Navaho Indian land. Flaming Gorge and Glen Canyon were very high and created long lakes that would catch as much runoff as possible.

By 1967 all four of the major dams had been built and twelve participating projects were either completed or under way. Two other projects, authorized in 1962, were also under way, both on the pattern of the Colorado–Big Thompson. One, the San Juan–Chama, was designed to transfer water of the San Juan River, stored in Navajo reservoir, over the Divide to an upper branch of the Rio Grande. The other, the Fryingpan–Arkansas project, was to lift water from the Fryingpan, a tributary of the Colorado, into a reservoir on the western slope, from which it would flow via a six-mile tunnel into a reservoir on the upper Arkansas. It would descend thence through seven mountainside power plants, including one at Pueblo, Colorado, generating 2.5 billion kilowatt-hours of energy a year. It would deliver 777,000 acre-feet of water to the Great Plains for irrigation and for use by such growing cities as Pueblo and Colorado Springs. The theme of President John F. Kennedy, when he came to Pueblo in October 1963 to inaugurate the project, was that it would help both "farm and factory."

Projects involving the diversion of water from one system to another through a tunnel necessitated technical equipment, as well as congressional financing. The technical equipment to meet this need was the mechanical "mole," a massive rotary, which pierced hard rock at unusually high speed. It was guided, as it moved forward, by a laser beam that produced a boring. The work proceeded from both ends and, when the breakthrough came, the junction was virtually perfect. A cement lining gave assurance against water leakage.

While these developments were taking place in the upper basin, the contest between Arizona and California concerning allotment of water was finally resolved. In 1952 Arizona had filed a suit against California in the United States Supreme Court. It charged that California was absorbing more of the water reserved to the lower-basin states than it was entitled to under the agreements of 1922 and 1944. The Court referred the case to a special master, who early in 1961 submitted a report upholding the Arizona claim. He held that, of the 7,500,000 acre-feet of mainstream water that Congress had allotted to the lower-basin states, California was to have 4,400,000 acre-feet, Arizona 2,800,000, and Nevada 300,000. California had sought 5,362,000 acre-feet, including a share in the water of the Gila. Arizona had maintained that it controlled all of the Gila water, since the river lay wholly within its borders; that this had been the intent of Congress in endorsing the 1922 Colorado River Compact; and that this intent had been reaffirmed in 1944. Arizona's position with respect to the Gila water was supported in the report of the special master.

The Supreme Court approved the master's report in a decision of June 3, 1963, by a vote of 7–1. Chief Justice Earl Warren, who had once been a governor of California, took no part in the case. Arizona acquired thus a secure right to 2,800,000 acre-feet of the annual flow of the Colorado River, plus all of the Gila water.

The Court decision freed Arizona to win congressional authority in 1968 for the Central Arizona Project. An essential part of this venture was the transfer of water from the Colorado River, over rough country, halfway across the state to the Arizona plateau. An early plan was to obtain hydroelectric power for the purpose from two dams constructed in parts of the Grand Canyon of the Colorado. But this produced an outcry against drowning out one of the scenic wonders of the world, and it had to be abandoned. In the substitute plan a great aqueduct was authorized to carry water from Havasu Lake behind Parker Dam to an aqueduct over the Salt River, a tributary of the Gila. From the Salt-Gila aqueduct the water was to be lifted to reservoirs at the level of the Arizona plateau. The power for the project was to come from a coal-fired plant, built by private industry, with the help of $100 million prepayment for the power by the federal government. The plant was to be at Page on the northern border of the state, where coal was available and a power system was already in place. The water so delivered was to flow by gravity to the irrigable lands, and to Phoenix and Tucson. The legislation of 1968 also authorized five additional participating projects in the upper Colorado Basin. This package, estimated to cost over a billion dollars, was approved by President Johnson, and construction began.

Viewed in its entirety, the reclamation of the basin of the Colorado River was an upgrading of inferior resources. Just as new technology made available low-grade mineral resources, so new engineering skills, by making water more available, converted soils that were fertile, but desert, into oases. Food was produced there of higher value per acre than some of the staples of the subhumid and humid areas, vegetables needing abundance of water, such as sugar beets, onions, lettuce, and cucumbers. Additional crops were fruits of many varieties, and fibers, such as the long-staple cotton of the Gila Valley. By the harnessing of the Colorado a great service was

99. Colorado River Storage Project (from *The New York Times*)

performed in flood control, especially in the Imperial Valley. The augmented water supply not only created a new frontier in agriculture but accelerated industrial expansion, particularly in southern California and Colorado. California became the leading industrial state of the Far West; Colorado was second in rank. Not least, the reservoirs and lakes produced by dams provided recreation to city dwellers of the region and of the nation.

But reclamation projects in the Colorado Basin also produced problems. These were financial, environmental, and international. The non-reimbursable costs of the projects were added to the national debt; the industrial concentration drawn to the area created degeneration of the environment; and the returned water from irrigated fields raised salinity issues with the government of Mexico.

Mexico had rights to Colorado River water established long before the Boulder Canyon Project Act of 1928. Her water rights came to least 600,000 acre-feet, the amount that had been in use on her side of the boundary. These rights the United

States was bound to respect. In 1944 a treaty was concluded whereby Mexico was allotted 1,500,000 acre-feet. This seemed a generous settlement, but was less so than it appeared. Part of the agreement was that the state of Texas receive from Mexico rights to more water from the Rio Grande River than the United States could properly claim. The treaty was, however, of world interest and was acclaimed as setting an example of the peaceful division of the waters of an international stream.

But the waters of the Colorado were special in a sense. They were tainted by salts of acid or alkaline nature, drawn up by capillary attraction from the semi-arid soil of the area drained by the river. The salinity became more decided with the spread of irrigation in the Imperial Valley. The return flow of irrigation water caused an intensification of the salinity problem already present in the Mexicali Valley, the Mexican extension of the Imperial Valley. An even greater degeneration followed the spread of irrigation in the Gila Valley's Wellton-Mohawk Irrigation District, after the diversion there of water from the main stem of the Colorado in 1961. The soil of that district was unusually impregnated with salt, and the drainage of its returned irrigation water into the lower Colorado brought calamity to thousands of Mexican farmers who used the river's waters in their production of vegetables and long-staple cotton. Mexico's initial protest came in 1962 after severe damage in the Mexicali Valley from the drainage waters of the Wellton-Mohawk District.

The first step to pacify Mexico was taken by the American government in the autumn of 1965, when an agreement between the two countries was signed to study the location of a desalting plant on the lower reaches of the Colorado. No positive action followed, however, owing to the absorption of American energies in the Vietnam War. The problem became increasingly emotional in Mexico and in the summer of 1972 President Echeverria carried the case to a joint session of the American Congress. The next year a pledge was given by the Nixon administration to find an early solution to the problem. On April 30, 1973, an executive agreement was reached providing that 11,000 acre-feet of drainage waters from the Wellton-Mohawk District would annually be discharged into the Colorado below the Mexican dam at Morelos, and that an equal volume of desalinated waters would be substituted above the dam.

On June 24, 1974, the Colorado River Basin Salinity Control Act was adopted by Congress and signed by President Nixon. It authorized the construction by the American government of the world's largest desalting plant at Yuma, Arizona, to clean the waters from the Wellton-Mohawk District before they entered Mexico. The plant is to treat 129 million gallons of water daily. A bypass drain to carry reject waters into the river below the Morelos dam is to be constructed. The cost of this portion of the project, which was set at $121.5 million, is to be assumed by the American government.

For salinity control on the upstream waters of the Colorado the act authorized four projects, two to be located in Colorado, one in Utah, and one in Nevada. They were to intercept and desalinate surface water from irrigated land and local salt springs and treat saline ground water. The costs of these projects were set at $125 million, three-fourths of which was to be assumed by the federal government. Construction of the five units of the whole desalting program was expected to be completed by 1979.

The act, in its international aspects, was a response essentially to moral needs. It recognized an obligation to do justice to a nation that in the preceding century had suffered grievously from the United States. In the course of the debate on the act the argument was advanced in the House that Mexico had no legal right under the treaty of 1944 to more than a specified quantity of the waters of the Colorado, that the quality of the water delivered had not been guaranteed. Congress rejected that argument. The act gave assurance that the quality of the water which flowed into Mexico would be not lower than it had been when the treaty dividing the waters was signed. The act also gave satisfaction to the many users of Colorado River water within the United States. It promised them rescue from the effects of saline waters in the Colorado Basin, both natural and man-made in origin.

The Columbia Basin and Central Valley Projects

RECLAMATION PROJECTS on a scale vaster than that of the Colorado River basin were set in motion before construction in the Southwest had been completed. They were in the Pacific West—the Columbia Basin Project and the Central Valley Project in California. They set new standards of construction not only in scope but in their multiplicity of purpose.

The Columbia Basin Project was designed to tame and put to useful work the mightiest river, next to the Mississippi, in North America. The headwaters of that river and of the Snake, its great southern tributary, lie in the Rocky Mountains. Each spring they released floods that had shaped the history of the region. A principal purpose of the project was to overcome that menace. Another was to produce a system of inland navigation for large craft. A third and major purpose was reclamation. The Columbia Basin Project was to be the greatest irrigation enterprise ever financed by the federal government. It would reclaim the eastern portion of the state of Washington—the region known as the Big Bend country.

Reclamation of the Big Bend region was an undertaking of great promise. The soil is rich—it is disintegrated lava—and the climate is favorable, except for the lack of rainfall. With an average of rainfall and snowfall less than ten inches a year the region was almost a desert. It is bordered at the south by the Columbia River, carrying immense quantities of water. But the water was out of reach, flowing 500 feet below the riverbanks through a giant gorge.

Correction of that defect of nature was a challenging goal of the project. The level of the river was to be raised 350 feet by a giant dam. A further boost was to be given the water by a set of massive pumps operated by power generated at the dam. The water was to be raised into a reservoir already created by nature. In the Ice Age the river had been plugged by ice at the point where the channel turns abruptly north. It had cut itself a new channel. With the passing of the Ice Age the plug had disappeared and left an immense dry basin, the Grand Coulee. This was an ideal reservoir for the future to use.

Grand Coulee Dam was authorized in 1935 as a Bureau of Reclamation project. It was completed near the beginning of World War II. It is a massive structure, almost a mile in length and three times the size of Hoover Dam. At the time of its completion it was the largest dam in the world. It raises the level of the river 350 feet, forming, as shown in the photograph, Lake Roosevelt (100). The second photograph shows the water raised another 280 feet, by power created at the dam, through twelve huge pipes each six or more feet in diameter (101). From the pipes the water flows by gravity in a canal into the natural reservoir. The third illustration shows the project spread out in an engineer's relief map (102). Note the dam, the river backed up behind it, the reservoir on high land above the dam, and the Columbia Basin Project, where land is now being irrigated by a network of canals. The next illustration depicts the project in diagrammatic form (103).

An administrative form was given the project by a political party that had an opposite philosophy of government from Herbert Hoover's. It was formulated in terms of the New Deal philosophy of Franklin D. Roosevelt, who had no fears of governmental operation of such a system. The one fear the President had was of profiteering at government expense by big landholders whose property lay in the path of the project.

Eighty percent of the lands there were possessed by a relatively few big holders who had acquired them cheap for pasturing cattle or for dry-land farming. The lands were without rights to irrigation water. They differed in that respect from land in the Imperial Valley. Their value would be enormously increased if irrigation water was

100. Grand Coulee Dam

101. Pipes Raising Water to the Coulee Reservoir

made available to them. Unless preventive action was taken by Congress the owners would get rich at public expense. In 1937 Congress passed the Columbia Basin Anti-Speculation Act, drawn up by the Reclamation Service. Its purposes were strengthened by an amendment in 1943.

The act placed a restrictive limit on the amount of water any irrigator could take from the project. If the individual was unmarried the limit was water for 40 acres; if he was married, water for 80 acres.

Any person holding land beyond these limits was declared to possess "excess" land. His ownership could not be rescinded. But he could get no project water for the excess. If he wished to sell the excess he must offer it first to the federal government, and at a dry-land figure fixed by the Reclamation Service. Under this authority the Service was empowered systematically to draw up contracts with owners of excess lands for purchase of them at dry-land values.

Under the terms of the act the land so acquired was to be made ready for irrigation by the Reclamation Service. It was to be leveled off, and subsidiary irrigation ditches to it were to be dug. Then it was to be sold to settlers. The terms of sale were made very favorable to them. The price was to be the dry-land cost of the land—the price at which the government had bought it. Part of the cost of the irrigation works was added. For Class I land an average of $85 an acre was to be paid,

102. Columbia Basin Project, Engineer's Relief Map

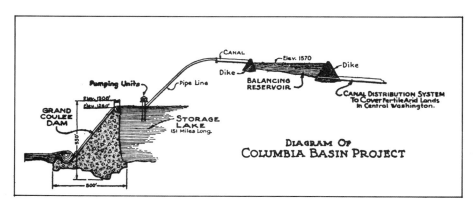

103. Profile of the Columbia Basin Project (from *Harper's Magazine*)

which included part of the cost of reclamation. The actual cost of reclamation was $445 an acre. The difference between the $85 and $445 was to be a loan made to the settler by the government out of the power profits of the project. Each settler was to have 40 years in which to repay the loan. Also he was to make annual payment for water used—$2.50 for each acre irrigated.

Applicants for lands had to meet specified tests of eligibility. They had to have farming experience, a minimum amount of capital, and the character to succeed. Those tests were designed to prevent the kind of failures that had occurred on earlier federal reclamation projects. Applicants who were veterans of World War II were given preference.

Distribution of land on a small scale began in 1948 at Pasco. The larger work of making the land ready for cultivation was done later. In the meantime the towns that were to be the marketing centers of the region—Pasco at the south and Ephrata at the north, were laid out. They became boom towns, bursting with frontier optimism and energy. Ultimately a million acres of land were put under irrigation.

The production of electric power greater than that needed to lift water into the Grand Coulee reservoir was another purpose of the project. It was a major purpose. Grand Coulee Dam was to be the greatest single power producer in the world. Another major power producer was to be constructed on the river at the head of tidewater—Bonneville Dam. Power could be manufactured at these dams cheaply because of the immense volume of water in the river and its steady flow. The philosophy embodied in the project as a whole was public production and sale of power. There was to be no partnership here with private capital as had been arranged by the Hoover administration in California. It was a New Deal concept.

The power generated at these dams became a great defense asset during World War II. It fueled defense industries, especially an aluminum industry, which is still a major one, and a great atomic plant at Hanford. The power generated at the two dams provided 42 percent of the output of the Pacific Northwest during the war.

A large part of the power was consumed by the cities and industries of the region. Only a tenth was consumed by the giant pumps. The demand belied the scoffing prediction, while the project was under debate, that if the project materialized, the government would be making power for jackrabbits. The output of the two great plants created its own demand. Major industries were drawn by it to the Pacific Northwest. In spite of the enormous quantity generated, the section persistently suffered power shortages and new units had to be added to the system on the main river and on the Snake tributary. On the main stream, between Bonneville and Coulee dams, 20 other dams, great and small, were built, including those on the Snake. They served a drainage basin of 259,000 square miles, not including the area north of the international boundary. They brought irrigation water to 100,000 acres of land, in addition to the million acres irrigated from the Grand Coulee, and generated 40 million kilowatts of power.

An issue marking the debate over the construction of the later dams was whether all should be built by the government, or whether the lesser ones should be left to private enterprise. It was precipitated by controversy over the Hell's Canyon site on one of the Snake tributaries. Conservatives wished the lesser dams to be left to private enterprise. In the Eisenhower administration a single high dam was proposed, but this was resisted, and a change was made to three lesser dams. The decision was that those dams be left to private enterprise.

The Columbia River has its origin in British Columbia. Of its annual flow, 15,500,000 acre-feet are Canadian. The provincial government was determined to share in the benefits of this project, and a treaty with Canada was concluded in 1964 to that end. It provided that Canada would construct three dams on Canadian waters. The United States would pay Canada $64,400,000, in recognition of the flood-control benefits thus contributed. Canada would also receive half the downstream power profits of its waters. One of the upstream tributaries of the Columbia, the Kootenay, rises in Montana, but flows for a distance through British Columbia, before entering the main stream. Under the treaty a dam was to be built on the stream by the American government on its side of the line, but provision was made that half the power benefits of this stream, as well as of the other waters contributed by Canada, should go to her (104).

Under the treaty the management of the power to which the United States was entitled was assigned to the Bonneville Power Authority, which Congress had established in 1937 in the Department of the Interior. A like function was given to a nonprofit combination of Canadian utility companies, which paid its government in advance for the privilege of selling the Canadian share of the power for a period of 30 years. The payment enabled the Canadian government to finance the construction of

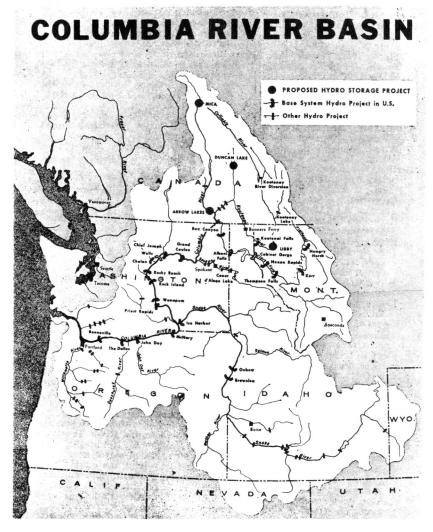

104. Columbia Basin Treaty with Canada, 1964 (from *Congressional Hearings, Foreign Relations*)

the new dams on its waters. The agreement was a demonstration to other countries of international cooperation in water use.

A valuable feature of the Columbia Basin Project was its conversion of the river into a stream navigable by deep-draft vessels almost to the Canadian border. The dams on the main stream and on the lower Snake were provided with locks for navigation. They were provided, also, with salmon ladders to permit the Chinook salmon, for which the river was famous, to ascend its waters for the seasonal spawning.

Yet another mighty undertaking of the same era was the Central Valley Project of California. Originally a state project, it received federal financial aid and Bureau of Reclamation direction after 1935. It was designed to remake the water system of the interior valley. In northern California an enormous potential of water existed. Snow falls on the slopes of the Sierra Nevadas to an annual height of 35 to 40 feet. In the spring this ran off in floods—sometimes destructive. On the other hand, in the San Joaquin Valley to the south, water scarcity had circumscribed progress from the beginning of occupancy.

Underground water was resorted to there in the early years of the 20th century. It got underground naturally through layers of sand and gravel in the beds of streams, and, in some cases, was made to sink in greater quantity by widening the mouths of canyons. It was pumped to the surface later where needed. But pumping was an expensive operation, and became uneconomical as the water level fell through increased use.

The purpose of the Central Valley Project was to transfer water from the northern valley, where it was almost an embarrassment, to the southern, where it was a growing need. The mechanism to do it is depicted in the illustration (105). The picture is so realistic that it creates the illusion of photography. It is a photograph of a model.

The key structure in the system is the giant Shasta Dam in the northern Sierra Nevadas, which holds back the spring floodwaters of the upper Sacramento River that used to run to waste. The stored waters are held in the reservoir of beautiful Shasta Lake; they are released as needed. Part of them are used in the Sacramento Valley. The rest flows down the channel as far as the river's delta. There the water is diverted into a cross-channel, which takes it to Tracy in the San Joaquin Valley, where it is lifted by six giant pumps a height of 200 feet into a canal that runs southward—the Delta-Mendota Canal. The canal, at an altitude higher than the Mendota Pool, carries the water into the pool, from which it turns northward, irrigating the parched lands of the San Joaquin Valley.

At the southern end of the Central Valley near Bakersfield the land is irrigated by water drawn from a tributary of the San Joaquin, the Friant, and stored at Friant-Kern Dam, and then sent southward by an irrigation canal. The whole system is a miracle of engineering.

The project was officially set in operation in 1951, when the station at Tracy began to pump water into the Delta-Mendota Canal. A segment completed in 1969 was the San Luis Project, consisting of a tap on the Delta-Mendota Canal, a dam and reservoir to hold the water drawn, and a canal to carry it as needed to southern California.

The construction cost of the project was $440 million, advanced by the federal

105. Central Valley Project (from *Life* Magazine)

government as a loan to the state of California and the Bureau of Reclamation. It was to be repaid in part from the profits of power generated at Shasta Dam. Another part (42 percent) was to be repaid from the sale of water to irrigators over the next 60 years. The rest was charged off to flood control, assumed by the federal government.

A controversial issue was raised by the project similar to that decided in the Columbia Basin Project. It was whether the big landowners in the Central Valley should be permitted to profit from major government expenditure of money. Nearly all the irrigable acreage in the valley was private land, first acquired in the Mexican era as cattle country. Early irrigation in the Sacramento Valley had been of the surface type, while in the San Joaquin Valley it had been by the use of underground water raised by pumping.

Much of the San Joaquin Valley was held by corporations in extensive tracts. The Di Giorgio Fruit Company owned 12,300 acres; Anderson and Clayton, the biggest cotton factors in the world, held 54,000 acres; the Kern County Land Company, a cattle outfit, owned 240,000 acres, of which 140,000 were irrigable. The Standard Oil Company possessed 79,000 acres in the Bakersfield area, originally acquired for oil prospecting. Twenty-three percent of the land in the Central Valley was owned in blocks large enough to bring them within the category described by the federal government as "excess lands."

From the beginning of federal reclamation the law was clear on that issue. In the Newlands Act of 1902 a provision appeared that on any federal irrigation project no private landowner could take water for more than 160 acres. In California, however, enforcement of that provision had been weak, partly for lack of enforcement machinery.

In 1916 it was further weakened by an administrative ruling of the Secretary of the Interior that when a husband and wife each held 160 acres of land on a federal project, each could take water from it for 160 acres. In 1926 Congress belatedly provided enforcement machinery for the law. It provided that local irrigation districts should take responsibility for water distribution and the enforcement of irrigation law.

This evolution was common knowledge in California when the Central Valley Project was brought before Congress. It was unquestionably known to corporations holding land in the Central Valley. No objection was raised to it in Congress while the valley project was under debate, but as soon as Congress had committed itself, opposition to the limitation appeared. A nationwide campaign was opened to exempt the Central Valley from the limitation. Three main arguments were advanced. One was that efficient farming required large-scale operation on truck farms, cotton plantations, and orchards, and that 160 acres was too small a unit. Another was that in the northern half of the Central Valley, in the Sacramento, enforcement of any limitation on water use of this sort would be impracticable, because big landowners had prior rights to irrigation water. If, to get more water, they would have to break up their holdings, they would simply refuse to take the added water. A third line was that in the San Joaquin Valley the limitation would be unenforceable. Its large landowners were already obtaining much water by pumping. They would refuse to take surface water from the federal project if it meant breaking up their holdings. They would simply make more use of underground water. They could be sure that their underground water would not get exhausted, for it would be constantly replenished by water seeping into the ground from the big quantities brought in by the federal project. Underground water could be used with impunity because, there, no distinctions could be made as to the origin of the water. The fight to gain exemption from the 160-acre limitation was not supported by all elements in California. It was frowned on by small landowners and by labor unions. They believed in the limitation as a protection to the ideal of the family-sized farm.

In Congress the fight for exemption of California from the law was unsuccessful. The principle of the 160-acre limitation on the use of federal water by an unmarried individual, or a 320-acre limit by a married one, was repeatedly reaffirmed in legislation of the 1930's and 1940's. An owner of excess acreage could keep the land but could not get project water for it. If he sold the excess the price must be no higher than the appraised value of the land before project water had become available, plus any buildings or other improvements on it. The contract of sale had to be recorded with the Reclamation Service. The irrigation district had to see to it that no excess land, and no land transferred contrary to law, got any project water.

The law allowed a period of ten years after project water had become available to dispose of excess land. Since project water became available only in 1951, the excess owners had until 1961 to divest themselves of their excess holdings. Few of the big owners or corporations took the necessary action. They got project water for 160 acres or 320 acres, as the case might be, and relied on pumped water for the rest.

In 1953 Douglas McKay, the Secretary of the Interior in the Eisenhower administration, handed down a ruling on an irrigation project similar to that of the Central

Valley, which undercut the 1902 principle of the 160-acre limitation on water use from federal irrigation projects. The ruling bore the name "lump-sum prepayment." If an excess owner would make a "lump-sum prepayment" of the irrigation charges on his land, he would be exempt from the 160-acre limitation. In the following year Secretary McKay announced his disapproval of the 160-acre limitation.

A striking difference is evident in the answers given in the Eisenhower and Roosevelt administrations to the problem of the excess owner. The answer of the one was the "lump sum" principle; of the other, the Anti-Speculation Act of 1937. The difference is to be accounted for partly in terms of the divergent philosophies of government of the two Presidents. But it was the result also of differences in the two projects. In that of the Central Valley the excess holders were in a stronger position to resist pressure than those in the Columbia Basin. They had underground water and the powerful influence of the California delegation in Congress to rely on. They believed that Congress would ultimately relent and exempt their project from the requirements of the Newlands Act of 1902. They relied also on the spotty enforcement given to that law. The issue is even yet not settled.

In 1955 an ominous condition was reported to the United States Geological Survey regarding the Central Valley. It was a sinking of land at the rate of a foot a year in wide stretches of the valley. In the counties of Merced and Fresno the subsidence had reached as much as eight feet. The explanation given for the phenomenon was not definitive. But the chief factor seemed to be overpumping of underground waters by the growers. Were this to continue it would disrupt the maintenance of canals, irrigation systems, highways, railroads, and other construction. The report had an obvious bearing on the problems related to exploitation of the land by excess holders in the valley.

The Tennessee Valley
Authority and Its Role as
Model for Western River
Basin Development

IN THE ERA OF THE far western projects for uplifting river basin societies, a major eastern project of similar purpose took shape and became a challenge to the West. The scene was the valley of the Tennessee, whose tributaries rise in the highest mountains of the eastern half of the United States—the Great Smoky range and the Alleghenies. In these mountains the rate of rainfall and snowfall is almost the highest in the nation, about 70 to 80 inches a year. This volume is carried into the Ohio River by a steep descent. Such a combination of volume and slope was the dream of hydroelectric engineers.

Projects to build dams and exploit the combination appeared in Congress in the early 1890's in the form of bills for private exploitation of a site at the Muscle Shoals in the Alabama portion of the river. In 1903 Congress passed such a measure, but it was vetoed by Theodore Roosevelt. He and his advisers, especially Gifford Pinchot, wished a public development of the resources of the Tennessee. They had the concept of an integrated, multipurpose development of all the rivers of the nation. They believed that the Tennessee could also be made a valuable channel of interstate commerce, provided dams with locks were built that would put water over rough places in the river. They wished the dams to produce power that would help to defray the costs of the project.

In 1916 an urgent need arose for the power the river could produce. The nation faced the prospect of being dragged into World War I, then raging in Europe. The War Department urged stockpiling of high explosives, especially nitroglycerine, of which nitrates are the base. But no nitrates of good enough quality for high explosives were available in the United States. They had to be imported from Chile.

The military planners were alarmed at this dependence on a foreign state for an essential military material, especially after the opening of the German campaign of unrestricted submarine warfare. They urged synthetic production of nitrates in the United States by means of an air-fixation process. For such a process electric power in great amounts was needed, and the undeveloped power resources of the Tennessee River seemed the obvious answer to the need. In 1916 a National Defense Act was passed by Congress, which authorized the construction of a government dam in the Tennessee River at Muscle Shoals, and adjacent to it, a power plant and a nitrate-fixation facility.

This measure was allowed to pass without much challenge. Under ordinary circumstances it would have been resisted on the ground that the government should not engage in power production or nitrate production in competition with private business. The building of the federal project began in 1917 and was still under way when the war ended a year later.

With the end of the war a fight opened in Congress at the instance of the private power and nitrate interests to prevent government operation of the power and nitrate plants. It continued for 21 years—from 1918 to 1939. In the Harding administration these interests demanded the liquidation of the whole Muscle Shoals project by sale. They urged in Congress the sale of the dam, the powerhouse, and the nitrate plant, which had cost $69 million, to Henry Ford for the sum of $5 million. The proposal was defeated by the liberal forces in Congress under the leadership of Senator George Norris of Nebraska. In the Coolidge administration Congress adopted a compromise plan—that the government should continue to produce power and nitrates at Muscle Shoals, but leave the retail distribution of them to private interests. This was too radical for Coolidge, who pocket-vetoed the bill. In the Hoover administration (1930) Congress worked out a new compromise that the government should continue to produce and sell power at the Muscle Shoals, but should lease the nitrate plant to private enterprise. To Hoover this seemed too socialistic and was vetoed in a vehement message.

In 1932 a presidential campaign was fought over these issues, not only over the issue of Muscle Shoals, but over the larger question of government control and regulation of private power utilities. Muscle Shoals was a symbol of the larger issue. On that issue, among others, Franklin Delano Roosevelt won the election.

But the power issue was only one phase of the larger problem of the Tennessee River. Flood control was another. Every year, in the months of February and March, floods occurred on the Tennessee as rain and snow went off the Great Smokies in a rush. The water rose to spectacular heights. The low-lying regions in the valley and especially the city of Chattanooga were in danger of being drowned out. The floodwaters were also a danger elsewhere than in the Tennessee Basin. They were a menace on the lower Ohio, of which the Tennessee is a tributary, and also on the lower Mississippi. The combined waters of the Tennessee, the Ohio, the upper Mississippi, and the Missouri annually threatened the lower valley with disaster. In the 1920's a new urgency was given to the flood problem. Record crests of waters were being established every few years. This was the result of the destruction of forests on the headwaters of the rivers and the plowing up of the land. Levees on the lower river had to be raised repeatedly.

In 1927 a record crest on the lower Mississippi was established. Levees were once again raised. But the Army Engineers gave warning that the limit of levee raising had been reached. Along critical stretches of the river, if additional yardage had been piled on the levees, the weight would have been so great that the foundations would have caved into the river. Also, the pressure of floodwaters was such that water was forcing its way under the foundations, coming out on the land side and producing the so-called sand boils, which were a symptom of grave danger. The conclusion of engineers was that the basic solution for these problems was to build storage dams on the upper tributaries to hold back floodwaters.

Another need was improvement of navigation on the river. In its natural state the river was almost useless for navigation. The channel was broken by many shoals, especially at Muscle Shoals, which was a 37-mile stretch of impassable waters. For generations this had made the river unusable for navigation, though otherwise the river might have been as useful a highway as the Ohio.

In 1930, in the Hoover administration, a navigation measure was adopted by Congress. It provided for a series of low dams, equipped with locks, that would put nine feet of water over the shoal stretches of the river, especially over Muscle Shoals. That measure was approved by Hoover, but no construction followed—the act came too near the end of his administration.

A further problem demanded action in the Tennessee Valley—its run-down physical condition. In some ways this was the most serious problem of all. The hill and mountain lands of the valley had become tragically eroded as a result of exploitive farming. Farming had ceased to be profitable and standards of living in the rural areas of the valley were distressingly low—almost the lowest in the United States.

In 1933, soon after the triumph of Roosevelt, a measure was carried through Congress by the Administration for the creation of the Tennessee Valley Authority. An authority was established in the form of a government corporation, with the right to operate the power and nitrate plants at Muscle Shoals, and to build and operate dams and power plants elsewhere on the Tennessee River. The act provided for the unified development of the river, combining flood control, power production, navigation, nitrate manufacture, and a number of other purposes. TVA was to be an example to the nation of a comprehensive, integrated development of a river as a means of rehabilitating a regional society.

In the debate over the measure the original issue of government manufacture of power was no longer central. That matter had been settled by the election. The issue was whether the government should also sell at retail the power it would produce at Muscle Shoals. The spokesmen for the private utilities took the position that at least the distribution of the power should be left to them, that in their hands it had been good, and could not have been otherwise, inasmuch as it had been under the supervision of state regulatory commissions.

The answer of the Roosevelt administration was that the distribution of power by the utilities had been bad, that the rates had been excessively high, that regulatory commissions had been ineffective protectors of the public interest, that the only result of orders to reduce rates or to improve service had been interminable litigation in the courts. The only effective solution of the power problem, so the Administration held, was public distribution as well as public production of power.

One private utility in the valley—the Alabama Power Company—was at the center of this discussion. It had been selling power, produced partly by its own steam plant and partly by the government plant at Muscle Shoals. It had been the only outlet the government had for its power. The company had a reputation for exorbitant rates. In general, private power companies had such a reputation. This was the period of the scandals arising out of the collapse of the Insull system in the Middle West.

The question of rural distribution of power was brought into the debate on the TVA act. This was urged by the Roosevelt administration as a means of rehabilitating the farming society of the basin. Private utilities had been uninterested in rural electrification, on the ground that it would not pay for itself.

In the TVA act Congress conferred a sweeping authority on the agency to distribute power—that is, to sell at retail. It conferred also the right to grant preferential rates to nonprofit organizations such as rural cooperatives and municipalities. It also gave the agency the power to help rural cooperatives and municipalities acquire distribution systems of their own.

The adoption of the measure was followed by a long court fight. For six years, from 1933 to 1939, the act was fought in the federal courts on the ground of unconstitutionality. Throughout these years TVA was kept in a state of uncertainty and handicapped in its operations.

In 1936 a famous decision was handed down by the Supreme Court in a case brought by a stockholder of the Alabama Company—the Ashwander case. The decision was that the federal government had the constitutional right to produce hydroelectric power, a right derived from its control over interstate streams; also, that it could administer this power as an incident to the right to produce it. In 1939 came another decision, one by a lower federal court, which the Supreme Court refused to alter—*Tennessee Electric Power Company v. T.V.A.* —which upheld the entire program of the act.

After these decisions the private utilities recognized the hopelessness of continuing the fight and agreed to sell their systems for transmitting and distributing power to joint organizations consisting of TVA and municipalities. Thus the Nashville distribution system of the Tennessee Electric Power Company was sold to TVA and the city of Nashville; the Chattanooga system was sold to TVA and the city of Chattanooga. By 1942 practically every municipality of any size in Tennessee, and most of those in adjacent states, owned and operated their systems jointly with TVA and bought their power from the system.

In rural areas the program of electrification was also pressed forward. In some cases TVA built distribution systems and sold them to rural cooperatives under an arrangement whereby repayments were spread out over a long period of years. In accordance with the act of Congress preferential rates to rural cooperatives and municipalities were granted at once, and they became the policy of the future. Low rates were passed on by the distributors to home owners under the supervision of TVA. The rates to home users were about half the average in American cities.

A new theory of rates—the promotional theory—was developed by TVA. It was that increased use of power machinery and equipment would add to the effectiveness of labor on the farm and in the home, and ought to be encouraged. The cost of delivering electricity is mainly that of installing and maintaining equipment, such as poles and wiring, and the expense of administration. These would decrease per unit as the amounts delivered increased.

One of the purposes of TVA was the improvement of farming on the hill and mountain lands of the Tennessee Basin. Farmers on these lands were to be induced to turn from corn and tobacco farming, from row crop farming, which invited soil erosion, to livestock farming, which would permit sloping lands to be put under grass or clover. The means of persuading farmers to make the change was fertilizer produced and distributed to this end cheaply. Nitrates and phosphates were the ones especially advocated, both essential to successful growing of grasses and clovers.

Nitrates were first emphasized. This was, in part, an aftermath of the early emphasis on nitrates for military purposes. Later phosphates were advocated. This was, in turn, an aftermath of emphasis on military production in World War II. Phosphorus was needed for the manufacture of the incendiary bombs dropped on Japanese cities. The raw materials for the phosphate industry were found in the phosphate rock deposits of Tennessee and Florida.

The scientific staff of TVA made advances in developing types of fertilizer that were economical to apply. It developed especially the concentrated superphosphates, which permitted the elimination of large percentages of inert matter that had been present before in such fertilizers. From the outset a principal purpose of fertilizer distribution was education. The recipients were normally demonstration projects in the basin of the Tennessee and elsewhere. Gifts of fertilizer for educational purposes were authorized by the act of 1933.

Selected demonstration farmers were chosen as recipients in all the counties of the Tennessee drainage basin. The selections were left to the local communities under the direction of a county agent of the Department of Agriculture. Each recipient agreed, in return for free fertilizer, to do his farming in accordance with a plan of conservation farming that the county agent and TVA helped to construct. Each farmer agreed to reduce the percentage of land he had in soil-exhausting or soil-eroding crops and increase the percentage in grass and soil-conserving crops. The primary objective was building up the soil. Each recipient agreed to keep accounts of his operations and permit them to be inspected by his neighbors. The demonstration farm became, thus, a kind of schoolroom for the neighborhood. In 1946 there were 38,000 demonstration farms in the drainage basin of the Tennessee using TVA fertilizer, and other farmers were responding to the conservation lessons. However, the program was open to criticism on the ground of duplicating the work of county agents of the Department of Agriculture and of state agricultural colleges. The fertilizer given to demonstration farms gradually decreased, therefore, and sales of it to cooperative associations increased.

TVA turned to practical modes of converting farmers to cover crops and to cattle raising. Its engineers developed a special machine that enabled farmers to maintain clover, yet to drill seeds of small grains into the clover without injuring it. Farmers were able thus to harvest some grain while keeping the soil covered. Also, farmers were encouraged to grow strawberries as a cover crop, for which quick freezers were designed, to put the berries into marketable form. More important, the growing of soybeans was stimulated in the hill areas in later years and became one of the region's main crops.

Forest protection and reforestation were important parts of the TVA program. Reforestation was a means of preventing erosion. For land suited to permanent forestry, TVA furnished farmers millions of free saplings. This program was also part of the program of protecting reservoirs against siltation. As a result of such reforestation the reservoirs of TVA were not in danger of early siltation. The interrelation of the soil conservation, flood control, and reforestation aspects of the program were taught in a slogan: "Keep the land out of the river and the river off the land."

A principal outcome of the TVA program was the conversion of a predominantly agricultural region into one mainly industrial and commercial. The chief industries were fertilizer, appliances, aluminum—which became a major military resource—and the production of power for atomic fuel at Oak Ridge, part of the secret Manhattan Project. The manufacture of steel for the building of new power plants was another segment of the valley industry. Twelve new power plants were put under construction in the valley during the war. The Cumberland River, which lies north of the Tennessee Basin, was added to the TVA system in order that favorable sites for added dams and power plants could be used. Coal-fired plants were constructed, initially to firm up hydroelectric power, then to increase the total power.

A major contribution of the TVA system was the virtual elimination of the flood problem of the river. The valley was made safe from inundation, particularly the city of Chattanooga, which had been more particularly a problem because of its exposed location. A contribution was made by the system, also, to the control of floods on the lower Ohio and on the lower Mississippi. The dams hold back Tennessee waters when the Ohio and Misssissippi are at crest. The most important single structure, from the point of view of reducing the flood crests on the Ohio, is the giant Kentucky Dam, which is near the point where the Tennessee enters the Ohio.

In the months of February and March—the months of prospective floods—all the storage reservoirs on the main Tennessee, and some on the tributaries, are kept in a drawn-down condition. Space is provided for expected floodwaters. In April and through the rest of the spring the reservoirs are allowed to fill up in preparation for the dry summer season. A constant watch is kept on weather conditions in the mountains so that floodwaters may be anticipated and preparations made to handle them.

Another major contribution made by the TVA system was that the Tennessee River became navigable; the river was converted into a new highway of commerce. Nine feet of water were put over such rough places in the river as Muscle Shoals. This transformation of the river was brought to completion by the construction of Kentucky Dam, which tied together the channels of three rivers, the Tennessee, the Ohio, and the Mississippi. Navigation was improved even on the Mississippi River. When the stage of water on the middle Mississippi is low, water to raise it is released from the stored waters of the Tennessee.

Transportation by barges became a vital part of the economic life of the valley. The commodities carried are those of bulk—raw materials such as coal, coke, lumber, grain, petroleum, sand, and gravel—and finished products such as fertilizers and automobiles. Fleets of barges are maintained by corporations in the valley and by public agencies.

A big recreation and tourist business was built up in the valley in connection with the reservoirs. That was one of the most important effects of the TVA enterprise. The recreation and tourist business created local markets and profits for the farmers of the valley—the same combination that brought prosperity to the irrigation farmers of the far western projects. The tourist and recreation businesses became among the greatest assets of the Tennessee Valley.

One of the health achievements of TVA was the virtual eradication of malaria from the drainage basin of the river. This was the result of mosquito-control measures carried out over a series of years, chiefly by the sudden lowering of the level of reservoirs at times when mosquito larvae were breeding along the edges.

But TVA raised major questions of policy. It not only touched the sensitive issue of goverment versus private sale of power. It also called for an immense expenditure of public money. Conservatives sharply raised the question whether TVA was financially sound, or a subsidy to a section financed by the taxpayers of the nation. An answer to the question required a survey of the costs of TVA in its several functions: flood control, navigation improvement, power production, and chemical plants. Such a survey would mean allocating the costs—all land takings, every dam constructed, every power plant built, plus other items—to each of its various functions. This was a complicated technical exercise.

The allocation shown here was made in 1953 by the engineers on the TVA staff. (The individual amounts have been rounded off.) It was declared fair by the Federal Power Commission and by dispassionate public-utility experts who publicly analyzed it.

Flood control	$182,000,000
Navigation improvement	156,000,000
Power plants	924,000,000
Chemical plants	56,000,000
	$1,319,000,000

To the investment made in flood control no revenue could be attributed. Flood control by its nature produces no revenue. It is preventive only. It has never been considered by the federal government to be a revenue producer. But the return in savings to the community, and indirectly in tax returns, has been large. The savings were estimated for the Tennessee Valley alone to be $51 million. And since disaster losses may be written off in income-tax returns this was indirectly a revenue saver. For the Ohio and Mississippi valleys the savings effected by TVA in flood prevention were even greater. According to the Army Engineers, they were well over the entire allocated cost of flood control.

On the investment in improvement of navigation the revenue was not large either. Federal internal improvements have not normally been revenue producers. They have not been undertaken for that purpose, but have always been regarded as subsidies in the interests of commerce and national development. Early federal highway construction, every improvement of rivers and harbors, land grants to railroads, subsidies to airlines—all these have been of this character. An expenditure of $156 million on the navigation improvement of the Tennessee River would probably not have met with any criticism at all if it had not been in association with the contentious question of public power.

The expenditure on navigation improvement was justified on the ground that an important new outlet had been provided for an area that was potentially a center of industry. Cheap transportation is an essential need of industry, and the Tennessee Valley, like the Great Lakes region, steadily became more important industrially.

In Europe, river and canal transportation by barge had long been a vital factor in industrial life. In the United States it had not been as important, chiefly because of the efficiency of railroads in long-distance hauling. But on the Ohio and the Tennessee, barge transportation helped to make possible the rise of industry. Also, by the time of the TVA allocation, the creation of an inland waterway as an alternative to railroads was deemed a security measure. In wartime, if an atomic attack were to paralyze the great railway centers of the nation, waterways would be essential alternative routes.

The investment in power facilities of TVA was in 1953 $924 million. This outlay of capital involved costs which require itemization. A large part of them was the charge for interest on the investment, which was set at the annual rate of 3 percent, a higher rate than the government paid on its current bonds. This was not actually paid by the TVA to the Treasury but it was the basis for fixing rates on the power sold. Another item repayable was amortization of capital. Under a 1948 act of Congress repayment of all funds invested in power production had to be made within 40 years of the time a unit went into operation.

A third item was depreciation—the rate of deterioration on items such as plant equipment and loss of storage capacity in reservoirs. The rate set by TVA was regarded adequate by public-utility experts. Payments in lieu of taxes to states and municipalities were another item. Such payments were also made by TVA's distributing agencies. They were roughly equivalent to the taxes paid by private utilities to state and local governments. A fifth item was operating costs—wages, repairs, materials, and bookkeeping.

Taking all these costs into account, TVA was a self-liquidating, indeed a profit-making enterprise. In the twenty-year period from 1933 to 1953 it earned on its power investment, despite the low rates it charged for power, net revenues averaging 4 percent a year. In some years, such as 1950, when water was especially plentiful, it earned nearly 6 percent. In its first six years, while it was harassed by court proceedings, it operated at a deficit. The 4 percent average over twenty years included those early years. In 1953 TVA was far ahead on its schedule of repayments to the Treasury.

TVA's profit from its power operations totaled $226 million for the years 1933 −53. This impressive record was the result of the efficiency of the plant, the program of power sales, and the enormous demand for power during World War II, the Korean War, and the ensuing rearmament program. The disposition made of the revenue earned was the payment of $50 million to the Treasury for amortization, $31 million for the retirement of special bonds issued on its behalf by the federal government, and $145 million for investment in new power facilities.

The swift expansion of TVA power plants aroused anxiety in private utility circles. It set off an attack in Congress on the financial structure of TVA. Under the terms of the statute of 1933 the revenues derived from the power and fertilizer plants were left in the project. They were to be used as a revolving fund, which meant self-sufficiency for the project. In March 1942 Senator Kenneth D. McKellar of Tennessee introduced a measure into the Senate that would have required TVA to remit its annual revenues to the federal Treasury. It was the first of a series of proposed amendments to the act of 1933 limiting the freedom of TVA by establishing a dependence on annual congressional appropriations. McKellar was the ranking member of the powerful Senate Committee on Appropriations. He had earlier been a supporter of TVA and his new stance was a symptom of gathering opposition. The attack was not well timed. It came shortly after the Japanese assault on Pearl Harbor and the American entrance into World War II, which emphasized the need for all the power TVA could produce. The attack had little support in the Tennessee Basin, where TVA was popular.

Resistance to the expansion of TVA appeared, also, in the Budget Bureau in the Eisenhower administration. It was manifested against legislation proposed in April 1955 by TVA which would have authorized the issue of its own bonds to finance new construction and would have removed in that way uncertainty in its operations. The counterproposal of the Budget Bureau was that each new emission of bonds have prior congressional approval, and the TVA measure was defeated. After four years, however, in August 1959, an act was approved by Congress and the President meeting the wishes of TVA though setting a ceiling on the bond emissions at $750 million. In 1966 the ceiling was lifted to $1.75 billion, and in 1970 to $5 billion.

By 1973 TVA was a mature institution. Its annual report marking the fortieth year of its growth was a glowing statistical record. Its interconnected dams and power plants, as illustrated on the map (106), formed one of the greatest in the world. The power system embraced 48 hydroelectric plants and 11 coal-fired steam plants. Its output of power was 103.5 billion kilowatt-hours. Its output from coal-fired plants not merely supplemented but far surpassed that of the hydroelectric plants. Not only industry but home owners thrived on low-cost power. The rate to home owners was 60 percent of the national average. Savings to the valley in the form of flood prevention were reckoned at more than a billion dollars, nearly five times the investment in flood control. A navigable channel for commerce of 650 miles in the main stream had been established for vessels of nine-foot draft. Depleted soils in the uplands had been restored and extensive areas had been reforested. The system's reservoirs formed the means for recreation, which meant improved health and prosperity for the valley. The number of visits to them in the preceeding year had been 14 million.

TVA was a government unit of a sort unknown to the farmers of the Constitution. It was an administrative agency entrusted with an unusual concentration of im-

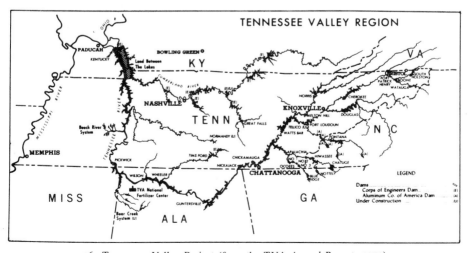

106. Tennessee Valley Project (from the TVA *Annual Report,* 1973)

portant powers which for the rest of the nation were distributed among separate agencies. Thus it had charge of flood control and dam construction, which, elsewhere in the nation, lay with the Army Engineers. It had charge of soil conservation, which elsewhere lay with the Soil Conservation Service. It directed reforestation, which lay with the Forestry Service. Such a concentration of authority seemed to Congress essential to the success of TVA. It produced extraordinary unity and flexibility of operation. It did, to be sure, create a duplication of services, but this was minimized by informal cooperation between TVA and the regular federal agencies. Thus TVA employed the Army Engineers to design and supervise the building of dams, and cooperated with the Department of Agriculture in its soil conservation and reforesting programs.

TVA was an innovation—a corporation entrusted with powers of government. It was comparable to the colonizing corporations of the early colonial period. Its central board of directors was composed of three members appointed by the President. Thus it had the initiative and efficiency of a business organization. It was attacked on the ground that this was not democracy. It was not even obliged to come to Congress for ordinary appropriations.

The TVA statute of 1933 had been framed to remove the institution as far as possible from Washington domination. The headquarters designated in the act was Muscle Shoals in Alabama. Later Knoxville, Tennessee, became the chief headquarters and here it has remained. Also its governing board was authorized to appoint managers and employees "without regard to the provisions of the Civil Service laws applicable to officers and employees of the United States." The persons employed by TVA were largely technicians, selected under its own merit system, designed not merely to minimize politics but to minimize the routine that is a drag on departments in Washington and that stifles individual initiative.

TVA was popular with the people and with the local authorities of the region it served. Its board made informal cooperation with them a guiding principle. They responded by warding off attacks on it in Congress. When President Eisenhower remarked in 1953 that TVA was an example of "creeping socialism," he stirred up such a storm in the valley that he soon found occasion to say that he had not meant that TVA was creeping socialism, but only that some parts of it were in conflict with his own philosophy.

The achievements of TVA were so impressive that enthusiasts had early sought the extension of their pattern to other river basins. In 1937 Senator Norris brought before Congress a bill proposing a nation of seven divisions, each to be patterned after TVA. The bill was supported for a time by President Roosevelt. But in and outside Congress it had little support. Its weakness was oversimplification.

The far western projects, including those encouraged by the New Deal, were not modeled on TVA for reasons peculiar to themselves. They lay in states of semi-aridity, where the prerogatives of the Bureau of Reclamation in constructing works of irrigation had congressional authority. Here also the Army Engineers had prerogatives under congressional authority for constructing works of flood control and navigation. There was, in fact, a duality of authority in western river-basin planning and construction, one that became formalized in 1944, when Congress authorized the largest of river-basin developments, that of the Missouri.

The Missouri and Arkansas Basin Projects and the Water Resources Planning Act of 1965

THE MISSOURI RIVER BASIN is comparable to that of the Tennessee in the opportunities and problems it presented. The river is one of the mightiest in the United States. It is 2460 miles in length and its basin covers parts of ten states. It seemed to Congress to be too diverse in its needs and interests to be entrusted to a single authority of the TVA type. Part of the upper basin is semi-arid, where irrigation is the prime need. Here small dams on the tributaries to store water for irrigation were the chief need, and these were the province of the Bureau of Reclamation. The basin of the middle and lower river needed flood control and stabilization of navigation rather than irrigation, and big dams on the main stem were the prime need—the domain of the Army Engineers. Advocates of states' rights entered the debate. The states were accustomed to join in shaping policy in areas requiring irrigation and demanded participation in the formulation of policy in an interstate project.

Rivalries between federal departments and agencies were normal. The Reclamation Service and the Army Engineers were fearful that a single agency would be set up by Congress. To head this off they entered a temporary alliance and recommended a fusion plan which Congress approved in the Flood Control Act of 1944. This was the Pick-Sloan plan, named for L. A. Pick of the Army Engineers and W. G. Sloan of the Bureau of Reclamation. The act gave blanket authorization for a series of dams to be constructed by each agency.

While the Pick-Sloan plan was under discussion in Congress, the Chief of the Army Engineers, the Commissioner of Reclamation, the Federal Power Commissioner, and a representative of the Department of Agriculture met frequently as a group. The objective of this interagency group was not only to fend off the creation of an authority for the Missouri Valley patterned on TVA, but also to promote a multi-purpose basin development program using existing agencies. This group was in touch with the governors of the Missouri Basin states, who had earlier formed a committee to promote a Missouri Basin development program. In 1945 the federal interagency group, by an informal agreement, set up a Missouri Basin Inter-Agency Committee (MBIAC), whose function was to coordinate the activities of field operatives of the four agencies in the basin, and to mesh them with comparable ones at the state level.The MBIAC, resting solely on an interagency agreement, was without congressional authorization. By later agreements its membership increased until the federal departments and agencies represented on it included, in addition to the original four, Health, Education and Welfare, Commerce, and Labor, while all ten governors were included in the membership. The MBIAC was in sharp contrast to the unity and coherence of the TVA. Its cumbersomeness was criticized by the two Hoover Commissions set up by Congress in 1949 and 1953–55 and by two appointed by President Truman. One of the latter, the Missouri Basin Survey Commission, urgently proposed that a legally constituted authority be established for the basin, with dominant control in Missouri Basin leadership.

Despite criticism of the MBIAC and its lack of authority, the wide scope of its membership was a recognition of the need for joint planning of land and water resources, combined with social needs. Moreover, out of the very size and complexity of the Missouri Basin, a model emerged for planning and coordinating the water resources of the entire nation, one used and improved upon in the significant Water Resources Planning Act of 1965.

In 1951 and 1952 destructive floods occurred in the basins of the Missouri and its Kansas tributary, despite the dams that were under construction there. The flood on the Missouri was the most destructive in the recorded history of the river and gave a terrible urgency to the completion of the big flood-control dams. By 1955 the principal main-stream dams were either in place or in the process of construction. They numbered six and made the middle and lower river basin relatively safe for the future (Map 107). Navigation also was transformed, and hydroelectric power was being generated on a vast scale. Five of the main-stream dams —Garrison, Fort Randall, Oahe, and Big Bend in the Dakotas, and Gavin's Point on the South Dakota–Nebraska line—were constructed under the Pick-Sloan plan. The sixth, at Fort Peck in Montana, a 1933 PWA dam completed in 1937, was initially a flood-control and power project. As storage for flood control and navigation was taken over by downstream dams, the function of Fort Peck became primarily irrigation and power. Storage at Garrison and Fort Randall was also available for irrigation when the lower dams were completed.

In the mid-1960's Congress became uneasy about the blanket authorizations it had earlier given for construction of units of the Pick-Sloan program. Expenditures needed to be brought under more direct control. A cancellation was therefore ordered of blanket authorization for units that had not begun construction before August 14, 1964. Reauthorization became necessary for starts beyond that date. The total project cost was then estimated to be $1,790,000,000. The ultimate cost was estimated to be $4,771,000,000.

Irrigation was a late participant in the allocations of the Pick-Sloan plan. The Garrison Diversion unit in North and South Dakota, initially authorized in 1944, was reauthorized in 1965 for reclamation. The reauthorization contained a provision reflecting a problem of growing concern to the nation. For ten years no part of the

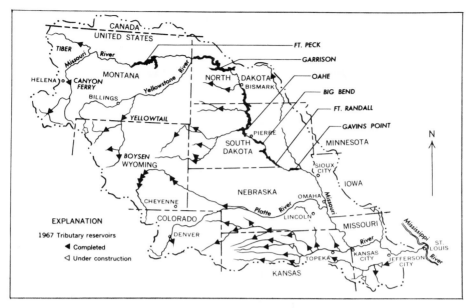

107. Missouri Valley Project (from the U.S. Water Resources Council)

newly irrigated lands could be used for crops that were on the list of the Agriculture Department as in surplus. By the early 1970's 25 of the irrigation sub-units of the project had begun to produce crops that were not restricted.

Hydroelectric power was a major objective of the Missouri Valley project. It was the paying partner as usual of such projects. It was supplied to municipal, industrial, and cooperative agencies. By agreement with the Corps of Engineers and the Bureau of Reclamation it was distributed by the two agencies on the basis of the investment in plants of each. This allocation was in keeping with the Pick-Sloan plan, which recognized that the dams built by each would be producers of power beyond their own needs.

A transformation of navigation on the Missouri River was achieved by 1973. According to a report of the Army Engineers, not only flood damage of more than $800 million had been prevented since 1955, but a river channel, stabilized by levees and open from mid-March to mid-November, had been created to a depth of nine feet from Sioux City in Iowa to St. Louis. Downstream traffic consisted largely of grain; upstream, it was mostly fertilizer, cement, iron ore, and gasoline. The carriers were principally barges, often as many as eight linked together and pushed by so-called towboats.

While the Missouri Basin project was unfolding, another of major dimension applied for federal aid. It came from the basin of the Arkansas River, the last of the principal tributaries of the Mississippi to be an applicant to Congress. The tardiness reflected prior commitments of the government and uncertainty about the project. The Arkansas is a meandering stream taking its rise on the eastern slope of the Rocky

Mountains in Colorado, whence it flows through Kansas, Oklahoma, and Arkansas to a junction with the Mississippi opposite the delta region of the Yazoo.

A principal need for improving it was its high potential of destructiveness. Floods on it were frequent and brought calamity that was widespread. In the great flood of 1927 half the state was under water. Rescue vessels steamed beyond the river channels to pick stranded families out of treetops. Cattle to the number of many thousands were lost and vast property was destroyed. In 1936 the state was hit again by floods, and again the next year, when the levees on the lower river broke and 100,000 acres of the valley were inundated. The river's banks were notoriously unstable. They caved in during and after floods, changing the course of the main stream and converting it into a succession of sandbars and shallow pools. For navigation, the river was useless except locally.

The waters of the river were polluted, partly by salt, partly by runoff from the Oklahoma oil fields, partly by industrial wastes, and partly from raw sewage dumped into it by cities along its banks. Like the Missouri, it was facetiously described as "too thick to drink, too thin to plow." It could not be used even for irrigation, according to an official engineering report, unless a dam and reservoir were constructed at Keystone, which would induce the settling of its impurities. In industry the waters were used, but only in operations in which quality was no factor, such as washing gravel for concrete. For municipal purposes the water was unusable all the way from the line separating Oklahoma and Kansas to Little Rock, except that some cities purified it as a supplement to ground water.

The resources of the basin, if unequal to those of the Missouri or Tennessee, were large. They included a wide variety of minerals—bauxite, copper, lead, zinc, and coal. In Oklahoma were major deposits of oil and gas that insured a petrochemical industry. Timber was available in the Ozarks in quantity inviting export. The soils of the basin invited irrigation if the water could be improved. Later, on irrigated land in central Oklahoma, alfalfa was raised, while in the White Valley in eastern Arkansas extensive rice and soybean crops were grown under irrigation. These resources had brought to the basin a share of the federal funds for protection against floods provided in the general flood-control legislation of 1938.

After the close of World War II, Congress adopted two general measures to improve the major river basins of the nation, including the Arkansas, which went for signature to President Harry S. Truman. One was a rivers-and-harbors measure, proposing an ultimate expenditure of a billion dollars for navigation improvement, flood-control, and power production. The other was a flood-control measure to cost nearly a billion dollars. Neither provided funds for construction. The President signed both, making clear, however, in a special statement that he did not expect an early appropriation and that he did not anticipate asking for funds before July 1, 1947. He indicated reservations as to the form of the measures, which would need to be resolved, and referred to inflationary pressures in the economy, which should be avoided. It was clear he adhered to the theory of compensatory spending—spending reserved for times of slack economy.

In 1949 Congress appropriated funds for the long-deferred Arkansas Basin Project. The first expenditures were for stabilization of the river's banks at critical points, an essential preliminary to construction, for a sudden flood might rearrange the channel and the banks and undo construction in process. Another delay was caused by the Korean War. But by the mid-1950's two key dams, Keystone and Eufaula, were under way west of Tulsa, Oklahoma. They were located where they would best control the flooding and siltation of the lower river. Keystone was completed in October 1963 and dedicated by President Kennedy. The high Oologah Dam on the Verdigris in Oklahoma was completed about the same time. Its purpose was to store surplus water against any future shortages. In Arkansas the first dam was finished in 1966 at Dardanelle, about 80 miles east of the Oklahoma-Arkansas boundary, where its purpose was chiefly power.

Thirteen dams and locks for navigation, with their powerhouses, were completed between 1963 and 1973 (Map 108). Unlike the dams for flood and siltation control, which were built first in Oklahoma and later lower on the river, construction of navigation facilities began downstream and moved upward. By 1973 it was possible to travel on the same vessel from New Orleans to central Oklahoma. By that year the Arkansas project had cost about $1,200,000,000.

Two years after President Kennedy went to Oklahoma to dedicate Keystone Dam, a major piece of legislation, which he had helped to start, passed both houses of Congress and was signed by his successor, Lyndon B. Johnson. This was the Water Resources Planning Act of 1965. A new framework to facilitate river-basin planning was set up. River Basin Commissions, to be created by executive order, would be composed of one member from each state wholly or partly in a basin and one member from each federal agency having a substantial interest in the project to be undertaken. The chairman of each commission would be a federal member designated by the President. Testimony taken in the course of planning was to be under oath. Completed river-basin plans were to be reviewed by a Water Resources Council composed of the Secretaries of the Interior, Agriculture, Army, Health, Education and Welfare, and the chairman of the Federal Power Commission. In addition to reviewing basin plans

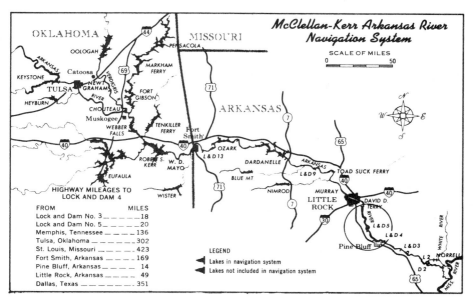

108. Arkansas Valley Project (from the U.S. Army Corps of Engineers)

and forwarding them with recommendations to the President for review and transmittal to Congress, the Council was to prepare a biennial assessment of the adequacy of water resources in each basin. Finally the act authorized grants of $5 million a year for nine years, to be apportioned among states involved in any approved program, and $400,000 annually for administration of such grants.

The concept of Seven TVA's—of the nation as a union of river-basin societies—had been discarded, partly because of the diversity of social and economic conditions in river basins. Yet the integrity of a basin for purposes of water and land-related resources was preserved. For two decades following the Pick-Sloan plan, the water resource agencies of states and field representatives of federal agencies had developed a sophisticated coordination, which was available when the 1965 act was passed. At the same time, the act set up a central council with a Washington office, and authorized it, in the manner of other agencies, to employ a Civil Service staff with specified continuing functions. Thus permanence in river-basin planning was to be maintained in the future. This act—the first statutory measure as distinct from temporary congressional or presidential commissions on the subject—was a tribute to the vision of George Norris.

Soil Conversation

THE NORTH AMERICAN continent as revealed to Europeans at the end of the 15th century was a world of rich resources. It contained vast areas of fertile land, together with some poor land, magnificent forest coverage, enormous wealth in minerals, above and below the surface, and natural means of communication in rivers and lakes that tied the sections together. In the portion of the continent destined to pass to the United States the aborigines were primitive in culture and able to do little more than scratch the surface of the land they occupied.

The newcomers, to whom these resources passed, were more energetic, but also more exploitive in developing them than the natives. The exploitation began at Jamestown in the form of single-cropping of tobacco. It continued on other frontiers in the growing of food and fiber. Single-cropping was an advantageous form of farming on the frontier. This was because the soil was the cheapest of the elements used in producing crops. Capital and abundant labor would have been required to maintain fertility, and both were more expensive than the soil. From the point of view of quick profit the using up of fertility was the cheapest and best farming. After years of single-cropping in tobacco, cotton, wheat, or corn, the soil ceased to yield abundant returns. It was then disposed of to later comers, and the same process was repeated on a new frontier. Exploitive farming was relied on until it became a habit. The habit persisted after the frontier stage had passed, when more conservative farming would have been more profitable,

A problem more serious than soil depletion was soil erosion. Erosion was a natural occurrence on steep hillsides and on mountains. It occurred especially where rain came down in pelting storms. Where rain falls in prolonged drizzles, as in New England, erosion of soil is unlikely. But over wide stretches of the United States the combination occurs of steep slopes and rain that comes in pelting downpours.

The South was more subject to erosion from water than the North. Its heaviest rains and runoff occurred in the late winter—in February and March—when topsoil on steep hillsides, left uncovered after harvest and thawed by mild weather, was washed down the slopes and carried off to sea. The Piedmont Plateau of the southern Atlantic states, the southern portion of the Allegheny Plateau, and the Ozark Mountain region became tragically eroded areas.

Three stages occur in the process of erosion by water. In the first stage the soil is exhausted of its humus. This is the element that ties the soil together. It consists of decayed matter of various kinds and rootlets of plant growth, all of which act as a binder. When this element becomes exhausted by exploitive farming the soil is like sand; it is lifeless. The second stage of water erosion is what is known as ''sheet'' erosion, which is the horizontal peeling off of the topsoil, the portion of most value. That stage took place so gradually in many parts of the United States that it was hardly known to have happened. Sheet erosion can be ascertained only when comparisons can be made of land levels where grass cover is retained, as in cemeteries, and the levels of adjacent cropland. The final form of water erosion is gullying, or perpendicular washing—the cutting of deep gashes or gorges in the soil.

Wind as well as water is an instrument of soil erosion. It is destructive especially in the dry western parts of the United States, notably on the Great Plains. It operates after prolonged droughts. In the springtime high winds come up from the southern Plains, pick up soil that has become powdery after years of drought, carry it far to the north, then turn eastward toward the Atlantic seaboard. That was notably the case in the duststorms of the 1930's, the ''black blizzards'' as they were called. The same phenomenon occurred in the mid-1950's and the mid-1960's.

Some soils are carried off more easily by winds than others. The light soils—the so-called soft soils—which become pulverized in prolonged droughts, are especially volatile. Unfortunately on the Great Plains much of the terrain is soft soil, especially in the ''dust bowl'' areas of the Texas Panhandle and the areas adjacent to it in eastern Colorado and western Kansas. Soil of that kind became a hazard when plowed. It should have been kept permanently under a protective grass cover. In the black blizzards of the 1930's as much as two inches of topsoil over entire states are estimated to have been lost in a single year.

The local loss is not the only damage from water and wind erosion. Loss is inflicted where the debris, carried by water or wind, is deposited. Channels of rivers and harbors become clogged with silt, and, to restore their usefulness, costly dredging becomes necessary. Irrigation reservoirs in the semi-arid West lose their storage capacity. An example is Lake Mead, behind Hoover Dam, in which deposits of silt have become a problem. The channel of the lower Arkansas is another illustration. To retard the process of sedimentation, construction of dams on the upper waters of river systems becomes necessary to catch and hold the silt.

The problems of soil destruction did not trouble the American public deeply in the period when land was free and abundant. No active public opinion could be aroused, though disastrous results of soil destruction were pointed out by specialists, especially by those in agricultural colleges. The attitude of the ordinary farmer was that soil erosion is bad, but is an inevitable process of nature and has to be endured. In the days of Theodore Roosevelt some conservation sentiment developed in the United States, but was directed more to the saving of forests than conserving soil. Conservation of the soil became an issue in the presidential campaign of 1932, in which Franklin D. Roosevelt urged the project of a Civilian Conservation Corps, partly as a relief to unemployed youth. Following his election the CCC camps were established, and, in the same year, an Emergency Soil Erosion Service was set up in the Department of the Interior.

In 1934 a presidential commission, the National Resources Board, directed that a broad survey be made of the erosion problem. The spectacular conclusion of its erosion report was that approximately 35 million acres of formerly cultivated land had been ruined by gullying, that, in addition, an area nearly four times as large had been stripped of its topsoil, and that additional millions of acres had been damaged. A map, submitted with the report, exhibited in shadings of black and gray the location and severity of the loss (109). The area that gullying had destroyed was about the size of Pennsylvania, Massachusetts, and Connecticut combined. The heaviest losses lay in the South. They were in the Piedmont of the southeastern states, the Allegheny Plateau west of it, and the Ozark Mountains.

Compounding the loss of soil by erosion were the losses where erosion debris was deposited. They were described in generalized terms in the report. The damage was to water-power locations, to municipal water supply systems, to irrigation projects, and to channels of navigation in rivers and harbors. The damage reduced the usefulness of works of construction upon which the federal and state governments had invested billions of dollars of public funds. Also, on the Great Plains duststorms scattered their debris far and wide. Drifts blanketed fields and houses and choked rivers and lakes. Part of the loss was redeemable. New storms blew soils back in place. The Great Plains have been for ages a land of instability, with soil blown back and forth across it. But part of the soil blew into rivers and lakes and was beyond reclaiming.

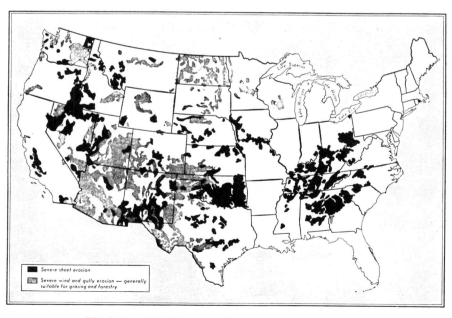

109. Distribution of Erosion, 1934 (from the National Resources Board)

The data gathered in preparing the soil-erosion report and map were challenged as to their reliability. They were said to have exaggerated the extent of the losses. The damage in the windstorms of the Great Plains was, in particular, challenged. The director of the report, Hugh H. Bennett, was an internationally known scientist in the field, and, though the report and map were drawn up in haste, and contained exaggerations, both have stood up well in the light of later studies.

In April 1935 Congress adopted the Soil Conservation Act, by which the Soil Conservation Service was established in the Department of Agriculture. In the act Congress for the first time accepted as a national responsibility the prevention of soil erosion. Bennett was made the head of the Service, and the functions relating to it, previously in the Interior Department, were transferred with him.

The functions of the Service were primarily educational. The principles and techniques of soil conservation were particularly stressed. Among the agency's publications was a periodical, *Soil Conservation*, which had wide circulation. It was a manual of methods and techniques, helpfully accompanied by illustrations. Practical exemplifications of method followed. Demonstration projects to the number of 150 were set up by the Service in various parts of the United States to teach methods of meeting regional conservation problems. They were developed in cooperation with agricultural colleges.

The methods taught were, for the most part, simple and inexpensive. For the preservation of soil fertility the methods emphasized were well known but too often neglected—crop rotation, the growing of cover crops, manuring and fertilizing, and also green manuring—the plowing of green crops into the soil. For the prevention of soil erosion, the methods were similarly plain and inexpensive. They differed from place to place depending on the conditions of slope and climate. Where land had a marked slope, terracing was recommended. The variety most widely practiced was inexpensive—merely a shifting of soil with a tractor and a heavy wing plow. The objective was the relocating of soil so as to slow runoff in rainstorms. The slower runoff reduced the cutting and washing power of the water. Terracing of a more costly sort, involving retaining walls, was also encouraged where necessary.

A vital technique, taught for sloping land, was contour plowing. This is horizontal plowing, the furrows so produced remaining constantly at the same elevation. The furrows serve as parallel gutters on the slope and check the runoff. Furrows cut by plowing up and down a slope, to conform with fencing, become runways for water and invite gullying.

Another method of protecting soil on sloping land taught by the Conservation Service was strip cropping. This was the planting of strips of hay or oats alternately with strips of row crops, such as corn, requiring cultivation. The strips of hay or oats served to check the runoff of water. They held and absorbed or at least they strained the water as it passed through.

For sloping pastureland, contour ridging was advocated by the Conservation Service. The sod was slightly raised, or ridged, on the contour. The ridges caught the rain and held it long enough to permit the water to soak in. Liming of pastures was emphasized with the same object in view. New cover crops were introduced, especially to the hill lands of the South. A Japanese variety of clover, lespedeza, was brought there, which became popular. From Switzerland was brought ladino, a broad-leaved clover. In gullies a Japanese vine was introduced—kudzu—the annual growth of which was 50 to 60 feet, which rendered service both as cover and fodder.

The problem of gullied land, particularly in the Piedmont, was met in the New Deal era and later by the construction of check dams in gullies already so deep as to discourage a uniform use of the land for pasturage. The building of such dams was a prominent part of the CCC program of the New Deal. The sides of the gullies were planted with protective vines such as kudzu, or clovers of one sort or another.

On the Great Plains various measures were developed to check duststorms. Where the soil was soft and likely to blow the advice was to maintain grass as a cover. In Colorado, in 1951, a compulsory grass ordinance was adopted to apply to areas especially subject to blowing. Nurseries were established by the Soil Conservation Service to grow seeds of various grasses, which were distributed to farmers virtually free.

In areas where soil was hard and where grain could be grown without undue risk, farmers were taught to let the stubble of wheat or sorghum remain after harvest as protection to the soil until just before a new crop was seeded in. The stubble held the soil in place and protected it against the wind. In such areas lister ridging also was employed. This was done by a special tool, called a lister, which ridged the earth while not disturbing the stubble. The ridges kept the finer earth particles in place. On the Plains the soil blows back and forth much of the time. If dust is held in place by lister ridging it can be worked back into the land in a subsequent year. A season's crop may be lost in a storm, but at least the soil has not blown off. Other practices, such as alternate years of fallowing, were urged to preserve moisture in the subsoil.

One of the notable adventures in soil conservation on the Great Plains was the "shelterbelt project." This was the planting of trees on the treeless, semi-arid plains for breaking the velocity of winds. The concept originated on the Russian steppes, where climate and soil resemble those on the Great Plains. Windbreaks of trees were already established in Texas as the result of local initiatives. As a national effort, the shelterbelt project was announced in January 1934 by President Roosevelt. In an executive order he designated a zone 100 miles wide, running from northwestern North Dakota to north central Texas, just west of the line of semi-aridity, within which owners of land were encouraged to plant trees in belts along the borders of their property. The trees were, in part, to be deciduous and drought-resisting—cottonwoods, American plum, chokecherry, box elder, willow, burr oak, American elm, ash, sycamore, Chinese elm, and Osage orange. In part, they were to be evergreens, useful as windbreaks—blue spruce, western white spruce, pine, Rocky Mountain juniper, and eastern red cedar. Soil factors were to dictate the plantings, both as to the kind of tree and its location.

In its early years the project was dogged by disbelief in its feasibility and by divisions of interest and authority. The climate of the western Great Plains and the age-long absence of forest there raised skepticism as to its feasibility. The interest of cattlemen in keeping the area closed to settlers and the differences of outlook between the Forestry Service and the Soil Conservation Service added to the disbelief. In 1934 the project began under the supervision of the Forestry Service. In 1936, when funds for the project were withheld by Congress, the WPA met the emergency with funds and men from the CCC. In the following year funds were voted to the Forestry Service to aid farmers in tree planting, though without specifying wind-erosion control among the objectives sought.

In the meantime the Soil Conservation Districts on the Plains had been encouraged to plant trees for wind-erosion control. In 1942 the Department of Agriculture withdrew from the Forestry Service the aspect of tree planting that had erosion control as its purpose, and transferred it to the Soil Conservation Service. With this clarification came the first direct appropriation for tree planting as a method of soil-erosion control. In the period 1934–42 nurseries of the Forestry Service had provided 14 million saplings to farmers, a large part of which were for protection from wind erosion.

In the 1930's debate was continuous as to the outcome of tree planting on the western Plains. The year 1941 happily brought the best rains in a decade and the survival rate of trees was 70 to 80 percent, depending upon the region. The discussions of the 1930's drew upon the past history of the Plains. Those sponsoring the project maintained that, even in the dust bowl, trees would survive. They had grown there until fires and drought destroyed them. Persistent doubters, especially cattlemen, maintained that the survival rate of the trees was due to the fact that the dry cycle had worn itself out. As wind erosion lessened, some doubters maintained that the explanation was contour plowing.

Whatever the role of trees in reducing wind erosion, no one doubted that, if they could be grown on the Plains, they would be of value, simply as trees. They would intercept snow on farms in the winter and increase thus the moisture in the spring; they would beautify the land; and they would attract birds that would, in turn, control harmful insects.

In the decade of the 1950's the survival rate of trees planted on the Plains continued to be 70 to 80 percent. By 1964 over 200 million trees had been planted and the project had won recognition as a contribution both to forestry techniques and to an effective mode of rescuing the Plains from soil erosion. In 1965 approximately 40,458 acres of the Plains had been converted into forest land in the form of tree belts. What had been a controversial New Deal project, described as one of the "most ridiculous ever submitted to the American people," turned out to be a success.

Thus, by a variety of soil-conservation methods, wind erosion on the Plains was put in check. In 1964 drought was severe, but soil-conservation practices, fostered by generous congressional and state grants, and used by informed farmers in the late 1950's and early 1960's, blunted the effects of the wind. Those who remember the duststorms of earlier drought periods remarked upon the difference. Control of wind erosion was a 20th century adventure in the winning of the West.

An essential adminstrative unit employed throughout the nation by the Service was the Soil Conservation District, operating under state charters. A standard form, distributed by the Department of Agriculture, was approved by Congress in 1937. Its principle was that the boundaries of the districts conform with natural features, rather than with county lines. The first of such districts was set up in 1937. By 1965 the number was 2989, almost as many as the counties in the continental United States. By 1972, 90 percent of the farmland of the nation was included in these self-governing Soil Conservation Districts. Each district was run by a board of directors consisting of farmers elected by farmers.

For each district a basic erosion-control plan was drawn up embodying local knowledge of the terrain and the technical expertise of agents of the Soil Conservation Service. The plans were not compulsory, but could be made so by vote of the resident farmers. The Service also devoted much time to drawing up conservation plans for individual farmers. In the mid-1960's nearly a million and a half basic plans for individual farms were in existence. On the Great Plains 60 percent of the farms had such plans; in the Southeast, 40 percent. Conservation measures too big for individuals or groups to undertake are left to the district to carry out with the aid of heavy equipment loaned by the Soil Conservation Service. The advice of the Service is free, and the costs are shared by the government and the farmers.

In 1936 Congress undertook to advance the work of soil conservation by means beyond those of the Soil Conservation Service. It offered payments to farmers for practicing soil-conservation principles, provided they cooperated also, in other agricultural programs of the government. This was done in the Soil Conservation and Domestic Allotment Act, popularly known as SCADA. It was a program, continued in later legislation, to induce farmers engaged in growing basic crops to agree to restrictive allotments of output, as well as to adopt soil-conserving practices. This was an aspect of production control and is deferred to later chapters. But the earlier concepts of the soil-conservation movement of the 1930's endured during the subsequent years. The spectacle of a nationwide destruction of the soil in visible forms had, from the mid-1930's onward, worked its way into the conscience of the American public.

Agricultural Overproduction and Production Control to 1941

WITH THE ADVANCE of population across the dry-farming and irrigation areas of the West an immense increase occurred in the production of American food and fiber. The production greatly exceeded what could be disposed of. This was an old American problem. It was present in the colonial period in the form of the problem of unsold tobacco. In the national period it took the form of the overproduction of food and fiber. The normal market course was that the demand in Europe for American farm produce was high in wartime, prices responded, and farmers in the United States prospered. With the return of peace demand fell off heavily and American farmers were in trouble. That correlation was illustrated strikingly in the early national years by the record of the Napoleonic wars. The demand for American food was insatiable during the wars, prices rose, and American farmers prospered. Then the wars ended and so did the prosperity. A like correlation appeared in the era of the 1850's. A great expansion occurred in European industry and was sustained by American food and fiber. Then the American surplus proved greater than even the need of Europe, and the twenty years from 1877 to 1897 were, for American farmers, a tale of woe. The woe was exhibited in such manifestations of farmer distress as Grangerism and Populism.

In the early years of the 20th century American farmers seemed at last to have become free of dependence on the European market for their prosperity. From 1898 to the outbreak of World War I a swiftly growing urban population in the United States and an expanding industry absorbed a larger and larger part of the American production of food and fiber. The European market was less and less essential. A happy balance was established domestically between production and consumption. The golden age of American agriculture seemed to have arrived in the period 1909–14. Prices of farm produce were stable and on a par with the prices paid by farmers for what they had to buy. The value of farmland in the country as a whole doubled in this period.

Then came World War I, and the balance between production and consumption was again upset. An enormous European demand for American food and fiber was built up. The powers fighting Germany relied chiefly on the United States and Canada for food. They could draw little from South America or from Australia because of distance and the problem of German submarines. They could get none from Russia after the Revolution. After 1917, when the United States entered the war and sent an army to Europe, the American government shipped even more food abroad.

The acreage planted to crops in the United States increased correspondingly. About 40 million acres of pastureland were plowed up for wheat, chiefly in the dry-land area, and 5 million acres of forest were turned to farming. Exports of wheat, pork, and pork products multiplied. The old heavy reliance on the European market to absorb the farm surplus was re-established.

With the close of the war the overseas demand declined. Europeans were too poor after the war to pay for American produce. Instead of wheat, they ate cheaper black bread; instead of lard, they consumed vegetable oils. Of meat, they simply ate less. In an attempt to acquire self-sufficiency European governments raised tariff and currency barriers against American food. They also tended to buy food where they sold their manufactures. They were unable to sell sufficient manufactures to the United States because of American tariffs.

For a brief time after the war the American government kept up an artificial market for food in Europe. It did so by substantial loans to its allies. Of the loans a third were used for the purchase of American farm produce. When the loans ceased the market for American produce shrank. When the market shrank American farmers reduced production.

But elsewhere a wheat expansion occurred, largely in the dry-land areas of Canada, Australia, and Argentina. A greater amount of meat was produced in South America and in Australia; a great cotton expansion developed in Brazil, India, and Egypt. Europe, to a large extent, became free of the old dependence on the United States for food, cotton, and tobacco. American farmers were confronted not only by a shrunken European demand for their produce, but by competition from other parts of the world. Their surplus fell back on the home market.

The home market for food grew somewhat after the war. But the rate of growth was slower than normal. The reason was a decline in both immigration and the American birth rate. The rate of the population increase in the years 1925–30 was less than half that of the preceding five years.

At the same time the home market for grain was diminished by another development. Horses and mules were disappearing in the cities and on the farms. They were giving way to autos, trucks, and tractors. Land previously used to grow feed for horses and mules was used to produce grain for humans. The result of all these forces was a collapse in agricultural prices in the 1920's and 1930's.

An accompaniment of the depression in prices was a major shrinking of cropland. Between 1919 and 1929 more than 32 million acres were withdrawn from cultivation and put into pasture, chiefly in the eastern half of the country. Most of the retired land was of marginal fertility and, from an economic point of view, was wisely withdrawn. Unfortunately no reduction in output followed, for while eastern acreage was withdrawn, more than an equivalent was put under the plow in the semi-arid Plains, devoted to dry farming.

Overproduction is a more stubborn affliction in agriculture than in industry. In industry, when it occurs, management closes factories. In farming, closing down involves loss of subsistence, often loss of land and home, through foreclosure of a mortgage or eviction for nonpayment of taxes. Wheat and corn farmers were bound to those crops by the specialized nature of their equipment. If they undertook to offset low prices by higher output, the result was merely further depression of price. What was especially hard to bear was that the farmer was helpless both as to what he produced and what he bought. What he produced was sold at the world price. What he bought was paid for at domestic prices.

In 1921 the so-called farm bloc was formed in Congress. It was a small group of senators and representatives recruited from both parties, chiefly from the Middle West and the Great Plains. In the Harding administration it held the balance of power in the Senate and steered a good deal of farm legislation to enactment. It obtained the Packers and Stockyards Act of 1921, which empowered the Secretary of Agriculture to prevent manipulation of prices by meat packers. It won, also, the Grain Futures Act of 1922, which conferred on the Secretary of Agriculture like powers over grain traders. In 1923 the Agricultural Credit Act was adopted, which eased the terms on which farmers could borrow money. In 1922 the Capper-Volstead Act was passed which exempted farmers' cooperatives from prosecution under the antitrust laws. But these measures failed to lighten the depression in agriculture.

Measures of congressional relief became more and more direct to rescue American farmers from the surpluses. The manner of rescue was set forth in the McNary-Haugen bills. The rescuer was to be an export commission which would buy up the annual surpluses of specified American farm commodities at a price higher than the world price and unload them in Europe at whatever they would bring. The losses incurred in the process would be assessed on growers' associations—on those engaged in growing wheat or other staples that were in trouble. By removing the surpluses, domestic prices of farm produce would be raised and, once raised, would be kept so, behind a high tariff wall.

Throughout the years 1924–28, McNary-Haugen bills were before Congress. But they merely aroused sectional clashes. In the East they were resisted on the ground that lifting food prices for farmers would raise living costs arbitrarily for city workers. In the South they were opposed, partly on constitutional grounds, partly because in the original bills tobacco and rice were overlooked.

In 1927 a revised measure including tobacco and rice was brought into Congress. Southern planters were now in such distress that they swallowed their constitutional scruples and voted for the bill. The West gave the bill complete support, except for isolated recusants in Kansas and Colorado. The one in Kansas had already announced he was not a candidate for re-election. The Colorado dissenter—a newspaper publisher—was soon sent into retirement.

The approved bill was promptly vetoed by President Calvin Coolidge. His argument was that if farm prices went up the wages of eastern factory workers would have to follow. The sale of American manufactures in Europe would drop, especially if Europeans were able to buy American raw materials and food at cut-rate prices. The only safe cure for what ailed American farmers was reduction of their output. The veto was not overridden, and the same fate awaited a similar bill passed in 1928. This repetition of defeat was salutary only in that it stressed the need for production control.

In the Hoover administration another temporary expedient was tried in the form of the Agricultural Marketing Act of 1929, the first major farm-support program in American history. A Federal Farm Board was established, to which was entrusted a loan fund of $500 million. Two types of loans to farmer organizations were authorized, one to cooperatives, to enable them to construct better storage facilities, the other to "stabilizing corporations" formed by cooperatives on a statewide basis, to enable them to buy and store surpluses until prices had improved. The theory animating the program was that the surpluses were a temporary phenomenon that would disappear if lifted off the market. Domestic prices did rise somewhat above world prices for two years, but that led to a prompt increase in the amount of cropland harvested and prices again collapsed. Ultimately a large part of the wheat stored under the act was given to the Red Cross for famine-stricken China, some was bartered to Brazil for coffee, and the rest was gradually sold. The loss to the government in three years of operation under the act was $329 million of the $500 million in the loan fund. Also, in the 1930's, the eastern industrialized seaboard succumbed to depression, and its capacity for absorbing the surpluses of the West and South departed.

In 1933 Congress, urged by the Roosevelt administration, passed the Agricultural Adjustment Act, a new plan for meeting the farm-surplus crisis. The idea was to restrict crop production. Farmers would make contracts with the Department of Agriculture whereby the number of acres in a farm devoted to any specified crop would be reduced. The contracts were to be administered by county growers' associations. Seven crops were named: wheat, corn, hogs, cotton, tobacco, rice, and dairy products. All were affected by world market prices; all had to undergo some sort of processing before consumption. With reduction in the acreage devoted to these crops, prices were expected to rise to the level of the five golden years preceding World War I. Farmers would once again be prosperous and the nation would recover from the Great Depression.

To induce farmers to agree to reduction in acreage, money payments were to be made to them. The payments were to be financed by a so-called processing tax, levied on initial processors. In the case of wheat, the tax was to be levied on flour millers; in the case of cotton, on textile mills; and so on. Ultimately the tax would be passed on to the American consumer.

The act proved effective. Contracts to reduce acreage were made by wheat growers for 80 percent of their acreage in the season of 1933–34. With cotton growers about a quarter of their acreage was taken out of cultivation. Farmers were not eager to curtail, but they needed the payments. Nature came to the aid of the plan. A severe drought struck the farming West, which drastically reduced wheat harvests. A great improvement occurred in the prices of wheat and cotton. They almost doubled in the year 1933–34. The results of the act were so encouraging that in 1934 Congress took a more radical step. It applied to cotton, in the Bankhead Cotton Control Act, a compulsory, rather than a voluntary, acreage restriction.

In an act of August 1935 Congress encouraged exports of United States agricultural surpluses to foreign countries, and inhibited imports of foreign primary and processed agricultural commodities. Section 32 of the act provided that in each fiscal year 30 percent of gross customs receipts be maintained in a separate fund by the Secretary of Agriculture. The fund was ''to encourage the exportation of agricultural commodities . . . by the payment of benefits in connection with [losses] in the exportation thereof.'' Section 22 of the act was an authorization to the President, with the advice of the Tariff Commission, to limit the importation of any article that would ''interfere with any program . . . undertaken, or reduce the amount of any processed article from any commodity, with respect to which an adjustment program is in operation.'' Thus Congress protected the price of agricultural commodities sold at home, while encouraging farm exports to world markets. In other words, a two-price system was set up.

In 1936 the whole domestic crop-restriction program ran afoul of the Supreme Court. In the case of *United States v. Butler*, brought on behalf of a Massachusetts textile corporation (Hoosac Mills), the Court declared the processing tax unconstitutional. By a 6–3 vote it declared that Congress could tax only for the general welfare and that the processing tax was for state welfare, since agriculture was under state control. Moreover, contracts made by the federal government with farmers to reduce acreage were an unconstitutional interference with the rights of states to regulate agriculture. Because of the power of Congress to regulate foreign trade, there was no challenge to the law of 1935 concerning export and import measures to keep domestic agricultural prices above the world level.

The Court decision made necessary new legislation to achieve acreage reduction. In 1936 Congress adopted the Soil Conservation and Domestic Allotment Act (SCADA). It was framed to circumvent the Supreme Court. The devices used to do so were three. The purpose of the act was declared to be soil conservation, clearly a national purpose. Invitations were sent to farmers, instead of contracts—invitations to reduce plantings in designated crops, and to put the acres into soil-conserving crops. Payments to farmers would come out of appropriations from general Treasury funds. No special tax would be levied.

The act was made completely Court-proof, but it was not effective as a method of acreage reduction. It did not offer big enough payments to attract farmers, and an actual increase in wheat and cotton acreage took place in 1937. Some farmers took only their poorer land out of cultivation and greatly increased their yield on more fertile acres by applying more fertilizer and planting better seed. They were able to collect payments from the government and at the same time raise crops almost as large as before.

In 1938 Congress adopted the Agricultural Adjustment Act of 1938, a thoroughgoing crop-restriction measure. It dealt with five staples—cotton, wheat, corn, tobacco, and rice—which were in great oversupply. The Secretary of Agriculture was to make an estimate, well before the growing season, of the amount needed of each staple. It was to include home and foreign demand, and as much carry-over as was desirable. On this basis the aggregate acreage necessary to produce the amount was to be reckoned. An acreage allotment was then assigned to individuals and any producer of staples who agreed to remain within his allotment was to receive conservation payments.

The act provided for two classes of conservation payments. The payments made to producers of the five staples was one class. These farmers received conservation payments for performing conservation practices on their allotted acreage and staying within their allotments. The other class of payments were to go to all farmers who carried out soil-conservation practices. In those respects the act was an affirmation of SCADA.

But the act went further. For each of the specified staples a "parity price" was to be announced that would, if attained, give the commodity a purchasing power for articles that a farmer had to buy equivalent to the purchasing power of the commodity in the base period, August 1909 to July 1914. A government corporation, the Commodity Credit Corporation (CCC), was created by the act, and authorized to store the five specified farm commodities and make loans to farmers on them as security. A farmer could store a portion of his crop, for instance wheat, if the market price was low, and receive a loan on it. The Secretary of Agriculture was given the authority to change the level of loans from time to time, but within upper and lower limits set by Congress. The amount of a loan might be as high as 75 percent of the parity price of a commodity or as low as 52 percent. This flexibility was designed to insure an "ever normal granary," as described by Henry A. Wallace, Secretary of Agriculture. If the Department anticipated a carry-over too low in a given year, the amount of the loans was to be set high. If the actual carry-over proved so high as to depress prices, the amount of the loans was to be kept low to discourage planting. In either case farmers would be assured of support to carry on essential operations and would have assurance of stable prices.

Almost as an afterthought the act provided for direct "parity payments" in addition to conservation payments and price-support loans. They were to compensate producers of the five staples for the difference between current prices and "parity prices." They did not continue for any length of time. They were the work of farm lobbyists and were opposed by the Roosevelt administration. Something comparable to them was to be set up many years later.

The act of 1938 was not compulsory. But a farmer who did not comply with his acreage allotment received none of the conservation or parity payments. He became ineligible likewise for loans on stored commodities. The inducements to comply were high. The loans on stored crops were non-recourse in character. If the market price of a stored commodity rose after a loan, the farmer was privileged to pay off the loan, recover his commodity from storage, and sell it at the favorable market price.

If, on the other hand, the market price fell below the level at which the loan had been made, the farmer had the privilege of allowing the commodity to pass to the government. The government, in effect, bought the commodity at the loan price, which was higher than the market level. Thus the loan price became the "support price." This crop-loan–price-support mechanism was one of the most enduring of the agricultural reforms of the New Deal.

The act of 1938 also provided for marketing quotas for the five specified commodities. These were to be established by the Agriculture Department, if the prospect of a depressingly large harvest in any of the five commodities appeared on the horizon. In that case a referendum would be held among farmers of that crop as to whether marketing quotas should be applied. If two-thirds of the farmers, in wheat for example, voted to accept marketing quotas, all wheat farmers would be assigned a marketing limit. If a farmer were to market more than his quota he was to be taxed on the excess. As a method of crop limitation the marketing quota was superior to acreage limits. It was directed to a finite quantity—the amount of produce that would move to market. Acreage limitation had left the outcome open to such uncertainties as weather, insect pests, soil fertility, or the amount of fertilizer applied. Marketing quotas could be based on interstate commerce, whereas acreage allotments were within states and subject to their laws. Marketing quotas were also superior in that they left the outcome to a vote—a two-thirds acceptance by those affected. In 1939 the constitutionality of the marketing quota came before the Supreme Court in the case of *Mulford v Smith*. The Court had been remade by President Roosevelt in his own image, and by a 7–2 vote it upheld the constitutionality of the tobacco quota involved in the case.

But the act as a whole was not effective in meeting the problem of overproduction. The number of acres planted declined, without an equivalent decline in harvests. Millions of acres were taken out of cotton production, but the harvest remained distressingly high. Cotton planters took the payments of the government. They then bought fertilizer and better seed, and on their allotted acres increased their production. Corn farmers did the same.

The payments distributed to farmers were staggering in amount. They totaled in the year 1939 $709 million. The loans made to farmers by the Commodity Credit Corporation were backed by enormous quantities of produce. The ever normal granary threatened to overflow. Loans were made to farmers on grain sealed in their own barns. But the barns were insufficient to hold all the grain that was security for loans. Temporary sheet-metal bins were widely built to hold wheat and corn. Abandoned school buildings and old churches were filled with grain. In the early 1940's the Commodity Credit Corporation owned or had loans on 519 million bushels of wheat (1942), 477 million bushels of corn (1941), and 10.7 million bales of cotton (1940). The government held close to an entire year's crop of cotton on loans. Then Providence or Satan intervened. World War II arrived and the vast stores of the Commodity Credit Corporation became a godsend.

But the basic problem—how an ungovernable surplus was, in normal times, to be dealt with—was far from solved. Cynics, who had witnessed the intervention of war as a solution of the peace-time problem, ironically observed that the only way to solve the overproduction evil was never to permit peace to rage too long.

Agriculture and
Farm Policy
During and After
World War II

WHEN WORLD WAR II began with Hitler's invasion of Poland in 1939, the initial effect was a severe crisis in the American rural economy. Exports of farm products abruptly fell off—they dropped by a third in the year following the invasion. The agricultural depression remaining from World War I was greatly intensified. A major domestic crisis would have occurred except for the mammoth expenditures of the American government in rearmament, which brought a high rate of employment and encouraged domestic consumption.

The adverse initial impact of the war was due to the closing of the markets for American farm surpluses on which the American economy relied. The British, who had normally taken about half of these exports, had to cut their purchases. They were denied credit for purchases because American neutrality legislation denied credits to foreign buyers at war, as a result of experiences in World War I. Such cash as the British commanded they had to use to buy American munitions and steel. They purchased wheat from Canada and cotton from India or Egypt, where it could be done on credit. Germany, which had been taking a third of American farm exports, was no longer able to buy. Her ports were immediately put under blockade by the British fleet. France had been a less important market.

This initial phase of the war came to an end in 1940–41 with a series of events that shook the world. The German Army overran Denmark and Norway. Then with devastating power it swept over France, Belgium, and Holland. The British Army almost went down at Dunkirk. British cities were showered with German bombs. The British Isles were almost cut off from overseas help by German submarines and mines.

In January 1941, President Roosevelt appeared before Congress and asked that American neutrality laws be suspended, that they be replaced by a policy of Lend-Lease. Lend-Lease was urged as a means of rescuing the imperiled democracies of the world from Hitler and his associated dictators. In March 1941, Congress adopted the recommendation, and the immense sum of $7 billion was authorized as an initial aid to the democracies.

The Lend-Lease Act was one of the turning points in the war. It marked the active intervention by the United States in the conflict. Its title was "an act to promote the defense of the United States." Its real purpose was to align the United States with the powers fighting the dictators by making available to them the agricultural and industrial resources of the United States. It was intended to rescue, especially, the democracies of England and France, and later China.

In December 1941 came the Japanese attack on Pearl Harbor, partly in retaliation for Lend-Lease. This was followed by the German declaration of war on the United States. By the end of 1941 the United States was in the midst of the fighting. American farmers entered a new era. They no longer had unsalable surpluses, ruinously low prices, or government restrictions on output. They were taken into an era where the one great objective was to produce enough. Enough had to be raised for three great markets—the expanded market of a civilian population in the United States earning high wages, the market of the American armed forces overseas, and the immense markets of the Lend-Lease program.

To that opportunity they rose with enthusiasm. They produced record-breaking crops year after year. An increase of 35 percent over all previous totals of farm production was scored in the United States. American farmers demonstrated that in agriculture an increase of production is much easier to achieve than a decrease.

A combination of forces helped to produce the spectacular increase. One was the high prices the government paid for food. Another was the direction it gave to farmers. Each year the Department of Agriculture specified how much it needed of the important crops. It allocated production goals to states, counties, and individual farmers. It used the machinery of the Agricultural Adjustment Act of 1938 for this purpose. The machinery designed for restriction of output became the vehicle for increase.

Technical improvements were of high importance in increasing the output. Artificial fertilizer was used on American farms in quantities never before approached. A nationwide use was made of improved seed. The use of hybrid corn seed, which Henry A. Wallace helped to perfect, was important in the corn records that were established. The wheat "papooses" were of similar effect on the Plains. The scientific feeding of cattle was emphasized. Control of insects and pests was stressed. An example of this was the use of DDT for beetle control in the Maine potato fields. These new techniques constituted a consolidation of a decade of technological advance, a revolution in farming. A final important factor was favorable weather, especially in the semi-arid Plains; an extraordinary succession of good years of rainfall occurred there. St. Peter fought on the side of the Allies.

In earlier wars an increase in the mechanization of farming had been an important element in farm production. In the Civil War and in World War I this had been the case. It was not, however, the case in World War II. No great upsurge of mechanization occurred. The explanation is that the government clamped priorities on steel, and that the big farm-machinery plants devoted themselves to producing army tanks. But existing machinery was put to increased use by extension of working hours.

No great increase occurred in the acreage under crops. There was no general plowing up of lands on the Great Plains such as had occurred in World War I.

The amount of land used for crop production remained relatively stationary. The same amount of land, worked by 8 percent less farm labor, but with much more highly developed techniques, produced the record-breaking crops of the war.

An immense quantity of produce was sent to the allies of the United States. It was sent in highly concentrated forms, as soon as the Lend-Lease Act had passed. The big items were meat, fats, oils, dairy products, and eggs. The concentration was made as high as possible. Meat was sent in canned form, eggs were sent as powder, milk as dried milk or cheese. The reason for emphasis on high concentration was partly the great shortage of shipping and partly the wishes of the Allies, who asked to be saved the labor of converting half-finished foods into concentrated foods. Since Lend-Lease was virtually a gift, the Allies could afford to take their foods in this concentrated, expensive form.

Some critical shortages appeared. The most critical was the shortage of fats and vegetable oils, the result of territorial conquests made by Germany and Japan early in the war. Germany was able to seize the great fat-producing regions of Europe, the dairy areas of Holland and Denmark, the pork areas of the Balkans, the Ukraine, and Poland. The Japanese occupied the leading oil-seed areas of the Far East: Manchuria, the world's great soybean producer; the Philippine Islands, with its great production of coconuts; and the East Indies, another major center of coconut and palm oil. Japan thus controlled more than half the world's supply of vegetable oils.

In any economy, whether in peace or war, fats and oils are indispensable. They are a major food. They go also into industrial production: fats, for instance, into tin plate and high explosives; oils into paint and soaps. Measures had to be taken therefore to make good the losses of fats and oils. The measures were special incentive payments to hog and dairy farmers, to soybean farmers in Illinois, to flaxseed farmers in the Red River valley, and to southern farmers for the production of cottonseed oil and peanut oil. Enough new fats and oils were produced in this way, and by the saving of fats in homes, to meet all essential American needs and those of the Allies.

In contrast to the importance of fats and oils, wheat, which in other wars had been an export of enormous significance, was of little consequence in World War II, chiefly because shipping space could not be given it. Wheat was in such abundance in the United States throughout the war that much of it was used for the manufacture of alcohol. No shortage of wheat appeared in the world until after the close of the war. Then the United States and Canada saved the world from famine. The postwar years were more critical in some respects than the war years. The same urgency existed then, as during the war, for greater production of food and fiber.

The consequences of the war and of postwar urgencies on American farming were far-reaching. One was a transformation in the financial status of farmers. The debts which the depression of the 1930's had left were largely cleared away. Another evidence of financial improvement was the decline of farm tenancy.

A nationwide shifting of the rural economy and population were other results of the war. Already under way before the war, these changes were accelerated by it. A major part of the change occurred in the cotton country of the South. The Piedmont of the Carolinas and Georgia had long been in decline as a producer of cotton. Its hill farms were small and patchy, unsuited to thorough mechanization, unable to compete with the mechanized regions to the west. They were converted to pasture and cattle production, which involved a siphoning off of a large part of their population, partly to eastern cities. In a like quandary were the hill areas of eastern Mississippi and western Alabama, which also changed to pasture and cattle raising.

The tidewater of the South underwent the same transformation. Its soil, which was not rich or durable, had become worn over wide areas. It moved into truck gardening, sweet potatoes, and fruit. The war merely hastened a shift already under way. Even in the Black Belt of Alabama, which is comparable to the tidewater, the soil was eroded. The white chalk of the subsoil was showing through. The area had become a "gray belt." It turned to peanut production and cattle raising. Only in the floodplain of the Mississippi and in the Black Prairie of Texas were cotton producers holding their own in the old areas.

In the floodplain of the Mississippi, more especially in the Delta country, all conditions made for success. The soil was fertile and took fertilizer well, though it needed little. The plantations were big and made use of scientific knowledge and high-yield seed. The costs of production were low. The level land was mechanized more intensively than any other part of the cotton belt. Its plowing, seeding, weed control, and picking were all done by machinery. It produced more than a bale of cotton to the acre and the quality was high. The picking was done by means of mechanical "spindle fingers" that selected the white fiber out of the open bolls, twisting it loose and feeding it into blowers, and from blowers into "cages." These operations were all accomplished by mobile units in the fields.

The second of the old cotton areas that continued to prosper was Texas. Its centers of production were partly the rich areas of the Black Prairie. But the most striking development was in the Panhandle—the region of semi-aridity extending into southwestern Oklahoma. These areas had many of the advantages of the Delta country, especially the flatness of the terrain. But, in addition, they had the semi-aridity of the climate, which protected them against many of the pests afflicting the East. The great expansion of cotton in West Texas came with the phenomenal development of irrigation from underground pools. Texas was, in the 1940's and 1950's, the greatest cotton producer in the Union.

A new cotton kingdom was rising in the Far West. In the Imperial and San Joaquin valleys of California, the new production was a response to the engineering miracles by which the waters of the Colorado and the Sacramento were brought to them. These valleys attracted the footloose of the Middle West and Southwest. In Arizona the valley of the Gila was another segment of the cotton kingdom. It produced a long-staple cotton, known as Pima SI, with a lustrous fiber an inch and a half long, that was used for the manufacture of thread and specialty fabrics. It relieved American textile manufacturers of dependence on Egyptian cotton. These fields, especially those in California, were the attraction that drew domestic and alien migrants. The California fields were also the focal point of the increasing mechanization of agriculture in the postwar years, and of the migration of the cotton plant from the Atlantic tidewater to the Pacific. A more rapid withdrawal of cotton from the eastern seaboard would have occurred if the government had withdrawn its price supports, which enabled cotton farmers in the Piedmont to survive. In the last analysis, the government was subsidizing there a soil-destroying industry. The migration of cotton into areas of highest efficiency was accompanied by an overall decrease in land devoted to its production. The total cotton acreage in 1956 was the smallest in three-quarters of a century of American history, and yet the production was so large as to be a headache to the federal government.

Coinciding with the shift of cotton production to the Pacific West in the war and postwar era was the westward flow of population. The growth of population in California in the decade 1940–50 was 53.6 percent; in Oregon it was 59.3 percent; in Washington, 45.8 percent. The California upsurge reflected the Central Valley Project, but also the development of the aircraft industry. In Oregon and Washington the upsurge was the result chiefly of industrialization—of aluminum and atomic-energy developments drawn by the Columbia Basin Project.

Arizona and Nevada also registered big increases of population. In Nevada the growth was the result of new discoveries of copper ore and their development by the flotation process. The increase reflected likewise the discovery of precious metals and of lead, zinc, and tungsten ores. Together they brought greater riches than those of the Comstock lode. In Arizona the upsurge of population was chiefly the result of the development of the Morenci copper mine.

In the wheat and corn country of the Great Plains the population and economy declined. The census of 1950 revealed an actual loss of population in North Dakota and Montana. In South Dakota there was no loss, but virtually a standstill. In Nebraska and in Oklahoma there were losses.

Yet in this decade a sensational rise occurred in rural land values. For the nation as a whole they rose from $33.6 billion to $75.2 billion. In the North the increase was from $18.9 billion to $38.4; in the South, from $9.7 to $22.9 billion; in the West, from $5.0 to $13.8 billion. The principal forces in the increase were the need for food, the supports given by the government to farm produce, and the added increments of efficiency given to production by greater use of machinery and chemical fertilizers. The rise meant fortunes for landholders.

Other effects of the war and the postwar years were the creation of an enormous capacity for the production of farm staples, the re-creation of a heavy dependence on the overseas market, and a decline of interest in soil conservation. The pressure for food, especially in the postwar years, was greater than the pressure for soil conservation.

The war brought significant changes also into American diet. As a side effect of the shortage of fats, oleomargarine, a product of vegetable oils, including cottonseed oil, come into favor on American dinner tables. By 1957 the consumption of oleomargarine in the United States equaled that of butter, and by 1971 it was more than twice as high. This led to clashes between dairy and cotton farmers over the federal tax on oleomargarine. In 1950 the tax was repealed, after which oleo sold at a price of 30 cents a pound. Thereafter, with butter at a price of 80 cents or more, housewives bought oleo and the government acquired the butter and put it into cold storage.

But while cotton farmers triumphed in regard to oleo, they suffered elsewhere. The war enormously stimulated the manufacture of synthetic fibers, especially rayon and nylon. Rayon was an essential military product. In the form of rayon cord it went into heavy-duty tires for jeeps and for airplanes. It went also into coverings for gasoline tanks on airplanes to make them self-sealing. Nylon was used for parachutes and mountain tents. These two textile synthetics became firmly established during the war and have since invaded cotton markets everywhere. Rayon could be manufactured more cheaply than cotton could be grown. The combined production of rayon and nylon in the United States by the 1950's was almost the equal of 10 million bales of cotton—not far from a year's cotton crop.

The war also increased the number of foreign producers of cotton, especially those of Brazil, India, and Egypt. They were able during the war, and even more after it, to invade markets the United States had once dominated. In an earlier era 65 to 70 percent of the world's cotton production was located in the United States. By 1950 the figure had fallen to 40 percent. The increase in foreign production created problems for even the most efficient American cotton producers, but especially for small farmers of the South.

The price-support policies of the federal government were fundamentally affected by the war. These policies ultimately became highly controversial. Their evolution from peace to wartime is instructive. The support program in effect at the opening of the war was based on the Agricultural Adjustment Act of 1938, which encouraged farmers to withhold major staples from the market by storing them with the Commodity Credit Corporation as security for loans. This price support was cautious. It embraced only a few staples and the loans were on a sliding scale— between 52 and 75 percent of a parity price. This price support was considered in the best interest of the nation. It would protect farmers from such an utter collapse as had occurred in the 1920's and early 1930's. It gave farmers the same sort of protection that tariffs provided industry and that minimum-wage legislation afforded labor.

In 1941 and 1942, as a consequence of the war, this policy was transformed. In March 1941, as an aid to the imperiled democracies, Congress adopted the Lend-Lease Act, and the Secretary of Agriculture asked farmers to increase their production of essential foods. In July, Congress directed the Secretary to make eligible for price support, at 85 percent of parity, all commodities of which increased production was requested. This meant that not only the basic staples but others, including perishables, became eligible for loan support. Between 1941 and 1945, by proclamations under this authority, approximately two-thirds of the nation's farm produce became eligible for support loans.

In January 1942, after the United States entered the war, Congress adopted the Emergency Price Control Act to stabilize prices and wages. In October, in response to a special message of President Roosevelt, it adopted an amendment to that act, offered by Representative Henry Steagall of Alabama, giving rigid price support at 90 percent of parity to farm commodities that would be proclaimed eligible. That rate was to remain in force for the rest of the war and for two years after the war had been formally declared at an end.

This legislation reversed the principle of flexible price support. It established the principle of high and rigid supports for specified farm commodities for the duration of the war and for two years thereafter. The fighting ceased in the summer of 1945. But the war was not formally declared ended by President Truman until December 31, 1946. Under the Steagall amendment fixed supports would thus remain in effect until December 31, 1948.

In the meantime the congressional elections of 1946 gave control of Congress to the Republicans, who had no taste for rigid controls, but could not terminate them until the end of 1948. In July 1948, urged by the Farm Bureau Federation, they adopted the Hope-Aiken Act, which would have restored the prewar principles of flexible price supports between 60 and 90 percent of parity. But they agreed to an extension to December 31, 1949, of the high, rigid supports of the Democratic legislation of 1942.

The Hope-Aiken Act was resented by farmers who wished a perpetuation of the war levels of price support. It was resented especially by corn and cotton farmers. They bided their time until the Republicans came asking for votes in the presidential election of 1948. Then they gave the Republicans an election-day spanking. They ensured the re-election of Truman and gave the Democrats control of Congress. The punsters of the press chortled after the election that the Aiken Act had produced "achin'" for the Republicans all over the spanked end.

In October 1949, the Aiken Act was replaced, before it was scheduled to go into effect, by the Gore-Anderson Act. Officially known as the Agricultural Act of 1949, this was the work of western and southern farm lobbyists. It restored rigid price support at 90 percent of parity to six basic staples until January 1951. To another six non-basic commodities, including such perishables as milk products and potatoes, it gave support varying from 60 percent to 90 percent of parity.

The act was lax in heading off excessive production. The Secretary of Agriculture and the President wanted to deny a farmer eligibility for price support if he made only a nominal compliance with crop-control measures—if he reduced acreage in a staple that was in oversupply but diverted it to another crop also in oversupply. They wished a provision making a farmer eligible for support only if he made a "cross-compliance" with all crop-reducing measures. Congress refused such a statutory brake on excessive production. It gave the Department of Agriculture only administrative authority in such matters, which was insufficient. If Congress itself would not apply the brakes, the Department would not do it, for fear of being wrecked in the process. The Gore-Anderson Act was the triumph of a pressure group.

During this struggle the Department of Agriculture had been in search of a program that would satisfy both the farmers and the public. In 1949, Charles Brannan, the new Secretary, prepared a plan designed to do this. The Brannan Plan, as it came to be called, was a combination of old and new ideas. One old idea was rigid support at 90 percent of parity for the six basic staples. This was defended on the ground that farmers should know in advance of the planting season how much support they could count on, and thus how much they must plant to make a living. The 90 percent level was defended on the ground that it was a fair compromise. Some farm spokesmen were demanding much more. Senator Allen Ellender of Louisiana wanted 115 percent on cotton. A 90 percent level, Brannan maintained, would not lead to overproduction. A lower level would lead to overproduction inasmuch as farmers would have to raise more to survive.

A new idea in the Brannan Plan dealt with perishables, which were to go to market without government support. Their price was to be allowed to fall to any level the market would establish. But if the level was below a fair standard worked out by the government, subsidies covering the difference should be paid the farmer. Arguments for this proposal were that if perishables fell to a low level, they would be freely bought. Consumers would have the benefit of low-priced milk, butter, eggs, and fruit, which was better than storing them at the risk of spoilage. Perishables were essential to proper diet and their sale was important to farmers. Half or more of the income of farmers came from perishables. Because the system of price support was costly to the government, Brannan felt that a plan of direct subsidies would cost no more and would bring better results. The subsidy concept was opposed by Republicans on the ground that overproduction would result and would be almost impossible to head off.

An important new idea in the Brannan Plan was that government price support be allowed only to family-sized farms. No farmer or corporation engaged in farming whose sales of produce amounted to $25,000 or more a year should be eligible for price-support loans. In 1950 farms in this category produced 26 percent of the total national production. The argument of Brannan was that big operators needed no such aid, that by reason of their highly mechanized production they could succeed without it. According to a study published in 1954 by the Department of Agriculture, loans of a million dollars each went to several California operators and to others averaging $650,000 each. In Mississippi five loans were made to cotton operators averaging $480,000 each. In the state of Washington five loans to wheat producers averaged $216,000 each. Some capitalistic farms for years were producing not for the market at all, but for disposal of their crops to the government for support loans.

The Brannan Plan became immediately the football of party politics. Its proposals were unacceptable to controlling elements in both parties and it was never enacted. In the meantime the Gore-Anderson Act brought a torrent of surpluses upon the government. It piled up surpluses in amounts that staggered the nation. The Commodity Credit Corporation, which administered the crop-loan–price-support program, was overwhelmed. In April 1950, it held 900 million bushels of corn, 9 million bales of cotton, 192 million pounds of butter, and dried eggs and powdered milk in terrifying quantity.

Under existing law no item in this huge surplus could be sold except for 105 percent of the parity price, plus carrying charges, unless the stuff was spoiling. The result was that perishable items such as potatoes, acquired at $1.25 per 100 pounds, finally had to be furtively sold when they got old, as cattle feed, or exported at a cent a bag.

The Department of Agriculture, as far as it could, tried to keep surpluses from becoming completely uncontrollable. It put all six of the basic staples covered by the law under acreage allotments; it also put three of them under marketing quotas. But the quantities of produce pouring in on the Commodity Credit Corporation continued to be stupendous. The Corporation's funds proved inadequate. They had to be increased to $6,750,000,000. Never before in the nation's history had the surplus problem been so staggering or so bewildering.

Then came deliverance. In June 1950, the North Koreans invaded South Korea, and the United States and the United Nations intervened. Communist China sent in its armies. A third world war seemed in the making. Immense defense preparations were voted by Congress. The surpluses of the Commodity Credit Corporation melted away. Once again, as in 1941, deliverance from the farm surplus problem came in the form of a world disaster.

In July 1952, during the Korean War, Congress extended the support levels of the Gore-Anderson Act for two years. The renewal was put through Congress by a combination of Democrats and Republicans seeking support in that year's presidential campaign. During the campaign, Dwight D. Eisenhower, the Republican candidate, electrified the middle western farmers by two speeches in which he declared that the Republican party was pledged to help the farmer to get 100 percent of parity. His precise words were later in dispute. Whatever he said, he left the impression that he and a Republican Congress would be willing, if elected, to continue for a time price supports at 90 percent of parity.

The Republican victory at the polls, the close of the Korean War, and the appointment of the conservative Ezra T. Benson as Secretary of Agriculture, made clear that there would soon be a return to the principle of flexible price supports, and that new policies regarding farm surpluses were in the making. In July 1954, Congress adopted and the President approved the Agricultural Development and Assistance Act (Public Law 480). Its declared purpose was to reduce the farm surplus by sales to friendly countries that would agree not to re-export the commodities to unfriendly (Communist) countries. Both the Commodity Credit Corporation and private commercial companies who would purchase from the CCC would do the exporting. The latter would be reimbursed for any losses incurred in the transactions. Sales were to be managed so as not to derange world prices.

In payment for the surplus farm commodities the CCC, and private exporters co-operating with it, could accept local currencies from the purchasing countries. Such payments could be converted into local strategic materials for stockpiles maintained by the United States, or could be used to meet costs of maintaining United States educators and technicians in these countries. The act also provided for donations of food to friendly nations in case of famine or other emergencies. These clauses were to run for three years. An expenditure of $700 million was authorized to reimburse the CCC for losses in connection with its sales, and $300 million more for outright gifts of food. These transactions came to be known as the ''Food for Peace'' program.

A third section of the law dealt with the disposal of CCC food surpluses inside the United States and its possessions. The food could be released at cost to local, state, and federal agencies to meet emergencies or help needy persons. Among the recipients were nonprofit school lunch programs. Costs of delivering the food to these agencies were to be borne by CCC.

Six weeks after the enactment of the Food for Peace legislation Congress adopted the Agricultural Act of 1954, which related chiefly to price supports. It restored flexible, though still high supports for the basic commodities, and flexible, less high supports for non-basic commodities. In addition to according milk, butter-fat, and their products support between 75 and 90 percent, Congress authorized the CCC to open markets for these products in schools and veterans' hospitals. Hoping that lower levels would discourage production, Benson gradually reduced the loan levels to the lowest point permitted.

A section of the act dealt with the specific commodities to be set aside for the purposes of Public Law 480. They were wheat, cotton, cottonseed oil, butter, nonfat dry milk, and cheese. The amount of each in the ''set aside'' was to be over and above the annual carry-over, plus what was needed for normal annual marketing operations. The total value of the ''set aside'' was not to exceed $2.5 billion at any one time.

The outcome of the act was disappointing. The surplus problem grew steadily bigger. The CCC had to be given $12 billion in funds. Its wheat holdings rose to over a billion bushels. Not only were all government storage facilities filled, but also 422 vessels of the mothball fleet. The grain was stored wherever it could be kept dry.

Farmers were urged to build additional storage of their own, and were aided in this by the government. Wheat cannot be kept without deterioration for longer than three years and much of it in storage was two years old. The situation in regard to cotton was as bad.

Farm prices in the meantime continued to decline, partly because Benson cut the support rates to some extent, partly because in some cases no further storage was available and produce not adequately housed could get no support. Discontent with the act became widespread, but the principle of government price support of agricultural staples at 90 percent of parity, which had dominated American farm policy during World War II and after, was not easily put to rest even as late as 1956. Congress approved a measure restoring that level, but it was vetoed by President Eisenhower. Something had to be done for farmers in an election year, however, and an administrative increase in price supports went into effect for some staples, contrary to all Republican theory.

Just prior to the 1956 presidential election Congress adopted the Soil Bank Act, which the President signed. It embodied two principal concepts. One was the "acreage reserve," a four-year program to remove from cultivation 15 million to 20 million acres of good cropland that had been producing basic staples. Any farmer who entered the plan was to let part of such land lie fallow. He was to receive from the government annual payments equal to the net amount he would have earned if the land had been planted and harvested. The payments were to be in cash, or in produce from the government's surplus.

A second concept was the "conservation reserve," a program to remove from cultivation 20 million to 25 million acres of submarginal cropland and plant it to grass or to forest. If planted to grass it was to remain so for a minimum period of three years, or, if planted to trees, for a maximum of fifteen. A farmer adopting the program would recover from the government the bulk of the cost of establishing the cover, and, in addition, would receive an annual rent as compensation for the crops not grown. The project was designed to conserve land resources for the future, to put them in a "soil bank." The annual cost of maintaining the two kinds of reserves was estimated to be $1.2 billion. The act ran out in 1962, but the portion of it compensating farmers for converting submarginal land to other uses than crops was continued by later administrations in new legislation.

Two other measures of the Eisenhower administration became parts of the program of the Soil Conservation Service. The Watershed Protection and Flood Protection Act of 1954 encouraged local initiation of watershed proposals. With state approval of plans, the federal government would provide technical assistance and cost sharing in building dams to contain floodwaters on small streams. State cooperation was in keeping with the Benson philosophy.

The second measure, the Great Plains Conservation Act of 1956, was impelled by disastrous duststorms that had swept the Great Plains earlier that summer. The act was directed specifically at the prevention of wind erosion. It provided for long-term contracts not to exceed ten years with farmers and ranchers of the Great Plains to make changes in land or water use and to install, with the technical assistance of the Soil Conservation Service, any needed facilities. During the contract period the government would share the cost of whatever material and labor were necessary. The cost sharing would be in addition to government payments to which the farmer was entitled. The contract holder would forfeit payments if he failed to follow a scheduled plan of changes, or failed to observe soil-conservation practices. By July 1961 nearly 7000 such contracts were in effect in 366 counties of the Great Plains. One of the achievements of the program was the return to grass of large acreages ill-suited to crop cultivation. But these constructive measures received little publicity in the closing years of the Eisenhower administration. Public attention was directed instead to the problem of the costs of the crop-loan–price-support program.

World War II and the postwar years had effects on American agriculture and on government farm policies that were enormous. While the record-breaking crops of the war period were due less to increased acreage than to better fertilizer and improved weed and pest control, acreage did expand in the postwar years. Wheat returned to sections of the Great Plains that had been relegated to grass. Cotton was revived in portions of the Piedmont that had been converting to cattle production. Thus when cropland should have been shrinking for reasons of soil conservation, it was becoming greater. The opening of new cotton areas outside of the United States during the war produced a decline in world cotton prices, while the support price in the United States remained high. This meant enormous differential payments to exporters by the government. The high supports maintained by the government for non-basic commodities, including perishables, meant heavy Treasury losses. A conspicuous example was potatoes, which remained unsold in government storage too long and had to be destroyed. The public conscience was shocked by the spectacle of food being destroyed at a time when starvation was widespread in the world.

One of the most significant consequences of the war and its aftermath was the government's high price support of farm commodities, their enormous accumulation in government storage, and the resulting cost to the taxpayer. The financial report of the Commodity Credit Corporation in 1960 revealed $7.3 billion invested in farm commodities and $2.1 billion in price-support loans. This total of $9.4 billion was publicized as "investment in price support." The inventory of price-supported commodities was approximately the equivalent of a two years' supply for the nation. The cost of these surpluses to the American taxpayer was given nationwide publicity. Stressed also was the belief that the chief benefits went to corporate farmers in no need of them. These were the lessons taught by World War II and its aftermath to the American public and they shaped the farm policy of the next administration.

The Kennedy-Johnson Years in Farm Policy

A PORTENT OF CHANGE in farm policy was John F. Kennedy's naming of Orville L. Freeman to the critical post of Secretary of Agriculture. A liberal in politics, Freeman had been governor of Minnesota, a farm state, since 1956 and knew agricultural problems at close range. He held his new post for the eight years of the Kennedy-Johnson administrations.

Freeman's first objective was to reduce agricultural production to the amounts needed for domestic consumption, for foreign trade, and for an adequate carry-over. High, flexible price supports were to be continued, but would be combined with greater restrictions on output. Effective reduction in output could not be accomplished by simple limitations in acreage. Improved technology and more effective fertilizers and pesticides were producing more crops per acre than ever before. Greater emphasis was therefore required on the amount of a commodity produced — on the "bales and bushels."

Feed grains were part of the surplus problem. Unlike grains for human use, they could not easily be subjected to marketing quotas since they were largely consumed on the farms where grown. Another problem was that feed grains (except for corn) were not subject to acreage-allotment limitations. Corn farmers were diverting to such alternatives as sorghum, barley, or oats. This trend resulted in overproduction of feed grains and a lowering of all feed-grain prices. The extension of acreage restrictions to producers of sorghum, barley, and oats was therefore desirable.

The initial farm legislation of the Kennedy administration was an "emergency" feed-grain act. Grain sorghum and "any other feed grain which the Secretary of Agriculture may designate" were made subject to acreage allotments and eligible for price supports for at leat 65 percent of parity. If the complying farmer diverted acreage formerly in corn or sorghum to an approved "conservation use," he would receive negotiable certificates issued by the Department of Agriculture equal to 20

574

percent of the value of his corn or sorghum production in previous years. This and later feed-grain acts effectively reduced the surpluses in these grains and diverted more cropland to soil-conserving crops than did the Soil Bank Act of 1956. It was also hoped that the inclusion of grain sorghum under price supports might induce some wheat producers to divert to this grain.

An important administrative change in the Department of Agriculture took place at the same time. The service that had directed the acreage-control and crop-loan programs was given jurisdiction over the payments made to farmers for soil-conservation practices, and was renamed the Agricultural Stabilization and Conservation Service (ASCS). The Soil Conservation Service, dating back to 1935 with its large body of scientific and technical personnel, continued to serve farmers with respect to conservation practices.

In 1962 Congress passed a comprehensive agricultural act. It continued the "conservation reserve" feature of the Soil Bank Act of 1956, namely government payments to owners of cropland for diverting part of their land to approved conservation uses. But now ten-year contracts for this purpose were authorized. The act introduced a new feature, replacing the "acreage reserves" of the Soil Bank Act. This was a ten-year experimental program for turning cropland into recreational, wildlife, and reforestation uses. Under the old "acreage reserves" a farmer received annual payments for simply letting land lie fallow. The philosophy behind the new feature was that constructive action should take place on such land, rather than leaving it idle, causing economic losses to nearby communities. Federal funds were authorized to help defray the costs of making such changes. The ten-year contracts had their precedent in the Great Plains Conservation Act of the Eisenhower administration. Their duration, whether for conservation uses or the experimental program, permitted time for the completion of major projects.

A reduction in the wheat surplus was another objective of the act. The means would be the marketing quota, a device that had been set up for all basic commodities in the Agricultural Adjustment Act of 1938. It had not been effective for wheat because the law prohibited a reduction in wheat acreage below 55 million acres. The 1962 act directed the Secretary of Agriculture to estimate the number of bushels that would be needed in 1964, taking into account all projected needs. The tentative figure was one billion bushels, for which only about 48 million acres would need to be planted. If marketing quotas were set, this meant that every wheat farmer's acreage would be proportionately reduced.

If a shift to mandatory marketing quotas was to be made, wheat farmers had the right to vote on it. The 1938 act had provided that marketing quotas could be mandatory on all farmers in a given commodity if two-thirds of them, in a referendum, agreed. Thus the 1962 act ordered a nationwide wheat farmers' referendum. In the event that mandatory controls were accepted in the referendum, the act authorized the Secretary of Agriculture to issue "wheat certificates" showing the number of bushels a farmer marketed. The number certified could not exceed his marketing quota. The act also mentioned that "certified" wheat would have a support level between 65 and 90 percent of parity. Since that high level was dependent upon the success of mandatory controls it was only tentative. It was put in the act as an inducement for a yes vote. If the referendum failed, the support level would remain where it was, at about 50 percent of parity.

The referendum was held after a heated campaign in May 1963. The conservative American Farm Bureau Federation led the opposition, printing placards maintaining that a yes vote would mean that the government would become the "co-manager of your farm." Proponents of mandatory control on the other hand contended that such control would sustain farm income without involving the federal government in the costly loan and storage aspects of the price-support system. In the referendum the proposal for mandatory controls did not get even a majority, indicating that most wheat producers were willing to receive low price supports, rather than accept mandatory marketing controls. The most unfavorable vote came from Republican areas.

The Kennedy administration also took measures to aid agricultural and other exports. After World War I the Reciprocal Trade Act of 1934 had empowered the President to lower tariffs by bilateral treaties in return for reductions by other nations, so after World War II the United States had joined in efforts to revive international trade. In 1947 at Geneva the General Agreement on Tariffs and Trade (GATT) was signed by 23 nations, providing for periodic, multilateral trade talks. The United States participated in the subsequent GATT meetings, but, after the formation of the European Common Market in 1957, it was eager for a more active role in GATT. Congress in 1962 passed the Trade Expansion Act, giving the President wide powers in foreign trade, and Kennedy took the lead in convening a new round of GATT talks in Geneva.

All types of exports were of concern to the United States during these talks, but attention was focused on agricultural commodities. Of the ten major countries which imported United States farm commodities, more than half belonged to the Common Market, and Common Market countries were expected to take a unified, protectionist position with respect to agricultural imports. The GATT meeting, which convened in response to the initiative of Kennedy, did not actually get under way until 1964, after his death. But this round of talks came to be known as the Kennedy Round.

In the meantime the Johnson administration came to grips with two major agricultural problems that were both domestic and foreign in nature. One, the cotton problem, was complex. Under existing legislation exporters bought raw cotton in the United States at the domestic support price and sold it abroad at the lower world market price. The difference between the two prices was made up to the exporters by a federal subsidy. Foreign textile firms could buy American cotton at the lower world price and convert it into textiles at less cost than could be done in the United States. Since the American tariff was low, it was possible for foreign textiles, including those made of American cotton, to undercut American textiles. Cotton manufacturers resented having to pay the support price for the raw cotton, while the government was in effect subsidizing foreign competition in its own markets. They applied to the Tariff Commission for a higher duty on imported textiles, but were refused.

This cotton problem and the continuing wheat surplus were challenges to the Johnson administration in an election year. The President and Orville Freeman were eager for congressional action on both fronts. The result was the Cotton-Wheat Act of 1964. The cotton portion of the act provided for payments to textile manufacturers equal to the difference between the domestic and world price of raw cotton. The act thus added to the already established subsidies for the producers and exporters of raw cotton, a third, for manufacturers. It was agreed to after reminders in congressional hearings that manufacturers could convert to synthetic textiles and make cotton farmers even worse off than they were.

The wheat portion of the 1964 act authorized a marketing tax on each bushel purchased by primary wheat processors or their agents; the procedure was as follows. At the time of purchase a negotiable certificate was issued, indicating the number of bushels taxed and the amount of the tax paid. The certificate was transferred to the farmer, from whom the wheat had been bought, and was the equivalent of a direct cash payment from the government. The certified bushels for which the farmer received payment could not exceed the marketing quota that had been assigned to him. These certificates came to be known as wheat certificates and were designed to induce farmers to reduce wheat plantings in the coming season. Ninety percent of the wheat farmers complied with this arrangement. Its mode of voluntary compliance with marketing controls achieved what the 1963 referendum could not deliver. In 1968 the wheat carry-over was 819 million bushels, as compared with 1.3 billion in 1960. This was about the level of normal carry-over.

In 1965 the heavy Democratic majority in Congress enacted a four-year farm program. The successful wheat processing-tax certificates were continued. Higher payments were authorized for feed-grain producers who diverted their acres to other uses. In order to correct continuing surpluses in cotton and to achieve a simpler solution to the problem of competing foreign textiles, cotton farmers were required to cut their alloted acreage by 15 percent if they wished to be eligible for price supports. At the same time the support price for raw cotton was reduced to 90 percent of the world price, virtually eliminating any need for subsidies to cotton exporters and textile interests, both of whom could now buy cotton at a price competitive with world prices. Cotton farmers who complied with allotments would, in compensation for the lower support price, receive direct payments. Small cotton farmers were permitted to remain eligible for price supports without making any reduction in their current allotments.

A Long-Range Crop Adjustment Program in the 1965 act authorized conservation contracts of not less than five nor more than ten years for farmers carrying out conservation practices, or diverting cropland to non-crop uses. Annual payments were not to be more than 40 percent of the average value of a farmer's previous crop. The act specified conservation purposes to which cropland could be diverted. Thus the needs of farm policy and the desires of conservationists would be met. Closely related to this program were other measures for soil protection and assistance to rural communities. One of them, the Appalachian Rural Development Act, appropriated $17 million in aid to landowners for combating erosion and shifting cropland to pasture. The act contained an early attempt to offset the ravages of strip mining through restoration of soil and vegetation.

Simultaneously with the passage of the agricultural act of 1965, Johnson appointed a National Advisory Commission to report on agricultural policy. The four-year term of the act gave the commission time to make a careful study of the existing legislation and to propose changes. Commission members included leaders in agricultural economics, the food industry, schools of agriculture, farmers' cooperatives, conservationists, and others. Its 1967 report, entitled *Food and Fiber for the Future*, was far from unanimous.

In the meantime there was a visible result of the Kennedy-Johnson policies. The

Quonset huts and other structures used as government storage bins were coming down or being auctioned off. In 1957 the CCC had owned, on land rented from farmers or county governments, from 200,000 to 250,000 such structures in 24 states, chiefly in the Middle West. In 1959 its assets in stored farm commodities had reached nearly $9 billion. By the end of 1966 the number of states providing storage bins had fallen to 15, representing a reduction of storage capacity by a third in less than a decade. In about the same period the government assets in farm commodities had dropped almost 50 percent.

The years 1965 and 1966 were the best years for farm income in a decade. Increasing exports, in response to food needs abroad, helped to shrink the surplus and raise prices. For the 1967 crop, allotments in wheat were increased by 15 percent, to assure at least a year's reserve supply. More acreage was allowed in feed grains to meet the steadily increasing livestock economy in the United States. The domestic and export demand for corn brought the price of the grain well above the federal support level.

By 1966 the Food for Peace program (Public Law 480), inaugurated under Eisenhower, was in need of overhauling. Some changes had already been made. One was that transportation costs for the exported food must be paid by the recipient countries. Another was legislation permitting the extension of long-term dollar credits to these countries, with a view to phasing out sales in local currencies. Prodded by public opinion, the Johnson administration pressed Congress for other changes. One was a correction of the impression that United States sales to developing countries were solely to get rid of surpluses. Another was that exports be made conditional upon a greater effort by the recipient countries to develop their own agricultural potential.

This urging of "self-help" was a reflection of the serious oversupply of cotton in the United States. Between 1954 and 1965, wheat, sent primarily to India and Egypt, had accounted for two-thirds of all P.L. 480 exports. But in 1965, after the passage of the Cotton-Wheat Act, wheat surpluses were being reduced, while those in cotton rose from less than 3 billion bales in 1960 to 12 billion in 1965. Congressman William R. Poage of Texas joined cotton oversupply with self-help as follows: "Why shouldn't we say to India, 'You should take 30, 40, or 50 percent of your cotton acreage and put it into something that would feed your peoples'? Then why not send them cotton from our surplus, instead of food?"

As renewed in November 1966, P.L. 480 contained definitions of self-help, such as more use of improved fertilizers and machinery and the training in those countries of farm technicians. A matter clearly related to their food problems was the need for population control. This was cautiously included in the revised act among the several types of self-help for which United States funds might be utilized.

For the period of the original Food for Peace program, 1955 to the end of 1966, the total United States agricultural exports amounted in dollar value to approximately $61,190,000,000. Of this amount $43,302,000,000 were exports by private commercial companies. The remainder ($17,898,000,000) were exports under government programs. Of these, $2,179,000,000 was exported under the Mutual Security and Foreign Assistance Acts, while $15,719,000,000 was exported under P.L. 480. Thus the activity of the Commodity Credit Corporation accounted for almost 26 percent of all foreign trade in agriculture for those years. The benefits derived from

P.L. 480 had been widely distributed. It was an important contribution to the economy of several developing nations, and an important factor in the level of American farm income.

President Johnson's budget for 1967–68 included $1.77 billion for a "new Food for Freedom Program." Of this amount $243 million was for technical grants connected with food production in developing nations. The size of the program reflected the United States involvement in Southeast Asia. At the same time an interagency committee on Food for Freedom was established, composed of representatives of the Departments of Agriculture, Treasury, Commerce, and Defense, the Budget Bureau, and the Agency for International Development located in the State Department. The creation of this committee was partly the result of public dissatisfaction with the Department of Agriculture's cutbacks in wheat acreage in the face of world hunger. In 1966, when 60 million acres were either idle or diverted from crop use, the report of a presidential advisory committee on foreign assistance had stressed the inconsistency of the cutbacks.

A practical method of deflecting this criticism was to encourage other food-exporting nations to increase their shipments to developing nations. In April 1967 a joint congressional resolution, authorizing technical aid to India and a donation of 3 million tons of grain, included a proviso that the gift of food be "appropriately matched." The proviso was designed to encourage the formation of a consortium of nations that would agree on proportions of food each would give to the developing nations.

An opportunity to accomplish this purpose was at hand in the GATT negotiations in Geneva that began in 1964 and were not yet completed. A stumbling block in these negotiations had been the failure of the United States to obtain tariff concessions for its principal agricultural exports. The European Common Market countries were particularly resistant. Technological advances in European farming had resulted in farm underemployment, and protection against United States imports would help lesson the impact of the changes. Ultimately, in August 1967, the United States negotiators, under instructions from the State Department, agreed to less than had been desired for United States agricultural exports, in return for the setting up of a consortium of food-exporting nations. The principal members of the consortium were the United States, the Common Market, Canada, and Australia. The amounts of food agreed upon, to be donated or sold to developing nations, ranged from the highest proportion by the United States downward in the above order. This agreement brought the Kennedy Round to a close.

The plight of the rural poor in the United States in this era was a major problem. In a special message to Congress in 1968, President Johnson pointed out that 40 percent of the nation's poor, defined as having an annual income of less than $3,000, lived in rural areas, more than half in the South. Three out of four were white, but the poorest were black. Johnson's emphasis on more aid for the rural poor was a response to a 1967 report by a National Advisory Commission on Rural Poverty, entitled *The People Left Behind*. It showed that between 1940 and 1965 approximately 25 million people from rural areas had migrated to cities, one of the great migrations of world history. The flight to the cities was the result of mechanized farming and of the neglect of small farmers in the agricultural programs authorized by Congress for 30 years.

The migration from the farms left nearby rural towns stagnating. To lessen the flow into crowded cities from farms and rural towns alike, Johnson made two types of proposals: financial aid to small farmers to help them convert to profitably sized farms or to non-agricultural enterprises, and economic assistance to rural towns for better housing and community development. Rural non-farm population was then about three times greater than farm population. Earlier efforts on behalf of the rural poor had centered on retraining small farmers and farm laborers for new occupations in the cities. Johnson's message marked a significant shift in its concern for rural non-farm communities that suffered from the changes in agriculture. His proposals resulted in congressional acts to aid rural non-farm communities, including an authorization of loans by the Farmers' Home Administration to small towns as well as to farmers.

A characteristic of the Kennedy-Johnson administrations was the use of direct payments to farmers. Price-support loans became progressively less, while direct payments increased in amount and in kind during these years. A brief survey of the history of direct payments may be useful. Among them were the Agricultural Conservation Program payments (ACP) dating back to the Soil Conservation and Domestic Allotment Act of 1936. They had been established for the combined purposes of soil conservation and production control in basic crops. Other direct payments were those paid to sugar producers from 1948 onward, and those paid under the Soil Bank Act of 1956 to farmers for conservation practices and for taking some good cropland and much marginal land out of cultivation. The types of new direct payments introduced by the Kennedy-Johnson administrations were the wheat certificates, the short-term payments for diverting wheat, feed-grain, and cotton acreage to non-restricted crops, and the long-term payments for converting cropland to non-crop uses. In 1968 wheat certificates amounted to $746 million and the payments for diverting wheat, feed-grain, and cotton acreage to non-restricted crops amounted to $885.2 million. The total of these two forms of direct payments exceeded the amount ($1,421,000,000) expended in 1968 for price supports.

In the meantime the ACP payments were increasing in amount and came under fire in the Johnson administration. They were paid to all types of farmers for carrying out practices certified by the Soil Conservation Service. Some payments were on an annual basis; others, over a period of years, for which contracts were made with the government. According to one estimate, ACP payments over the period 1936 to 1963 amounted to $5,800,000,000. The ACP report for 1968 showed a cost to the government for that year of $209,547,000 for payments and cost sharing. It showed that per-unit costs were highest for making sod waterways, erosion-control dams, wells for livestock, and wildlife ponds, while the largest percentage of the total cost that year went for permanent ground cover to prevent wind erosion. The number of farms receiving ACP benefits in 1968 was 951,331, located in 695 counties.

In the 1967 report of President Johnson's Commission on Food and Fiber, critics maintained that the ACP payments encouraged too many farmers to make technical changes, which in turn increased the personnel of the Soil Conservation Service too much; that farmers ought not to be paid for practices they would perform anyway; and that the payments were illogical in encouraging farmers to produce more while other programs encouraged them to produce less. Defenders of ACP payments said that they had been useful in reducing basic cropland acreage; that the type of agriculture encouraged by these payments was very different from the basic-crop agriculture that was being brought under control; and that the value of the payments in conserving natural resources was a benefit to the nation.

The soundness of the new direct payments introduced in the Kennedy-Johnson administrations was also examined. On the positive side, they were more effective in reducing surpluses in basic crops than any previous measures. A wheat farmer who routinely kept within his acreage allotment was not likely to step up his per-acre production if he also received negotiable certificates for keeping within marketing limits. He would be even less likely to do so if he received, in addition, benefits for diverting some cropland to non-restricted crops or to non-crop uses. Direct payments also facilitated more accurate Budget Bureau predictions in preparing the agricultural budget. When government expenditures for farmers' income had been estimated chiefly on CCC loans, budget making was difficult since loans fluctuated with market prices. A third advantage of direct payments was the reduced cost of storing farm commodities.

A major criticism of the direct payments introduced in the 1960's was that they went chiefly to large producers. This development received as much public disapprobation in the last years of the Johnson administration as the size of loans and bursting storage bins had received at the end of the Eisenhower years. Another criticism of direct payments was that they unbalanced land values. They had to be geared either to acreage or to production. If they were geared to curtailed crop acreage in compliance with an allotment, or to acreage diverted to a non-restricted crop, the effect would be to increase the value of the land affected beyond what it otherwise would have been. If payment was made for curtailment of production, the size of the payment was a proportion of the value of the previous production of a farm. If the farm was large, the payment would be large. The effect was to augment the farm's value. Critics and defenders alike recognized that by 1968 production was concentrated on about one-third of all United States farms, and that "concentrated benefits were almost inevitable in a concentrated agriculture."

Two important developments in the farm situation in the 1970's were traceable to the increased reliance upon direct payments in the 1960's. The emphasis on "income support" through direct payments made easier a specific limitation on the amount of benefits per farm. Efforts in Congess to limit payments had been defeated in the 1960's by powerful farm interests. At length, by the Agricultural Act of 1970, signed by President Nixon, a limit of $55,000 was put on total annual payments to any person participating in the wheat, feed-grain, and cotton programs. "Person" was defined to include corporations and cooperatives. The types of payments affected were those in connection with price supports; those for acreage not planted to wheat, feed grains, and cotton; those for diverting former wheat, feed-grain, and cotton cropland to approved uses; and marketing certificates. Some farmers were receiving benefits in two or more categories.

Another effect of direct payments was that they made possible adjusting the level of domestic support prices to approximately world price levels. This development, together with the increasing foreign demand, led a leading agricultural economist to comment: "For the first time in nearly 30 years, farmers in the 1960's came to have a clear view of the value of commodities in peacetime world markets," an essential view in a country "which is a legitimate agricultural exporter."

Farm Tenancy
and Its Decline:
A Century of Change

ONE OF THE BASIC characteristics of American rural life in the era preceding the Civil War was the farm-owning status of the tillers of the soil. This marked especially the rural life of the northern states. It was in contrast with the tenant status of farmers in the greater part of Europe, as reformers in those countries noted with bitterness. American farmers were the lords of the earth; those in Europe were renters of the rich or they were serfs of the nobility. America, as a result, was a land of plenty; Europe was, for the masses, a land of poverty and periodic famine. The contrast was emphasized especially in the famine years of the mid-1840's.

However, even before the Civil War, a change was taking place in the American Eden. The diseases of the Old World were appearing in the farm life of the New, especially in the southern states, where tenancy was increasing among white farmers as early as the 1850's. Among all rural whites in the South the birth rate was high. Surplus boys in southern families did not move to the cities as they did in the North. Cities were less numerous and were smaller than in the North. Sons chose to rent land as they grew to manhood, either from parents or from others, and slipped easily into the tenant class.

During the Civil War came the disorganization of southern life, and after it, the wholesale emancipation of the slaves. Freedom came to the blacks, but no land. The owners of the land were left without capital to finance wages over a growing season. The blacks were less attracted by wages than by the feeling of freedom and independence that came from working for themselves. So plantation lands were divided into tenant holdings, each let out to a Negro on a basis of sharecropping. By 1880, when the first notice of tenancy was taken in the census, from 30 to 40 percent of all southern farmers, black or white, were tenants.

The distribution of tenancy in the South in the census years 1880 and 1930 is seen on the maps (110) showing on a statewide basis the counties where at least half the

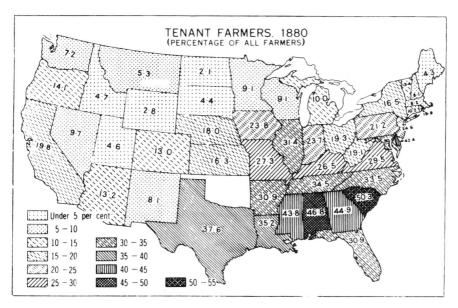

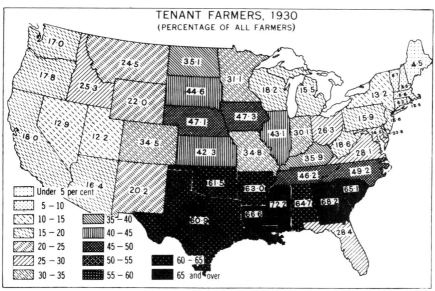

110. Farm Tenancy, 1880, 1930 (from Paullin)

farms were tenant-operated in those years. They show, especially, the swift growth of tenancy in the South in that half-century.

In the state of Mississippi the percentage of farmers who were tenants in 1880 was 43. By 1930 it had increased to 72. In Louisiana, the 1880 figure was 35 percent; in 1930, 66 percent. In Georgia, the 1880 figure was 44 percent; in 1930, 68 percent. In the South as a whole the tenant percentage of all farmers in 1930 was 55 percent.

Three types of tenant farmers were established in the South in 1880. One was cash tenants, who rented land and paid the landlord cash. They normally owned equipment and farm stock, which meant mules. They were in the best position of any southern tenants. But they were the least numerous. A second type was share tenants, who paid as rent a share of their crop. They usually owned part of their equipment such as mules and the seed they planted. For the remainder of their equipment and fertilizer they relied on the landlord. They paid the landlord a fourth of the cotton they raised and a third of any other crop, as rent. Croppers were another type. They ordinarily paid half their cotton crop as rent. They had to pay especially high rates because they rented not only the land but all the equipment they used. They relied on the landlord for the mules, for seed, and for fertilizer. They were hardly distinguishable from farm laborers.

While the crop was growing they relied on the landlord, or on a local storekeeper, even for the groceries their families consumed and the clothing worn. They got such necessities under a system known as "furnishing" or "advancing," wherein they agreed to make payment for the furnishings after the harvest was in. They would repay out of their half of the crop. The furnishings were paid for at a higher price than would have been the case if the goods had been bought for cash. That was especially true in the case of Negroes, who normally kept no records of their borrowing arrangements.

Throughout this system risks were taken by those who extended credits, the landlord or the local storekeeper. If the cotton crop should fail on account of bad weather or a boll-weevil invasion, or if the price of cotton remained persistently low, as it did during much of the 1920's and 1930's, the landlord might recover at the end of the season only part of what he had advanced. To compensate for the risk he charged high interest rates on the furnishings—commonly 25 percent a year, or more.

The capital tied up in these furnishings was often a considerable sum. It might be more than the landlord himself possessed in fluid form. In that case he had to borrow from a local factor or banker, who took a risk. If the crop failed or the price of cotton was low, he might not recover his loan. He therefore required from the landlord a high rate of interest. Thus the whole system of furnishings rested on a pyramid of borrowings. Whenever there was a succession of cotton failures, as at the time of the boll-weevil invasion, or if the price of cotton was ruinously low, as in the 1890's or in the 1920's and 1930's, the banker, the landlord, and the cropper would all go into bankruptcy together.

In the tenant system it was an advantage to the landlord to subdivide his acres into as many small holdings as possible. If the holdings were small, the land would be worked more intensively and the total rent collected would amount to more. The landlord set the size of the holdings at about 25 or 30 acres. On such a patch of land the tenant raised a crop often no larger than eight or ten bales of cotton. He netted as his half of the crop not much more than a few hundred dollars. According to a 1954 report of the Southern Regional Council, half the southern Negro farm families had an annual income of not more than $1000 a year and many had less.

The living standards of croppers, whether white or black, were the lowest in America. The diet consisted of cornmeal mush, molasses, and salt pork—the so-called three M's. It lacked milk and green vegetables. The croppers might have raised green vegetables in some cases, but were too careless to do so. They suffered the diseases of an unbalanced diet—rickets and pellagra. Homes were shacks, un-screened against mosquitoes. The malaria rate in the early years was high, as was that of typhoid fever and tuberculosis, due to unclean homes and poor sanitary facilites. The effect of such conditions was that the croppers became a spiritually defeated and debilitated class.

Most croppers were whites. In 1930 the census showed that in the South 1,100,000 whites were in the tenant class, most of them croppers. This was 46.7 percent of all white farmers in the South. Of Negro farmers in the South 700,000 were tenants, virtually all croppers. There were also 4,500,000 Negro farm laborers in the South. Croppers and farm laborers were almost indistinguishable.

The forces swiftly increasing southern tenancy in the first third of the 20th century may best be analyzed by areas, in the successive census reports of that period. In 1910 a great increase was reported in the rich Black Belt area of Alabama and in the floodplain of the Mississippi River. The decade was one of high cotton prices. The owners of plantations were dividing their lands into smaller plots and, to enable tenants to survive, providing them with fertilizer lavishly. The result was a sharp increase in the number of tenants. The 1920 returns revealed a marked increase in the Yazoo delta region of the lower Mississippi, where there had been a major reclamation of land by drainage, the land being divided among tenants. In the Piedmont region by 1920 a great increase had occurred, a result, as elsewhere, of lavish use of fertilizer and consequent subdivision of plantations. In the 1930 returns, the lower Mississippi Valley showed an even greater increase, as a result of the success in combating the boll-weevil, and consequent redivision of plantations.

In these returns a decrease in tenancy in some areas was reported and analyzed. In the first decade of the 20th century a big decrease occurred in the Alabama Black Belt. This was the period of the boll-weevil infestation, before farmers knew the method of dealing with it, which was to start the growth of cotton early so that the plant could reach maturity before the pest matured. Early planting was, however, difficult to achieve in the Black Belt because the soil is heavy and slow to warm up in the spring. Landlords were forced to consolidate tenant holdings and so the number of tenants declined. In the period 1920–30 tenancy fell off in South Carolina and in Georgia. This was the result partly of soil erosion and partly of the arrival there of the boll-weevil. In general it is safe to conclude that where decreases in tenancy occurred the reason was that tenant holdings had been consolidated or had gone out of cultivation.

The grain-growing Middle West was, next to the South, the portion of the Union in which tenancy prevalence was high in the half-century 1880–1930. The rate of increase was even higher than it was in the South. In Illinois, where it had been 31.4 percent in 1880, it was 43.1 percent by 1930. In Iowa, where it had been 23.8 percent in 1880, it was 47.3 percent in 1930. In Nebraska, where it had been 18 percent in 1880, it was 47.1 percent in 1930.

The explanation of this rapid growth was in part the rising value of middle western farmland. Purchase of land became increasingly difficult and renting the only feasible beginning for a man without capital. Another factor was the growing maturity of the West. As the original homesteader reached the retiring age, if he wished not to sell, he rented out his land. Tenancy was a development of age; it grew as the frontier stage receded. A third factor was the agricultural depression of the 1920's and 1930's.

In periods of agricultural depression farmers burdened with mortgages lost their farms and became tenants.

An added force in the increase of tenancy in the north central states was the activity of individuals intent on acquiring large agricultural holdings. Such individuals, in the frontier period, were of two groups. One was the so-called cattle kings, who were buyers of federal lands, paying for them chiefly with military bounty warrants, and using them for the production and fattening of cattle for the eastern market. They were the predecessors of the cattle kings of a later period on the Great Plains. Their holdings were converted into tenant farms after the cattle industry had shifted westward.

In the same category were capitalists who came West to establish estates that would be operated by tenants. One of them was William Scully, the scion of a family in Ireland that held extensive tenant-operated farms. In 1850 he migrated to Illinois and for the remainder of his life devoted his energies to creating there and elsewhere in the West tenant-operated holdings. The center of his activities was Logan, Grundy, and Livingston counties in Illinois, but he also acquired extensive holdings in Missouri, Kansas, and Nebraska. He purchased some 230,000 acres of prairie land, much of it from the federal government, for which he paid $1,350,000. All was let out to tenants on lease. The terms were cash rent and taxes to be paid by the tenant and collected as part of the rent before any of the crop could be sold. Normally leases ran for five to six years, and were renewable to approved tenants. Improvements such as fences, houses, and barns had to be built at the tenant's expense. The cash rent that Scully and other landlords required had merits, but it left to the tenants the risks and hardships attending any collapse in crop prices. Scully was as notorious in the nation as his family was in Ireland for rent exactions. But a redeeming feature in his rent policy of later years was his requirement that the soil be protected from depletion.

Middle western tenants were in a better state than those in the South. They normally owned part of the equipment they used and the stock they needed. Some were in a class important enough to be recognized by the census, owning a farm and renting adjoining land. Tenants on the Great Plains in this class were often big operators. But everywhere tenancy was considered an evil, a cancer formed on rural society.

It had a strong predilection for land of high fertility. Its greatest prevalence was in areas of the most fertile soil, and particularly where land was devoted to the commercialized raising of grain or cotton. This is shown clearly on the accompanying map of cropland harvested by tenants in 1934 (111). The map is particularly accurate in its location of tenancy prevalence, since it shows on a county basis the location of cropland harvested by tenants. The areas of heaviest tenancy prevalence are the corn kingdom of the Ohio Valley, the wheat kingdom in the Red River valley of the North, the eastern portions of Nebraska, Kansas, and Oklahoma, and the Spokane district of Washington. The cotton kingdom stands out in the South—the Black Belt of Alabama and Georgia, the floodplain of the Mississippi, the Black Waxy of Texas. This map could almost serve as a soil map of the United States. When the Great Plains became profitable for wheat growing by the technique of dry farming, tenancy promptly established itself there.

The concentration of tenancy on land that was fertile and devoted to single-crop agriculture is readily explained. Such land was too costly to be bought by a man of

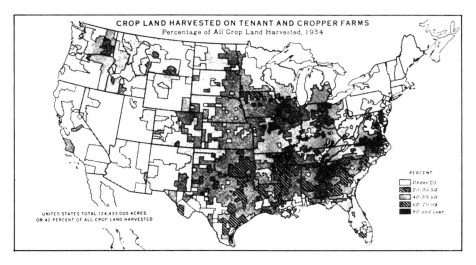

111. Crop Land Harvested on Tenant and Cropper Farms, 1934 (from the Dept. of Agriculture)

little means. Wheat and corn farms require costly equipment, and a farmer of little means found it advantageous to invest what he had in equipment and to rent the land. Conversely, the owner of wheat or corn land who permitted renting on shares found attractive the easy convertibility of his share of the crop into cash.

On the other hand, tenancy did not become established on rich land devoted to dairy farming, which required an owner's interest and care. In the rich dairy country of southern Wisconsin and eastern Minnesota there was little tenancy. Also, in fruit-growing areas tenancy was not easily established. In southern California the fruit lands were the property of capitalists who looked to migrant labor for their work force. Tenancy was not easily established, either, in truck-gardening areas or in areas of mixed farming. There was little tenancy on poor or marginal soil, such as the hill regions of New England and of the Northeast. It fell off there steadily in the 20th century. The explanation is that on poor soil the surplus was too small to permit payment of rent to a landlord.

The spread of farm tenancy created dismay in American society and excitement in rural areas. The excitement found expression particularly in periods of agricultural distress. In the Populist era it expressed itself over the issue of alien ownership of land. One middle western target of it was William Scully. In at least ten western states, laws were passed limiting ownership of land by aliens. Among the limitations adopted was the denial of the right of permanent ownership of land inherited from aliens. A prominent plank in the Populist platform of 1892 was a demand for laws prohibiting all alien ownership of land in the United States and a ''plan to obtain all lands now owned by alien and foreign syndicates.'' Scully grasped the meaning of this rural temper and in 1895 he took out naturalization papers, followed by citizenship in 1900. Until then he had used his alien status as a shield protecting his ownership of American lands. The huge property left to his heirs is still maintained, for the most part, in tenant operation.

Tenancy, and its hold on the American rural economy, persisted for the half-century following the Populist revolt. Its increase is graphically revealed in the map published in 1934 by the Department of Agriculture (111). The area of the most startling increase was the semi-arid Plains. Land there was farmed to the best advantage in large units well equipped with machinery. Large units were achieved by adding rented to owned land.

In the dismal decade of the 1930's nearly 1,750,000 farmers in the United States as a whole lost their farms by foreclosure or by tax sales, and became tenants. Forty percent of all farmers in the nation had become tenants, which was felt by idealists to constitute a caving in of American democracy. Books of disillusionment appeared such as John Steinbeck's *Grapes of Wrath* (1939) and A. F. Raper's *Sharecroppers All* (1941). The question was raised whether the fate which the American Indian had suffered under the administration of the Dawes Act awaited the American farmer. Had the free-enterprise system as to land ownership been wise? A proposal had been made by Horace Greeley and others, when a Homestead measure was before Congress in the 1850's, that a restriction on the right to alienate a homestead should be incorporated in the law. It had not been adopted. A question was raised in the 1930's: which is worse, an ownership of land so hedged about by restrictions as to stifle initiative, or an ownership so unrestricted as to end in loss of land? A consequence of separating the husbandman from ownership of his means of production would be as disastrous as separating the artisan from his workshop. Both were roads to instability and to class conflict.

One effect of separating the farmer from ownership of the soil, especially in the South, was incessant shifting of tenants from farm to farm and area to area. Among southern croppers the length of stay on a rented farm was seldom longer than a year or two. Nearly a million tenant farmers annually moved in the depression years of the 1930's. What that meant to the social and educational life of tenant families hardly needs to be pointed out. Another effect of frequent tenant shifting was depletion of the soil. The one interest of tenants was to take as much as possible out of the soil.

Contracts of tenancy could have been devised to safeguard the welfare of families and of the soil. In Great Britain and in Ireland such contracts were required in reform legislation. But in the United States such matters lay within state jurisdiction and tenancy contracts were not regulated. In the South contracts were likely to be oral.

On the other hand, farm tenancy had beneficent potentials. In the South it was sometimes used to give supervision to careless and undisciplined workers. On big southern tenant holdings supervision was an early development, taking the form of "riding bosses," employed by landlords, who were as constant in their supervision as overseers had been in prewar days. In the North some tenant contracts were drawn to give protection to the soil as well as to the tenant. They specified leases of five to six years and spelled out soil preservation in such terms as crop rotation and use of lime and clover. In the semi-arid Plains and in the Middle West, large farms relying on mechanization could conveniently be established by renting, or, as was often done, by owning some land and renting more that was adjacent. Tenancy was defended in some circles as a means of ascending the ladder to ownership.

To cope with the tenancy problem the federal government went into action early in the New Deal. In 1936 President Roosevelt appointed a Committee on Tenancy, which, in the following year, laid bare the extent of the problem's evils. A year later

Congress adopted the Bankhead-Jones Farm Tenancy Act, the first federal legislation in the field. The act established the Farm Security Administration as a bureau in the Department of Agriculture, with the function of providing financial aid to tenants and other low-income farmers. Government loans to aid in the purchase of farms were authorized to tenants, selected by county committees under the supervision of the Farm Security Administration. The loans, limited to $12,000 to any one person, were to run for 40 years. Their carrying charge was often less than the rent that had been paid to the landlord. Eligibility for them was hedged about with restrictions. The farm to be purchased had to be large enough, and its soil good enough, to support decently a man and his family. The recipient of the loan had to agree to a soil-conservation program. The project, experimental at first with a congressional authorization of $50 million a year for loans, was continued under new legislation in 1946, when the Farmers' Home Administration replaced the Farm Security Administration. Forty-year loans at low interest, conservatively administered, were continuing to be made in the 1970's, and most of them have been repaid.

A second type of loans was authorized by the Bankhead-Jones Act—the so-called rehabilitation loans. These were designed to aid tenants and other low-income farmers to buy equipment, livestock, and fertilizer. They were short-term loans, running for 5 to 10 years and carrying an interest charge of 5 percent. Eligibility for such loans was carefully restricted. The recipients needed to have high recommendations, a written rent contract meeting the specifications of an enlightened lease, and must agree to a program of diversified farming. By 1952 more than a million tenants and low-income farmers had received loans amounting in total to a billion dollars, and the repayment rate was fairly good.

A third type of loan was made under the Pope-Jones Water Facilities Act of 1937 for the semi-arid region of the West. It was designed to aid low-income farmers to improve their water facilities. It was aimed at the drilling of wells and the building of storage ponds.

Congress passed a consolidating act in 1946 to attract private capital into the financing of tenant ownership loans. It provided for a government guarantee of such loans, and permitted loans to be made to an amount equaling 90 percent of the value of the farm bought by the tenant. The bank interest charge would be 3 percent a year, plus 1 percent to reimburse the government for the cost of guaranteeing the loan. All these federal measures were New Deal experiments to preserve the ideal of farm ownership by the tillers of the soil.

In the second half of the 20th century the dimension of the farm-tenancy problem shrank dramatically and so did its gravity as a political issue. Farm tenants in the nation, who had numbered 6,812,350 in 1935, had declined by 1969 to 2,730,250. In the same period the ratio of tenant farmers to all farmers declined from a high of 42 percent to a low of 13 percent. By 1969 the ratio of tenant farms to all farms was, as the census noted, "the lowest ever recorded in a census."

In sectional terms the decline in tenancy was equally striking. In the North Central states it was from 2,263,543 to 1,151,884 in the period from 1935 to 1969. In the South it was from 3,421,923 to 1,161,399. In the West it was from 570,959 to 265,101. The decline among non-white tenants in the South was especially striking. From 815,947 it fell to 90,141 in 1969. Non-white tenants had always been fewer than white tenants in the South. In 1969 they seemed to be disappearing.

The census of 1969 offered a limited explanation of the marked decline in the number of farm tenants. It noted that the total of persons employed in farming had fallen off greatly in number. They had left the farms for the cities. This was especially true of tenants, North and South, whether white or non-white. Many low-income tenants remaining in agriculture had moved into the ranks of owners, as a result of the federal program of aid to them. Prosperity in agriculture during the period of World War II and the Korean War had had the same effect. The growing mechanization of agriculture and the increase of corporate farming had also been major forces in reducing the number of low-income tenants. But the last-mentioned factors, though diminishing tenancy, contributed to the growth of another equally grave problem, that of migrant farm labor.

Migratory Farm Labor, 1900 – 75

BY THE CLOSE OF THE 19th century migrant labor was a recognized phase of agriculture on the Great Plains. In was part of the harvesting of wheat. For winter wheat harvesting began in Texas in the spring. From Texas it moved northward with the ripening of the grain to the Canadian border and across the border into Manitoba and Saskatchewan. After the harvest the migrants flocked to the lumber camps of the Pacific Northwest, or they holed up in cheap boardinghouses in the cities of the Middle West. As footloose nationals, white and black, they traveled without family. Their total number in the period prior to World War I was estimated to be in the neighborhood of 200,000.

With the advent of World War II a massive use of aliens, especially Mexicans, began in the United States in temporary farm work. It was a response to an acute shortage of labor that growers and the government felt obliged to meet. On the part of the Mexican government it represented an effort to relieve itself of unemployment. An executive agreement, concluded in 1942, legalized and protected such labor, which was followed by an act of Congress to the same end the next year. The act exempted the transients from the provisions of an immigration law of 1917 forbidding the importation of contract labor. It classified them as non-immigrants. The act was repeatedly extended after the war emergency had passed. In 1951 a formal treaty was negotiated with Mexico further regulating the terms of labor of Mexican aliens temporarily employed on American farms. In July 1951, Congress enacted Public Law 78, which confirmed the new agreement. This law, as well as the executive agreement, was renewed several times.

Mexicans entering the United States by agreement were known as braceros. They were to be paid the prevailing wage of the locality in which they worked. The prevailing wage was the one proclaimed by state authorities. In Texas it was 50 cents an hour; elsewhere in the Southwest it was 60 to 75 cents. If, because of bad weather or because crops ripened later than anticipated, work was delayed, the workers were entitled to receive, for a guaranteed number of days, three-fourths the amount they would have earned if they had worked. They were protected, also, as to housing and care in case of illness, accident, or death. Protections such as these, not guaranteed to native-born migratory workers, seemed to the native-born discriminatory, and were resented.

More numerous than the braceros were illegal entrants into the United States from Mexico—the so-called wetbacks. Their name was an allusion to the belief that they waded or swam the Rio Grande in crossing the border. Actually a major part of them crossed the border west of the river. They came for the most part from the Mexican states adjacent to the United States, where unemployment was especially critical. They had been told by returned braceros of the wonderful wages that could be earned in the United States. They made contact with smugglers, the so-called coyotes, who were familiar with the routes and arts of underground travel. The charge for crossing the border and conveyance to mid-Texas in the early 1970's was $200 per person; for conveyance as far as Chicago it was $300 per person. The earnings on a truckload of passengers were a tidy sum.

Wetbacks were without treaty protections. They were particularly vulnerable to exploitation because of the illegality of their presence in the country. They were preferred for precisely that reason as harvest hands by many of the farmers in the Southwest. According to the testimony of a church committee interested in the problem, there was a widespread conspiracy among large-scale producers to attract and exploit such labor. The wages paid wetbacks were as low as 25 to 30 cents an hour in the 1940's and early 1950's. Such pay seemed tempting to Mexicans in the interior provinces where an entire day's labor often brought no more than 25 or 30 cents.

The annual entrance of wetbacks increased steadily during World War II and thereafter. In the early 1950's wetbacks were estimated to have numbered a million, or even two million. In 1953, 900,000 of them were caught and were deported by the border patrol. Twice that number were estimated to have succeeded in entering the United States.

The American and Mexican governments had unlike interests in bracero and wetback labor. The American government, while at war, urgently needed both types to harvest food and fiber produced on its farms. The Mexican government welcomed the bracero program as a relief to unemployment, but frowned on the exploitation of wetbacks by American growers. It wished terms and conditions of labor to be accorded to its nationals in the United States consonant with those accorded American farm labor. With regard to wetbacks it objected to the cost of receiving those expelled and restoring them to their villages. It wished penalties to be imposed by the American Congress on those who employed wetbacks. In the United States no penalties were imposed on employers except forfeiture of the right to employ legal Mexican labor. By Texan and other employers this would hardly have seemed a penalty.

Migratory labor consisted of an eastern as well as a western segment of the rural economy of the United States in the 20th century. It numbered fewer persons in the eastern states than in the western but was found all along the Atlantic seaboard from Florida to Maine. Its centers were Delaware, New Jersey, Pennsylvania, and Maine. In the 1940's this segment comprised a force of from 100,000 to 150,000 individuals.

A large part of the eastern migrants were Negroes from the southern states. Other considerable portions were Puerto Ricans and British West Indians. At the North were French Canadians, laboring in the potato fields of Maine. Puerto Ricans came to the United States by right of citizenship. The British West Indians and French Canadians came by virtue of executive agreements. The island workers were enlisted and transported by recruitment agencies operating in the islands in conjunction with labor contractors and crew leaders in the United States. The transportation of the workers from job to job was done by crew leaders, who spoke Spanish and owned trucks to carry the men from job to job. They were paid from the wages of the workers.

The Puerto Ricans arrived in the United States early each April. They were brought by airplane to the middle Atlantic states to engage in harvesting asparagus. Their importation came to be known as the "asparagus airlift." At the conclusion of the asparagus season they engaged in the stoop work of other vegetable production. Then they moved into peach and apple harvesting.

Their wages were 65 to 75 cents an hour, depending on the minimum-wage requirements of the states in which they labored. This was better than the wages paid wetbacks in the West. They were charged $12 to $13 a week for board and lodging, a registration fee to the labor contractor, and a trucking fare to the crew leader. They paid, also, an airplane ticket amounting to $125 for the round trip to Puerto Rico. They returned to the island in the late autumn in time for the sugar harvest. Many of the Puerto Ricans were carried to the Great Lakes region during their stay on the continent, especially to the sugar-beet region in Michigan. There they competed with imported Mexicans for the stoop work American farm laborers preferred to avoid.

The flow of migrant farm labor was determined by the season and by the nature of the crop in the several sections of the United States. The pattern of the flow changed during the three periods of the growing season—April, July, and October. In April, Puerto Ricans came to the middle Atlantic states for the harvesting of vegetables. In the lower Rio Grande Valley the work was the chopping of cotton; in southern California, it was cotton and fruit. In southeastern Colorado it was cantaloupes.

In July, harvesting was in full swing, and migrant labor provided extra hands to gather it. In the Central Valley of California it was used for fruits and vegetables. In the Willamette Valley the crop cared for was berries and fruit. In eastern Washington it was peas and wheat. In northern Colorado it was sugar beets; in southern Minnesota, peas and onions; in southern Wisconsin, peas; in the Delta country of the Mississippi, cotton cultivation; in Georgia, peaches and peanuts.

In October extra labor was needed most widely for fruits. In southern Idaho it was used for potatoes; at the Red River of the North, for sugar beets and potatoes; in the Great Lakes region, for vegetables and fruits; in the cotton kingdom, for cotton. Along the Texas and Louisiana Gulf line, it was used for rice and sugarcane.

One of the features of this migrant labor was that it was grouped into segments. The Pacific West was one; the intermountain plateaus of Idaho and Colorado was another; the Great Plains, a third; the cotton South and West, a fourth; the Middle West, a fifth; and the middle Atlantic seaboard states, a sixth.

Normally migrants confined their work to some one of these segments. They preferred to do so. They got adjusted to the kind of work and the conditions in one area. In each, however, the problem was the same: short-term jobs, constant moving from job to job, low wages and standards of living, especially in housing, that were the worst in the United States.

Migrant housing in Texas was especially bad, consisting for the most part of shanties in shack towns at the edges of cities, auto courts, and even tents. Much of the housing contained no plumbing except a cold-water tap. In California in the 1930's, when the problem was beginning to be serious, labor camps were built for migrants by the federal government, which contained plumbing and were considered ideal by John Steinbeck. Unionizing the migrants was almost impossible. They were too temporary, too constantly on the move, and too disorganized to be easily unionized.

One of the most serious aspects of the migrant problem, from the point of view of migrants traveling with families, was the plight of the children. Children were estimated to comprise a fifth to a fourth of the American portion of the migrants. They grew up virtually without education, exploited in spite of child-labor laws, and reared under the disintegrating influences of a roving life.

The public demanded reform. A Commission on Migratory Labor was appointed by President Truman in 1950 to report on the problem and to recommend remedies. The Commission responded in the summer of 1951 in a notable report. It recommended that in crop emergencies of the future no measures be adopted to increase the number of alien laborers beyond the level of 1950, and that no certificates of scarcity of domestic labor be issued by the Immigration and Naturalization Service unless domestic labor had first been offered wages and conditions as favorable as those prescribed by agreement with Mexico for foreign labor. It urged that the wetback invasion be halted.

As for domestic farm workers, the Truman Report recommended minimum-wage legislation to be extended to all farm workers, migratory and non-migratory, and, in addition, unemployment compensation, federal and state. It urged federal and state cooperation to ensure decent housing for migratory labor, and vigorous enforcement of child-labor legislation. It proposed prohibition of the employment of children under the age of fourteen and cooperation of federal and state agencies for the education of all migrant children. The report was an indictment of conditions found among migrant workers in the nation. It was an ill fate that it appeared shortly after the Korean crisis had exploded into war, involving the United States, which was to prolong for at least another quarter-century the evils the report was designed to remove.

During World War II and the Korean War machinery was increasingly displacing manual labor on farms. Mechanical spraying and airplane dusting were coming into use for the control of pests. For control of weeds row cultivation by machine and chemical spraying were found cheap and effective. For harvesting grain, combines were growing in size. Cotton was harvested by mechanical pickers, and fruit and vegetables were gathered by collectors, all powered by tractors. The age was marked increasingly by corporation farming of cropland—the corporations owning thousands of acres of rich land and investing millions in labor-saving machines.

An early example of such farming was the Delta and Pine Land Company, operating in the Delta region of the Mississippi floodplain. Organized in 1919 by British capitalists, it held 35,000 acres of land, and farmed it with specialized machinery. It was the epitome of agricultural capitalism, including skilled management and diversified farming that did not impoverish the soil. Later examples of capitalistic farms were the big outfits in the Central and Imperial valleys of California, engaged in producing fruit, vegetables, and cotton.

The first half of the 20th century witnessed a significant change not only in the methods of food production but in public opinion regarding food consumption. The public was being taught to insist on daily consumption of fresh fruit and green vegetables. This necessitated the maintenance of rapid transportation of perishables from section to section, the extension to homes of mechanical refrigeration, and the development of a nationwide system of deep freeze of foods. The section of the United States profiting more particularly from such changes was the irrigated area of the Southwest, where fruit and green vegetables were grown throughout the year. This was the section that had been making the greatest use of migrant labor— domestic and foreign.

On behalf of domestic migratory labor, reform legislation had been adopted in some states by 1950. States on the northeastern seaboard had done more than those of the West and South. They more effectively enforced minimum-wage laws and required better housing for migrants. They also gave migrants help by charting seasonal employment opportunitites and information so that workers could be steered quickly to places where work was to be found. Finally these states took steps to control labor contractors and crew leaders by putting them under license.

At the national level in 1951 and 1952 two laws were passed which were responses in some degree to the *Report on Migratory Labor* of the Truman Commission. The first was Public Law 78, a confirmation of the executive agreements permitting the bracero program. It came during the Korean War, when pressures mounted for increasing agricultural production. In response to labor, the law placed the recruitment of temporary alien labor directly under the Department of Labor. Also, alien workers might enter only those areas where the Secretary of Labor had certified that insufficient domestic labor was available and where alien employment would not adversely affect wages and working conditions of domestic workers. The law was biennially renewed in succeeding years in response to grower demands.

Temporary alien labor was not the only threat to domestic farm workers. Equally feared was the immigrant alien laborer who was qualified to enter and remain in the country under existing immigration laws. This fear found expression in certain clauses of the Immigration and Naturalization Act of 1952 (McCarran Act). As in earlier laws, no quota was set in the McCarran Act for immigrants from countries of the Western Hemisphere. But such aliens seeking to do skilled or unskilled labor had to be certified by the Secretary of Labor as well as by the Secretary of State and the Attorney General.

Between 1954 and 1959 renewals of P.L. 78 brought into the country annually approximately 425,000 braceros. After that the numbers declined. The last renewal in 1963 was for only one year. Mexico would have liked the program to continue, but it was allowed to lapse on December 31, 1964. By that time its attractiveness to growers had somewhat subsided because the mechanization in agriculture had reduced the need for manual labor, notably in harvesting cotton. Other reasons for the decline of grower interest in the renewal of the program were the Labor Department's enforcement of the protective features of the program on behalf of braceros, and the limitation of braceros to locations where they would not adversely affect domestic labor.

After the demise of P.L. 78 some growers, especially those producing the less easily mechanized crops, sought ways to obtain the equivalent of braceros. The McCarran Act listed several categories of "special immigrants" not subject to the general provisions of the act. Class A were natives of Western Hemisphere countries "who had fulfilled all admission requirements," and for whom there was no quota. Class B were aliens who already had resident status in this country (many were former braceros) and were privileged to leave and return without a State Department visa each time. All that was needed for their re-entry was a permit issued by the Immigration and Naturalization Service. Both Class A and Class B were "aliens of immigrant status," in contrast to braceros, who were non-immigrants. The privileges of the aliens of immigrant status made them attractive to growers but not to organized labor and their sympathizers.

Under pressure from domestic labor organizations, Congress passed legislation setting limits to alien farm workers of immigrant status. In October 1965 it amended the McCarran Act by placing a quota for the first time on immigrants from Western Hemisphere countries and, for those entering within the quota, strengthened the earlier requirement that farm workers be certified by the Secretary of Labor that they would not adversely affect domestic labor. This limitation, and the limitation in numbers, would gradually reduce labor competition from new immigrants from the Western Hemisphere.

But the act made no change with regard to the category of Class B special immigrants—those who already qualified for permanent residence and were permitted to re-enter the country "after a temporary visit abroad" by showing an Immigration and Naturalization permit, a "green card." This practice was frowned upon by many in Congress, but was allowed to continue. In 1969 a congressional investigation showed that daily commuters from Mexico were 42,000, of whom 25,000 were engaged in non-agricultural work. Daily commuters from Canada numbered 10,000. Seasonal commuters were 8300. Daily commutation across the border had long been customary, but after the demise of the bracero program in December 1964, there was an increasing amount of seasonal commutation.

This development was challenged in a Washington, D.C. District Court by the United Farm Workers and the AFL-CIO. The plaintiffs asked the court to issue an injunction to stop the Immigration and Naturalization Service from issuing its "green card" permits to seasonal commuters. The government won its case in the District Court. The plaintiffs appealed, and gained a reversal in the Appeals Court. The government then carried the case (*Saxbe v. Bustos*) to the Supreme Court and won a 5–4 decision in November 1974. This was a victory for the growers because a commuter, once he had qualified for resident status in the United States, could return to Mexico and later re-enter the United States without a new visa. A visa, if required for each re-entry, would also have necessitated a new certification by the Secretary of Labor. After this decision a public information officer of the Immigration and Naturalization Service said, "As a practical matter our counsel believes this decision leaves things exactly where they are. We plan to go on classifying aliens this way and issuing new green cards."

An official publication of the Department of Agriculture, *Agricultural Statistics* for 1973, revealed a striking decline in migratory farm workers in the United States, from 477,000 in 1959 to 184,000 in 1972. These statistics included only native farm migrants. It did not include alien migrants, legal or illegal. These could not be accurately reported, but their number was known to far exceed domestic migrants.

Illegals were estimated already in the early 1950's to number 1 million or more. (In 1953, 900,000 were caught by the border patrol, but twice that number were thought to have evaded the patrol.) In 1973 the number caught was 515,448, but the Immigration and Naturalization Service estimated that in 1973 between 1 and 2 million made it into the United States.

By 1975 the total of illegals in the United States was estimated by the Service to be more than 7 million. In the press the number was estimated to be an additional million. This constituted 8 percent of the total labor force of the nation. It was increasing, according to the Immigration and Naturalization Service, at a phenomenal annual rate.

In geographical location, the principal center of the illegals had once been the Southwest—the region adjoining Mexico, where travel back and forth was relatively easy, and the best of both worlds was available. But in more recent years the illegals increasingly remained in the United States after the harvest season had passed, and vanished into the barrios of such cities as Los Angeles, Chicago, and New York, where they were used in industry. The industrialized cities of California were the major centers of them in 1975. But New York State, especially metropolitan New York City, came next. Florida, Texas, and Illinois followed in that order. In metropolitan New York, according to the Immigration and Naturalization Service, the number of illegals in 1975 was a million.

In like proportion were the problems attending the invasion. One was the undercutting of wages in the lower income brackets of farm and city labor despite minimum-wage laws. Another was the frauds on welfare and Medicaid programs perpetrated by the illegals, especially in the larger cities. A third was the overburdening of educational facilites. The children of illegals could have been screened and excluded, but this would have been at the cost of applying tests of admissions that school boards and their communities shrank from adopting. An even greater evil was the increase in crime brought by the illegals to metropolitan centers, especially the trade in narcotics.

In origin the illegals were predominantly Mexican. Ninety percent were estimated to be Mexicans. Those with families remaining in Mexico were able to send home savings from their earnings, estimated by Congressman Peter Rodino of New Jersey to amount to more than a billion dollars annually. None of this income paid taxes except indirectly. Some of the illegals were natives of other parts of the world. They were likely to be tourists to the United States who overstayed the time limits of their visas. Enforcement of time limits was not feasible. In a good many cases illegals came to their new abode with professional training, which they were able to put to profitable use.

Attempts to halt and reverse this alarming flow into the country began to be seriously pressed in 1972. The remedy was, or seemed, simple—to penalize all employers found to be knowingly employing illegals. This would be an effective cure, for it would shut off the attraction that had been luring the illegals to come and stay. Such legislation had been proposed to the American government by the Mexican at an earlier day. A bill of this nature was brought into the House of Representatives after a careful committee investigation in the spring of 1972. It was passed by a resounding voice vote but was blocked in the Senate. A comparable bill, introduced into the House the next spring, was passed by a recorded vote of 297–63. Again it was blocked in the Senate.

The remedy contained in the bill raised basic problems of civil rights. If such a law were adopted employers would be obliged to apply to every holder of a job or applicant for a job tests of citizenship. A screening system would be needed that would resemble the documentary apparatus of a police state. For that reason opposition to the bills adopted by the House was marshaled by civil rights, ethnic, and religious groups. In the Senate such legislation was opposed also by spokesmen of employers who stressed the need to offset the competition of imports produced by cheap foreign labor.

In the Senate the chairman of the Judiciary Committee and of the subcommittee on immigration, to whom such bills came, was James O. Eastland of Mississippi, owner of a large cotton plantation, who was interested in preserving the bracero program and to whom bills to penalize employers of illegals were anathema. The problems of illegal aliens, already almost out of control, seemed in 1975 destined to grow in gravity as long as the lure of American wages drew the underpaid of foreign lands to the farms and cities of the American Arcadia.

American Indians, 1934 – 74

A NATIONWIDE RE-EXAMINATION of the Dawes Severalty Act came with the advent of the New Deal. The attack was led by John Collier, a Columbia University anthropologist, whom President Roosevelt appointed as head of the Bureau of Indian Affairs. He believed the whole concept of the Dawes Act had been a mistake, that the tribal organization should have been preserved and used as a means of advancement of the race, that it was the only form of society the Indian really understood. It had the same moral and spiritual values for the Indian that individualism had for the Anglo-Saxon, and served as a stabilizing force in the same way. Community effort was the traditional form of Indian economic existence. Properly guided, it should have been made the basis for communal farming, herding, and forestry. Improvement for the Indian lay in this direction, not in seeking to instill in him the sense of individualism and ownership of land in severalty, which were white man's incentives and foreign to the Indian spirit. The same thesis was set forth as to the social and spiritual life of the Indian. The tribes had been the focus of the Indian arts and crafts and religious ceremonial, and should have been kept alive.

Collier proposed a reconstruction of Indian tribal life. Properly reconstructed, the tribe should be given local self-government, substituted for the paternalism and the bureaucracy of the Indian Office. These points of view were embodied in a radical new measure, the Indian Reorganization Act, or Wheeler-Howard Act, adopted by Congress in 1934. Under this act any tribe of sufficient size was permitted to organize itself into a tribal community and receive a charter tailored by the Indian Office to suit its particular needs. The charter gave the tribe economic, social, and political functions, while the federal government retained a guardianship role.

The most important of the tribe's economic functions was the management of land. Any undistributed reservation land still left to the tribes, and any land that had been allotted in trust to individual Indians but had not yet been converted to full possession, was to be returned to the control of the tribes. These lands were to be perpetually held by the tribal communities under federal safeguards. The Dawes Act was repealed.

The lands recovered for the communities were to be enlarged by land donated by the federal government. They were to be consolidated into compact holdings, so that they could be advantageously used for grazing, forestry, or farming. The amount of land the Indian Office thought would be needed to support the tribal communities was about 95 million acres. To reach this total, lands were to be acquired by the federal government, at a cost of up to $2 million a year for a series of years, and donated to the communities. All tribal lands, including those restored and donated, were to be permanently exempt from federal, state, and local taxes. Ultimately about 6 million acres were acquired and given the tribes under this program, chiefly marginal lands.

With regard to the tribal trust funds not yet dispersed, the act provided that they should be permanently preserved. Each tribe's funds were to be administered, under federal supervision, by the tribal community. The money was to be used for projects chosen by the tribal community from a list authorized by the Bureau of Indian Affairs.

A system of tribal or community government was to be established, and the communities were gradually to absorb the powers of the Bureau. Courts of Indian affairs were established for each tribe with jurisdiction over civil and most criminal cases. The social life and education of the Indians were entrusted to the tribal communities, subject to federal supervision. Tribal arts and crafts, tribal ceremonials and traditions were to be encouraged and strengthened.

In Congress vigorous objection was made to the reorganization measure, even by groups in the various Indian rights associations. These elements took the position that the principles embodied in the Dawes Act, and especially the distribution of tribal property to the Indians in severalty, had been correct and ought not to be abandoned; that the only mistake made had been administrative—the premature giving of full title to land to Indians; that tribalism should not be resuscitated; that Indians should not be encouraged to remain permanently apart from their white neighbors in their economic, social, and political life; also, that exemption of Indian lands from state and local taxes was unjust to neighboring whites, especially in sparsely settled areas. It would put the burden of supporting schools, roads, and health wholly on the whites, and tend to alienate the whites from the Indians. On religious grounds the reorganization measure was denounced as anti-Christian and an encouragement of heathenism. Finally, the measure was denounced because it would encourage a form of communism in the nation.

Under the Wheeler-Howard Act each tribe could decide for itself whether it would come under it or stay out. Their decision was unmistakable. Eighty-five percent of the tribes, including those in Alaska, voted to agree to its provisions.

The act left some problems unsolved. One was the marked growth in Indian population, which increased from about 325,000 in 1934 to 425,000 at the end of the 1950's, exclusive of Alaska. The "vanishing race" had taken on new life. Its rate of growth was much higher than the nation's, partly as a result of the lowering of the mortality rate.

While the tribes grew in numbers, their resources did not, except for the few that possessed oil or coal lands. The Navaho tribe is a striking example of a plight resulting from overpopulation and insufficient resources. By the late 1940's the tribe's situation had become so desperate that Congress was obliged to authorize a ten-year plan of relief and rehabilitation for it at a cost of $88,500,000. The enlargement of reservations by donations from the federal government provided in the Wheeler-Howard Act came to a halt because of the outbreak of World War II and its costs. The rise in reservation population was to some extent offset when some Indians found occupations during the war in the cities of the Northwest. But on the whole the effort to drain off excess reservation population encountered too many difficulties, chiefly because nearly all the Indians were unskilled for occupations in industry, and many of them, especially the full-bloods, constituting half the Indian population, did not speak English.

Educational costs were another problem. Education of American citizens was a state responsibility, and all Indians had become citizens under the Snyder Act of 1924. Yet Indians on reservations paid no taxes, and the states were reluctant to bear all the costs of educating them. Congress was obliged to extend aid to states to defray such expenditures. Health problems on the reservations remained. Indians had a marked susceptibility to tuberculosis, which their mode of living and lack of food intensified.

Because such problems persisted, sentiment developed at the end of the Truman administration, and even more actively in the first Eisenhower term, for reversing the policy of the Indian Reorganization Act and putting in its place a policy of "termination." Eisenhower's Commissioner of Indian Affairs, Glenn Emmons, a banker rather than an Indian expert, made termination the keynote of his policy. In 1953 under his guidance Congress adopted Concurrent Resolution 108 by an overwhelming majority, stating that Congress intended to make the Indians "subject to the same privileges and responsibilities as are applicable to other citizens." The resolution specified the tribes, within named states, that should be freed "at the earliest possible time from Federal supervision . . . and from all . . . limitations specially applicable to Indians."

The policy was bitterly resisted by John Collier, then in retirement, and Oliver La Farge, president of the Association of American Indian Affairs. They charged that the forces behind the new policy were predatory interests looking for power sites on Indian reservations, or timber, or mineral or grazing lands that the tribal communities still possessed. Most Indians resisted the policy, considering termination as a mode of setting them adrift—"freedom" to lose what little they had.

A few days after the policy statement, Congress enacted a law authorizing states to extend their civil and criminal law over Indian reservations. The states cited were Wisconsin, Minnesota, Nebraska, California, and Oregon, but other states were offered the same authority. Eisenhower signed the law, though it did not contain a provision he had recommended requiring the states to obtain Indian consent before acting. Not until fifteen years later was an amendment to the law adopted, requiring states to obtain Indian consent before acting under the law.

In pursuance of the Concurrent Resolution, Congress in 1954 passed six laws with respect to the tribes consenting to termination. Over the next five years their termination was implemented. The outcome was what had been predicted by the reformers. The tribes sold lands, no longer a trust of the government, to the amount of 1,600,000 acres, and the proceeds were distributed to the tribal members. Two tribes, the Klamath in Oregon and the Menominee in Wisconsin, had valuable stands of timber, which they sold to whites. The case of the Menominee attracted special notice and protest. The tribe had made a profitable living by logging and milling of timber. When the question of termination arose, its representatives voted acceptance, without fully understanding its implications. The reservation was converted into a county of Wisconsin and its members became subject to taxation. They briefly enjoyed a period of affluence, but for most of them this was followed by indigence and dependence on welfare. Congress ultimately had to give financial assistance to the tribe.

In the 1954 congressional elections the Democrats were successful, and defeated any further termination laws. But Commissioner Emmons was able, administratively, to curtail Bureau services for other tribes than those terminated by Congress. The public outcry was such that termination, whether by legislation or by administrative order, was renounced in the 1956 Republican platform. But Emmons continued the policy, as much as he could, until nearly the end of the second Eisenhower administration. By then the services of the Indian Bureau to 61 tribes had been curtailed.

When a tribe was legally terminated, not only did its lands cease to be a trust of the United States, but its tribal funds also ceased to be a trust and went to the tribe. These funds, like the proceeds from land sales, could either be retained by the tribe or distributed to its members.

The tribes that were terminated in the six states were small or relatively small. They had been selected as a first phase of a larger plan which came to a halt. The 101 reservations enumerated in the census of 1970 were nearly all fragments of earlier reservations. They comprised about 52 million acres, as amplified under the Indian Reorganization Act. Much reservation land was poor in agricultural quality.

A parallel development respecting tribal funds related to awards given certain tribes by the Indian Claims Commission, established by Congress in 1946. Its assignment was to adjudicate claims, brought by tribes between 1946 and 1951, against the federal government for treaty violations, frauds, and other injustices in its past land dealings with Indians. The Commission received 580 claims. As of June 30, 1967, it had decided 256 cases, of which 133 were rejected, and 123 had resulted in awards totaling $208 million. Some tribes voted to hold the money as tribal property, and invested it in ways that would bring future financial returns. In the case of tribes selected for termination that might receive awards, Congress decreed that the money be divided among its members. For this reason some tribes selected for termination were split in their vote on the procedure.

In the Kennedy administration the Indian Bureau policy was reversed. As nearly as possible the Collier ideal was restored. A reformer, Stewart Udall, was appointed Secretary of the Interior. A re-evaluation report became the guiding principle of the Bureau. It proposed a return to the tribal land base, with an effort to enlarge it by acquisition of more land. The report favored attracting industries to the reservations, especially those that featured Indian arts and crafts, to give employment to the surplus population, and to preserve Indian tradition and cultural values. Education was to be emphasized. One purpose of the educational program was to prepare those who would later meet the problems of urban life. The general direction was not assimilation, but integration of the Indian into the national community.

This program was adhered to in the Kennedy-Johnson era, and its aims were in part realized. The program for the enlargement of the land base lagged, but that of preparing Indians for urban life progressed. In 1960 the Indian Bureau estimated that

40 percent of the Indian population was urban. Of the reservation Indians who migrated to Pacific coast cities during World War II, some remained and succeeded as urban dwellers; some became stranded in an alien society; others returned to the reservations. Under the Kennedy-Johnson program future migrants to cities were to be screened and only those believed to have a good chance of adjustment to a new life were encouraged to go.

Another trend in the Johnson administration was an increasing involvement of federal agencies, other than the Indian Bureau, in Indian matters. The Department of Health, Education and Welfare extended its health services to the reservation Indians. The Office of Economic Opportunity included reservation Indians in its vocational training and other programs. Indians came to think of themselves as part of the national community, rather than as members of tribes.

Between reservation Indians and urban Indians who were able to make their way on or off the reservation, a gulf of difference appeared. The reservations themselves seemed secure, but among urban Indians support for ultimate ''termination'' could be found. A reincarnated Tecumseh would still find in the Indians of the 1970's the same divisiveness that had balked his own crusade for unity that was the hope of the future.

Land-Use Planning

THE PROCESS BY WHICH a transcontinental wilderness was converted into a civilized society was in one respect like the work of the elements. It was unplanned. Lands were permitted to pass into private possession regardless of their potentiality for farming or the wisdom of allowing them to be used for crop production.

In New England much of the interior hill country had a soil so thin and stony as to be unsuited for crop farming. Those areas would have been better left under forest, and closed to settlement. They had, however, a surface fertility and were cleared and put under the plow. In a short time their soil had been depleted. Then began a hopeless struggle against poverty which continued generation after generation and ended in defeat. In the course of this struggle the land, and the people on it, suffered. In the interior hill country of New England are to be seen today thousands of open cellar holes and endless miles of stone fences, all shrouded by forest, marking farms that were hopefully begun in an earlier era and then abandoned. A large part of interior New England—about two-thirds—is again wooded. Most of the growth is, however, of little commercial use. Except in northern New England, it is a scrub forest, exploited only for cordwood if cut at all.

In the Piedmont region of the South, land so steep that it could not safely be cultivated was distributed to settlers and put under tobacco and cotton. Much of it became a line of soil erosion and of human erosion. The human erosion is described by Erskine Caldwell in his depressing novel *Tobacco Road*. A gradual conversion to pasture for cattle needed to take place there. But it required siphoning off a large part of the rural population, a major operation both for the people living there and for the taxpayer of the United States. The hill and mountain area of the Tennessee Basin is another example of settlement made without plan, with subsequent problems of soil erosion, human deterioration, and rescue expenditures by the nation.

In the northern Great Lakes area large tracts of forested sandy soil were allowed to pass into the hands of capitalist lumbermen. The lumber was logged off. The naked land was sold to local or Chicago real estate dealers or land speculators. It was palmed off on immigrants who did not know their way around and made a bare living for a time by combining farming with logging in adjoining areas. As soon as all the adjoining timber had been cleared, and the soil alone had to be relied on, poverty set in. This cut-over region became one of the dreariest areas in the United States, a home of stranded families, an area requiring constant aid from relief agencies, a region of physical and spiritual decay.

In the semi-arid Plains and in the intermountain plateaus, lands so dry and so subject to duststorms as to be unsafe to farm were allowed to pass into the hands of farmers under such legislation as the Enlarged Homestead Act of 1909 and the Stock Raising Homestead Act of 1916. About 15 million acres of land so distributed was later abandoned. Much of the remainder supported a society that had to be helped by federal rehabilitation loans or similar aids of other kinds.

Other lands which should have been kept in public possession were those at the headwaters of streams, where the logging off of timber meant floods over low-lying valley lands. For over three centuries this planless and indiscriminate disposal of the public domain went on, leaving in its wake rural problems that later plagued the American people. It may be asked why was this improvident policy so long tolerated, why was it that in so vital a matter, reform could come only after nearly all the more valuable public lands had been put into private possession?

The answer lies in a combination of forces. One was the spirit of laissez-faire that dominated American thinking in the earlier years. The public was confident that the best way of getting the public domain settled was to leave the matter to the self-interest and judgment of the settlers. In no sphere of American life did rugged individualism have as free a rein as in the sphere of public land disposal. Another explanation was the need of state and federal governments throughout the early period of American history for revenue from the sale of public land. A third force was the eagerness of the federal and state governments to have the country settled rapidly for economic and nationalistic reasons. The pressure of land speculators and the eagerness of railroad companies in the trans-Mississippi West to sell their lands and develop traffic were other factors. An urban factor was the eagerness of city chambers of commerce and related organizations to stimulate settlement as a means of stimulating city business. An important element was lack of public interest in soil conservation while there was an abundance of virgin land remaining in the West. The same indifference was shown with regard to the forests and mineral resources. The wilderness was considered a province to conquer rather than to conserve for posterity.

Finally, an important factor was lack of scientific knowledge of soil. Soil now known to have been unfit for settlement often had a surface fertility that was deceptive. In upland New England settlers for years believed that the land was good. Frontiersmen were not always sound judges of the potentialities of virgin land. They did not have, as the historian who judges them has, the advantages of hindsight. However, even land recognized to be of inferior quality was allowed to pass into settlers' hands. Illustrations of legislation under which land of low quality was distributed to the public are the Graduation Act of 1854 and the Homestead Acts of 1909 and 1916.

Ultimately the consequences of this planless settlement were brought home to the American public. They became clear in the period of farm collapse and depression that followed the close of World War I. They came home in various dramatic and painful forms.

One was a staggering relief problem. In all the areas of marginal and deteriorated land, where farmers had hardly been able, even when prices were high, to make a decent living, distress became acute as soon as the Great Depression arrived. Relief had to be given not merely to individual families, but to whole communities that could no longer maintain schools or roads or health services. The relief had to be extended over years; it became a subvention for rural slums, a subsidy to keep them going.

A second painful problem was chronic tax delinquency, affecting whole areas and extending over periods of five to ten years. In the cut-over region of the northern Great Lakes 20 million acres of land became chronically tax-delinquent during the 1920's and 1930's, and in six southern states an equal area was chronically tax-delinquent.

A third manifestation of unwise settlement was a series of dramatic disturbances of nature in the chief trouble areas. On the arid Great Plains duststorms occurred on a scale never known before. On the Mississippi and other rivers floodwaters rose to unprecedented crests. In many of the hill regions gullying of land reached canyon dimensions that could no longer be ignored.

These penalties led to the new concept of land-use planning after World War I. National and state governments began to plan the use to which land should be put. They applied planning to areas which they still owned, and also introduced it to areas that had passed into private possession. In 1931, in the Hoover administration, a national land-use planning committee was organized in the Department of Agriculture. In 1934, in the Roosevelt administration, the National Resources Board directed a National Planning Committee to set in motion a comprehensive program of planned land use. State governors set up planning boards at the suggestion of the National Planning Committee. In 46 states—all of the 48 except Delaware and Louisiana—such boards were appointed to work in cooperation with the national committee. Interstate planning boards were also organized.

In 1935 the National Planning Committee issued a landmark report in government resources policy. The report identified the chief distress areas and recommended a course of action for each. It was the charter of a new rural society in the United States.

One recommendation was that much private land should be restored to public possession. The types to be recovered were: land steeply sloping which was being destroyed by washing and gullying, land that was being destroyed by duststorms, land with a productivity so low that it could not support a decent standard of living, and land that lay at the headwaters of important streams and regulated stream flow. The amount of land in these categories which should be restored to public ownership was set in the report at 75 million acres. Of this amount, 20 million acres was land then in farms; 35 million acres was land then in pasture; and 20 million was land that was wooded.

The accompanying map (112) shows roughly the location of lands unsuited to farming: those in the Appalachian Mountains from New England to Georgia; in the Allegheny Plateau particularly in Kentucky and the Highland Rim of Tennessee; in the region of cut-over lands in the Great Lakes area; in the Ozark Plateau; and lands

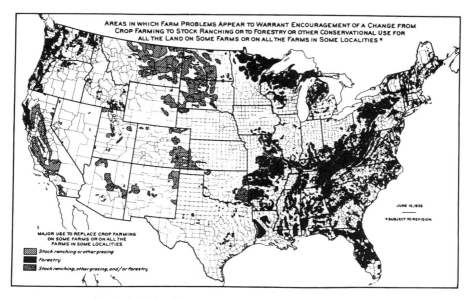

AREAS IN WHICH FARM PROBLEMS APPEAR TO WARRANT ENCOURAGEMENT OF A CHANGE FROM CROP FARMING TO STOCK RANCHING OR TO FORESTRY OR OTHER CONSERVATIONAL USE FOR ALL THE LAND ON SOME FARMS OR ON ALL THE FARMS IN SOME LOCALITIES *

112. Areas Unsuited to Farming, 1935 (from the National Resources Board)

subject to blowing in the Great Plains and Intermountain Plateaus. The areas shown were partly government-owned and partly privately owned.

A government land purchase program was recommended, to be spread out over fifteen years. Areas not suitable for farming were to be converted to grass or forest, or used for wildlife refuges. The people on such land were to be resettled where they could make a decent living. This program was carried forward under various federal authorities until the early 1940's. Altogether about 16 million acres were bought. The land was paid for at the rate of $5 or $6 an acre. Special communities were established for some of the families whose lands had been purchased. The program was virtually halted by the outbreak of World War II, and by the increase in land values, which the war brought about. The difficulty of this program was that little public land of good agricultural quality remained. Soil of good quality on irrigation projects required capital and irrigation expertise, and most of the uprooted families had neither.

In some states reacquisition of inferior land also occurred in the 1930's, but by involuntary process, in the form of chronic tax delinquency. An example of the process is found in the state of Michigan, where much of the northern cut-over land reverted to state ownership. The location of it is shown on the map as of 1934 (113). More than half the cut-over area of northern Michigan became state-owned, a large part through tax reversion. The same pattern applied to northern Wisconsin.

In some states the tax-reverted lands were not dealt with imaginatively. They were resold to speculators and again unloaded on inexperienced immigrants. But in Michigan, Wisconsin, and Minnesota a more constructive program was adopted. Most of the tax-reverted lands were permanently withdrawn from crop use. They were allowed to reclothe themselves with forest—aspen and jack pine, for the most part, which are usable for pulpwood.

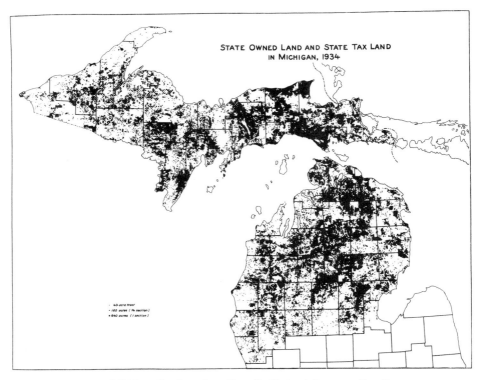

113. Michigan Cut-Over Area (from the National Resources Board)

In Wisconsin another advanced step was taken. In 1929 a rural zoning law was adopted by the state legislature, which authorized local governments to close to settlement areas so inferior that they could not support decent standards of living, or so isolated that they could not be provided with schools or public health services. Farmers already established in such areas were not evicted, but were encouraged to sell out to some state or federal agency as soon as possible, or to exchange their lands for better ones elsewhere. Under this law 37 counties in Wisconsin, mostly in the cut-over area, put rural zoning into effect. A total of 5 million acres of land was closed to farming. Lands acquired from farmers were put into forest or into recreational uses (Map 114).

In 37 other states, including Michigan and Minnesota, similar enabling legislation was adopted, authorizing local governments to adopt rural-zoning ordinances which would restrict the use that could be made of land in designated farming areas. This growth of rural zoning was one of the most promising of land reforms of the past half-century.

While the federal and state governments were struggling with the consequences of planless settlement, a new problem threatened to arise in the intermountain plateaus. In 1934 there was still in this region, and in the semi-arid parts of the Plains, a large amount of public land open to homesteading under the Stock Raising Homestead Act of 1916—a total of 165,695,497 acres. The location of this land is shown

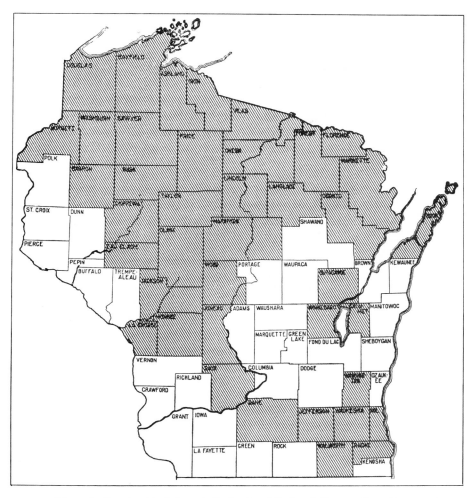

114. Wisconsin Counties (shaded areas) Having Rural-Zoning Ordinances (from Carstensen)

on map 115. The map was made in 1923, when the quantity of land in that area open to homesteading was about 20 million acres more than in 1934.

The land was good for little except grazing, often poor grazing. It was open range that was being exploited by cattlemen and roving sheepmen. It was being rapidly spoiled by overgrazing. It had lost from 40 to 50 percent of its productivity as range and in some sections erosion had set in. Yet in 1934 the federal government had 7741 applications for grazing homesteads on this land, a reflection of the desperate economic conditions of the period. These applications, if approved, would have created new problems for the future, but they were all rejected.

Instead, Congress passed the Taylor Grazing Act in 1934, which provided that 80 million acres of land should be withdrawn immediately and permanently from the possibility of private entry. The land was to be organized into grazing districts, and

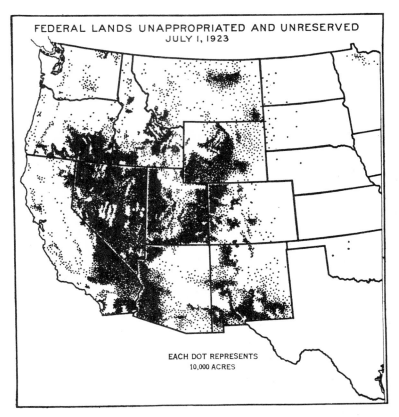

FEDERAL LANDS UNAPPROPRIATED AND UNRESERVED
JULY 1, 1923

EACH DOT REPRESENTS
10,000 ACRES

115. Federal Lands Unappropriated and Unreserved, 1923 (from the *Yearbook of Agriculture*, 1923)

leased at a grazing fee to stockmen under the supervision of the Department of the Interior. In 1934 and 1935, 65 million acres more of this land—virtually all the remaining public domain open to homesteading—were withdrawn by executive orders, later approved by Congress.

The Taylor Grazing Act stemmed from a combination of influences. One was the new public interest in land-use planning. Others were the support of the measure by the Roosevelt administration and that of some large-scale stockmen and sheepmen of the intermountain plateaus who had come to realize that only federal control could save the range from destruction. Opposed to the measure were sheepmen who had acquired, or hoped to acquire, grazing homesteads and intended to operate from them as a base.

The authorized grazing districts were administered by a new agency in the Interior Department, the Grazing Service. Initially it worked in informal cooperation with local associations of stockmen. Cooperation was in a sense a necessity, for the stockmen had the knowledge and experience required for a successful administration of those lands.

In 1939 this cooperation was formalized. An amendment was added to the Taylor Grazing Act authorizing advisory boards of local stockmen to be set up in every grazing district, to cooperate with officials of the Interior Department in operating the districts. Those advisory boards soon became not merely advisory but local machinery for carrying out grazing policies. Here was another illustration of the many federal controls that evolved from earlier informal settlers' controls. The advisory boards were organized not merely on a local, but on a statewide basis, and they became a political power in Washington.

In 1946 a lobbying committee of stockmen and sheepmen was formed to influence national grazing policy—the Joint Livestock Committee. This and the advisory boards came more and more to dominate federal administration of the grazing lands. Their influence was great enough to defeat Grazing Service efforts to increase grazing fees on the land—efforts to lift the fees to a level commensurate with the costs of federal range supervision. The fees even yet hardly pay the costs of range supervision. The lobby also sought to prevent reduction in the numbers of cattle and sheep on the range to levels the Grazing Service would have liked. It also influenced Congress to hold down appropriations for the Grazing Service as a means of preventing adequate staffing. The strategy of starving the Grazing Service into ineffectiveness was worked out in cooperation with Senator McCarran of Nevada. On the next map the grazing districts organized under the provisions of the Taylor Grazing Act are shown (116). The districts included considerable state and private lands that were operated with the federal lands under cooperative arrangements.

The Taylor Grazing Act and the executive orders extending it ended the era of public land distribution by homesteading. It brought to an end the open West. The era ahead was one of planned use of the remaining public domain. Besides the newly created public grazing land, the federal lands then embraced forest reserves, national parks, fish and wildlife preserves, land reserved as potential sites of federal irrigation works, and mineral reserves. Of arable land, capable of being cultivated without extensive outlay of capital, there was little left even in Alaska.

Grazing land withdrawn from entry under the Taylor Grazing Act was in 1971 organized into 52 grazing districts, containing 157,298,847 acres. Since 1946 these lands have been administered by the Bureau of Land Management (BLM) in the Department of the Interior. The Bureau had been created in that year by a merger of the Land Office and the Grazing Service. Its gross receipts in 1971 from grazing fees amounted to $6,223,449. Its per-acre fees were well below the economic value of the forage. The Bureau's primary interest was protection of the range from overgrazing, a factor in soil erosion.

The forest reserves were even more extensive. The first reservations of forest land followed a codification of land laws ordered by Congress in 1891. Into that code had been slipped an inconspicuous provision which gave the President authority to withdraw forest areas from private entry at his discretion. This was taken advantage of with characteristic energy by Theodore Roosevelt, one of the outstanding conservationists of American history. He withdrew during his presidency 141 million acres of forest land. By 1974 the National Forests—which included grazing areas—had grown to 184,276,463 acres. Both types of land were in charge of the Forestry Service in the Department of Agriculture.

By comparison with these figures, privately owned timberland amounted to about 340 million acres, which provided the bulk of lumber used in industry. Only a tenth of the lumber produced in the United States in 1971 came from the forest

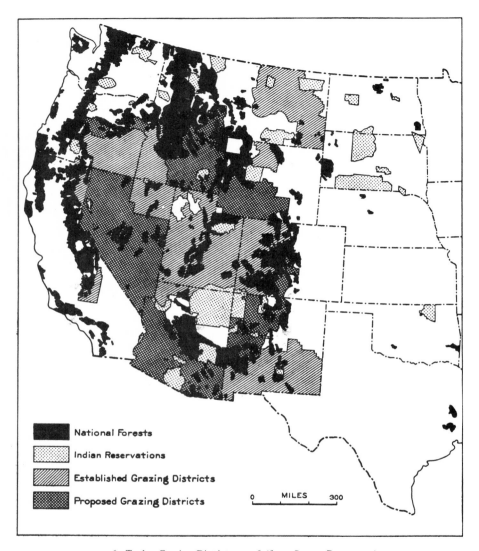

116. Taylor Grazing Districts, 1936 (from *Senate Documents*)

reserves. One evidence of the public acceptance of the concept of land-use planning is the attitude now shown by the big private timber holders. Such giants as the Weyerhaeusers and Crown-Zellerbach of California and Canada now cut on a re-placement basis. Timber cutting and replacement are now in balance in the United States.

A third category of public land in the United States is the National Parks, dating from March 1, 1872, when Congress ordered the formation of the Yellowstone National Park in Wyoming, the first and then the largest of national parks in the world. It embraces 2,213,000 acres. Before 1900 three other National Parks had been created: Yosemite, Sequoia, and Mount Rainier. Their selection was based on unusual natural beauty or geologic or other scientific interest. In 1971 the National Park System contained approximately 30 million acres. Besides 36 parks created for outstanding scenic or scientific interest, the system included about 250 smaller units, established for historical, recreational, scenic, or scientific purposes. The use of the National Parks for the logging of timber for commerical purposes is forbidden. The public response to the National Park System is millions of visits a year.

A comparable category of national reserves are those under the United States Fish and Wildlife Service, which in 1971 embraced 27,907,000 acres of land. Formed first in 1871, they were a remnant of the wet and undrained land that remained to the federal government after states had chosen large amounts of such land, donated to them under the Swamp Land Act of 1850. In 1975 these reserves contained 350 wildlife refuges, 100 fish hatcheries, and 35 research stations.

More diffused, more hidden, but equally important are the mineral reserves of the federal government, which lie chiefly in Alaska and in the National Forests and Taylor Grazing Act districts of the Cordilleran West. In addition, the mineral reserves include about 60 million acres of subsurface land in the Plains states, where mineral rights were reserved to the federal government when surface land, mainly Stock Raising Homesteads, passed into private ownership.

The federal government makes a distinction between two main types of its mineral lands. On those containing the metallic minerals enumerated in the basic mining acts of 1866 and 1872 (a list somewhat expanded since), an individual or a group may prospect, and "locate" a claim, anywhere on public land except in the National Parks. As soon as a claim is commercially productive, the claimant is entitled to purchase the land involved and receive a government patent conveying legal title. Over the years, such lands were constantly passing from the public domain and into the hands of well-known private companies who now produce most of the nation's output of such metals as copper, silver, lead, and mercury. Public lands containing metallic minerals are still passing from the public domain to private companies. In 1973, 2496 acres went to patent in this way.

By contrast, the Mineral Leasing Act of 1920 reserved to the federal government all of the second type of its mineral lands—those containing coal, oil, oil shale, natural gas, phosphate, and sodium. All federal lands, except National Parks, were open for prospecting for these resources, and their private development, under lease, was encouraged. Since 1920 periodic sales of leases of fuel-mineral lands have been held at the urging of private concerns. In 1965, 64 million acres of federal land was under lease for oil and gas, mostly in the eleven states of the Cordilleran West. The same year between 6 and 7 percent of the national oil production, valued at $570 million, came from leased federal lands.

The Bureau of Land Management handles the mineral leases on land administered by other public land agencies, as well as those on land under its own care. In the 1950's Congress enacted legislation to prevent mineral leases from conflicting with the surface uses of federal lands. Conversely, surface users had to recognize the right of lessees to use the surface to enter the subsurface area. This legislation was an illustration of multiple land-use planning in the public sector.

The benefit to the national Treasury from the leasing of mineral lands—plus timber sales and forage fees from the nation's forests and grasslands—was the result of a 20th century reversal of the 19th century expansionist assumption that the "highest use" of the public domain lay in its ultimate disposal. In 1972 a third of the nation's land was still federally owned—a total of 751,300,000 acres—slightly more than half of it in the High Plains and Cordilleran West, with the remainder in Alaska.

Another federal territory of vast mineral potential is the outer continental shelf beyond the three-mile-wide state "tidelands." This belt adjoins the tidelands on two oceans and in the Gulf of Mexico. For a distance of 50 miles or more it forms an extension of the sovereignty of the nation, subject to an eventual international treaty on the law of the sea. From an early date it was known to contain petroleum and gas resources. The parts of it off the Gulf coast and off the coast of southern California have been exploited for years under lease from the federal government. The belt off the Atlantic shore was also believed promising, especially the Georges Bank Basin east of Cape Cod, the Baltimore Canyon off the middle Atlantic states, and the Southeast Georgia Embayment.

In 1969 the federal government brought before the Supreme Court (*United States v. Maine et al.*) the issue of claims of the Atlantic seaboard states to the resources underlying the shelf. (*Et al.* were the other Atlantic coast states except Connecticut, whose shores are on Long Island Sound.) Each of the states claimed a right or title to its relevant area, which allegedly interfered with the rights of the United States. A special master was appointed by the Court to analyze these claims and submit a report and judgment on them.

After a prolonged investigation the special master made a report denying all the state claims. It was unanimously adopted by the Supreme Court, which ruled on May 17, 1975, that the federal government had exclusive right to the oil, gas, and other mineral resources under the outer continental shelf. The decision validated the Outer Continental Shelf Lands Act, which (shortly after the tidelands act) declared the shelf federal property and conferred on the Secretary of the Interior authority to regulate mining there. Oil and gas leases were to be awarded by the Bureau of Land Management on a competitive basis. They were to be paid for either by a cash bonus with a fixed royalty of not less than 12½ percent of the value of production, or on a royalty basis with a fixed cash bonus.

The so-called proved reserves of the outer continental shelf were reckoned in June 1968 to be 2.9 billion barrels of oil and natural gas liquids, and 30.3 trillion cubic feet of gas. Estimates of undiscovered resources were from 34 billion to 220 billion barrels of liquids and from 170 to 1100 trillion cubic feet of gas. Other minerals are known to be present there.

Between 1953 and 1975 the Santa Barbara and Gulf of Mexico fields of the outer continental shelf yielded over 3 billion barrels of oil, 19 trillion cubic feet of natural gas, 13 million long tons of sulphur, and over 4 million long tons of salt. In 1973 the daily yield of the shelf was 1,081,000 barrels of oil and 8.9 billion cubic feet of natural gas. The contribution of the shelf to the federal Treasury, from the sale of leases, rentals, and royalties as of June 3, 1968, amounted to $2.7 billion. The resources of the shelf's known reserves, added to those of the Alaska fields and those hoped for from the Atlantic portion of the shelf, are relied upon to release the nation from dependence on the oil of the Arab states.

The land-use planning concept of the National Resources Board found expression, for public land, in the Taylor Grazing Act of 1934. For private land it found expression in the Soil Conservation Act of 1935, which encouraged farmers to plan and practice conservation on their own land. Subsequent congressional measures carried forward the theme of conservation in land use. Demonstration areas in land-use planning, created in the 1930's, were continued in succeeding years.

With respect to federal lands, the theme of land-use planning was stressed again in the 1950's and 1960's, the result of environmentalist pressure and of criticism of the cumbersome and conflicting federal land laws. In 1964 these pressures brought about the creation by Congress of the Federal Land Law Review Commission.

The Commission's 1970 report, *One Third of the Nation's Land,* contained 137 recommendations. Some were bitterly attacked, especially the willingness to be flexible about "modest" disposals of federal land at their market value. On the other hand, the report contemplated acquisitions. If any public lands were to be sold or acquired, the sole criterion would be the public interest. On balance, the public land acreage would remain approximately the same. The need for better land classification was stressed. The report suggested that the Treasury was not receiving an adequate return from the economic value of its lands. Better classification of timberlands, for example, would bring larger returns from the National Forests. User fees should be greater. Obsolete and conflicting land laws should be repealed. New laws were needed emphasizing environmental quality as a prime objective of public land management. Mineral lease holders on public lands must restore the natural environment they disturb. Thus, both enhancement of the economic capability of federal resources and an ecological point of view—development and conservation—were balanced in the report.

The Commission recommended coordination of land planning at all levels of government, notably where federal and state or private lands adjoined each other. In 1970 this general recommendation resulted in a proposal to amend the Water Resources Planning Act of 1965 so as to establish a nationwide system of grants from the federal government to state and interstate agencies to encourage land-use planning. In June 1973, the Senate passed a stronger proposal providing for an eight-year $1,066,000,000 program to induce states to devise plans for urban, suburban, and rural land use, based on federal guidelines. A government agency would administer the program with access to detailed information on land supply and needs. Eligibility for grants would be made subject to a state's compliance with the federal guidelines. A similar bill was introduced into the House in 1974, but no action was taken. Stumbling blocks have been the old issue of states' rights versus federal dominance and those arising from the protection of privately owned property. The problems inherent in national land-use planning are more numerous and complicated than those affecting water-resources and clean-air planning, where legislation setting up national planning has won congressional approval.

Despite Congress's failure to pass a general land-use planning act, state legislatures have been receptive to the idea and have been meeting innumerable environmental issues. During 1975 at least seventeen states enacted bills requiring county land planning. Many states have strengthened wetland-protection laws and many have enacted regulations on strip mining. Citizen groups are emphasizing the need to apply technology, not for exploitation, but for careful husbandry of the public land resources still remaining under federal custodianship.

Afterword

THE WESTWARD MOVEMENT across the continent was not merely prolonged, but massive. It brought uncounted millions from the Old World to the New, and from the shores of the Atlantic to the Pacific. It was the greatest migration of peoples in recorded history.

It was magnificent in its achievements. It replaced barbarism with civilization. It unlocked the bounties of nature and made them a blessing to mankind. It bent reluctant and unfriendly forces of nature to man's will and control. It created a nation that by 1975 contained a population of over 213 million, and that has given leadership to the free peoples of the world. It gave the nation many of its fundamental democratic institutions. It helped shape American literature, sectional and national. It imparted emotional and spiritual values to successive generations. To them the open West was the land of promise, the Utopia of their dreams.

Some aspects of the movement were less attractive. Conquest, speculation, exploitation, and violence were all part of this crusade into the wilderness. They were the harsher realities of the movement, and the source of some of the nation's present problems. They were a reflection of a society, dynamic, determined in the face of resistance, rising on successive frontiers from youth to maturity.

The end of the movement occurred at a date which has called forth differences of definition. In 1890 the Director of the Census drew attention to the fact that the frontier as a continuous line no longer existed. That observation was the point of departure for the great essay of Frederick Jackson Turner, "The Significance of the Frontier in American History." The essay was misread. By some it was thought to say that the frontier in all its aspects had ended. What it said was that the line of the continuous frontier had ended. In one sense the frontier persisted to the date of the Taylor Grazing Act. In a sense it still persists in the third of the national domain held by the federal government in the Far West, and in Alaska, and in a further domain under the sea.

Increasingly, however, the open frontier has become one in the realms of science and technology, of man's control over the environment, and of the relations of man to his fellow man. This is the frontier now challenging the national energies. The hope of the future is that all the optimism, all the indomitable will to overcome obstacles, all the love of freedom and of democratic process, and all the determination to make things better for the future, which the old frontier nourished and symbolized, will remain part of American thought and aspirations.

FURTHER READING
SOURCES OF ILLUSTRATIONS
INDEX

FURTHER READING

CHAPTER 1

Willey, Gordon R. *An Introduction to American Archaeology, North and Middle America,* Englewood Cliffs, N.J.: Prentice-Hall, 1966.

Driver, Harold E. *Indians of North America,* Chicago: University of Chicago Press, rev. ed. 1969. First edition, 1961, contains valuable portions omitted in the revised edition.

Hodge, Frederick W. *Handbook of American Indians North of Mexico,* 2 vols., Washington, D.C.: Bureau of American Ethnology, Government Printing Office, 1907, 1910.

Swanton, John R. *Indian Tribes of North America,* Washington, D.C.: Bureau of American Ethnology; Government Printing Office, 1952.

CHAPTER 2

Washburn, Wilcomb. *The Indian in America,* New York: Harper & Row, 1975.

Josephy, Alvin M. *The Indian Heritage of America,* New York: Alfred A. Knopf, 1968.

Underhill, Ruth M. *Red Man's America: A History of Indians in the United States,* Chicago: University of Chicago Press, rev. ed. 1971.

Mangelsdorf, Paul C. *Corn: Its Origin, Evolution, and Improvement,* Cambridge: Harvard University Press, 1974.

CHAPTER 3

Craven, Wesley F. *White, Red and Black: The Seventeenth Century Virginian,* Charlottesville: University Press of Virginia, 1971; *Dissolution of the Virginia Company,* New York: Oxford University Press, 1932; *Southern Colonies in the Seventeenth Century,* Baton Rouge: Louisiana State University Press, 1949.

Morton, Richard L. *Colonial Virginia,* I, Chapel Hill: University of North Carolina Press, 1960.

Gray, Lewis C. *Agriculture in the Southern United States to 1860,* I, Washington, D.C.: Carnegie Institution, 1933.

Robert, Joseph C. *Tobacco Kingdom,* Durham, N.C.: Duke University Press, 1938.

Smith, Abbot E. *Colonists in Bondage: White Servitude and Convict Labor in America, 1607–1776,* Chapel Hill: University of North Carolina Press, 1947.

Campbell, Mildred. "Social Origins of Some Early Americans," in Smith, James M., ed. *Seventeenth Century America,* Chapel Hill: University of North Carolina Press, 1959.

Beverley, Robert. *The History and Present State of Virginia* (1705), edited with an introduction by Louis B. Wright, Chapel Hill: University of North Carolina Press, 1947. Beverley warned that the one-crop system would ruin Virginia.

Wertenbaker, Thomas J. *The Planters of Colonial Virginia,* Princeton: Princeton University Press, 1922. Contains Governor Nicholson's rent roll of planters, 1703.

CHAPTER 4

Crane, Verner. *Southern Frontier, 1670–1732,* Durham, N.C.: Duke University Press, 1928.

Phillips, Paul C. *The Fur Trade,* I, Norman: University of Oklahoma Press, 1961.

Abernethy, Thomas P. *Three Virginia Frontiers.* Lecture I, Baton Rouge: Louisiana State University Press, 1940.

Washburn, Wilcomb. *The Governor and the Rebel: A History of Bacon's Rebellion in Virginia,* Chapel Hill: University of North Carolina Press, 1957.

Craven, Wesley F. *The Southern Colonies in the Seventeenth Century,* Baton Rouge: Louisiana State University Press, 1949.

CHAPTER 5

Adams, James T. *The Founding of New England,* Boston: Little, Brown, 1921.

Vaughan, Alden. *New England Frontier, 1620–1675,* Boston: Little, Brown, 1965.

Akagi, Roy H. *Town Proprietors of the New England Colonies,* Philadelphia: University of Pennsylvania Press, 1924.

Bidwell, Percy W., and John I. Falconer. *History of Agriculture in the Northern United States, 1620–1860,* Washington, D.C.: Carnegie Institution, 1925.

Powell, Sumner C. *Puritan Village: The Formation of a New England Town,* Middletown, Conn.: Wesleyan University Press, 1963.

CHAPTER 6

Andrews, Charles M. *The Beginnings of Connecticut, 1632–1662,* New Haven: Yale University Press, 1934.

Buffinton, Arthur H. "New England and Western Fur Trade 1629–1675," *Publications of the Colonial Society of Massachusetts,* XVIII, Boston: The Colonial Society, 1917.

Mathews, Lois K. *Expansion of New England.* Boston: Houghton Mifflin, 1909.

Clark, Charles E. *The Eastern Frontier: Settlement of Northern New England, 1610–1763,* New York: Alfred A. Knopf, 1970.

Leach, Douglas E. *Flintlock and Tomahawk: New England in King Philip's War,* New York: Macmillan, 1958.

Woodward, Florence M. *Town Proprietors in Vermont: The New England Town Proprietorship in Decline,* New York: Columbia University Press, 1936.

CHAPTER 7

Alvord, Clarence W., and Lee Bidgood. *First Explorations in the Trans-Allegheny Region by Virginians, 1650–1694,* Cleveland: Arthur H. Clark, 1912.

Abernethy, Thomas P. *Three Virginia Frontiers,* Lecture II, Baton Rouge: Louisiana State University Press, 1940.

Bassett, John S., ed. *The Writings of Colonel William Byrd,* New York: Doubleday, 1901.

Knittle, Walter A. *Early Eighteenth Century Palatine Emigration,* Philadelphia: University of Pennsylvania Press, 1936.

Faust, Albert B. *German Element in the United States,* 2 vols., New York: Steuben Society, rev. ed. 1927.

Ford, Henry J. *The Scotch-Irish in America,* Princeton: Princeton University Press, 1915.

Green, Fletcher M. *Constitutional Development in the South Atlantic States, 1776–1860: A Study in the Evolution of Democracy.* Chapel Hill: University of North Carolina Press, 1930.

CHAPTER 8

Brebner, John B. *Explorers of North America, 1492–1806,* New York: Doubleday, 1955.

Thwaites, Reuben Gold. *The Jesuit Relations and Allied Documents, 1610–1791,* Cleveland: Arthur H. Clark, 1896–1901.

Parkman, Francis. *La Salle and the Discovery of the Great West,* Boston: Little, Brown, 1880.

McDermott, John Francis, ed. *The French in the Mississippi Valley,* Urbana: University of Illinois Press, 1965.

Rich, Edwin E. *Montreal and the Fur Trade,* Montreal: McGill University Press, 1966.

Trelease, Allen W. *Indian Affairs in Colonial New York: The Seventeenth Century,* Ithaca, N.Y.: Cornell University Press, 1940.
Gipson, Lawrence. *Zones of International Friction: The Great Lakes Frontier, Canada, the West Indies, India, 1748–1754,* 2 vols., New York: Alfred A. Knopf, 1939–42.

CHAPTER 9
Parkman, Francis. *Half Century of Conflict,* Boston: Little, Brown, 1892.
Peckham, Howard H. *The Colonial Wars, 1689–1762,* Chicago: University of Chicago Press, 1964.
Wallace, Paul A.W. *Conrad Weiser, 1696–1760, Friend of Colonist and Mohawk,* Philadelphia: University of Pennsylvania Press, 1945.
Gipson, Lawrence. *The Great War for the Empire, 1754–1763,* 3 vols., New York: Alfred A. Knopf, 1949–56.
Wright, J. Leitch. *Anglo-Spanish Rivalry in North America,* Athens: University of Georgia Press, 1971.
Corkran, David M. *Cherokee Frontier, 1740–1762,* and *Creek Frontier, 1540–1783,* Norman: University of Oklahoma Press, 1962 and 1967.
Jacobs, Wilbur R., ed. *Indians of the Southern Colonial Frontier: The Edmond Atkin Report and Plan of 1755,* Columbia: University of South Carolina Press, 1954.

CHAPTER 10
Peckham, Howard H. *Pontiac and the Indian Uprising,* Princeton: Princeton University Press, 1947.
Alvord, Clarence W. *The Mississippi Valley in British Politics,* Cleveland: Arthur H. Clark, 1917.
Sosin, Jack. *Whitehall in the Wilderness, 1760–1775,* Lincoln: University of Nebraska Press, 1961, and *Revolutionary Frontier, 1763–1783,* New York: Holt, Rinehart and Winston, 1967.
De Vorsey, Louis, Jr. *Indian Boundary Line in the Southern Colonies, 1763–1775,* Chapel Hill: University of North Carolina Press, 1966.
Flexner, James. *Mohawk Baronet, Sir William Johnson,* New York: Harper and Brothers, 1959.
Alden, John R., *John Stuart and the Southern Colonial Frontier, 1754–1775,* London: Oxford University Press, 1944.
Neatby, Hilda. *The Quebec Act: Protest and Policy,* Scarborough, Ontario: Prentice-Hall of Canada, 1972.
Gipson, Lawrence. *The Coming of the Revolution, 1763–1775,* New York: Harper & Row, 1954.

CHAPTER 11
Semple, Ellen C. *American History and Its Geographic Conditions,* Boston: Houghton Mifflin, 1903.
Bakeless, John. *Daniel Boone,* Harrisburg, Pa.: Stackpole, 1939.
Abernethy, Thomas P. *Three Virginia Frontiers,* Lecture III, Baton Rouge: Louisiana State University Press, 1940.
Woodward, Grace S. *The Cherokees,* Norman: University of Oklahoma Press, 1963.

CHAPTER 12
Abernethy, Thomas P. *Western Lands and the American Revolution,* Charlottesville: University Press of Virginia, 1937.
Bailey, Kenneth P. *The Ohio Company of Virginia, 1748–1792,* Glendale, Calif: Arthur H. Clark, 1939.
Mulkearn, Lois, ed. *George Mercer Papers Relating to the Ohio Company of Virginia,* Pittsburgh: University of Pittsburgh Press, 1954.
Wainwright, Nicholas B. *George Croghan, Wilderness Diplomat,* Chapel Hill: University of North Carolina Press, 1961.

Sosin, Jack. *Whitehall in the Wilderness, 1760–1775,* Lincoln: University of Nebraska Press, 1961.
Livermore, Shaw. *Early American Land Companies,* New York: Commonwealth Fund, Oxford University Press, 1939.

CHAPTER 13

Flexner, James T. *Mohawk Baronet, Sir William Johnson,* New York: Harper and Brothers, 1959.
Thwaites, Reuben G., and Louise P. Kellogg. *Frontier Defense on the Upper Ohio,* and *Documentary History of Lord Dunmore's War,* Madison: Wisconsin State Historical Society, 1912 and 1905.
Quaife, Milo M., ed. *The Conquest of the Illinois,* Chicago: Lakeside Press, 1920.
James, James A. *Life of George Rogers Clark,* Chicago: University of Chicago Press, 1928.
Graymont, Barbara. *The Iroquois in the American Revolution,* Syracuse: Syracuse University Press, 1972.
O'Donnell, James H. *Southern Indians in the American Revolution,* Knoxville: University of Tennessee Press, 1973.
Alden, John R. *A History of the American Revolution,* New York: Alfred A. Knopf, 1969.
Sosin, Jack. *Revolutionary Frontier, 1763–1783,* New York: Holt, Rinehart and Winston, 1967.
Brown, Richard M. *Strain of Violence: Historical Studies of American Violence and Vigilantism,* New York: Oxford University Press, 1975. Chapter 3.
Morris, Richard. *The Peacemakers: The Great Powers and American Independence,* New York: Harper & Row, 1965.

CHAPTER 14

Jensen, Merrill. "Cession of the Old Northwest" and "Creation of the National Domain," *Mississippi Valley Historical Review,* XXIII (1936) and XXVI (1939).
McLaughlin, Andrew C. *Confederation and Constitution,* New York: Harper and Brothers, 1905. Includes useful maps.
Haskins, Charles H. *Yazoo Land Companies,* New York: Knickerbocker Press, 1891.
Magrath, C. Peter. *Yazoo: Fletcher v. Peck in Its Socio-Economic Setting,* Providence, R.I.: Brown University Press, 1966.

CHAPTER 15

Jensen, Merrill. *Articles of Confederation: An Interpretation of Social and Constitutional History, 1774–1781,* Madison: University of Wisconsin Press, 1940, and *The New Nation: A History of the United States during the Confederation, 1781–1789,* New York: Alfred A. Knopf, 1950.
McLaughlin, Andrew C. *Confederation and Constitution,* New York: Harper and Brothers, 1905.
Ford, Amelia C. *Colonial Precedents of Our National Land System.* Madison: University of Wisconsin Press, 1910.
Gates, Paul W. *History of Public Land Law Development,* Washington, D.C.: Government Printing Office, 1968. Chapters 3–5.
Turner, Frederick Jackson. "Western State Making in the Revolutionary Era," *American Historical Review,* I (1895–96).
Williams, Samuel C. *The Lost State of Franklin,* New York: Pioneer Press, rev. ed. 1933.
Jellison, Charles A. *Ethan Allen, Frontier Rebel,* Syracuse: Syracuse University Press, 1969.

CHAPTER 16

Hulbert, Archer B., ed. *Records of the Original Proceedings of the Ohio Company,* Marietta, Ohio: The Marietta Historical Commission, 1917.
Cutler, William P. *Reverend Manasseh Cutler,* 2 vols., Cincinnati, 1888.
Livermore, Shaw. *Early American Land Companies,* New York: Commonwealth Fund, Oxford University Press, 1939.

Sakolski, Aaron M. *Great American Land Bubble*, New York: Harper and Brothers, 1932.

Higgins, Ruth. *Expansion of New York*, Columbus: Ohio State University Press, 1931.

Evans, Paul D. *Holland Land Company*, Buffalo: Buffalo Historical Society, 1924.

McNall, Neil. *Agricultural History of the Genesee Valley, 1790–1860*, Philadelphia: University of Pennsylvania Press, 1952.

Cross, Whitney R. *The Burned-over District: The Social and Intellectual History of Enthusiastic Religion in Western New York, 1800–1850*, Ithaca, N.Y.: Cornell University Press, 1950.

Buck, Solon J., and Elizabeth H. Buck. *The Planting of Civilization in Western Pennsylvania*, Pittsburgh: University of Pittsburgh Press, 1939. Includes a section on Pennsylvania's land policy and on land speculation.

CHAPTER 17

Campbell, John C. *The Southern Highlander in His Homeland*, Lexington: University Press of Kentucky, 1921, reprinted with a new introduction, 1969.

Posey, Walter B. *Religious Strife on the Southern Frontier*, Baton Rouge: Louisiana State University Press, 1965.

Wallis, Charles L., ed. *Autobiography of Peter Cartwright*, Nashville: Abingdon Press, 1956.

Cole, Arthur C. *Whig Party in the South*, Washington, D.C.: Carnegie Institution, 1913. Maps in color show distribution of Whig and Democratic votes in the South, including the Allegheny Plateau, in elections 1836 through 1852.

CHAPTER 18

Whitaker, Arthur P. *The Spanish-American Frontier, 1783–1795*, Boston: Houghton Mifflin, 1927.

Bemis, Samuel F. *Pinckney's Treaty: American Advantage from Europe's Distress, 1783–1800*, New Haven: Yale University Press, rev. ed. 1960.

Lyon, E. Wilson. *Louisiana in French Diplomacy, 1759–1804*, Norman: University of Oklahoma Press, 1934.

Savelle, Max. *George Morgan*, New York: Columbia University Press, 1932.

Jacobs, James R. *Tarnished Warrior*, New York: Macmillan, 1938. (James Wilkinson.)

Caughey, John W. *McGillivray of the Creeks*, Norman: University of Oklahoma Press, 1938.

Wright, J. Leitch. *William Augustus Bowles, Director-General of the Creek Nation*, Athens: University of Georgia Press, 1967.

Holmes, Jack D. L. *Gayoso*, Baton Rouge: Louisiana State University Press, 1965. Gayoso was the Spanish governor in the Mississippi Valley, 1789–99.

CHAPTER 19

Stevens, Wayne E. *Northwest Fur Trade, 1763–1800*, Urbana: University of Illinois Press, 1928.

Manning, William R. "The Nootka Sound Controversy," *Annual Report of the American Historical Association*, 1904.

Wildes, Harry E. *Anthony Wayne*, New York: Harcourt, Brace, 1941.

Ritcheson, Charles R. *Aftermath of Revolution: British Policy Toward the United States, 1783–1795*, Dallas: Southern Methodist University Press, 1969.

Bemis, Samuel F. *Jay's Treaty*, New Haven: Yale University Press, rev. ed. 1962.

Combs, Jerald A. *The Jay Treaty: Political Battleground of the Founding Fathers*, Berkeley: University of California Press, 1970.

Burt, Alfred L. *United States, Great Britain and British North America*, New Haven: Yale University Press, 1940.

Perkins, Bradford. *The First Rapprochement: England and the United States, 1795–1805*, Philadelphia: University of Pennsylvania Press, 1955.

CHAPTER 20

Adams, Henry. *History of the United States in the Jefferson and Madison Administrations*, New York: Scribner's, 1889–91.

Perkins, Bradford. *Prologue to War, 1805–1812*, and *Castlereagh and Adams, 1812–1823*, Berkeley: University of California Press, 1961 and 1964.

Tucker, Glenn. *Tecumseh*, Indianapolis: Bobbs-Merrill, 1956.

Cotterill, Robert S. *The Southern Indians*, Norman: University of Oklahoma Press, 1954.

Horsman, Reginald. *The War of 1812*, New York: Alfred A. Knopf, 1969.

Brown, Wilbur S. *Amphibious Campaign for West Florida and Louisiana*, University: University of Alabama Press, 1969.

CHAPTER 21

Turner, Frederick Jackson. *The Rise of the New West*, New York: Harper and Brothers, 1906.

Pooley, William V. *Settlement of Illinois, 1830–1850*, Madison: University of Wisconsin Press, 1908.

Schafer, Joseph. *Four Wisconsin Counties*, Madison: Wisconsin State Historical Society, 1927.

Curti, Merle. *The Making of an American Community*, Stanford, Calif.: Stanford University Press, 1959.

Prucha, Francis P. *Broadax and Bayonet: The Role of the United States Army in the Development of the Northwest, 1815–1860*, Madison: Wisconsin State Historical Society, 1953, and *The Sword of the Republic: The United States Army on the Frontier, 1783–1846*, New York: Macmillan, 1969.

Cole, Cyrenus. *I Am a Man: The Indian Black Hawk*, Iowa City: Iowa State Historical Society, 1938.

Mathews, Lois K. *The Expansion of New England*, Boston: Houghton Mifflin, 1909.

Stilwell, Lewis D. *Migration from Vermont, 1776–1860*, Montpelier: Vermont Historical Society, 1948.

Hansen, Marcus L. *Atlantic Migration*, Cambridge: Harvard University Press, 1940.

Wright, James E. *Galena Lead District, 1824–1847*, Madison: Wisconsin State Historical Society, 1967.

CHAPTER 22

Scheiber, Harry N., ed. *The Old Northwest*, Lincoln: University of Nebraska Press, 1969.

Buley, R. Carlyle. *The Old Northwest, 1815–1840*, 2 vols., Bloomington: Indiana University Press, 1950.

Gates, Paul W. *The Farmer's Age*, New York: Holt, Rinehart and Winston, 1960.

Schafer, Joseph. *History of Agriculture in Wisconsin*, Madison: Wisconsin State Historical Society, 1922.

Hutchinson, William T. *Cyrus H. McCormick*, 2 vols., New York: Century Press, 1930–35.

Henlein, Paul C. *Cattle Kingdom in the Ohio Valley, 1783–1860*, Lexington: University Press of Kentucky, 1959.

Clark, John G. *Grain Trade of the Old Northwest*, Urbana: University of Illinois Press, 1966.

Berry, Thomas S. *Western Prices before 1861: A Study of the Cincinnati Market*, Cambridge: Harvard University Press, 1943.

CHAPTER 23

Swanton, John R. *Indians of the Southeastern United States*, Washington, D.C.: Bureau of American Ethnology, Government Printing Office, 1946.

Bassett, John S. *Andrew Jackson*, Garden City, N.Y.: Doubleday, Page, rev. ed. 1925.

Foreman, Grant. *Indian Removal*, Norman: University of Oklahoma Press, rev. ed. 1953.

Cotterill, Robert S. *Southern Indians*, Norman: University of Oklahoma Press, 1954.

Green, Fletcher, ed. *The Lides Go South and West: The Record of a Planter Migration in 1835*, Columbia: University of South Carolina Press, 1952.

Young, Mary E. *Redskins, Ruffleshirts and Rednecks*, Norman: University of Oklahoma Press, 1961.

Smith, Alfred G. *Economic Readjustment for an Old Cotton State, 1820–1860*, Columbia: University of South Carolina Press, 1958.

CHAPTER 24

Gray, Lewis C. *Agriculture in the Southern United States to 1860,* II, Washington, D.C.: Carnegie Institution, 1933.

Sitterson, J. Carlyle. *Sugar Country,* Lexington: University Press of Kentucky, 1953.

Atherton, Lewis. *Southern Country Store,* Baton Rouge: Louisiana State University Press, 1949.

Woodman, Harold D. *King Cotton and His Retainers,* Lexington: University Press of Kentucky, 1968.

Cole, Arthur C. *Whig Party in the South,* Washington, D.C.: Carnegie Institution, 1913.

CHAPTER 25

Phillips, Ulrich B. *American Negro Slavery,* New York: Appleton, 1918.

Stampp, Kenneth M. *The Peculiar Institution: Slavery in the Ante-Bellum South,* New York: Alfred A. Knopf, 1956.

Franklin, John Hope. *From Slavery to Freedom: A History of American Negroes,* New York: Alfred A. Knopf, rev. ed. 1956.

Gray, Lewis C. *Agriculture in the Southern United States,* II, Washington, D.C.: Carnegie Institution, 1933.

Genovese, Eugene D. *Political Economy of Slavery,* New York: Random House, 1965.

Sydnor, Charles S. *Development of Southern Sectionalism, 1819–1848,* Baton Rouge: Louisiana State University Press, 1964.

Wiltse, Charles M. *John C. Calhoun, Nullifier,* Indianapolis: Bobbs-Merrill, 1949.

Russel, Robert R. *Economic Aspects of Southern Sectionalism, 1840–1861,* Urbana: University of Illinois Press, 1924.

Olmsted, Frederick Law. *The Cotton Kingdom: A Traveller's Observations on Cotton and Slavery in the American Slave States,* New York and London: 1861; edited with an introduction by Arthur M. Schlesinger, New York: Alfred A. Knopf, 1953.

CHAPTER 26

Taylor, George R. *Transportation Revolution, 1815–1860,* New York: Holt, Rinehart and Winston, 1951.

Scheiber, Harry N. *The Ohio Canal Era: A Case Study of Government and the Economy, 1820–1861,* Athens: Ohio University Press, 1969.

Shaw, Ronald E. *Erie Water West,* Lexington: University Press of Kentucky, 1966.

Hunter, Louis C. *Steamboats on Western Waters,* Cambridge: Harvard University Press, 1949.

Johnson, Arthur, and Barry Supple. *Boston Capitalists and Western Railroads,* Cambridge: Harvard University Press, 1967.

Bassett, John S. *Andrew Jackson,* Garden City, N.Y.: Doubleday, Page, rev. ed. 1925.

Gates, Paul W. *The Illinois Central Railroad,* Cambridge: Harvard University Press, 1934.

Goodrich, Carter. *Government Promotion of American Canals and Railroads,* New York: Columbia University Press, 1960.

CHAPTER 27

Taussig, Frank W. *Tariff History of the United States,* New York: Putnam, 8th rev. ed. 1931.

Hofstadter, Richard. *The American Political Tradition and the Men Who Made It,* New York: Alfred A. Knopf, 1948.

Wiltse, Charles M. *John C. Calhoun, Nullifier,* Indianapolis: Bobbs-Merrill, 1949.

Bassett, John S. *Andrew Jackson,* Garden City: N.Y.: Doubleday, Page, rev. ed. 1925.

Freehling, William W. *Prelude to Civil War: The Nullification Controversy in South Carolina, 1816–1836,* New York: Harper & Row, 1966.

CHAPTER 28

Gates, Paul W. *History of Public Land Law Development,* Washington, D.C.: Government Printing Office, 1968.

Robbins, Roy M. *Our Landed Heritage,* Princeton: Princeton University Press, 1942.

Rohrbough, Malcolm. *The Land Office Business: The Settlement and Administration of American Public Lands, 1789–1837,* New York: Oxford University Press, 1968.
Zahler, Helene S. *Eastern Workingmen and National Land Policy, 1829–1862,* New York: Columbia University Press, 1941.
Stephenson, George M. *Political History of the Public Lands, 1840–1862,* Boston, 1917.
Smith, Elbert B. *Magnificent Missourian: The Life of Thomas Hart Benton,* Philadelphia: Lippincott, 1958.
Turner, Frederick Jackson. *The United States 1830–1850: The Nation and Its Sections,* New York: Henry Holt, 1935.

CHAPTER 29

Powell, John W. *The Lands of the Arid Region of the United States,* Washington, D.C.: Department of the Interior, Government Printing Office, 1878.
Webb, Walter P. *The Great Plains,* Boston: Ginn, 1931.
Kincer, Joseph. "Temperature, Sunshine and Wind" in *Atlas of American Agriculture: Part 2, Climate,* Washington, D.C.: Department of Agriculture: Government Printing Office, 1922.
Kraenzel, Carl. *The Great Plains,* Norman: University of Oklahoma Press, 1955.

CHAPTER 30

Oglesby, Richard E. *Manuel Lisa and the Opening of the Missouri Fur Trade,* Norman: University of Oklahoma Press, 1963.
Sunder, John E. *Fur Trade on the Upper Missouri, 1840–1865,* Norman: University of Oklahoma Press, 1965.
Morgan, Dale. *Jedediah Smith and the Opening of the West,* New York: Bobbs-Merrill, 1955; and Dale Morgan, ed. *The West of William H. Ashley . . . recorded in diaries of Ashley and his contemporaries, 1822–1838,* Denver: Old West Publishing Company, 1964.
Phillips, Paul C. *The Fur Trade,* II, Norman: University of Oklahoma Press, 1961.
Cleland, Robert C. *This Reckless Breed of Men: Trappers of the Southwest,* New York: Alfred A. Knopf, 1944.
Weber, David J. *The Taos Trappers: The Fur Trade in the Far Southwest, 1540–1846,* Norman: University of Oklahoma Press, 1971.
Gregg, Josiah. *Commerce of the Prairies,* 2 vols., New York, 1844. One-vol. ed., Max L. Moorhead, ed. Norman: University of Oklahoma Press, 1954.
Hafen, Leroy. *Old Spanish Trail,* Glendale, Calif.: Arthur H. Clark, 1954; and *Mountain Men and the Fur Trade of the Far West: Biographical Sketches,* Glendale, Calif.: Arthur H. Clark, 1965–72. Vol. I is a useful introduction to the set.

CHAPTER 31

Birkbeck, Morris. *Notes on a Journey in America,* London: Severn and Company, 1818.
Dickens, Charles. *American Notes.* First American ed., New York, 1842.
Clemens, Samuel L. *Life on the Mississippi.* First ed., Boston, 1883.
Rollins, Phillip A. *Discovery of the Oregon Trail: Robert Stuart's Narrative of His Overland Trip Eastward from Astoria in 1812–13,* New York: Edward Eberstadt and Sons, 1935.
Billington, Ray A. *Far Western Frontier, 1830–1860,* New York: Harper and Brothers, 1956.
Stewart, George R. *The California Trail: An Epic with Many Heroes,* New York: McGraw Hill, 1962.
Ghent, William J. *The Road to Oregon: A Chronicle of the Great Emigrant Trail,* New York: Longmans, Green, 1929.
Alter, J. Cecil. *James Bridger, Trapper, Frontiersman, Scout and Guide,* Salt Lake City: Shepard Book Co., 1925; rev. ed., Norman: University of Oklahoma Press, 1962.
Jackson, W. Turrentine. *Wagon Roads West: A Study of Federal Road Surveys, and Construction in the Trans-Mississippi West, 1846–1869,* Berkeley: University of California Press, 1952, reprint: New Haven: Yale University Press, 1965.

CHAPTER 32

Bannon, John F. *Spanish Borderlands Frontier, 1513–1821,* New York: Holt, Rinehart and Winston, 1970.
Barker, Eugene C. *Stephen F. Austin,* Nashville: Cokesbury Press, 1926.
James, Marquis. *The Raven: A Biography of Sam Houston,* Indianapolis: Bobbs-Merrill, 1929.
Binkley, William C. *The Texas Revolution,* Baton Rouge: Louisiana State University Press, 1952.
Callcott, Wilfred H. *Santa Anna: The Story of an Enigma,* Norman: University of Oklahoma Press, 1936.

CHAPTER 33

Hall, Claude H. *Abel P. Upshur, Conservative Virginian,* Madison: Wisconsin State Historical Society, 1963.
Wiltse, Charles M. *John C. Calhoun, Nullifier,* Indianapolis: Bobbs-Merrill, 1949.
Chitwood, Oliver P. *John Tyler, Champion of the Old South,* New York: D. Appleton-Century, 1939.
Merk, Frederick. *Fruits of Propaganda in the Tyler Administration,* Cambridge: Harvard University Press, 1971; and *Slavery and the Annexation of Texas,* New York: Alfred A. Knopf, 1972.
Jarvis, Edward. "Statistics of Insanity in the United States," *Boston Medical and Surgical Journal,* September 21, 1842.
Bemis, Samuel F. *John Quincy Adams and the Union,* New York: Alfred A. Knopf, 1956.

CHAPTER 34

Smith, Justin. *The Annexation of Texas,* New York: Baker and Taylor, 1911.
Pletcher, David. *Diplomacy of Annexation: Texas, Oregon, and the Mexican War,* Columbia: University of Missouri Press, 1973.
Merk, Frederick. *Slavery and the Annexation of Texas,* New York: Alfred A. Knopf, 1972.
Smith, Elbert B. *Magnificent Missourian: The Life of Thomas Hart Benton,* Philadelphia: Lippincott, 1958.
Gambrell, Herbert. *Anson Jones, the Last President of Texas,* Austin: University of Texas Press, rev. ed. 1964.

CHAPTER 35

Cook, Warren L. *Flood Tide of Empire: Spain and the Pacific Northwest, 1543–1819,* New Haven: Yale University Press, 1973.
Rich, Edwin E. *Hudson's Bay Company, 1670–1870,* 3 vols., Toronto: Macmillan, 1961.
Howay, Frederick W. *Voyages of the "Columbia,"* Massachusetts Historical Society *Collections,* LXXIX, Boston, 1941.
Porter, Kenneth W. *John Jacob Astor, Business Man,* 2 vols., Cambridge: Harvard University Press, 1931.
Merk, Frederick ed. *Fur Trade and Empire: George Simpson's Journal, 1824–25,* Harvard University Press, rev. ed. 1968; *Albert Gallatin and the Oregon Problem,* Harvard University Press, 1950; *The Oregon Question; Essays in Anglo-American Diplomacy and Politics,* Harvard University Press, 1967.
Bemis, Samuel F. *John Quincy Adams and the Foundations of American Foreign Policy,* New York: Alfred A. Knopf, 1949.
Bemis, Samuel F., ed. *The American Secretaries of State and Their Diplomacy,* New York: Alfred A. Knopf, 1927–29. Vol. V of this series deals with the Oregon diplomacy of Webster, Upshur, Calhoun, and Buchanan.
Moore, John B., ed. *Works of James Buchanan,* VI and VII, Philadelphia: Lippincott, 1909.
Quaife, Milo M., ed. *Diary of James K. Polk during His Presidency,* 4 vols., Chicago: A. C. McClurg, 1910.

Sellers, Charles G. *James K. Polk*, II: *Continentalist, 1843–1846*, Princeton: Princeton University Press, 1966.

Graebner, Norman. *Empire on the Pacific*, New York: Ronald Press, 1955.

CHAPTER 36

Flanders, Robert. *Nauvoo: Kingdom on the Mississippi*, Urbana: University of Illinois Press, 1965.

Morgan, Dale L. *Great Salt Lake*, Indianapolis: Bobbs-Merrill, 1947.

Arrington, Leonard J. *Great Basin Kingdom: An Economic History of the Latter Day Saints, 1830–1900*, Cambridge: Harvard University Press, 1958.

Lass, William E. *From the Missouri to the Great Salt Lake: An Account of Overland Freighting*, Lincoln: Nebraska State Historical Society Publications, 1972. Covers period 1848 to 1870's.

O'Dea, Thomas F. *The Mormons*, Chicago: University of Chicago Press, 1957.

Geddes, Joseph A. *The United Order among the Mormons*, Salt Lake City: Deseret Press, 1924.

Mulder, William. *Homeward to Zion: Mormon Migration from Scandinavia*, Minneapolis: University of Minnesota Press, 1957.

Peterson, Charles S. *Take Up Your Mission: Mormon Colonization along the Little Colorado River, 1870–1900*, Tucson: University of Arizona Press, 1973.

CHAPTER 37

Cleland, Robert G. *From Wilderness to Empire: A History of California, 1542–1900*, New York: Alfred A. Knopf, 1944.

Bolton, Herbert E. "The Mission as a Frontier Institution," *American Historical Review*, XXIII, October 1917.

Engelhardt, Fr. Zephyrin. *The Missions and Missionaries of California*, 4 vols., San Francisco: James H. Barry Company, 1908–16.

Chevigny, Hector. *Russian America*, New York: The Viking Press, 1965.

Dana, Richard H. *Two Years Before the Mast*, New York: Harper and Brothers, 1840.

Robinson, Alfred. *Life in California*, New York: Wiley and Putnam, 1846.

CHAPTER 38

Cleland, Robert G. *From Wilderness to Empire: A History of California, 1542–1900*, New York: Alfred A. Knopf, 1944.

Moore, John B., ed. *Works of James Buchanan*, VI, VII, and VIII, Philadelphia: Lippincott, 1909.

Nevins, Allan. *Frémont, Pathmarker of the West*, New York: Longmans, Green, 3rd ed. 1955.

Spence, Mary Lee, and Donald Jackson, eds. *The Expeditions of John Charles Frémont*, II, Urbana: University of Illinois Press, 1974.

Royce, Josiah. *California . . . 1846 to 1856*, Boston: Houghton Mifflin, 1886. Reprinted with an introduction by Robert G. Cleland, New York: Alfred A. Knopf, 1948.

CHAPTER 39

Quaife, Milo M., ed. *Diary of James K. Polk during His Presidency*, 4 vols., Chicago: A. C. McClurg, 1910.

Cole, Arthur C. *Whig Party in the South*, Washington, D.C.: Carnegie Institution, 1913.

Adams, Charles F., ed. *Memoirs of John Quincy Adams*, XII, Philadelphia: Lippincott, 1877.

Wiltse, Charles M. *John C. Calhoun, Sectionalist*, Indianapolis: Bobbs-Merrill, 1951.

Merk, Frederick. *Manifest Destiny and Mission in American History*, New York: Alfred A. Knopf, 1963; and "Dissent in the Mexican War" in Samuel Eliot Morison, Frederick Merk, and Frank Freidel, *Dissent in Three American Wars*, Cambridge, Harvard University Press, 1970.

Pletcher, David. *The Diplomacy of Annexation: Texas, Oregon, and the Mexican War*, Columbia: University of Missouri Press, 1973.

CHAPTER 40

Morrison, Chaplain W. *Democratic Politics and Sectionalism: The Wilmot Proviso Controversy*, Chapel Hill: University of North Carolina Press, 1967.
Wiltse, Charles M. *John C. Calhoun, Sectionalist*, Indianapolis: Bobbs-Merrill, 1951.
Schurz, Carl. *Henry Clay*, Boston: Houghton Mifflin, 1899.
Dalzell, Robert F. *Daniel Webster and the Trial of American Nationalism*, Boston: Houghton Mifflin, 1973.
Hamilton, Holman. *Prologue to Conflict*, Lexington: University Press of Kentucky, 1964.
Rayback, Joseph G. *Free Soil: The Election of 1848*, Lexington: University Press of Kentucky, 1970.
Woodford, Frank B. *Lewis Cass*, New Brunswick, N.J.: Rutgers University Press, 1950.
Berwanger, Eugene. *Frontier against Slavery*, Urbana: University of Illinois Press, 1967.

CHAPTER 41

Ray, Perley O. *Repeal of the Missouri Compromise*, Cleveland: Arthur H. Clark, 1909.
Johnson, Allen. *Stephen A. Douglas*, New York: Macmillan, 1908.
Milton, George F. *The Eve of Conflict: Stephen A. Douglas and the Needless War*, Boston: Houghton Mifflin, rev. ed. 1963.
Nevins, Allan. *Ordeal of the Union*, II: *A House Dividing, 1852–1859*, New York: Scribner's Sons, 1947.
Thayer, Eli. *Kansas Crusade*, New York: Harper and Brothers, 1889.
Johnson, Samuel A. *Battle Cry of Freedom: The New England Emigrant Aid Company*, Lawrence: University Press of Kansas, 1954.
Smith, Elbert B. *The Presidency of James Buchanan*, Lawrence: University Press of Kansas, 1975.

CHAPTER 42

Kutler, Stanley L. *Dred Scott Decision*, Boston: Houghton Mifflin, 1967.
Swisher, Carl L. *Roger B. Taney*, New York: Macmillan, 1935.
Fehrenbacher, Don E. *Prelude to Greatness: Lincoln in the 1850's*, Stanford, Calif.: Stanford University Press, 1962.

CHAPTER 43

Nevins, Allan. *Ordeal of the Union*, III and IV: *The Emergence of Lincoln*, New York: Scribner's Sons, 1950.
Potter, David M. *The South and Sectional Conflict*, Baton Rouge: Louisiana State University Press, 1968; and *The Impending Crisis, 1848–1861*, New York: Harper & Row, 1976. Two final chapters are by Don E. Fehrenbacher.
Thomas, Benjamin P. *Abraham Lincoln*, New York: Alfred A. Knopf, 1952.
Johannsen, Robert. *Stephen A. Douglas*, New York: Oxford University Press, 1973.
Kirwan, Albert. *John J. Crittenden: The Struggle for the Union*, Lexington: University Press of Kentucky, 1962.
Knoles, George H., ed. *The Crisis of the Union, 1860–1861*, Baton Rouge: Louisiana State University Press, 1965.

CHAPTER 44

Paul, Rodman. *California Gold: The Beginning of Mining in the Far West*, Cambridge: Harvard University Press, 1947; and *Mining Frontiers of the Far West* [to 1880], New York: Holt, Rinehart and Winston, 1963.
Wright, William (Dan De Quille). *Big Bonanza*, Hartford, Conn.: American Publishing Co., 1877; reprint, New York: Alfred A. Knopf, 1959.
Jackson, W. Turrentine. *Treasure Hill: Portrait of a Silver Mining Camp*, Tucson: University of Arizona Press, 1963.

Greever, William. *Bonanza West: The Story of Western Mining Rushes, 1848–1900,* Norman: University of Oklahoma Press, 1963.

Shinn, Charles M. *Mining Camps: American Frontier Government,* New York: Scribner's, 1884; reprint, with an introduction and footnotes by Rodman Paul, New York: Harper & Row, 1965.

Trimble, William J. *Mining Advance into the Inland Empire,* Madison: University of Wisconsin Press, 1914; reprint, with an introduction by Rodman Paul, New York: Johnson Reprint Corp., 1972.

Spence, Clark C. *British Investments and the American Mining Frontier, 1860–1901,* Ithaca, N.Y.: Cornell University Press, 1958; and *Mining Engineers and the American West: The Lace-Boot Brigate, 1849–1933,* New Haven: Yale University Press, 1970.

CHAPTER 45

Meyer, Roy W. *History of the Santee Sioux,* Lincoln: University of Nebraska Press, 1967.

Hyde, George E. *Red Cloud's Folk: A History of the Oglala Sioux,* Norman: University of Oklahoma Press, 1937.

Berthrong, Donald J. *Southern Cheyennes,* Norman: University of Oklahoma Press, 1963.

Ewers, John C. *Indians of the Upper Missouri,* Norman: University of Oklahoma Press, 1968.

Spicer, Edward H. *Cycles of Conquest: The Impact of Spain, Mexico, and the United States on the Indians of the Southwest, 1533–1960,* Tucson: University of Arizona Press, 1962.

Foreman, Grant. *The Five Civilized Tribes,* Norman: University of Oklahoma Press, 1934. Their history from removal to 1860.

Priest, Loring B. *Uncle Sam's Stepchildren: The Reformation of United States Indian Policy, 1865–1887,* New Brunswick, N.J.: Rutgers University Press, 1942. Includes the Dawes Act.

Otis, D. S. *The Dawes Act and the Allotment of Indian Lands,* Norman: University of Oklahoma Press, 1973. An account written in 1934 by a historian employed by the Bureau of Indian Affairs, edited with an introduction by Francis Paul Prucha.

CHAPTER 46

Bogue, Allan. *From Prairie to Corn Belt: Farming on the Illinois and Iowa Prairies in the Nineteenth Century,* Chicago: University of Chicago Press, 1963.

Merk, Frederick. *Economic History of Wisconsin during the Civil War Decade,* Madison: Wisconsin State Historical Society Press, 2nd ed. 1971.

Babcock, Kendric C. *The Scandinavian Element in the United States,* Urbana: University of Illinois Studies in the Social Sciences, 1914.

Drache, Hiram M. *Day of the Bonanza: Farming in the Red River Valley of the North,* Fargo: North Dakota Institute for Regional Studies, 1964.

Hoffman, George W. *Future Trading,* Philadelphia: University of Pennsylvania Press, 1932.

Buck, Solon J. *The Granger Movement,* Cambridge: Harvard University Press, 1913.

Unger, Irwin. *The Greenback Era,* Princeton: Princeton University Press, 1964.

Scheiber, Harry N. "The Road to Munn," *Perspectives,* V, Cambridge, Mass.: The Charles Warren Center, 1971.

CHAPTER 47

Kuhlman, Charles B. *Flour Milling Industry in the United States,* Boston: Houghton Mifflin, 1929.

Smith, Alice E. *Millstone and Saw,* Madison: Wisconsin State Historical Society Press, 1966.

Merk, Frederick. *Economic History of Wisconsin during the Civil War Decade,* Madison: Wisconsin State Historical Society Press, 2nd ed. 1971.

Larson, Agnes M. *History of the White Pine Industry in Minnesota,* Minneapolis: University of Minnesota Press, 1949.

Hidy, Ralph, et al., *Timber and Men: The Weyerhaeuser Story,* New York: Macmillan, 1963.

Gates, William B. *Michigan Copper and Boston Dollars,* Cambridge: Harvard University Press, 1951.

Wirth, Freeman P. *The Discovery and Exploitation of the Minnesota Iron Lands,* Cedar Rapids, Iowa: Torch Press, 1937.

Temin, Peter. *Iron and Steel in Nineteenth Century America: An Economic Enquiry.* Cambridge, Mass.: Massachusetts Institute of Technology Press, 1964.

CHAPTER 48

Osgood, Ernest S. *The Day of the Cattleman,* Minneapolis: University of Minnesota Press, 1929.

Abbott, Edward C., and Helena H. Smith. *We Pointed Them North.* Norman: University of Oklahoma Press, rev. ed. 1955.

Haley, J. Evetts. *The XIT Ranch of Texas,* Norman: University of Oklahoma Press, rev. ed. 1953.

Atherton, Lewis. *Cattle Kings,* Bloomington: Indiana University Press, 1961.

Dykstra, Robert. *Cattle Towns: A Social History of the Kansas Cattle Trading Centers,* New York: Alfred A. Knopf, 1968.

Gressley, Gene. *Bankers and Cattlemen,* New York: Alfred A. Knopf, 1966.

Jackson, W. Turrentine. *The Enterprising Scot: Investors in the American West after 1873,* Edinburgh: University Press Publications, 1968.

Smith, Theobald, and F. L. Kilbourne. *Investigations into the Nature, Causation, and Prevention of Texas Fever,* Department of Agriculture, Bureau of Animal Husbandry, Bulletin No. 1, Washington, D.C.: Government Printing Office, 1893.

Robbins, Roy M. *Our Landed Heritage,* Lincoln: University of Nebraska Press, rev. ed. 1976. Includes fraudulent enclosures by cattle interests.

Savage, William W., Jr. *The Cherokee Strip Livestock Association,* Columbia: University of Missouri Press, 1973.

Oliphant, J. Orin. *On the Cattle Ranges of the Oregon Country,* Seattle: University of Washington Press, 1968.

CHAPTER 49

Fite, Gilbert. *The Farmers' Frontier, 1865–1900,* New York: Holt, Rinehart and Winston, 1966. Includes agriculture in California and Pacific Northwest.

Hedges, James B. "The Colonization Work of the Northern Pacific Railroad," *Mississippi Valley Historical Review,* XIII (December 1926). The settlement of Minnesota and Dakota railroad lands.

Overton, Richard C. *Burlington West: A Colonization History of the Burlington Railroad,* Cambridge: Harvard University Press, 1941. Detailed discussion of the company's advertising of its lands and their settlement.

Bogue, Allan G. *Money at Interest: The Farm Mortgage on the Middle Border,* Ithaca, N.Y.: Cornell University Press, 1955.

Rister, Carl C. *Land Hunger: David L. Payne and the Oklahoma Boomers,* Norman: University of Oklahoma Press, 1942.

Lamar, Howard. *Dakota Territory 1861–89,* New Haven: Yale University Press, 1956.

CHAPTER 50

Hicks, John D. *Populist Revolt,* Minneapolis: University of Minnesota Press, 1931.

Saloutos, Theodore. *Farmer Movements in the South,* Berkeley: University of California Press, 1960.

Wright, James E. *Politics of Populism: Dissent in Colorado,* New Haven: Yale University Press, 1974.

Woodward, C. Vann. *Origins of the New South, 1877–1913,* Baton Rouge: Louisiana State University Press, rev. ed. 1971; and *Tom Watson,* Savannah: Beehive Press, rev. ed. 1973.

Glad, Paul W. *McKinley, Bryan, and the People,* Philadelphia: Lippincott, 1964.

Coletta, Paolo E. *William Jennings Bryan,* I: *Political Evangelist,* Lincoln: University of Nebraska Press, 1964.

Pollack, Norman. *The Populist Response to Industrial America,* Cambridge: Harvard University Press, 1962.
Durden, Robert F. *Climax of Populism: Election of 1896.* Lexington: University Press of Kentucky, 1965.

Chapter 51

Hargreaves, Mary W. *Dry Farming in the Northern Great Plains,* Cambridge: Harvard University Press, 1959.
Kraenzel, Karl. *Great Plains in Transition,* Norman: Oklahoma University Press, 1955.
Malin, James C. *Winter Wheat in Kansas,* Lawrence: University Press of Kansas, 1944.
Hewes, Leslie. *Suitcase Farming Frontier: A Study of the Historical Geography of the Central Great Plains,* Lincoln: University of Nebraska Press, 1973.
Ottoson, Howard W., et al. *Land and People in the Northern Plains Transition Area,* Lincoln: University of Nebraska Press, 1966.

Chapter 52

Rickard, Thomas A. *Concentration by Flotation,* New York: Wiley, 1921.
Elliott, Russell. *Nevada's Twentieth Century Mining Boom,* Reno: University of Nevada Press, 1965.
Gibson, Arrell. *Wilderness Bonanza: The Tri-State District of Missouri, Kansas, and Oklahoma,* Norman: University of Oklahoma Press, 1972. The world's leading producer of lead and zinc, 1850–1950.
Hogan, William T. *Economic History of the Iron and Steel Industry in the United States,* IV, Lexington, Mass.: D. C. Heath, 1971.
Davis, Edward W. *Pioneering with Taconite,* St. Paul: Minnesota Historical Society, 1964.
Williamson, Harold, et al. *The American Petroleum Industry,* II: *The Age of Energy, 1899–1959,* Evanston, Ill.: Northwestern University Press, 1963.
Enos, John L. *Petroleum Progress and Profits: A History of Process Innovation,* Cambridge, Mass.: M.I.T. Press, 1962. Describes the cracking process.
Nash, Gerald D. *United States Oil Policy, 1890–1964: Business and Government in the Twentieth Century.* Pittsburgh: University of Pittsburgh Press, 1969. Includes development of the natural-gas industry.
History of Standard Oil Company (New Jersey),
   Vol. I. Hidy, Ralph and Muriel E. *Pioneering in Big Business, 1882–1911,* New York: Harper and Brothers, 1955.
   Vol. II, Gibb, George S., and Evelyn H. Knowlton. *The Resurgent Years, 1911–1927,* New York: Harper and Brothers, 1956.
   Vol. III, Larson, Henrietta M., et al. *New Horizons, 1927–1950,* New York: Harper & Row, 1971.
Larson, Henrietta M., and Kenneth W. Porter. *History of Humble Oil and Refining Company,* New York: Harper and Brothers, 1959.
Swenson, Robert W. "Legal Aspects of Mineral Resources Exploitation," in Paul W. Gates, *History of Public Land Law Development,* Washington, D.C.: Government Printing Office, 1968.

Chapter 53

Golzé, Alfred R. *Reclamation in the United States,* New York: McGraw-Hill, 1952.
Kleinsorge, Paul L. *The Boulder Canyon Project,* Stanford, Calif.: Stanford University Press, 1941.
Cole, Donald B. "Transmountain Water Diversion in Colorado," *The Colorado Magazine,* XXV (March and May 1948).
U.S. Department of the Interior. *The Story of the Colorado–Big Thompson Project,* Washington, D.C.: Government Printing Office, 1962.
Pollak, Franklin S., ed. *Papers of the Western Resources Conference, 1959,* Boulder: University of Colorado Press, 1960.

Terrell, John U. *War for the Colorado River,* 2 vols., Glendale, Calif.: Arthur H. Clark, 1965.
Hundley, Norris. *Dividing the Waters: A Century of Controversy between the United States and Mexico,* Berkeley and Los Angeles: University of California Press, 1966.
Hundley, Norris. *Water and the West: The Colorado River Compact and the Politics of Water in the West,* Berkeley and Los Angeles: University of California Press, 1975.

CHAPTER 54

Warne, William E. *The Bureau of Reclamation,* New York: Praeger, 1973.
Funigiello, Philip J. *Toward a National Power Policy: The New Deal and the Electric Utility Industry, 1933–1941,* Pittsburgh: University of Pittsburgh Press, 1973. Includes chapters on the Bonneville Power and the Rural Electrification administrations.
McKinley, Charles. *Uncle Sam in the Pacific Northwest,* Berkeley: University of California Press, 1952.
U.S. Congress. Hearing on a bill (S2172) to prevent speculation in lands in the Columbia Basin, Washington, D.C.: Government Printing Office, 1937.
Krutilla, John V., and Otto Eckstein. *Multiple Purpose River Basin Development,* Resources for the Future, Inc., Baltimore: Johns Hopkins Press, 1958.
Richardson, Elmo. *Dams, Parks, and Politics,* Lexington: University Press of Kentucky, 1973.
De Roos, Robert. *Thirsty Land,* Stanford, Calif.: Stanford University Press, 1948.
Taylor, Paul S. ''Excess Land Law,'' *Yale Law Journal,* LXIV (February 1955).

CHAPTER 55

Lowitt, Richard. *The Persistence of a Progressive, 1913–1933,* Urbana: Illinois University Press, 1971. Vol. II of a biography of George Norris.
Lilienthal, David E. *T.V.A.: Democracy on the March,* New York: Harper and Brothers, 2nd ed. 1955.
Droze, Wilmon H. *High Dams and Slack Waters: T.V.A. Rebuilds a River,* Baton Rouge: Louisiana State University Press, 1965. An increase in internal commerce was the result.
McCraw, Thomas K. *T.V.A. and the Power Fight, 1933–1939,* Philadelphia: Lippincott, 1971.
Directors of Tennessee Valley Authority. *Annual Report for 1973,* Knoxville, 1974.
McKinley, Charles. ''The Valley Authority and Its Alternatives,'' *American Political Science Review,* XLIV, No. 3 (September 1950).
Commission on Organization of the Executive Branch of the Government, Herbert Hoover, chairman. *Water Resources and Power,* Washington, D.C.: Government Printing Office, 1955. Part of the Commission's report to Congress.

CHAPTER 56

Terrel, Rufus. *The Missouri Valley,* New Haven: Yale University Press, 1947.
Missouri Basin Interagency Committee. *Missouri River Basin Development Program,* Washington, D.C.: Government Printing Office, 1952.
Ridgeway, Marian. ''Missouri Basin's Pick-Sloan Plan,'' *Illinois Studies in the Social Sciences,* XXXV, Urbana, 1955.
Kerr, Senator Robert S. *Land, Wood, Water,* New York: Fleet Publishing Corp., 1960.
Mapes, Ruth B. *Arkansas Waterway,* Little Rock: University of Arkansas Press, 1972.
Pealey, Robert H. *Comprehensive River Basin Planning: The Arkansas-White-Red Interagency Committee Experience,* Ann Arbor: University of Michigan Press, 1959.
Armstrong, Ellis L., ed. *History of Public Works in the United States, 1776–1976.* Chicago: American Public Works Association, 1976.
Smith, Stephen C., and Emery Castle, eds. *Economic and Public Policy in Water Resources Development,* Ames: Iowa State University Press, 1964.
Moss, Senator Frank E. *The Water Crisis,* New York: Praeger, 1967.
U.S. Water Resources Council. *The Nation's Water Resources: The First National Assessment,* Washington, D.C.: Government Printing Office, 1968.

CHAPTER 57

Bennett, Hugh. *Soil Conservation*, New York: McGraw-Hill, 1939.

Morgan, Robert J. *Governing Soil Conservation*, Baltimore: Johns Hopkins Press, 1965.

Held, R. Burnell, and Marion Clawson. *Soil Conservation in Perspective*, Resources for the Future, Inc., Baltimore: Johns Hopkins Press, 1965.

Nixon, Edgar B., ed. *Franklin D. Roosevelt and Conservation, 1911–1945*, 2 vols., Hyde Park, N.Y.: Franklin D. Roosevelt Library, 1957.

Johnson, Vance. *Heaven's Tableland: The Dust Bowl Story*, New York: Farrar, Straus, 1947.

Droze, Wilmon H. "New Deal Shelterbelt Project, 1934–1942," in Droze, W. H., et al., *Essays on the New Deal*, Austin: University of Texas Press, 1969.

CHAPTER 58

Saloutos, Theodore, and John D. Hicks. *Agricultural Discontent in the Middle West, 1900–1939*, Madison: University of Wisconsin Press, 1956.

Shideler, James H. *Farm Crisis, 1919–1923*, Berkeley: University of California Press, 1957.

Socolofsky, Homer E. *Arthur Capper: Publisher, Politician, Philanthropist*, Lawrence: University Press of Kansas, 1962.

Fite, Gilbert. *George N. Peek and the Fight for Farm Parity*, Norman: Oklahoma University Press, 1954.

Rowley, William B. *M. L. Wilson and the Campaign for the Domestic Allotment*, Lincoln: University of Nebraska Press, 1970.

Schapsmeier, Edward L. and Frederick H. *Henry A. Wallace: The Agrarian Years, 1910–1940*, Ames: Iowa State University Press, 1968.

Campbell, Christiana M. *The Farm Bureau and the New Deal: A Study in the Making of National Farm Policy*, Urbana: University of Illinois Press, 1962.

CHAPTER 59

Wilcox, Walter W. *The Farmer in the Second World War*, Ames: Iowa State University Press, 1947.

Rasmussen, Wayne. *A History of the Emergency Farm Labor Supply Program, 1943–1947*, Agricultural Monograph 13, Bureau of Agricultural Economics, Washington, D.C., September 1951.

Street, James H. *The New Revolution in the Cotton Economy: Mechanization and Its Consequences*, Chapel Hill: University of North Carolina Press, 1957.

Green, Donald E. *Land of the Underground Rain: Irrigation on the Texas High Plains, 1910–1970*, Austin: University of Texas Press, 1973.

Matusow, Allen J. *Farm Policies and Politics in the Truman Years*, Cambridge: Harvard University Press, 1967.

Rich, Spencer A. *United States Agricultural Policy in the Post-War Years, 1945–1963*, Washington, D.C.: Congressional Quarterly Service, 1963.

Davis, John H., and Roy Goldberg. *A Concept of Agribusiness*, Boston: Division of Research, Harvard Graduate School of Business Administration, 1957.

Soth, Lauren. *Farm Trouble*, Princeton: Princeton University Press, 1957.

Benedict, Murray R., and Oscar Stine. *Agricultural Commodity Programs, Two Decades of Experience*, New York: Twentieth Century Fund, 1956.

Schapsmeier, Edward L. and Frederick H. *Ezra Taft Benson and the Politics of Agriculture: The Eisenhower Years*, Danville, Illinois: Interstate Printers and Publishers, 1975.

CHAPTER 60

Tweeten, Luther. *Foundations of Farm Policy*, Lincoln: University of Nebraska Press, 1970. This book is both historical and analytical.

Hathaway, Dale. *Government and Agriculture: Public Policy in a Democratic Society*, New York: Macmillan, 1963.

Humphrey, Don D. *United States and the Common Market: Background Study*, New York: Praeger, rev. ed. 1964.

President's National Commission on Food and Fiber. *Food and Fiber for the Future,* Washington, D.C.: Government Printing Office, 1967.

Hardin, Charles M. "Food and Fiber in the Nation's Politics," in *Technical Papers,* Vol. III, President's National Commission on Food and Fiber, Washington, D.C.: Government Printing Office, 1967.

President's National Commission on Rural Poverty. *The People Left Behind,* Washington, D.C.: Government Printing Office, 1967.

National Farm Institute. *Corporate Farming and the Family Farm,* Ames: Iowa State University Press, 1970.

Baker, Gladys, and Wayne Rasmussen. *The Department of Agriculture,* New York: Praeger, 1972.

Schnittker, John A. "Distribution of Benefits from Existing and Prospective Farm Programs," in Heady, Earl O., ed., *Benefits and Burdens of Rural Development,* Ames: Iowa State University Press, 1970.

CHAPTER 61

Brandfon, Robert. *Cotton Kingdom of the New South,* Cambridge: Harvard University Press, 1967.

Conrad, David E. *Forgotten Farmers: Sharecroppers in the New Deal,* Urbana: University of Illinois Press, 1966.

Stein, Walter F. *California and the Dust Bowl Migration,* Westport, Conn.: Greenwood Press, 1973.

Bogue, Margaret B. *Patterns from the Sod: Tenure in the Grand Prairie,* Springfield: Illinois State Historical Society, 1957.

Gates, Paul W. *Landlords and Tenants on the Prairie Frontier,* Ithaca, N.Y.: Cornell University Press, 1973.

Baldwin, Sidney. *Poverty and Politics: Rise and Decline of the Farm Security Administration,* Chapel Hill: University of North Carolina Press, 1968.

CHAPTER 62

Craig, Richard B. *The Bracero Program,* Austin: University of Texas Press, 1971.

McWilliams, Carey. *Ill Fares the Land: Migrants and Migratory Labor in the United States,* Boston: Little, Brown, 1942.

Rasmussen, Wayne. *A History of the Emergency Farm Labor Supply Program, 1943–1947,* Agricultural Monograph 13, Bureau of Agricultural Economics, Washington, D.C., September 1951.

President's Commission on Migratory Labor. *Migratory Labor in American Agriculture,* Washington, D.C.: Government Printing Office, 1951.

Samora, Julian. *Los Majados: The Wetback Story,* Notre Dame, Ind.: University of Notre Dame Press, 1971.

Matthiessen, Peter. *Sal Si Puedes: Cesar Chavez and the New American Revolution,* New York: Random House, 1969.

Bishop, Charles E., ed. *Farm Labor in the United States,* New York: Columbia University Press, 1967.

Hawley, Ellis. "The Politics of the Mexical Labor Issue, 1950–1965," *Agricultural History,* July 1966.

United States Reports, October term, 1974: *Saxbe v. Bustos.*

CHAPTER 63

Debo, Angie. *A History of the Indians of the United States,* Norman: University of Oklahoma Press, 1970. Includes a chapter on Alaska Indians.

Hagan, William T. *American Indians,* Chicago: University of Chicago Press, 1961.

Philp, Kenneth R. *John Collier's Crusade for Indian Reform, 1920–1954,* Tucson: University of Arizona Press, 1977.

Washburn, Wilcomb. *Red Man's Land/White Man's Law,* New York: Charles Scribner's Sons, 1971. Includes the work of the Indian Claims Commission. See also Wilcomb Washburn, ed. *The American Indian and the United States: A Documentary History,* IV, New York: Random House, 1973.

Watkins, Senator Arthur. ''Termination of Federal Supervision: Removal of Restrictions over Indian Property and Persons,'' *Annals of the American Academy of Political and Social Sciences,* May 1957. The author was a chief proponent of termination.

Tyler, S. Lyman. *History of Indian Policy,* Washington, D.C.: Government Printing Office, 1973. Explains termination in terms of Collier's failures.

Josephy, Alvin M., Jr. *The Indian Heritage of America,* New York: Alfred A. Knopf, 1968.

Driver, Harold E. *Indians of North America,* Chicago: University of Chicago Press, rev. ed. 1969. The final chapter contains a summary and chart of legislation relative to Indians, 1900–68, including portions of the Civil Rights Act of 1968.

Levine, Stuart, and Nancy O. Lurie, eds. *The American Indian Today,* Deland, Fla.: Everett Edwards, 1968.

United States Bureau of the Census. *Census of Population, 1970, Subject Reports, American Indians,* Washington, D.C.: Government Printing Office, 1973.

CHAPTER 64

Ottoson, Harold W., ed. *Land Use Policy and Problems in the United States,* Lincoln: University of Nebraska Press, 1963.

Carstensen, Vernon. *Farms or Forests: Evolution of a State Land Policy for Northern Wisconsin,* Madison: University of Wisconsin, College of Agriculture, 1958.

Peffer, E. Louise. *The Closing of the Public Domain: Disposal and Reservation Policies, 1900–1950,* Stanford, Calif.: Stanford University Press, 1951.

Schlebecker, John T. *Cattle Raising on the Plains, 1900–1960,* Lincoln: University of Nebraska Press, 1963.

Clawson, Marion. *The Bureau of Land Management,* New York: Praeger, 1971.

Foss, Phillip. *Politics of Grass,* Seattle: University of Washington Press, 1960.

Frome, Michael. *The Forest Service,* New York: Praeger, 1971. Especially useful is the chapter on timber harvesting on the federal domain.

Hidy, Ralph W., et al. *Timber and Men: The Weyerhaeuser Story,* New York: Macmillan, 1963.

Ise, John. *Our National Park Policy: A Critical History,* Resources for the Future, Inc. Baltimore: Johns Hopkins Press, 1961.

Udall, Stewart. *The Quiet Crisis,* New York: Holt, Rinehart and Winston, 1965.

Bartley, Ernest R. *Tidelands Oil Controversy,* Austin: University of Texas Press, 1953.

Public Land Law Review Commission. *One Third of the Nation's Land,* Washington, D.C.: Government Printing Office, 1970. Included in this report are revenues and statistics of oil and gas production from the outer continental shelf, as well as the revenue from other federal lands. Pocket map.

Nathans, Harriet, ed. *America's Public Lands: Politics, Economics and Administration, Conference on the Public Land Law Review Commission Report,* Berkeley, Calif.: Institute of Government Studies, 1972.

SOURCES OF ILLUSTRATIONS

1. Driver, Harold E., *Indians of North America*. Chicago: University of Chicago Press, 1961, map 37.
2. Based on Francis O. Allen, *History of Enfield*. Vol. 1. Lancaster, Pennsylvania, 1900.
3, 4. Mathews, Lois K., *Expansion of New England*. Boston: Houghton Mifflin, 1909.
5. McLaughlin, Andrew C., *The Confederation and the Constitution*. New York: Harper & Brothers, 1905, p. 300.
6. Maps by Herbert Friis in *Geographical Review,* Vol. 30. New York: American Geographical Society, 1940.
7. Farrand, Max, "The Indian Boundary Line." *American Historical Review,* 10 (1904–1905).
8. U.S. Geological Survey, map in "Southern Appalachian Forests." *Professional Papers,* 37. Government Printing Office, 1905. Cross section of Appalachians is from A. K. Lobeck, *Physiographic Diagram of the United States.* New York: Columbia University, 1922.
9. Courtesy of the National Park Service, Middleboro, Kentucky.
10. Avery, Elroy M., *A History of the United States.* Vol. 5. Cleveland: The Burrows Brothers Company, 1904–15.
11. Ranck, George W., *Boonesborough*. Filson Club Publications, 16. Louisville, Kentucky, 1901.
12. Roosevelt, Theodore, *Winning of the West*. Vol. 1. New York: G.P. Putnam's Sons, 1889–1896.
13. McLaughlin, p. 14.
14. Based on Paullin, Charles O., *Atlas of the Historical Geography of the United States*. Washington, D.C.: Carnegie Institution of Washington, 1932, plate 89.
15. McLaughlin, p. 108.
16. Cartwright, John, *American Independence, the Interest and Glory of Great Britain*. London, 1775. Reprint. New York: Burt Franklin, 1970.
17. Barrett, Jay A., *Evolution of the Ordinance of 1787*. New York: G. P. Putnam's Sons, 1891.
18. Winsor, Justin, *Westward Movement*. Boston: Houghton Mifflin, 1897, p. 498.
19. Sakolski, Aaron M., *The Great American Land Bubble*. New York: Harper & Brothers, 1932.
20. Brown, Ralph H., *Historical Geography of the United States*. New York: Harcourt Brace & Company, 1948.
21. Based on Paullin, plate 102.
22. Dodd, William E., *Expansion and Conflict*. Boston: Houghton Mifflin, 1915.
23–25. Maps by Frederick Jackson Turner, Huntington Library, San Marino, California. Published in Frederick Jackson Turner, *The United States, 1830–1850*. New York: Henry Holt and Company, 1935, pp. 413, 485, 529.
26, 27. Paullin, plate 76.
28. Bidwell, Percy W. and Falconer, J. I., *History of Agriculture in the Northern United*

States, 1620–1860. Washington, D.C.: Carnegie Institution of Washington, 1925, p. 339. All illustrations from this volume were originally made from U.S. Census reports by the Bureau of Agricultural Economics in the Department of Agriculture.

29. Gray, Lewis C., *History of Agriculture in the Southern United States to 1860*. Vol. 2. Washington, D.C.: Carnegie Institution of Washington, 1933, p. 729. All illustrations from this volume were originally made from U.S. Census reports by the Bureau of Agricultural Economics.

30. Gray, p. 890.

31. Map by Frederick Jackson Turner, Huntington Library, San Marino, California, published in Turner, p. 443.

32. Wilson, Frazer E., *The Treaty of Greenville*. Piqua, Ohio, 1874.

33. Paullin, plate 76.

34. Based on maps in U.S. Department of the Interior, Bureau of Ethnology, *18th Annual Report* for 1896–7. Part 2. Washington, D.C.: Government Printing Office, 1899.

35. Leverett, Frank, "Diagrammatic Representation of the Ice Border of the Great Lakes at Successive Positions," in Department of Interior: *Monographs of the U.S. Geological Survey*. Vol. 53. Washington, D.C., 1915, p. 62.

36. Paullin, plate 76.

37–40. Bidwell and Falconer, pp. 321, 322, 343, 348.

41, 42. U.S. Department of Agriculture, *Yearbook of Agriculture* for 1923, p. 236.

43, 44. Paullin, plate 76.

45–52. Gray, pp. 653–5, 684, 890–1.

53. Map by Frederick Jackson Turner, Huntington Library, San Marino, California. Published in Turner, appendix.

54. Robbins, Roy M., *Our Landed Heritage: The Public Domain, 1776–1970*. Rev. ed. Lincoln: University of Nebraska Press, 1976, p. 344.

55. Based on map in "Physiographic Regions of the United States" by John Wesley Powell in *The Physiography of the United States*. New York: The National Geographic Society, 1896.

56. Drawn by Frederick Merk.

57. Kirkland, Edward C., *A History of American Economic Life*. 3rd ed. New York: Appleton-Century-Crofts, 1951, p. 448.

58. *Yearbook of Agriculture* for 1921, p. 423.

59. Based on Eugene C. Barker, *Stephen F. Austin*. Nashville and Dallas: Cokesbury Press, 1925. Drawn by Frederick Merk.

60. Binkley, William C., *The Expansionist Movement in Texas, 1836–1850*. Berkeley: University of California Press, 1925.

61. Paullin, plate 115.

62. Based on map by Frederick Merk.

63. Based on map by Frederick Jackson Turner. Courtesy of the Huntington Library, San Marino, California.

64. Paullin, plate 115.

65. Based on map by Frederick Merk.

66. Based on map by Frederick Jackson Turner. Courtesy of the Huntington Library, San Marino, California.

67. Department of the Interior, Bureau of Ethnology, *18th Annual Report*. Part 2, map 22.

68, 69. Paullin, plates 35 and 36.

70–73. Photographs of original maps made by U.S. Bureau of Agricultural Economics. Courtesy of the National Archives.

74. *Yearbook of Agriculture* for 1923, p. 237.

75. *Scribner's Statistical Atlas of the United States*. New York, 1885, plate 16.

76. Brown, p. 350. Based on Paullin, plate 140.

77. Dale, Edward Everett, *Range Cattle Industry*. Norman: University of Oklahoma Press, 1930.

78. For cattle in 1860: Paullin, plate 143. For cattle in 1880: photograph of an original Bureau of Agricultural Economics map, the National Archives.

79. Paullin, plate 78.
80, 81. *Yearbook of Agriculture* for 1933, pp. 141, 142.
82. *Yearbook of Agriculture* for 1921, p. 173.
83. *Yearbook of Agriculture* for 1915, p. 349.
84. Paullin, plate 79.
85. Based on *Yearbook of Agriculture* for 1921, p. 389.
86. Based on Paullin, plate 108.
87. Paullin, plate 79.
88. *Yearbook of Agriculture* for 1923, p. 435.
89–91. Photographs of original maps made by the Bureau of Agricultural Economics. Courtesy of the National Archives.
92. Paullin, plate 142.
93. Photograph of an original map made by the Bureau of Agricultural Economics. Courtesy of the National Archives.
94, 95. Kennecott Copper Company illustrations owned by the author.
96. Brown, p. 537. Based on *U.S. Census* of 1890, vol. 3.
97. Original photograph by the Bureau of Reclamation, Lower Colorado Region.
98. Department of the Interior, *Story of the Colorado–Big Thompson Project.* Washington, D.C.: Government Printing Office, 1962.
99. *The New York Times,* March 4, 1956.
100. Original photograph by Frederick B. Merk.
101. Original photograph by Frederick B. Merk.
102. Postcard published by Ellis, 1942, owned by the author.
103. *Harper's Magazine,* Vol. 174, February 1937.
104. *Congressional Hearings, Foreign Relations.* Vol. 1, 87 Cong., 1 sess. (1961), "Columbia Treaty."
105. Engineer's Model of the Central Valley Project. *Life* Magazine, Vol. 31, August 20, 1951.
106. Tennessee Valley Authority, *Annual Report* for 1973.
107. U.S. Water Resources Council, *The Nation's Water Resources: The First National Assessment.* Washington, D.C.: Government Printing Office, 1968.
108. U.S. Army Corps of Engineers, Little Rock District. Information folder of about 1970.
109. National Resources Board, *Report.* Washington, D.C.: Government Printing Office, 1934.
110. Paullin, plate 146.
111. U.S. Department of Agriculture, *Miscellaneous Publications* for 1936, number 261.
112. National Resources Board, Land Planning Committee, *Report.* Part 6. Washington, D.C.: Government Printing Office, 1935, frontispiece.
113. National Resources Board, Land Planning Committee, *Report.* Part 7. Washington, D.C.: Government Printing Office, 1935, p. 46.
114. Carstensen, Vernon, *Farms or Forests: Evolution of a State Land Policy for Northern Wisconsin, 1850–1932.* Madison: University of Wisconsin Press, 1962.
115. *Yearbook of Agriculture* for 1923, p. 522.
116. *Senate Documents,* 74 Cong., 2 sess. (1936), Doc. 199, p. 32.

INDEX

Aberdeen, Lord, alleged plot of, 282; denial of interference in Texas, 286; reproves Elliot, 305; Secretary for Foreign Affairs, 322; draws Oregon instructions for Pakenham, 324; Oregon offer of, 326; peace propaganda of, 328

Adams, Charles F., on Mexican War, 364, 368

Adams, John, American peace negotiator, 93

Adams, John Quincy, on Indian removal, 186; on federal aid to internal improvements, 219; proposes new tariff, 227; on committee for amending the Constitution, 295–6; on joint resolution, 301; first annual message to Congress on Oregon issue, 314; instructions to Gallatin, 314–16; non-colonization doctrine of, 316–17; in Mexican War, 366, 368

Addington, Henry U., questionnaire of, 313; recommendation of, 314; instructions to Ashburton from, 323

admission of foreign territory to the Union, issue of, 297

Agricultural Act, of 1954, 571–2; of 1962, 575; of 1965, four-year farm program provided by, 577; of 1970, government payments limited by, 581

Agricultural Adjustment Act (1933), 559

Agricultural Adjustment Act (1938), 560–2

agricultural commodities measure of 1935, encourages export of, and limits primary and processed imports of, 559–60

Agricultural Conservation Program, payments evaluated, 580–1

Agricultural Credit Act (1923), 558

Agricultural Development and Assistance Act (1954), 571–2

agricultural machinery, development of, 433

Agricultural Marketing Act (1929), 559

Agricultural Stabilization and Conservation Service, 575

Alabama, legislation on Indians residing in, 186

Alabama Power Company, 535

Alamance, battle of the, 54

Alamo, defense of, 275; battle at the, 360

Alaska, discovery of oil field near Prudhoe Bay, 506

Albany, British fur trading base, 60

Algonquian, linguistic stock, tribes belonging to, 5

Allegheny Front, barrier to the interior, 74

Allegheny Plateaus, 77

Allen, Ebenezer, on interference in Texas affairs, 306

Allen, Ethan and Ira, seek Vermont statehood, 108

Allen, Sen. William, excluded from conference committee, 326

American Farm Bureau Federation, 576

American party, in 1854, 402–3; in 1856, 404

Amherst, Lord Jeffrey, policy of, 65

Anti-Corn Law League, peace crusade of, 328

antihelminthic drug, 183

Anti-Masonic party, in western New York, 121

Appalachian Mountains, linear ridges of, barrier to the interior, 74

Appalachian Rural Development Act (1965), 577

Archer, William S., on federal aid to internal improvements, 220; on admission of Texas, 297, 299–300

Arizona, action of, with respect to equality of new states, 111; copper mining in, 497

Arizona v. California (1963), 519

Arkansas Basin, resources of, 546; flood problem of, 546

Arkansas Basin project, storage and navigation dams of (1973), 547

Arkansas River, pollution problem of, 546

Armijo, Antonio, initiator of Santa Fe trade to California, 258

Articles of Confederation, land cessions provision of, 98

artificial fertilizers, use of in World War II, 564

artisan class, in the South, 202

Ashburton, Lord, mission of, 322–3

Ashley, William H., fur trader, 253

Astor, John Jacob, Astoria post of, 310

Astoria, fur trade establishment, 252; sale of, to North West Company, 310

Atchison, David R., and Kansas-Nebraska Act, 384

Atocha, Col. Alexander, emissary of Santa Anna, 369

Austin, Moses, Spanish grant to, 138; empresario grant to, 267

Austin, Stephen F., empresario, 268; arrested, 274

Bacon, Nathaniel, rebellion of, 31–2

Baltimore, Md., market for wheat, 118

Baltimore-Ohio Railroad, 218

Bancroft, George, on census errors, 292

Bankhead Cotton Control Act (1934), 559

Bankhead-Jones Farm Tenancy Act (1937), 589

barley, drought resistant, 489

Bastrop, Baron, Spanish grant to, 138

Battle of Bad Axe, 171

Battle of New Orleans, 160

Batts, Thomas, explorer, 55

Baylies committee, report on Oregon issue, 314

Baynton, Wharton and Morgan, fur trading and land speculating company, 72

Bear Flag Republic, proclaimed, 357

Bear Flag revolt, 357–8

beaver, significance of, 250–1

Becknell expedition, 256

Beef Slough War, on the Chippewa River, 450–1

Belser, James E., proposes joint resolution of annexation, 294

beneficiated ore, defined, 500

Bennett, Hugh H., report on soil erosion by, 552; heads Soil Conservation Service, 552

Benson, Ezra T., Secretary of Agriculture, 571–2

Benton, Thomas Hart, on Foot resolution, 231–2; advocate of graduation, 235; speech of, 287; proposes joint resolution of annexation, 294; exposes speculation in Texan land and debt, 298–9; conversion of, on Texas annexation, 299–300; views on Oregon of, 315–16; on leasing law, 414

Berkeley, Sir William, regime of, 31–2

Big Bend region of Columbia Basin, reclamation of, 523

Biloxi (Indian tribe), 8

bimetallic system of coinage, 479

Bingham, Utah, copper mine at, 496–7

Black Hawk War, 169–71

Blair, Francis P., of Washington *Globe,* supports joint resolution, 300

Bland-Allison Act (1878), 445–6, 481

Blue Grass region, 77–8

Blue Ridge Mountains, barrier to the interior, 74

bond issues, in Civil War, 444

Bonneville Dam, 527

Bonneville Power Authority, 528

Book of Doctrine and Covenants, 333

Book of Mormon, history of, 332–3

Boone, Daniel, explorer, 78; Spanish grant to, 138

Boonesboro, founded, 83

Boston, Mass., settled, 33–4

Boston and Albany Railroad, construction of, 218

Boulder Canyon Project Act (1928), 513

Boulder Dam renamed, 513

Bowles, William A., intrigues of, 140

Bozeman Trail, 421

braceros, employment of, 591–2

Bradburn, Col. John, uprising against, 273

Braddock, Gen. Edward, defeat of, 63

Braddock's Road, 76, 83

brandy, in the fur trade, 57–8

Brannan, Charles, plan of, 569–70

Brant, Joseph, Mohawk chief, 90–1; peace advocate, 144; conservative influence of, 149

Breckinridge, John C., in presidential campaign of 1860, 400; vote for, in 1860, 404, 409–10

Bridger, Jim, adviser of Brigham Young, 336

brigade technique in fur trade, 253, 255

Briscoe, Andrew, incident of, 274

British Columbia, gold mining in, 417–18

British Navigation System, 23–4

British Orders in Council, in Anglo-French war, 147

Broughton, William A., explorer, 252

Brown, John, 391–2

Brown, Milton, proposes joint resolution of annexation, 294; proposes to leave to Texas its lands and debt, 299–300

Bryan, William Jennings, nominated, 482

Bryant and Sturgis, California trade of, 354

Bryant, William C., of N.Y. *Evening Post,* supports joint resolution, 300

Buchanan, James, presidential candidate, 179; on British Oregon offer, 326–7; instructions to Larkin, 357; on Trist treaty, 372

buffalo, on the Great Plains, 249–50

Buffalo, N.Y., as forwarder of internal commerce, 222

Bureau of Dry Land Agriculture, 489

Bureau of Land Management, 611, 613

Burke Act (1906), evaluation of, 426–7

Burke, Edmund, on committee for revising the Constitution, 296

Burnt-Over-District, 119

Burr, Aaron, expedition of, 266

Burton, William, inventor, 502

Butler, Col. John, western Tory, 90

Butte, Mont., gold discovery at, 413

Byrd, Col. William, fort of, 48

Calhoun, John C., conservative influence of, 130; approves war declaration, 161; on removal of Indians, 187; defends slavery, 207; on federal aid to internal improvements, 219–20; approves tariff of 1816, 225; on tariff of 1828, 227; nullification doctrine of, 227; Texas program of, 282; appointed Secretary of State, 285; instruction of to Benjamin E. Green, 286; letter of, to Pakenham, 286; exploits correspondence with American minister in France, 290; exploits census errors, 291–2; on admission of Texas by joint resolution, 297; letters of concerning Duff Green, 287, 303; in Oregon negotiation of 1844–45, 324; opposed to Mexican War, 364; on Mexican acquisitions, 369; leader of secession movement, 375; *Address* of, 375; on territorial clause, 377–8; in crisis of 1850, 379–80

California, physical character of, 347; land grants in Upper, 353–4; hide and tallow trade of, 354; overland pioneers to, 355; administration of, 355–6; conquest of, 358; desired by Whigs, 372; significance of gold discovery in, 378

California Trail, 263–4

Cambridge, Mass. (Newtowne), 39

Camden, Lord, jurist and land speculator, 80, 82

Camden-Yorke opinion, on land title in India, 82

Cameron, Alexander, incites Cherokee to war during Revolution, 89

Camfield et al. v. U.S. (1895), 464–5

Campbell, Hardy W., exponent of dry land farming, 489

Canning, George, characterized, 313; objectives of in Oregon Country, 313–14, 316

Capper-Volstead Act (1922), 558

carbon 14, 3

Carey Act (1894), 510

Carnegie, Andrew, acquires iron ore lands, 456

Carolina Piedmont, expansion over to 1780, 48–51

Carondelet, Baron de, governor at New Orleans, 139

Carroll, Charles, 100

Cartwright, Edmund, inventor, 199

Cartwright, John, British pamphleteer, defender of colonial autonomy, 107

Cartwright, Peter, circuit rider, 132

Cass, Lewis, doctrine of, 375–6; on territorial clause, 378

Catawba (Indian tribe), 8

cattle, "long drive" of, 458–60

cattle industry, 49

census of 1840, errors in, 291–2; Calhoun's use of, 291–2

Central Arizona project, 519

Central Valley project of California, 529–31

Champlain, Samuel de, founder of Quebec, 55

Chandler, Zachariah, entrepreneur, 454–5

Channing, William E., on three-fifths clause, 295

Charleston, S.C., pelt center, 48, 60

Chase, Salmon P., on Compromise of 1850, 380

Chase, Samuel, 100

Cherokee, 5–6; line of boundary of, 69; sale of land to Richard Henderson, 80, 82; in Revolutionary War, 91–2; domain of, 183–4; advances in education and economy, 184; appeal to federal government against laws of Georgia, 185; pressured to cede lands in Georgia, 185; division over removal, 189; forced removal of, 190

Cherokee Nation v. Georgia (1831), 185

Cherokee Strip Livestock Association, tribal land lease to, 425

Cherry Valley, massacre in, 90

Chesapeake and Ohio Canal, 218

Cheyenne and Arapaho, 5; war with, 420–1

Chicago, meat-packing center, 431; railroad center, 433, 438; distributor of lumber, 453; livestock market, 466

Chickamauga, attack Nashville settlement, 92

Chickasaw, 8; domain of, 183–4; economic advances, 184; agree to removal, 189; removal of, 190

Chickasaw Bluffs, Spanish fort at, 138

China, trade to, 310

Choate, Rufus, on unconstitutionality of admission of Texas, 297

Choctaw, 8; domain of, 183–4; economic advances, 184; agree to removal, 188; removal of, 190

Chouteau, Augustin, fur trader, 253

Civilian Conservation Corps, 550–1

Clark, George Rogers, in Revolutionary War, 91; contribution to peace negotiation, 97

Clay, Henry, on removal of Indians, 186; stand on slavery, 206–7; American System of, 217; on federal aid to internal improvements, 220; proposes new tariff, 227; opposes immediate annexation of Texas, 287; in election of 1844, 288–9; on Whig votes in the Mexican War, 366; compromise proposals of, in 1850, 379

Clayton, John M., on Mexican War bill, 364; vote on Mexican War bill, 364

Clean Air Act (1970), effect on deep coal mines, 505

Cleveland, Grover, opens Oklahoma to settlement, 467; repudiated, 482

climate, domination of, over far western provinces, 245

climatic cycles, on the Great Plains, 247, 472–4

Clinton, Governor George, heads land commission, 113

closure, Spanish policy of, at New Orleans, 135–7

Coahuila-Texas, establishes empresario system, 268; Texans desire separation from, 271; gradual emancipation of slaves by, 272; limits introduction of slaves as indentured workers, 273

coal, location of reserves of, in U.S., 504–5

Coercive Acts, challenged in the colonies, 106–7

coinage act (1834), ratio provision of, 479

Collier, John, on Indian tribalism: program of, 599–600; opposes "termination," 601

colonial autonomy, doctrine of, 107

Colorado-Big Thompson project, 517–18

Colorado Plateau province, 241–3

Colorado River, distribution of power generated at Hoover and Davis dams on, 514–15

Colorado River Basin Project Act (1968), 519

Colorado River Basin Salinity Control Act (1974), 521–2

Colorado River Compact (1922), terms of, 515–16; participants in, 515; Arizona postpones ratification of, 516

Colorado River Storage Project Act (1956), 517, 520

Columbia Basin Anti-Speculation Act (1937), 525–7

Columbia Basin project, objectives of, 523–4; uses of power, 527

Columbia Basin Treaty (1964), with Canada, 527–9

Columbia Plateau, geology of, 241

Columbia River, discovery of, 310

Commission on Migratory Labor, recommendations of, 594

Commodity Credit Corporation (1938), established, 561; surpluses held by, 570–1; role in Food for Peace program, 571; holdings of, in 1960, 573; shrinkage of holdings, 578; exports of, 578–9

compact of Upper Colorado basin states, 516–17

Compromise of 1850, origin of, 179; adoption of, 381

Comstock lode, 412, 414, 416

Concurrent Resolution (1954), adopted by Congress, 601

confederation program, of Spanish with Indians, 139

congressional election, of 1854, 402–4; of 1858, analysis of, 404–5, 408

Connecticut River towns, founded, 39; population in 1637, 39

Connecticut Western Reserve, sale of, 114

Constable, William, land speculator, 114

Constitution, federal, vote on ratification in New England, 46–7; principle of equal statehood in, 106; Article IV, Section 3, 110, 376–7, 395, 397

Constitutional Union party, sectional character of, 405, 410

contour plowing, mode of soil conservation, 552

Convention of Joint Occupation, renewed, 321

convict labor, 20

Cook, Capt. James, explorer, 252

Coolidge, Calvin, McNary-Haugen bills of 1927 and 1928 vetoed by, 558

Cooper, William, land developer, 117

copper, migration of, 1860–1954, 497–8

copper production, *see* charts, 498

Cordilleran West, significance of mining in, 418

corn, evolution of, 11–12; initial frontier crop, 126; in the Blue Grass region, 126; migration of, 174–7, 469; production center of, 431–2; in World War II, use of, 564

Corn Law crisis, effect on Oregon treaty, 328

Corwin, Thomas, on Mexican War, 367

Cotton, John, 39

cotton, concentrations of, 126; westward movement of, 196–9; Sea Island long-staple, 197–9; inland short-staple, 197; Mexican upland, 199; shipping of to northern ports, 211; collapse in price of, 476; migration of to Plains, 492–4; advantages of dry land farming for, 494; shifts in areas of production of, 565–7; effect of synthetic textiles on market for, 567; effect of foreign competition on market for American, 567; subsidy to exporters of, 576

cotton factors, functions of, 211

Cotton-Wheat Act (1964), 576–7

coureurs de bois, 55–7, 59

covered wagons, 50

Coyle v. Smith (1911), 111

Creeks, 8; line of boundary of, 69; barrier to interior, 77; Spanish alliance with, 139; divisions among, 157, 159; obtain arms in Pensacola, 159; domain of, 183; treaty ceding lands in Georgia, 184; agree to removal, 189

Creoles, in southern Louisiana, 202

Crittenden, Sen. John J., introduces conciliatory form of notice, 326; views on Mexican War, 363–4

Croghan, George, fur trader, 62

Crompton, Samuel, inventor, 199

Crown Point, fortress at, 61

Crozat, Sieur Antoine, fur trade capitalist, 56

Culpeper, Lord, grant to, 30

Cumberland Compact, framed, 85–6

Cumberland Gap, pass to the interior, 75–6

Curtis, Justice Benjamin R., dissenting opinion of, in Dred Scott case, 397

Curtis Act (1898), 427, 429

Cushing Treaty, 1844, 356

Cutler, Rev. Manasseh, lobbyist, 104–5

Dane, Nathan, 233

Danville, Ky., convention at, 140

Dargan, Edmund S., congressman, proposal of, on Oregon issue, 326

David Franks & Company, land speculators, 72

Davis, Garrett, on committee for revising the Constitution, 296; speech of, 363

Davis, Jefferson, on Trist treaty, 372

Davis, Sen. John, on Wilmot Proviso, 370

Dawes Act (1887), provisions of, 425–6

Delta and Pine Land Company, capitalistic farm of, 594

Delta-Mendota Canal, segment of Central Valley project, 529

Democratic party, concentration of, 127–9; divisions of, in the South, 203; divided over Mexican War, 365; convention of in Charleston in 1860, 400; convention of in Baltimore in 1860, 400; in 1854, 402; in 1856, 404; split in, 482

Democrats, southern, views of on Oregon, 326; vote of in Mexican War, 363–4

demonetization of silver, 481

dengue, 183

Department of Agriculture, disagreement with Interior Department on reclamation projects, 512

depression, in American agriculture, causes of in 1920's and 1930's, 557–8

Deseret, squatter state organized, 338

Desert Land Act (1877), fraudulent use of, 464; terms of, 509

Des Groseilliers, Timothy, *coureur de bois, see* Radisson, Pierre

De Smet, Pierre Jean, adviser to Brigham Young, 335

Dickens, Charles, describes frontier turbulence, 261

diet, changes in American, 595

Dingley Tariff Act (1897), adopted, 482

direct agricultural payments, policy of, 580–1

Disciples of Christ, geographic origin of, 119

Distribution-Preemption Act (1841), terms of, 234

Dixon, Archibald, and repeal of Missouri Compromise, 385

Dodge, Henry, resident of lead-mine region, 260

Donelson, Andrew J., American chargé in Texas, urged by Houston to use his influence, 304

Donelson, John, surveyor, 71

Doniphan, Col. Alexander W., occupies Chihuahua, 368

Dorchester, Lord, memorandum of, 145–6; provocative address of, 147

Douglas, James, governor in British Columbia, 417–18

Douglas, Stephen A., presidential candidate, 179; favors Illinois Central grant, 222; on Compromise of 1850, 380; on Kansas-Nebraska Act, 383–5; on Lecompton Constitution, 393; Freeport doctrine of, 399; disrepute of, 399–400

Douglas Democrats, in election of 1860, 405

Drake, Sir Francis, 252

Dred Scott v. Sandford (1858), first suit for freedom in state of Missouri, 394; lines of argument in, 395–7; consequences of Supreme Court decision, 398

Drew, Daniel, drover, 216

Driftless region, unglaciated, 163

dry land farming, zone of, 484–5; techniques of, 484, 486–9; advantages of, for wheat, 491–2; expansion of, 557

Duer, Col. William, land speculator, 105, 114; bankruptcy of, 116, 118

Du Pont de Nemours, Pierre, 141

dust storms, problem of, on the plains, 494

Eastland, Sen. James O., on problem of illegal immigrants, 598

Echeverria, Alvarez, president of Mexico, meets with Richard M. Nixon, 521

Edmunds Act, bans polygamy, 344–5

Edwards, Hayden, rebellion of, 270

Eisenhower, Dwight D., on revenues from offshore drilling, 503; on farm price supports, 570–2; Agricultural Development and Assistance Act (1954) approved by, 571

Eisenhower administration, on TVA, 541–2; soil conservation measures of, 572

elevators, grain, development of, 435–7; operation of, 440

Ellet, Charles, program of, 182

Elliot, Charles, British chargé in Texas, 304; mission of, to Mexico, 304–5

embargo, limited to thirty days, passed by Congress, 147

Emergency Price Control Act (1942), amended, 568; post-war effect of amendment, 568–9

Emergency Soil Erosion Service, 551

Emmons, Glenn, Indian policy of, 601–2

empresario contracts, described, 267–8; to Americans, 269–70

Enclosed Basin, 241–3, 330–1

Enclosure Act (1885), against fencing public domain, 463

Enfield, Ct., 35–6

English bill, 393

Enlarged Homestead Act (1909), 489

Erie (Indian tribe), 5

Erie Canal, construction of, 217; significance of, 168

European Common Market, 576, 579

Evans, George H., proponent of homestead legislation, 236

Everett, Edward, opposes Indian removal, 187–8; dispatch to Upshur on interview with Aberdeen, 283; American minister in London, consulted in Oregon negotiation, 324; in Oregon crisis, 328

Exeter, N.H., riots in, 47

expansion of Mormonism, mode of, 337

expatriation of Negroes, failure of, 206

extension of nation's area, 1845–49, 381

fall line, insulator between sections, 48, 51, 53

Fallam, Robert, explorer, 55

Fallen Timbers, battle at, 149

farm bloc, components of, 558

Farm Bureau Federation, 568

farm machinery, types of on the Plains, 491–2

farm tenancy, in the South, growth of, 582–5; in the Middle West, growth of, 585–6; forces producing, 586–7; and alien ownership of land, 587; effects of, 588; in semi-arid Plains, 588; and soil depletion, 588; shrinkage of, 589–90

farmers' alliances, formation of, 477

Farmers' Home Administration, grants of, to small towns, 580

fat and vegetable oil production in World War II, 565

Federal Land Law Review Commission, created, 615; report of, 615

federal mineral reserves, 613

Federalist party, in New England, 47; in western New York, 120

Feed Grain Act (1961), 574–5

fencing, illegal: *see* diagram, 465; *see also* Enclosure Act (1885)

Fillmore, Millard, presidential candidate, 179; approves Illinois Central grant, 222; in favor of Compromise of 1850, 381

Finley, John, explorer, 78

Fish and Wildlife Service, 613

Five Civilized tribes, location of, 1860 and 1866, 421–2

Flaming Gorge Dam, purposes of, 517–18

Fletcher v. Peck (1810), 115

Flood Control Act (1944), authorizes dams, 543

Floridas, the, boundaries of, 68; returned to Spain, 97

flour milling, technological development of, 447–9

Floyd, John, Oregon bill of, 314

Food and Fiber for the Future, report of National Advisory Commission, 577

Food for Freedom, program of, 579

Food for Peace program, 571; overhauled, 578

Foot, Sen. Samuel H., resolution of, 231–2

Forbes's Road, 83

Force Bill, adopted by Congress, 228

Ford, Gerald, vetoes of strip mining bills, 505

forests, in the Gulf Plains, 183; in the Far West, 249

Forsyth, John, declines Texan offer of annexation, 279; on unconstitutionality of admitting an independent state with treaty obligations, 297

Fort Augusta, fur trade center, 60

Fort Beaubassin, 61

Fort Beauséjour, 61

Fort Confederation, on Tombigbee River, 139

Fort Duquesne, settlements at, 83

Fort Frontenac, 56

Fort Henry, trade post, 48

Fort Malden, British fort, 152

Fort Mims, settlement at, 158; massacre at, 159

Fort Moore, fur trade center, 60

Fort Okfuskee, fur trade center, 60

Fort Peck dam, functions, 544

Fort Stanwix, Indian cessions at Congress of, 68–9

Fort Stoddert, settlement at, 157

Fort Vancouver, fur trade center, 252–3; site of, 312

Foster, Sen. Ephraim H., proposes joint resolution of annexation, 294

France, in peace negotiations of 1782–83, 92–5; revolution of 1848 in, 290

Franklin, Benjamin, land speculator, 79, 100; American peace negotiator, 93

Franklin, proposed state of, 108

Freeman, Orville L., program of, 574

Free-Soil party, in western New York and Ohio, 122; platform of, 376

Frelinghuysen, Theodore, opposes Indian removal, 188

Frémont, John C., presidential candidate, 179; explorer and reporter, 255; writings of, used by Brigham Young, 335; activities of, in California, 357; receives message and letters via Lt. Gillespie, 357; later career of, 358

French and Indian War, in New England, 40; bounties for scalps, in, 41

French Creek, significance of, 62

Friant-Kern Dam, segment of Central Valley project, 529
frontier, closing of, 470–1, 483
frontier station, community shelter, 87–8
froth-flotation, discovery and development of, 495–500
Fryingpan-Arkansas project, 518
fugitive slaves, return of, 375
fur trade, French mode of, 56–7; rivalries in, 252–5; of the Oregon Country, 310
futures trading, significance of, 437–8

Gaines, Gen. Edmund P., affair of, 361
Gallatin, Albert, on annexation of Texas by joint resolution, 297; Oregon negotiation of, 314, 318–321; on Mexican War, 365
Galloway, Joseph, land speculator, 79
Gardner, Johnson, trapper, 254
Gardoqui, Don Diego de, instructions of, 135
General Agreement on Tariffs and Trade (1947), ''Kennedy Round'' negotiations (1964–67) of, 576, 579
Genesee Valley, wheat growing center, 118
Georgia, cession of land claim by, 101; sale of western claim, 115; on removal of Indians, 184; legislation curbing resident Indians, 185
Germans, early settlers, 49; as emigrants, 168; in campaign of 1860, 401–2
Gerry, Elbridge, in Constitutional Convention, 110
Gerstäcker, Friedrich, cited, 261
Giddings, Joshua R., on Mexican War, 366–8
Gillespie, Lt. Archibald, courier, 357
Gilmer, Thomas W., letter of, on Texas annexation, in *The Madisonian*, 281; death of, 285; report on elimination of three-fifths clause, 295; speculator in Texas lands, 298
Gist, Christopher, fur trader and explorer, 62, 78
Glen Canyon Dam, part of Colorado River Storage project, 517–18
Glenn-Fowler expedition, 256
gold, mining of in California, 414–15; output of, 418
gold-silver ratio, *see* chart, 481
Gold Standard Act (1900), 483
Goliad, executions at, 274, 360
Gore-Anderson Act (1949), 569; extended for two years, 570
graduation, proposal of sliding scale in price of lands, 235
Graduation Act (1854), terms of, 235
Grain Futures Act (1922), for regulation of grain traders, 558
Grand Coulee Dam, 524–7
Grand Ohio Company, organized 1769, 79
Granger cases, decisions in, 441–2; modifications of decisions, 442

Granger movement, to control transportation and elevator companies, 440–1; contributions of, 442–3
Grant, Ulysses S., hard money advocate, 445
grasses, varieties of, in the Far West, 249
Gray, Lewis C., thesis of, 208–9
Gray, Capt. Robert, discovers mouth of Columbia, 252; trader, 310
Grazing Service in Interior Department, established, 610
Great Britain, Oregon claim of, 310; alleged designs of, on California, 356
Great Lakes, cut-over lands of, 604–5; tax delinquency in cut-over region, 606
Great Plains, description of, 240, 242–3; high winds of, 248; purity of atmosphere, 248; treelessness of, 248; as cattle country, 457–62; settlement of, 467–72; population decline in, 468, 474–6; dust storms on, 605–6
Great Plains Conservation Act (1956), 572–3
Greate Charter, 27
Greeley, Horace, editorials on the Mexican War, 364–6
Green, Duff, 1841 mission of, to England and France, 282; 1843 mission of, to England, 281–2; letter of to the press, 287; as consul in Texas, 302–3; Del Norte Company of, 302–3
Greenback party, objectives of, 445–6
Greenback-Labor party, 446
greenbacks, issued, 443; depreciation of, 443–4; redemption of, 444–6; limitations on use of, 478
Greenbrier Land Company, grant to, 79
Greenbrier River, settlement of valley of, 83
Gregg, Josiah, authority on Santa Fe trade, 257
Grenville, George, minister of Crown and land speculator, 80
Guerrero, Vicente, President of Mexico, decrees abolition of slavery, 273
Guizot, François, P. G., collaborates with Aberdeen on Texas issue, 290
Gulf Plains, description of, 181; occupation of, 190–2, 195
Guthrie, Okla., settlers rush into, 467, 469
Gutierrez-Magee expedition, failure of, 266

Hamilton, Alexander, land speculator, 104; assumption of state debts by, 117–18; in Nootka Sound issue (1790), 146; in crisis of 1794, 147–8, 151; proponent of tariff protection, 223
Hamilton, Gen. Henry, incites Indians, 91
Hammond, George, proposals of, 147–8
Hanford, Wash., atomic plant at, 527
Hanna, Mark, campaign manager, 482
Hard Labor, S.C., conference at, 69

Harmar, Gen. Josiah, in Indian war, 146
Harrison, William H., election of, 130; Indian
     program of, 153; Indian treaty of, 169;
     death of, 280
Harrodsburg, Ky., founded, 83
Hartford, Ct., founded, 39
Hartford, so-called treaty of, 112
Hawaiian Islands, trade to, 310–11
Hayne, Robert Y., in nullification crisis, 228
Haywood, Sen. William H., proposes joint
     resolution of annexation, 293
heavy-media separation, process in iron
     production, 501
Helper, Hinton R., on slavery, 210
Hell's Canyon, Snake River Valley, controversy
     over, 527
Henderson, Gen. J. Pinckney, in annexation
     negotiation, 285
Henderson, Judge Richard, Transylvania project
     of, 80, 82–3; Kentucky government of, 85
Hertford, Lord, land speculator, 80
Highland Rim, 77
Hite, Justus, early pioneer, 49
Holland Company, purchase by, 113; lands of in
     Pennsylvania, 114; extensions of credit to
     settlers, 117; profits of, as a land developer,
     118
homestead legislation, background of, 236;
     retarded by clash over Wilmot Proviso, 236;
     approved in the House, 236; Homestead Act
     (1862), 236; plank favoring, in 1860, 401;
     significance of 1862 Act, 433; use of
     1862 act to acquire iron ore lands,
     455–6
Hooker, Thomas, 39
hookworm, 183
Hoover, Herbert, initiator of Colorado River
     project, 513
Hoover Dam, 513–14
Hope-Aiken Act (1948), 569
Horseshoe Bend, battle at, 159
House rule 25, rescinded, 296–7
Houston, Sam, military tactics, 275;
     recommendation to Texas Congress, 285;
     authorizes Van Zandt to open negotiation,
     285; on joint resolution of annexation, 304;
     shifts position on annexation, 306–7; on Trist
     treaty, 372
Hudson's Bay Company, formation of, 59; grant
     to, 59; possessions of, in 1821, 311;
     monopoly of trade in Oregon Country,
     311
Hunt, Memucan, 279
Huron (Indian tribe), 5
Huskisson, William, associate of George Canning,
     313, 318

illegal immigrants, as harvest hands, 592; numbers
     of in the United States, 592, 596–7; problems
     presented by, 597–8
Illinois and Michigan Canal, construction of,
     218–19
Illinois Central Railroad, grant to, 221–2
Illinois Confederacy, 5
Illinois country, French residents of, united with
     Quebec, 72
Illinois Wabash Company, land purchase of, 72;
     speculative project, 100
immigration, importance of, 431; restriction of,
     proposed, 478
Immigration and Naturalization Act (1952), 595
Imperial Valley, flood problem and control in,
     512–13, 520; irrigation of, 515–16
indentured servants, contracts of, 18–20; numbers
     of, 19–20
India, donation of grain to, 579
Indian archaeology, dating techniques in, 3
Indian Claims Commission, 602
Indian Office, maladministration in, 420–1, 423–4
Indian Peace Commission, recommendations of,
     421–2
Indian population north of Mexico, estimates of at
     contact, 8–9
Indian removal, encouraged by state legislatures,
     185–6; preparation for in trans-Mississippi,
     187–8
Indian Removal Act of 1830, 187–8
Indian Reorganization Act (1934), 599–600
Indian reservation period, 422–3
Indian reserve, British proposal of, 147
Indian society, a mosaic of cultures at time of
     European contact, 10–11; factors in
     breakdown of, 13–14
Indian treaties, of Fort Stanwix (1768), 69; of Hard
     Labor (1768), 69; of Lochaber (1770), 71; of
     New York (1790), 139–40, 157; of Greenville
     (1795), 150–1; of Fort Wayne (1803), 153; of
     Vincennes (1803), 154; of St. Louis (1804),
     154; at Grouseland (1805), 155; of Fort
     Wayne (1809), 155–6; of Fort Jackson
     (1814), 159; of Fort Laramie (1851), 419–20;
     replaced by agreements (1871), 424
Indians, Asiatic origins of, 1–2; migrations of, 2,
     5; movements of in the New World, 3–5;
     linguistic stocks of, 5, 7–8; food of, 11–12;
     assets in intertribal trade of, 12–13; diseases
     among, 13; in Confederation period, 144;
     western, wars with, 419; government
     rationing of, 423–4; loss of land of, 427;
     dispersion of trust funds of, 427–8; numbers
     of in 1950's, 600
Indians of eastern woodlands, 11
Indians of Northwest coast, culture of, 12

Indians of Plains, 12

Indians of Southwest, intensive agriculture and irrigation developed by, 12

Ingersoll, Charles J., proposed joint resolution of annexation, 294

Ingersoll, Joseph R., on committee for revising the Constitution, 296

Innes, Judge Harry, 136

insect control, improved methods of used in World War II, 564

interbasin transfers, equipment for, 518–19

internal commerce, means of, 214

internal improvements, demand for, 217; federal aid to, 219

internal trade, volume of, 216–17; mechanisms of, 217

Irish, as immigrants, 168

iron, ore deposits of Lake Superior region, 453; production of in Lake Superior region, 500–1

Iroquoian linguistic stock, 5, 7

Iroquois, wars of, 7; League of, 7; a factor in trade war, 60; cession of land between Ohio and Tennessee Rivers, 69–70; barrier to interior, 77; in Revolutionary War, 89–91

irrigation, early instances of, 507; potentiality of Utah for, 336–7; mode of in Salt Lake Valley, 338–9; code of developed in Utah, 338–9; advances of, from Utah, 507; location of in 1889, 510; types of enterprises in (1919–29), 508; relief measures, 510–11

Jackson, Andrew, Creek campaign of, 159; occupies Pensacola, 159; unsympathetic to Cherokee appeal against Georgia, 185; on Indian removal, 187; on federal aid to internal improvements, 221; elected president, 227; action on nullification, 228; declines offer of annexation, 279; encourages Texan expansion, 276; favors annexation, 306

Jackson, Helen Hunt, author, 424

Jacksonville District, mining code of, 415–17

Jarvis, Dr. Edward, exposes census errors, 291–2

Jay, John, American peace negotiator, 93; negotiates with Gardoqui, 135; negotiates with British, 151

Jay-Gardoqui plan, defeat of, 135

Jay Treaty (1794), 151

Jefferson, Thomas, plan of, for future states, 108–9; role in Louisiana Purchase, 141–2; Indian policy of, 153; on slavery, 206; on tariff protectionism, 224; on constitutionality of Louisiana Purchase, 297; expects an independent Pacific Coast republic, 315

Johnson, Guy, incites Iroquois against frontier, 89

Johnson, Lyndon B., appoints National Advisory Commission to report on agricultural policy, 577; on rural poor, 579; supports Food for Freedom program, 579; Indian policy of, 603

Johnson, Sir William, 68; land speculator, 79

Johnson v. McIntosh (1823), 82

Joint Livestock Committee, lobby, influence of, 611

Joint Occupation, convention of, *see* Oregon Country

Joint Resolution Annexing Texas, summarized, as passed, 301; Texan leaders dissatisfied with, 304–6

Joliet, Louis, explorer, 55

Jones, Anson, on joint resolution, 304; valedictory address, 308; tragic death of, 308

Jones, Commo. Thomas ap Catesby, seizure of Monterey by, 356–7, 361

Kansas, sources of settlement of, 390–1; violence in, 391–2; two governments in, 391–3

Kansas-Nebraska Act, 382; political consequence of, *see* diagram, 387

Kearny, Brig. Gen. Stephen W., follows traders' trails in Mexican War, 258; completes conquest of California, 358

Kennedy, John F., dedicates river basin dams, 518, 547; administration of, 574–6

Kentucky, land speculation in, 84; government in, 85; statehood acquired by, 106

King, Richard, ranch of, 458

King, William R., American minister in France, 289

King George's War, 60–1

King Philip's War, 40

King William's War, 59

Klamath Indians, consent to termination, 601

Klondike, discovery of gold in, 482

Know Nothing party, 387–8

Knox, Gen. Henry, land speculator, 113–14; Secretary of War, 139; instructions to commissioners, 148

Korean War, effect of on farm surpluses, 570

Koster site, 11

kudzu, soil conserving vine, 553

ladino, 552–3

La Farge, Oliver, opposes "termination," 601

Lake Michigan, lumber area, 452–3

Lamar, Mirabeau B., expedition of, 277

Land Act of 1800, 230

Land Act of 1820, 231; *see also* Relief Act (1821)

land disposal, peaks in 1817–18, 1836, 1852–56, 236–9

land laws, liberalization of, in periods of economic depression, 239

Land Ordinance of 1785, principles established by, 102–4, 230; sale terms under, 104

land policy, of North Carolina in Revolutionary War period, 84; of Virginia in Revolutionary War period, 84

land sales, acreage of, under Graduation Act, 235; periods of collapse in, 237–9

Langlade, Charles de, expedition of, 63

Larkin, Thomas, consul, 354; confidential instruction to, conveyed by Lt. Gillespie, 357

La Salle, Cavelier, Sieur de, explorer, 55; fur trader, 56–7

Laulewasika, the Prophet, views of, 156

Lawrence, Kans., sacked by border ruffians, 263, 392

lead, deposits of, 166; mining of, 414

lead-zinc mining, process of froth-flotation applied to, 498–9

Lecompton Constitution, 392–3

Le Moyne, Sieur de Bienville, expedition of, 62–3

Lend Lease Act (Mar. 1941), 563–5

lespedeza, soil conserving clover, 552

levees, on the Mississippi, 182

Lewis and Clark expedition, explorations of, 252, 310

Lincoln, Abraham, presidential candidate, 179; elected president, 179–80; on race problem, 206; in Mexican War, 366; on Dred Scott decision, 396; in Lincoln-Douglas debates, 399

Lincoln-Douglas debates, theme of, 399

line of semi-aridity, described, 245

Linn, Lewis F., proposal of, 323–4

Lisa, Manuel, fur trader, 253

Liverpool, Lord, cabinet of on Oregon issue, 313, 317

Livingston, Robert, role in Louisiana Purchase, 141–2

lode mining, method of, 413–15

Logan, John, Delaware chief, 89

logging, component of lumbering, 449; techniques of, 452

London Company, grant to, 15

Long, James, expedition of defeated, 266–7

Long-Range Crop Adjustment Program, 577

Lord Dunmore's War, 87–8

Louis-Philippe (King of France) gives assurances to American minister, 289–90

Louisiana, ceded to Spain, 64; colonization of by Spain, 137; retrocession to France, 140–1

Louisiana Purchase (1803), 106, 142

L'Ouverture, Toussaint, 142

Lowndes, William, approves tariff of 1816, 225

Loyal Land Company, grant to, 79, 83

lumbering, center for, in Great Lakes basin, 449; techniques for, 449–50

Mackenzie, Alexander, explorer, 252, 310

Macomb, Alexander, land speculator, 113

Madison, James, role in Louisiana Purchase, 141; on race problem, 206; on federal aid to internal improvements, 219; on territorial clause, 377

Maine boundary controversy, settled, 280

malaria, 183

Manifest Destiny, doctrine of, 263; climax of sentiment for, 368

Marquette, Jacques, explorer, 55

Marsh, Dr. John, pioneer settler and land speculator, 354–5

Marshall, John, Chief Justice, decisions in *Cherokee Nation v. Georgia* and *Worcester v. Georgia,* 185

Maryland, signature of Articles of Confederation by, 100–1

Massachusetts Bay Company, grant to, 34

Massachusetts legislature, elimination of three-fifths clause proposed by, 295; resolutions of on Mexican War, 367

Matamoros, incident at, 362

Mathews, Gen. George, seizes Fernandina, 160

Maumee rapids, British post at, 149

Maysville Road bill, veto of, 221

McDuffie, George, on tariff of 1828, 227; proposes joint resolution of annexation, 293

McGillivray, Alexander, Creek leader, 138–9

McKellar, Sen. Kenneth D., proposal on TVA, 540

McKinley, William, nominated, 482

McLane, Louis, in Oregon negotiation, 1845–46, 326

McLean, Justice John, dissenting opinion of in Dred Scott case, 397

McNary-Haugen proposals, resistance to, in East and South, 558

Mead, Elwood, of Bureau of Reclamation, 513

meat packing, centers of, 216

Mendota Pool, segment of Central Valley project, 529

Menominee, 5; consent to termination, 601–2

Merritt, Alfred and Leonidas, entrepreneurs, 455–6

Mesabi Range, iron ore of, 453

Mexican Colonization Law of 1823, 267; Law of 1824, 267, 353

Mexican garrisons in Texas, an irritant, 272

Mexican Law of July 13, 1824, prohibits slave trade, 272

Mexican law of 1830, prohibits further American colonization, 270–1; effect of, 271; on further introduction of slaves, 273

Mexican secularization acts (1833–34), 352

Mexican tariff, a factor in Texan revolution, 271

Mexican War, ultimate consequences of, 372–3
Mexicans, as migratory farm laborers, 593
Mexico, revolt of, 256; claims of U.S. against, 359–60; war with announced by Polk, 359; Slidell's mission to, 361–2
Miami, in Revolutionary War, 91
Miami and Erie Canal, construction of, 218
Michigan, northern, tax-delinquent land in, reverts to, 607
Middle Atlantic states, views on land policy, 230; favor tariff protectionism, 224
migratory farm labor, in World War II, 591; segments of, 592–3; seasons of, 593
Military Bounty Act (1847), 238
Military Bounty Act (1855), 238
military town, institution of, 40
military tracts, in western New York, 113
Millerites, geographic origin of, 119
Mineral Land Act (1866), 415–16
Mineral Land Act (1872), 454
Mineral Land Act (1873), 455
Mineral Leasing Act (1920), 504–5; 613–14
minimum principle of valuation, frauds under, 226
Minneapolis, Minn., flour milling center, 449
Minnesota Sioux, war with, 420–1
Miró, Don Esteban, governor at New Orleans, 136
missionaries, function of in New France, 58
missions, frontier institution in California, 348–9; economic activity of, 349; units of, 349
Mississippi, legislation of, on resident Indians, 186
Mississippi Land Company, organized to purchase land in Illinois, 72
Mississippi River, in peace negotiations, 95, 97; navigation rights on, 134; Spanish fortifications on, 138; flood-plain, 181–2
Mississippi Sound, 160
Mississippi Territory, organized, 106
Mississippi Valley, as recruiting ground, 259; turbulence in, 259–62
Missouri Basin Interagency Committee, membership in, 544
Missouri Basin project, Pick-Sloan plan for, 543, 545; as model, 544; irrigation in, 544–5; mainstream dams of, 544; improvement of navigation by, 545; inter-agency cooperation in power distribution, 545
Missouri Compromise, state equality an issue in, 110; origin, 179; debate over, 207; elements of, 207; repeal of, 385; constitutionality of, questioned, 396–7; held valid in dissenting opinions, 397
Missouri River Basin, diversity in, 543
Mohonk Conference, reforms advocated by, 424
molasses, in internal trade, 215
monopoly, in northwestern transportation, 439

Monroe, James, role in Louisiana Purchase, 142; orders withdrawal of troops from East Florida, 160; on Indian removal, 187; on federal aid to internal improvements, 219; on territorial clause, 378
Montreal, fur trade center, 56–7
Morgan, Col. George, venture of, 137–8
Mormon Church, geographic origin of, 119; hierarchical organization of, 346
Mormons, expulsion of, from Illinois and Missouri, 262, 334–5; land allotment system of, 337; land adjustments of to Homestead Law, 338; missionary activities of, 345
Morris, Gouverneur, in Constitutional Convention, 110; land speculator, 114
Morris, Robert, land speculator, 84, 100, 104, 113; bankruptcy of, 118
mountain parks, description of, 240–1
Mulford v. Smith (1939), constitutionality of marketing quotas, 562
Muscle Shoals, Tenn., dam at, 534; nitrate plant at, 534
Muskogean linguistic stock, 8
mustangs, significance of, 250

Narragansett Bay settlements, 40
Narragansetts, 40
Nashville, Tenn., founded, 83
Nashville Basin, 77
National Advisory Commission on Rural Poverty, report of, 579–80
national bank notes, 478
National Currency Acts of 1863 and 1864, 444
National Defense Act (1916), dam and nitrate plant at Muscle Shoals, authorized by, 534
national forests, acreage in 1974, 611
National Intelligencer, on Mexican War, 365
National Land Planning Committee, report of 1935, 606
National Parks, creation of, 612–13
National Resources Board, report on erosion by, 606; *see also* soil erosion
National Road, line of demarcation, 125; construction of, 215
nationalization of railroads, proposed, 478
nativism, 401–4
Nauvoo, Mormon settlement at, 334–5
Navajo Dam, 517–18
Navarro, Martin de, Spanish intendant, 136
navigation, on Columbia River, 529
Negroes, as migrant farm laborers, 593
neutrality, American violations of, 360–1
Nevada, statehood accorded, 412
New Almaden, Cal., mine at, 414
New England, land speculation in, 41; two societies formed in, 42–4; migration from,

New England *(continued)*
118; views on tariff, 244; views on land
policy, 229–30; interior of, 604
New England Emigrant Aid Company, 117,
390–1
Newlands Reclamation Act (1902), 511; defying
and weakening of 160-acre limitation of,
530–2
New Madrid, colony at, 137–8
New Orleans, founding of, 55; French fur trade
center, 60; commerce of, 135, 137; battle of,
160; loses trade, 222; first U.S. mint in West
at, 258
New River, significance of discovery of, 48
New Ulm, massacre at, 420
New York, cession of land claim by, 98; land
speculation in northern, 113–14
Nicholson letter, 376, 378
Nicolet, Jean, explorer, 55
Nipmucks, 40
Nixon, Richard M., signs Colorado River salinity
control measure, 521
Nolan, Philip, expedition of, 266
non-colonization doctrine, applied to British in
Oregon Country, 316–17
Nootka Sound affair (1790), 145–6
North Carolina, land policy in Revolutionary War,
84; Washington County of, 85; Davidson
County of, 86; land cession by, 101
Norris, Sen. George, defeats proposed government
sale of Muscle Shoals, 534; proposes "Seven
TVA's," 542, 548; vision of, 548
Northeastern boundary controversy, Webster's
plan to settle, 280
Northwest, favors tariff protectionism, 225
northwest boundary, defined, 143
North West Company, merger of, 311
Northwest Ordinance of 1787, principles of,
105–6; evolution of, 105, 107–8; cited in
Dred Scott case, 396
Northwest Posts, location of, 143; Indian problem
of, 144
Nueces River, boundary of Texas set at, 359
nullification ordinance, adopted in South
Carolina, 228

Ogden, Peter S., trapper, 254
Ogden, Samuel, land speculator, 113
Ohio, regional pattern of population elements, 118
Ohio Company (1748), grant to, 79
Ohio Company (1786), land speculating venture,
104–5; sale to, 114
Ohio and Erie Canal, construction of, 218
oil shale, conversion of, 503–4
Oklahoma, opening of, 467, 469
Omaha, livestock market, 466

Omaha platform (Populist), monetary planks in,
477–9
Oneida, in Revolutionary War, 90
One Third of the Nation's Land, report of Public
Land Law Review Commission (1970), 615
Orderville form of Second United Order of Enoch,
342
Ordinance of 1784, 108–9
Ordinance of 1787, *see* Northwest Ordinance of
1787
Oregon, negotiation of 1826–27, 314, 318–21;
issue of "notice resolution," 325–6, 328;
influence of pioneers on treaty, 327
Oregon Country, described, 309; joint occupation
convention, 311, 318–21; divided opinion on
worth of, 316; American conception of stakes
in, altered, 321–2
Oregon Trail, 263–4
Oregon Treaty (1846), 329
Oregon "triangle," 311–12
Oswego, British trading fort at, 60
Ottawa (Indian tribe), 5
Outer Continental Shelf Lands Act (August, 1953),
614
outer continental shelf, production in 1973, 614;
proved reserves of, 614
overproduction, agricultural, 473

Pacific Coast province, 241–4
Pacific Northwest, geology of, 246
Packers and Stockyards Act (1921), to prevent
price manipulation, 558
Pakenham, Richard, in Oregon negotiation with
Calhoun in 1844, 324
Panic of 1857, effect on campaign of 1860, 401;
exploited by Republicans, 404
Panic of 1893, halted, 482
Panton, Leslie & Company, fur traders at
Pensacola, 139
Paredes, Gen. Mariano, revolution by, 362
Paris peace negotiations (1782–83), 104–7
parity payments, in act of 1938, 561
Parker Dam, function of, 513
Parkman, Francis, on Jesuits, 58–9
Payne, David L., association of, 467
Pearl of Great Price, 333
Pearl Harbor, Japanese attack on, 564
Peel, Robert, in Oregon crisis, 328
pellagra, 585
pemmican, production of, 250
Pendleton, George H., plan of, 444–5
Pennsylvania Canal and Portage Railway,
construction of, 218
Pensacola, Spanish fur trade center, 60
People Left Behind, The, 579
Pequot war (1637), 40

Personal Liberty Laws, adoption of, 386

petroleum, discovery of, 501; components of, 501–2; "cracking," 502; catalytic cracking, 502; off-shore drilling, 503

Phelps & Gorham, purchase by, 113; sale to, 114; permitted to return part of their purchase, 118

Phillips, Ulrich B., thesis of, 207–8

Pickawillany, Miami town, fur trade center, 62–3; destruction of, 63

Piedmont, soil deterioration, 604

Pierce, Franklin, approves Kansas-Nebraska Act, 385

Pierre's Hole, fur trade rendezvous, 254

Pinckney Treaty (1795), terms of, 140

Pinkney, Sen. William, on equality of new states, 110

Pitt, William, leadership in Seven Years' War, 63; resignation of, 64

placer mining, method of, 413

Plan of 1764, described, 68; abandoned, 71

Plan of Union (1801), 119

plantation economy, development of, 200–1

Platte Country, physical character of, 382–3; railroad connection for, 383–4; Indian tribes of, 383

Plymouth, settlement of, 33

Plymouth Company, grant to, 15

Point Pleasant, battle of, 89

Polk, James K., wins election of 1844, 289; on Tyler's haste in implementing the joint resolution, 303–4; interference in Texan affairs by, 306; on Texan annexation, 307; Oregon commitment of, 324–5; inaugural address of, 325; on Oregon issue in annual message (1845), 325; overture to Pakenham, rejected, 325; on British Oregon offer, 326–7; on Mexican War, 367; objectives of, 369–71; on Wilmot Proviso, 370–1; on Trist treaty, 371

poll tax, 30; in southern colonies, 54

polygamy, revelation to Joseph Smith, 334, 343; prohibited by Congress, 344; renounced by President Wilford Woodruff, 345

Pontiac's War, origin of, 66

Pope-Jones Water Facilities Act (1937), 589

population shifts during World War II, 567

Populist party, public land plank of, 478; silver plank of, 478, 482; on alien ownership of land, 587

Populists, sub-treasury plan of, 478; vote in 1892, 479–80

post technique in fur trade, 253, 255

potatoes, price support of, 573

Prairie Plains, glaciation of, 163

prairie province, diversity of populations in, 167, 176–9

preemption, applicable to selected areas, 233–4; provisions of, in Distribution-Preemption Act of 1841, 234; frauds under, 455

presidential election of 1836, in the South, 128

presidential election of 1840, in the South, 203

presidential election of 1844, in the South, 203

presidential election of 1848, in the South, 203–4

presidential election of 1856, 388, 392; analysis of, 404, 406

presidential election of 1860, issues in, 400; analysis of, 409–10; outcome of, 410

Prince Rupert, organizer of the Hudson's Bay Company, 59

prior appropriation, code of, 338–9; doctrine of, 515

Proclamation of 1763, terms of, 67–8

Prohibition movement in campaign of 1860, 402

Prophetstown, Tecumseh's headquarters, 156; destroyed, 157

protective tariff, held to be a form of exploitation, 211

public domain, extent of, 229

public lands, sectional interests in, 229–30

Puerto Ricans, as migrant farm laborers, 593

Puget Sound Agricultural Company, settlers of, 322

Pulteney, Sir William, capitalist, 113; land developer, 117; profits of, as land developer, 118

Putnam, Gen. Rufus, surveyor, 104

quarantines, European, against American meats, 473–4

Quebec Act, terms of, 71–2; purposes of, 72; as factor in Revolutionary War, 73; Roman Catholicism extended by, 73

Quebec province, boundaries of (1763), 68

Queen Anne's War, 59

Quintuple Treaty, defeat of, 282

racemization, use of, 3

Radisson, Pierre, and Des Groseilliers, Timothy, *coureurs de bois,* discover Grand Portage, 55; enlist British support, 59

rafting, techniques of, 452

railroads, in prairie economy, 174; spread of, 216; construction of northern, 219; significance of, 433, 435; domination of state governments by, 439–40; land colonization by, 472

Randolph, John, on protectionism, 226; on tariff of 1828, 227

range ranching, history of, 464–6

range rights, on federal land, 461; fencing of, 463

range wars, nature of, 464

Rayneval, Gerard de, map of, in peace negotiation, 93

Reciprocal Trade Act (1934), 576
reclamation, *see* irrigation
redemptioners, described, 20
reforestation of cut-over lands, 607
Regulators, 54
Relief Act of 1821, 231
religion, in areas of New England expansion, 119; in upland areas, 132; as factor in Texan revolution, 271
remonetization of silver, 481
Reorganized Church, Mormon dissenters, 344
Republican party, origins of, 386; exploits violence in Kansas, 392; tactics of, 400–2; in 1854, 402; in 1856, 404; in election of 1860, 405, 410
Reserve Mining Company, Minn., production of, 501
reservoirs of surplus, in internal trade, 215
Resumption Act (1875), 445
revivalism, on frontier, 132–3
Reynolds v. U.S. (1878), bans polygamy, 344
Rigdon, Sidney, Mormon leader, 335, 341
right of deposit, issue of, 134
Rio Grande River, alleged boundary of U.S., 359
Rives, William C., on unconstitutionality of admission of Texas, 297
Robertson, James, 137
Rochester, N.Y., flour milling center, 118
Rockefeller, John D., acquires iron ore lands, 456
Rocky Mountain Fur Company, operations of, 253–5
Rocky Mountains, description of, 240, 242–3
Rogers Rangers, 42
Rolfe, John, 22
Roman Catholicism, extended by Quebec Act, 73
Roosevelt, Franklin D., farm legislation of, 559
Roosevelt, James, land speculator, 114
Roosevelt, Theodore, limits sale of federal forest lands, 611
roundup, institution of, 462
Royal African Company, 21
rum, in the fur trade, 57–8
Rupert's Land, granted to Hudson's Bay Company, 59
rural cooperatives, as distributors of federal power, 536
Russell, Lord John, in Oregon crisis, 328
Russia, claims on Pacific coast of North America, 310; cedes Oregon claim, 310–11
Russian-American Company, 310

Sacramento Valley, 244; climate of, 348
sage brush, in intermountain plateaus, 249
St. Clair, Governor Arthur, Indian treaties of, 145–6; defeat of, 146; effect of defeat, 146

St. Lawrence Seaway, 501
St. Louis, fur trade center, 252–3; flour milling center, 448
St. Lusson, Daumont de, at Sault Ste. Marie, 55
Saligny, Alphonse de, French chargé in Texas, 304
salinity problem in Mexicali Valley, 521
Saluda Gap, pass to the interior, 75–6
Sample, Samuel C., on committee for revising the Constitution, 296
San Diego mission, established in Upper California, 349
Sandusky, Ohio, Indian council at, 149
Sandys, Sir Edwin, 27–8, 33
San Francisco, harbor of, 348
San Jacinto, battle of, 275
San Joaquin Valley, 244; climate of, 348; underground sources of water in, 529; problem of declining water table of, 529; irrigation by Central Valley project, 529–30
San Juan-Chama project, 518
San Luis project (1969), segment of Central Valley project, 529
San Pasqual, battle of, 358
Santa Anna, Gen. Antonio López de, becomes president of Mexico, 274; anti-clerical, 352; boundary agreement of, with Texas, 359; proposal in peace negotiation with Trist, 371
Santa Fe, trade center, 256–7
Santa Fe Trail, 256–7
Sauk and Fox, 5
Sault Ste. Marie Canal, outlet of, 454
Saxbe v. Bustos (1974), 596
Scandinavians, as emigrants, 168
Schurz, Carl, reformer, 425
Scioto Land Company, 114; purchase by, 116
Scotch-Irish, early emigration to U.S. of, 49; compared with German settlers, 50
Scott, Gen. Winfield, in Mexican War, 368, 371
Scully, William, activities of, 586–7
sea otter, mode of hunting, 310
sea power, in Oregon crisis, 327
Sebastian, Judge Benjamin, pensionary of Spain, 136
Second United Order of Enoch, in Utah, 341–2
secularization, issue of in Spain and Spanish America, 350–2; in Mexican politics, 350–1; results of, 352
Sells, Cato, commissioner of Indian Affairs, 427–8
Seminole, 8; war with, 189
Seven Years' War, European origin of, 61; zones of friction in North America, prior to, 61–2; British cabinet divided on gains, 63–4; treaty of peace following, 63–4; results in America, 64–6
Sevier, John, in Revolutionary War, 92; dalliance with Spain, 136

Seward, William H., on Compromise of 1850, 380

Shasta Dam, segment of Central Valley project, 529

Shawnee, barrier to interior, 77; in Revolutionary War, 91; wars of, 155

Shawnee War (1774), causes of, 88–9; results of, 89

Shays's Rebellion, 47

Shelburne, Earl of, policy of, 71; in peace negotiation, 95

Shelby, Evan, Indian fighter, defeats Chickamauga, 92

Shelbyville moraine, sectional division along, 176–9

shelterbelt project, established, 553; criticized and justified, 553–4

Sherman Silver Purchase Act (1890), 481; repeal of, 481–2

Sierra Nevadas, 241–4

silting, a result of wind and water erosion, 550

silver, in Santa Fe trade, 257

Simcoe, John G., proposes British mediation, 148

Simpson, George, methods of, 311–12; proposes line of partition, 312–14; on potentiality of contested area, 313–14

sintering, mining process, 500

Siouan, linguistic stock, 8

Sioux, 420

slavery, in Virginia, 22; region of compromise on, 179; advance of, 190–5; in the colonial period, 205; as a race problem, 205–6; revitalized, 206–7; costs of, 208–9; inelasticity of, 209–10; as unifier of southern sections, 210–11; defended as a positive good, 280; in District of Columbia, 374–5

slaves, increasing number of, 202

slave trade, southern agitation to reopen, 212

Slidell, John, mission of, 361–2

Smith, Ashbel, Texan chargé in London, 283; Everett's conference with, 283

Smith, Hiram, death of, 335

Smith, Jedediah, fur trader and explorer, 255; rediscovers South Pass, 264

Smith, Capt. John, acting governor of Virginia, 17

Smith, Joseph, religious experiences of, 332–4, 340; leadership role of, 333–4; death of, 335

Smith, Dr. Theobald, 460

Smith, Sir Thomas, 27

Snively Expedition, episode in Texan expansionism, 278

Soil Bank Act (1956), two concepts in, 572

soil conservation, urged by Franklin D. Roosevelt, 550; in Eisenhower administration, 572; neglected, 605

Soil Conservation, periodical, 552

Soil Conservation Act (1935), 552

Soil Conservation Districts, principles of, 554; numbers of, 554

Soil Conservation and Domestic Allotment Act (1936), 555, 560

Soil Conservation Service, established 1935, 552

soil erosion, by water, 549–50; by wind, 550

sorghum, varieties of, 488–9

South, alleged vassalage of to North, 211–12; demand for political independence, 212; views of seaboard on land policy, 230

south Atlantic states, oppose tariff protectionism, 224

South Carolina, electors chosen by state legislature, 130

South Pass, discovery of, 264; first wagon transit through, 264

southern boundary, in peace negotiations of 1782–83, 95–7

Southwest, on tariff protectionism, 225

Spain, in peace negotiations of 1782–83, 92, 94; mercantile policy of, 135; territorial claim of, 252; cedes Oregon claim, 310

Spanish secularization law (1813), 350

Spanish Trail, route of Santa Fe-California trade, 257–8

specie circular, July 11, 1836, effect of, 238

speculation, in Texas land and debt, Benton on, 297–8

Spiritualists, geographic origins of, 119

Spotswood, Alexander, governor of Virginia, 49

Sprague, Peleg, opposes Indian removal, 187

Springfield, Mass., founded, 39

statehood, issue of equality of new states, 108, 110

Steagall, Henry, proposes agricultural amendment to Emergency Price Control Act, 568

steamboats, in internal commerce, 214

steel, concentration of industry in Great Lakes ports, 454

Steuben, Baron Friedrich von, applies for land grant from Spain, 138

Stiles, Charles W., 183

stock raising, in the South, 201

Stock Raising Homestead Act (1916), terms of, 489; lands still open (1934) under terms of, 608

Stockton, Capt. Robert F., interference in Texas, 306

Storrs, H. C., opposes Indian removal, 188

Stowe, Harriet Beecher, novel of, 382

Strader v. Graham (1851), cited in Dred Scott case, 395, 397

Strang, James J., contender for headship of Mormon Church, 335

stratification of southern society, 201–4
strip cropping, mode of soil conservation, 552
strip mining, process of, 504
Stuart, Col. John, Indian superintendent, 68; conference held by, 69; incites Cherokee to war during Revolution, 89, 91
Stuart, Robert, discoverer of South Pass (1811), 264
Sublette, Milton, fur trader, 254
Submerged Lands Act (May, 1953), on tidelands, 503
sugar, developments in sugar cane production, 200–1; production of in Louisiana, 197, 200–1
suitcase farmers, 492
Sullivan, Gen. John, in Revolutionary War, 90–1
Sumner, Charles, on Mexican War, 364, 367
Survey Bill (1824), terms of, 220–1; debate and vote on, 220
Susquehanna War, 31
Sutter, Capt. John A., 353–5
Swamp Land Act, 182
Symmes Tract, land purchase, 115

taconite, lean ore of Mesabi Range, 453; mining and processing of, 500–1
Tallmadge, James, proposal of, 207
Taney, Chief Justice Roger B., in Dred Scott case, 395–7
Taos, fur trade center, 253
Tappan, Sen. Benjamin, betrays treaty to the press, 287
tariff, of 1816, 224–5; sectional attitudes on, *see* chart, 224; of 1824, 225; of 1828, 226–7; of 1832, 227–8; Compromise, of 1833, 228; provision in Distribution-Preemption Act of 1841, 234; in campaign of 1860, 401; of 1857, 404; Dingley Act of 1897, 482
"Tariff of Abominations," 227
Taylor, Gen. Zachary, march of, 361–2; conquests of in Mexican War, 368; Whig candidate, 376; elected president, 376; recommendation on the territorial issue, 379; opposes Compromise, 381
Taylor Grazing Act (1934), 609–11
Tecumseh, vision of Indian confederation, 152; program of, 156; confrontation with Harrison, 156; tour of the South, 157; second visit to South, 158; slain, 161
tenancy, *see* farm tenancy
Tennessee, statehood acquired by, 106
Tennessee Basin, soil deterioration in, 604
Tennessee Electric Power Company v. T.V.A. (1939), 536

Tennessee Valley Authority, created, 535–6; power production authorized, 535; issue of power distribution by, 535; promotional theory of rates, 536; fertilizer promotion by, 536–7; reforestation program of, 537; flood control by, 534, 538; navigation improvements of, 538; role in industrialization of Tennessee Valley region, 537–8; recreation and tourist business resulting from, 538; survey of costs and profits of (1953), 539–40; costs of fertilizer promotion by, 539–40; costs of power production by, 540; Annual Report (1973), 541; unity of administration of, 541–2; merit system of, 542
Terán, Manuel de, report of, 270
"termination," policy of, 601–2
Teton Sioux, war with, 420–1
Texan revolution, propaganda during, 275; joined by American volunteers, 275; land bounties offered during, 275
Texas, expansionism of, 262, 276–7; geographic provinces of, 265–6; Spanish missions in, 266; American proposals to buy, 270; alleged British plot to abolitionize, 282; annexation desired by its public, 285; terms of proposed annexation treaty with, 286; rejection of treaty with, 288; boundary issue in annexation of, 299; Congress of, and special convention of, approve joint resolution, 307; boundary claim of, 359–60, 374; land policy of, 458; *see also* Joint Resolution Annexing
Texas fever, control of, 460
"Texas fund," 298
Thayer, Eli, *see* New England Emigrant Aid Company
three-fifths provision of the Constitution, problem of, 294–7; failure of effort to eliminate, 296
Timber Culture Act (1873), fraudulent use of, 464
tobacco, indigenous to the New World, 22; depression in, 22–4; trade in, 22–5; concentrations of, 126
Totten & Crossfield, land speculators, 114
Tower, Charlemagne, entrepreneur, 456
town planning, method of, 34–7
town proprietors, 34–8
Trade Expansion Act (1962), 576
Trans-Alaska Pipeline Act (1973), 482
Transylvania, project of, 80
Treaties
    Utrecht (1713), on Rupert's Land, Nova Scotia, and Newfoundland, 59, 61
    Paris (1763), British cabinet discussions on, 63; terms of, 64

Jay (1794), 151

Pinckney (1795), 140

San Ildefonso (1800), news of, 140–1

Ghent (1815), 161; silent on maritime issues, 161; significance of *status quo ante bellum* in Oregon Country, 161–2; ends freedom of British fur traders within U.S., 162

Oregon (1846), 329

Guadalupe Hidalgo (1848), 371–2

with Mexico (1944), division of water rights, 521

Columbia Basin Treaty (1964), with Canada, 527–9

See also Indian treaties

triangular trade in internal commerce, 215

Trist, Nicholas P., peace negotiation of, 371–2

Truman, Harry S., views of on river basin projects, 546; reelection of, 569; appoints Commission on Migratory Labor, 594

turnpikes, era of building, 215

Tuscarora, 5

Tyler, John, becomes president, 280; ambitions of, 280–1; letter to Edward Everett, 281; authorizes annexation negotiations with Texas, 283; evasive letters of, 287; proposes joint congressional action on annexation of Texas, 288–9, 293; invites Texas to join the Union, 301–2; responses to queries on Duff Green, 303

Udall, Stewart, returns to Collier ideal, 602

United Order of Enoch, established by Joseph Smith, 340; regulations of, 341

United States Steel Company, acquires iron ore lands, 456

United States v. Butler (1936), 560

United States v. California (1947), 503

United States v. Maine et al. (1975), 614

Upshur, Abel P., appointed Secretary of State, 281; action on plot charge, 282; dispatches of to Everett, 283; annexation negotiation pressed by, 284–5; death of, 285

Utah, copper mining in, 496

Utah-Idaho Sugar Company, 340

Van Buren, Martin, 130–1; opposes immediate annexation of Texas, 287; Free-Soil candidate, 376

Vancouver, Capt. George, 252

Vandalia, projected colony, 80; collapse of projected colony, 100

Van Zandt, Isaac, Texas minister in Washington, 284; declines annexation negotiation, 284; directed to open annexation negotiation, 285

Vergennes, Comte de, in peace negotiation, 93

Vermillion Range, iron ore in, 453, 456

Vermont, statehood demanded by, 108

Virginia, London Company, 15; Virginia Company, 16, 28; *Nova Britannia* (Johnson), pamphlet, 16, 19; plantations in, 22, 25–7; royal colony, 28; headright system and speculation in, 28–9; quitrents in, 29–30; land grants to Crown favorites in, 29–30; poll tax in, 30; two 17th century societies in conflict, 30–1; expansion over Piedmont, 48–51; land disposal by, in Seven Years' War, 65; land policy in Revolutionary War period, 84; land claims of, as state, 98; Military Tract reserved by, 101; land cessions by, 100–1; land warrant system of, 103

Wabash and Erie Canal, 218–19

Walker, Robert J., *Letter Relative to the Annexation of Texas,* a factor in election of 1844, 288; exploitation of census errors by, 292; resolutions of, 300

Walker, Dr. Thomas, explorer, 78

Walnut Hills, Spanish fort at, 138

Walpole, Thomas, British banker and land speculator, 80

Wampanoag, 40

War of 1812, summary of issues of, 161; appraisal of results of, 161–2

Ward, Nancy, Indian, warns Watauga settlers, 91

Warfield, Col. Charles, expedition of, episode in Texan expansionism, 277

Washington, George, at battle of Great Meadows, 63; land speculator, 104

Watauga, valley of, occupied, 83; attacked in Revolutionary War, 91; warned by Nancy Ward, 91

Watauga Association, compact of, 85

Water Resources Planning Act (1965), 547–8; proposals to amend, 615

Watershed Protection and Flood Protection Act (1954), 572

Watson, Thomas E., Populist, 477

Wayne, Anthony, campaign of, 149

Weaver, James B., 446; nominated, 479

Webster, Daniel, early opposition to high tariff, 224; Secretary of State, 280, 322; resigns as Secretary of State, 281; on unconstitutionality of admitting an independent state with treaty obligations, 297; negotiation with Ashburton, 323; effort to obtain Upper California, 356; tri-partite proposal of, 323, 356; a Cotton Whig, 365; on territorial clause, 377; on Compromise of 1850, 380–1

Webster-Hayne debate, 232–3

weed control, improved methods used in World War II, 564

Wentworth, Benning, grants by, 41

West Feliciana, seized, 158

West Florida, northern boundary of, 134; American claim to, 158; expansion in during War of 1812, 162

Western Reserve, dairy center, 118

Westsylvania, intrigue of, with Spain, 108

"wetbacks," *see* illegal immigrants

Wethersfield, Ct., founded, 39

Weyerhaeuser, Frederick, lumber king, 451

Wharton, Samuel, partner in fur trading firm, 79, 80; land speculator, 100

wheat, migration of, 174–6, 434, 469–70; production center of, 431, 433–4; drought resistant varieties, 484, 486–8; spring varieties and cultivation, 486–7; winter varieties and cultivation, 486–7; in World War II, 565; marketing quotas of, 575–6

Whig party, in western New York, 121–2; concentration of, 127–9; in the South, 202–4; divided over Mexican War, 365

Whigs, Oregon views of, 326; vote of in Mexican War, 363–4

White, James, in pay of Spanish, 136–7

Whitney, Asa, railroad promoter, 384

Whitney, Eli, inventor of cotton gin, 199

Wickliffe, Charles A., interference in Texas by, 306

Wilderness Trail, marked out, 83–4

Wilkinson, James, memorial by, 136; annual Spanish pension of, 136; seizure of Mobile, 158

Willamette Valley, 244; occupation of, 323

Williams, Roger, 40

Williamson, Charles, land developer, 117

Wilmot, David, on Mexican War, 370

Wilmot Proviso, terms of, 370; debate on, 374

Wilson, James, land speculator, 100, 104; bankruptcy of, 118

Wilson, John, challenges preemption, 235

Windsor, Ct., founded, 39

Winthrop, Governor John, 34

Winthrop, Robert C., on admission of Texas, 297; elected Speaker of the House, 368

Wisconsin, rural zoning law adopted, 608

Wisconsin Drift Border, 164

Wise, Henry, cited, 262; on Texan expansionism, 276; allegations of, 285–6

Wood, Capt. Abraham, 48

Woodward, John, speculator in Texan land and debt, 298

wool, migration of, 176; production center of, 178, 433, 435

Worcester v. Georgia (1832), 185

World War I, effect on American agriculture, 557

World War II, effect on American agriculture, 563–8

Wyandots, in Revolutionary War, 91

Wyoming Valley, massacre in, 90

Wyoming v. Colorado (1922), 515

XIT Ranch, 458

Yeardley, Governor George, instructions to, 27

Yell, Archibald, interference in Texas, 306

Young, Brigham, characterized, 335; gives theological rationalization of polygamy, 343–4; appointed governor of Utah territory, 338

Yuma, Ariz., desalting plant in, 521

Zion's Cooperative Mercantile Institute (ZCMI), organized, 340; development of, 340

A Note About the Author

One of America's great historians of the West, Frederick Merk was Gurney Professor of History at Harvard. Born in Milwaukee, he received his A.B. at the University of Wisconsin and his Ph.D. at Harvard. He served on the editorial staff of the Wisconsin State Historical Society for five years and it was there that he developed an interest in American frontier society that brought him under the influence of the seminal historian of the frontier, Frederick Jackson Turner. He followed Professor Turner to Harvard, first as Turner's student and then, as instructor in history, taught the second half of the westward movement course, while Turner continued to teach the first half. When Turner retired in 1924 Professor Merk took over the entire course—which among Harvard students became known as "Wagon Wheels"—and taught it until his retirement in 1957.

He wrote a number of books, including *Manifest Destiny and Mission in American History* (1963), *The Monroe Doctrine and American Expansionism, 1843–1849* (1966), *The Oregon Question* (1967), *Fruits of Propaganda in the Tyler Administration* (1971), *Slavery and the Annexation of Texas* (1972), and *Economic History of Wisconsin During the Civil War Decade* (rev. 1971). He was editor of *Fur Trade and Empire: George Simpson's Journal, 1824–25* (rev. 1968), and co-author of *Dissent in Three American Wars* (1970).

Professor Merk was president of the Agricultural History Society and the Organization of American Historians, and served on the Council of the American Historical Association. He was also a member of the Massachusetts Historical Society, the American Antiquarian Society, and a fellow of the American Academy of Arts and Sciences. He was awarded a Litt.D. by Harvard, and L.H.D. degrees by the University of Wisconsin and Clark University. Married to Lois Bannister Merk, he was father of a son and a daughter. He died in 1977 at the age of 90.

A Note on the Type

The text of this book was set in Times Roman, a VIP version of a Linotype face. Times Roman was designed by Stanley Morison for *The Times* (London), and first introduced by that newspaper in 1932.

Among typographers and designers of the twentieth century, Stanley Morison has been a strong forming influence, as typographical adviser to the English Monotype Corporation, as a director of two distinguished English publishing houses, and as a writer of sensibility, erudition, and keen practical sense.

In 1930 Morison wrote: "Type design moves at the pace of the most conservative reader. The good type-designer therefore realises that, for a new fount to be successful, it has to be so good that only very few recognise its novelty. If readers do not notice the consummate reticence and rare discipline of a new type, it is probably a good letter." It is now generally recognized that in the creation of Times Roman Morison successfully met the qualifications of this theoretical doctrine.

This book was composed by Typesetting Services of California, Pleasant Hill, California, and printed and bound by The Haddon Craftsmen, Scranton, Pennsylvania.

Typography and binding design by Leon Bolognese.